FROM THE MATERIAL TO THE MYSTICAL IN LATE MEDIEVAL PIETY

The German mystic Gertrude the Great of Helfta (ca. 1256–1301) is a globally venerated saint who is still central to the Sacred Heart devotion. Her visions were first recorded in Latin, and they inspired generations of readers in processes of creative rewriting. The vernacular copies of these redactions challenge the long-standing idea that translations do not bear the same literary or historical weight as the originals on which they are based. In this study, Racha Kirakosian argues that manuscript transmission reveals how redactors serve as cultural agents. Examining the late medieval vernacular copies of Gertrude's visions, she demonstrates how redactors recast textual materials, reflected changes in piety, and generated new forms of devotional practices. She also shows how these texts served as a bridge between material culture, for example, in the form of textiles and book illumination, and mysticism. Kirakosian's multifaceted study is an important contribution to current debates on medieval manuscript culture, authorship, and translation as objects of study in their own right.

Racha Kirakosian is Professor of Medieval German at the Albert-Ludwigs-Universität Freiburg. She previously taught at Harvard University and the University of Oxford. A scholar of historical text, medieval spirituality, and church history, she is the author of *Die Vita der Christina von Hane: Untersuchung und Edition* (2017) and of *The Life of Christina of Hane* (2020).

FROM THE MATERIAL TO THE MYSTICAL IN LATE MEDIEVAL PIETY

THE VERNACULAR TRANSMISSION OF GERTRUDE OF HELFTA'S VISIONS

RACHA KIRAKOSIAN

CAMBRIDGE
UNIVERSITY PRESS

University Printing House, Cambridge CB2 8BS, United Kingdom

One Liberty Plaza, 20th Floor, New York, NY 10006, USA

477 Williamstown Road, Port Melbourne, VIC 3207, Australia

314–321, 3rd Floor, Plot 3, Splendor Forum, Jasola District Centre, New Delhi – 110025, India

103 Penang Road, #05–06/07, Visioncrest Commercial, Singapore 238467

Cambridge University Press is part of the University of Cambridge.

It furthers the University's mission by disseminating knowledge in the pursuit of education, learning, and research at the highest international levels of excellence.

www.cambridge.org
Information on this title: www.cambridge.org/9781108841238
DOI: 10.1017/9781108893657

First published 2021

Printed in the United Kingdom by TJ Books Limited, Padstow Cornwall

A catalogue record for this publication is available from the British Library.

Library of Congress Cataloging-in-Publication Data
NAMES: Kirakosian, Racha, 1986- author.
TITLE: From the material to the mystical in late medieval piety : the vernacular transmission of Gertrude of Helfta's visions / Racha Kirakosian.
DESCRIPTION: I. | Cambridge, United Kingdom ; New York, NY, USA : Cambridge University Press, 2020. | Includes bibliographical references and index.
IDENTIFIERS: LCCN 2020022770 (print) | LCCN 2020022771 (ebook) | ISBN 9781108841238 (hardback) | ISBN 9781108810128 (paperback) | ISBN 9781108893657 (epub)
SUBJECTS: LCSH: Gertrude, the Great, Saint, 1256-1302. | Manuscripts, Medieval–History and criticism. | Transmission of texts.
CLASSIFICATION: LCC BX4700.G6 K57 2020 (print) | LCC BX4700.G6 (ebook) | DDC 248.09/02–dc23
LC record available at https://lccn.loc.gov/2020022770
LC ebook record available at https://lccn.loc.gov/2020022771

ISBN 978-1-108-84123-8 Hardback

In memoriam parentum optimorum

Zohair Kirakosian (1949–2005) & Heilani Ayoub (1956–2017)

CONTENTS

ILLUSTRATIONS

FIGURES

Color plates are to be found between pages 174 and 175.

MAPS

ACKNOWLEDGEMENTS

Perhaps every scholar of the historical past is trying to tell a story, trying to fill a gap that, due to various factors, has never been filled or even noticed before. We may oscillate – depending on whom we are speaking to – between contending that our object of study does not require justification, indeed moves in a realm beyond it, and claiming the indisputable importance of our research topic for the understanding of humanity. I have found myself applying both these rhetorical strategies, and to be honest, not believing in either. Why should anyone care for what late medieval minds may have made (or not made) of the personal visions of a thirteenth-century religious woman, who was so attuned to her faith that it came to affect and infuse every inch of her being? How can we even begin to approach devotional practices that lie more than half a millennium back in time, when leaving a written record of one's thought was neither a chore nor a joy, but destiny? The word, so holy in that world, considered to be the incarnation of God, was sacrosanct in all its forms; whether imaginary as in the Book of Life, in which all saved souls would be listed, or physically in a quire of parchment, which needed years of care for cattle and reliable trading networks for ink to be produced, the word itself manifested the desire for the approximation of eternity. Maybe, certainly unintendedly, I have bestowed a little of that approximation on some of the redactors of Gertrude's visions by discussing their writing activities in this book. I hope that my readers will be intrigued by the scribal nature of late medieval piety, where material culture and mysticism were intertwined, where the perceiving and retelling of visions functioned as a creative outlet.

The first time I seriously dedicated time to researching the medieval texts associated with Gertrude of Helfta was during my DPhil years at Oxford, when I was working on Christina of Hane, a Premonstratensian canoness who belonged to a generation of mystics living before Gertrude. Yet the *Life* of Christina, transmitted only much later, is somewhat influenced by the Helfta mysticism, to which, along with Gertrude's visions, those of Mechthild of Magdeburg and Mechthild of Hackeborn belong. The texts of these Helfta women radiated an unparalleled force of inspiration for future scribes, even when the latter copied and redacted seemingly unrelated and older material like that of Christina of Hane. I realised then that turning my attention to the scribal culture of redaction and its implications for devotional practices would be my next project; and encouraged by my dissertation supervisor and dear friend Almut Suerbaum, I took the first steps towards it. The vernacular transmission of Gertrude's visions offered itself almost immediately: with a plethora of manuscripts from the late Middle Ages – almost entirely unresearched – the German redactions of the Latin writings connected with Gertrude of Helfta contain beautiful examples of how book production and devotional culture intersect. Vivid visions grounded in the material world of the late thirteenth century, and abundant with rich images of objects such as textiles, continued to be charged with meaning by generations of readers. Seen over the period of a couple of centuries – and it is vital to respect the pace of medieval communication – the collective effort of redacting the artistic energy of Gertrude and her cowriters becomes the fulfilment of her mystical programme, which was to engender new experiences of transcendence.

Moving to the United States, I took the project with me to Harvard, where it was awarded the Harvard Medical School William F. Milton Fund, which facilitated my archival work in subsequent years. Further financial support came from Harvard University's Anne and Jim Rothenberg Fund for Humanities Research and the Arts and Humanities Dean's Office. In the summer of 2015, I worked with the holdings of the Herzog Ernst Library in Gotha, having the honour to do so as a research fellow of the Fritz Thyssen Stiftung. In 2016, a scholarship of the Gerda Henkel Foundation enabled me to spend three months in Oxford in order to study the historical context of the reform movement as well as consult manuscripts at the Bodleian. The next project stage was reserved for studying the material aspects of medieval books and textiles: the first stop was the Huntington Library in San Marino California, where I was a Mayers Fellow in the spring of 2017; the second stop led me to Dumbarton Oaks, where, invited by Jan Ziolkowski as the Director's Scholar, I received important input from colleagues working on Byzantine artefacts and saints' lives. Many other fora and workshops advanced my research on material culture and mysticism, as I had the opportunity to present and discuss different book chapters, for example: at UC Berkeley with Niklaus Largier; at Yale University (Medieval Studies Lecture Series) at the invitation of Brianne Dolce; at the Anglo-German Colloquium in Saarbrücken with Sarah Bowden, Stephen Mossman, and Nine Miedema; at Cornell University (Institute for German Cultural Studies) with Peter Gilgen, Leslie Adelson, Patrizia McBride, and Paul Fleming; at the University of Berne (Doktoratsprogramm der Westschweizer Universitäten) with Michael Stolz and Seraina Plotke; at Augsburg University (Oberseminar) with Freimut Löser; at Somerville College Oxford with the college-based medieval research group; at Heidelberg University at the invitation of Stefan Seeber, Tobias Bulang, and Ludger Lieb; at the LMU Munich with Beate Kellner, Susanne

Reichlin, Julia Zimmermann, Michael Waltenberger, Holger Runow, Margreth Egidi, Frank Bezner, and Kathrin Gollwitzer; at the University of Fribourg (Medieval Institute) with Elisabeth Dutton, Cornelia Herberichs, Michele Bacci, and Marion Uhlig; at Notre Dame with Ann Marie Rasmussen and Fiona Griffiths at the invitation of CJ Jones; and at the International Congress on Medieval Studies in Kalamazoo in 2018 at the invitation of the Cistercian Order. My ideas have matured in these communities of scholars as new perspectives were opened and explored; I thank all of them sincerely.

In the past years I had the fortune to be around colleagues who nourished my work with their lucid and perceptive attention: my heartfelt gratitude goes to Jeffrey Hamburger, whose expertise and generosity of knowledge keeps me awe-inspired, and to Amy Hollywood, Kevin Madigan, Nicholas Watson, and Luis Giron Negron, who are the best sounding boards for all things medieval and mystical that one could wish for. It has been a great pleasure to discuss my work also with Barbara Zimbalist, Jessica Barr, CJ Jones, Nigel Palmer, Jan Ziolkowski, Leah Whittington, Almut Suerbaum, Barbara Newman, Ann Marie Rasmussen, Kathryn Starkey, Laura Nasrallah, Annette Volfing, Henrike Lähnemann, Markus Stock, Jim Schultz, Stephen Jaeger, Jackie Jung, Eva Schlotheuber, Richard Fasching, Kathrin Chlench-Priber, Alison Frank Johnson, Catherine Brekus, Nicole Sütterlin, Miri Rubin, Judith Ryan, Sean Gilsdorf, Susanne Köbele, Burkhard Hasebrink, Regina Schiewer, Christian Kiening, Mireille Schnyder, Sally Poor, Caroline Emmelius, Cornelia Oefelein, and, last but by no means least, Balázs Nemes. My thanks extend to my students who, with their optimism and hard work, are a constant source of inspiration. The fabulous and inimitable quintet of Hans Pech, Jonas Hermann, Lydia Shahan, Eleanor Goerss, and Philip Liston-Kraft deserve special mention here. I am also grateful to Linus Möllenbrink for his dedication.

Going back to the primary sources was the uncompromised premise of my research project, and it would not have been possible to comply to it were it not for the generous and professional help of libraries, museums, archives, convents, and the wonderful people who work or live at these institutions. My sincere thanks go to all of them, although I will mention but a few: special thanks go to Pater Otmar Wieland of St Stephan in Augsburg, Soror Maria Magdalena Zunker and Abbess Hildegard Dubnick of St Walburg in Eichstätt, archivist Damásdi Zoltán of the Pécs Diocesan Archives, the Fratres of Muri-Gries, the Sorores of St Hildegard Abbey, and the Sorores of Kloster Helfta.

During this book's publication process I was a Fellow at the Swedish Collegium for Advanced Study (SCAS) in Uppsala: the calm and collegial atmosphere there made the last stage most enjoyable. My gratitude towards Christina Garsten, Director of SCAS, is endless; and I am also indebted to

Björn Wittrock, Raine Daston, Karin Jensen, Fredrik Charpentier Ljungqvist, Ewan Jones, Barak Kushner, Boris Lenin, Mikhail Khorkov, Peter Mancina, Merja Polvinen, Laurent Guéguen, Michael Puett, Eric Cullhed, Hazem Kandil, Ruth Tatlow, and Peter Schroeder-Heister. I heartily thank the magnificent Beatrice Rehl, Publisher, Religious Studies & Archaeology at Cambridge University Press, who never failed to believe in the book and its author. Her support and enthusiasm were decisive for making this book a fact in print.

Next to administrative and intellectual backing, the emotional support of friends has helped me to carry this project through: I want to thank Francesca Southerden, Anna Horakova, Monika Studer, Claudia Lingscheid, Lisa Lochner, Bobbi Paley, and Ed Jones for their time and patience. Finally yet foremost, I owe more than I can express to my husband David William Hughes: your commitment and confidence make everything seem possible, thank you so much.

NOTE ON THE MAPS

The two distinct maps aim to visualise the reception of the *Legatus* in late medieval Germany. Map 1 portrays the discernible centres of transmission for the reception of the vernacular redactions, *ein botte der götlichen miltekeit* and the *Trutta*-Legend. The actual dissemination of these texts was much broader than the depiction on the map, on which only places that certainly or very likely held text copies are indicated. The geographical span is still accurate. The same is true for Map 2 which shows the provenances for text witnesses of the Latin *Legatus*, including the recently discovered *Leipzig Legatus* from the Benedictine abbey in Pegau. Helfta is included on this map as a point of reference; however, it is marked in parentheses because no actual text witness originating in Helfta survives. Whether a convent was a male monastery or a nunnery is not indicated, the maps' purpose being the illustration of the identified geographical dissemination and the diversity of the religious orders. Please consult Chapters 1 and 3, and the list of manuscripts in the "Appendix" for more information on the transmission history.

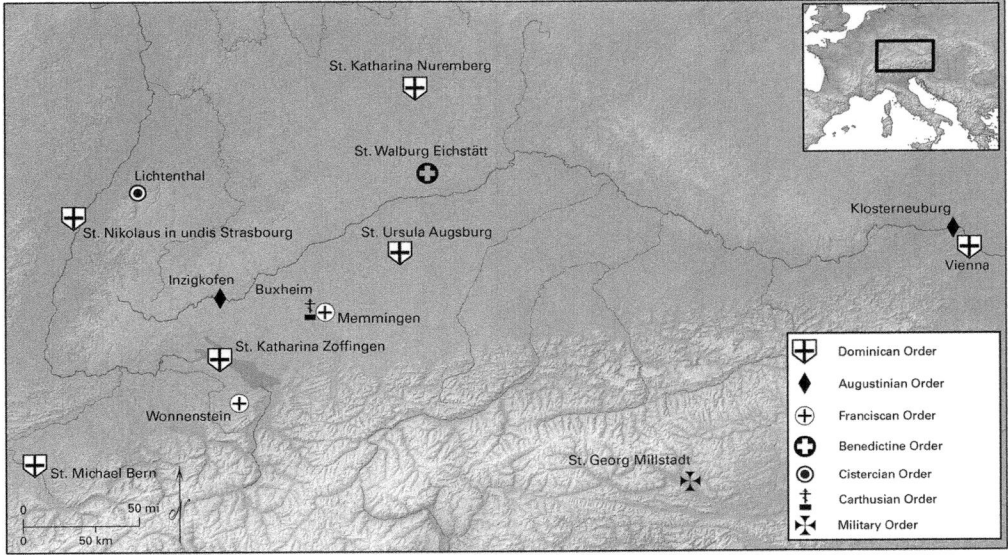

1 The Vernacular Reception of the *Legatus*

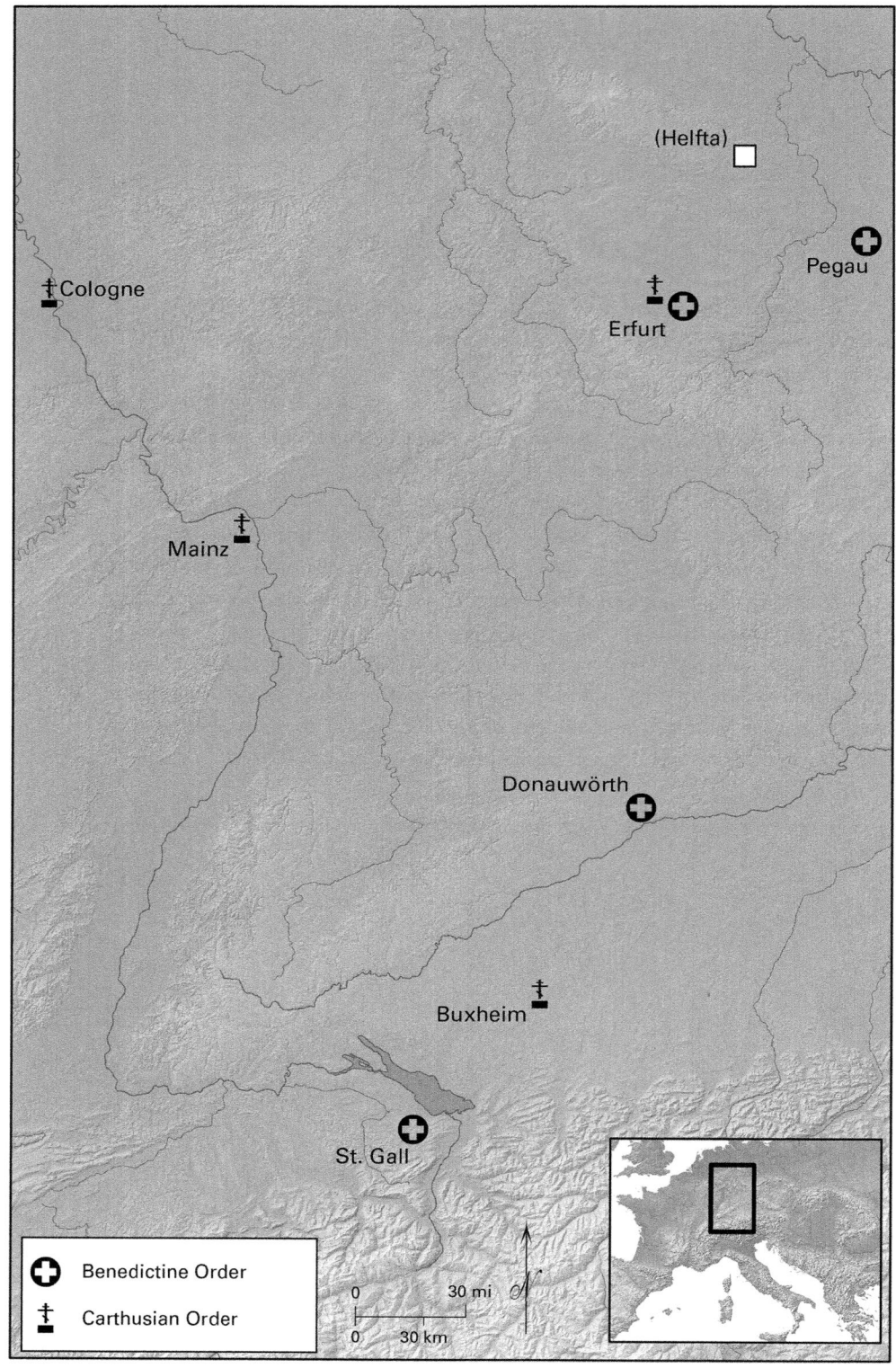

2 The Latin Reception of the *Legatus*

INTRODUCTION

Visionary writing was popular with both women and men in the Middle Ages,[1] and it has never ceased to attract the interest of scholars and believers alike. The German mystic Gertrude the Great of Helfta (ca. 1256–1301) is, to this day, globally venerated in the Catholic Church as a saint central to the Sacred Heart devotion. The earliest account of her life, the *Legatus divinae pietatis* (*Legatus* for short), partly written by herself, deals primarily with her revelations, prayers, and teachings; it is one of several mystical and hagiographic texts originating from the Saxon convent of Helfta. Written around 1300, it gives an account of a visionary culture practised by liturgically orientated and exegetically sophisticated religious women living in monastic communities.[2] The history of its reception serves as a mirror – in the medieval sense of an 'example' – to the development of devotional culture. This study looks at the emergence and reception of the German redactions of the *Legatus*, illuminating the text material from a variety of angles, including historical, codicological, and literary aspects. The chronological focus of this book is the late thirteenth to fifteenth centuries, a period marked by a revival of mystical devotion, monastic reform, and – significantly, for the purpose of this study – an intense increase in pious book production. With this study, I hope to raise awareness of the late medieval resonances the *Legatus* had in vernacular contexts and to show its broader implications for our understanding of late medieval rewritings of Latin material more generally. My driving questions, from which a number of other questions follows, are: how was the *Legatus* read in late medieval vernacular contexts, and what do these readings tell us about how collaborative aspects of medieval text production as processes of translation, abbreviation, and redaction emerged from within a culture of hagiographic and mystical rewriting?

GERTRUDE'S VOICE IN THE LATIN *LEGATUS*

Knowledge of the Latin source – on which the German redactions are based – is essential when answering questions about the German reception of the *Legatus* and its paradigmatic significance for medieval writing culture. Gertrude's voice in the *Legatus* can be characterised as self-reflective, loving, and rooted in a specific time, place, and community. Gertrude also expresses the ineffable, using images and figurative speech; this aspect of her voice is exceptionally important for the German reception of the *Legatus*.

Gertrude's voice is expressed in the first-person account of the second book of the *Legatus*:

> When I called to mind the freely-given blessings your loving mercy gave me, unworthy though I am, I decided that it would be quite wrong if I were to pass over in this account, as if through ungrateful forgetfulness, the gift which the wonderful generosity of your most amiable loving-kindness gave me one Lent.[3]

The opening of this chapter on 'the accomplishment of the beatific vision' (*de effectu visionis divinae*) presents the reader with a soliloquy, spoken to the divine 'thou'. Different time levels are unfolded: an instant at which the 'loving-kindness' (*amicissima pietatis*) was received, a time of reflection about the necessity of reporting this (marked by the past tense of the intent), and the very moment (*in hoc*) in which the account is written. As a preamble, this opening is rhetorically clever; the speaker, identifiable as Gertrude from the context, justifies her account while creating the impression of an intimate conversation with God. The self-reflection about what should rightfully be done – that is to pass on what was generously granted to her – prepares the way for the narration proper:

> On the second Sunday in Lent, while they were singing at mass before the procession the responsory beginning 'I have seen the Lord face to face', my soul was illuminated by a miraculous and priceless flash. In the light of divine revelation I saw what seemed to be a face, right up against my own, as described by Bernard: 'Not the recipient but the giver of form, not affecting the eyes of the body but rejoicing the face of the heart, pleasing not by its outward appearance but by its gift of love'. In this vision, flowing with honey, I saw your eyes which are like suns directly opposite my own and I saw how you, my sweet darling, were then acting not on my soul alone but also on my heart and all the parts of

my body, as you alone know how. As long as I live I shall render you humble service for this.[4]

The tone is loving when describing Gertrude's face-to-face experiences with God. To be faced by God, to face God, is known as the beatific vision. According to medieval theology, it is the state in which saved souls will dwell in eternity, a state which on earth can be achieved temporarily through the mystical union of soul and God. Gertrude describes this union in a seemingly paradoxical way: on the one hand, the inwardness of the vision is underscored by referring to Bernard of Clairvaux's *Sermons on the Song of Songs* in which he urges his readers to aim for a union in the spirit, detached from the body;[5] on the other hand, she repeatedly stresses the act of seeing and the effects on her heart and limbs (*cor meum cum omnibus membris*). She recalls the encounter in affectionate words, still addressed to God, her 'sweet darling' (*dulcedo mea*), creating a dialogical space in which the reflection of the lovers' encounter can evolve.

Gertrude's vision is anchored in a particular moment of time and space; she remembers it to have taken place in a collective setting in the past, during mass. Because of the liturgical frame, the demarcation of 'we' and 'they' is one that allows the 'we' — Gertrude and her 'darling' God — to be folded into the 'they' — the community of worshippers. The intertextual intensity reinforces a sense of participation despite the personalised narrative: the mentioned responsory 'I have seen the Lord face to face' (*Vidi Dominum facie ad faciem*), based on Genesis 32:30, comes from the gospel reading for the second Sunday of Lent. The fact that the same passage is read on the Feast of the Transfiguration is somewhat reflected in Gertrude's subsequent words 'my soul was illuminated by a miraculous and priceless flash' (*mirabili quodam et inaestimabili coruscamine illustrata anima*).[6] Readings of the Scriptures and the study of patristic and theological literature were communal activities, so Gertrude's words must have evoked a sense of shared experience in her readers' minds.

Gertrude explicitly engenders a community when she goes on to mention her readers and her account's spiritual effect on them:

> Although in springtime the rose is far more delightful when, fresh and blooming, it gives off a sweet scent than it is in winter when, long since withered, people say that it did once smell sweet, nonetheless recalling the past does seem to kindle some small pleasure. For this reason I too long to offer a description, with what imagery I can muster, of what my littleness perceived in that most delightful vision, with your praise in mind. Then if some of my readers have perhaps received similar or greater favors, my account may stimulate them to give thanks. May I myself, by frequently recalling it, keep in check a little, through thanksgiving, the dark cloud of my negligence by this reflecting mirror which glitters with the sun.[7]

The relationship built between Gertrude and 'those who read' (*quis legentium*) is established through spiritual experiences which in remembrance can still incite praise and thanksgiving.[8]

Images – such as the rose in this passage – play a central role in the account of devotional acts in the *Legatus*: they are not only discussed but brought forward themselves by the use of other images. The recollection of sensorial experiences – here scent and vision – is used to negotiate memory and aspects of temporality. Allegory and sensorium are involved but the rose in Gertrude's account is neither simply a symbol nor a visual mirage; rather, the image serves to illustrate a figurative mode of speculative perception.[9] Figuration creates a virtual space for sensory effects which allows the divine to be perceivable in aesthetic experiences. Speculation, in thirteenth-century philosophy, is not restricted to spiritual introspection; it encompasses all phenomena, 'those of nature and those of grace' meaning all things worldly ('visible') and sacred ('invisible').[10] Both Hugh and Richard of St Victor highlight the role of images in the contemplative practice of figurative speculation.[11] Gertrude's reflections and rhetorical techniques engage with these contemporaneous ideas on contemplation when she explains and illustrates how reading her account may create new opportunities for the encounter with the divine, using images to do so.

Images are also used to describe the experience of union with God, when Gertrude plunges back into the description of the beatific vision, which is presented as a light entering her body through her eyes, 'a light which came from your deifying eyes, a light beyond price, bringer of sweetness, which penetrated all my inner being and seemed to produce an extraordinarily supernatural effect in all my limbs'.[12] The union of soul and God is played out in bodily terms, applying hypothetical proximations – for example, 'it seemed to empty my bones of their marrow' (*quidem quasi evacuans omnes medullas ossium meorum*) – as well as corporeal sensations – 'then, too, the bones themselves and my flesh melted away into nothingness' (*hinc etiam ipsa ossa simul cum carne annihilans*).

Figurative speech is another way for Gertrude to express the ineffable. Gertrude asks: 'What more am I to say of that sweetest of visions, as I must call it?'[13] Experiencing and then recalling the experience is a way to overcome the insufficiency of language to describe the mystical union:

> For to tell the truth as I see it, the combined eloquence of all tongues throughout my entire lifetime would never have persuaded me of the existence of this dazzling mode of seeing you, even in the glory of heaven, had not your generosity, my God, the one and only salvation of my soul, introduced me to it through personal experience.[14]

The beatific vision, so personal and 'experienced again and again' (*saepius experta sum*), is – despite its supposed ineffability – still communicated. The exclusiveness is shared as a 'sweetness' – a form of embodied understanding – which 'one person instills into another'.[15] Gertrude's self-reflected account aims to function as a trigger for her readers to gain new experiences with the divine.

The *Legatus,* which deals with the spiritual life of Gertrude as a model for Christ's mystical bride, also contains Gertrude's instructions for the spiritual and educational care of her fellow nuns and the readers at large; artistic reflections on objects from Gertrude's world; creative commentaries on the Scriptures, the patristic writings, and the liturgy; and numerous instances of direct communication with God. The intensity of Gertrude's words, the complexity of her thought-building, and her inexhaustible capacity for drawing images of the imageless have attracted countless readers to her writings. This study looks at their late medieval reception, that is when the translated and redacted books of the Latin *Legatus* found a vernacular readership that, dealing with Gertrude's legacy creatively, reshaped and revisited the transmitted material to match its devotional needs.

VERNACULAR REWRITINGS

There are very few medieval saints who – like Gertrude – are only known through their writings.[16] We know a little more about Gertrude's contemporaries Mechthild of Hackeborn and Mechthild of Magdeburg, the two other mystics connected to the convent of Helfta, than we do about Gertrude herself.[17] While Mechthild of Magdeburg wrote in her mother tongue, a Northern-German dialect, Gertrude of Helfta, Mechthild of Hackeborn, and unnamed fellow writers opted for Latin as their written language. Much ink has been spilled about the community of Helfta, and scholarship has begun to address the nuns' Latin compositions as transmitted in late medieval manuscripts.[18] Their earliest vernacular reception, however, has received only a little attention – despite a burgeoning body of research into the reform movement (in which the *Legatus* was read and copied), and the role of vernacular theology in the late Middle Ages – and it deserves more.[19]

Gertrude's spirituality, which testifies to her robust knowledge of the Scriptures, the patristic tradition, and contemporaneous scholasticism, has rightly been described as theology.[20] This attribution has more gravity than it may seem at first glance; religious women active in writing are more often described as visionaries and/or mystics. Vernacular rewritings in this regard seem then even further removed from what is conventionally considered to count as original theology. The translation of Gertrude's ideas and visions into the vernacular faces some of the problems with which medieval religious texts are often confronted.[21] What is at stake becomes evident when we flip the coin and consider, for a moment, the attention translated texts receive whenever a supposed original is lost: we may think of Greek material that has come down to us solely through Latin, Arabic, Syriac, or Persian transmission. We may likewise think of Mechthild of Magdeburg's *Flowing Light of the Godhead*, of which Middle Low German fragments were discovered only very recently.[22] All of these texts are greatly valued despite their status as translations. Often the loss or non-existence of originals is bemoaned but the independent value of a text is still underscored. This does not quite hold true for vernacular translations of texts that continued to circulate in Latin; in this discrepancy of judgment (translation is the only transmission versus original is still extant) lies the real bias against vernacular rewritings from the Middle Ages.

Indeed, late medieval Germany has an embarrassment of riches when it comes to vernacular writings, which remain under-explored. 'The German-speaking regions can boast, perhaps more than any other modern region, of a long history of book production and preservation', one which allows exploration of 'the work that nuns were doing from the eighth through the sixteenth centuries'.[23] Reasons for the neglect of vernacular (re-)writings have often been implicit; as outlined above, translations of Latin texts are seldom studied because of underlying assumptions about 'originality'. In addition, in scholarship on the late medieval reform movement, vernacular texts have mostly only been considered whenever reformers or other male theologians authored them as programmatic writings for communities undergoing observant changes,[24] whereas vernacular redactions have been regarded as mere translations serving a technical end (such as a copying practice) rather than conveying creative devotional significance. This problem (translation versus original) occurs notably with religious textuality where poetological aspects are often deemed secondary to theological content.[25] In research on courtly literature, for example, the same problem does not arise; German epics based on French romances are never termed translations, and instead, their independent literary composition is highlighted.[26] Yet, many religious texts in the late Middle Ages, based on prior Latin texts, also developed independent lines of transmission and ought to receive the same critical attention.[27]

In the middle of the fourteenth century, courtly literary production in Germany decreased drastically, in contrast to mystical texts being continuously produced and copied in predominantly Dominican female communities.[28] Vernacular religious texts are currently being revaluated, using concepts such as vernacular theology and mystical lives,[29] in studies that prove a prevailing Latin literacy among scribes and readers who were, in fact, bilingual.[30] Writing in the vernacular language was more of a choice than a necessity – a condition which results in a 'self-reflectiveness' of vernacular religious texts.[31] This 'self-reflectiveness' needs to be explored in detailed analyses in order to understand vernacular writing and reception in the late Middle Ages, but research into concrete cases has been slow to catch on.

The current study fills this vacuum by exploring the vernacular reception of one of the most successful female-authored religious texts, the *Legatus divinae pietatis*. In subsequent chapters, I consider the German reworkings of the *Legatus* from both manuscript and cultural standpoints, tracing the production and reception contexts of the vernacular redactions. What interests me most is not *what* had changed in the redactions – that is to say, the editorial details in each extant manuscript – but rather *how* the *Legatus* was reshaped for different purposes, *how* the hagiographic material was revisited for new audiences who would be invited to reimagine Gertrude's life and visions. This shift in analytical approach moves away from the notion of 'author' to explain collaborative authorship with women's attempts to generate authority pushing instead towards the more accurate concept of 'redactors'. The German continuation of the *Legatus* tradition does not represent discontinuous productions but a continuation of collective redactorial processes. More broadly seen, the reception and transmission of Latin visionary writing in predominantly fifteenth-century vernacular literary culture was a creative playground for adopting and adapting devotional tropes of the thirteenth and early fourteenth centuries.

Studies on vernacular theology have been able to lift some of the often stigmatic judgment attached to non-Latin religious texts, emphasising the innovativeness of late medieval religious culture which included processes of translating and compiling.[32] Yet, regarding the situation on the European continent, much work remains to be done as assumptions about the supposed lack of 'original text production' prevail. In this book I contend that this assumption is misplaced and is aggravated if terms such as 'originality' and 'authorship' are overused for analysing translations which emerge in the context of a dynamic manuscript culture that evades the stable notion of a 'single author-work production'. What makes this argument distinctive is that it focuses not on the act of translating itself, but on the effects of redacted texts as embedded in a culture of devotion: hagiographic and mystical writings were constantly reshaped and revised according to the spiritual needs of their readers. By emphasising a body of writing which, as a result of our unexamined assumptions about the nature of religious text production, is still relatively unknown to the modern reader, I hope to illuminate the intricate situation of vernacular writing.

As the *Legatus* was adapted and translated into early modern European languages – for example, a French version (*L'image de noblesse*) printed in Paris in 1612, and an Italian life (*La vita della b. vergine Gertruda*) printed first in Venice in 1562 – the Latin version continued to be distributed and read, mostly in shorter redactions and excerpts.[33] The story of the rewriting of the *Legatus* in other languages begins, however, in the fourteenth century in Germany, with the text known as *ein botte der götlichen miltekeit* (the *botte* for short). Examination of this earliest vernacular redaction of the *Legatus* allows us to study its reception in late medieval contexts in which monasticism, under the influence of flourishing lay religious communities, underwent important reforms that affected the devotional culture of the time.

The *botte* and its further redaction, the *Trutta*-legend, are not simply abridged translations; they are rewritings and at the same time text creations, worthy of being considered distinctly and in their own right, just as they were received autonomously in their historical contexts. Studying these vernacular texts allows us to trace various reception histories which consider redactions of texts and challenge modern understandings of medieval processes of translation.[34] The vernacular redactions of the *Legatus* teach us how medieval readers generated devotional meaning in new contexts. These new contexts were influenced by fourteenth-century German mystics such as Henry Suso, who wrote long after Gertrude of Helfta had died and whose notions on meditation via images came to impact the way Gertrude's visions were read.[35] Central to these new readings is the concept of 'corporeal image', which in the *Legatus* and the *botte* ties back to material culture, allowing us to speak of imaginary material objects in Gertrude's visions.[36] That in such 'corporeal images' materialities are represented rather than presented does not alter the fact that the reader is invited to imagine them in a sensorial way, just as material objects can be seen, touched, and smelled.[37] The inner sensorium, according to medieval philosophy, mirrors the outer sensorium; so through the process of reimagining, Gertrude's 'corporeal images' gain quasi-material qualities.[38]

Combined with the *Legatus'* inherent programme of 'corporeal images',[39] late medieval devotional culture enhanced the understanding of the *botte* as a dynamic text susceptible to processes of rewriting and reimagining. This dynamic quality continued with manuscript copies of the *botte* being produced up to the seventeenth century, but print versions in the early sixteenth century changed the patterns of dissemination as reception in wider circles became possible. The following analysis focuses on the German manuscript transmission because the *botte* itself emphasises a dynamic book culture where the process of copying is analogous to the transformation of the soul into the bride of Christ. The *botte* demonstrates a dynamic manuscript culture in multiple ways – which are explored in the next six chapters – as it forms part of an increase in production of vernacular texts in the late Middle Ages.

A significant challenge in studying the German reception is how little we know about the historical contexts for some of the manuscripts. My examination of the vernacular transmission thus involves two parallel and complementary aims: first, to broaden the scope of study regarding medieval visionary culture to include translations (treating them as creative rewritings in another language) by introducing the German redactions of the *Legatus*; and second, to explore new ways of understanding this repertoire from different interpretative angles, focussing less on individual text witnesses in various manuscripts than on a set of images that they hold in common. Exploring central images which evoke manuscript culture (the book), the human body (the heart), and textile culture (festive garments) – motifs that are linked to the liturgy, illuminations and miniatures, objects, sermons, scholastic works, and mystical texts – allows for a more complete sense of how Gertrude's visions activated meaning for generations of pious readers, and it reveals the contours of late medieval devotional practices in which reading and writing were understood as holy services and salvific acts. My aim is to show that vernacular redactions, no less than their Latin models, deserve our attention.

My intervention in scholarship on vernacular writing culture via the reception of Gertrude of Helfta's visions in medieval Germany comes in three parts. First, I offer critical and historical contextualisation of the writing culture and book history of the *Legatus*: I delve into previously unstudied archival material for both the German *botte* (Chapter 3) and its Latin sources (Chapter 1). As I explain in Chapter 1, the writing culture and the religious life at Helfta form together an important background for the understanding of the reception of the *Legatus*. Two further chapters investigate the topic of the status of the *botte* from two distinct perspectives: after discussing the concept of redaction with historical examples (Chapter 2), I turn to literary constructions in the *botte* and the implication for its textual status, for which book metaphors and writing imagery are central (Chapter 4). Finally, I trace the revisited understandings of Gertrude's visionary images in the vernacular reception, focussing in particular on images relating to the heart (Chapter 5) and textiles (Chapter 6) as I study their literary, liturgical, and artistic contexts.

STRUCTURE OF THE STUDY

The first chapter ('The Helfta Scriptorium') investigates Helfta's intellectual and scribal culture, and intervenes in current debates on gendered authorship by suggesting collective writing scenarios that evade notions of authorial originality. New insights into how the scriptorium at Helfta was managed, with the names of the sisters writing and illuminating manuscripts, suggest a nuanced image of the convent's book culture. Consideration of a recently discovered alternative version of the *Legatus*, now the oldest known text witness (Leipzig, Universitätsbibliothek, Ms 827), brings to light a dynamic manuscript culture in which parallel versions of 'one text' coexist. In Chapter 1 I argue that the scriptorium at Helfta was characterised by collaborative processes of writing, rather than the site of three individual authors, Mechthild of Magdeburg, Mechthild of Hackeborn, and Gertrude of Helfta.

The second chapter ('Redactions within a Dynamic Textuality') examines questions about vernacular redactions and updates previous research on the *botte* as I suggest that the *Legatus* was redacted into the *botte* by Carthusians and that the *Trutta*-legend emerged first in the Dominican nunnery of St Katharina in Nuremberg. This chapter takes the *botte* as a paradigmatic example of late medieval cocreative writing processes which were fuelled by a self-reflective vernacularity. I propose using the term 'redactor' to capture the specific textuality engendered by the Helfta mystics. By defining the concept of redaction – with reference to Bonaventure and others – I argue that the translation of the *Legatus* is another – a redacted – version of it. Inspired by approaches developed under the flag of Material Philology, Chapter 2 moves away from rigid binaries between author and scribe, or original and translation, demonstrating instead that production of writing is a multifaceted process, in which there can be a spectrum of approaches to writing, adapting, and copying.

In the third chapter ('Manuscript Transmission History') I address the vernacular reception history – 'Überlieferungsgeschichte' – of the *Legatus*, which demonstrates 'textual flexibility', seen in both the *botte*'s rearrangement and its manuscript transmission. Drawing on the methods of Material Philology, I introduce each of the manuscripts rather than attempting to establish stemmatological dependencies.[40] The *botte* circulated in hagiographic, visionary, and mystical miscellanies. Comprehensive text witnesses, excerpts (often consisting of prayers), as well as the *Trutta*-legend were read, reshaped, and copied, mostly by nuns, but also by lay communities and individual devotees. The manuscript transmission history discusses newly unearthed manuscripts and exposes intricate networks within the reform movement and beyond it.

Chapter 4 ('The Book's Self-Reflectivity') offers an innovative way of contextualising the codicological findings of the preceding chapters within a discussion on affective literacies. The examination of book and writing metaphors in the *botte* reveals an attentiveness to how the *botte* comes into being through processes of reading, rearranging, and copying. Reading and imagining with the help of 'corporeal images' – a term asserted in the *Legatus* – become holy acts and means to embody the bride of Christ. Such ontological effects are partly embedded in the *Legatus* but they become programmatic in the vernacular redaction, which draws authoritative assertion from salvific mechanisms associated with scribal activity. I put forward that the reworking of the *Legatus* in the vernacular positions itself, and thus the activity of the redactor, alongside that of the original as a holy book, placing greater emphasis on the processes of reading and copying, rather than on production and authorship.

The sacred heart, which has always been seen as the hallmark and innovation of Gertrude's spirituality, is the focus of the fifth chapter ('The Scriptorial Heart'). Instances of the sacred heart need to be seen in a wider context of writings which, inspired by Richard of St Victor's concept of *amor vulnerans*, consider processes of wounding and their affinity with writing. Heart imagery takes us back to Helfta's writing culture, where the cross-pollination of ideas meant that Mechthild of Magdeburg's understanding of the divine heart, and how it relates to her writing, had an effect on the visionary world of Gertrude. Studying the vernacular reception of the *Legatus* in this regard, I explore correlations of visions and corporeal imagery in the *botte*, where Christ's Passion is aligned with text production. Comparison to other fourteenth-century texts – for instance, Otto of Passau's *The Twenty-Four Elders* – suggests that Gertrude's visions were widely appealing to a late medieval devotional culture in which meditative images were thought to create a mental gateway to the divine.

In the sixth and final chapter ('Imaginary Textiles'), I move from a review of historical research on the status and function of textiles within late medieval monastic culture to the way in which such cultures formed the basis for an imaginary transformation within literary creation. In Chapter 6, I situate a vision of Gertrude's life as a garment within discourses of materiality and temporality; the way that processes of imagination are connected to material culture becomes evident in textile imagery. The earliest portion of the *botte* that has come down to us (Gotha, Forschungsbibliothek, Chart. B 269) transmits this vision of Gertrude on Easter Monday, in which an imaginary textile translates aspects of temporality onto spatial coordinates; both past and future collapse into the presence of a visionary garment. An imaginary collective visibility is evoked in performative ways and harks back to late medieval social practices in which crafting a textile and saying or writing a prayer were part of one spiritual act. So-called craft-prayers, while popular in the German South-West in the fifteenth century, built upon older textile traditions especially in female monasteries, evidence of which can be seen in the numerous textile visions recounted in the texts from Helfta. Surviving textiles from Gertrude's lifetime suggest close connections between the material and the mystical which together formed the ground for the visions' figurative language. Fabricating textiles and composing texts come full circle in a material culture where the salvific word is both embodied in the book and ever fluid in the reader's imagination.

ONE

THE HELFTA SCRIPTORIUM

This chapter addresses the late thirteenth- and early fourteenth-century writing culture at the convent of Helfta and its implications for the ideas about how divine matters are communicated that are contained in the resulting texts. The 'Helfta phenomenon' is marked by an intense period of written production towards the end of the thirteenth century, which led to the emergence of some of the most popular mystical texts in the Western tradition: *The Flowing Light of the Godhead*, the *Liber specialis gratiae*, and the *Legatus divinae pietatis*. Although no autographs of these texts have survived – unless they remain undiscovered – we can be certain that the mystical texts attributed to the Helfta nuns were composed in collective settings, mostly at the convent of Helfta itself. Discussions of collective authorship and gendered writing can lead to a new understanding of the crossover of textual transmission and the social practices of writing and reading, using the production of writings at Helfta and the text material related to Gertrude of Helfta's life, in particular the Latin and German traditions, as examples for wider phenomena of scribal culture in the Middle Ages.

The concept of medieval authorship has been critically discussed and constantly reviewed, ever since Alastair Minnis's work on *auctor* and *auctoritas*.[1] In addition, in the past thirty years feminist studies have unearthed cases of female authorship that had been ignored or dismissed in scholarship.[2] With the case of Helfta, we can further develop the notion of medieval authorial writings by highlighting the inherently collective nature of monastic text production.

The collaborative nature of the texts produced in Helfta was not necessitated by a want for authority, but rather was fostered by a vibrant intellectual community. This observation holds true also for the German redactions of the *Legatus,* which represent the continuation of the kinds of collaborative and editorial processes that produced the Latin versions of the *Legatus* in the first place.

The ensuing exploration of manuscripts – including ones recently discovered – relating to the Helfta scriptorium marks an intervention in the debate on medieval authorship, by highlighting the specifically collective and intergenerational nature of Helfta's writing culture. The historical and predominantly chronological overview of the literary activities at Helfta is followed by the analysis of collective writing scenarios and coexisting alternative text versions, before I finally turn to the issue of gendered writing. I argue that collaborative writing fostered a sense of community and offered a creative outlet for the nuns' spiritual engagement with the intellectual input they received by reading scholastic works and the Scriptures, celebrating the liturgy, and being involved in other daily practices such as contemplation as well as producing images and objects.

THE CONVENT'S WRITING CULTURE

Gertrude of Helfta, commonly called Gertrude the Great, lived during the second half of the thirteenth century (c. 1256–1301). She stands in close connection with two other female mystics of her time, namely Mechthild of Hackeborn (d. 1299) and Mechthild of Magdeburg (d. 1280/90).[3] Mechthild of Magdeburg, who entered the convent of Helfta late in her life, joined a community deeply engaged in writing, where Gertrude and Mechthild of Hackeborn would later thrive.[4] As Gertrude is the most recent of the three known mystics of Helfta, studying her case comprehensively requires the consideration of the two older Mechthilds and indeed – to the extent this is possible – of the entire community.

In 1229, the convent was founded in Mansfeld in the diocese of Halberstadt by Count Burchard of Mansfeld and his wife, Countess Elisabeth of Schwarzburg. Seven nuns from the convent of St Jacobi in the nearby city of Halberstadt started the community, which in 1234 moved from the Mansfeld residence of Thal-Mansfeld to Rodersdorf. Because of difficulties with the water supply, the nuns moved to Helfta in 1257 (and not in 1258 as has been assumed in scholarship until recently),[5] where they remained until the mid-fourteenth century, when, due to the ravages of war in the region, the convent had to move to outside the city walls of Eisleben (Neu-Helfta).[6]

Only a few documents relating to the history of the convent survive. The convent library of Neu-Helfta – mostly consisting of incunabula, eighteen of which are identified – remains little researched.[7] Cornelia Oefelein, who has begun to study this library, draws attention to a surviving cartulary from 1521.[8] This cartulary, however, is not complete when it comes to documenting the convent's history. Comparing the texts in the cartulary to the historical synopses recorded by the theologian and chronicler Cyriacus Spangenberg (1528–1604), Oefelein is able to show that Spangenberg had access to a Latin convent chronicle and to other historical documents, all of which are lost today.[9] The extant cartulary certainly draws from this non-extant convent chronicle as does an anonymous historical preamble to the 1503 imprint of the *Liber specialis gratiae* (which deals with the life and revelations of Mechthild of Hackeborn).[10] A third reference tells us about a convent chronicle that was produced in Helfta, as Oefelein demonstrates: in a letter dated to 10 January 1451, Abbess Sophia of Stolberg (1409–1459/63) reported to the mother convent St Jacobi in Halberstadt about the convent's history using information 'from our chronicle' (*ex nostra cronica*).[11] That the sisters produced a chronicle – when exactly, and under whose supervision, is not known – means that they had the skill, knowledge, and motivation to engage in a historiographical project which would also give them a sense of collective identity. This sense of belonging expanded over generations, if we may assume that the chronicle was written before the governance of Sophia of Stolberg. It becomes clear that the sisters of Helfta were active and self-conscious writers.

A convent chronicle helps to situate a community in history, to understand its place in the diocese, and to explain and confirm spiritual affiliations to other convents. In this regard Helfta, though a Cistercian foundation, was never firmly incorporated into the order.[12] The nuns followed the Benedictine rule and by the end of the fifteenth century took part in the Benedictine reform movement of Bursfelde.[13] By the early fourteenth century, Helfta had become part of an interregional prayer community initiated by the Benedictine convent of St Peter in Erfurt.[14] The approbation of the *Legatus divinae pietatis* – transmitted in some *Legatus* manuscripts – certainly attests to important connections to Dominican and Franciscan readers, namely to the Erfurt-based Dominican hagiographer Dietrich of Apolda (d. 1302).[15] Nonetheless, the Cistercian Order remained a point of reference for the nuns.[16] At the same time, close ties to the Dominicans of the city of Halle were maintained.[17] These affiliations and contacts tell us about the nuns' elaborate network outside their own convent walls; they also illustrate how in the Middle Ages belonging to one order or another was not as strictly regulated as we might imagine.[18] Female convents especially seem to have enjoyed a relative freedom in adapting statutes to their needs.[19] Since Cistercians understood themselves as a reformed branch of the Benedictine Order, there was more flexibility when it came to the incorporation in the Order as Eva Schlotheuber has shown in the case of the female convent Heilig-Kreuz near Braunschweig.[20] For the

Helfta nuns, the possibility of choosing one constitution over another at different times and hence remaining somewhat flexible was more than a matter of spirituality: it meant a relative independence from governance by the Order – as a bishop's foundation, it was subject to diocesan control – and allowed for strategically motivated alliances.

The convent was economically successful from its beginning, and this contributed to its geopolitical strength. Early on, the Counts of Mansfeld and other noble families of the region such as the families of Hackeborn, Querfurt, and Schraplau, had donated land to the convent. In exchange, girls of the aforementioned families would receive tuition from the convent's nuns. These family ties formed a somewhat closed network, as the vast majority of the abbesses (15 out of 18) were actually family members of the regional nobility.[21] One of these abbesses stands out, because it is when she is in office that we can observe the short but intense production of mystical texts in Helfta: Gertrude of Hackeborn (d. 1292), who was abbess from 1251 to 1292.

Gertrude of Hackeborn and her younger sister Mechthild had entered the convent as young children when it was located in Rodersdorf. It was under Gertrude's governance that the convent moved to Helfta, then commonly called Helpede. They saw the convent grow, but it was not until the older of the Hackeborn siblings took over the leadership of the convent that a time of consolidation and thriving was established.[22] This new era came hand in hand with increased religiously motivated literary activities. In Book VI of the *Liber*, Gertrude of Hackeborn's investment in education is portrayed as a project from which the entire community profited: new books were acquired and the sisters were encouraged to copy books. Gertrude's main reason for this attention to learning and writing was that the sisters should maintain a thorough understanding of the Scriptures which would inform their devotional practice, principally in reciting the liturgy.[23] Similarly, in the *Legatus*, Gertrude of Helfta is depicted as 'collecting and writing down everything which she thought might sometime be of use to anyone,' and 'where she knew there was a special shortage of the sacred books, she willingly did what she could to get hold of the necessary copies, so as to win everyone for Christ.'[24] Abbess and nuns invested together in the acquisition and transmission of knowledge. Repeated references to wax tablets and styli attest to a sophisticated and confident writing culture.[25]

In addition to these text-internal references to the nuns' book management, further sources provide us with important historical evidence for manuscript production and an autonomous literary workflow in Helfta. Two daughters of Count Hermann II of Mansfeld are attested to have been active in what could be described as the convent's scriptorium at the time of Gertrude of Hackeborn's governance. These were, as the 1503 preamble to the *Liber* imprint has it, Sophia, 'a good scribe who wrote many good and useful books for the convent,' and Elisabeth, 'a good artist (*Maler*) who with her drawings (*Malen*) eagerly adorned the books and other things belonging to the divine service.'[26] Here we have historiographical evidence for a – if not an architecturally defined, then still managerially – well-organised scriptorium at Helfta, where the tasks were divided and where sisters collaborated on various multimedia projects. When reading the mystical texts that were produced or completed at Helfta, we ought not to understate this institutional framework which enabled their recording and/or compiling. The reality of Helfta's book management could even influence the recorded visions more profoundly; for example, one of Gertrude of Helfta's visions is triggered by an image of the cross that she contemplates in a book.[27] Perhaps a book that was produced by the nuns *sur place*? Maybe Elisabeth of Mansfeld was the illuminator? No matter how personal the revelations and lives of some of the sisters appear in the transmitted hagiographic and mystical accounts, these texts came into being in dialogue with material culture and in a collective environment, which had an impact on how they were shaped and transmitted.

One case that differs slightly from the normal circumstance of collective production, is that of Mechthild of Magdeburg. When Mechthild arrived in Helfta in 1270, Gertrude of Hackeborn's intellectual reform was very likely in full swing, meaning at least that Mechthild's engagement in writing fell on fertile soil.[28] Where exactly Mechthild of Magdeburg had come from, what she had done before, we do not know for certain. Despite many narratives about Mechthild's life before Helfta, some of which are more plausible than others, there are near to no historical traces that would furnish additional details of her former life. All biographical details are drawn from her own work *The Flowing Light of the Godhead*. Even whether she actually lived in Magdeburg or not remains contested.[29] What we do know is that Mechthild did not come empty-handed to Helfta; she brought a manuscript of her own writings to the convent. The first six books (out of seven) of the so-called *Flowing Light of the Godhead*, originally composed in what would have been Mechthild's tongue (i.e. Middle Low/Central German), had been written before Mechthild's entrance to Helfta.[30] The surviving primary copies (both German and Latin) are organised into books and chapters according to scholastic ordering principles; but it is impossible to establish at what stage of the transmission the ordering of the material or even the rubrication in the manuscripts took place.[31] There are attempts to extrapolate a writing pattern from the *Flowing Light*, which would suggest that Mechthild wrote and disseminated her text in instalments, but other than literary observations in the text itself there is no evidence for such a staggered and methodical publication process.[32] While the later Latin *Lux divinitatis* is not directly based on the extant *Flowing Light*, there is evidence that it is indeed a translation of a version of Mechthild's text.[33] The order in which the different versions came into being is the following: Mechthild's Middle Low/Central German text was translated into Latin at the end of the thirteenth century (the Latin *Lux divinitatis* was later translated into the Alemannic dialect of Middle High German);[34] then in 1345, the Middle Low/Central German text was translated into Middle High German (Einsiedeln manuscript, and other manuscripts with excerpts only).[35] The final evidence for a Middle Low/Central German version has come to us with the recent discovery of a manuscript fragment in Moscow, whose dating from around 1290 places it very close to Mechthild's alleged autograph.[36] Although we cannot be absolutely certain, it is very likely that the first six books of the *Flowing Light* were written by Mechthild as a single author (certainly with the encouragement of others and in intellectual exchange with Dominicans)[37] while the last book was the product of a collective effort, a communal project fostered by the Helfta nuns.[38]

Indeed, the seventh book of the *Flowing Light* differs from the preceding books in both style and content;[39] its structure is influenced by the daily office and the liturgical year. Monastic elements were very likely added by an unnamed scribe, in scholarship referred to as Sister N (d. after 1301), who would continue to play a key role in Helfta's 'mystical scriptorium.'[40] A newly discovered manuscript (Leipzig, Universitätsbibliothek, Ms 827) which emphasises the collective nature of the genesis of the *Legatus*, further highlights the scribal and editorial responsibilities of Sister N.[41] As the oldest known *Legatus* manuscript that has come down to us, Leipzig, Universitätsbibliothek, Ms 827, unlocks a new set of questions concerning the Helfta scriptorium.

Kurt Ruh argues that Sister N was also responsible for the noting down of some of Mechthild of Hackeborn's revelations. Together with Gertrude of Helfta, she wrote down those visions that Mechthild did not record herself. Until the age of 50, Mechthild would keep her visions private; then bedridden due to bodily afflictions, in rapture, and unaware of her physical environment, she started to voice what she saw. Should we believe the story of the genesis of the text presented in the resulting work – the *Liber specialis gratiae*, which they were encouraged to write by their new abbess Sophia of Querfurt-Mansfeld (d. after 1303, abbess 1292–1298) – Mechthild's fellow sisters started to record the visions they heard from her directly.[42] This enterprise lasted seven years without Mechthild realising that Gertrude of Helfta and other nuns had been active in writing. It is commonly assumed that Mechthild was able to influence the editing of the final *Liber*. Mechthild had served the convent as a *magistra* and *cantrix*, that is, she was in charge of education, and she led the divine office. The biographical details drawn from the Helfta writings suggest that, in 1261, the five-year-old Gertrude of Helfta was put into her care.[43]

Gertrude's family background is unknown, and everything we know about her person or education is derived from the visionary hagiography originating from Helfta.[44] Gertrude of Helfta, who together with Sister N compiled Mechthild's visions into what forms the *Liber*, stands herself at the centre of the *Legatus divinae pietatis*. This third work from Helfta is mainly concerned with the mystical life of this one nun, Gertrude of Helfta, in relation to the community, and it presents, again, a text produced collectively in different stages.

The content of the *Legatus* may be described as visionary hagiography, which in parts is autobiographical. It comprises five extensive books composed in Latin, only the second book of which presents itself as being written by Gertrude; it is narrated from a first-person perspective. It is very likely that Sister N was the main force behind the compilation of the *Legatus*: Ruh points out that Books III–V, mainly recounting Gertrude's visions, are different in style from Book II, which in his opinion authentically represents Gertrude's spirituality. In Book I, Sister N proves her skills as a hagiographer, and the style in all the visionary books except Book II is identical to Mechthild of Hackeborn's *Liber*. It is plausible to deduce that the *Liber* and the *Legatus* were edited by the same person (Sister N). The German term 'Werkgeschichte', used by Ruh to describe this writing situation, aims to portray the deliberate 'composition' of these 'works' as a carefully supervised enterprise.[45] Yet, even if the editorial work cannot be categorically attributed to Sister N, it would not be surprising that the hagiographic and pastoral parts of the *Legatus* reverberate with Mechthild of Hackeborn's *Liber* since both emerged in the same context and were hence concerned with similar issues.[46] Also, that Book II testifies to Gertrude's individual spirituality, whereas the rest are more communally orientated, may not necessarily hint at a single authorship in this context. In fact, Gertrude is never explicitly named as the author. While the first-person perspective alone cannot be taken as a guarantee of single authorship, especially not in the case of Helfta where several nuns were active in the composition of Latin writings, the style of Book II of the *Legatus* is distinct from the rest,[47] which in turn suggests that the multilayered and collective writing process of the *Legatus* allowed Gertrude's voice to come through nevertheless.

It is uncertain, whether Gertrude authored the *Exercitia Spiritualia* conventionally attributed to her, although it is possible. The Carthusian John of Landsberg printed these ever popular prayers and chants alongside his 1536 edition of the *Legatus* without indicating any source that would justify Gertrude's authorship or even its affiliation to Helfta.[48] As John is usually meticulous in naming his sources for the *Legatus*, he leaves room for doubt about the genesis of the *Exercitia*.[49] The *Spiritual Exercises* were certainly inspired by the *Legatus* and other writings from Helfta, but since there is no textual tradition to refer to, other than Landsberg's edition, claiming Gertrude's authorship is hypothetical.[50] Ruh, however, has no doubts about Gertrude's authorship of the *Exercises* because, he argues, they are similar in style to Book II of the

Legatus, for which he also does not question single authorship.[51] Still, how difficult would it have been for John of Landsberg, or someone before him, to have taken a narrated prayer from Book II and changed it into a spiritual exercise, that is into a prayer in an appellative mode? Such transformations occurring in the transmission processes of hagiographic texts are common,[52] and to apply a modern concept of authorship to this phenomenon somewhat ignores creative forms of medieval text reception. To pin down a single author for any text produced in a pre-modern setting is not only difficult; it also often shifts the focus to the notion of an individual creator, which in many cases is ahistorical.

Exploration of Helfta's writing culture shows that the nuns, around 1300, consciously regarded themselves as historiographers and hagiographers in the service of their community. This self-understanding was framed by the intellectual reform begun by Gertrude of Hackeborn and continued by Sophia of Querfurt-Mansfeld, and was motivated by the primary objective of ensuring profound spiritual knowledge among the nuns. The sisters' choice of writing in Latin is not surprising then, given that all liturgical and most devotional readings they engaged with would have been in Latin. The writing, copying, and embellishing of books was regarded as a collective activity. The distribution and organisation of tasks facilitated long-term and large-scale writing projects at Helfta.

REVISITED WRITING SCENARIOS

From the many self-reflective references in the *Legatus* we know a relatively large amount about how it was written and edited. External factors are harder to determine but the transmission of manuscript itself offers supplementary clues as to how the *Legatus* came into being. The following investigation combines these two approaches, internal (text-based) and external (manuscript transmission), in order to reassess the production of writing at Helfta. I show that Gertrude and her coauthor Sister N were aware of complex writing processes and that the coexistence of alternative versions of the *Legatus* may be understood as evidence for these processes, in which text material was not produced in a straightforward fashion, but rather constantly revised, edited, and rearranged.

The *Legatus* can be described as 'a conglomeration of texts'.[53] According to the narrative expounded in the prologue of the *Legatus*, it was produced in different stages. Book II would have been written before 1289, while Books III–V and Book I were composed during a period starting no later than 1292 and continuing up to Gertrude of Helfta's death in 1301.[54] Like Mechthild of Magdeburg's *Flowing Light* and Mechthild of Hackeborn's *Liber*, the *Legatus* is indebted to the bridal mysticism of Bernard of Clairvaux, and follows a predominantly liturgical structure that characterises all of the writings from Helfta (apart from the *Flowing Light*'s first six books).[55] In Helfta, we can observe an intricately woven net of interdependencies spanning all three mystics and beyond: genealogical links (the Hackeborn siblings; that Mechthild of Magdeburg and Gertrude of Helfta are related to the Hackeborns cannot be ruled out either); the confident handling of Latin and vernacular (possible translation processes from the visions' presumably vernacular oral report to its recording);[56] the cross-pollination of visions (for example, when one nun figures in another's vision or when visions of different nuns have clear parallels); and compellingly entangled writing scenarios (with sisters editing and writing for themselves and for one another).

The transmission history of the Helfta texts, as reconstructed from the manuscripts that have come down to us, continues this tradition of connected minds, since the *Liber* and the *Legatus* were often copied together as early as the fourteenth century. However, the transmission of both the *Liber* and the *Legatus* is detached from that of the *Lux divinitatis* or the vernacular *Flowing Light of the Godhead*. Whether this circumstance means that 'Mechthild of Magdeburg never belonged to the 'official' corpus of revelations that originated at Helfta in either German or Latin,'[57] is a question that remains hard to answer. Nevertheless, the transmission history underlines the intricate relationship between text production, dissemination, and reception. In the light of recent discoveries of new manuscript material related to Helfta, the generally assumed scenario of how the *Legatus* came into being needs to be redressed. The picture we have of the local text production and its subsequent tradition is also complicated through the recent discovery of an alternative edition of the *Legatus*, commonly called the *Leipzig Legatus*.

Before we turn to the *Leipzig Legatus*, a few words about the manuscript situation will help to situate it within the transmission history of the *Legatus* at large. When the last scholarly edition of the *Legatus* was published in the latter half of the twentieth century (1968–1986), the editors – the Benedictine brothers of Solesmes – considered five manuscripts in total. Since then, many more text witnesses have been discovered.[58] Judging from the transmission known to us today, there are three discernible centres where the *Legatus* was read and in some cases also copied (see Map 2): Erfurt, the Middle Rhine area, and Swabia. In all these regional centres, the Carthusians were at the forefront when it came to the dissemination and reception of Gertrude's *Legatus*. Strikingly, all of the Latin text witnesses originate from male convents. What has come down to us is certainly only a fragment of the *Legatus'* actual dissemination. The library catalogue of the Erfurt Charterhouse, for example, refers to a complete copy of the *Legatus* and to a series of manuscripts that contained excerpts from it, most of which are not extant today.[59]

There is one newly discovered manuscript that stands out from the rest: Leipzig, Universitätsbibliothek, Ms 827, which contains a hitherto unknown version of the *Legatus*, including a special prologue. Produced in the first quarter of the fourteenth century, this 'special' *Legatus* – also named the 'Leipzig Special Edition' after its place of preservation by Balázs Nemes and Almuth Märker (*Leipziger Sonderausgabe*, here: *Leipzig Legatus*) – dates from Gertrude's lifetime or very shortly thereafter. Nemes and Märker name the Benedictine convent Pegau (only 43 miles from Helfta) as the manuscript's likely place of origin.[60] This proposition is sound not only because the codex was formerly held at the Benedictine Abbey of Pegau, but also because the Benedictine monks in Erfurt had created a link between Helfta and the double monastery in Pegau through their prayer community network.[61] This network, established in the first quarter of the fourteenth century, most likely facilitated the dissemination of the *Legatus*.[62] Leipzig, Universitätsbibliothek, Ms 827, includes an alternative prologue to the *Legatus*, different from that which is transmitted in other, younger, text witnesses; it was probably compiled by so-called Sister N of Helfta. The narrator of the *Leipzig Legatus* specifies that she is the same scribe who was active in collecting and coauthoring Gertrude's visions; thus she implicitly identifies herself as Sister N. Although the term she uses, the Latin *conscribere*, usually describes a copying activity, Sister N was certainly not simply a copyist. Sister N held the editorial position and the power inherent therein; she not only comments and selects, but also has the final say in the form of the finished book.[63] A comparison between the two different versions highlights the technical detail with which the *Legatus* was compiled and, on a more theoretical level, showcases the collective genesis of texts in the Helfta scriptorium.

The writing scenario in which the text was produced is invoked in both the 'standard' *Legatus* and the *Leipzig Legatus*. In the prologue to Book I of the 'standard' *Legatus*, we hear that 'one part [was] written down eight years after her [Gertrude's] reception of grace, and the second part [was] completed about twenty years later.' The first-person voice in this account tells us that Gertrude does not want anyone to see what is written 'in this little book', that is, the aforementioned second part. Gertrude dedicates the first book to the Lord in humble devotion. Her repeated prayer, begging to be allowed to stop writing the second book, is answered by God who commands it to be written: 'I will encourage the scribe and support her faithfully; and that which is mine I will preserve unsullied.' This incident happens one night 'while the second part was being written to the great delight of God's will'. Gertrude recognises that 'it would please the Lord to bind both parts together': upon her enquiry, God lets her know how to compile the different parts, 'after He had declared Himself to distinguish the different parts by different titles, as noted before'. The work is divided into five books for 'the readers' estimation and comprehension' (*Legatus* I, 1).[64]

While it seems undoubtedly to be Gertrude who in the narrated world receives these messages from God, the specification that she was also compiling her own work seems to suggest that she assisted Sister N in putting the five books together. The narrator's voice in the prologue is not that of Gertrude, yet the visions and revelations are positively attributed to Gertrude. The 'standard' *Legatus* remains ambiguous in this point of editorial work; but it is very likely that we hear Sister N's voice in the following passage:

> I have therefore recorded in the margin what my simple wit and inexperienced understanding could recall on the spur of the moment, in the hope that if anyone of keen wit and experienced understanding should come across it, he would be able to cite far more credible and appropriate witnesses.[65]

While the writing scenario is usually depicted from Gertrude's perspective, the text itself initially does not clearly identify who compiled it. At numerous instances throughout the *Legatus*, chiefly in Books III–V, reference is made to an anonymous sister who takes part in the writing process and who even reflects on her role as scribe.[66] Considering this deeply involved editor, it may well be that it is not Gertrude who receives the instructions from God about how to compile the material, but that the text production scenario refers – if not entirely, then partly – to Sister N. She heavily edited whatever Gertrude told her or had passed to her in writing; for example, Sister N mentions the bypassing of certain aspects 'for the sake of brevity' (*Legatus* V, 1), or, in another instance she fears that a longer account might weary the reader (IV, 27).[67] As Nemes notes, '[t]he material selected is [...] what she – not Gertrude – considers useful'.[68] Weaving into the *Legatus* the testimony of an eyewitness as well as quotations from the Bible and the Church Fathers, Sister N enhances the authorial character of the *Legatus* with important theologically invested strategies of justification. By providing an eyewitness account and buttressing the meaning of Gertrude's visions with theological arguments, the text participates in certain hagiographic discourses which depict the production of the text as being part of the divine grace shared with the saint. This aspect of a saintly writing is illustrated when, following a vision of the Heart of Jesus, Gertrude recognises that 'it pleases the Lord that everything should be written down for the benefit of all' (*Legatus* III, 30). In this way, the scribal work of Sister N is indirectly authorised through the same authoritative instance from which Gertrude receives her visions.[69] She is a coauthor. These scattered indications about the text production convey a complex coming into being of the *Legatus*, one that involved several writers at different times. Nevertheless, we get the sense of one dominating hand, that of Sister N.

The hypothesis of an active editor for the *Legatus* is corroborated by specifications about the text production made in the newly discovered

Leipzig Legatus. The text transmitted in the Leipzig manuscript has a different structure to that of the hitherto known *Legatus* and it also lacks parts, such as the list of approvers, the *commendatio*. It furthermore offers a relatively high proportion of new material: many visions that the 'standard' *Legatus* does not contain.[70] In the *Leipzig Legatus'* prologue, we get important details about the production of the text: 'This book is divided into three parts, the first of which was written by she who was worthy enough to receive it from the giver of all grace with her own hands, eight years after she had received the grace on Maundy Thursday' (Leipzig Ms 827, fol. 25v).[71] The *Legatus*, normally divided into five books, is here described as consisting of three parts; part one, written by Gertrude herself, corresponds to Book II of the 'standard' *Legatus*. The anonymous author of the prologue continues to explain the production of the other parts: 'the Lord advised her to choose one person to whom she should uncover her secrets in order to increase God's praise' (Leipzig Ms 827, fol. 26r).[72] Forty days later, after resistance and hesitation, Gertrude 'at an occasion produced by God, uncovered some things to me – because only I was present with her'; but Gertrude's speech on this occasion is hardly comprehensible, and she trembles violently with her whole body, 'making it obvious to anyone who saw her that she revealed these things against her own human will' (Leipzig Ms 827, fol. 26r).[73] This instance is described as the beginning of a 'long period of time' in which Gertrude's secrets are recorded by the confidential sister and author of the current prologue. When the abbess finds out about this collaboration, Gertrude is taken by a strong fever, again interpreted as a sign of her discomfort with the recording of her 'secrets'. The anonymous scribe and editor assures the reader that she too has since shared the suffering.[74] Her own writing is therefore portrayed in a similar light to Gertrude's 'received grace' or rather, it is the writing which is precarious and which makes both sisters uncomfortable. At the same time, the expressed awareness as writers gives us important insights concerning the historical reconstruction of writing processes at Helfta.

The information given about the third part in the *Leipzig Legatus*, now called the third booklet (*libellum*), is very precise as it specifies both the social situation in the convent as well as concrete codicological information about the manuscript production. Here we learn that the third booklet consists of 'the final five quires of four bifolios each' (Leipzig Ms 827, fol. 26v).[75] We are also told that Abbess Gertrude (of Hackeborn) suffers from a 'severe ailment', which means that the writing project cannot be supported any longer. This motivates the anonymous scribe to find a 'worthy end approved by several people' to that 'fine book that I love so much' (Leipzig Ms 827, fol. 26v–27r).[76] At this point, it becomes obvious that the scribe is actively invested in the project. So as not to disturb the dying abbess, the book is finished secretly and discreetly. The scribe and editor affirms that the abbess herself had entrusted this book to her and that it should finally be handed over to God; Gertrude (of Helfta) and her editor agree on this procedure. The prologue ends in the tone of a typical colophon, with the scribe dedicating the book to the divine heart as long as Gertrude lives – literally until her death – but guarding it and hoping that she should be rewarded for all the troubles she suffered, which were 'as many as there are letters in this book' (Leipzig Ms 827, fol. 27r–v).[77]

These details about the completion of the book give us a glimpse of literary production at Helfta. Gertrude's scribe in the *Leipzig Legatus*, which is so striking for its technical tone, advances to the position of being a 'scribal agent' who is coauthoring and managing the work. She is most likely the same anonymous sister, who in scholarship about the 'standard' *Legatus* is generally called Sister N. While the enterprise of writing down Gertrude's visions seems precarious, the two sisters – Gertrude herself and her confidential scribe/editor – rely on the support of Gertrude the abbess. The discomfort they still experience does not just satisfy the humility topos, but it is very likely an honest uneasiness; in the convent context, any individual projects would need the approval of the community. We should therefore not mistake the expressed nervousness as a purely rhetorical anxiety; obedience sworn to the abbess was taken very seriously in the monastic community.[78] Why then did they keep it a secret? Would we not expect that the Helfta nuns, who were so familiar with writing projects, stand united behind this one too? Perhaps, because two other sisters had already been gifted with visions, Gertrude's case would have needed considerable justification? However, the depiction of the abbess's feebleness as the reason why this project had to be kept secret makes more sense, since she would not have been in a viable position to defend it.[79] Also, postponing the sharing of the book until after Gertrude of Helfta's death meant that any direct confrontation or questioning could be avoided.

The manuscript transmission mirrors the complex production scenario that is so vividly painted in the texts. Observations about the structures of the two *Legatus* versions reveal that during the production process of the *Legatus*, text material was already not uniform and consistent. The *Leipzig Legatus* is divided into different production stages: the first refers to Gertrude's book itself, the second to the collaboration between Gertrude and her scribe/editor, and the third to the completion by the scribe/coauthor. Although one is inclined to align the five books of the 'standard' *Legatus* to these three parts/writing stages, i.e. part one equals Book II, part two equals Books III–V, and part three equals Book I, the actual make-up of the Leipzig manuscript reveals that such alignment is impossible. Not only are additional passages included, but passages known to us from the 'standard' *Legatus* do not follow the same order. Two conclusions could be drawn from the comparison between the two different Latin versions: either the text transmitted in the Leipzig manuscript relies on an early text of the *Legatus* which was then reworked into the version of the 'standard' *Legatus* (which was then more widely disseminated); or both versions – the 'standard' *Legatus* and the *Leipzig Legatus* – existed side-by-side. While these two conclusions are not mutually exclusive, preference has been given to the first one on the basis that the Leipzig manuscript is older than all other manuscripts transmitting the *Legatus*.[80]

Be that as it may, this analysis leads us to reconsider the prevalent image of the coming into being of the *Legatus* as it could have occurred in Helfta. The writing scenario of the *Legatus* is considerably better known with the Leipzig manuscript filling in important gaps in our knowledge of its production, even telling us about the physical composition of the text in separate quires. Its discovery demonstrates how our view of the actual text production is limited by the sources that are available to us, and how the slightest addition of new material may change our assumptions. Rather than assuming – as has hitherto often been the case – that inconsistencies in the transmission of the *Legatus* go back to a sense of immediacy created through the direct dictation of the visionary to her scribe, we can now see that the writing at Helfta occurred in a much more complex, deliberate, and self-reflective fashion. Now that there is textual evidence for the editorial and authorial work of Sister N, who explicitly speaks of rearranging and rewriting, we may infer that we have several distinct versions of the *Legatus*, and, most importantly, awareness of these different versions during the earliest writing process. With this newly gained knowledge, it is now possible to reconsider the nature of collective authorship in Helfta, including the question of female authorship.

WOMEN WRITING COLLECTIVELY

A point of contention in scholarship has been how to assess authorship in the cases of Helfta mysticism.[81] This can be done from different angles – including a theological perspective (for example, highlighting the importance of God as author and the mystic as mediator), transmission history (for example, examining the earliest manuscripts for scribal clues), and literary devices (for example, considering topoi of authority and other rhetorical conventions).[82] Questions of gender complicate the debate about authorship for several reasons, one of which is the fact that formulations of male approbation can be found alongside the transmission of the presented texts (most often prepending the book proper). Leaving the specific yet formulaic approbations aside, each of the three mystical texts that were produced or edited in Helfta – the *Flowing Light*, the *Liber*, and the *Legatus* – understands itself to be a written work, a book;[83] and they all to some extent tell the story of (or rather a story about) their genesis. On the texts' surface God appears to be the author, the visionary is a 'medium or instrument'.[84] Yet, hints about the actual writing processes allow us to discern literary activities that could be counted as authorship, were we to apply a broad definition of the term.[85]

One central purpose of this book is to establish the importance of collective writing in the ensuing transmission history of the *Legatus*, and to explore the spiritual meaning of collective work embedded in the vernacular redactions. The *Legatus* was so popular among generations of communities, I argue, because the story of its collective and communal writing in Helfta is palpable in the text. This intervention thus concerns debates about authorship, including gendered authorship since a female form of writing has repeatedly been discussed specifically for the writings of Helfta. In the following examination I study the problem of authorship by critically questioning the historical situation of Helfta's writing culture with discursive issues on gendered writing, arguing that collective authorship springs from the reality of communal life and that, as such, it impacts the content of a text and how it is written less than a gender-specific style does. In other words: communal authorship is not an inherently gendered phenomenon.

While each of the Helfta texts has an individual woman at the centre of its interest, the texts' production as well as reception are conceived of as collective.[86] Writing in Helfta was always communal. That the nuns supported each other in recording and editing visions becomes obvious in the text production of Mechthild of Hackeborn's *Liber* and Gertrude of Helfta's *Legatus*; and yet, there seems to have been tension and uneasiness about the recording of visions. For Sister N, who compiles, edits, and coauthors the *Legatus*, this is not simply a rhetorical device to confirm her humility but a real concern: she needs the approval of the abbess because writing could be a breach of obedience. The collective character of sharing visions therefore plays out on different planes: it begins with Gertrude seeking confidentiality – this step, too, is portrayed as submission to God's will, that is, obedience – and goes on to both Gertrude and Sister N being nervous about the knowledge of their common writing project among other sisters. The justification of their writing is put into terms of emotional discomfort as if to demonstrate their unwillingness to keep it secret from the community while exposing it as a necessary consequence of obedience. They are extremely concerned with reactions within the community, which may explain why the individual mystic recruits an accomplice: not having a single author mitigates any anticipated negative effects.

The fact that individual experiences could hardly ever be proven meant that anyone – regardless of their gender – who was involved in sharing mystical experiences needed to be sure they were standing on solid ground. The resulting claims of authority in mystical texts mean that the question of authorship is even more complicated than in other literary genres.[87] Of the literature emerging from clerical and monastic scriptoria, mystical texts were potentially the most difficult to integrate into any canonical corpus. If the mystical outlook of a text largely determines the discourse on authority presented in it, what place does gender hold in a discussion of authority? The question arising for Helfta's writing projects is then: to what extent are textual strategies of authorisation determined by gender-specific qualities?

The kind of concern that Helfta mystics and their helpers express has often been interpreted as a distinctly female way of writing, assuming that women writers had to justify their literary agency.[88] While acknowledging the significance of authorial justification, I want to propose a different explanation for the communal writing culture at Helfta – my purpose is rather to show that religious women involved in text production opted for collective work environments because of the fundamentally collaborative nature of their spiritual lives, and that this was not an exclusively female experience.[89]

In order to understand what a collective writing culture means for questions of authority, our terminology needs to be scrutinised first. In research on medieval authorship, the disparity between historical reality and modern terminology becomes evident as the terms 'author' and 'authorship' are borrowed from analytical studies on modern texts, while medieval textuality is inherently more intricate due to theoretically different concepts of authority and the complexities of the transmission of texts. Attention has been drawn to the inadequacy of a classical 'author-work paradigm' when dealing with premodern textuality.[90] In this regard, Michel Foucault's definition of authority, more distanced – but not absolutely detached – from a historical individual and defined through conventions in textual discourses, is valuable since it allows a certain flexibility in understanding authorship other than in the strict sense of an individual creator.[91] The concept of an 'aura of personal-bibliographical "auctoritas"', first introduced by Ursula Peters, stands in this tradition of a discursive understanding of authorship and acknowledges characteristics of modern authorship for medieval texts without confining them to modern implications about single authors.[92] Major differences of opinion between scholars dealing with historical authorship – the two extremes being taking biographical hints at face value, or understanding any authorial voice as a literary construct – have increasingly been smoothed out by refining our understanding of authorship and authority.[93] Sara S. Poor, for instance, in her work on Mechthild of Magdeburg's *Flowing Light of Godhead*, lays out why a 'single-author mentality' misses the point when talking about the *Flowing Light* and similar bodies of texts originating from a female context, showing how many presuppositions about female authorship are more broadly due to modern misconceptions of medieval literacy.[94]

One of these misconceptions concerns language itself, where Latin is thought of as learned and male, in contrast to the supposedly unlearned register of the vernacular. Yet medieval scholars like Meister Eckhart used the vernacular with confidence and deliberation. The opposite is also true: Mechthild of Hackeborn and Gertrude of Helfta chose to have their visions written in Latin in accordance to the convent's tradition of writing in the 'Church's language'. In both cases – whether Latin or the vernacular was preferred – the choice of language had theological implications.[95] Emphasising the 'choice' that some women had – in Poor's terms 'agency' – the stereotype of the unlearned female mystic who does not know Latin and therefore must write in the vernacular, is certainly often constructed to justify this choice (rather than necessitating it).[96]

However, while undoubtedly '[t]he scriptural proscription against women teaching and speaking [...] made writing a more dangerous enterprise for women',[97] linking the problem of authorship to gender, essentially to the female body, as has been attempted in scholarship, is complicated and entails many underlying assumptions about somatic mysticism, and discourses about sexed bodies.[98] A brief overview of the relevant debate elucidates the caveats implicit in linking gender to the act of mystical writing.[99]

Many studies that explore mystical texts through the lens of gendered bodies are influenced by Caroline W. Bynum's idea of gendered mysticism, which draws attention to the bodily nature of late medieval spirituality. Bynum argues that certain elements found in mystical writings concerning or written by women, such as eating and fasting, were not coincidental but are witnesses to female conditions .[100] The idea of gendered mysticism is accompanied by a discursive reasoning according to which images are applied differently by men and women respectively, in order to construct the 'female'; Grace Jantzen, for example, sees gendered mysticism as inherited from the fifth-century theologian Pseudo-Dionysius who bequeathed a 'mysticism of the intellect' to male church officials, thereby perpetuating a 'gendered aspect of mysticism'.[101] Amy Hollywood further develops a critical distinction between women's writings and the writings of men *about* women, in which the key aspect is the body itself and the gendered differences in how to refer to it.[102] Hollywood also emphasises that questions of authorship need to be addressed independently from the actual writing scenarios since mystical texts in particular construct complex male and female relationships.[103] This intervention is crucial as it distinguishes the historical setting from the discursive level. Patricia Dailey adds a poeto-theological aspect to the discussion on discursivity by inquiring into 'how embodiment relates to gendered practices, nuancing the expression of the theological'[104], and speaking of 'embodied poetics'.[105] With Poor's work, attention has been drawn to the manuscript transmission of the texts in question, and only recently have scholars distanced themselves from 'somatising' medieval women authors, focusing on the 'text body' instead.[106]

In the debate on female authorship of mystical texts, dichotomies between Latin versus vernacular, and body versus mind have played major roles. Indeed, strict male–female discourse boundaries can seldom be maintained; historical reality shows intricate networks in writing projects between religious men and women.[107] In monastic writings, we find that there is often a mixed-gender genesis of texts, meaning that male and female identities, constructions, and conceptions of authorship get intertwined.[108] We know many examples of male–female collaborations on mystical texts: for example, Angela of Foligno and her spiritual confidant Brother A.; Christine Ebner and an anonymous collaborator; Henry Suso and Elsbeth Stagel; and Dorothea of Montau and Johannes Marienwerder. Nevertheless, textual constructions of authority play with supposed gender attributions, as Fiona Griffiths and Julie Hotchin have shown.[109] In some cases, interactions between religious men and women had long-lasting effects on the texts they were producing: Jessica Boon, for example, infers from Ruusbroec's reading of Hadewijch that he accepted her 'as a fully equal theologian'; she influenced not only his style and metaphorical expressions but also his theology.[110] As Ruusbroec and other male writers were influenced by women in their use of imagery, so women writers were influenced by male-authored texts, for instance by Bernard of Clairvaux's widely disseminated *Sermons on the Song of Songs*, to name just one important source for mystical writings such as Gertrude of Helfta's *Legatus* and Mechthild of Hackeborn's *Liber*.

To determine clear gender-specific discourses in mystical writings is also problematic because of genuinely complicating theological concepts on the one hand and the transmission histories of the texts in question on the other. The grammatically inherent feminine character of the soul (Lat. *anima*), for example, involves a whole set of feminine attributes such as the virginity of the soul and the pregnancy of the soul, both of which metaphors can be applied to women and men alike. The impact of this kind of grammatically gendered language on theological concepts can be seen with Meister Eckhart and Richard Rolle.[111] The latter uses gendered language and gendered tropes 'but it would appear that gender-specific discourse features throughout the writings in order to feminise both the reader and Rolle's own authorial self in acknowledgement of the soul as conceptually feminine'.[112] However, when it comes to the question of Rolle's ministry to women, '[t]extual evidence is lacking in the English treatises to suggest such a gendered reading'.[113] Claire Elizabeth McIlroy points out that in his work *The Commandment*, 'Rolle appears to have been influenced by both the gender and spiritual maturity of his initial audience, but on the whole the implied audience is not explicitly gendered.'[114] The same is arguably true for Meister Eckhart, despite the fact that many of his German sermons are transmitted in books originating from nunneries as, in his role as a Dominican spiritual supervisor, he frequently preached to nuns. Especially when we accept the transmission of manuscripts as a form of collective writing expanding over time, the collaboration between men and women evinces that gendered writing can sometimes be a misleadingly vague and unhelpful category for questions of textual authority.

Regardless of historical realities and theological concepts, which complicate the question of a gendered writing, it is still debated whether a distinct female style exists that differs from a male one. In these debates, mystical writings originating from female contexts have often been described in terms of somatic and affective mysticism.[115] Yet, sensory images and affective language were not exclusively used by women writers such as Hildegard of Bingen or Marguerite Porete; they are first and foremost found in works authored by men, including Gregory of Nyssa and Bernard of Clairvaux, later also Richard Rolle, as well as the German mystics Henry Suso and Friedrich Sunder. It is for this reason among others that no gender can be definitely attributed to the anonymous author of the *Cloud of Unknowing*. Any mystic faced problems when it came to authorising their writings; what they communicated needed to be legitimised because of a lack of authority when speaking about the divine and their encounter with it. The so-called apophatic discourse, inherited from Pseudo-Dionysian negative theology, is an expression of this circumstance of falling short in communicating divine matters. Formulations that target the insufficiency of language belong to this apophatic discourse; '[m]ale and female mystical writers alike shared the difficulties of grappling with what Porete called "the thing which one cannot say" and all were agreed that appeals to authority, reason or learning were of no assistance.'[116] The complications inherent in discussing gendered authorship and authority in mystical texts highlight the caveats for determining writing scenarios when historical evidence is scarce and when literary conventions play into textual strategies of authorisation.

What does this mean for the mystical texts originating from Helfta? Can we say anything about whether their collective authorship is innately female, and what would that mean? The Helfta texts are special because they emerge in a collaborative context where male hagiographers have little or no place.[117] There was no gendered conflict concerning the mystical authority of the women writers of Helfta.[118] The commendations of male readers, usually clerics, are later additions to the different text witnesses of the *Legatus* and *Liber*. This absence of male hagiographers in the first place underlines the need for the question of gendered writing to be looked at in conjunction with transmission history.[119] This kind of study, which takes the transmission of texts into account, has been conducted for Mechthild of Magdeburg with the conclusion that 'gender matters in some instances of reception while in others it does not'.[120] Yet, gendered authority becomes an evasive concept in the reception history of mystical texts as they were read and copied by both women and men alike.

Whether authorship is meant in the sense of individual agency or in the sense of a discursive aura of authorship in the transmission history, conclusions about historical scenarios can shift on the basis of the sources available to us. This is illustrated in the case of the *Legatus*: now that the coauthorship of Sister

N is consolidated through the Leipzig manuscript, the aspects of 'agency' and 'authority' appear even more communal than they already had before. In general, books in the Middle Ages, no matter what 'secrets' they contained, were rarely objects assigned to one individual – and this is true for both the production and the reception.[121] Writing scenarios were diverse, even in cases where one can determine one single mind behind a writing project.[122] Although Gertrude is undoubtedly not only the protagonist of the *Legatus* but also the initiator of its coming into being, Sister N has an equally important role in the text production because of her 'literary independence', 'autonomous authorial activity', and 'editorial approach to the material'.[123] Sister N's influence certainly had an impact on the content, too, as a facilitator of the communication of visions. In addition to the named and unnamed individuals involved in the writing projects, the institutional frame in which the writing happened was just as important. The intellectual vibrancy in Helfta promoted by Gertrude of Hackeborn made the scriptorium's prolific text production possible. Just like the *Liber*, the *Legatus* is a communal project executed by a collective of writers, regardless of any communal conflicts that might have existed at the time of its production.

Characterising the *Legatus'* text production as collective does not categorically entail a gendered dimension. Granted, the given social context meant that Helfta was a community of women, and social relationships in both the *Liber* and the *Legatus* relate to friendships among women, but whether this female milieu influenced the actual theology found in these texts or not is another issue that cannot be addressed here.[124] When it comes to the actual writing process, however, we get a sense that although Mechthild of Hackeborn and Gertrude of Helfta were close friends, there were tensions between the two sisters in spirit;[125] rivalries between the two can also not be ruled out. This dynamic relationship was shaped by a hierarchical setting as Mechthild was someone Gertrude looked up to within the convent hierarchy as well as personally, while Gertrude of Hackeborn, the abbess, might have acted as some kind of a mediator. With this social background in mind, Gertrude and Sister N's concerns about the actual writing, as laid out in both *Legatus* versions known to us, are more understandable. Indeed, Sister N's uneasiness may have left traces in her report as her prose style is not only distinctive from that attributed to Gertrude (presented in Book II) in that it is 'somewhat labored and not as fluent'; she also inscribes her hesitations into her language by distancing herself from the visions. Alexandra Barratt observes that Sister N 'is always reluctant to state that Gertrude "saw" something and prefers to use more ambiguous expressions such as "it seemed to her" [. . .]. And she likes to nuance her account of Gertrude's visions by using similes (introduced by "as if") rather than direct description and then sometimes further modifying them by phrases such as "as it were".'[126] We may, therefore, understand these reservations not just as rhetorical expressions (for example the humility topos arguably dependent on female authorship) but as consequences of the social context in which the actual writing first took place. The collaborative nature plays out on many levels, that of production as well as that of textual composition and style. This means that the communal context also came to influence the way the *Legatus* was written.

★ ★ ★

To sum up, the Helfta scriptorium teaches us that scribal authority in the Middle Ages did not necessarily stem from a single person but was rooted in a community's intellectual culture. Individuals and their ideas were still emphasised but always in relation to the community. In an atmosphere of women writing collectively, even initially single-author projects would turn into communal projects. Editing, writing, copying, and indeed embellishing manuscripts belonged to one greater endeavour, which was to uphold religious knowledge and an awareness of the community's history. The notion of collective writing as a communal effort is reflected in the texts produced.

In tracing the vernacular reception history of the *Legatus*, the following chapters turn further away from a primary emphasis on individual authority and gendered writing, focusing rather on the historical modes of collective copying, reading, and editing. At first sight the process of translating appears to add a layer of complication to the question of authority. However, in a manuscript culture, texts are prone to change without it necessarily causing a problem of authority. This adaptability included shifts in language. In the course of the transmission history of the *Legatus* – as the next two chapters show – a mediating function of the redactor (as held by Sister N) was readapted and reinterpreted. This shift happens in exciting ways in the German main redaction of the *Legatus*: based on the Latin text, the *botte der götlichen miltekeit* demonstrates 'textual flexibility' in both the rearrangement of the material and its manuscript transmission. The vernacular manuscript transmission opens new avenues for understanding how medieval readers used and adapted Gertrude's life and revelations in different contexts.

TWO

REDACTIONS WITHIN A
DYNAMIC TEXTUALITY

Redactorial activities continued to influence the transmission of the *Legatus*; although the vernacular 'community' of redactors did not live together in a convent nor even necessarily at the same time, the composition of the different texts is as collaborative, iterative, and myriad as the Latin text versions – of which we now know more than one. Having discussed Helfta's writing culture, I now turn to the question of the textual status of the vernacular redactions of the *Legatus*, first revisiting previous research on the *botte* before moving on to discuss new insights into multilingual activities in late medieval female convents, and their interest in copying the *botte*. On the basis of critical observations of texts and sources, I contend that the *Legatus* was rendered into the German *botte* by Carthusian monks in the fourteenth century (the *Trutta*-legend as a redaction by Dominican nuns will be discussed in Chapter 3 where I examine the reform context). In the current chapter, I look at theoretical issues which accompany the study of the *botte* and contextualise the concept of redaction in its literary tradition by referring to medieval ideas about literary activities, especially those developed by Bonaventure (1217–74). With the focus of inquiry on conceptual problems, this exploration is not intended to be exhaustive but rather generative as it invites debates on the status of vernacular redactions. In the latter half of this chapter, I suggest a new approach to the *botte* – inspired by ideas from Material Philology – which highlights the dynamic nature of a manuscript culture. Taking in particular Christopher Baswell's notion of a generative readership into account, I argue that we ought to think of the *botte* as a 'redaction' in the sense of the medieval term, which encompasses improvement, interpretation, and innovation. The term 'redaction' has already been employed to describe the *botte*; investigating the term's meaning for the status of a translation in relation to its Latin model evinces innovative ways to think about vernacular texts in the late Middle Ages highlighting their dynamic textuality.

In the past 20 years of German scholarship, the term *Redaktion* has somewhat fallen out of fashion, with preference being given to the term *Fassung*.[1] Nevertheless, the derived forms of *Redaktor* and *redaktioneller Eingriff* ('redactorial intervention') continue to be used even though they might relate to what is circumscribed as *Fassung*, so the line between the terms remains blurry.[2] German scholars often translate *Fassung* as 'redaction' and *Redaktion* as 'version';[3] while in English scholarship, the technical term 'recension' more accurately captures what the German *Fassung* means.[4] Following the work of Joachim Bumke,[5] scholars in the early 2000s discussed different editorial conceptions, attempting to distinguish a redaction, in the sense of any reworked text material, from a version, which implies a hierarchical structure between text witnesses.[6] Editorial techniques were revisited since questions of interdependencies complicate the reconstruction of transmission history where stemmata are often misleading due to lost material.[7] In this context, Hans-Jochen Schiewer pleaded for the equal consideration of any reworked text in the transmission history to be part of 'the polyphony of premodern textuality'.[8] The reverberations of the impact of New Philology could be sensed in this discussion, which is by no means concluded; in fact, text editions in German scholarship, especially from the religious sphere, have begun to return to the terminology of *Redaktion*.[9] My exposition, far from being able to contribute to the complex debate in German scholarship, aims to enhance the concept of 'redaction' in its English use, arguing that revised text material in a manuscript culture bears cultural significance and that translations belong to the reception history of the texts they are based on.

One of the reasons why the *botte* has not traditionally been considered alongside the *Legatus* is that it has not been regarded as part of the reception history of the *Legatus*. To determine the *botte*'s status as a distinctly authoritative text means to understand where it came from and in what tradition it stands; it also means to acknowledge that it stands in relation to the *Legatus*. The broad transmission of the vernacular rewritings of the *Legatus* gives testimony to a redactional openness of the text, which is reshaped in new constellations. The vernacular redactions of the *Legatus* circulated primarily in female monastic circles; or, put differently, the intellectual shift which 'marks the rise of the female interest in vernacular books' is a historical development which coincides with the *botte*.[10] In the rich and complex engagement with the transmitted material, readers – both male and female – in the late Middle

Ages were not just consumers but active producers of texts. This engagement with 'textual transfer of knowledge through the production of books' was not restricted to creative compositions but included the compilation of different texts in miscellanies – examples of which are given in the next chapter on the manuscripts' transmission history.[11]

Implicit assumptions about the status of translations more generally have inhibited research on the *botte*: seen as secondary to texts in their original language, translations are often dismissed as unworthy of attention.[12] For a long time in the study of medieval texts, Latin was considered learned and scholastic, in contrast to the vernacular.[13] Recent studies have shown that the lines of authoritative discourse between Latin and vernacular languages became increasingly blurred in the later Middle Ages so that topics and genres that were formerly reserved to scholastic circles were renegotiated in the vernacular in the late medieval period.[14] This shift is also true for the *botte*, where dialects of the language 'Middle High German' brought about new emphases – and in some instances new meanings – that need to be discussed separately from the Latin sources,[15] as I do in the final chapters of this book.

In providing a definition for the term 'redaction' in this chapter, I discuss the theoretical underpinnings of this book's enterprise, which is to reassess the reception of Gertrude of Helfta's visions in the vernacular tradition but I also want to make clear that there are boundaries to what can be adduced about the historical text genesis of the *botte* and the *Trutta*-legend. When it comes to establishing links between the emergence of German redactions of the *Legatus* and the reform movement, we arrive at limits when trying to pin down correlations between institutional contexts and literary production, although there is no doubt – as the transmission history proves – that reading the *botte* was considered suitable for nuns living in enclosure. Despite those limitations, the *botte*'s composition as a fluid text and the notion of several redactors – rather than one 'author' – may serve as a paradigmatic approach for how to tackle medieval vernacular texts that were based on readings of Latin texts, more generally.

In reassessing transmission history and updating previous research, I intend to show that the study of the *botte* opens up new ways for understanding vernacular texts that were based on Latin models. I argue that the collective settings in which these texts were copied and received enhanced their status as authoritative texts rather than weakened it, demonstrating that processes of redaction were self-conscious and cocreative literary activities. In this way, what was formerly deemed to be 'merely a translation' becomes the focus of scholarly interest in its own right, just as the medieval reader handled a vernacular redaction – manifested in the book copy they held in their hands – as an authoritative text.

EXISTING RESEARCH REVISITED

Before diving into the research discussion, a few words about how scholars have characterised the *botte* helps to explain why manuscript studies are essential when studying medieval textuality. Our ideas about texts are shaped by the manuscripts that contain them and by the historical and cultural environment they are set in.

With the discovery of the earliest German portion of the *botte*, the date for a vernacular written reception of the *Legatus* can now be placed in the four-teenth century, rather than the fifteenth as was assumed before.[16] This oldest surviving translation presents a vision from the *Legatus* and can be found in a miscellany of Bavarian origin, today kept at the Herzog Ernst Research Library (known as Forschungsbibliothek) in Gotha, West Thuringia (see Figs. 1 and 2). The lengthier version of the German redaction, *ein botte der götlichen miltekeit*, which has come down to us in several manuscripts and an early imprint from 1505 (commissioned by Lady Sidonie, Duchess of Meißen, and printed in Leipzig by Melchior Lotter), presents itself as one book and contains material from all five books of the 'standard' *Legatus*, with the majority stemming from Books III–V. The *botte* offers a carefully reordered and rewritten selection of chapters from the 'standard' *Legatus*. Ernst Hellgardt defines it as an 'adaptation of the Latin *Legatus*, abbreviated according to a clearly recognisable plan in three stages'.[17] What Hellgardt continues to expound are, however, less stages than organisational principles, which neither depend on nor develop from each other (as stages would). He observes that while the headings have been taken over from the Latin text, 'the adapter had least interest in the passages from the "Legatus" which dealt mainly and specifically with Gertrude,' con-centrating instead on 'the fate of the deceased and the effect on them of intercession on their behalf'.[18] For Hellgardt, this depersonalising principle conflicts with the mode of speech in parts of the *botte*, in which Gertrude's first person voice from *Legatus* Book II is largely retained. Yet, the focus on the community is a prominent feature in the *Legatus* already and not newly introduced; even if it appears more accentuated in the *botte*, it does not diminish Gertrude's singularity, since the community itself is always established in relation to Gertrude, hence making her both the centre of the text and the decentraliser through her prayers for, and connections to, others. Therefore, to have a first-person account in a text concerned with communal salvation is not contradictory but rather a way to combine both the singularity of one person and the well-being of a group.

Hellgardt's last principle, the considerable abridging of *Legatus* chapters, had previously been identified by the *botte*'s editor, Otmar Wieland.[19] Wieland pays meticulous attention to the material, juxtaposing the *Legatus* with the *botte*. For large parts of the *botte*, he concludes that 'the intentions of the

25

[Middle High German manuscript text in a late-medieval cursive hand, fol. 25r]

iiii

1 Easter Vision, corresponding to *botte* 93 (1375–1400)
Gotha, Herzog-Ernst-Forschungsbibliothek, Chart. B 269, fol. 25r
Copyright: Forschungsbibliothek Gotha der Universität Erfurt

2 Continuation: Easter Vision, corresponding to *botte* 93 (1375–1400)
Gotha, Herzog-Ernst-Forschungsbibliothek, Chart. B 269, fol. 25v
Copyright: Forschungsbibliothek Gotha der Universität Erfurt

translator are not fully comprehensible'. Indeed, the shortening of the text material does not align with a thematic selection, rather it seems genre-specific: exegetical and interpretative passages contained in the *Legatus* are largely missing in the *botte*. This creates the effect of a series of vignettes, in contrast to the theologically loaded chapters of the Latin *Legatus*. In addition, the regrouping of several visions (which appear in different years in the Latin *Legatus*) onto one feast day in the *botte* leads to a less repetitive and more concentrated account, one that can more easily be used in the rhythm of the liturgical year. In this way, the *botte* creates a closed unit that is somewhat more coherent than the *Legatus*. The German redaction is hence more than just a summary, it is a new text. At the same time, the *botte* itself was also copied in excerpts, allowing single vignettes to stand on their own.

The following reflections address statements made about the *botte* in scholarship in order to discuss challenges that occur when working with the German redactions of the *Legatus*. Existing research on the *botte* concerns its (a) composition, (b) mystical content in comparison to the *Legatus*, (c) devotional themes, (d) reception, and (e) questions of authorship. A methodological problem in the comparison of the *botte* with the *Legatus* has been that conclusions were drawn on the basis of working with modern editions rather than manuscripts, an issue that needs addressing (f). In unearthing implicit presuppositions, which have led to discarding the *botte* as a kind of watered-down *Legatus*, it becomes apparent that the *botte* needs to be studied in itself and not solely as dependent on the Latin sources.

(a) Ringler pleaded for understanding the *botte* as a reworking ('*Bearbeitung*') rather than a translation, although many parts are closely translated from the Latin. For him, it is mainly because of the rearrangement of chapters that the *botte* must be considered a 'work' ('*Werk*') in its own right, a 'new composition' ('*Neukomposition*'). This is one of the reasons why he speaks of an 'author' of the *botte* and not of a 'translator', employing in fact two German words for 'author': '*Autor*' and '*Verfasser*'.[20] When it comes to the designation of 'author', Ringler discusses this characterisation, pointing out that only an author and not a translator would have taken as much liberty to change the text, given the many apparent discrepancies between the *Legatus* and the *botte*.[21] The other reason for attributing an authorship to the *botte* has to do with its style, which shows a profound knowledge and 'feeling' for the German language. Metaphors and distinct phonetic features are adapted from Latin into German with expertise, conferring a poetic tone to the text, accomplished through a distinctly German rhythm, sound, and vocabulary.

A phrase from *Legatus* III, 18 serves Ringler as a paradigmatic example for this kind of poetic rendering: *Amor proprii cordis facit quod amici verba sunt suavia.*[22] The *botte* offers for this phase a rhythmically intricate vernacular version: *Die minne des hertzen machet, das die wort des lieben fründes süsse duncken*.[23] Just as the Latin phrase alternates between dark and bright vowels, in the German text the bright vowels /i/ and /ü/ in the words for 'love' (*minne*) and 'sweet' (*suesse*) are contrasted with the dark vowels /a/, /o/, and /u/ in *wort*, *fründes*, and *duncken*. The phrase's iambic meter begins with an unstressed upbeat, and the inverted subclause continues this iambic rhythm flawlessly. Whoever wrote the *botte* understood that the *Legatus* is vested with a poetic language, and was eager to provide a German version that would be in no way inferior. Thus, the language encountered in the *botte* is not simply representational; it has performative effects too, on a phonetic level as well as on an imaginary visual plane where images evoke staged experiences of encounters with the divine.[24] Indeed, it is programmatic for the *botte* to apply a performative language in which images are central, as is announced right at the beginning of the *botte*, where 'corporeal images' help the reader to imagine 'divine miracles'.[25]

The kind of ordered interpretation of material from the *Legatus* that we see in the *botte* means that text material has not been curtailed randomly; Ringler stresses: 'whoever handles a text in this way, does not intend to abridge it but to set certain emphases'.[26] In the *botte*, different chapters have been collated to create a 'new book', one that was not so much about the accurate recounting of visionary scenes in all their complexity but rather about general themes and motifs. Ringler recognises structural principles of a mystical ascent up to Ch. 63 of the *botte*, after which, as he explains, the chapters more closely follow the Latin text in their order. He explains this sudden change in the reworking of the material as intentional: Ch. 63 marks the climax of Gertrude's mystical development; once the soul's mystical maturity is reached, the interest in new events diminishes, as 'life only expands in width and depth'; 'the space' rather than 'the path' becomes significant.[27] Ringler explains this narrative of a postclimatic stability with Gertrude's age, and aligns it to any human's life, which, according to him, has a recognisable development up to the age of 30, after which less compelling changes occur even though there is no lack of excitement.[28] In terms of portraying a mystical life, such a trajectory up to the age of around 30 is entangled with the principle of *imitatio Christi*; after the age of Christ's crucifixion (33 years) the mystic dwells in a state of anticipation of death and fulfilment of eternal life where the soul will perpetually be reunified with her bridegroom Christ. While this is certainly not the case for the timeline of every mystical life, the *botte* supports the idea of the soul's development in imitation of Christ's life.

Focusing on Gertrude's visions and less on the exegetical explanations expounded in the *Legatus*, the *botte* presents a concentrated reworking of the *Legatus*, worthy to be thought of as a new text. The fact that the *botte* still forms part of the reception of the *Legatus* does not alter its status as a composition in its own right. The statements on the *botte* as a 'new composition' are not always self-consistent, but they are nonetheless deeply revealing as more questions about its revisited content arise.[29]

(b) Gertrude is often celebrated for her distinct mystical ideas expressed from her individual perspective. Has this individual 'voice' been altered in the *botte*? This question preoccupied Ringler, a philologist and historian of the book, and Gertrud Jaron Lewis, a scholar of theology. Lewis concentrates on the religious content, comparing the *botte*'s mysticism to that of the *Legatus*. Ringler, on the other hand, questions the status of the *Legatus* as a mystical text to begin with. Mysticism, in his view, is only 'authentic' and 'original' if it appears in 'individual language' and deals with 'unmediated experience'.[30] According to this strict definition of mysticism, the *Legatus* itself barely counts as a mystical text, the elements of hagiography outweighing mystical elements that might meet Ringler's criteria. In his earlier work on late medieval hagiography, Ringler had opted for the term '*Gnadenvita*' in order to categorise the lives of mystical women, finding the designation of a mystical life too vague.[31] Ursula Peters, in her critique of this term, warned of ring-fencing hagiographic texts that emerged from female convents between 1300 and 1360 in this way, since the transmission reality of these texts is often more complex than a narrow definition would allow.[32] As Ringler remarks himself, the 'author' ('*Verfasser*') of the *Legatus* did not distinguish between mystical experience, scholastically informed theological reflection, and pastoral edification. Given the various transmission contexts, the reception of the *Legatus* – both in Latin and in German – reveals that Gertrude's life was considered a type of 'mystical life'. The ample – and since Ringler's work considerably better-known – transmission of the vernacular text shows that the reception of the *botte* was diverse and was understood to be mystical, which explains why several manuscripts transmit the *botte* alongside other mystical texts.

The fact that scholars have doubted the mystical nature of the *Legatus* has implications for the *botte* too. Ruh defended the position that only Book II of the *Legatus*, which presents itself as written from Gertrude's own perspective, gives testimony of her individual mystical spirituality, while the other books are either hagiographic or pastoral in their nature.[33] He therefore holds that the *Legatus* is not as much about Gertrude and her mysticism as it is about spiritual life in the convent. Although Ringler too asks what kind of mysticism one may speak of given the collective tone of the *Legatus*, he goes on to conclude that it was not the nuns of Helfta, who struggled to edit Gertrude's revelations,[34] but the 'author' of the *botte* who was able to 'find the most convincing solution in terms of mysticism'.[35] Praising the *botte* for its elegance as a masterpiece of mystical literature, Ringler still stresses that it does not represent Gertrude's mysticism.[36] In doing so he underlines the importance of acknowledging the *botte* as a 'new composition', also in terms of its mystical contents.

By contrast, Lewis is interested in showing how removed the German *botte* is from what she understands to be Gertrude's original spirituality. Lewis finds that the *botte*, while stylistically impeccable, is – compared to the *Legatus* – impoverished in theological content, and that, in this way, Gertrude's individual spirituality is lost or misrepresented. The underlying presupposition is that Gertrude's individual spirituality can be found in Book II of the *Legatus*, which is written from an autobiographical standpoint. This assumption overlooks the fact that the *Legatus* largely portrays itself as written by another nun.[37] With no autographs having survived, we cannot rule out that Gertrude, even while she herself wrote Book II, was not heavily influenced by others in her writing. As we can tell from similarities between all the mystical texts of Helfta, the sisters influenced each other in the imagery of their visions as well as in their writings; I caution that it is difficult to attribute an individual spirituality to Gertrude since the *Legatus* is embedded in an environment of a collective mystical culture.[38] Be that as it may, Lewis focuses on the analysis of devotional themes in order to show how the *botte* departs from central motifs that form part of Gertrude's supposed individual spirituality.

(c) One thematic difference between the *Legatus* and the *botte* that has been emphasised in scholarship, indeed overemphasised, concerns Marian devotion, as – in comparison with the *Legatus* – the *botte* has fewer allusions to the Virgin Mary. The comparison of *Legatus* III, 20 with *botte* 38 reveals a clear contrast, the theme of the passage in question concerns the conflict between focusing on Christ as bridegroom whilst also venerating the Virgin Mary. In the *Legatus*, Gertrude refuses to hail an image of Mary, to which Christ reacts by assuring her that he will accept the praise to Mary as if it had been offered to him.[39] The *botte* does not include Christ's final words, instead the chapter ends with Gertrude's refusal to worship anyone else. Furthermore, the *botte* adds one phrase – not found in the *Legatus* – which characterises Christ as 'someone who loves to hear from his beloved betrothed that she loves him more than anything else'.[40] The narrative is changed drastically at this instance. More importantly, we can discern a deliberate principle of rearrangement and revision in the *botte*.[41] With this careful shift to a focus on the veneration of Christ, perhaps intended to be adapted to late medieval piety, we see that vernacular rewritings 'generate their own systems'.[42] By adding one sentence and removing another, the German redaction offers an entirely new solution to Gertrude's conflicting interests, and makes her more radically orientated towards Christ.

Marian devotion may be seen as a subset of the veneration of saints more generally. What can be inferred from differences between the *botte* and the *Legatus* regarding the cult of saints? The *botte* does not include *Legatus* IV, 4; IV; 16; IV, 34; IV 48 – chapters in which the special relationship between St John the Apostle and Mary is highlighted, nor can one find the vision with

St Catherine from *Legatus* IV, 57. However, many other saints feature prominently, including St John the Evangelist (*botte* 62), St Agnes (*botte* 113), and St Elisabeth (*botte* 126). Looking more deeply at how these saints are invoked, we find that they are mentioned to confirm the superiority of Gertrude's relationship with Christ. For example, St Agnes is known as the saint who yearned to have Christ as her spouse, and St Elisabeth confirms to Gertrude in a vision that it is not suitable to sing for the saint's honour but only for God's honour on Elisabeth's feast day. In contrast to the *Legatus*, St Dominic and St Francis are not mentioned at all in the *botte*, while St Bernard and St Augustine remain very central. Gertrude's visions of these two latter figures are even included in some late medieval *Saints' Lives*.[43]

The cult of saints in the *botte* is less pronounced than in the *Legatus*, the reason being a matter of quantity rather than quality; after all, some saints are included in the German redactions. Mary is not worshipped as much in the *botte* as in the *Legatus* but she still features in many visions as an important figure. The figure of Mary has in fact a strong presence in the festive and musical vision of *botte* 62. Other instances also make clear that the Virgin Mary is not absent or neglected in the German redactions, even though she does not have the same prominence as in the *Legatus*.[44]

Other than saintly devotion, Lewis claims that central themes contained in the Latin *Legatus* are absent from the German *botte*, namely the femininity of the deity, the Sacred Heart, the Eucharist, Christological symbols like the Pelican, priestly authority, and worship in hymns. In addition, Ringler remarks that scenes from the convent's everyday life – which are often quite amusing to read in the *Legatus* – are absent from the German *botte*, making the *botte* somewhat more serious and solemn.[45] Moreover, according to Lewis, 'the "botte" not only eliminates most of what is characteristic of Gertrud's hymnic book of praise, but also refrains from portraying the saint herself'; the conclusion being that in comparison to the Latin 'original', it omits many themes and passages from the *Legatus* and moves away from Gertrude's spirituality.[46]

The concern that reverberations of the liturgy – in Lewis's words, a 'hymnic tone' – are entirely missing in the *botte*,[47] needs checking. In fact, *botte* 62 – by far the lengthiest chapter of the entire text – recounts the so-called 'Gertrude-Messe' in great detail. Drawing from *Legatus* IV, 59 but extending it considerably, this depiction of a celestial celebration of the mass, in which Gertrude partakes, is abundant with descriptions of liturgical sound.[48] A 'hymnic tone' is present in the dense description of the liturgy with detailed references to anthems, responses, and the way angels and saints worship.[49] It also cannot be claimed that Eucharistic notions connected to the Sacred Heart image as found in the *Legatus* were entirely cut in the *botte*.[50] Again, *botte* 62 as well as 63 offer intricate images of the Eucharist associated with the divine heart. In Ch. 62, a golden altar emanates from the divine heart:

Gertrude's pain and hardship suffered in body and mind are offered in the form of a chalice and brought to the altar by a high prince who is her own guardian angel, and all the saints lift up their hearts to the chalice with golden tubes which receive what emanates from the chalice. The offering on the altar is an image for the juxtaposition of the relationship between the divine heart and Gertrude's own ailment which is suffered for the benefits of others (at the time of the vision she is ill).[51] In Ch. 63, Christ tells Gertrude that he has given everyone golden tubes to draw in whatever they desire from his divine heart.[52] Both chapters include many details about singing hymns and sequences, and reciting the psalter.[53] Other parts of the *botte* also refer to the golden tubes of the divine heart; for example, in Ch. 135, each golden tube connected to the heart of Christ has a golden cup in which whatever is sucked from the heart accumulates.[54] To sum up, all four themes – the divine heart, the Eucharist, Mary, singing and celebrating the liturgy – are present in the *botte*, albeit not as prominently as in the *Legatus*.

(d) Concerning the reception history of the *Legatus*, to which the *botte* belongs, it has been argued that in the late medieval period not much care was taken to disseminate the Helfta mysticism, so that the reception of the *Legatus* only took off 200 years after the convent's destruction in 1343, when the printed works of Gertrude of Helfta and Mechthild of Hackeborn, as commissioned by the Duchess of Meißen, Lady Sidonie of Saxony (1449–1510), received a broad reception.[55] The promotion of saintly figures in the sixteenth-century Counter-Reformation Church and the ensuing seventeenth-century Catholic reforms in Spain and France were decisive in making Gertrude a highly venerated saint known beyond the German-speaking realm; she was the only thirteenth- or fourteenth-century German mystic who made it to the altar ranks of Catholic churches all across Western Europe. In contrast to women mystics from the Low Countries (especially the Beguines) and Italy (for example Catherine of Siena), the Helfta writings did not emerge in an urban context – a circumstance which certainly made the dissemination of the *Legatus* and *Liber* comparatively slow. The mobility of texts related to the *Legatus* – and this includes the vernacular redactions – was defined through convent, rather than interurban, networks. With new manuscripts complementing and updating previous research on the transmission of the *botte* – as presented in Chapter 3 – we see that a late medieval vernacular reception of the mysticism connected with the *Legatus* existed as early as the fourteenth century and that it was widely disseminated, mainly in South-German nunneries.

(e) The *botte*'s medieval readership has been generally thought to have been solidly female. In previous research this observation was not based on the extant manuscripts and their provenance, but rather on the fact that the *botte* was a German adaptation of the *Legatus*, the underlying assumption being that a vernacular religious text must have been intended for women.[56] Taking the artificial divide of vernacular-female and Latin-male one step further and combining it with the belief that the *botte* only emerged in the latter half of the fifteenth century, it was then speculated that a male reformer had been the 'author' of the *botte*: Lewis and Ringler both speak of a male author of the *botte*.[57] The rationale behind assuming a male author is that the *botte* would have been composed by a fifteenth-century reformer – who would have been able to understand the Latin source in order to translate it – with its dissemination in nunneries in mind. The suggestion that the *botte* was authored by a fifteenth-century male reformer from the observant movement was brought forward by Lewis with much zeal, referring to the *botte* as a 'pastoral manual', 'a useful booklet of practical spiritual and moral advice' transformed from the *Legatus* to fit the model of a '*Gnadenvita*'.[58] The status of a mystical text was thus denied to the *botte* by Lewis, who saw in it less an expressive account of 'first-hand mystical experiences' than an instructive description of mystical thought.[59] The thematic omission of 'female priesthood' in the *botte*, for example, served as an indicator – in addition to the 'tone of the "botte"' – to conjecture that 'the author was male and probably a clergyman'.[60]

While it is quite possible that the *botte* was written by one or several men (as I will suggest further on in this chapter on the grounds of transmission history) the reasons held in previous research for the assumption of a male authorship stand on shaky ground. To answer the issue of a gendered 'tone' first, we may counter that the *botte* remains a female-cantered text. Knowledge about and from God is communicated through female voices, and no male mediator reveals himself as the crucial missing link to share this knowledge with the reader. This is to say that even if the *botte* was written by men, there are certainly no traces left in the text that would suggest a gender-motivated curtailing of the *Legatus* material.[61]

Ringler is convinced that the German adaptation evinces an 'author' who has reflected on Gertrude's spirituality; however, in contrast to Lewis, he assumes an 'author' who wanted to protect the *Legatus* from misinterpretations and therefore decisively put Christ into the centre of his work. This *botte* 'author', again, a male reformer, would have found the veneration of Mary and the saints, as encountered in the *Legatus*, to be exaggerated, old-fashioned, and in general far too sensual, posing the danger of misapprehension.[62] Ringler next suggests reading the *botte* as an apologetic text ('*Rechtfertigungslehre*'), which aims to emphasise trust in God.[63] The notion that you can confess your sins in your heart rather than to a priest, expressed in *botte* 116, fits for Ringler into the apologetic genre. Yet, the notion of inner confession was not invented in the fifteenth century, nor in the fourteenth century; rather, it was a by-product of the long twelfth century, when internal penitential processes were increasingly seen as canonically sound.[64] That Gertrude in the *botte* should still require affirmation from St John for confessing in her heart whenever there is no confessor present, corroborates the convention of inner confession rather than defending it as a new practice. Elements such as the inner confession are already present in the *Legatus*. Although it is an important hypothesis that the *botte* 'author' pitched his revisions to his own time, it is problematic to deduce authorial intentions from it because many of the mentioned concerns of the alleged male author who wrote for reformed, and specifically Dominican nuns, refer to elements that are ingrained in the *Legatus* and not newly integrated into the *botte*.

(f) A final point of contention rounds up the discussion on previous research: judgements about the *botte* have been made on the ground of comparing one edition (Wieland's *botte* edition) against another (the *Legatus* edition of the Solesmes brothers). Drawing hard conclusions about medieval textual history while working with modern editions – which at best can capture a fragmented image of the past while creating the impression of a stable text that never existed – is dangerous. The shortcoming in showing discrepancies by comparing the Latin to the German edition is that there is a silent assumption that whoever wrote the medieval German redaction had exactly the same Latin text in front of them that scholars use today: the edition published in Paris between 1968 and 1986. Of course this is a known dilemma; modern editions are useful and necessary, but they seldom reflect textual transmissions accurately. Using editions for the comparison between different texts is inevitable, but it becomes problematic when conclusions are drawn about the authorial status of texts.

The Latin and vernacular transmission of the *Legatus* provides an optimal case study for the demonstration of this problem: the current critical edition of the *Legatus* is based on five text witnesses in manuscripts from the fifteenth century (four of which are from the latter half of the century), and on several early modern prints. Today, more than fifteen additional manuscripts have been identified to contain portions from the *Legatus*. In addition, there are speculations about a lost German version, which was used for the 1536 printed *Legatus*: Carthusian scholar John Justus of Landsberg mentions a German text that he needed to reconstruct the Latin of the prologue and of Book I. Hellgardt supposes that this German text could not have been the *botte*: 'since the retranslation corresponds closely to the Latin original, it appears that the German translation of the "Legatus" used by Landsberg corresponds more closely to the Latin original then the '[b]otte der götlichen miltekeit'.[65] Such an assumption leaves out, however, the possibility of an intermediary text or even several layers of text redactions in the *botte* transmission. The Gotha manuscript, for example, contains a phrase translated from the Latin *Legatus*, which cannot be found in any other *botte* text witness, therefore suggesting an additional transmission layer that we cannot fully retrace today

(Gotha, Forschungsbibliothek, Chart. B 269). It is not inconceivable that Landsberg used a *botte* version that has simply not come down to us; just as it is also possible that there existed yet another German version. A Karlsruhe manuscript transmits a German translation altogether different from the *botte* (Karlsruhe, Badische Landesbibliothek, Lichtenthal 89).[66] In fact, how can one presume that the writer of the *botte* had a full copy of the Latin *Legatus* if we do not even know what a full copy would have looked like? Since the discovery of what seems to be the oldest known *Legatus* text witness (the *Leipzig Legatus*), previous assumptions about a stable *Legatus* text need also to be revised.[67]

Previous research has rightly highlighted the great liberty with which the *Legatus* was translated into German. Manuscript transmission has, however, not yet played a role in the discussion of the *botte*'s reception and its textual status. Reassessing the transmission history allows us to shed light on the literary environment of the *botte*, where mystical and devotional texts were increasingly available in the vernacular, and where the book management in literate circles impacted the way Gertrude's visions were transmitted and received in the late Middle Ages.

NEW INSIGHTS

In 2008, an early fourteenth-century manuscript containing the so-called *Leipzig Legatus* was unearthed: the manuscript most likely belonged to the Benedictine convent at Pegau, 43 miles to the South East of Helfta.[68] This codex (Leipzig, Universitätsbibliothek, Ms 827) is older than any other known *Legatus* witness; it clearly shows that there was a fourteenth-century reception of the *Legatus* in the area around Helfta.[69] The vernacular reception, as it is known to us, reaches back into the last quarter of the fourteenth century as the Gotha miscellany of Northern-Bavarian origin, which contains Gertrude's Easter Monday vision portion of the *botte*, testifies (Gotha, Forschungsbibliothek, Chart. B 269). It is nevertheless true that the vast majority of the texts associated with the *Legatus* – whether Latin or vernacular – date from the fifteenth century and later. The smaller the reception was, the more likely the material is lost to us today; this does not mean that a reception did not exist, rather that it has not come down to us. Precisely because in the fifteenth century we can observe an increase in the dissemination of both the *Legatus* and the *botte*, we must infer that texts were circulated, redacted, and copied in the preceding century. Reassessing the manuscript transmission history of the *botte*, I suggest that the earliest German redaction of the *Legatus* emerged in a Carthusian context; but we still need to surmise collective writing scenarios, not least because of the many textual layers folded into the manuscript transmission.[70]

In studies of Gertrude of Helfta's mysticism and its impact, the vernacular tradition has received little to no consideration, because the Latin *Legatus* has traditionally been judged original and superior to subsequent adaptations. This assessment has been made even though the genesis of the *Legatus* is intricate and complex – eluding notions of originality – and despite the fact that the German manuscript transmission – with the exception of Leipzig, Universitätsbibliothek, Ms 827 – is as old as the Latin one. The *Legatus* cannot be considered the only valuable primary source when it comes to the reception history of the writings related to Gertrude the Great. In order to allow the transmission history to give us glimpses of what an early reception may have looked like, we first need to accept the *botte* as being as authoritative as the Latin *Legatus*. This entails exploring the question of why the *botte* happened to be more successful in female convents than its Latin counterpart – given that nuns were invested in vernacular learning as well as Latin. The reassessment of transmission history looks at: (a) the multilingual literary activities in late medieval female convents, (b) the interest which reformed convents took in copying and redacting the *botte*, and (c) the inclusion of new material in the *botte*'s final chapters for communal reasons which reflect developments in late medieval piety.

(a) The vernacular *botte* enjoyed a wide reception in the observant movement, where it often appears to have been copied in reformed nunneries. From this circumstance, it seems logical to conclude that women's writing in the late Middle Ages was intrinsically connected with the vernacular, bearing the implication for historical text studies 'that if a codex was written in the vernacular, it was meant for women and that, in the absence of a named female scribe, manuscripts were written by men'.[71] As a matter of fact, the supposition of a male author of the *botte* builds on this traditional view, which has been shaped by research in the 1980s and 90s about the observant reform as a movement that was decisively administered by fifteenth-century male reformers supplying female convents with spiritual literature.[72] In more recent years, scholars have addressed this hypothesis by acknowledging women's engagement in reform and text production.[73] For example, Anne Winston-Allen has highlighted women's agency in literary discourses,[74] and studies by Antje Willing and Simone Mengis have demonstrated that the female convents' prolific book production was largely managed by the women themselves.[75] Moreover, Claire Taylor Jones, who discerns that 'the interference of male [o]bservant reformers in the fifteenth-century dissemination of fourteenth-century mystical literature' has been overstated, calls for an understanding of female observant networks as 'reflecting the women's own concerns and preferences at least as much as the guiding hand of the male reformers'.[76]

An issue that appears repeatedly in research concerns precisely the tension between Latin and vernacular, often judged as a question of gender which assumes that women could only express themselves in the vernacular. In this sense, we still find the general assumption in scholarship that women writers who named themselves referred to a command from God to write in order to justify their writing activity.[77] When it comes to the question of writing in the vernacular being gender-specific, namely female, the *Legatus* in itself is of course a witness against this assumption. Indeed, the *Legatus* and its vernacular rewritings provide a formidable example for how language cannot be held as an arbiter for a gendered practice of authorial writing. Writing or reading in the vernacular cannot be held to indicate Latin illiteracy, since literacy generally – and more concretely the ability to write – was linked to knowledge of Latin.[78] In the thirteenth century when the *Legatus* was written, as well as in the fifteenth century when it was most frequently copied, we move in a multilingual culture where writing in one language or the other was not a necessity but a choice. This also meant that the overlapping reception of text material in several languages was common.[79] This multilingual culture favoured parallel versions of a text, a variability which allowed the *botte* to stand not beneath but beside its Latin counterparts.

Nuns before and during the reform managed their own libraries, a task which demanded an active engagement with Latin and vernacular texts. Historians of the text have shown that 'in the absence of other literature, older works were copied together with texts [...] of the reform' which meant that '[o]ften the content of the older texts was adapted to meet the needs of the doctrine of the [o]bservance [m]ovement'. Regina Dorothea Schiewer reminds us that such revisions 'were very probably the work of women themselves', employing 'the technique of compilation to restructure and reorganize material which they either found in the libraries of their convents or borrowed from other – mostly women's convents'.[80] Older material was also copied without alteration thus preserving, for example, mystical texts of the thirteenth and fourteenth centuries. 'And it is not until the second half of the fifteenth century that we find more and more texts that were especially written for nuns of the Dominican [o]bservance movement.'[81] The fact that, in reformed nunneries, we only ever find the German *botte* being copied – no Latin *Legatus* is known to have been kept in a late medieval women's convent whereas some male houses read both – is telling; not because women would not have been interested in the Latin text, but because – as I would like to propose – the Latin *Legatus* had never reached them.

Gertrude's visions fitted the ambitions of the observant reform, precisely because all of the texts associated with her – those produced in Helfta or redactions of the Helfta texts – take the liturgy as the 'point of departure'.[82] The primary aim of the observant reform was to promote the understanding of the liturgy; in practical terms, this translated into the correction of liturgical books as a first step. The 'acquisition of appropriate vernacular devotional literature was a secondary concern'.[83] Considering the Latin proficiency that many nuns had, and that prose texts were marginal for the reformers' devotional programme, why was the *Legatus* not more widely disseminated in their circles?[84]

We can confirm that Latin literacy existed among women in the fourteenth and fifteenth centuries, further shedding doubt on the assumption that they would have not been able to deal with the Latin *Legatus*. For example, some of the fourteenth-century Dominican sisterbooks were originally written in Latin, although they were later translated, namely the sisterbooks of Unterlinden and Adelhausen.[85] Also, Latin quotations in vernacular sisterbooks reveal knowledge of non-liturgical Latin texts thereby proving that Dominican women engaged with Latin prose treatises and devotional literature beyond the Vulgate Bible.[86] Scholars have shown that Latin literacy in late medieval nunneries was much more nuanced than the male reformers (and some modern scholars) would have us believe.[87] In North-German nunneries, like that of Paradies bei Soest, nuns maintained high levels of Latin literacy.[88] In the South, too – despite the decrease in Latin book production – there was certainly enough Latin knowledge to follow the liturgy.[89] The Latin *Legatus* would have been understood at least by some; but its absence in nunneries suggests that it was never read there, perhaps because prose texts were 'irrelevant' to the friars who pushed for the apprehension of liturgical Latin in the reformed nunneries.[90] Taken all together – the bilingual literacy of medieval nuns, the transmission of the *botte* in nunneries, and the non-transmission of the *Legatus* – it seems very unlikely that the *botte*, which emerged before the reform had firmly taken root in the South-German houses in which it is transmitted, should have been translated by a man for the specific purpose of edifying nuns' souls.

(b) There is no doubt, however, that the *botte* circulated in these convents; the network of the reformed nuns of St Katharina in particular facilitated the *botte*'s transmission in the fifteenth century, as I will discuss in greater detail in the following chapter. Because writing and copying books was seen as a devotional activity, the observant movement favoured the dissemination of texts deemed worthy of the ambitions of the reform, and the *botte* was one of those favoured texts. In the period of late medieval reform, interest in all matters concerning community building meant that texts like those dealing with Mechthild of Hackeborn and Gertrude of Helfta were considered useful. As I have shown in Chapter 1, community aspects are at the heart of the *Legatus* in its production and also in terms of the content, which often puts the collective body of nuns in the foreground.[91]

Since late medieval reformed convents were deeply interested in the benefits its reading would bring, it remains a puzzle why the early reception of the *Legatus* was not more widespread – given that historical sources create the impression that the nunnery of Helfta maintained good relationships with

Cistercians, Benedictines, and Dominicans alike.[92] When it comes to inter-communal networks there was no social or economic exchange between Helfta and the South-German convents, where contemporary mystical movements led to the production of similarly community-orientated sisterbooks.[93] Rather, when exploring the transmission of these texts, it becomes apparent that the reception took some detours. Now that we are able to trace a more accurate *botte* transmission we see that, early on in the transmission history, the Nuremberg Dominican nuns of St Katharina held readings from a vernacular version. By this time – the early 1400s – the *botte* was established enough that it served for several readings during the year, with Gertrude featured next to older saints. The shorter redaction, commonly called the *Trutta*-legend, was very likely an outcome of refectory readings in St Katharina as I will explore in Chapter 3.

(c) The longer text witnesses of the *botte* transmit additional material – not extant in the *Legatus* – which speaks to communal monastic life and reflects on late medieval piety. The readings of and about Gertrude (and Mechthild of Hackeborn for that matter) were multifaceted; the communal aspect of these Helfta writings certainly came in handy in the reformers' pastoral programme. Although a single visionary figure – at times named, at times simply referred to as 'a pious person' – does not entirely disappear behind the concept of 'community', the community is held up high.[94] The communal aspect is particularly strong in the *botte* where text material beyond that which was written in Helfta is transmitted. Concern for the community is already embedded in the *Legatus*, where the majority of Book V recounts the lives of other sisters (and also those of befriended monks), some of whom have visions of Gertrude. While this part resembles South-German Dominican sisterbooks, it still functions as an account of Gertrude's afterlife; it depicts the ongoing impact that her pious life had on the community. In this extended narrative, one figure, called 'the daughter', occupies several chapters which recount a kind of mini-life as 'the daughter' follows in Gertrude's footsteps. The *botte* includes these episodes, and furthermore adds three final chapters (Ch. 171–173) on other religious women, none of whom is mentioned in the *Legatus*, at least not in the witnesses known to us.

The *botte*'s editor, Wieland, has been criticised for having included these extra chapters which are found in only some of the *botte* manuscripts.[95] *botte* 170 culminates in the unification of Christ and his bride (Gertrude's soul), in the text marked as a total *unio*: 'she became one thing in him like the iron melts in the fire'.[96] Still, Wieland had good reasons for including the additional chapters in his edition even though they do not correspond to the hagiographic account found in the *Legatus*. First, from a transmission point of view, all major *botte* manuscripts contain the additional material. In the Dresden manuscript (Dresden, Sächsische Landesbibliothek, Hs M 243), Ch. 171–173 appear separately from the rest of the text, but this irregularity has occurred because the quires have been mixed up in a binding mistake.[97] The final chapters can likewise be found in Vienna, Schottenkloster, Hs 308; Brussels, Bibliothèque Royale, cod. 8507–09; and Munich, Bayerische Staatsbibliothek, Cgm 5292. Early modern printers also decided to include them. Hence, the current edition respects the manuscript transmission, which dictates not what is 'correct' as judged by modern standards, but rather what is extant and thought to be inclusive by medieval copyists. Excluding several chapters would have been a major editorial intervention. Second, there is an explicit ending to the *botte* following Ch. 173 in the aforementioned Brussels and Munich manuscripts. After this final chapter, which draws from Gregory the Great's *Homilies* to recount the story of Blessed Rumela (in Gregory: Romula),[98] a final paragraph ends the entire book in a colophon-like manner:

> Here the book of divine loving kindness ends. Let us praise and thank our beloved Lord for his abundant gifts and grace that he has shared with his chosen friends so lovingly; and let us beg him also to have mercy on us poor ones, and to give us the rich treasure of his grace and mercy, so that we in this life may gain forgiveness for all our sins and receive his divine grace, and that he may bestow on us the eternal life after this life. All of this may his boundless mercy, goodness, and love bestow on us at all times. Amen.[99]

After the explicit end of the *botte*'s account in the passage's first phrase, there follows a prayer expressing thanks for the mercy God has shown to his chosen friends, coupled with a plea to extend his grace to 'us', that is those who pray to him, so that 'we' may gain eternal life. Seen within the *botte* as a whole, such an ending makes perfect sense because it concludes a text that presented one case (Gertrude) as standing for a larger community in a collective manner. By extension, all recipients of the text are invited to identify with the praying voice of the final passage. The *botte*'s overall structure describes the ascent of a mystical path that imitates Christ's life, as the bride does. By including her 'afterlife' – several stories of people from Gertrude's community and beyond – it is likewise modelled after Christ's impact on the community of believers as told in the Book of Acts, this narrative structure being generally adopted in hagiography. Taking all of these considerations into account, it becomes evident that while Wieland's edition may be criticised for different reasons, his decision to include what seemed to him the most complete *botte* version is justified and coherent with the *botte*'s emphasis on community.[100]

CARTHUSIAN INFLUENCE

The manuscript transmission of the *botte* and the *Trutta*-legend reveals their strong presence in reformed nunneries and shows that interest for them was high among lay communities and individual persons.[101] Who was responsible for the first vernacular renderings of the *Legatus*, however, is a different issue altogether. With the late fourteenth-century Gotha codex transmitting the earliest vernacular portion of the *Legatus*, we have a copy dating from before the reform, meaning that we need to call alternative genesis scenarios into consideration. In the following exploration, I suggest that Carthusians were responsible for the first translations of the *Legatus* into German.

Previous research has located the genesis of the *botte* and its intended reception in a Dominican reform context. Apart from the dating issue – that the oldest copy pre-dates the reform – another important factor weakens the hypothesis of a Dominican origin: visions of St Dominic recounted in the *Legatus* are entirely missing from the *botte*. At the same time, visions with patrons of other orders, namely St Augustine and St Benedict, are kept. Of course, we cannot be certain that whoever translated the *Legatus* had access to the material containing visions of St Dominic but it is still rather striking that there should be such a discrepancy of saintly figures mentioned in the *botte* if a Dominican were responsible for its redaction. If not a Dominican, who else could have had an interest in translating the *Legatus*?

The meditating role of the Carthusians in promoting the *Legatus* – and women's visionary literature at large – has been remarked upon by scholars.[102] A considerable number of *Legatus* witnesses have come down to us that originate from the charterhouses in Buxheim, Mainz, Cologne, and Erfurt. This in itself shows the genuine interest that the Carthusians held for the *Legatus*. Next to Latin learning, Carthusians made great use of vernacular sources in their teaching.[103] The influx of lay brothers to their communities increased the demand for vernacular texts, which the Carthusian monks in turn produced. The *botte* was most likely written under Carthusian influence, if not by a Carthusian monk. Several aspects buttress this hypothesis: the broad transmission of the Latin *Legatus* manuscripts in charterhouses; the Carthusian's mission as translators of theological and spiritual texts into the vernacular, together with their importance for the circulation of vernacular texts in the South-German lands;[104] the concomitant transmission of the *Legatus* and the *botte* in the Buxheim Charterhouse; and the earliest *botte* text witness in Gotha, Forschungsbibliothek, Chart. B 269, a manuscript that in its composition, and combination of Latin and vernacular sources might well have been a Carthusian miscellany or modelled after one.[105] Finally, the literary calibration of the *botte* may also hint at a Carthusian composition: the relative absence of exegetical passages in the *botte* creates a dense series of visionary vignettes which in their allegorical programme resemble meditational cycles, such as the Carthusians were most interested in.[106]

The *botte* redactor, like other Carthusian writers, had 'a sophisticated command of religious discourse in German', which was 'underpinned by familiarity with Latin monastic writing'. The same observation for a fifteenth-century cycle of prayers leads Nigel Palmer to believe that a male author with clerical training stood behind the so-called Ursula Begerin Prayers. Palmer acknowledges that male and clerical associations with medieval Latin texts need to be differentiated 'with regard to the tradition of meditational texts on the life of Christ', but nevertheless argues for a Carthusian author of the vernacular Begerin Prayers that are formulated from a feminine perspective.[107] A similarly controversial case concerns the Italian version of the *Meditationes vitae Christi*, a Passion treatise from c. 1300, for which Sarah McNamer considers a female author, while Michelle Karnes has reservations about a female authorship finding that '[i]t is more likely that the author was male'.[108] In all these cases, we can see that reconsiderations about a gendered authorship, though they have their limits, are important as they challenge assumptions about intellectual training and Latin learning. Medieval text production depended on skills that were undoubtedly more common among religious men than women in the Middle Ages. Yet, I do not suggest a Carthusian genesis for the *botte* because it is difficult to argue for a female authorship of the *botte* on the grounds of learning, but rather because all of the transmitted Latin text witnesses used to belong to male convents (the Helfta copies which belonged to the nuns are lost to us today). In addition, the Buxheim Charterhouse is the only discernible place known to have owned both Latin and vernacular redactions of the *Legatus*.[109]

Perhaps the Carthusians of Erfurt were responsible for the *botte*'s genesis: they were geographically close to Helfta, and, moreover, the Benedictines of St Peter in Erfurt were connected to Helfta through a prayer community in the early fourteenth century, meaning that the *Legatus* could have been passed on to them via this intercommunal network. One *Legatus* manuscript from the late fifteenth century survives from the Benedictine Abbey in Erfurt,[110] and one Erfurt citizen, Mathias Pahe, owned a shorter copy during the first quarter of the fifteenth century.[111] Even though no medieval library catalogue from the Erfurt Benedictines survives, scholars have shown that the monks interchanged texts – especially texts connected to the visionaries of Helfta – with the Erfurt Charterhouse.[112] By the end of the fifteenth century, Erfurt had a vibrant charterhouse in which mystical texts were highly valued;[113] the Erfurt Carthusians were keen on mystical and devotional texts, filling their library systematically with such books, including several fifteenth-century manuscripts with material from the *Legatus*.[114] Reference in the library catalogue, which was started in 1475 by Jakob Volradi and continued until the 1520s, shows that the Erfurt Carthusians had knowledge of a 'full copy' of a *Legatus* kept at the Eisenach Charterhouse: an anonymous collaborator (Brother N) noted the corresponding words *In domo Isenacensi habentur iste revelationes integraliter* next to the description of shelf mark I 8, which – the letter I (J) being reserved for revelations and devotional works – was allotted to extracts of the *Legatus*

(*Revelationes sancte virginis Trute, et videntur esse hic nisi quedam extracta*).[115] Carthusians with access to the Latin sources very likely translated the *Legatus* into the *botte*, for themselves, for their lay brothers, and for dissemination more broadly including to befriended convents in the South, such as the Buxheim Charterhouse.[116] If this argument holds true we must accept that the supposed first translations are lost or remain undiscovered today.

A CULTURE OF REDACTING

How then may we think of the transmission of the manuscript as it exists now? In light of what has come down to us, redactorial changes in the extant copies of the *botte* were probably not made by male reformers.[117] In the transmission of the *botte*, single text witnesses were shaped mostly by women who copied and rewrote their material. Women writers before and during the reform movement engaged creatively in text production;[118] this can be observed in the transmission of the *botte* and the likely emergence of the *Trutta*-legend at the Dominican nunnery of St Katharina in Nuremberg. By highlighting the continuous reshaping of text material, the concept of redaction turns our attention to cocreative processes of text production, and I argue that redactions enhanced the status of a text as authoritative.

Studying the diachronic state of medieval textuality, that is, considering the evolution of text over time, we deal with a plurality of redactors who reworked their material. In the manuscript material related to the *botte*, for example, the vast variety among the text witnesses is overwhelming. The transmission shows that processes of copying were never just mechanical but inherently creative and that we deal with a culture of redacting in which the outcomes of literary activities were considered authoritative, that is, effected by an *auctor*. The *auctor* was 'someone to be believed and imitated', someone whose account was thought to be bestowed with authority.[119] Whether they were named or remained anonymous, the authorial status is not affected since it is attached to the text or the artefact.[120] The literary history of redactions is as long as the history of any textual engagement, but for the purpose of this study I want to turn to the most prominent example of the High and Late Middle Ages as a point of reference, in order to elucidate the theoretical implications of the medieval concept of redaction: Bonaventure's *Legenda maior* on the life of St Francis.[121]

After being commissioned by the Rome Chapter of the Franciscan Order in 1257 to write a new and definite hagiographic account of Francis of Assisi (approximately thirty years after his death), Bonaventure set off to first gather and carefully study all of the existing accounts as a letter issued by the Paris General Chapter, written after the completion of the task, explains.[122] Charged to create a smooth text for use in the choir which would foster the sense of a monastic community in the relatively young order, Bonaventure redacted his earlier sources drastically, reducing, for example, Francis's 'relationship with women to a level of nonexistence'.[123] Interpolations that altered the meaning of Francis's visions were also made where Bonaventure deemed them necessary to make his version fit the changed needs of his spiritual brothers, for whom he was writing. As Jay M. Hammond demonstrates, such redactions were meant to be 'absolutely authoritative'.[124] Bonaventure also limited the range of sources he had access to by drawing primarily from two hagiographies produced by Thomas of Celano and Julian of Speyer, reinterpreting them within the tripartite theological framework of purgation, illumination, and perfection. He deleted some episodes from Celano and Julian and integrated new narrative episodes not found in earlier materials. Bonaventure appended a collection of miracle stories (*De miraculis*) to his *Legenda maior*, which was adapted from Thomas of Celano's *Treatise on the Miracles of St Francis*,[125] a decision which underscores the liberties taken on behalf of Bonaventure in deconstructing and recomposing the material he had at hand. Structural interventions were informed by his main goal of producing a text for the liturgy; in the prologue he specifies that 'he purposely ordered his "Legenda" according to a "thematic" schema rather than a chronological one'.[126] Indeed, Bonaventure at the same time also oversaw the 'compilation/redaction/correction' of the order's liturgical texts, the order's Constitutions, and a 'concise theology manual to help train the brothers in their pastoral care duties'.[127] His *Legenda maior* hence forms part of a larger liturgically orientated reform project, in which older materials were to be transmitted and preserved in a reassessed shape.

In fact, Bonaventure responded to Rome's call for a new *legenda* by submitting two: a *Legenda maior* and a *Legenda minor*.[128] The contexts for their respective reception were conceived as distinct as a prefatory note transmitted in two manuscripts clarifies:

> This major Life or Legend of Saint Francis may be kept in any place for the edification of the brothers. It can be read at table through the entire octave of the Death of Saint Francis. However, the minor Legend, which is excerpted from it, should be placed in choral books and read according to their distinctions in the feast of Saint Francis and through the octave of his Death. And it can be placed in portable Breviaries. Therefore, scribes are compelled to preserve the punctuations and text of the exemplar; and their errors are to be diligently corrected by the brothers according to the exemplar itself.[129]

The legends were to fulfil communal functions, for example as table readings, and also serve for individual meditations, inserted for instance into prayer books. Their various lengths made them apt for different liturgical and paraliturgical settings. The scribe of this note mentions the continuous copying of texts, in the course of which they could be improved by scribes who would eradicate errors. In the interest of the Order's agenda of liturgical reform, Bonaventure considered both the choir and the refectory as communal places where the life of St Francis would be read, as he attempted 'to move the brothers from an admiration and remembrance of Francis to an imitation of him'.[130]

The works of Bonaventure have been described as 'unquestionably among the most influential spiritual writings of the late Middle Ages'.[131] Less focused on the exact content, I want to stress the methodical implications of Bonaventure's literary activities. His spiritually minded redaction of texts continued to influence the practice of rewriting hagiographic dossiers in different contexts. The communal aspect remained essential to editorial enterprises as traditional saintly models were constantly adapted to contemporaneous interests.[132] New waves of devotional piety thus brought increased literary activities, which were often of a redactive nature.

For example, rearranging biographies of religious models for a devout reading was one of the main literary activities in the *Devotio moderna*, the religious reform movement which started in the 1370s in the Low Countries and spread all across North-Western Europe. Reorganising hagiographic material, the reformers deliberately planned the creation of 'coherent' books.[133] Restructuring and selections of older texts happened in order to recreate models of virtuous lives.

In this sense, translations – in the process of which a text's structure and content are altered and adapted – may count as redactions. To illustrate this point, we can consider *The Flowing Light of the Godhead*, which was reshaped to fit religious instructions and guidance for the pastoral care needed by Dominican friars when the Latin version (the *Lux divinitatis*) was made. The chapters were systematically rearranged and the language change brought new meanings.[134]

In addition to translations, any further reorganised and rewritten copy of a text may count as a redaction, authoritative in its own right. Nuns in the fifteenth century were not only aware of the status of edited texts but engaged themselves in rearranging and rewriting material, including activities such as structuring (for example with rubricated titles), selecting, and altering texts. For instance, Anna Eybin (or Ebin), the fifteenth-century provost of the Augustinian convent of Pillenreuth, employed many 'editing techniques' in her redactorial work on a collection of *Saints' Lives*.[135] Such editorial interventions are far from just being stylistic; they testify to deliberate choices and document how the hagiographic material was reshaped to fit the needs of a particular community.[136] Eybin attempted to improve the texts she was copying and rewriting, often changing their meaning 'to make more sense'.[137] In this way, redacted texts kept the same authoritative status their models possessed.

To summarise the exploration of the medieval concept of redaction, three key aspects of Bonaventure's work and its impact are essential for the term 'redaction' as it is applied in this study. Firstly, the content of earlier material is adapted to the historical situation, the resulting changes often bearing theological implications.[138] Secondly, structural alterations are deliberate, for example with the intent to match the liturgy thematically. Lastly, rewriting a text comprises editorial as well as compositional elements; interventions in existing material as well as inventions adding to existing material. These aspects enhance the authoritative status of any redaction.

The comparison between the Latin *Legatus* and the German *botte* shows that the process of translating the mystical hagiography was not only, or simply, the act of rendering it in another language, however necessarily interpretative, but that it actually meant a consequential engagement with the text, adding new layers of understanding.[139] The production scenario of the *Legatus* alone suggests a multilayered system of writing and revising, and its reworking into the vernacular may be seen as a continuation of such literary practices.[140]

The concept of redaction extends to any ensuing copy of a text which is altered in a systematic fashion by an active reader who engages with the text. The term 'redactor' indeed comprises the idea of a reader who is invested in shaping the text as an author would do.[141] In his prose prologue to the *Anticlaudianus*, written in the early 1180s, Alan of Lille commands the enraged reader (*lector*), discontent with the poem, to 'emend it with the file of correction, trimming what is superfluous, filling out what is insufficient'; the reader may also polish what is 'rough' and 'send back to the workshop, what is unskilfully done'.[142] Of course, Alan later continues to condemn the insufficiently educated reader who dares to 'scorn this work'.[143] More importantly for our study, though, is the depiction of the literary workflow which Alan draws as a revising scenario for his work. The reality of the workshop (*fabrica*), to which texts can be returned for alteration, is embedded in an active form of reception – no matter how ironic the use of this possibility may seem for Alan of Lille. From his description we may learn that a revised text also bears the connotation of an improvement.

While some may claim that the *botte* does not present an improvement compared to the *Legatus*, it is undeniable that the more comprehensive witnesses of the *botte* unite into one book what in the *Legatus* appears to be 'a conglomeration of texts', and this alone may be described if not as an improvement than as an act of skilful uniting.[144] Redacting comprises acts of uniting, organising, and ordering written documents into a whole unit.[145] A redactor may also insert new thoughts or material to a text; for example, new thoughts are introduced in the *botte* relative to the *Legatus*, and – as discussed – a few text witnesses include additional text material. Finally, the curtailing practice observed in the *botte* gives another reason to speak of a redactor; although we cannot ascertain what kind of *Legatus* material the first *botte* redactors used, they certainly abridged it – and this is a form of redaction as it refers to a process described in the Latin verb *redigere*, which can mean 'to reduce'.

Many of these redacting activities are indeed explicitly or implicitly exercised by Sister N in the *Legatus*, but the reflective writing process embedded in the *Legatus* differs from that in the *botte* (and the *Trutta*-legend for that matter). In the *Legatus*, the activity of compiling and editing is part of a concrete and historically determinable writing project. In the *botte*, writing is not necessarily urgent anymore; and uncoupled from concrete circumstances dependent on the mystic, writing takes on the more abstract meaning of text production and transmission. Here, the redactors – by cutting exegetical passages and descriptions of Sister N's struggles, by introducing new thoughts, and constantly finding new shapes for portions of the text material – achieve a reflective textuality, which becomes programmatic.

DYNAMIC TEXTUALITY

Moving away from the concept of a single author and their intended work, and towards the idea of many redactors of the *botte*, what is the place of manuscripts when studying text? In other words, how can we combine text criticism with source criticism? What implications do these reflections have for the study of *botte* manuscripts that were mostly read and copied by late medieval nuns? Theoretical reflections about the consequences of a holistic take on medieval primary sources lead us to new ways of thinking about the *botte*. I argue for the understanding of a dynamic textuality when dealing with the *botte* and do so by discussing manuscript studies in the wake of Material Philology, an active readership that decentralises single authorities (referring to so-called 'polyphonic' or 'multi-vocal' approaches to manuscripts), and the notion of continuous rewritings.

With New Philology, the importance of manuscript context has been widely recognised since the 1990s. In 1986, Hans Fromm deplored the clash between codicologists and philologists, describing the work of a philologist in aggressive terms: they tear apart what belongs together and withdraw from textuality that which keeps it alive.[146] This was an indirect appeal to transcend the boundaries between those who study the material and those who are interested in texts. The implicit call for any scholar of medieval texts was that the material evidence ought to be the primary source. More than thirty years (and a New Philological turn) have passed since Fromm's lament; in the meantime, countless studies combining codicology and literary scholarship have been published, further advanced by Ralph Hanna's call for a 'cultural move' in manuscript studies.[147] Those studies show that as soon as textuality is examined in its material context, the need to zoom in and to concentrate on primary source material emerges, which often leads to single case studies. Editorial works must be counted among such case studies since the modern editor of a medieval text makes careful decisions when presenting the text material, being aware that they are in a way 'recycling' (and redacting) it. Text, it seems then, is in constant change, is flexible, and can take different shapes. Manuscript culture has become a central aspect of medieval text studies.[148]

Despite Fromm's assessment in 1986, some of the methodological aspects proclaimed in the context of New Philology had already been practiced by scrupulous philologists and codicologists; arguably, a group of Germanists based in Wurzburg had been working with some central aspects of New Philology decades before it became important for Medieval Studies. Freimut Löser, in a comprehensive article, explicates the working principles of the Wurzburg school in comparison to Nichols' ideas, differentiating New Philology from *Überlieferungsgeschichte* by making the point that the latter follows an approach closer to a medieval textual practice than any poststructural theoretical claim could ever do. He critically asks whether the variants seen in medieval texts are a postmodern projection, since variance in medieval texts only exists in contrast to modern versions that require a narrow definition of an author. Finally, he recapitulates that New Philology, as prepared by Bernard Cerquiglini and announced by Nichols was not new after all.[149] Löser's discussion exemplifies the lack of communication between different research cultures, and the gap between theory and practical philology. Yet, it appears that the further development of New Philology into Material Philology is able to encompass areas that *Überlieferungsgeschichte* does not necessarily put to the forefront, in particular 'marginal voices' (on the manuscript page and in the text) and the importance of linking text interpretation to its material manifestation. Manuscripts, although physical in their nature, are – like texts – subject to change. They not only carry manifestations of text, music, and images, but also provide the space for a conversation with these, which in turn can lead to new manifestations arising, whether in the same manuscript (comments, annotations, etc.) or in others (copies, rearrangements, commentaries, etc.).

Producers, copyists, and consumers of medieval texts are not always clearly distinguishable, meaning that our sense for how texts were perceived needs to take a complex manuscript culture into account. Dynamic manuscript culture stands at the heart of New Philology where the so-called manuscript matrix includes 'marginal voices' and makes room for the concept of variance.[150] In the context of Material Philology – a derivation of New Philology which stresses the material transmission of texts – Christopher Baswell argued for a 'powerful margin of the medieval page' and 'its capacity both to challenge and to reform the centre it surrounds.'[151] The manuscript margin becomes the reader's 'locus of creative activities' from whence the page centre is challenged through the emergence of new text; in this way, the central authority is in constant danger of being attacked by conflicting 'voices' talking back to the text.[152] Variability, as it was originally conceived, targeted the dynamic character of textual transmission; in Baswell's words, variability is 'potentially generated each time the text crosses from manuscript to manuscript, [and] is more consistently explosive at points where the text crosses divides, such as the move from Latin to vernacular of most prose'. The notion of multiple text versions as a kind of variability, a term borrowed from Nichols' call to New Philology, is here adapted to the idea of multiple readings.[153] Readership, Latin *lectio*, had manifold meanings in antiquity and the Middle Ages, and encompassed 'the act of reading, reading out loud, the text which is read, its variants, its teaching and interpretation'.[154] Translations may be added under this umbrella of *lectio* as one may speak of a new redaction generated by a readership.[155]

Thinking along these lines, the German *botte* is undoubtedly a product of a readership of the Latin *Legatus* (just as the *Trutta*-legend began as a reading of the *botte*). Such redactions stand in conflict, and even in competition, with their models. Reading is always an act of interpretation,[156] and in the *botte*'s case this meant rearranging the text material to an extent that any notion of originality that may have clung to the *Legatus*, is overshadowed. If we treat the readership producing the *botte* witnesses as 'marginal voices', we may spin the idea further and argue that with the emergence of new redactions, any marginal reader becomes the centre. Hence, this now central 'voice' does not explicitly point towards an act of translation; instead it appears as the authoritative text. Yet, as natural as it may seem, this 'voice' is again constructed.[157] Medieval textual culture is grafted onto interactive modes which permit the reader to enter a dialogue with the text. This dramatic engagement creates a doubling effect of 'voices', a 'polyphony'.[158] The notion of polyphony in order to talk about variance stems again from Nichols' work; following the studies of Jacqueline Cerquiglini-Toulet, Nichols supported her suggestion to 'pluraliser l'origine', that is to recognise the different versions of a text.[159] Material Philology in compliance with textual criticism shall in this way provide a 'polyphonic account of the origins of our works'.[160]

Although New Philology in its beginnings was still very much indebted to the idea of an author and their intentions – a notion that is notoriously hindering when dealing with medieval collective writing scenarios – the concept of a reader-interpreter and consequently of a multitude of 'voices' provides a good way to think about the *Legatus* as well as its reception history. On the level of textual criticism, we may start investigating the different redactorial 'voices'. Literary activities of rewriting, rearranging, commenting, and restructuring text may then be referred to as written forms of 'multi-vocality'.[161] For example, as a redactor, the aforementioned nun Anna Eybin is more than just a scribe when she enters into a dialogue with her material by reworking it; her translations and revisions present productive/creative forms of writing.[162] Indeed, Eybin called herself a *scheyberin*[163] – a word that does not simply denote 'a scribe', rather, like its Latin counterpart *scriptrix*, a writer and author in the broader sense. In 1969 Klaus Grubmüller had already pleaded for an open approach to nuns' literacy, as sisterbooks were both written and rewritten in collective contexts.[164] Such an approach is helpful as long as it does not veil programmatic editorial changes that a redactor would deliberately make when reworking text material.[165] To accept the notion of a cocreative form of authorship for a redactor is even more impactful for the reform context, where women left their footprint in the texts that they were copying and altering for their own and other communities, as well as for their personal use.

Acknowledging a form of interpretation as a valid – that is authoritative – 'voice' next to or even in rivalry with earlier accounts is more than just a postmodernist approach, because it is closer to a medieval notion of readership than one thinks at first.[166] After all, in most cases the medieval reader would have only had one copy of a text, which would be the authoritative text by default. In cases where more sources were consulted and where an engagement with sources added new layers of textuality, the lines between producer and copyist, coproducer and user were blurred. This means that we need to understand medieval textuality as dynamic and fluid. When examining the transmission history of a text, both aspects, dynamic textuality and systematic redaction, are not mutually exclusive.[167] Constant rewritings mean that we deal with a multiplicity of redactors – with partly superposed textual layers – in the diachronic history of the *botte*'s transmission, as we move away from text genesis towards dynamic processes.

Because manuscript books are constantly in a process of reimagination as they circulate in dynamic networks,[168] the different text witnesses of the *botte*, embedded in this medieval manuscript culture, convey the notion of a fluid text. Processes such as compilation, translation, and redaction more generally, gave rise to opportunities for literary innovation; and authority was attached to texts re-composed in this way. As Rita Copeland has shown, the medieval genre of translation requires an 'inventive' reader who in turn becomes a 're-creative' writer. In this sense, vernacular (re)compositions acquire the potential to possess the same authoritative status as their Latin models.[169] The medieval redactors of the *botte* form part of a vernacular writing culture to which Paul Zumthor famously attributed the concept of *mouvance*.[170] Surviving vernacular texts suggest – more than Latin ones – 'a fluidity of the categories of "author" and "work" during the Middle Ages'.[171] The *botte*, for example, eludes these notions in all ways imaginable, including the category of 'single authorship', especially when considering its transmission over several centuries.

★ ★ ★

Because the *botte* and the *Trutta*-legend are several steps removed from an alleged original stable text – one that may never have existed given the different *Legatus* redactions – dealing with the German transmission liberates us from the idea of an authentic account with the primary intentions of a single author. This liberation is not read into the text material: it is something that the scribes and copyists were aware of. Translating into the vernacular did not mean neglecting accuracy but rather allowing room for a cocreative writing process. The *botte* invokes a writing culture conscious of its own potential for how to use language to disseminate ideas. Part of this writing culture is that the German text must act as if it was just as directly about Gertrude as any text could be. There is only one instance in which the status of the translation is implicitly evoked: while liturgical feast days and hymns are usually quoted with their Latin titles, at one point a Latin verse that Gertrude sings on Ascension Day is rendered in German, this process being specified as a translation (*Das sprichet zů tútsch...*).[172] At other instances at which Bible verses or hymns are quoted in German, there is no further explanation to reveal an active translation. The *botte*'s structure, in addition to its content, confirms that the German text is not a mimetic translation but a deliberate reworking. In no single witness – no matter how short – does the *botte* presents itself as lacking something. This should be the strongest argument for why it is important to treat it as an authoritative text: because it does so itself. Understanding the *botte* in its many redactive layers, variance, and variation of themes allows us to see its redactions not as a weakness but a strength.

THREE

MANUSCRIPT TRANSMISSION HISTORY

Embedded in a dynamic manuscript culture, the medieval book was a cultural artefact that enabled dynamic textuality.[1] Because we never deal with a stable text in a manuscript culture, each text witness is equally important for a study which looks at transmission history. The dynamic and adaptable nature of texts can be seen in the transmission of the *botte* and the so-called *Trutta*-legend. Therefore detailed analyses, not only of the individual manuscripts but also of their interconnections, are necessary in order to understand medieval texts. My approach uses a combination of Material Philology, involving 'an ensemble of practices and methods for the study of medieval culture broadly conceived',[2] and *Überlieferungsgeschichte*, which takes the full codicological production as well as the reception contexts into account.[3] This combined approach allows the manuscripts to be placed into their historical backgrounds, and to understand the transmitted texts within larger cultural contexts.[4] Special consideration is given to the relationship between the materiality of the texts' transmission and the devotional piety they evoked.

The fact that most of the manuscripts date from the fifteenth century – the latter period of this book's focus – reflects the 'sharp increase in the production of manuscripts, notably those that bound together religious writings meant for use in the devotional life of nuns and semi-religious' people at this time.[5] One major cultural frame for the German reception of the *Legatus* is the late medieval reform movement, which occurred in different orders and also influenced lay devotion. Neu-Helfta itself, for example, underwent a

Benedictine reform of strict observance in 1496–1497 following the model of the Bursfelde reform.[6] Other Cistercian convents joined in, and visitations of the reformed convents by both Benedictines and Augustinians were common.[7] Yet it is not in Helfta or its directly affiliated houses where the German reception of the *Legatus* is most clearly manifested, but in the German South, principally in Dominican reformed circles.[8] While the reforms differed from one another depending on the specific monastic rule, they all had in common strict observance, liturgical renewal, dedication to poverty, fasting, and other devotional exercises such as a profound communal and individual prayer practice.[9]

Links between the reform movement and the 'explosion' of literary production are important, although they are often overstated.[10] The reform itself was not homogenous and the literary landscape was complicated by further factors such as individual interests, group dynamics, family politics, and the fluctuating nature of library collections.[11] Debates about the significance and impact of the 'Reformbewegung' on the production and transmission of religious texts are currently shifting. In the burgeoning literature on the observant movement, the central role that was attributed to it by a previous generation of scholars has been questioned.[12] More recent studies have shown that reformed convents looked back on a tradition of text production, meaning that religious women continued to manage their libraries and scriptoria with relative freedom.[13] Furthermore – as the transmission history of the *botte* and the *Trutta*-legend demonstrates – the reform context was not the only cultural backdrop for the production and dissemination of devotional texts in late medieval Germany.

Networks among convents were not necessarily tied to reformed circles either; interregional prayer communities established in the fourteenth century for example connected different houses across the orders. One such prayer community linked Helfta with the Benedictines of St Peter in Erfurt as early as 1314.[14] This connection to Erfurt very likely contributed to the reception of the mystical texts from Helfta among the Carthusians. The importance of the Erfurt Charterhouse – for its collection of mystical texts – has already been highlighted in Chapter 2;[15] in the course of the fifteenth century, Benedictine convents especially – such as St Peter in Erfurt – sought the advice of Carthusians, who were known for their strict observance, in their implementation of the reform.[16] The Carthusians indeed remained pivotal when it came to disseminating not only the Latin *Legatus* but also its German counterparts, which is evident in extant copies from the Buxheim Charterhouse. The transmission of the *botte* and the *Trutta*-legend underlines that such intricate networks were boosted by the reform movement, not exhausted by it.

In the following analytical survey of transmission history, I draw evidence from the surviving manuscripts of the German redactions of the *Legatus*. Many copies can only be approximately dated, and for some the provenance is speculative; as Nicholas Watson has warned, 'manuscript survival is [. . .] far from being necessarily a reliable guide to the circulation (let alone the actual impact) of medieval texts, and ideally its evidence would be supplemented' by other evidence.[17] Looking into the historical and codicological contexts of the vernacular redactions of the *Legatus*, this chapter reveals the contours of late medieval devotional text production: we deal with Carthusians, lay communities, and nuns who interacted 'with their regional and supra-regional environment, for which, due to strict enclosure, writing played an important role',[18] and they copied and edited the vernacular *botte* and *Trutta*-legend. In the final part of this chapter, I show that new discoveries pertaining to the *Trutta*-legend hint to the Dominican nunnery St Katharina in Nuremberg as its place of composition. Reviewing supplementary information on the historical and cultural situations, and following the plurality of the sources, I regroup the manuscripts – rather than give a listed presentation (which can be consulted in the appendix) – according to transmitted material, provenance, types of manuscripts, and network relations, creating an organic map and shedding light on the complex circumstances of their production and reception.

For the purpose of facilitating the ensuing exploration, some key terms concerning textual criticism need to be defined: whenever I use the word 'manuscript' I refer to a source, which may be a hand-written book, a leaflet, or another form of physical writing; a 'text' concerns the content of a written account rather than its physical form and – in this study – is usually transmitted in manuscripts; a 'version' is an edited form of a text which may be a translation, an edition, or another form of adaptation; a 'redaction' – the focus of Chapter 2 – is also a version of a text, but with this term, the editorial character is highlighted; a 'recension' is a particular line of transmission of a text version; a 'text witness' is an extant copy of a text and forms one specific variant or reading when compared to other witnesses. A text is different from a text witness in that it is conceptualised and not a concrete copy; a critical edition is normally derived from a comparison and collation of witnesses of one text. Thus, when I refer to the '*botte* text', I mean the literary material at large and not a distinct witness or recension.

Next to many shorter text witnesses, there are two major lines of transmission – also called recensions – to which *botte* editor Otmar Wieland assigns the nominations X and Y, whereby only the X group transmits full versions of the *botte*, the Leipzig imprint from 1505 belonging to this group. Since Wieland's *botte* edition from 1973, more than ten additional manuscripts containing German redactions of the *Legatus* – or in those cases in which the books are lost, which contained them – have been identified. In light of the complex transmission history, it has been impossible to calibrate a stemma or to recreate recensions other than the ones already known. Rather than reproducing

Wieland's stemma,[19] which remains the most convincing one of several possible reconstructions of the transmission, I therefore choose to present each manuscript in its historical context of production and in a thematically structured order, an approach which permits new connections to be made among the text witnesses and hence among the different parties – mainly convent communities but also private persons – involved in the reception of the *botte* and eventually the *Trutta*-legend.

Starting off with the comprehensive text witnesses of the *botte*, which derive from a range of religious orders, we can see the variety of redactorial activities that shaped its transmission. I treat the extant copies that once belonged to the Buxheim Charterhouse independently for their creative engagement with the text material; for example, the Carthusians integrated Gertrude's devotional practice into a treatise on the Passion of Christ. A set of Carnival prayers (for the week before Lent) that caught the attention of the Buxheim readers was also popular among a series of further redactors: the third grouping in the following exploration contains those manuscripts that transmit these Carnival prayers, which reflect on urban culture and how monastic people reacted to it. The fourth and most wide-ranging grouping concerns devotional miscellanies; here, the *botte* finds itself embedded in mixed-media environments in which the material side of late medieval piety continues its lasting effects into the early modern period. Among these manuscripts we have the oldest known text witness which presents a single vision of Gertrude like a vignette amidst other texts, and the youngest manuscript which is partly based on printed text material and uses visualisation through copper plate miniatures. Links to Mechthild of Hackeborn's *Liber specialis gratiae* and the ongoing redactorial treatments of the Helfta corpus, with new vernacular translations from Latin sources, stand out among the devotional miscellanies. The different manuscripts and their relationships to one another elicit a South-German network in which – stimulated by connections spun between reformed nunneries – the vernacular reception of the *Legatus* was widespread. The final two subsections of this chapter look at the *Trutta*-legend which was integrated into a legendarium that was disseminated in the German South-East (centred around Vienna). On the basis of related entries in extant books from the Dominican nunnery St Katharina in Nuremberg, I contend that the *Trutta*-legend emerged here first in the early fifteenth-century.

COMPREHENSIVE TEXT WITNESSES

Several manuscripts transmit comprehensive text witnesses of the *botte*, that is they contain all or most of the overall known text material. An important one is Dresden, Sächsische Landesbibliothek, Hs M 243, which is discussed later in this chapter in the context of a South-German network of reformed convents.

The other manuscripts with comprehensive text witnesses – kept today in Brussels, Munich, Vienna, St Gall, and Solothurn – were originally produced and held by Dominican nuns, Augustinian canonesses, and Franciscan Tertiaries. The geographical area is that of the South-West German-speaking lands. Texts transmitted alongside these *botte* witnesses are theological, scholastic, mystical, devotional, and hagiographic. These collections underscore the *botte*'s versatility and integrability in the literary landscape of late medieval piety.

One manuscript transmits what can be considered the full version of the *botte* since it is the most comprehensive text witness; Brussels, Bibliothèque Royale, cod. 8507–09, which originates from the Dominican nunnery St Nikolaus in undis in Strasbourg, as indicated by the *ex libris* on fol. 363v (see Fig. 3).[20] This manuscript dates from the second half of the fifteenth century, and provides the main text witness on which Wieland's critical *botte* edition is based. Brussels, Bibliothèque Royale, cod. 8507–09, also transmits the life of Gertrude of Ortenberg (1275–1335), a Franciscan Tertiary who lived the last part of her life in Strasbourg,[21] and a German legend of St Catherine of Siena (1347–80).[22] The second fascicle on St Catherine contains two miniatures typical of the nuns at St Nikolaus (see Plates I and II) and was later bound with the first part on Gertrude of Helfta and Gertrude of Ortenberg into one codex.[23] The composition of this codex is telling for an active community like that of St Nikolaus in undis, as it combines the lives of three religious women that had one major aspect in common, that is, a spiritual and visionary life. The codex opens with the life of Gertrude of Helfta, who entered a Cistercian/Benedictine convent as a child and whose spiritual journey commenced just as early. Gertrude lived all her life as a nun in the community of Helfta. The second life contained in the Brussels codex is that of Gertrude of Ortenberg, a religious woman who came to the Franciscans as a widow after the death of her youngest (fourth) child. The inclusion of this text may be due to its apparent link to Strasbourg's devotional culture, since this Gertrude is said to have lived an intellectually vibrant life amidst mendicant preachers and devout lay people; her *Life* concludes: 'Gertrude went out into the cities and villages of this world. The words that she spoke struck right to the heart. With her mild admonition and virtuous power she often outdid the mendicants.'[24] Catherine of Siena provides yet another life model: her biographer Raymond of Capua draws the image of a publicly engaged young woman who managed to escape marriage and become a member of the Third Rule of the Dominicans whilst living outside of convent walls and being mixed up in one of the most debated political controversies of the time, the Great Schism (1378–1418).[25] We know that St Nikolaus was an important centre for literary book production in Strasbourg; the variety of the lives collected in the Brussels codex demonstrates just how widely the nuns' interest in spiritual matters

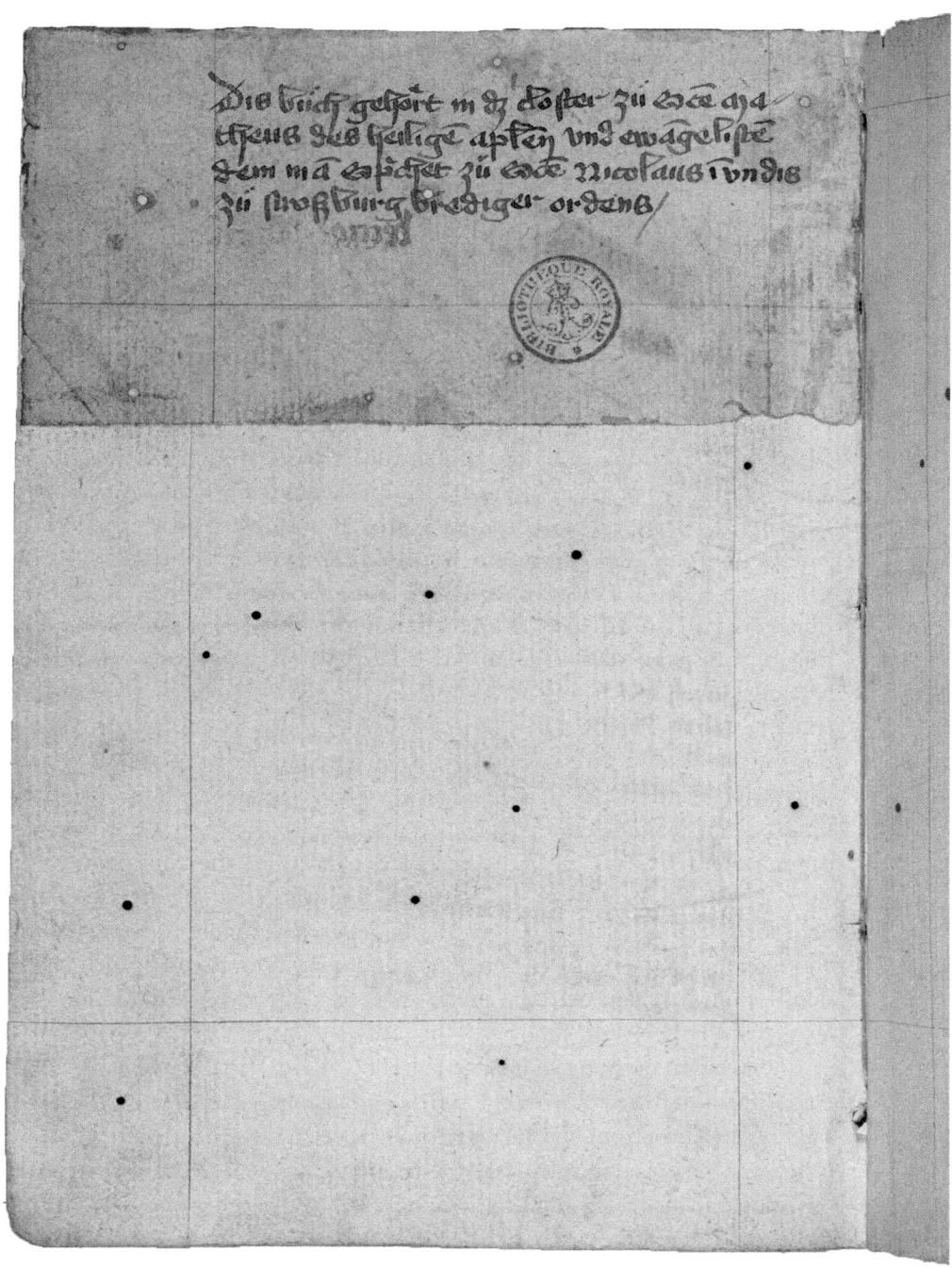

3 *Ex libris* (1450–1500)
Brussels, Bibliothèque Royale, cod. 8507–09, fol. 363v
Copyright: KBR

ranged.[26] The late medieval devotional atmosphere dominated by the reform movement in which St Nikolaus partook – the convent was reformed in 1431 – favoured these kinds of compilations, which were intended to intensify the relationship between text and devotion.

The *botte* text circulated not only in Dominican reformed circles, but also among the Carthusians, Franciscans, Cistercians, and Augustinians. One mid-fifteenth-century manuscript (Munich, Bayerische Staatsbibliothek, Cgm 5292) originated in the Augustinian nunnery in Inzigkofen, a reformed convent which was connected to Dominican circles. The codex was heavily used, as can be deduced from many marginal notes and tabs. One of these tabs, which protrudes from the book, marks the portion transmitting parts of the *botte* (see Figs. 4 and 5). The chapters highlighted in this fashion consist of exemplum-like vignettes which portray three episodes in which the Devil is described as profiting from any of Gertrude's deeds and prayers that are not done with diligence (*botte* 45–47). In this manuscript, the *botte* is twice interrupted by other texts consisting either of exempla – on Christ's Passion and on host miracles – or, in one instance, a short visionary text.[27] The final text in the codex is a short passage comprised of visions attributed to Christine Ebner (1277–1356) who as a Dominican nun was involved in the writing of the Engelthal Sisterbook; she wrote down her life and revelations, having been encouraged to do so by her male confessor Konrad of Füssen.[28] All of the texts contained in the Munich manuscript are written in a Swabian dialect and by one Gothic textura hand, which also dates the manuscript to 1448 (fol. 211r). This scribe identifies herself as Anna Jäck, who was prioress of Inzigkofen at the time. Several marginal notes, especially annotations on fols. 45v–46r specifying the calendar feast days, and structural notes concerning the number of Kyries, suggest that the manuscript had a paraliturgical function. It might have been used for refectory readings. Given the manuscript's contents – visionary texts and exempla – these liturgical markers underline the active engagement the nuns would maintain between private and contemplative devotion, and collective and liturgical prayer.

Another manuscript (Vienna, Schottentift, Cod. 308) connectable to the Augustinian nunnery of Inzigkofen by a partially erased *ex libris* on fol. 1r (see Fig. 6) dates from roughly the same time (1451). The contents of this miscellany are more varied than those of the manuscript in Munich, but generally are devotional in character, transmitting, *inter alia*, passages from the *botte* and also from various sisterbooks such as those of Kirchberg, Ulm, and Engelthal (written by Christine Ebner). It also contains the lives of the Dominican mystics Adelheid Langmann (1306–1375) and Friedrich Sunder (1254–1328). That the *botte* text in this manuscript, although having belonged to the same convent library as the manuscript in Munich, neither depends on – nor stands in a close relationship to – that text witness, means either that the two texts

der zit · dz man die rich hat · die mit gold
vnd mit edelm gestain geklait sind · oder
mit glas oder mit kupfer · Dz sind bos
gaist strässer · dz sy ir zit ze bald las
Er zit las si ze   vñ vñ dz spinnen
ainem mäl vnbedächteklich · Do kam d'
vient alles menschliches geschlächtes ·
Der tett als ob er ir spotet · vnd antrat
si vñ spch · Din schöpfer vnd din lieb ·
hät es wol an dir angeleit · dz er dir
ain als redlich gespräch het geben · also
dz du ain iegklich red zimlich gereden
macht · vñ dz du an dem götlichē dienst
also tagest · dz du als vil buchstaben vñ
sillab under wegen läst · wan do si den
psalmen las · Mirabilia · do las er ze sa —
men alle die buchstaben · die si nit vast
gesprochen het · vñ zogt ir sy · vñ do si
sah dz er die selben buchstabē vñ sylab ·
als eben gezelt het · Do vstund si wol ·
wen d' · 9 · Sin zit bald vñ vnbedähteklich

4 Reading help, text corresponding to *botte* 45 (1448)
Munich, Bayerische Staatsbibliothek, Cgm 5292, fol. 31r
Copyright: Bayerische Staatsbibliothek München/Bildarchiv

liſet· ſo behalt er es· dz er vns an dem
dez bas gerügen müg· Ze aine mål
do ſpan ſi· vñ enpfalh dem hren ir
werk· vñ do ſi die klainen knöbeh vñ
d' woll alſo hin warf· do ſah ſi dz der
vient die ſelben lök ze ſame las· als
ob ſi ain ſchuld dar an begange hett·
Do rüſt ſi got an ·ze hand kam er vñ
v'traib den böſen gaiſt· vñ ſträffet in vñ
ſpüh· wie er es getörſt wägen dz er ſich
miſthet in dz wh· dz ſ an de an dem an
vang enpfolhen wär   B geſchach
an ainer audn nacht· dz ſo vö gröſſem
tröſt· den ſi gehebt het· vö d' gegenwür
tihait dez herre krank ward· vñ öch
vö gaiſtlich ühüg· Vnd do äſſ ſi winber·
Vnd brächt ſi wider· in d' mainüg als
ob ſi den hren ſelb ſpiſen wolt· Daz
enpfieng er fründlich· Vñ ſpüh ith v'
gih dz du mir ietzund v'golten häſt
die bitterkait· die ith trank an dem

5 Reading help, text corresponding to *botte* 47 (1448)
Munich, Bayerische Staatsbibliothek, Cgm 5292, fol. 31v
Copyright: Bayerische Staatsbibliothek München/Bildarchiv

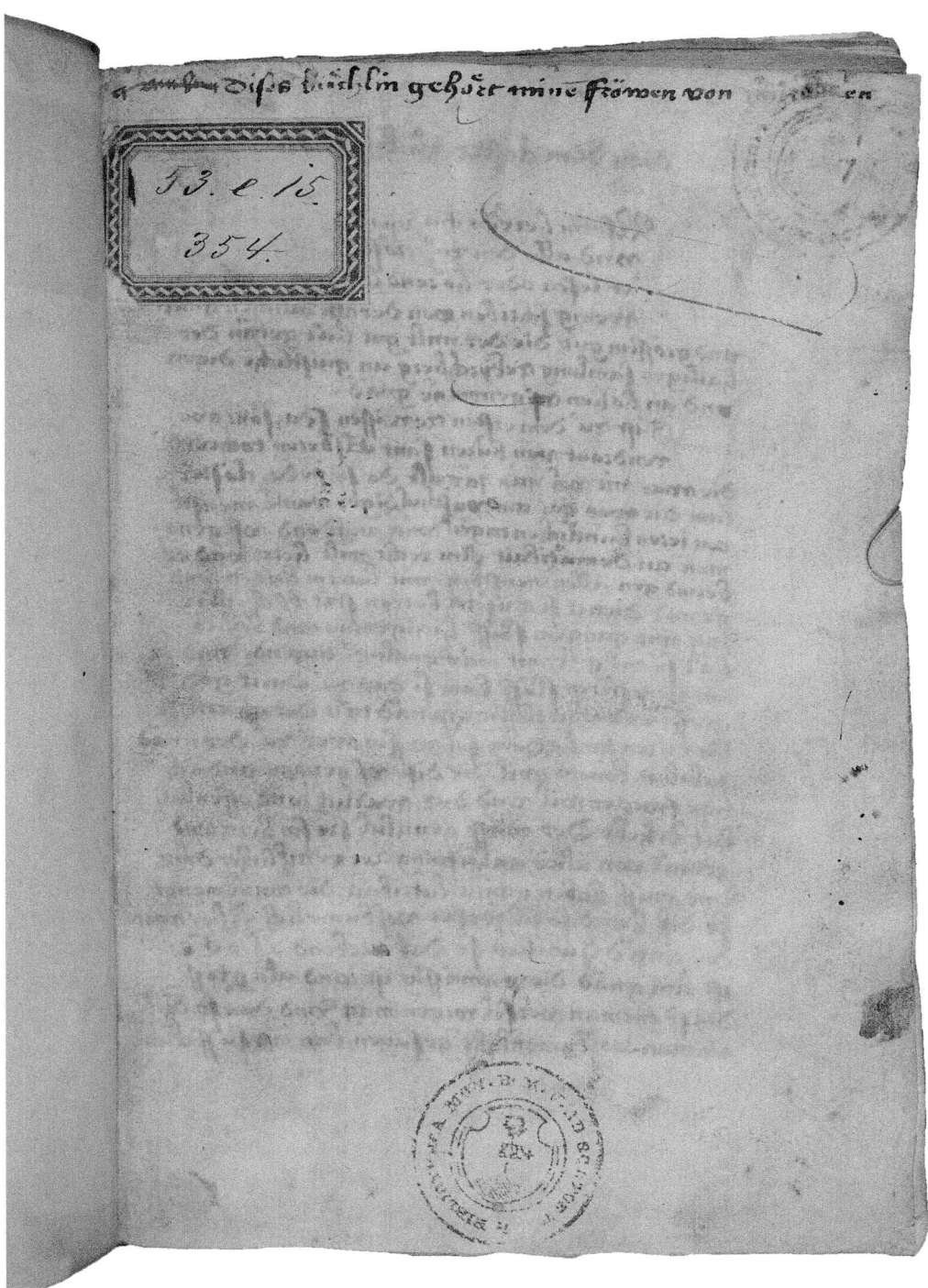

6 *Ex libris* (1451)
Vienna, Schottenstift, Cod. 308, fol. 1r
Copyright: Archiv des Schottenstifts Wien

might have been copied from different sources or that the scribes altered their copies substantially (though the dialect of both *botte* witnesses is Swabian). The first fascicle of the Vienna manuscript was most likely not produced in Inzigkofen, but instead came to the convent later where it would have been bound together with another fascicle produced in the convent scriptorium. The scribe of the first fascicle (fols. 1r–229r) identifies himself (on fol. 229r, see Fig. 7) as Hans Probst [bropstz], a townsman of Biberach, whereas the hand of the much shorter second fascicle is that of the prioress of Inzigkofen, Anna Jäck (fols. 230v–238r, and possibly also marginal annotations throughout the manuscript).[29] The exchange of devotional texts among orders was nothing unusual in the atmosphere of late medieval reform. In addition, at this point Inzigkofen – which had first been founded c. 1350 as a house of the Franciscan Third Order before adopting the Augustinian rule later in the 1390s – already maintained links to several orders.[30] Although the place of origin for the entire manuscript cannot be determined, we can be certain that the bound book belonged to the library of the Inzigkofen canonesses, who clearly had a strong interest in visionary and mystical texts regardless of the specific orders with which these texts were associated.

Actually originating from Franciscan Tertiaries is a manuscript (St Gall, Stiftsbibliothek, Cod. Sang. 973) dated to 1498 (pp. 404 and 475; see Figs. 8 and 9) that belonged to the convent of Wonnenstein (in the municipality of Teuffen near St Gall; provenance on p. 12; see Fig. 10).[31] This manuscript contains a variety of treatises, including a German translation of Bonaventure's *Regula novitiorum*, a register of manuscripts and printed works held in the convent library (pp. 1–9), as well as texts with mystical and visionary content.[32] Among the latter are visions attributed to Christine Ebner (pp. 485–486), Mechthild of Hackeborn (pp. 480–484), and Gertrude of Helfta (pp. 476–480). Indeed, the Gertrude portion in this manuscript transmits a unique version of the last two-thirds of Ch. 91 of the *botte*. In this version, a speech in which Gertrude is instructed on how to contemplate Christ's Passion is divided into sections according to the monastic hours. This added structure shows how flexible translations of the *Legatus* really were: clearly visible rubrics referring to the monastic hours (*Zu prym zitt, Zu tertz zytt, Zu Sext zitt*, etc.) transform a visionary narrative with edifying content into a set of devotional pieces. The rubricated title of the entire section is wrongly attributed to *sant eruten ain äpttissin Santt Beneditten ordens*, that is, Gertrude the abbess – a mistake that could and did easily occur, given that Gertrude of Hackeborn, the actual abbess of Helfta at the time the *Legatus* had been started, was well known among later religious communities (p. 476, see Fig. 11). The full version of *botte* 91 is made up of three different chapters from the *Legatus* (IV, 22; IV, 26; III, 42). Although the structure of the text found in the St Gall manuscript most closely resembles *Legatus* III, 42, in which the monastic hours also

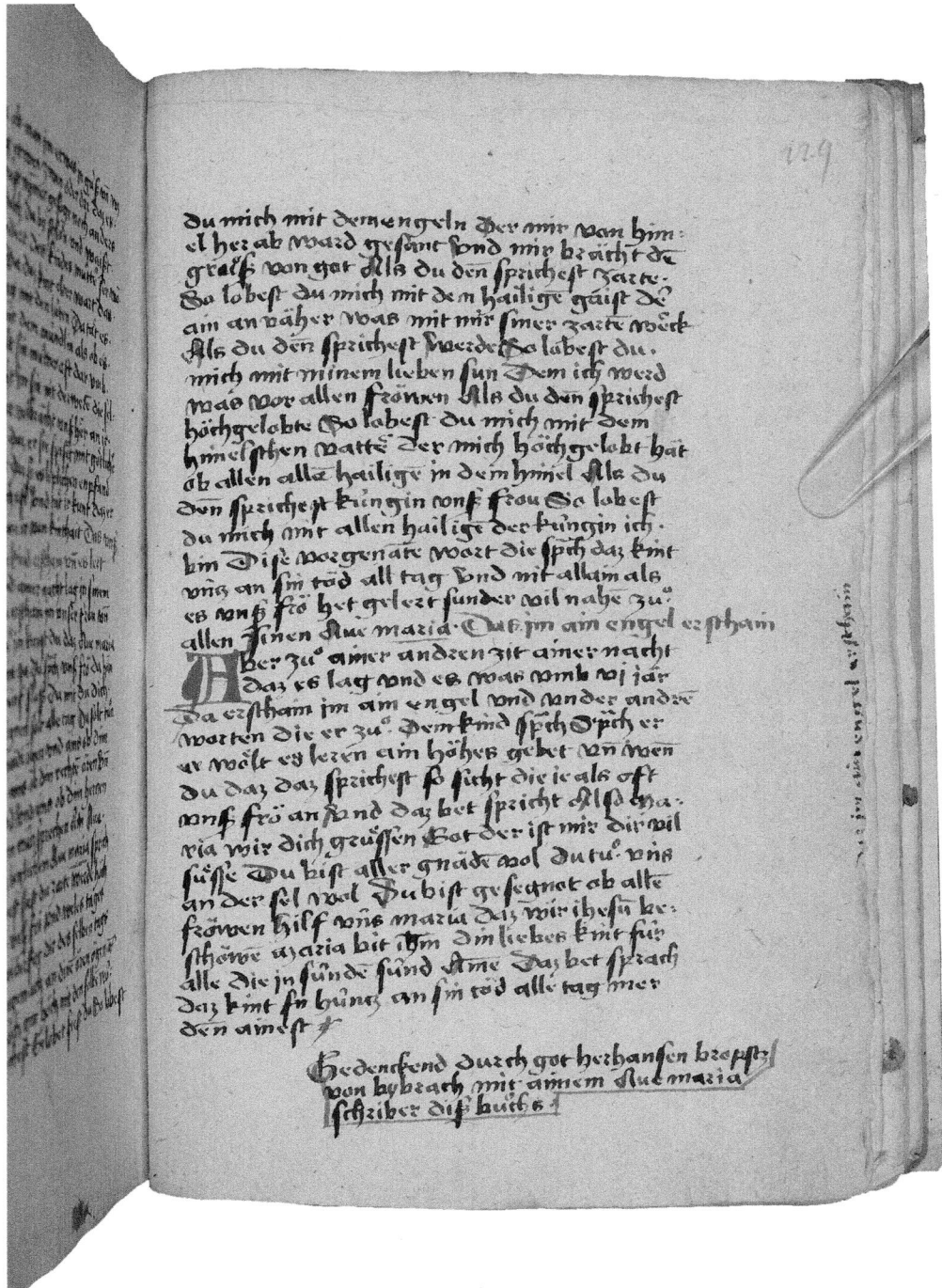

7 Scribal colophon (1451)
Vienna, Schottenstift, Cod. 308, fol. 229r
Copyright: Archiv des Schottenstifts Wien

8 Scribal colophon (1498)
St Gall, Stiftsbibliothek, Cod. Sang. 973, p. 404

9 Scribal colophon (1498)
St Gall, Stiftsbibliothek, Cod. Sang. 973, p. 475

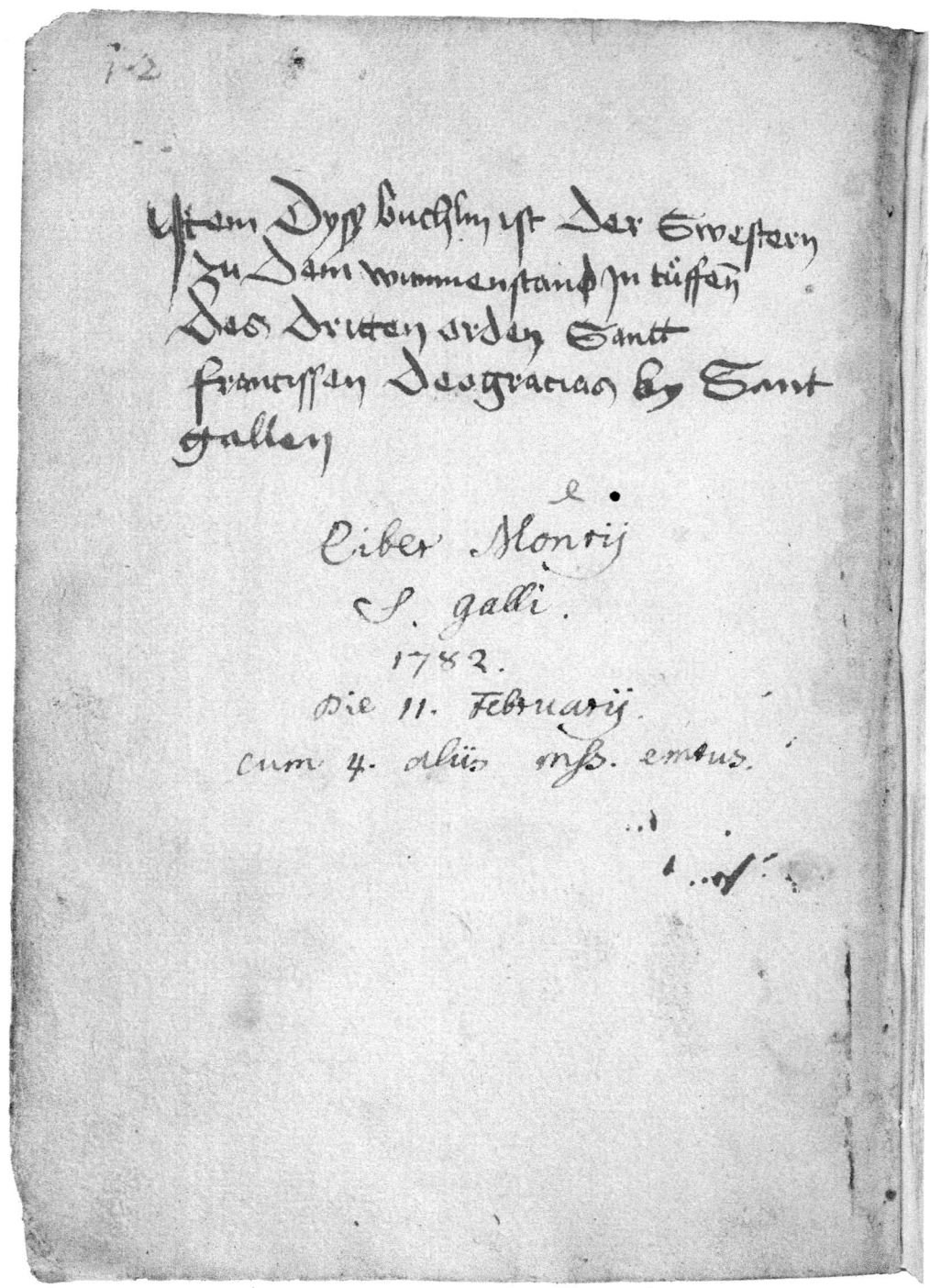

10 *Ex libris* (1498)
St Gall, Stiftsbibliothek, Cod. Sang. 973, p. 12

11 Text corresponding to the beginning of *botte* 91 (1498)
St Gall, Stiftsbibliothek, Cod. Sang. 973, p. 476
Copyright: Stiftsbibliothek St. Gallen

introduce each prayer section, the content is closer to the *botte* text when it deals with Christ's Passion. In contrast, the corresponding *Legatus* chapter (III, 42) is concerned with the adoration of Christ through his virgin mother. Therefore, it is impossible to ascertain whether the scribe of Cod. Sang. 973 used an alternative German version other than the ones known to us or whether they altered the passage, possibly comparing it to a Latin text witness. In any case, the structuring of the chapter hints at the paraliturgical use of the *botte*. Cod. Sang. 973 is also an example for the relative openness of tertiary houses when it came to identifying with a monastic order.[33] Diverse spiritual models – especially, but not only from Dominican-influenced sources – were adapted to the community as the nuns of Wonnenstein increased their library stock, which by 1500 would reach approximately 110 books.[34]

An early sixteenth-century miscellany (Solothurn, Zentralbibliothek, Cod. S 458) organised around feast days and hours of the day also transmits shorter liturgically structured selections from the *botte*. The Solothurn manuscript was written by several scribes, one of whom identified herself in the scribal colophon: *Diss büchlin hat geschriben S. Lucia von moss jn dem jor do man zalt xvc vnd vii jor, und wem es wirt noch minem tod, der bit got getrüwlich für mich* (fol. 187v; see Fig. 12). This scribe, a Dominican nun of the convent St Michael in Bern, is known to have died on 2 February, 1512, aged 88; at the time of copying the manuscript she must have been 82 or 83 years old. The contemporaneous binding and the Alemannic dialect in which the texts are composed suggest Bern as the manuscript's place of origin.[35] The structure of the collection – texts are assembled and arranged topically, meaning that a text like the *botte* is integrated partially and in four different places – and the care taken in its execution insinuate that this manuscript was made with a certain community in mind. Each time the *botte* is quoted, Gertrude's name is explicitly mentioned in the rubric (fol. 63v, see Fig. 13; 70v; 96v; 101r). As a product of the early sixteenth century, the manuscript bears traces of the interplay between manuscript and print culture.[36] A woodcut of the Annunciation has been glued onto one page (fol. 4v, see Fig. 14); another page (fol. 5v), which has been left empty in this otherwise meticulously planned collection, might have been intended to have accommodated another woodcut. In addition, transcriptions from the 1503 Leipzig imprint of Mechthild of Hackeborn's German *Liber* have found their way into the codex. The first portion of the *Liber* is highlighted with an 11-line initial (fol. 46r, see Plate III) imitating Burgundian manuscripts, in which this style of elaborate flourishes attached to ascenders and descenders (known as cadels) originated. By the early sixteenth century, such decoration was common.[37] All of these factors speak to a production context in which tradition was combined with individual touches in order to create a tailored collection for a specific nunnery. The front and rear paste-downs, parchment leaves from a

fröhch verdien mit dir zeleben
ran bit doch durch alles des ge
nemen dienstes vollen dines Ein
gebornen sines & du bit mit mir
tollest vo der gemigsame din
Göthchen genaden maller der
volkommenheit so dir gezimpt
ze geben mit als mir armen dir
ftigen gezimpt ze entphochen
Amē n

Diss biechtm hat geschriben
S hien vo moss indem jar do
man zalt xvc̄ vñ vij jor
vñ wem es wirt noch mi
nem tod der bit got getri
vohch für mich

12 Scribal colophon (1507)
Solothurn, Zentralbibliothek, Cod. S 458, fol. 187v
Copyright: Zentralbibliothek Solothurn

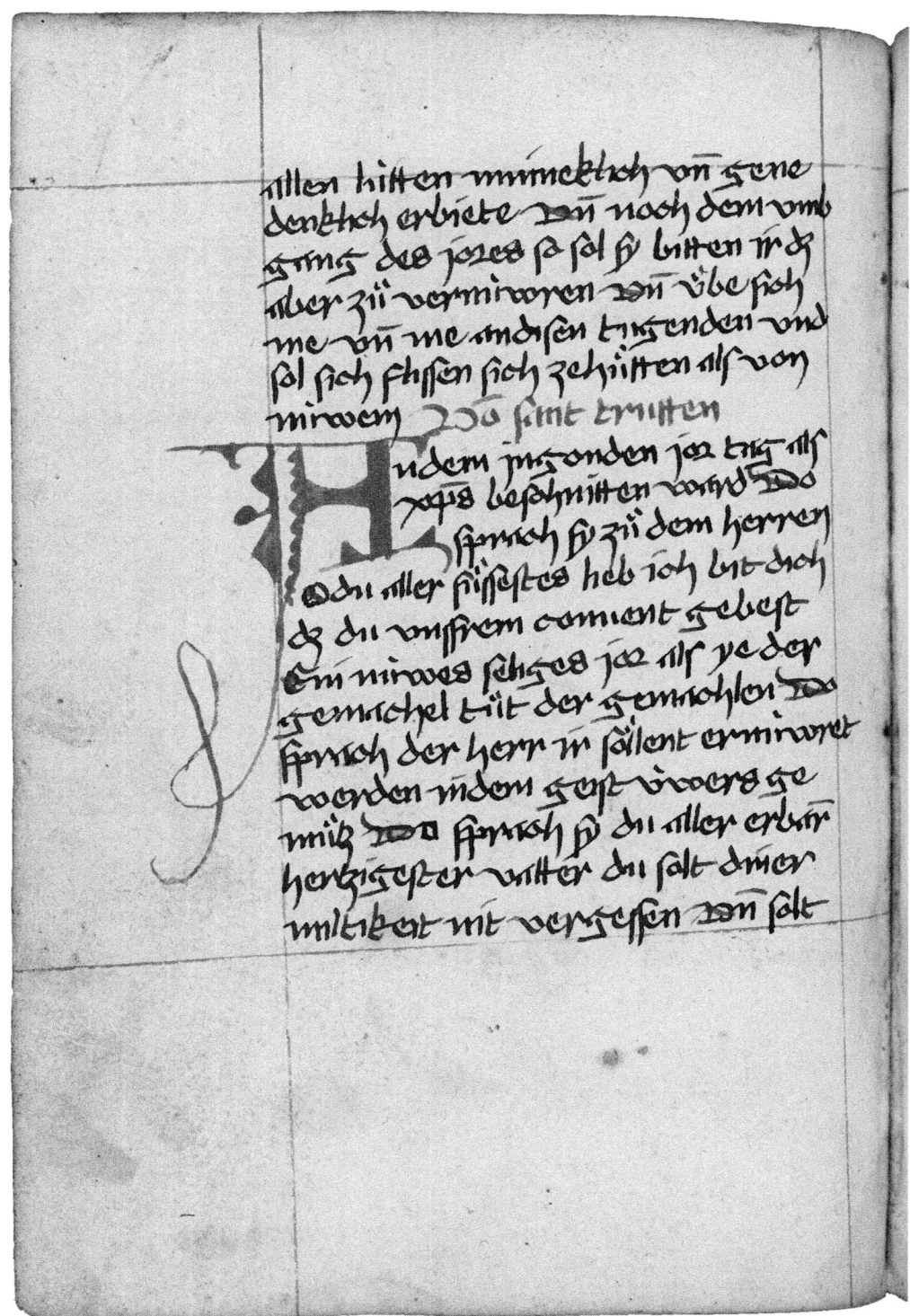

13 Text corresponding to *botte* 70 (1507)
Solothurn, Zentralbibliothek, Cod. S 458, fol. 63v
Copyright: Zentralbibliothek Solothurn

14 Woodcut depicting the Annunciation (1507)
Solothurn, Zentralbibliothek, Cod. S 458, fol. 4v
Copyright: Zentralbibliothek Solothurn

Carolingian Bible, transmit other material through repurposing (although, of course, transmission was hardly the purpose here).[38] The calibrated composition and the pristine presentation of the Solothurn manuscript attest to the prestige and prominence texts like the *botte* could occupy in a late medieval reformed nunnery.

The study of the Brussels, Munich, Vienna, St Gall, and Solothurn manuscripts exposes literary processes of compiling, copying, and editing, which shaped the way the *botte* was transmitted: the text witnesses vary from long entries to interspersed sections and modified passages, which could easily be fitted together with other texts, creating complex devotional miscellanies. The entire set of manuscripts presented thus far was produced and kept – albeit in collaboration with male scribes – by nuns. This is different for the following manuscripts which originate from the Buxheim Charterhouse.

THE BUXHEIM TEXT WITNESSES

The monks of the Carthusian Order, who combined eremitical monasticism with community life, were prolific book producers, the copying, editing, and translating of texts being one of the order's primary missions. Their libraries were well stocked and systematically organised.[39] A formidable example for the Carthusian excellence in book culture is the Charterhouse of Buxheim.[40] The oldest existing library catalogue from 1450 lists the title *Revelacio Gerdrudis* among devotional works; this could well have been a copy of the *Legatus* under the shelf mark F 2.[41] One longer copy of the *botte* was kept and used in Buxheim; it is held today by the Benedictine Abbey of St Stephan in Augsburg. There was possibly another copy which has not come down to us or remains undiscovered, as references in the Augsburg manuscript indicate. One annotator put Gertrude's visionary prayers, narrated in a third-person account, into a first-person mode, thus engaging with the text in a productive way. That the *botte* incited a cocreative readership is also shown by the inclusion of its material in a theological treatise, also from the Buxheim Charterhouse and today kept in London. The Swabian Carthusians were interested in vernacular as well as Latin versions of Gertrude's revelations. One complete copy of the *Legatus* and one shorter text witness (German: *Streuüberlieferung*) with portions from the Latin *Legatus* were kept at the Charterhouse of Buxheim, which was famous for its late medieval library.[42] Simultaneously we find the aforementioned *botte* material in this same convent, transmitted in London, University College, MS Germ. 24, and Augsburg, Benediktinerabtei St Stephan, Hs 38.

In the first of these vernacular Buxheim codices, a miscellany on Christ's Passion, the *botte* is partially quoted in a treatise-like theological florilegium on the contemplation of the Passion (fols. 11r–14r), a treatment for which there is no parallel.[43] In London, University College, MS Germ. 24, Gertrude's name appears next to those of Albert the Great and Bernard of Clairvaux; here, the mystical thought from Helfta associated with Gertrude the Great rises up into the ranks of scholastic theologians.[44] Deliberating on the spiritual purpose of contemplating Christ's Passion, the anonymous compiler of the florilegium recounts an episode from the *botte*, in which Christ recommends that Gertrude read the story of the Passion and 'write the deeds found in it down into that holiest place, and renew them frequently in prayers' in order to have his 'heart drawn to her in desire' (fol. 12v, see appendix for the transcription and translation of the text). This episode is based on *botte* 89. One peculiarity, however, distinguishes it from any other witness: according to the standard version (edited after the Brussels codex), Gertrude should search in Christ's Passion for the words that he had spoken on the cross, write those down, and recollect them frequently. The change from 'words' to 'deeds' (Middle High German: *wort* and *werck*) could well stem from a scribal error. Whether the scribe might have had another text witness to hand, from which the passage was drawn (rather than translating directly from the Latin *Legatus*), cannot be ascertained. The same scribe dated the fascicle to 1493 (fol. 42v).

As it happens, another fifteenth-century manuscript (Augsburg, Benediktinerabtei St Stephan, Hs 38) with an almost complete *botte* witness also belonged to Buxheim. This manuscript transmits nearly all of the known chapters, which, however, are interrupted and accompanied by several shorter independent stories (a Passion story and six host miracles).[45] Whether this witness, written in a Swabian dialect, provided the model for the florilegium in London, University College, MS Germ. 24, cannot be fully established; moreover, the aforementioned possible error does not occur in the Augsburg copy. Could there have existed yet another *botte* copy in Buxheim which has not come down to us? A marginal note in the Augsburg copy makes this possibility seem not so far-fetched. In the bottom margin of the page containing this manuscript's last portion of the *botte* (fol. 114r), the main scribe enters a correction of a crossed-out line above. Underneath this correction is an entry by yet another hand written in red ink referring to another book probably kept in the same library: *huc Vsque in alio libro in quarto MS. X. 80* (fol. 144r, see Figs. 16 and 17). The shelf mark *quarto M.S. X. 80* means that if the books were shelved by size, then the reference is to the quarto-sized bookshelf, case X number 80.[46] Yet, in monastic libraries of this period, books usually were shelved by genre, starting with Bibles. From that it follows that most (although hardly all) were the same size as their 'peers.' Be it as it may, the interlibrary reference occurs at a specific point in the *botte* text. The text on fol. 144r is *botte* 159, which may be seen as one possible end to Gertrude's life proper, the following chapters in longer text versions being mainly concerned with prayer practice. The reference to another codex with the text 'up to this point'

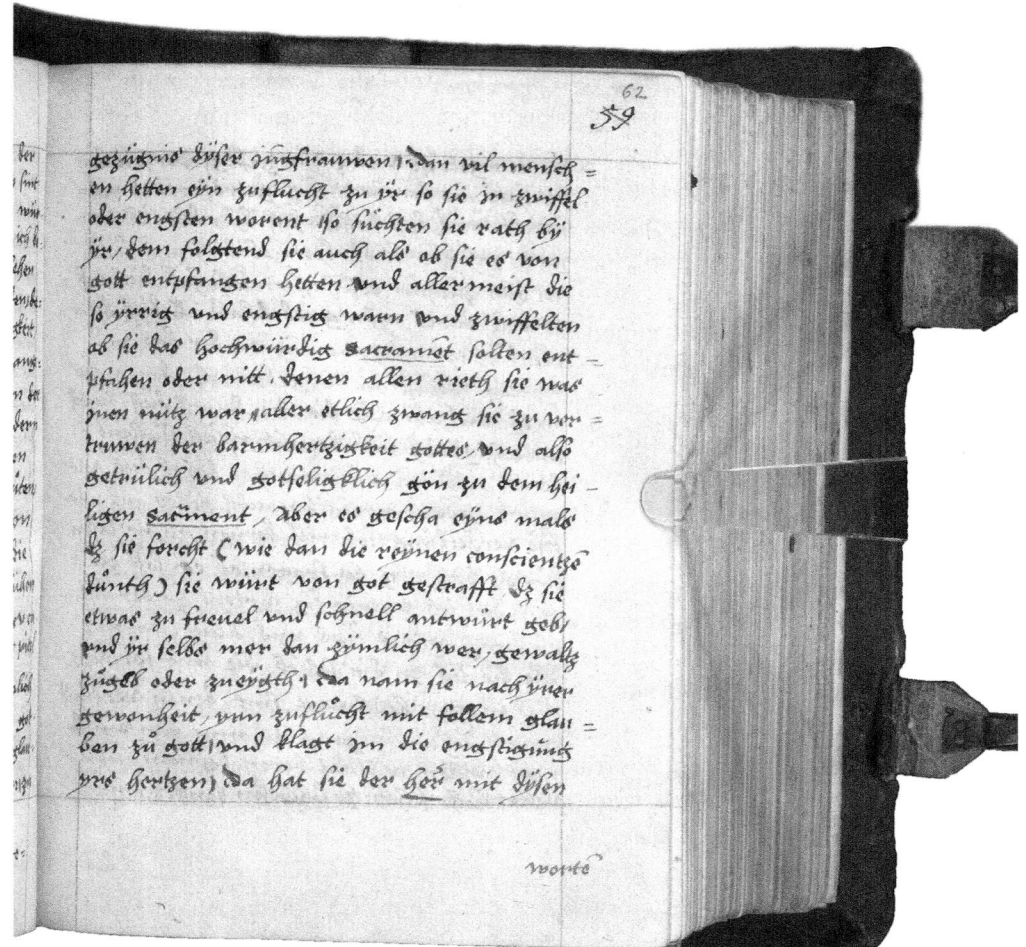

15 German text corresponding to *Legatus*, Book I (1566)
Karlsruhe, Badische Landesbibliothek, Cod. Lichtenthal 89, fol. 62r
Copyright: Badische Landesbibliothek Karlsruhe

(*huc Vsque in alio libro*) may well hint at an awareness that this *botte* copy was shorter than others. Alternatively, it may mean that it was compared to the Latin *Legatus*.[47] In any event, we get a sense for this copy as a part of a larger collection. The readers of this manuscript, the Buxheim Carthusians, put it in relation to other codices that they kept in their library.

Further indications of how Augsburg, Benediktinerabtei St Stephan, Hs 38, was used support the hypothesis of a historically concrete intertextual reception. The annotator found on fol. 144r reappears in other parts of the manuscript. Whereas the main body of text (apart from fols. 97r–100r, a John Chrysostomus legend which is not annotated at all) is written by one scribe, a second hand adds marginal notes throughout providing structural help and

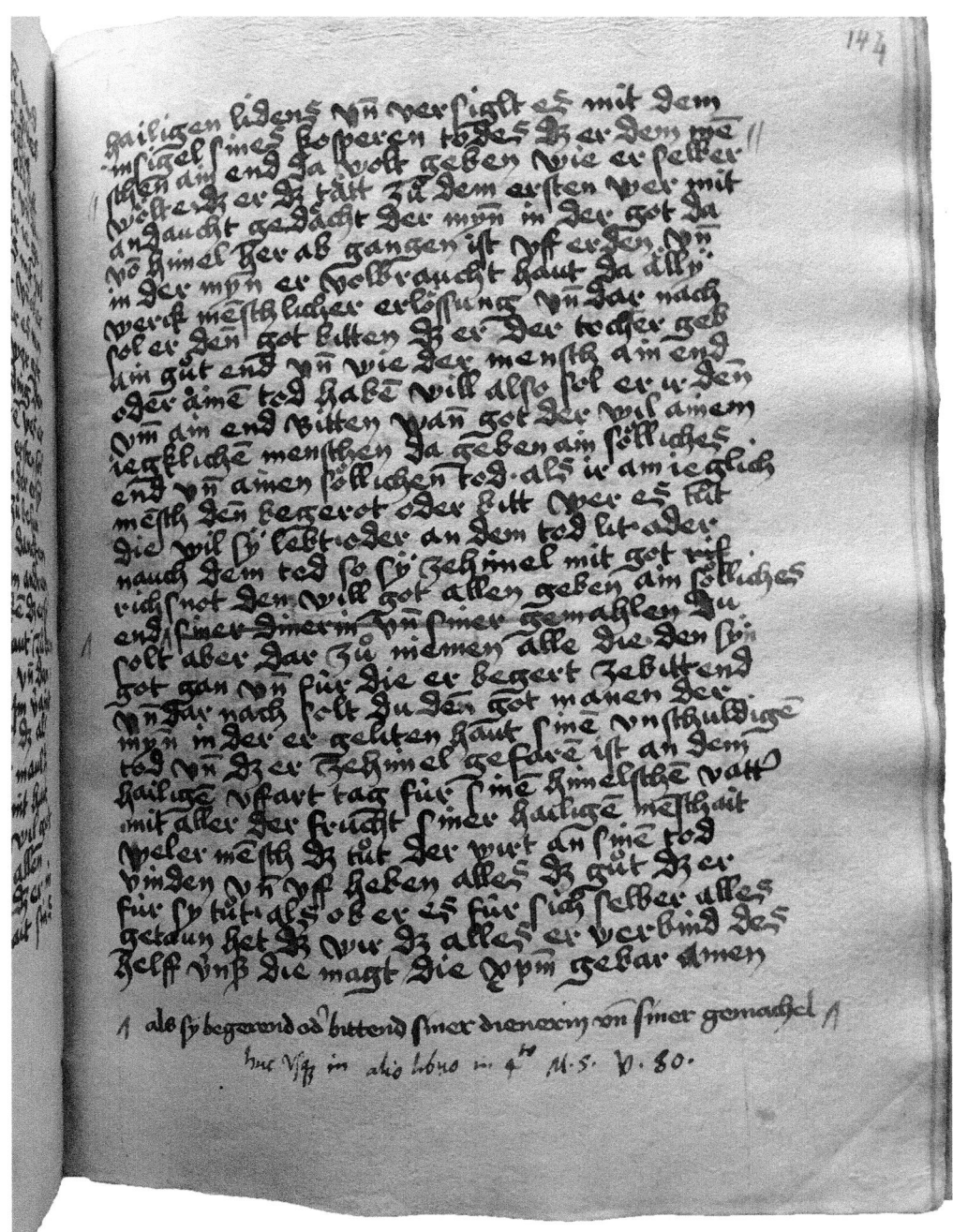

16 Text corresponding to the end of *botte* 159 (c. 1450)
Augsburg, Benediktinerabtei St Stephan, Hs 38, fol. 144r
Copyright: Klosterbibliothek Abtei St. Stephan Augsburg. Photo: Racha Kirakosian

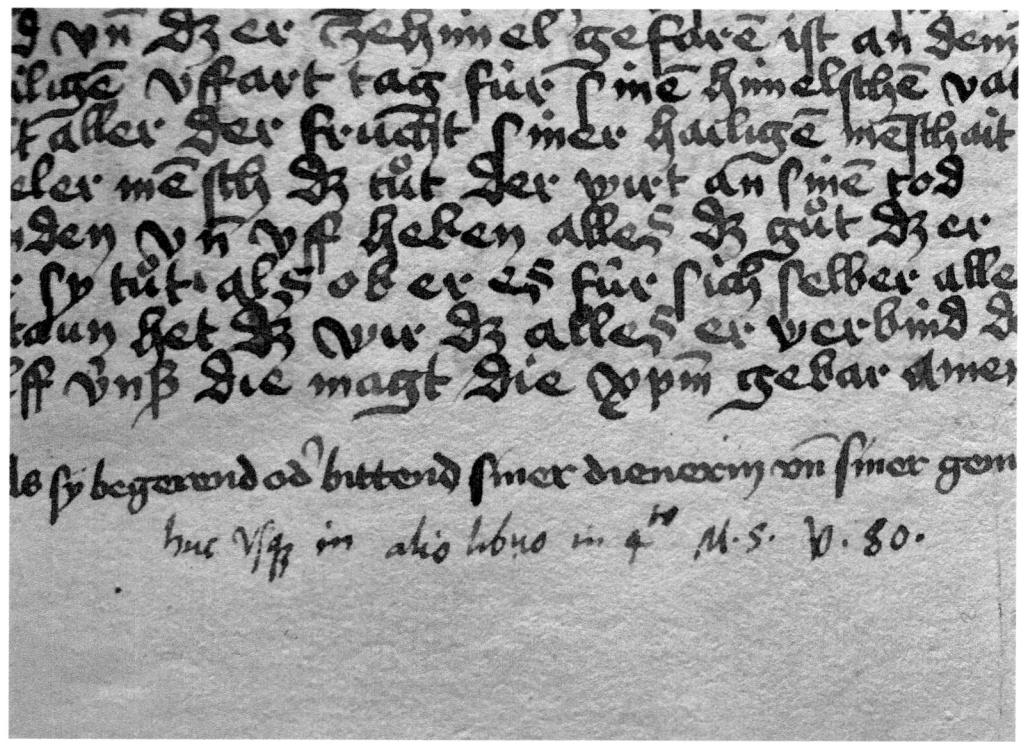

17 Marginal book reference: *huc Vsque in alio libro in quarto MS. X. 80* (c. 1450)
Augsburg, Benediktinerabtei St Stephan, Hs 38, fol. 144r
Copyright: Klosterbibliothek Abtei St. Stephan Augsburg. Photo: Racha Kirakosian

occasional Latin translations of Bible verses. The German annotations are illuminating, as the annotator summarises and comments on the main body of the text. One way to interpret these paratextual additions is from a performative angle, meaning that how to read the text was thus prepared and guided. For example, the commentator found it important to highlight *botte* 57, which deals with Gertrude's insomnia, noting next to the chapter title that this is 'a useful and handsome chapter'. Later on, next to the passage in which Christ tells Gertrude what she should pray if she wants to rest at night, he instructs the reader: 'when you cannot sleep call to God and say' (fol. 23r, see Fig. 18).[48] The annotations are partly associative. For example, in the same chapter, the commenting scribe provides a Biblical allusion relating the passage in which Christ explains to Gertrude that if someone does not get rest despite having prayed for it, it is for their improvement, specifically to make them more patient. The annotating scribe associates Christ's statement that a good friend would stay awake to provide company to another friend who cannot sleep with the vigil in Gethsemane (Matthew 26:31–46), supplementing in the margin: 'when on the Mount of Olives he told his disciples to sleep and rest now' (fol. 23v, see Fig. 19). The inter-text informs us of a potential

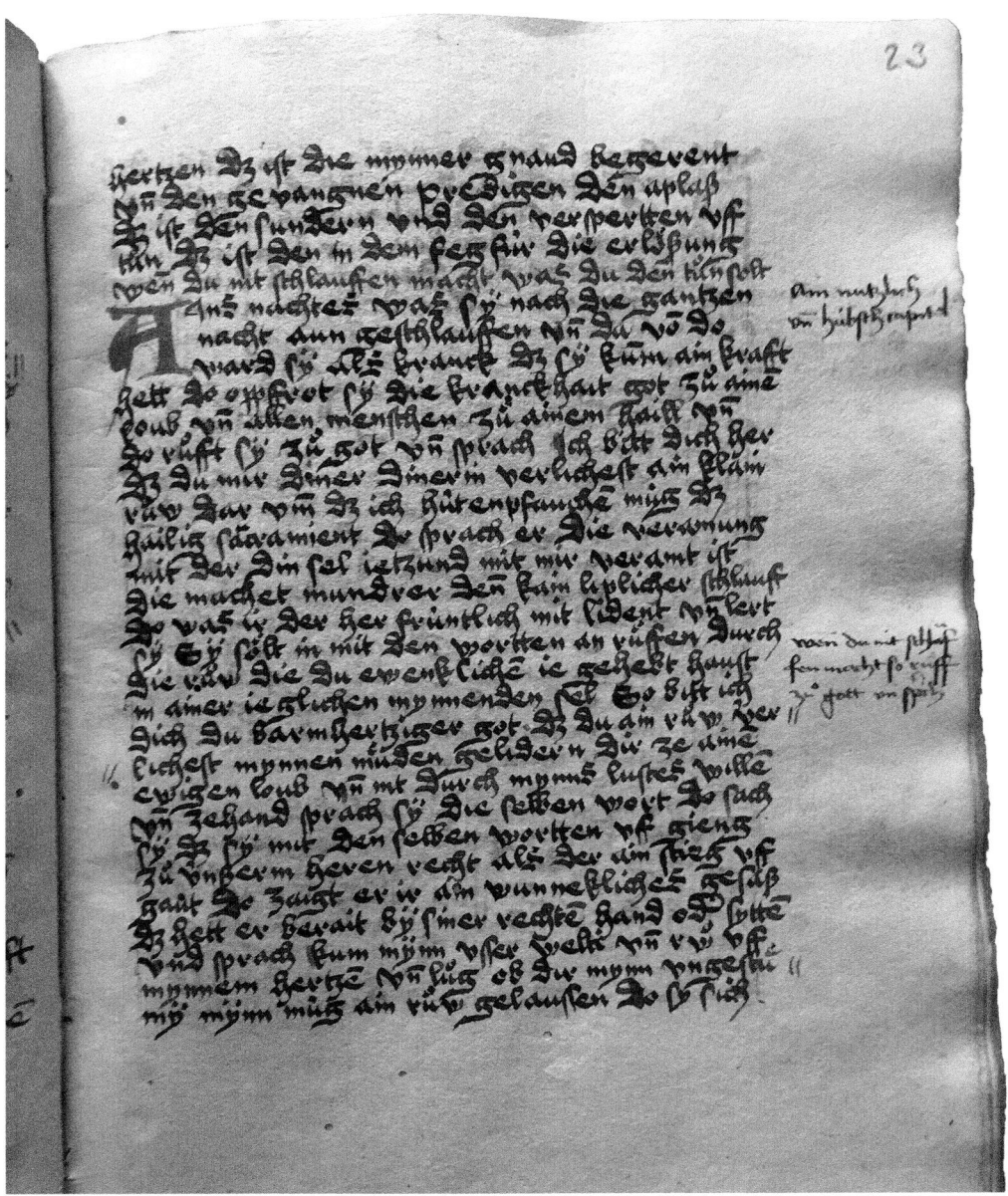

18 Marginal notes corresponding to *botte* 57: *ain nutzlich vnd hübsch capitel*; *wen du nit schlaffen macht so ruff zů gott vnd sprich* (c. 1450)
Augsburg, Benediktinerabtei St Stephan, Hs 38, fol. 23r
Copyright: Klosterbibliothek Abtei St. Stephan Augsburg. Photo: Racha Kirakosian

performative practice; it also indicates how the *botte* was perceived and put into relation with Scripture. Here and in many other places throughout the manuscript, an interpretive mode of text reception, which in some sense serves as an extension or coproduction of the text, is built into the manuscript matrix.

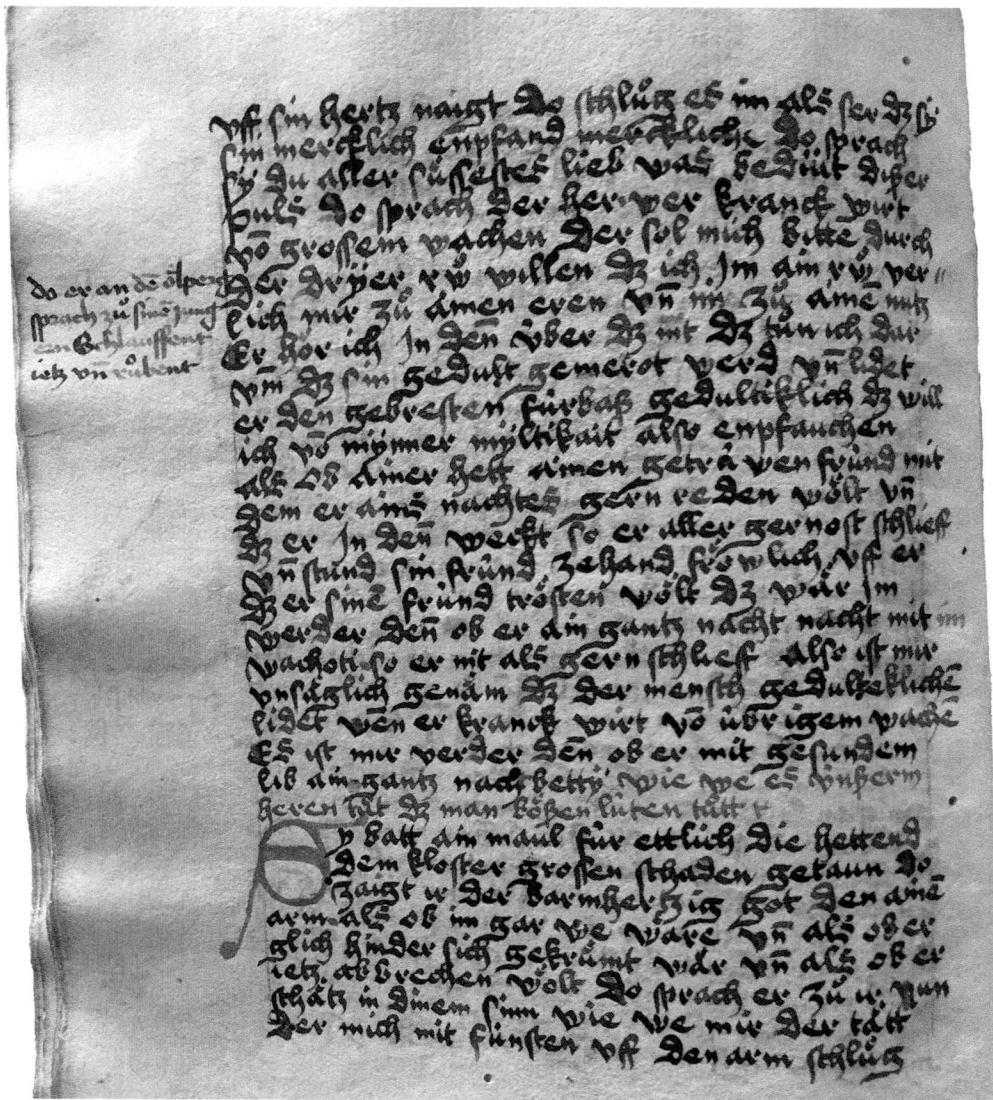

19 Marginal note corresponding to *botte* 57: *do er an den ölperg sprach zů sinen jungern Schlauffent ietz vnd růhent* (c. 1450)
Augsburg, Benediktinerabtei St Stephan, Hs 38, fol. 23v
Copyright: Klosterbibliothek Abtei St. Stephan Augsburg. Photo: Racha Kirakosian

That this second scribe maintains a coproductive relationship to the *botte* can be seen at the opening of the codex where he rewrote or copied a set of three prayers. Adapted to a first-person perspective from a third-person narrative, these prayers present a modified version of *botte* 77 (fol. 1r, see Fig. 20). Also, at the very top of the page the same scribe included a definition of the word 'gem' (*gymme*), laying out its use in the following *botte* text by listing various meanings, among them early buds on trees or glittering rain drops,

20 Note and prayers corresponding to *botte* 77 (c. 1450)
Augsburg, Benediktinerabtei St Stephan, Hs 38, fol. 1r

which represent rather surprising metaphorical interpretations of the precious stones which feature so prominently in both Scripture (especially in 'Revelation') and exegesis.[49] These additional meanings are unconnected to the *botte*, in which gems predominantly figure as images for virtues, prayers, and other acts of devotion.[50] The definition of 'gem' differs in its function from the prayers written below it, which are not so much a paratext as an instructive call to worship. These prayers define Christ's martyrdom and asceticism as a compensation for the sins related to the corruption of the flesh, in particular, eating and drinking. The alignment of human debauchery and Christ's reparation is better understood in the context of *botte* 77, in which these prayers are embedded in the narrative on Gertrude's discomfort prior to Lent, that is, during Carnival. On *Esto mihi*, the last Sunday before Lent, Gertrude desires to know how to redeem the sins committed during the three days 'when the world is so corrupted'. Christ replies to her in a command, teaching her what to pray: 'Whoever ever prays three Pater Noster for me is doing good towards me. With the first Pater Noster he shall offer to my celestial father the exercise of my innocent mouth...'[51] In the Augsburg manuscript, the same scribe who added the first-person prayers on fol. 1r also annotated Ch. 77 by marking in rubricated letters *vaßnacht* (i.e. Shrove Tuesday) in the margin (thereby echoing the chapter title, *An der faß nach Esto michi*, and the chapter beginning *An der vassnacht an dem sunnentag*), additionally drawing a – typical for Carthusian book culture – red circle and specifying: 'note the following two chapters and exercise yourself with special spiritual exercises in those three days' (*Merck die her nach geschriben ij capitel vnd üeb dich mit besonderen gaistlichen üebung die iij tag*, fol. 46v, see Plate V). The prayers on fol. 1r are linked to these marginal annotations in a variety of ways: materially, because they are executed by the same hand, and semantically because the prayers represent the enactment or realisation of the marginal instruction, which summons the reader to practice the exercise. The rewritten prayers' rubricated headings are imperatives (*Sprich ain pater noster...*) and as such they function as instructions to say the prayers, all of which are formulated from a first-person perspective (*Almächtiger hijmlischer vatter, jch vffopfren dir alle üebung...*, fol. 1r, see Fig. 20). The annotating scribe hence performs what is narrated in the main text of *botte* 77 ('Whoever ever prays...he shall offer') and reinforced in his own annotation ('...exercise yourself with special spiritual exercises...'). These direct prayers – a modified portion of the *botte* – possibly represent more than just a spontaneous transposing of a set of prayers from the narrative-appellative to a performative mode, as the same set of prayers is transmitted independently in several other manuscripts.[52]

The extant Buxheim manuscripts give us valuable insights into how the *botte* was read and used: theological ideas were integrated into short treatises creating associative connections between different texts; connections were also made between different codices by referring to related material in the library; commentators left instructive notes for an intellectual as well as devotional reading practice; scribes transformed narrated text into prayers allowing us to elucidate how visionary text translated into social practice.

A SET OF CARNIVAL PRAYERS

The set of prayers for the days leading up to Lent proved to be very successful in the transmission history of the *botte*, and they give us insights into the understanding of prayers as a quasi-currency for dealing with grace. From this line of transmission, predominantly connected to Dominican nunneries, we may infer that the Carnival prayers may well have circulated as a kind of subset of the *botte* text. Transmitted in six manuscripts, Gertrude's pre-Lenten prayers circulated in Swabia and Bavaria, and were copied by single devotees in reformed communities and possibly beyond since provenance cannot always be fully determined. One of these manuscripts reveals a close relationship between the meditative prayers and the material book (Munich, Bayerische Staatsbibliothek, Cgm 843). Another modifies the text to condemn late fifteenth-century Carnival practices such as cross-dressing (Bayerische Staatsbibliothek, Cgm 861). The transmission of Gertrude's Carnival prayers alongside related material proves that contemporaneous practices from both late medieval mysticism, as promoted by Henry Suso, and folkloric lay culture influenced a creative reception of the *botte*.

A small miscellany from the convent of Dominican nuns in Nuremberg (Nuremberg, Stadtbibliothek, Cod. Cent. VII, 62), which among other texts includes excerpts from Meister Eckhart's *Reden der Unterscheidung* (*Talks of Instruction*), transmits that part of *botte* 77 which concerns the three prayers before Lent commanded by Christ to be prayed.[53] The prayers are kept within the same narrative frame, but are shortened from how they usually appear in longer *botte* witnesses. The name of Gertrude, however, is removed. Christ simply speaks to a female-gendered third person. This anonymous account makes a reception outside the formal readings of saints' lives more likely. The soft binding of the manuscript, its composition (five hands in ten fascicles that were bound together), and traces of frequent use also indicate a semi-private reception of the texts contained within it. Mainly comprising prayers, some of which are fragmentary, this booklet of 117 folia belonged to one named sister, Felizitas von Watt, as indicated by an inscription on the front cover (see Fig. 21) as well as a note on fol. 117v. Felizitas probably copied a few of the texts that were bound in this booklet herself. If, as Karin Schneider has suggested, one specific hand can be identified with hers, Felizitas copied prayers and exempla alike.[54] By the second half of the fifteenth century, the time at which this book was assembled, the reformed convent of St Katharina

21 Front cover, ownership: *S[oror] felicitas von watt* (1450–1500)
Nuremberg, Stadtbibliothek, Cod. Cent. VII, 62
Copyright: Stadtbibliothek im Bildungscampus Nürnberg

had gained a reputation as a centre of book production. The Dominican nuns'
devotional activities radiated to other houses in the Teutonic province of the
Order, as they were regularly sent out to reform other convents. One of these
was the Dominican convent of St Katharina in St Gall; their 'convent book',
essentially a chronicle, recounts the reform of 1482 in detail, and letters
exchanged between the nuns in Nuremberg and those in St Gall show a close
friendship between the two houses. As a consequence of the successful reform

22 *Ex libris* (1497–98)
Überlingen, Leopold-Sophien-Bibliothek, Ms. 26, fol. 311r
Copyright: Leopold-Sophien-Bibliothek Stadt Überlingen. Photo: Racha Kirakosian

in St Gall, their nuns were sent out by the bishop of Constance in 1496/97 to reform the convent of Zoffingen in Konstanz.[55]

From the Dominican convent of Zoffingen (Canton Aarau) there survives another manuscript (Überlingen, Leopold-Sophien-Bibliothek, Ms. 26) containing a small portion of the *botte*, which, again, encompasses Ch. 77 (the provenance of Zoffingen is indicated on fol. 311r, see Fig. 22). In contrast to the Nuremberg text witness, however, Gertrude is mentioned by name (*Ain sälge closter frow genant Trutta...*, fol. 84vb). Consisting of a collection of sermons and devotional texts, the manuscript leads the nuns of Zoffingen through the liturgical year starting with the Annunciation. The link to the Dominican nuns of St Gall can be established on the grounds of paleography; Regina Sattler (d. 1522), who had entered St Katharina in St Gall in 1475, has been identified as the scribe of the Überlingen manuscript,[56] while the content exactly corresponds to Augsburg, Universitätsbibliothek, Cod. III. 1. 4° 30,[57] a codex which probably belonged to the female Franciscan convent of Memmingen and which also dates to the late fifteenth century.[58] The liturgically orientated texts in these two similar codices are interspersed with various exempla and with prayers accompanied by glosses. The portion from the *botte* functions like an exemplum for the time leading up to Lent as it follows a sermon for the last Sunday before Shrove Tuesday. Indeed, not only the first part of *botte* 77, that is, the one with the Carnival prayers is transmitted, but also the beginning of Ch. 78 (Gertrude's vision of St John the Evangelist writing a letter at Christ's feet). In comparison to the prayers' overall transmission, this additional material hints at a possibly independent copying process, meaning that interest in this portion of the *botte* might have developed simultaneously at different places. The perspective in which the prayers appear is again a third-person narrative in which Christ instructs a second person, Gertrude. The fact that this portion is explicitly attributed to Gertrude, whose name, *Trutta*, personifies the 'blessed nun', elevates the status of the visionary considerably as everyone else who is named in the same collection is either a Biblical figure or a Church Father.[59] Other visions and inspirations from the *botte* would have fitted equally well into the collection's liturgical structure, and yet the Carnival prayers seem to have attracted much interest. Rather than assuming a coincidental interest for the same passage, it is more likely that we are dealing with evidence for a specific transmission history which favoured these prayers.[60]

While the links connecting Nuremberg, St Gall, and Zoffingen forged during the Dominican reform suggest that the *botte* travelled the same way, one cannot exclude other means of transmission. For example, the Augustinian nuns of Inzigkofen, who through family relations maintained close ties to the Dominican nuns of St Gall in the late fifteenth century, owned at least one copy of the *botte* by the mid-fifteenth century (Munich, Bayerische Staatsbibliothek, Cgm 5292, and possibly also Vienna, Schottenstift, Cod. 308), which they might well have shared with the Dominican nuns in St Gall.[61] Moreover, the last mentioned Augsburg manuscript, and three additional manuscripts in which *botte* 77 is transmitted, complicate the sketchy picture of the text's transmission.

Moving into the sixteenth-century, a prayer book (Sarnen, Benediktinerkollegium, Cod. chart. 215) from the first quarter of the century contains a collection of devotional prayers, some of which include formulaic indulgences.[62] The collection does not fully match up with any of the other miscellanies which also contain portions from the *botte*; the insertion of the prayers based on *botte* 77, however, and the general interest in a devotional prayer practice aligns this codex to the manuscripts in the transmission line of the Carnival prayers. Here too, Gertrude is named but not further identified: *Ain sälgi closter frow hiess Trutta...* (fol. 59v) and the prayers are kept in the third-person narrative. While the provenance of the manuscript is not determined, the dialect points to the north-eastern Alemannic language region, in the centre of which St Gall is located. Given the similarities to the fifteenth-century prayer books which contain the Carnival prayer it is possible that the manuscript was copied in St Gall (where the reception of the *botte* is attested) or an affiliated convent in the area, which profited from the circulation of texts during the reform movement.

A compact booklet from the early 1500s, which belonged to the Dominican nun Barbara Leychtroeckin of St Ursula in Augsburg, also contains, next to various devotional texts, the prayers from *botte* 77.[63] As in the standard text, the narrative in Munich, Bayerische Staatsbibliothek, Cgm 861, remains in the third person, but one peculiarity makes this a unique text witness: the Carnival customs against which Gertrude is requested to pray are specified. For instance, Christ teaches the prayers in order to counteract cross-dressing, 'shameful songs', and treacherous monks (see appendix for the transcription and translation of the text in Munich, Bayerische Staatsbibliothek, Cgm 861).[64] Some of these details are only remotely alluded to in the Latin *Legatus*, in which gluttony and drunkenness in church are criticised (*Legatus* IV, 15). The zeal with which Carnival debauchery is described in the Munich manuscript is more suggestive of late medieval popular culture than that of Gertrude's time. Reflecting Carnival customs that by around 1500 had developed into popular urban festivals, the *botte* text was re-adapted to fit the contemporary atmosphere before Lent. This example shows how redactors functioned as cultural agents channelling and processing the information and atmosphere of their time. The diligently executed collection of devotional texts was very likely intended to be read in a semi-private setting in which one nun in a community kept a private prayer book that she occasionally lent to other sisters. We know of one additional reader ten years after this copy was made; a reader records that the prayer book was given to her on Saturday, St Servatius' day (i.e. 13 May) in 1514 (fol. 77r–77v).

Another prayer book (Munich, Bayerische Staatsbibliothek, Cgm 843) from the same period, in which portions of the *botte* are transmitted, likewise has the character of a devotional pocketbook, although it consists of twice as many folia and was written by at least twelve hands. The manuscript contains various prayers, exempla, and didactic texts, among which are excerpts from Suso's works, as well as Birgitta of Sweden's *Revelations*. This collection of various short devotional texts, which circulated in observant circles, clearly points to a reformed convent. Although the exact provenance cannot be determined, the dialect of almost all of the scribes indicates a Northern-Bavarian origin, perhaps an Augustinian house, since a miracle and other short texts related to St Augustine are included in the collection (fols. 62r–68v).[65] That this must be a nunnery can be deduced from a nearly faded note which mentions the name of a *soror* (*S. Clara Pampergerin 14...*, fol. 1r). Still, a nun called Clara originating from Bamberg is not traceable in any Northern-Bavarian Augustinian nunnery. A scribe whose hand does not reappear in the manuscripts has copied parts from the *botte* that correspond to passages from Ch. 77, 83, and 91 in Wieland's edition; the Carnival prayers (Ch. 77) are formulated – as on the first folio of Augsburg, Benediktinerabtei St Stephan, Hs 38 – in the first person. That they should be presented as enacted fits the manuscript context, since the *botte* prayers appear among other direct prayers presented from a first-person perspective; for example a fragmentary passion prayer precedes the *botte* passages (fol. 86r) and an *ars moriendi* prayer follows them (fols. 90r–95r). The Carnival prayers here combine the conventional Ch. 77 and the formulaic prayers from the Augsburg manuscript: the narrative frame is provided, albeit not personalised, while the three prayers are set directly, each introduced with the same phrase marked by an initial (*O herr himlischer vater, Ewiger got*, fol. 87r, see Plate VI). The invocations occur as spoken from the praying person's perspective, which conveys the practical use of this collection of texts. The contemplative use of the devotional prayers contained in this manuscript is furthermore highlighted by monograms of the holy name Jesus (*Ihs*) written in red and green ink in the top margin of some pages containing prayers. That the monograms, in three cases accompanied by the name of the Virgin Mary (*Maria*), should only appear on certain pages leads us to believe that at least the reader who executed these monograms used the actual book material meditatively, presumably as a kind of prayer practice. This interactive reception with the actual text not only reflects upon historical devotion but aims to leave a trace of it by means of sanctifying the materiality with the Holy Name. In this way, Gertrude's prayers receive a kind of superimposed meaning. The inclusion of the monograms on the manuscript pages may be related to the Dominican mystic Henry Suso (ca. 1295–1366), as this manuscript also contains texts by Suso who was most famous for engraving the IHS monogram on his chest.[66] The so-called '*Ur*-*Exemplar*' (Strasbourg, Bibliothèque Nationale et Universitaire, MS 2929) contains inscriptions related to the content of Suso's *Life*, where '[i]imitating Suso's handling of the sacred monogram, the annotator wrote the paired "nomina sacra" [IESUS.MARIA] in large, red display letters'.[67] The practice of inscribing the names of Jesus and Mary on the pages in Cgm 843 was perhaps inspired by reading Henry Suso's *Exemplar* and its manuscripts, even though the excerpts of Suso's texts in Cgm 843 do not include the emblematic scene from his *Life* in which he carves the sacred monogram into his flesh.[68]

The manuscript study of Cgm 843 shows that the *botte* and in particular its Carnival prayers formed part of a late medieval devotional culture in which prayers and their textual transmission stood in a material dialogue. The next excerpt, stemming from *botte* 83, fits into the narrow context as well as into the overall rationale of the collection, as it recounts a Lenten vision and deals with the compensational aspect of prayers. Christ instructs the reader that their life and martyrdom should be 'paid for' with thirty-three Pater Nosters. The subsequent longer passage from *botte* 91 also deals with the concept of paying back spiritual debts to Christ through contemplation.[69] These latter passages from the *botte* might have not lent themselves as well to a performative setting of prayers as the Carnival prayers seem to have done, but they too dramatise the personal relationship between any devout person (Gertrude is unnamed) and Christ in ways which allowed some readers to engage not only with the text but even with the material, as added monograms occur on these pages as well, suggesting a close relationship between the material and the meditational.

The transmission of a set of prayers for the days leading up to Lent demonstrates how versatile the *botte* material was. Mostly disconnected from the *botte*'s context, the Carnival prayers found their way into various prayer books and devotional booklets with mystical content. Some readers adapted the third-person account while others transformed it into what may be called an 'impassioned I'.[70] Interest in these prayers developed simultaneously in different places where the *botte* was read. Yet, it becomes apparent that the Carnival prayers also circulated independently meaning that there existed a separate recension. As far as we can tell with the extant copies, Gertrude was sometimes mentioned by name as the initial receiver of these prayers, but even then she would not be further identified. This relative detachment from a historical figure may well have contributed to the popularity of her prayers, which became adaptable to many contexts.

DEVOTIONAL MISCELLANIES

The *botte*'s transmission history shows that prayers and shorter excerpts were especially likely to be copied as part of seemingly eclectic collections of devotional texts. Most of the *botte*'s witnesses are integrated into devotional miscellanies, showcasing the many ways that the text was used, repurposed, and adapted. The study of these manuscripts, containing the earliest and the oldest witnesses, allows us to draw more connections between orders and to analyse how historical conditions shaped the itinerary of the text's transmission. Some of the following presented manuscripts have unidentified provenances, but, all in all, further connections between reformed circles and personal book ownership can be illustrated with them. Following the history of shorter portions of the *botte* also leads us into early modern continuations and in one case to an alternative vernacular redaction of the *Legatus*.

Firstly a codex, whose origin is uncontested; the collection Eichstätt, Abtei St Walburg, Ms germ. 23 – dated 1611 in a note that was added to the inside of the book cover – belonged to a woman called Eugenie Peiserin. Eugenie was a lay sister with the Augustinian Canonesses of Mariastein in Rebdorf; according to the necrology of Rebdorf (Augustinian Canons in the Diocese of Eichstätt) she died on 6 December 1618.[71] The relatively late genesis of this manuscript in the early seventeenth century allowed for a combination of older material reaching back to the fourteenth century, devotional prayers from the reform movement, and early modern prayers. All of the prayers are organised according to weekdays starting with the first day of the week, Sunday. A prayer from *botte* 160 falls under Sunday: concerned with the purification of the soul at the end of one's life through the blood of Christ, it is attributed to Gertrude of Helfta, here called *die heilig Trudina*, and it is largely congruent with the known *botte* texts (Abtei St Walburg, Ms germ. 23, fols. 58r–60r). The fact that one scribe was responsible for nearly the entirety of the manuscript (fols. 3r–400v, with a second scribe from 401r to 421r), careful handwriting, and a regular collation of quires of four bifolios each, are indicative of a planned and targeted manuscript production that may have well taken place under Eugenie Peiserin's direction, if not executed by her personally.[72] In addition to the written passages, a few small-scale copper plates pictorially matching the surrounding texts have been glued into the manuscript, some of which occupy nearly an entire page (for example, an image of Mary Magdalene facing a page with prayers dedicated to her, fol. 202r, see Fig. 23); others imitate elaborate *O*-initials as they are usually found in earlier

23 Inserted coloured copper-plate, S. MARIA MAGDALENA, Mary Magdalene with halo, holding crucifix and human skull in her hands (1611)
Eichstätt, Abtei St Walburg, Ms germ. 23, fol. 202r
Copyright: Abtei St. Walburg Eichstätt. Photo: Racha Kirakosian

manuscripts (for example, fols. 6ov and 27or, see Plates VII and VIII). The mixed-media production of this codex – manuscript with copper-plates coloured and fitted to match the page layout – shows the versatility of material culture when it came to devotional books. After Eugenie Peiserin's death, the prayer book was left to the Abbey community of St Walburg where it is still kept today.

After many attempts to withstand new rules, the Benedictine Abbey of St Walburg had been reformed between 1452 and 1456, and became part of interregional reform and prayer networks which included Benedictines in Nuremberg and Augustinian canonesses in Pillenreuth.[73] The Canons of Rebdorf joined the Congregation of Windesheim, that is, the Augustinian reform movement, in 1458. Thus, it is not surprising that the prayer book of Eugenie Peiserin contains prayers that circulated in reformed circles, including the prayers of Gertrude of Helfta and Mechthild of Hackeborn. Some of the prayers, however, are dedicated to the Sacred Heart of Jesus – a trope which the reformers did not much care about, but which developed later and flourished in the Counter-Reformation Church. However, it is hard to tell at what stage the Helfta mysticism made it to Rebdorf or nearby Eichstätt – a question that was first raised by Jeffrey Hamburger, who in his discussion of drawings produced around 1500 at Walburg saw 'fascinating analogies' between the *Legatus* and the 'patterns of prayer' suggested by one drawing from St Walburg. Hamburger concluded: 'The texts associated with Gertrude, however, cannot be regarded as the source either for the image or for associated devotional practices; there is no evidence to suggest that the nuns at St Walburg knew the *Legatus*.'[74] The Benedictine sisters in Eichstätt may not have known the *Legatus* before 1500, but with Ms germ. 23 (an early seventeenth-century copy), and with the reform link that connects Eichstätt and the nearby Rebdorf with reformed convents, we can now at least assume a reception of parts of the *botte* around St Walburg in the late Middle Ages. More importantly, Ms germ. 23 highlights the interplay between personal prayer books, lay communities, and reformed convent networks.

More manuscripts transmitting the *botte* reveal how widespread and adaptable the German reception of the *Legatus* was. Among these is the oldest known witness, which contains an Easter Monday vision in which Gertrude sees herself presented to God in a sumptuous dress. This excerpt, which correlates to *botte* 93, is found in a miscellany of Northern-Bavarian origin (Gotha, Forschungsbibliothek, Chart. B 269), which unites both Latin and German devotional and hagiographic texts.[75] Among other texts, the codex in Gotha contains excerpts from Birgitta of Sweden's *Revelations* as well as German translations of letters attributed to St Jerome. The portion from the *botte* (fol. 25r–v, see Figs. 1 and 2) is surrounded by a Latin reading guide to visionary texts (fols. 18r–21v) and by a German rendering of the *Visio monachi*

Eyneshamensis, *The Revelation of the Monk of Eynsham* (fols. 26r–53v). Gertrude is not mentioned by name; the visionary is referred to as an anonymous 'pious person' (*ain gut mensch*). That the vision should appear in such an unspecified manner enhances the appellative character of the text collection; the texts are not simply narrative but instructive, as the Latin guide to how to interpret visions exemplifies. Written by one late fourteenth-century scribe, who also rubricated the texts, the miscellany was produced for a religious person or community with an active interest in short devotional texts that varied in their genres (epistles, legends, miracles, visions, mystagogical texts, and blessings). The codex is given a title by its medieval scribe: *fegfewr puch*, that is *Book of Purgatory*.[76] The mixed text collection suggests that this codex might have been produced by Carthusians, who had a strong interest in visionary texts dealt with from many perspectives. One codicological feature supports this hypothesis: the scribe must have known the Latin text or a German redaction closer to it because he added a clause in the margin (*vnd ain klaines steublein maht niht verholen werden wann daz*) that cannot be found in any other, younger German text witness (fol. 25v, see Fig. 2) but that clearly goes back to the Latin source (*Nec aliquis saltem minimus pulvis aut punctus latere poterat*, *Legatus* IV, 28). The Carthusians, notably those in Erfurt, kept manuscripts containing the 'standard' *Legatus*; those at Buxheim, both Latin and German text witnesses. Given that the *botte* portion transmitted in this codex contains only one vision (corresponding to Ch. 93 in Wieland's edition) that, other than the marginal note, forms part of the *botte* transmission, means that an older *botte* text witness unknown to us today or a Latin text were consulted. The source for the whole passage or for the marginal note might have travelled southwards from one of the more northern charterhouses (Erfurt?), but the texts could also have been transmitted in the opposite direction (Buxheim?). The Northern–Bavarian dialect in Chart. B 269 hints at Franconia as a possible place of origin, yet the precise provenance remains unidentified.

Similarly, we cannot exactly locate a group of manuscripts written in Swabian dialects. Two of these manuscripts are closely tied in their manuscript transmission history: Freiburg im Breisgau, Universitätsbibliothek, Hs. 202, and Freiburg im Breisgau, Erzbischöfliches Archiv, Hs. 31. Both transmit the beginning and middle portions of the *botte* with a narrative on Christ's Passion and an exemplum on the Resurrection interposed between *botte* 91 and 92. On the basis of their respective papers' watermarks, Hs. 202 can be dated to 1474–1476, while Hs. 31 was written between 1476 and 1478.[77] Hs. 202 has later additions made by four sixteenth-century scribes that concern various prayers and short teachings (fols. 178r–191v);[78] but the older fascicle, which contains the *botte* along with a Passion story and an exemplum (fols. 1r–177v) was written by the same scribe who wrote the codex kept at the Archdiocesan Archives (Hs. 31). This fifteenth-century scribe employed a bastarda script and also rubricated the text with distinctive and greatly varying lombards (for example, G-lombard in Universitätsbibliothek, Hs. 202, fol. 8r, see Plate IX). Moreover, in these two miscellanies, the parts of the *botte*, their order, and the dialect (East Swabian) are identical.

The insertion of the Passion and Resurrection is meaningful since it follows a passage in which Christ teaches Gertrude the benefits of contemplating of his Passion. The text transitions seamlessly into the subsequent Passion narrative (*das ist von vnsers hern marter*), which functions as a performative echo of the *botte* text. The transition at the end of the passage is remarkable: the exemplum on Christ's Resurrection depicts souls singing in a meadow. This is then followed by Gertrude's Easter vision in which the sceptre of a *Christus majestatis* is adorned with blossoming flowers placed there through Gertrude's contemplative prayers.[79] At the beginning and the end, the Passion story and the Resurrection exemplum suspend the *botte* narrative, meaning that they themselves work as contemplative vignettes. The careful alignment of the various texts according to reading principles orientated at devotional practice means that whoever was responsible for the compilation and the text order deliberately chose this arrangement. The same arrangement, namely that between *botte* 91 and 92, in which space is opened up for a Passion story and a Resurrection exemplum, also appears in two manuscripts already discussed: Augsburg, Benediktinerabtei St Stephan, Hs 38, and Munich, Bayerische Staatsbibliothek, Cgm 5292. Indeed, all of these manuscripts form one recension group, which Wieland, who did not know Freiburg im Breisgau, Erzbischöfliches Archiv, Hs. 31, described as the Y-version of the *botte*.[80]

A fifth, much later text witness dated to 1643 (Freiburg im Breisgau, Universitätsbibliothek, Hs. 186) also belongs to this transmission group; it is incontestably a direct descendant of Munich, Bayerische Staatsbibliothek, Cgm 5292, since it not only contains the same selections from the *botte* text (with the exception of Ch. 1), but also the inserted collection of exempla before the final *botte* section that can also be found in Munich, Bayerische Staatsbibliothek, Cgm 5292.[81] In addition to the material found in the Munich manuscript, the sole scribe of Freiburg im Breisgau, Universitätsbibliothek, Hs. 186, also copied several shorter texts with devotional and legendary material. Siegfried Ringler suggests the Augustinian nunnery of Inzigkofen as this codex's place of origin and sees the entire Y-line of the *botte* transmission as possibly going back to a Nuremberg-Inzigkofen link.[82] Although the Swabian dialects of all these text witnesses and the Inzigkofen provenance of Cgm 5292, may support Ringler's theory, the Augsburg manuscript, which belonged to the Buxheim Charterhouse, complicates the transmission connexion between the Dominican nunnery in Nuremberg and the Augustinian nunnery in Inzigkofen, as it forms a triangle with the Carthusians. The connections between the different convents, especially those forged in the reform movement, can easily lead us to assign an unidentified manuscript to one convent or another, but the wide and scattered dissemination of the *botte* reveals that its transmission history unfolds beyond what is known about established convent networks. This becomes evident with the Carthusian elements in the transmission history.

A manuscript with a South-Rhine Franconian text witness of the *botte* (Heidelberg, Universitätsbibliothek, Heid. Hs. 33) dated 1516/1517, complicates this picture of the transmission history even further. The manuscript transmits only the last part of the *botte* (Ch. 133–170), and it also contains a German translation of passages from Mechthild of Hackeborn's *Liber* and other mystical texts by Henry Suso.[83] This mystical portion of the manuscript was written by one scribe (fols. 3r–269r), while a second fascicle with sermons and other theologically relevant short treatises was written in a second hand (fols. 275r–300v). Towards the end of the codex the first hand reappears in a treatise on praying (fols. 302r–317r). The first fascicle stands out, because its texts are structured in a scrupulous way: they are divided into short entries that are visually partitioned with rubrics and titles. The *botte* text also appears special in its layout since the chapters are broken into several paragraphs that sometimes are ordered in a dramatic way, meaning that the performative aspect of the narrative is displayed. For example, the headlines often take the form of *introit*-formulas so as to mark the beginning of a speech, hence labelling different voices and rendering them visible on the page (fols. 226r and 237r, see Figs. 24 and 25). This dramatic mode suggests a certain imaginative reception in which the visionary's account becomes a stage for the reader's own visualisation. One thus may speak of a process of revisioning manifested in the manuscript's materiality. Although the rubrications cease from fol. 243r onwards, the principle of dramatic headlines remains throughout the *botte* text. The text preceding the *botte* text – selections regarding spiritual instructions from the German *Liber* of Mechthild of Hackeborn copied from the print version of 1503 or 1508 – is similarly broken into paragraphs, some of which have dramatic headlines (for example, fol. 154r, see Fig. 26).[84] The juxtaposition of these two texts attributed to the Helfta mystics reveals the primarily communal objective of the Heidelberg codex; the selections from the *Liber* are mainly instructive and the chapters that were copied from the *botte* text exclusively concern stories about nuns other than Gertrude. These final chapters recount sisterbook-like episodes from the time after Gertrude's death. Indeed, in contrast to fuller versions of the *botte*, the Heidelberg codex does not mention Gertrude's name at all. This is not surprising considering that the selection itself is not concerned with Gertrude but rather with the community of the nuns. While this collective aspect opens up the possibility of a broader reception, as it is more adaptable to any given community, the concrete historical community of Helfta is mentioned at the beginning of the German

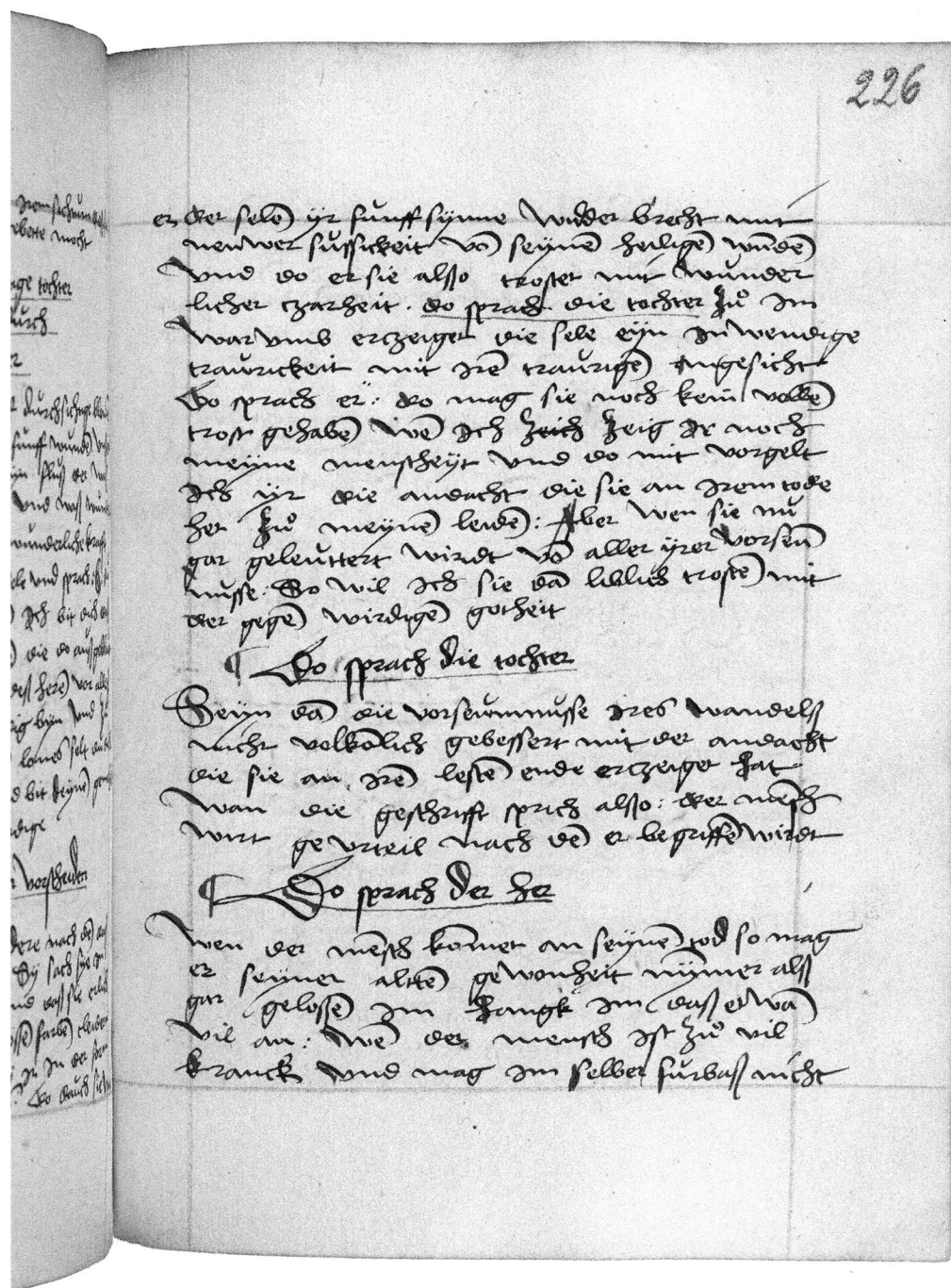

24 Text corresponding to *botte* 136 (1516–17)
Heidelberg, Universitätsbibliothek, Heid. Hs. 33, fol. 226r
Copyright: Universitätsbibliothek Heidelberg

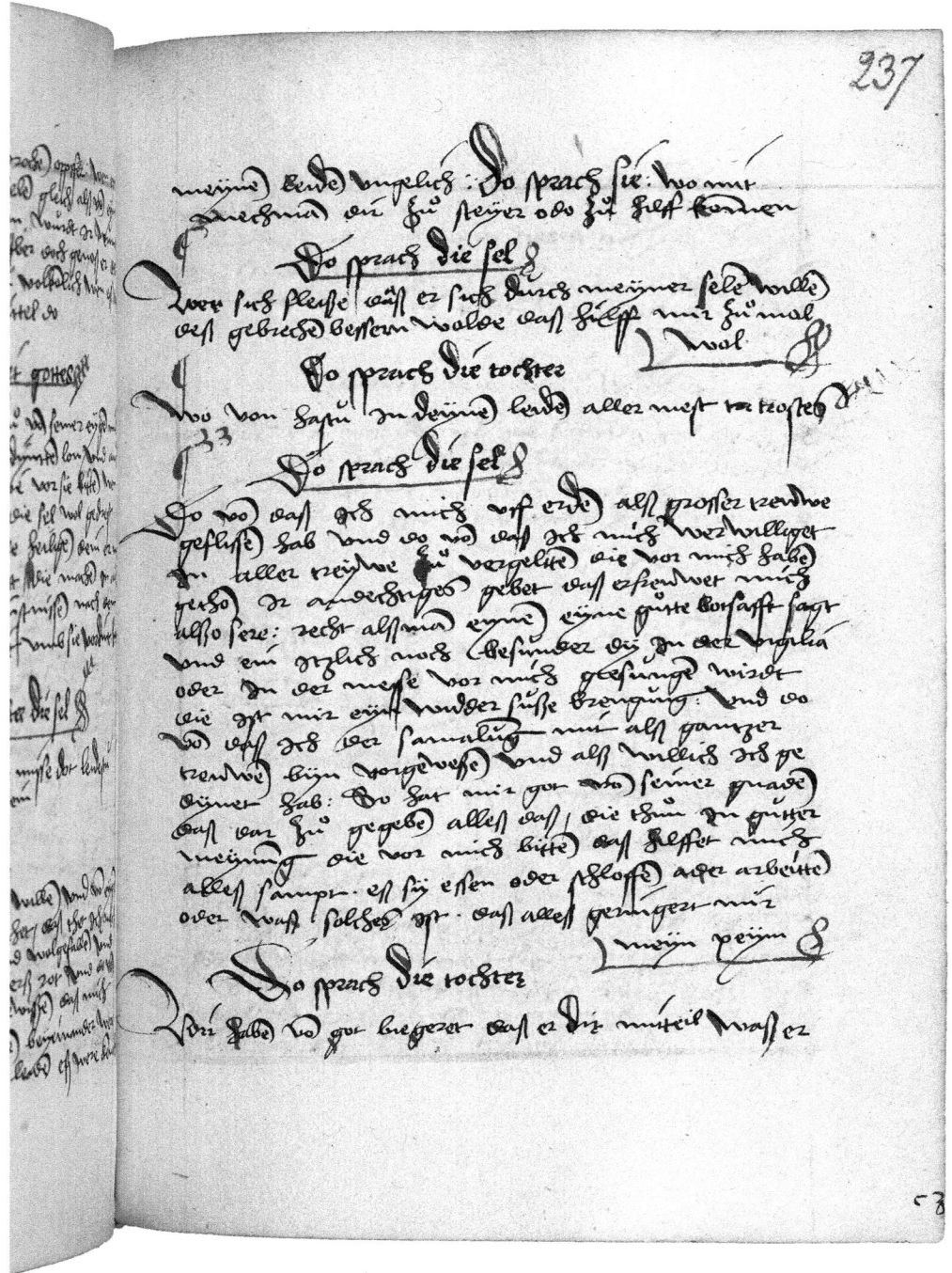

25 Text corresponding to *botte* 143 (1516–17)
Heidelberg, Universitätsbibliothek, Heid. Hs. 33, fol. 237r
Copyright: Universitätsbibliothek Heidelberg

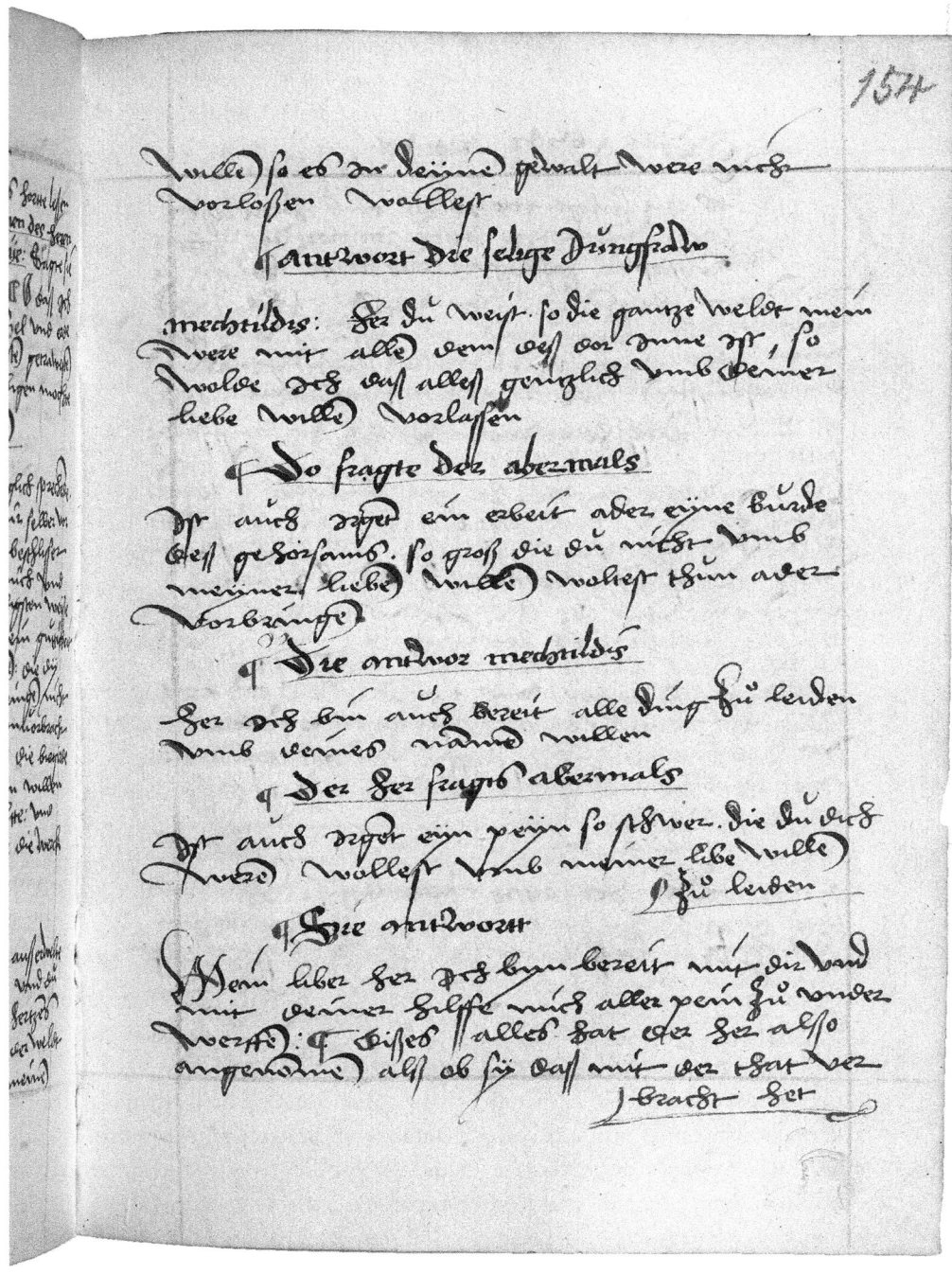

26 Text corresponding to *das búch geistlicher gnaden* (1516–17)
Heidelberg, Universitätsbibliothek, Heid. Hs. 33, fol. 154r
Copyright: Universitätsbibliothek Heidelberg

Liber in which the protagonist Mechthild and her convent are clearly identified (*das búch geistlicher gnaden. oder der offenbarúngen der selichen júngfrauwen mechtildis etwan closter júngfrauwen. dess closters helfede im lande zů sachssen beÿ Eissleben gelegen*, fol. 107r, see Fig. 27). Heidelberg, Universitätsbibliothek, Heid. Hs. 33, also transmits four exempla in the first fascicle containing the mystical texts; these can also be found in the *botte* imprint of 1505 as well as in a fifteenth-century manuscript from Nuremberg (Dresden, Sächsische Landesbibliothek, Hs M 243). This observation has led Wieland to believe that the Heidelberg *botte* was probably copied from the Leipzig 1505 imprint.[85] Be this as it may, the unidentified provenance of the Heidelberg codex also means that questions of its origin must remain unanswered. This relatively late copy and the hypothesis about the imprint it is based on underline the difficulties which one encounters in tracing manuscript transmission histories after 1500, at a time when printed books made texts more accessible and widespread.

Three manuscripts with Alemannic texts (Karlsruhe, Badische Landesbibliothek, Cod. Lichtenthal 89; Rastatt, Historische Bibliothek der Stadt im Ludwig-Wilhelm-Gymnasium, Cod. K 152; and St Gall, Stiftsbibliothek, Cod. Sang. 506) have only partially identified provenances. These codices differ substantially from one another, although two of them probably belonged to the Cistercian nuns at Lichtenthal.

By the early sixteenth century, the Cistercian nuns at Lichtenthal had access to a copy of the printed Latin *Legatus* which they translated into Alemannic. The resulting codex (Karlsruhe, Badische Landesbibliothek, Cod. Lichtenthal 89) deserves a few words as it shows that even centuries after the *botte*'s emergence, vernacular redactions of the *Legatus* were continuously produced, and processes of redacting the mystical text in new languages remained appealing to early modern devout communities. The Alemannic translation of the *Legatus*, contained in the Karlsruhe manuscript, is based on the John of Landsberg imprint of 1536.[86] It is thus not a text witness of the *botte* but a separate translation of the *Legatus*. While three scribes were active in the production of this German translation of the 1536 edition, the main scribe can be identified as the abbess of Lichtenthal, Barbara Veus (1551–1597).[87] The use and decoration of this manuscript reveal an interest in Gertrude's visions: markers in the margins and colourful initials indicate the beginnings of each book (for example, fol. 611r, see Plate IV), and key words are underlined in red, including Gertrude's and other saints' names as well as theological terms such as the 'sacrament' (for example, fol. 62r, see Fig. 15).

The manuscript at Rastatt, however, belongs to the *botte* transmission. The Rastatt codex is a book which comprises eight different imprints and two manuscripts, among which is a text witness spanning *botte* 1–77.[88] Wieland shows that certain linguistic features which are incongruent with the overall Alemannic dialect, such as the prefix *vor-* instead of *ver-*, mean that this

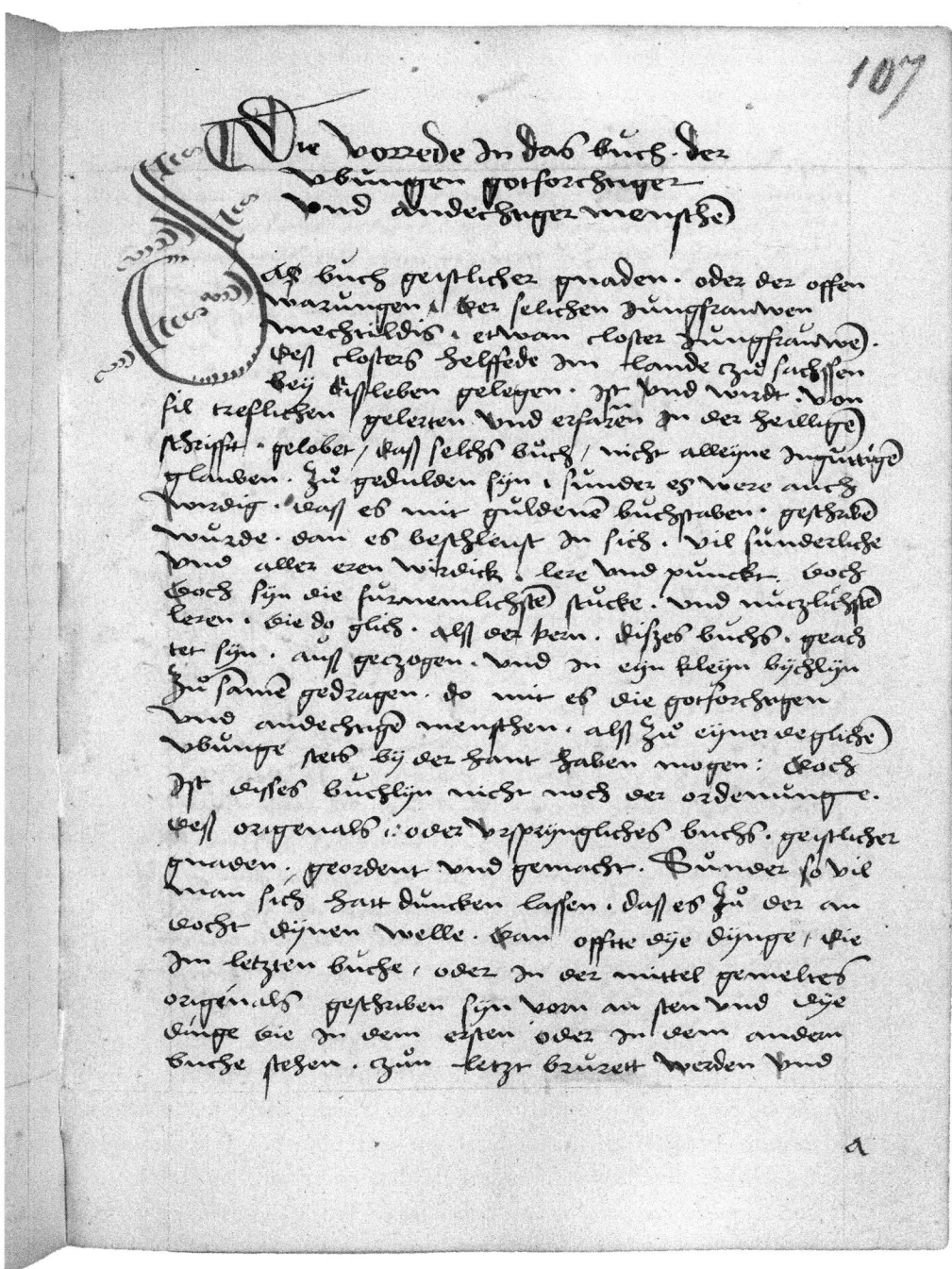

27 Text corresponding to *das búch geistlicher gnaden* (1516–17)
Heidelberg, Universitätsbibliothek, Heid. Hs. 33, fol. 107r
Copyright: Universitätsbibliothek Heidelberg

text witness is a copy of the 1505 imprint of the *botte*, in which one can find this special linguistic feature.[89] As Felix Heinzer has argued, several indicators point to its production in the early sixteenth-century at the convent of Lichtenthal.[90] If one accepts Lichtenthal as the place of origin for the manuscript in Rastatt, then Lichtenthal forms a particularly interesting part of the *Legatus* transmission in terms of media history; the creative reception of text included copying and translating between different languages in a mixed media environment of manuscripts and imprints. The overlapping of several vernacular redactions of the *Legatus* provides insight into the complexity of literary management in South Germany in the late medieval period.

The other Alemannic *botte* witness (St Gall, Stiftsbibliothek, Cod. Sang. 506) dates from the first half of the sixteenth century and probably belonged to a devout woman before it came to the Benedictine nunnery of St Georgen in St Gall.[91] Several fascicles were bound together to form a miscellany containing prayers, German translations of Psalms, and contemplative and proverbial texts. The first part of the manuscript (fols. 1v–93v) was written by one scribe and begins with an abridged German rendering of Mechthild of Hackeborn's *Liber* III, 18. The same German *Liber* text can be found in two manuscripts from the second half of the fifteenth century: St Gall, Stiftsbibliothek, Cod. Sang. 603 (pp. 442b–443b, see Figs. 28 and 29) originated at the Dominican nunnery of St Katharina in St Gall;[92] Zurich, Zentralbibliothek, Ms. C 162 (fols. 274r–275v) probably also belonged to St Katharina.[93] These two codices have in common that they also transmit *Liber* IV, 29; however, this latter text portion – each time preceding the selections from *Liber* III, 18 – is (wrongly) attributed to Gertrude (*Únser lieber her lert sant Trutten/trŭtta. . .*). In contrast, in St Gall, Stiftsbibliothek, Cod. Sang. 506, the portion from *Liber* III, 18 has no name attached to it; it is followed by abridged selections from the *botte* into which another portion from Mechthild's *Liber* is inserted (fols. 27v–42r). This time Mechthild is mentioned by name so that the alternation between episodes relating to Mechthild and Gertrude is marked (fol. 27v, see Fig. 30). Still, the arrangement suggests that the text collection is less about singling out one mystic or an other, but rather about gathering related material. This becomes more obvious when considering the actual content of the text portions and the transitions between them. Right at the beginning (fol. 1v), the portion from the *Liber* recounts how God advises a devout person (Mechthild) to say the psalm *Laudate dominum omnes gentes* three times (abbreviated translation of *Liber* III, 18). The topic of worship in prayers and song is picked up again in the inserted section (fols. 27v–42r). The final chapters of the *botte* selections that were included in this copy are also about reciting Psalm 116 (*Laudate dominum omnes gentes*).[94] In the St Gall manuscript, Gertrude reads the psalm 225 times rather than 125 times as is the case in other *botte* text witnesses. Hence, the Mechthild/Gertrude part of this manuscript comes full circle and

Junkfrowen maria
vnd darnach in all
engel vnd hailgen
vnd sol lessen ain pa
ter noster vnd das
opffren zu verainigung
des lobs got des vatte
rs mit dem mich him
el vnd erd vnd all
creaturen lobent vnd
wol sprechent vnd
bitten durch mich ihm
xpm gottes sun das
sin gebet genem we
rd durch den alles dz
geopffret got dem va
ter geopffret wirt
von in der höchsten ge
sellikait vff stigt vnd
also werdent all sund
vnd versumnus erfüst
vnd wer das tüt der
sol gütlich gloßen das
er die selben gnad
entpfacht von der
her spricht das vnmug
lich ist das der mensch
nit er folgt das er
gelobt oder hofft

de erst
ü ainem mal
do sij den here
bat für ain person
vnd in fragt was er
für gr versumnus
welt vff nemen En
pfieng sij ain söllicke
antwurt Sij solt täg
lich lessen iii lauda
te dominum omnes
gentes vnd sol neme
das kind ihs in ir
rechte hand vnd sol
in opffren got dem
vatter mit allen sine
werken siner kinthe
it vnd gutem zu erfül
ung aller gütter werk
die sij in ir kinthait
versumt hat
Den andren
laudate sol
sij lessen vnder der
meß vnd sol nemen
den heren ihm den
gemahel ir sel vnd
sol sich schuldig gebe
vor got dem vatter

28 German text corresponding to Mechthild of Hackeborn's *Liber specialis gratiae* III, 18 (1450–1500)
St Gall, Stiftsbibliothek, Cod. Sang. 603, p. 442
Copyright: Stiftsbibliothek St. Gallen

443

das sy ain sollichen ge-
machel wirdigen ge-
spincen billichliebe vn
triuw nie erzaigt hat
als sy solt vnd sol ge-
denken wie fil sy guit-
es vm sich von ym en
pfangen hät do sy arm
vnd schnöd was vnd
das er sy mit allem
güt vberflüssig gerich
et hät vnd sol got ~
dem vatter opfren die
brinenden min mit
der xps blügt vnd
grünet yn allen tug
enden yn siner kint
hait vnd gugent
en driten laud
ate sol sy lesse
am aubent vnd sol
nemen den heren ihm
xpm mit aller siner
folkomnen wandlung
vnd yn antwurte got
dem vatter für alles
das sy yn yrem leben
versumt hät vn sol
yn bitten das er all yr

vnfolkumenhait erfull
Darum ob sy all gab
gottes der sy übel gebru
cht hat oder yr versum
nis / yenigsamlich wi
der bringen will ~

29 German text corresponding to Mechthild of Hackeborn's *Liber specialis gratiae* III, 18 (1450–1500)
St Gall, Stiftsbibliothek, Cod. Sang. 603, p. 443
Copyright: Stiftsbibliothek St. Gallen

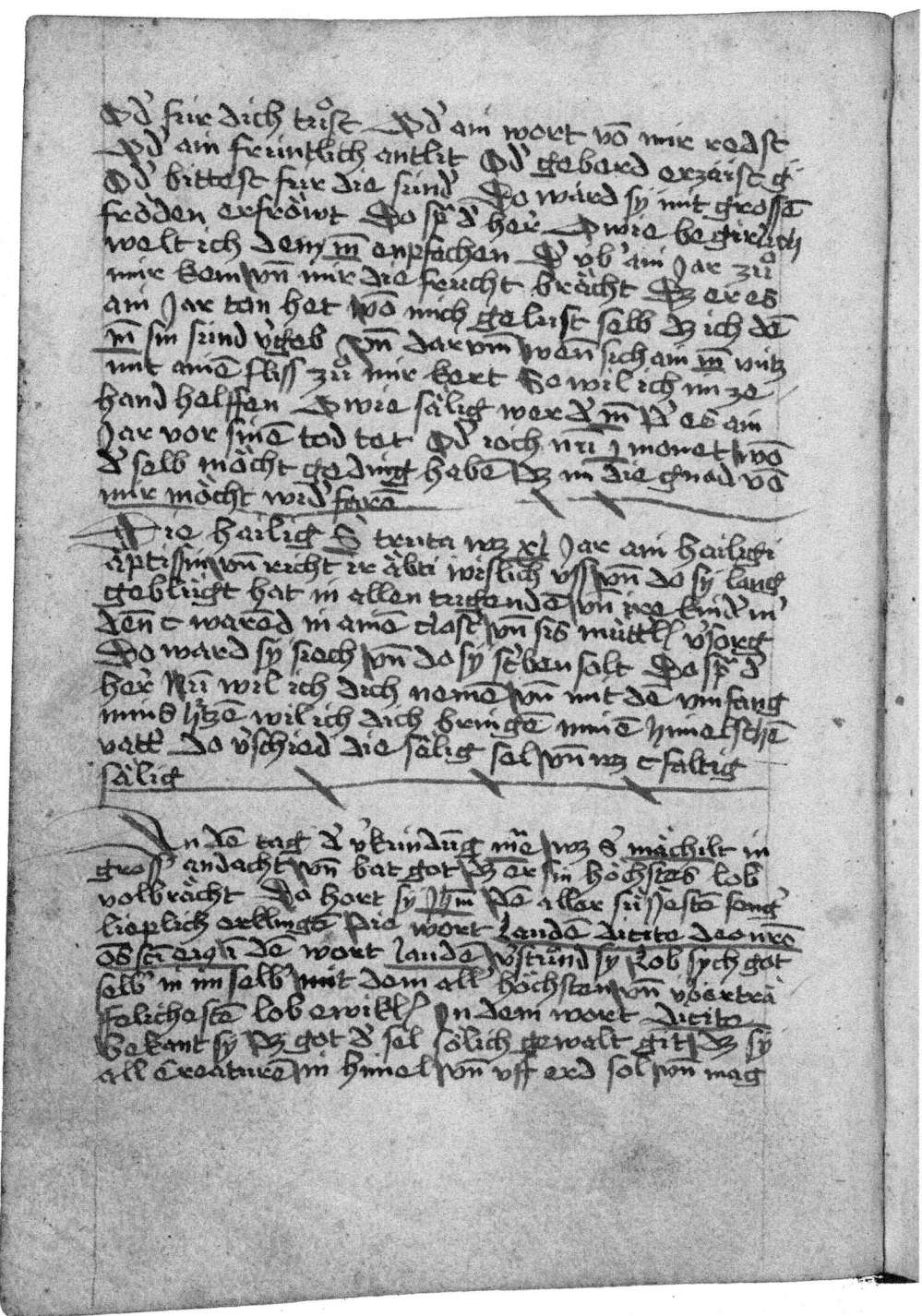

30 Transition between texts corresponding to the *botte* and *das búch geistlicher gnaden* (1450–1500)
St Gall, Stiftsbibliothek, Cod. Sang. 506, fol. 27v
Copyright: Stiftsbibliothek St. Gallen

forms a unit through bracketing the various visions and auditions with the motif of praying Psalm 116. Once more, scribal activity goes beyond mere copying and compiling, as it is invested in arranging and organising with regard to the content. Indeed, the *botte* selections in Cod. sang. 506 do not consist of entire chapters as they are known from other text witnesses even though they appear to have been copied from one of the more comprehensive text witnesses, namely, Dresden, Sächsische Landesbibliothek, Hs M 243.[95]

A SOUTH-GERMAN NETWORK

We can discern already that the *botte* found fertile ground in a South-German network where the majority of circulating devotional texts were written in the vernacular – in contrast to nuns in North Germany who continued to produce Latin texts.[96] The aforementioned Dresden manuscript (Sächsische Landesbibliothek, Hs M 243) dates from around 1435 and was very likely produced and kept at or around Nuremberg. The *botte* found in it is a relatively long text witness and can be placed in the context of the reform movement since the miscellaneous character of the entire text collection attests to a reformed devotional culture (for example, texts by Caesarius of Heisterbach are transmitted alongside saints' lives, miracles, and legends).[97] The manuscript in Dresden not only served as template for the St Gall manuscript, it also contains exempla that it has entirely or partly (*inter alia* stemming from the German version of the *Dialogus miraculorum* by Caesarius of Heisterbach) in common with the Heidelberg Codex, the Leipzig 1505 *botte* imprint, and one or two manuscripts from Inzigkofen (Munich, Bayerische Staatsbibliothek, Cgm 5292; and perhaps Vienna, Schottenstift, Cod. 308).[98]

As the oldest codex of this recension, the Dresden manuscript may help in drawing a concluding assessment of the *botte* transmission before turning to the *Trutta*-legend. On the basis of the dialect, Ringler and Wieland both suggested the area around Nuremberg for the provenance of this codex, but it was Hoffmann who first endorsed the Augustinian convent of Pillenreuth as place of origin.[99] Should the canonesses of Pillenreuth truly have been responsible for the Dresden codex (which, given the evidence, is very likely), it would mean that there was a South-German network of reformed female convents across orders which were deeply engaged with the mystical tradition associated with Helfta and in particular, that of Gertrude the Great. This network spanned both general *botte* recensions, X and Y. The historic links between the Dominican nunneries of Nuremberg, St Gall, and Zoffingen favour this theory.[100] In addition, the Dresden codex brings Pillenreuth near Nuremberg, which maintained strong ties with the Augustinian canonesses of Inzigkofen into the discussion: the convent of Inzigkofen had adopted statutes from Pillenreuth in 1431.[101] In studying Vienna, Schottenstift, Cod. 308, Ringler observed ties between Pillenreuth and Inzigkofen, especially in the transmission of late medieval sermons.[102] Furthermore, the convent of Rebdorf, which was connected to St Walburg from 1494 onwards, was part of the same network.[103] There is no doubt that the general transfer of books in the observant movement favoured the dissemination of the *botte*. The full transmission of the *botte*, however, is not tied to the reform, rather the reform promoted it; so the *botte* was part of the general increase in vernacular literacy that took place in the period.

SAINTS' LIVES

There is clearly one dominant branch of vernacular versions – the recensions of the *botte* – but at no time did the text material solidify. This is best demonstrated with the emergence of the so-called *Trutta*-legend, an extreme distillation of *botte* material revised, shortened, and stylised into a legend. It is not only the length and style that support the genre classification of a legend; the transmission context also shows that this concentrated version, essentially a redaction, was understood as a legend since it is transmitted as the final narrative in a number of legendaries. Five such legendaries are extant today: Graz, Universitätsbibliothek, Ms. 64; Graz, Universitätsbibliothek, Ms. 75; Vienna, Österreichische Nationalbibliothek, Cod. 3042; Pécs, Klimo Könyvtàr Bibliothek, AA. II. 21; and Klosterneuburg, Stiftsbibliothek, cod. 711. Updating and exploring the *Trutta*-legend's transmission reveals that the German reception of the *Legatus* continued in the late Middle Ages in different circles, including lay communities.[104]

The *Trutta*-legend forms part of a text collection of *Saints' Lives*, the so-called *Der Heiligen Leben*, which is divided into a summer half and a winter half, with entries according to the saints' days. The structure could vary and the selection of saints differed from context to context.[105] The sources are diverse ranging from passionals and books of martyrs to German prose legends. Within the overall transmission of the *Heiligen Leben*, only a few codices of Bavarian/Austrian origin include the *Trutta*-legend. A single codex would normally contain either the summer or the winter half, and the *Trutta*-legend can be found in volumes for the summer season. The legend's structure generally follows the chronology of the *botte*, but in a very selective manner, and with one significant exception: the legend's end is the *botte*'s beginning (*commendatio*). According to Wieland, the legend's redactor (he speaks of a 'compiler') followed an unsystematic yet 'mechanical' principle in 'his' choice of *botte* material.[106] A closer look reveals that the *Trutta*-legend includes some of Gertrude's most vivid visions and those passages that describe prayers in terms of monetary-like exchange. Also, the list of approvers in the *commendatio* includes a certain King Gottfried (*kunig Gotfridus*) who is not attested in any other vernacular witness, making this a revision with unique additions inspired by the *Legatus*.[107]

Gertrude's visions are concentrated in the *Trutta*-legend, which forms a story coherent in itself. Moreover, three of her visions are integrated into other saints' entries, namely St Mark (*botte* 115), St Bernard (*botte* 118), and St Augustine (*botte* 119). These visions of the respective saints appear as anonymous miracle-like accounts, with each vision being generically attributed to a 'pious' or 'holy' woman who maintained a special relationship to that particular saint. Hence, each of these single visions appears as an episode that demonstrates the accessibility of saints through devotion and prayer. The thematic assemblage of the collection follows more than just a structuring principle; rather, as the transmission shows, it accounts for an associative reading practice relevant for monastic as well as lay communities.

Both Graz manuscripts (Universitätsbibliothek, Ms. 64 and Ms. 75) contain the summer half of the *Saints' Lives*, date from the mid-fifteenth century, and were part of the library of the Military Order of St George in Millstadt (Styria), a lay community.[108] Although the script as well as the decoration in these two codices differ (for a comparison of the opening pages, see Plates X and XI),[109] the bindings reveal that they were most likely produced in the same professional workshop in Vienna, which would sell such copies commercially (for a comparison of the bindings, see Plates XII and XIII).[110] Also, the watermarks show that both codices use some of the same paper stock.[111] On the other hand, the paper of Vienna, Österreichische Nationalbibliothek, Cod. 3042, gives no clear indication as to where this codex was produced. Below the final legend (that is, the *Trutta*-legend), the scribe specifies the year of the copy (1442) and identifies himself in the colophon as Paulus of Nikolsburg (fol. 419v, see Fig. 31).[112] Although this scribe is attested in other manuscripts (one of which belonged to the Dominican nuns of St Lorenz in Vienna), the provenance of Cod. 3042 is not clearly identified.[113] More can be said about the provenance of Klosterneuburg, Stiftsbibliothek, cod. 711, since the chapter concerning legends about St Augustine is marked as being about 'our father': *Von sand Augustino dem heiling vnd grassen lerer vnßern vater* (fol. 386rb), thus clearly pointing to an Augustinian convent. The Klosterneuburg codex, which, due to a missing major initial on the opening page (fol. 2r, see Fig. 32), appears not to be as richly decorated as the two Graz codices might well have belonged to the canonesses of Klosterneuburg itself rather than to the canons, who assigned shelf marks to their books and attached braces for chains to them, none of which can be seen in late fifteenth-century Klosterneuburg, Stiftsbibliothek, cod. 711.[114]

The motifs and colours used on the opening page of Pécs, Klimo Könyvtàr Bibliothek, AA. II. 21, show that it was modelled after Graz, Universitätsbibliothek, Ms. 75, although the decoration is not quite as professionally executed (fol. 1r,

31 Scribal colophon (1442)
Vienna, Österreichische Nationalbibliothek, Cod. 3042, fol. 419v
Copyright: Österreichische Nationalbibliothek

32 Opening page of *Der Heiligen Leben*, summer half (1450–1500)
Klosterneuburg, Stiftsbibliothek, cod. 711, fol. 2r
Copyright: Stiftsbibliothek Klosterneuburg

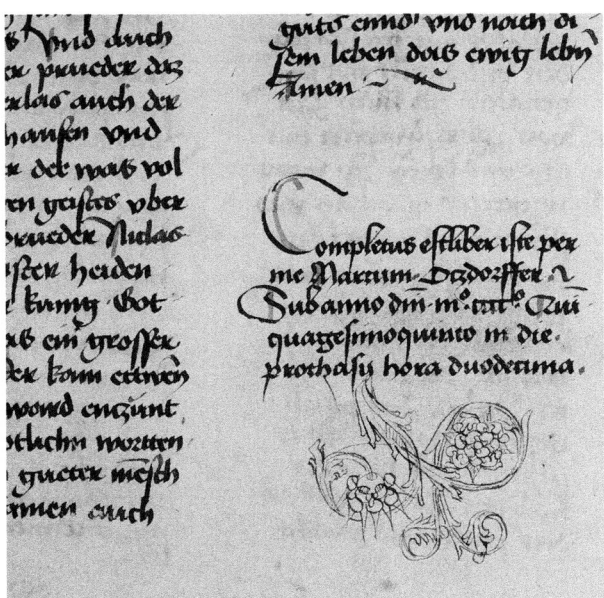

33 Scribal colophon (1455)
Pécs, Egyházmegyei Könyvtár – Diocesan Library, AA. II. 21, fol. 466v
Copyright: Pécsi Egyházmegyei Könyvtár

see Plate XIV). In the eighteenth century (the date of the current binding), the codex belonged to Bishop Klimo György Püspöki and, as clearly indicated by the *ex libris* and the shelf mark on the frontispiece, was kept in the diocesan library,[115] but the late medieval provenance remains unknown. The scribe of this copy provides the date of completion (1455) and his name: Marcus Oczdorffer (fol. 466v, see Fig. 33). Two more hands from the second half of the fifteenth century can be found in the last quires of the codex, copying, among other texts, a fragmentary sermon attributed to Nikolaus of Dinkelsbühl. Some of these later texts, including the aforementioned sermon, are also transmitted in Vienna, Österreichische Nationalbibliothek, Cod. 3042.[116] This recurrence of text material suggests that in the late fifteenth century the codex was originally kept at a convent or lay community somewhere near or in Vienna. The extant copies of the *Saints' Lives* reveal a reception in monastic as well as lay circles. In the following exploration, new material sheds light on the geographical origins of the *Trutta*-legend.

ST KATHARINA IN NUREMBERG

On the basis of library catalogues and intertextual references found in codices originating from St Katharina in Nuremberg, I want to corroborate the hypothesis that the *Trutta*-legend was probably composed in that Dominican nunnery. Due to the surviving manuscripts in which the *Trutta*-legend can be found, Grubmüller suggested that the legend originated in the area around

Vienna; after all, there undoubtedly existed an Austrian reception of the legend.[117] Contrary to this hypothesis, Williams-Krapp suggested that the legend, as an abridged adaptation of the *botte*, was written first in Nuremberg. This suggestion is based on the transmission, too, but argues from another standpoint, namely, that because there is no manuscript of Austrian provenance transmitting the *botte*, and because there are no indicators that should make us assume that a *botte* reception existed in South-Eastern German-speaking lands, the emergence of the legend in Vienna and the area around would be unlikely.[118]

There are other, positive, reasons to locate the legend's genesis further north, specifically in the Dominican nunnery of St Katharina in Nuremberg. In their registers regarding lunchtime reading in the refectory, the so-called lectionaries or lecture catalogues, there are several entries for readings from a book of *sant Druta*. These readings were usually taken from the *Saints' Lives*. That 'St Gertrude' is the mystic of Helfta rather than the martyr Gertrude of Nivelles becomes apparent when considering that the latter's legend is included in the winter half of the *Saints' Lives* and that the readings in question refer to the summer half, into which the *Trutta*-legend is integrated. None of the actual *Saints' Lives* from St Katarina of Nuremberg survive but a closer look into their lectionaries leaves no doubt that the Dominican nuns read a legend about Gertrude as early as the late fourteenth or early fifteenth century. Before they joined the observant movement in 1428, they owned a copy of the *Saints' Lives*: in the library catalogue, which the convent librarian Kunigunde Niklasin (d. 1457) put together between 1455 and 1457, the summer half of the *Saints' Lives* − from which certain chapters of Gertrude's legend would be read − is assigned the shelf mark *J. XXI*. In total 352 shelf marks are systematically registered, *J* standing for hagiography.[119] The lectionaries indicate that chapters from the *Trutta*-legend should be read on the following feast days: *Circumcisio domini* (01.01), *Dom. I. post Epiphaniam, Dom. I. post Octavam Epiphaniae, Estomihi, Invocavit, Palmarum, Cena domini, Ascensio domini*, and *Penetecoste*. Some of these references include short descriptions of the respective chapter and/or codicological details, for example, specifying the folio number and/or marks in the margin to guide the reading (. . .*stet an dem CCLV. plat und stet ein rotz kreucz dopey*).[120] Only one of these readings, that for Pentecost, is not attested in the extant version of the *Trutta*-legend but included in the *botte* text (Ch. 104). This observation suggests that in the early fifteenth century, the Nuremberg Dominican nuns had integrated a legendary redaction of the *botte* into their copy of the *Saints' Lives* and that this was later abridged as it has come down to us in five Austrian copies.

The Dominican nunnery St Katharina radiated an unparalleled energy of reform in the fifteenth century when their nuns travelled to other houses to implement observance, and when writing and copying took on a new dimension, one carried out in an extremely organised fashion and with missionary zeal.[121] All things considered – the reform movement network reaching into the South East, the fact that the Dominican nuns in Nuremberg owned at least one *botte* copy, and the numerous references to the legend of *sant Druta* integrated in the *Saints' Lives* – it is most likely that a redactor connected to the convent of St Katharina – if not one of the nuns themselves – was responsible for the rearrangement of the *botte* into a legend.

A devotional miscellany (New Haven, Yale University, Beinecke Rare Book and Manuscript Library, MS 968) provides further evidence for the hypothesis of St Katharina in Nuremberg as place of the original composition of the *Trutta*-legend. Written by Ursula Geiselherin (d. 1498),[122] a Dominican nun at St Katharina who wrote in a similar hand to her older convent sister Kunigunde Niklasin,[123] the Beinecke codex combines mystical texts and prayers by, among others, Christine Ebner, Dorothea of Montau, Mechthild of Hackeborn, and Birgitta of Sweden. As a note on the frontispiece clarifies, it was kept as a communal book: *Item Das puch schol nyemant auß dem Cor tragen on wissen der supriorin vnd der puchmeysterin* (frontispiece, see Fig. 34).[124] In a German translation of an excerpt from Mechthild of Hackeborn's *Liber*, the visionary Mechthild is not mentioned by her name *per se* but called *fraw Cantrix* and is identified via the 'Gertrude-legend': *Die heilig selig vnd gotliebe dy man nennt in der legent drudis fraw Cantrix oppfert eins mals got vm iiijc vnd lx pater noster dy het der Conuent gepett jn den eren der funff wunden Christi* (fols. 17v–18r, see Figs. 35 and 36). It may well be that any text attributed to Gertrude could be meant by the *legent drudis*; either the *Legatus*, the *botte*, or the *Trutta*-legend from the *Saints' Lives* would be candidates, as all of them predate this miscellany from 1466. Determining the exact reference, however, is not as important as the implications which come with this note: there is a certain familiarity in the way in which Gertrude and Mechthild are invoked and imagined side by side.

The community of Helfta functioned like a projection screen for late medieval observant activities, which were invested in contemplation and prayers. When exactly the *Trutta*-legend was added to the discussed recension of the *Saints' Lives*, before or after the reform, is, however, impossible to determine. Maybe the fact that it is the final legend in the extant copies means that it was added later in St Katharina too; but even so, to make the reform movement responsible for its composition is, though not inconceivable, not a given either. Considering their own role in fifteenth-century text and book production, it seems likely that the Dominican nuns of Nuremberg would identify with the wordy mysticism of Helfta. Without doubt, the Helfta scriptorium offered an ideal foil for advocating female scribal activities as a form of devotional exercise, as was one of the objectives of the reformers. In the fifteenth-century observant movement, writing and copying books served the reformers' ambitions in three ways: first, the scribal activity led to the

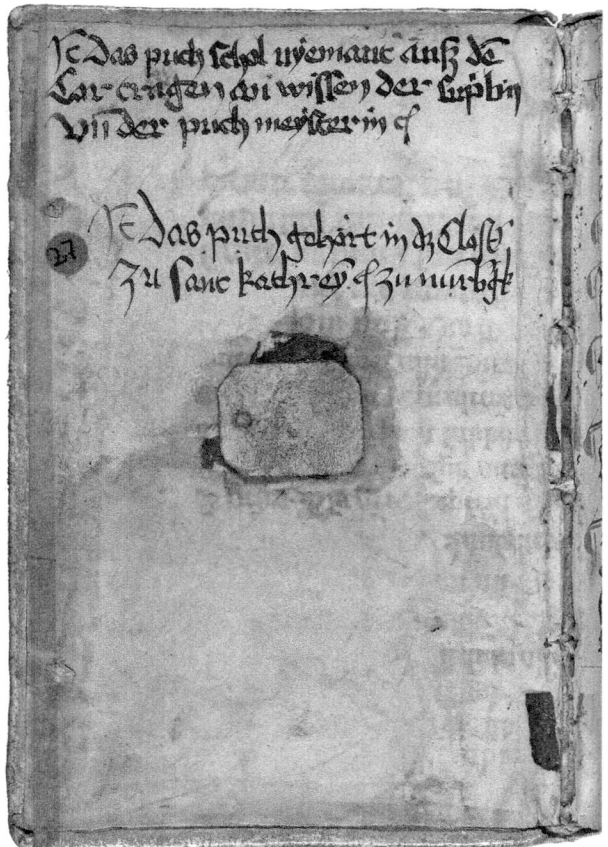

34 Library user note: *Item Das puch schol nẏemant auß dem Cor tragen on wissen der supriorin vnd der puchmeẏsterin etc.* (1456–66)
New Haven, Beinecke, MS 968, frontispiece
Photo Credit: Beinecke Rare Book and Manuscript Library, Yale University

updating and correcting of older texts (not least to the standardisation of liturgical procedures); second, writing itself was regarded as an act of devotion; and third, it kept the devout busy and far from the danger of falling idle.[125] These tendencies speak to a development that begun before the reform took hold of monastic institutions meaning that we need to see the genesis of the *Trutta*-legend as part of a broader culture of dynamic textuality.

To add a final complication to the *botte* and *Trutta* transmissions, however, a manuscript that was probably produced in Inzigkofen and is lost today needs to be taken into consideration. Dating from the late fifteenth century, it was last housed in Wrocław (Biblioteka Kapitulna; no shelf mark), where it had been transferred from the Diocesan Archives.[126] This was a devotional book which belonged to an early seventeenth-century woman: Countess Anna Dorothea von Hohenzollern-Haigerloch, who died on 8 February 1647. The surviving

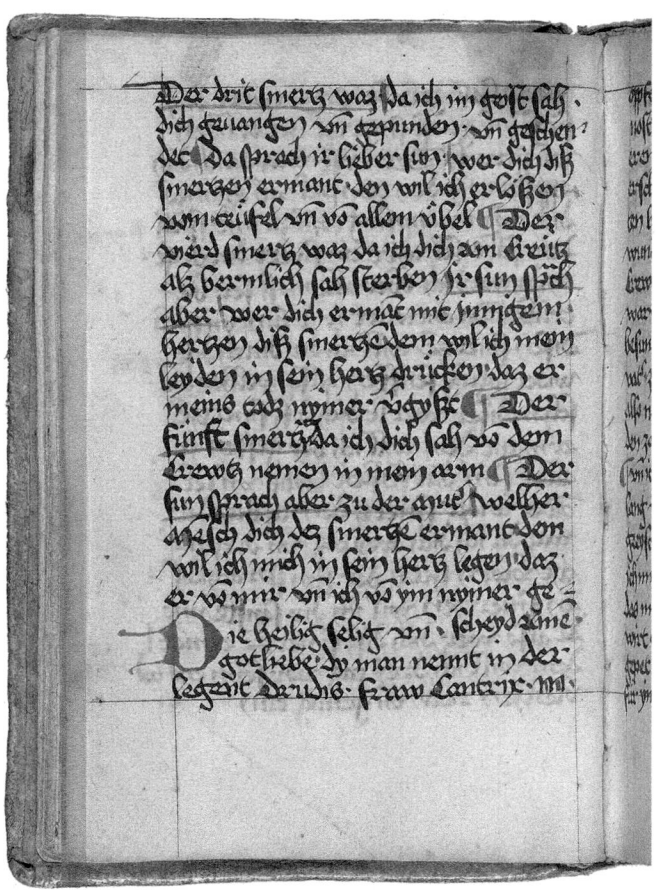

35 Reference to a Gertrude-legend in German text corresponding to Mechthild of Hackeborn's *Liber specialis gratiae* IV, 52: *Die heilig selig vnd gotliebe dy man nennt in der legent drudis fraw Cantrix* (1456–66)
New Haven, Beinecke, MS 968, fol. 17v
Photo Credit: Beinecke Rare Book and Manuscript Library, Yale University

evidence for this manuscript is a ten-page description of it made by Joseph Klapper in 1910.[127] Klapper's description indicates that the binding contained a note giving Anna Dorothea's name, followed by a dedication to the life of the Countess, in which she is referred to as a saint who lived a virtuous life. Anna Dorothea was one of the five children of Count Christoph von Hohenzollern-Haigerloch (1552–92), whose sons Johann Christoph and Karl died without male heirs meaning that this family line ceased to exist in 1634.[128] All three sisters had entered convents − an indicator of the financially precarious situation of the parents who were not able to supply three dowries − of which the youngest, Maria Sidonia, was a Clarissan nun at Söflingen near Ulm, while the two older sisters, Anna Dorothea and Maria Salome, were both at Inzigkofen. In addition, Anna Dorothea became prioress of the Augustinian convent. It is

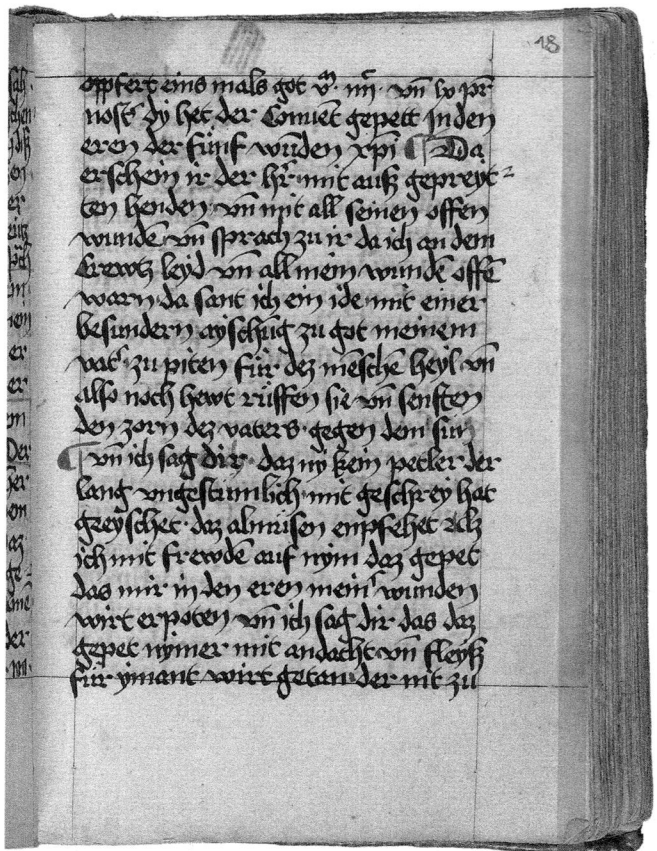

36 Continuation: German *incipit* corresponding to Mechthild of Hackeborn's *Liber specialis gratiae* IV, 52: *oppfert eins mals got vm iiijc vnd lx pater noster dý het der Conuent gepett jn den eren der fünff wunden Christi* (1456–66)
New Haven, Beinecke, MS 968, fol. 18r
Photo Credit: Beinecke Rare Book and Manuscript Library, Yale University

possible that the Wrocław codex was not produced in Inzigkofen, but only kept there in the seventeenth century. The circumstances, however, favour production in this convent where a *botte* copy was held already in the fifteenth century. Judging from Klapper's notes, the first text in the miscellany begins with *botte* 5: *Got hat sin erwelt gespons Sant truta geschaiden von der welt do sie nun v jar alt waz* (fol. 1r/p. 2 in Klapper's description). While the wording is identical with the *botte*, the fact that it begins with Ch. 5 correlates with the beginning of the *Trutta*-legend, which, while rewritten and shortened, introduces the same information about Gertrude entering the convent as a five-year-old. Klapper only records the *incipit* and then describes the further content: *Es folgen die Andachtsübungen, Visionen und Gebete der Hl. Truta* (p. 2). The next section in the manuscript description picks up at fol. 155r. Although we do not have the exact content for what is described as the 'devotional exercises, visions, and prayers of Saint Gertrude', we may infer that this first text portion spanning from fol. 1r to fol. 154v or 155r could not have been the *Trutta*-legend alone (that is, if it was the legend), which in the folio format of the *Saints' Lives* occupies up to seventeen double pages. In a quarto – the lost manuscript's recorded dimensions of 140 × 97 mm suggest this format – the legend could have occupied between 50 and 80 double pages depending on the script. Maybe this was a longer version of the *Trutta*-legend? Maybe Joseph Klapper laid eyes on a text that corresponded to the one which the lost volume of the *Saints' Lives* from the Dominican nuns of Nuremberg contained? To assume a longer version of the *Trutta*-legend, that is some kind of hybrid or intermediary version between the *botte* and the legend as encountered in the *Saints' Lives*, would mean that important manuscripts have been lost, especially some which would further strengthen the ties between Nuremberg and Inzigkofen. Nevertheless, it becomes obvious that Nuremberg was not the only major player when it came to the transmission of the German redactions of the *Legatus*. It was really the network between South-German convents (and less single centres), which in revising and rearranging the text material, kept it alive.

★ ★ ★

The *botte*-text, itself a vernacular reworking of the *Legatus*, proved to be highly flexible and easy to integrate into different environments, whether liturgical or devotional, collective or private. Redactors read and adapted the *Legatus*, layering new meanings onto it. Moreover, the structure and composition of the text underwent continuous transformations showing that the history of the dominant German redactions of the *Legatus* by no means ended with the 1505 imprint. As demonstrated, manuscript production persisted and only in some cases depended on the printed version. The manuscript transmission shows that the *botte* text material remained fluid at all times and that, despite discernible transmission lines for the German redactions of the *Legatus*, the reception in reality was as versatile as the interests of those who came in touch with it. Links between late medieval piety and the material transmission of texts underscore the status of books as sacred objects that were malleable in the hands of those who produced and used them. Just as the *Legatus* was a communal project, so too was the transmission and reception of its vernacular revisions: these were mainly, but not only, copied and read by reformed nuns. The *botte* and the *Trutta*-legend proved to offer formidable material with which to create intercommunal connections across religious orders and lay communities.

FOUR

THE BOOK'S SELF-REFLECTIVITY

All medieval writing is to some degree self-reflective, that is, it shows awareness of its own medial (pertaining to its physical materiality) and textual (concerning its contents) status. In a dynamic manuscript culture this means that any witness of a text takes on an authoritative status; this is the case for the transmitted witnesses of the *botte*. There are different ways to establish rhetorical authenticity in texts; the *botte* authorises itself through an internal narrative about its coming into being which is compared to the mystical ascent of the soul. The awareness that a sanctified textuality is made manifest in a book takes on a pivotal role in this alignment of internal narrative and the process of becoming Christ's bride. Textuality is negotiated within the *botte* in a way that evinces a sense for the existence of multiple text copies in which the core message, theoretically, is always the same. The use of book metaphors and writing imagery conveys that the understanding of text as dynamic is inherent to the *botte*, and that it forms part of its mystical programme which operates within so-called corporeal images underscoring the importance of embodying effects. Showing that the text's programmatic beginning follows a rationale according to which any reworking of the *Legatus* is just as salvific and holy as the alleged first book (as long as the copyist – who is also a reader – has good intentions), I argue that, in the *botte*, images of writing – relating to acts of copying and redacting – and imaginary reading scenarios are treated as embodied forms of becoming the bride of Christ.

Given that the transmission of the *botte*, including the reception of its various witnesses, is detached from the *Legatus* – an issue explored in the previous chapters – we may infer that even though an awareness of Latin sources may have existed in most late medieval reception contexts, the German redactions were regarded as authoritative texts in their own right. Just as this status of the *botte* can be established on the levels of historical and theoretical reflections, so too does the content propagate a sovereign understanding of the *botte*'s own literary composition. Self-reflectivity about its own textual status contributes to the understanding that the coming into being of the book is part of a mystical programme which itself aims to draw the reader into becoming the mystical bride. At the very beginning of the *botte,* writing and reading are set up as two sides of a conceptual process of salvation linked to an ontological dimension of the book. This highly self-conscious 'theology of the book' is most pertinent to those text witnesses that include most of the seven first chapters of the *botte*.[1] In relation to the transmission as a whole, these manuscripts – and one imprint – make up more than half of the *botte* text material that has come down to us. In order to facilitate the following study of the book's self-reflectivity, quotations are here mainly drawn from Wieland's edition of the *botte*, which is representative of the textual transmission in the relevant manuscripts.[2]

Writing, reading, voicing: all are portrayed in the *botte* as acts of salvation if done with the right intentions. They are acts of envisioning and reimagining, and, as such, are methods to newly embody the mystical bride. If one can become the bride through the reception of text – either read or copied – this means that the physical presence of the book is another form of the incarnated bride: the book as a 'medium of salvation' ('Medialisierung von Heil')[3] is both a material manifestation of, and a tool for the reader to reach, salvation; to become another bride. The imaginary act of reading, which I trace in this chapter, is a bridging act, located 'between body and script'.[4]

In recent years, researchers working on medieval German religious texts have highlighted the processual character of reading in the context of pre-modern textuality, suggesting it can be understood as an imaginative form of communicating salvation ('Heilsvermittlung'). In this debate, medieval texts have been shown to be self-reflective about their own status as dynamic texts.[5] Readers are embedded in devotional texts; they are set up to perform a transformative act of reading, in which the voicing of words may lead to the embodiment of the bride of Christ.[6] The medieval manuscript book and the act of voicing the words that are written within it create a complex between materiality and imagination, which lends itself to a Christological understanding of the incarnated word that brings salvation.[7] When the *botte* stresses the act of reading at the beginning of the text, it invokes this salvific notion and appropriates its alleged effects. What is special here, however, is that in comparison to the book's self-reflectivity in the *Legatus*, the *botte* introduces new ways of portraying continuous textual production as salvific by connecting writing imagery to becoming the bride of Christ.

WRITING IMAGERY

In order to understand how writing imagery in the *botte* is accompanied by an embedded notion of reception (more specifically by imaginary acts of reading) we need to compare it to the *Legatus*, where textual images with a salvific meaning are already present and where writing and reading are described as transformative processes. Scholars have drawn attention to the act of reading implanted in the *Legatus*.[8] As Anna Harrison has shown, the collective benefit of Gertrude's experiences is portrayed as a result of them being written down and communicated, so that others can share the grace she received, in their act of reading. Writing and reading have strong communal aspects, and these are reflected in images of writing in the *Legatus*.[9] Other studies have made observations on more interpretive levels, mapping between the *Legatus* and theoretical reflections on reading and writing. Jessica Barr, in her recent study on reading and embodying spiritual experiences in the *Legatus*, for example, demonstrates that while the 'text is the point of access to the divine', reading 'does not lead to a mimetic reproduction of Gertrude's spiritual experience'. Shifting the focus to the reader's own body, 'one is to conceive of reading the *Legatus* as a physical encounter with God'.[10] Bodily aspects such as respiration and also physical vulnerability (notably wounds) align 'salvific reading with the body's participation in textual activity'.[11] That reading should be seen as a cognitive – that is to say concerning the intellect – as well as affective act, generating meaningful devotional states, has been discussed from a more a general and theoretical viewpoint by Sarah McNamer and Mark Amsler.[12] In their respective studies, affective and cognitive processes are not put into opposition, as they 'more often complement each other in medieval texts than not' as Michelle Karnes clarifies.[13] Taking reading to be active spiritual work that leads to salvation means, as Barr emphasises, that the *Legatus* tries to 'bring the reader into a similarly intimate encounter with God' as Gertrude.[14] The key term here is 'similarly', as writings from Helfta repeatedly employ formulations of approximation (Latin *quasi*) rather than of identification when aligning the soul to God.[15] Despite an added distance brought by mediation, the *Legatus* encourages 'the reader to imagine an embodied encounter with God through the medium of the text'.[16] If reading is an embodied activity which can alter bodies as well as minds, as Karin Littau asserts,[17] then Barr's conclusion about the *Legatus*' textuality implying physicality is important for the understanding of how salvation in the *Legatus* works. By recalling the physical nature of divine experiences, reading becomes a way to 'transform lives through the imagery of embodied textuality'.[18]

While Barr identifies the target of epistemological incarnation to be the body of the mystic – which then through the mediated word is reflected in the reader's body – the following analysis suggests that in the case of the *botte*, the book – or the 'text's body' – itself functions as an embodied fulfilment of Gertrude's communications. Following the rationale of the *Legatus*, which aims to recreate intimate divine encounters through the act of transformative reading, the *botte* appears to be the product of such an embodied reading. The *Legatus* has been literally transformed into a new embodiment through a reader's – the *botte*'s redactor's – imaginative engagement. This embodying process is self-reflective in the *botte* where writing imagery adapted from the *Legatus* creates the foundation of and justification for the *botte*'s existence and its claim to salvific effects. The relationship between the *botte* and the *Legatus* in regards to writing imagery, however, is less one of structural equivalence between source and translation; rather, the *botte* makes use of the *Legatus* material in order to establish a more nuanced and more methodical self-reflectivity of the book which has ontological effects. By aligning the first seven *botte* chapters to the *Legatus* we can detect how, in contrast to all known Latin text witnesses, the German version (as edited by Wieland) expresses a programmatic self-reflectivity in its writing imagery via the use of deictic formulations, visionary justification, and the narrative of the book's approbation.[19]

The beginning of the *botte*, when compared to the extant copies of the Latin *Legatus*, shows how deliberately composed it is. In Wieland's *botte* edition, based on the codex that belonged to the fifteenth-century Dominican nuns in Strasbourg, the text begins with a title which mentions Gertrude and her supposedly Benedictine nunnery in Saxony.[20] There then follows the first chapter which is a *commendatio*, that is, an approbation of the 'book' by church officials and scholars who testify to the good effect that reading it had on them. Here, the *botte* is explicitly referred to as 'this book' (*dis bůch*). The second chapter, entitled the 'prologue of this book' (*der prologus dis bůches*), proceeds in setting up God's (unnamed) chosen mystical bride as a paragon for the *botte*'s reader: those who read it shall develop the desire to follow God's path in a celebration of 'reading, contemplating, and divine worshipping' (*feiern mit lesen, mit contemplieren und mit gőtlicher betrahtunge*). According to this participatory rationale of salvation, the collective benefit of the book necessitates the use of 'corporeal images' (*mit liplichen bildern*).[21] Although the first two chapters already list 'benefits of this book', the third chapter is called exactly that ('This chapter is about this book's benefits'):[22] it recounts the visions of a nun at a time, after 'the book' was written (*Do das bůch geschriben wart*). In these visions, Christ praises the scribal work, sanctifies the reading of it, and curses those who attempt to scrutinise and misread it.[23] *botte* 2 and 3 are based on the *Legatus'* final passages in Book V, 36 and V, 33–34, which deal with the scribal completion and divine sanctification of the recording of Gertrude's revelations. The *botte*'s arrangement then jumps back to earlier *Legatus* books: in *botte* 4, God addresses the aforementioned chosen bride for the first time in a dialogue in which the book is given a 'name'.[24] This passage is again concerned with the divine justification of the *botte* and the effects it aims to have on its readers.[25] It goes back to material from the prologue of the *Legatus* (I, 1). More authorising visions follow in the *botte*'s fifth and sixth chapters: a so-called Frowe M. Kantrix, who in the *Legatus* may be identified as the convent's cantrix Mechthild of Hackeborn, has a conversation with God about his chosen bride's – that is, Gertrude's – immaculate character.[26] Similarly, an unnamed monk praying for the chosen bride is told by God that the bride, separated from her biological family, may only be loved through what God works in her.[27] These visions authorising the writing and revelations of Gertrude stem from various chapters in the first book of the *Legatus* (I, 1; I, 11; I, 16). After what seems to be a lengthy prelude to the *botte* proper, the seventh chapter begins to recount Gertrude's mystical life with 'How she saw a young man in a vision' as the title, followed by the announcement that 'now she speaks of herself saying. . .'.[28] The subsequent vision is told in direct speech from Gertrude's perspective, and is indeed based on the autobiographically styled part of the *Legatus*. Ch. 7 of the *botte* thus introduces material from *Legatus* Book II, but the German chapter as a whole is composed of three different *Legatus* chapters: *Legatus* II, 1; II, 2 and II, 8. The rest of the *botte* largely follows – even if in a strongly edited manner – the general order of the 'standard' *Legatus* with occasional leaps between books and the addition of some new material (*botte* 100, and 170–173 are unparalleled). The material's rearrangement, chiefly at the *botte*'s beginning, indicates less a method of abridging than a thematic restructuring, a redaction that took place in the process of translating and rewriting the *Legatus*, thereby underscoring the deliberate work of the *botte* redactors as creative readers.

In more recent research the structural discrepancies between the *Legatus* and the *botte* have gone largely unnoticed or have been dismissed as an indicator of an imperfect process of translation, with scholars focussing instead on a comparison of the spirituality communicated in the *Legatus* and *botte* respectively.[29] The *botte* editor Wieland, however, had compared the arrangement of chapters in the *botte* to the *Legatus* sources and concluded that the German 'translator intended to recast the comprehensive Latin work as a compact booklet on spiritual matters (probably for convent women)' following a compositional principle that allowed for more flexibility.[30] As a consequence of this redaction, one of the strategies of justification for writing, namely the approbation or *commendatio*, was rearranged.

The *botte*'s opening – the book's *commendatio* – is contained in all longer *botte* text witnesses where it is consistently placed at the beginning, whereas in the Latin sources its transmission appears patchy. The *commendatio* in the *Legatus* is transmitted in only three of the text witnesses and in each instance placed at a different position in the text. In only one manuscript, dating from the fifteenth century, does it appear at the beginning (Trier, Stadtbibliothek, Cod. 77/1061). In another manuscript, the approbation note follows *Legatus* Book III and precedes Book IV (Vienna, Österreichische Nationalbibliothek, Cod. 4224), and in yet another it closes the *Legatus* as the last chapter following Book V (Munich, Bayerische Staatsbibliothek, Clm 15332).[31] In terms of content, the German version of the *commendatio* does not mention the date of Gertrude's revelations (in contrast to the Latin version which indicates the years around 1300) and it also leaves out the name of the Saxon Dominican and author of a *Life of St Dominic*, Dietrich of Apolda, who appears as a major authority in the Latin approbation as 'he often conversed with her and fully approved these writings in terms of style and teaching'.[32] Where the approbation of the *Legatus* should be placed is indicative for the reading process; the modern editors of the *Legatus* have recognised this and chose to position the *commendatio* at the very start before the prologue, even though only one manuscripts actually transmits it thus.[33] The medieval reader had similar sentiments about the book's opening as we can see in the *botte* which keeps the *commendatio* at the front.[34] In this way, the justification for the writing functions like a declaration for everything that is following.

Although the structural shift in the *botte* with regards to the *Legatus* (placing the *commendatio* at the front) was remarked upon, no one has yet engaged with the effects that the calibrated beginning of the *botte* might mean for its self-reflectivity as a book. In the Latin sources containing a *commendatio*, it comes mostly as an appendix even though its position may not be at the end of *Legatus* Book V. The approbation functions as an additional document to the main text meant to authorise the writing; the *commendatio* is not part of the narrative about how the book came into being. Instead, the ontological narrative is laid out in the prologues of both the 'standard' *Legatus* and the *Leipzig Legatus*, and in the final chapters of Book V as transmitted in the 'standard' *Legatus* (not contained in the *Leipzig Legatus*) where the finished book is depicted as sanctified by Christ. In both instances – prologues and final chapters – the text production is thematised in visions in which the divine authority approves scribal as well as editorial activities, furthermore granting beneficial effects on the book's readers.[35] Moreover, the Latin prologues to Books II and III of the 'standard' *Legatus* describe the text's production as one that is fulfilled in different stages. What thus appears scattered throughout the *Legatus*, adding to a 'particularly complex' explanation of its own literary composition,[36] is condensed in the *botte* and placed right at the beginning making it a coherent narrative of how 'this book' came about and how it was approved.

By combining the prologue to *Legatus* Book I with the final chapters of Book V, the *botte* blends two sets of approbation by interlocking the respective visions. The result is that the *botte* starts with a finished book rather than ending with it as the *Legatus* does. In the *botte*, there is no specification as to how the book was actually, that is physically, produced in Helfta. Also, the deep concern of Sister N in the *Legatus* that comes with her scribal responsibility, finds no place in the *botte*. The divine approbation which Sister N receives through the vision of yet another nun who sees Christ bending down to her as she presents the finished manuscript (*Legatus* V, 34), appears then different in the light of a narrative about the book's genesis in which the text production is already concluded.

In the *botte*, the words of Christ sanctifying the writing can be understood to be valid for any copyist or editor despite being directed to the diegetic scribe:

> In the same love that I had commissioned you to write this book I shall recommend it to the reader who will hear it thanks to you. And I will arrange and make sure that whoever writes it will write all things according to my well-pleasing.[37]

The corresponding Latin wording from the 'standard' *Legatus* V, 33 is significantly different:

> With the same love, with which I in my freely given grace poured out all that is written in this book, I also committed it to the memory of the one who listened to you, who collected and ordered it all to my greatest delight.[38]

In the Latin version, Christ refers to the finished book when he blesses the scribal work; the invoked writing scenario is that which happened in the community at Helfta and it is consequently kept in the past tense since the present scene evolves after the book project has been finished. The German *botte* on the other hand, projects a future interaction with the text: here, Christ's words are directed to subsequent reading and scribal activities marked by the future tense of the sentence. Indeed, the medieval German word 'schriben' may also be translated as 'copying', meaning that Christ would literally endorse all future copied redactions in his role as guiding editor (*das wil ich selbes rihten und orden*). It becomes evident that the *botte* not only contains an alternative order of chapters but that temporal implications regarding book production have an effect on the interaction with the text. The idea of an already completed book, ripe to be copied and reworked, remodels its medial self-reflectivity conceptually. It shifts the mode of communication from the hard-copy of the book to the fluidity of the text.

The vernacular *botte* opens a retrospective view upon the book's production while accentuating its potential as a dynamic text. The writing that follows this beginning – Gertrude's life and revelations – is already approved and blessed before the account proper has even started. References to 'the book' in the *botte* are not bound to the copy in the narrated world, but the notion of the physical book is expanded to include any copy that is based on the diegetic book which Christ blesses in the visionary account. In this sense, the way the book came into being at Helfta is more of a prerequisite. No details about the collaboration between scribe and mystic are expounded; instead the idea of an already finished book that is available for copying is fully fleshed out. This shift in narrating how the book emerged adds a new understanding to the *botte* in two regards: firstly, what the *botte* redactor writes and restructures is through Christ's authorisation an activity as sanctified as the narrated scribal activity; and secondly, the potential salvation radiating from the book is in every copy, including redacted copies. The scribe's blessed work is not just that of the Helfta nun who puts it all together but of any editing scribe or copyist.

CORPOREAL IMAGES AND IMAGINATION

The conceptual elements raised in the *botte*'s first chapters are programmatic; they fashion the idea of a self-reflective book which reaches into the realm of reception and, on a theological level, maintain eschatological claims about salvation. The *botte*'s opening is set up to create a participatory mystical programme by connecting the individually experienced mystical revelation to the potential of salvation for many by reception, including creative forms of reception which lead to new redactions. The grace experienced by Gertrude is shared in this continuous process of codification through the use of 'corporeal images' (*lipliche bilder*).[39] This term is taken from the prologue of the *Legatus* where the use of imagery is justified as a means of approximation, when specifying that God:

> poured out his grace on her [Gertrude], through visions of physical likeness as well as through purer enlightenments of her thoughts, all the same he wished to have described in this little book visions of physical likeness, for human understanding.[40]

'Through visions of physical likeness' (*per imaginationes corporearum similitudinum*), God is said to manifest himself in order to be intelligible to humans. In the *Legatus*, Christ reassures Gertrude that 'this particular form of imaginative experience, rooted in the senses, constitutes a legitimate form of revelation';[41] in other words, 'the theological doctrine of images receives visionary sanction directly from Christ'.[42]

By contrast, the corresponding passage in the *botte* has the reader engage in the act of imagining 'corporeal images' as the bride of Christ is said to be 'raised' by God:

> to his private chambers by means of imagination, as if climbing up steps, that she may gain great divine wonders, which we would not be able to understand had he not shown them to her in corporeal images.[43]

The *botte*'s use of 'corporeal images' for the Latin words *per imaginationes corporearum similitudinum*, removes the distance of 'likeness' and instead makes the images themselves the gateway to the 'great divine wonders' that can be thus communicated. In the *botte*, the indicative formulation of the corporeal images being the way to access the divine imparts an act of corporate imagining to the reading experience; the reader is invited to partake in the process of establishing Gertrude as the bride of Christ. Based on the very last chapter of the *Legatus* (V, 36), *botte* 2 joins the understanding of a completed book and its effect to the use of the reader's imagination, that is, the reader is to imagine the book copy as an outcome of God's outflow.[44] The key concepts 'imagination' (*bildunge*) and 'corporeal images' (*lipliche bilder*) are not merely mentioned in the *botte*'s introduction, they are also instantly applied to the text's own materiality – to its bookness – hereby deploying the character of images as being immaterial and yet corporeal. This is a performative, nearly pedagogical, approach to the method of imagination, aiming to stimulate the reader's intellectual pleasure.[45]

What kind of figurative ideas are invoked with 'corporeal images' given that they appear in text and can only be generated by a process of 'imagination'? Different forms of medieval devotion – whether meditation through reading or prayer – basically depended on two methods, one relying on physical pictures or objects, the other not.[46] Mental images in this regard nonetheless operated like material images as they were summoned before the inner eye and functioned as an imagined materiality. Figurative language, in medieval literary theory, is seen as a method of eschewing the insufficiency of speaking of the divine. For example, in Alan of Lille's *Anticlaudianus*, personified Theology portrays transcendent meaning through 'God's claim to all names', which works through 'the agency of metaphor and the rule of figuration'; imagery is here seen as a necessary step in the ascent to God.[47] While physical images were not recommended for prayer in late medieval devotional culture, mental images occupied a less controversial place.[48] The *botte* redactor uses the association between devotion and image when establishing the imagining of corporeal images as programmatic.[49] The process of imagination is central to the figurative aspect of images; corporeality in this sense means imaginary materiality, with imagination being a practice of ascent to the divine.[50]

With this programmatic concept of images in mind, we return to the *botte*'s narrative of its coming into existence and the ensuing textual imagery. In the *botte*, any text copy is collapsed with the notion of salvation – figuratively designated as the 'book of life' – in a reading process akin to imagination:

> These [the corporeal images] are abundantly proven in this book by the divine love in order to bring salvation to the afflicted, that they shall gain hundredfold fruit from it, that they may be worthier of being recorded in the book of life.[51]

The subsequent sentence is about pleasure: 'because all those who read it [the book] cannot do differently than derive pleasure from this book of divine love'.[52] The Book of Life assigns a scriptural imagery to the idea of predestination and salvation. The image of the Book of Life is also a Christological metaphor based on that of the scroll with seven seals from John's Book of Revelation (Apocalypse). As '[t]he symbiosis between Jesus and the book' dates back to 'at least the early fifth century',[53] the *botte* stands in a long tradition of Christological book metaphors. On a meta-level, too, Christ becomes the *materia* of the book – a thought which is in line with formal biblical exegesis.[54] What is special about the *botte*'s dealing with the Book of Life is that the notion of salvation is transferred from Christ to the actual text physically present in a book. Under this condition, the work of a scribe is that of a mediator between the soul and God, and this function of a coredemptor has a bearing on the book as 'holy matter' – to borrow a fitting term from Caroline Walker Bynum.[55] The physical book – the *botte*'s material manifestation – becomes a gateway through which the reader can access the Book of Life, which, according to the *botte*'s rationale, is Christ. The book imagery takes on some of the qualities of a relic (through its physical materiality) but there is no hierarchy of the book over the text. Instead, there is an awareness for the fluidity of the text. In order to understand the tension between book and text better we need to pay closer attention to scribal activity as mentioned in the *botte*.

GOD, THE AUTHOR, AND HIS SCRIBES

In the *botte* – like in the *Legatus* – Christ appears to be the author of the book. Scribal activity is portrayed as only completed with the 'miraculous help of the divine grace' thereby assigning God a decisive part in the book's coming into being.[56] There is one detail, though, which makes the *botte* stand out: the same divine authority extends from the current book to any text copy, no matter if redacted. In *botte* 4, Christ emphasises his relationship to the scribe, giving assurance that he will send 'arrows of my divine love' to them who write (or copy) the book in devotion of God. The explanation for this image follows in the account; it is Christ who directs what needs to be written, the outcome is his 'work' (*werg*):

> Moreover, to whomever writes [or: copies] it [the book] with devotion and by grace, I will send as many arrows of my divine love shot from the sweetness of my divine heart as things that are written in the book, these arrows moving and enlivening the pleasure of divine sweetness in his heart. For I incite him and arrange that it gets written. And so I will loyally sustain this [that it gets written] as I will protect my work to remain uncorrupted.[57]

The whole passage, spoken from Christ's perspective, is kept in the present tense, alluding to simultaneous or future scribal activity. Here, not a unique and historically determinable scribal activity is meant, but any copying process is Christ's 'work'. The idea of the book being produced and copied in a dynamic manuscript culture – for example, similar to what we can find in Suso's *Büchlein der ewigen Weisheit* (*Little Book of Eternal Wisdom*) – is thus embedded within the *botte* text.[58] Medieval writers 'used writing and the authorship of a text as metaphors for creation, in which one could read the "writing" of its divine author',[59] and the *botte* redactor deploys the visionary material found in the *Legatus* to authorise their own text version; by stating that Christ is the creator of the text, it advances to be not only divinely approved but also divinely authored.

In this way, visions containing book images potentially refer to any text version manifest in a book copy. The vision of an anonymous nun, in which Christ appears to press the finished book against his heart, links the transubstantiation of the Eucharist to the manuscript book, making the latter the manifestation of the word made flesh and hence bestowing it with Christological power.[60] While on the diegetic level the visionary book is the finished product of the scribe's work in Helfta, Christ's speech act in the vision expands this to any copied redaction by means of its deictic formulation. The reference to 'the book' radiates outside the narrated world and into the reader's world, where 'the book' is the physical manifestation of the *botte* in a manuscript:

> I have pressed this book onto my heart so that I may drench each and every letter written in it with the sweetness of my divine love – similar to someone who dips a soft bun into a sweet mead – so that everyone who reads in it to my praise and in humble devotion, will gain the fruit of eternal salvation.[61]

The simile of a drenched bun seems striking as it is borrowed from what seems to be a remarkably mundane routine of how to consume a bread roll. Such everyday images for describing theologically complex issues are common to Mechthild of Hackeborn's and Gertrude of Helfta's mysticism, and are even more present in the Latin writings of Helfta than in the *botte*.[62] The latter includes the distinct image of the mead-drenched bun in the context of authorising the writing. In the subsequent narration, the scribe begs Christ to protect the book from being misunderstood and of being changed and falsified. We have already seen – in Chapter 2 – that medieval authors such as Alan of Lille and Bonaventure were very conscious of the process of textual alteration in scriptorial activities. Such awareness continued to exist in the late Middle Ages and included translated redactions as well.[63] In the *botte*, the awareness of a text's susceptibility to alteration is used to the advantage of its status; by narrating Christ's blessing of the book with the sign of the cross while uttering a further speech act in which the writing is declared to be as beneficial as the communion, the *botte*'s own precarious status as an altered text is suspended. In a manuscript book culture in which copying and reproducing meant that a text was dynamic, the *botte*'s 'authenticity' as God's intended 'work' is confirmed.

The insistence on the text's mutability shows an awareness for a processual manuscript culture, that is a manuscript culture in which the processes of copying and editing result in constantly newly rearranged and recomposed redactions.[64] When Christ in the vision of the unnamed nun finally affirms that he will punish those who aim to 'discern and pervert the book' (*das bůch erforschen und verkeren*), the possibility of a 'bad copy' is implied.[65] In the vision, Christ gives the assurance that he will not allow this to happen, instead saying that all future copies will have just as beneficial an effect on their readers as 'the book' does in the narrated world. In the *botte*, the word 'book' can either mean the physical manuscript copy or the text. This multilayered alignment helps us to understand the tension between book and text; the two concepts of a physical book and a text are not in opposition but belong together. This conceptual overlap is central for the establishment of the *botte* text to be on equal standing with 'the book' in the narrated world.[66] On this ground, the *botte* sets up a salvific effect of any text copy when read. Writing and copying texts become equally sacred activities.

The notion of the continuation of God's approbation of the copied text – even when it is only read and not necessarily written – is not unique to the *botte*, but also appears in another translation of a text related to Helfta, in the Latin translation of Mechthild of Magdeburg's *Flowing Light*, the *Lux divinitatis*. Roughly based on Mechthild's wish to bless the scribe who records the *Flowing Light* for her,[67] the newly added prologue to the *Lux divinitatis* has anyone who copies and anyone who reads 'this book' receive comfort and mercy from God, as long as they write or read it with pious intentions: *Sic etiam omnes qui hunc librum scripturi uel lecturi sunt, si tamen pia intenderint, incrementum consolationis et gratiæ spiritus, sicut in ipso promissum est a Domino, consequentur.*[68] Whether the translator Heinrich von Halle wanted to thus legitimise his project, or whether this statement is meant to encourage readers and copyists to approach the

Lux divinitatis with the right attitude, or both, is hard to tell. In any case, it shows a reflected awareness for a dynamic manuscript culture in which reading and writing habits are considered in their spiritual dimension.[69] The extension of the salvific efforts of text production and text reception to future generations also means that the text itself, manifested in the book that the reader/ scribe holds in their hands, becomes the medium of salvation.

In the *botte*, the solemn avowal that the writing of the book is part of a salvation plan is heightened by allusions to sensual experiences of the divine, especially in terms of sweetness in taste as Christ confirms that:

> [t]he work of the scribe, who writes the book, makes me as joyful as if someone gave me as many fine flasks of fragrance as letters written in it; because each separate letter gives me threefold pleasure as I taste in them the ineffable sweetness of my divine love, from which all words written in the book have flown.[70]

Christ maintains a sensual relationship to the scribal work, one which highlights his human nature in its physicality as its invokes the senses of taste and smell. Fine flasks filled with fragrant oils are pictorially associative of ink wells such as those that medieval scribes would have used. Indeed, the explanation as to why the letters please Christ underpins the imagery of the scribal ink well since Christ says that all the words written in the book 'flowed out' of his divine love. Consequently, the good intention of the scribe is described as the reflection of God's grace, once more marking the correspondence between salvation and writing.[71]

The analogous identification of God's grace with scribal activity harks back to the image of the honey-drenched bread roll as Christ wants to 'soak' through every letter. This image plays with Eucharistic notions of the incarnated Word. In her work on the Leipzig *botte* imprint from 1505, Beatrice Trînca, looking at this correlation, explains that the codex functions as a substitute for the Eucharist which allows an even more intimate time with Christ than the communion does, because of its tactile proximity.[72] Even though Trînca's analysis is primarily based in the medium of print, her observations regarding the salvific aspect of copying texts are equally valid for the earlier, that is manuscript text, witnesses of the *botte*.[73] Very cautiously she formulates the hypothesis that it is 'as if' Christ's blessing of the scribal work extends to more than just the initial 'original' work. Translations and copies of 'an ever disappearing original' are 'embodied substitutes'.[74] For Trînca, the importance of the first book recedes into the background, and, in addition, no version of the text is ever exceptionally relevant.[75] This rationale is indebted to a *res/signa* understanding according to which the idea of an original copy and the book that is talked about in the text as being this original copy belong to one another. Yet, another aspect needs consideration: in the *botte* there is the notion of a mutable text which gets still referred to as the incarnated word as it is physically present in a manuscript copy. As a consequence, when Christ blesses the book in the narrated world, the salvific claim of the writing extends virtually to any copy, any text witness – including redactions. Because scribal work is presented in the present tense with future implications, and because there is a clear awareness for a dynamic text culture, the very material side of the writing is included in this conceptual fusion of manuscript original and text copy. The notion of an abstract textuality does not diminish the physicality of the manuscript; on the contrary, it strengthens it as it is embedded in a manuscript culture in which redactions hold an authoritative status.[76]

VOICING THE WORD

Salvation through reception implies reading as a mode of contemplation and meditation of the divine. According to the *botte* this will lead the reader to taste (in the words of the Psalmist) 'how sweet the Lord is'.[77] Sensory modes of reception are further explored in terms of voicing and breathing. Breath as an enlivening spirit is embedded in the final vision of the *Legatus*, where Christ is said to want to blow his divine breath into the book's reader (*Legatus* V, 34). The *Legatus* contains a considerable amount of language to do with breathing, but it is, arguably, not programmatic for its own textual status. Exploring voicing as a respiratory exercise which leads to new embodiments of the bride of Christ, I argue that the sensorial re-enactment of textuality in the *botte* is defining for its own self-reflectivity as a book.

It is the act of imagination that allows the text of the *botte* to be embodied. The methodological background to this argument is that the concept 'voice' bears an ontological dimension, its phenomenological quality being one of presence.[78] Paul Zumthor has highlighted the importance of voice and of vocality as traces of the body in medieval texts.[79] In my analysis, 'voice' is understood to be an expressive and performative mode of textuality, one which, by activating the sensorium in the reading process, enables embodiment.[80] The sensorium in the medieval understanding is the 'combination of the outer sensory instruments and the inner sensory faculties'.[81] Reading by lending a voice to the words of a text becomes a bodily devotional practice. Understanding through embodying operates through imagination, which, according to Karnes, 'made a unique contribution to the process by which sensory knowledge became intellectual apprehension'.[82] To combine this with observations made about the book' self-reflectivity, Gertrude's corporeal images function in two bodily ways: they are corporeal as they represent physical appearances perceived by Gertrude,[83] and they cause the reader's body to be activated. The bridge between the two is imagination, as the reader 'imagines' Gertrude's 'corporeal images'.

The *Legatus divinae pietatis* is peppered with instructions for how to read it, which may not come as a surprise given the emphasis that the Rule of St Benedict (which was followed by the Helfta nuns) placed on 'several literacy competencies to engage in contemplative practices'.[84] In the reception contexts of both the Latin and vernacular traditions of the *Legatus*, reading habits have the effect of fostering a sense of community. In late medieval reform convents, where the *botte* was read, enclosure meant that reading was promoted more and more. Silent reading is just one historical form of reading in a monastic setting where 'reading was a community activity, not just in service, but at table and for collations'.[85] Mystical experiences of visionaries were regarded as appropriate for sharing in the community as the visions 'ought to be socialized'.[86]

As an illustration of the social effect of reading mystical texts, we may look at one vision in the *botte* which connects the book and its reading to the communal celebration of the Eucharist, the central act of daily devotion present in the lifeworld of the monastic readers of the *botte*. In one of the first visions recounted in the *botte*, Christ, while making the sign of the cross over the book, says that he blesses 'all words written in this book' with his celestial blessing just as he has 'changed during mass today wine and bread into my holy body'. In doing so, he aligns the Eucharist with the written word,[87] 'so that those who read in it may partake in eternal salvation'.[88] Although still in the preterit, Christ's blessing is introduced with the temporal adverb '*zühant*', meaning 'immediately' in a present progressive mode. This adds a dramatic dimension to the scene and collapses the sense of time. Christ's lengthy speech exploits this dramatic space as it ties itself back to the celebration of the Eucharist, which itself is a moment in which past, present, and future theoretically fall into a timeless singularity. The transubstantiation is applied to the words contained in the book, that is to the text; just as the Eucharist transforms into the blood and body of Christ, so the words written in the book become the incarnated Christ. This transformation occurs through the performative act of reading. The implicit background of this ontological process is the Gospel of John. The incarnation of Christ – 'the word was made flesh', John 1:14 – and the salvation through his martyrdom, remembered in the celebration of the Eucharist, stand in a quasi-typological relationship to the book Christ blesses, and, by extension, to the performative act of blessing. This is also true for the subsequent text redactions that derive from the process of copying the book. That all subsequent redactions are also blessed is conveyed by Christ's reassurance that he will guarantee that all things are written according to his will. As a consequence, the late medieval reader is able to identify with the quasi-Eucharistic transformation of the words they are reading, since their text copy is just as sanctified as the one described in the diegetic world. The transformative effect is achieved through the bridging of visionary account and textual presence in the manifest book; reading of Gertrude's experience is thus meant to substantially shape the reader's own spiritual life.

Other instances in the *botte* show that reading is an integral part of the book's self-reflectivity. In the vision in which the scribe and compiler (in the *Legatus*, historically identifiable as Sister N) offers her work to God, the act of reading appears in an intimate situation: Christ wants to sit on the reader's lap to show them with his finger 'what is most useful'.[89] The book imagery within the text means that there is a double reinforcement of the materiality that works both inside and outside the diegetic world. André Schnyder, working on book imagery in medieval texts, stresses the level of self-reflectivity that is achieved with such imagery.[90] Famous examples of couples reading together are Francesca and Paolo in Dante's *Inferno*, Canto 5, and *Tristan and Isolde* in Gottfried of Strasbourg's verse epic; in these acts of reading, the lovers both kindle and recognise their desire for each other. Reading, here, is a harbinger or trope for the consummation of love. The *botte*'s intimate reading situation is similarly charged with tropes of desire as it uses affective formulations akin to those from the Song of Songs. The critical difference to the affective reading situations, as encountered in the *Inferno* or in *Tristan and Isolde*, is that the book Christ and the reader are holding in their hands contains theoretically the same text that the actual reader is supposed to read. This is where the book, which functions as a material manifestation of the text, allows the visionary and the imaginary to become one and the same.

Books being read within the story also point to complex relationships between orality and literacy.[91] The link between writing and voicing is not merely present but programmatic in the *botte*. In the vision with Christ and the reader reading the book, Christ specifies: 'And I will be so close to him [the reader] as if I wished to kiss him, and I will breath on him the breath of my sweet divinity which is like that of the human who is filled with fragrant things.'[92] Compared to the formulations in the *Legatus*, the detail in the *botte* about God's breath smelling of fragrant things poses a conundrum. In the Latin, the breath is connected to the two substances at communion (*diversis speciebus saturatus*).[93] Could this be an instance where the *botte* redactor made a translation mistake? This is unlikely for several reasons: the redactor having fully understood the *Legatus* would not have had a problem with a word like *speciebus* so central to the Eucharistic sacrament.[94] More importantly, the qualification of the divinity as being sweet points to a sense-based acquisition of knowledge which has less to do with pleasure or actual taste than with the positive effects achieved through sensory perception. Medieval Latin and vernacular writers – as Mary Carruthers has shown – employed 'sweetness' to refer 'to a definable sensory phenomenon'.[95] In the *botte*, the respiratory element of reading, the voiced word, implies that the breath can be smelled; and the better the reading, the more 'fragrant' that smell. Reading hence appears particularly meditative where it is put in terms of a sense-orientated contemplative mode.

That the olfactory theme is not just a random insertion but buttresses a deliberate notion of affective reading becomes more obvious when further on in the *botte* the visionary, Gertrude, recounts a dialogue with Christ, and concludes that from 'henceforth I rejoiced in a new spiritual joy and followed him in the fragrance of his good balm'.[96] Subsequently she prays directly to Christ, picking up the olfactory theme and combining it with an auditory quality: Christ is a clear note on the 'sweetest string instrument' and his breath is a perfume 'better than any spice'.[97] The olfactory aspect harks back to the breath of Christ and his word being re-enacted by the reader of 'this book'. The life of the mystic, lived 'in the fragrance of his good balm', like the act of reading, is encapsulated in an affective mode. This affective 'reading' highlights the programmatic dimension of the *botte*'s self-reflectivity. The *botte* is a product of affective reading that does not lack authority when it comes to making claims to salvific effects. Rearranging and modifying material from the *Legatus*, the *botte* constantly heightens the intensity of the reading programme by referring to its own coming into being through the act of reading.

In this regard, voicing is central to the *botte*'s programmatic affective reading as it relies on a participatory mode of engagement with the text. This affective reading is not part of a depersonalised type of affect as often proclaimed in affect theory based on Deleuze and going back to Spinoza.[98] Rather, this affective reading is attached to bodily feelings and sensory experiences,[99] as the medieval tradition of *affectus* is shaped in relation to monastic reflections of practice and habitus. The *botte* employs affective reading advantageously to establish its own status as a book that is as equally blessed as the one appearing in the vision of the *Legatus*, in which the Helfta compiler's work is approved. This authorisation through affective reading is nuanced in *botte* 4, where the chapter's title specifies that the subsequent account explains the book's name. For the first time, divine speech is addressed directly to the mystical bride, that is to Gertrude:

> I will suck in the breath of him, who wishes to read in this book in a devout manner, as if he read in it from between my hands. And doing so I will join him [in his reading] so that two are reading in one book, one sensing the breath of the other. In this way, I will suck in the breath of his desire for so long until the bowels of my love will get stirred about him. In addition, I will breathe the breath of my divinity at him for so long until he is transformed in my spirit.[100]

Sensing the breath of the other (*einer des anderen otem entpfindet*) concerns the sensory side of reading, or, in other words, its enactment by voicing. Christ joining the respiratory flow leads to the transformation – literally renewal – of the reader. This effect is a performative way to divinely justify the book and to prove its salvific significance. The point of reference for Christ's engagement can itself be taken as influenced by an affective and Bernardian reading of the Song of Songs: the voicing of the words stirs up Christ's intestines just as, in the Song of Songs, the bride's heart, or bowels, begin 'to pound for him' when her 'beloved thrusts his hand through the latch-opening' (*dilectus meus misit manum suam per foramen et venter meus intremuit ad tactum eius*, Ct 5:4).[101] In the *botte*, this rich imagery borrowed from the Song of Songs is applied to a reading practice which is intended to lead to loving Christ through reading Gertrude's life and visions. The joint reading – the very intimate reading situation of Christ holding the book and sitting on the reader's lap – highlights a participatory reception. In this vision Christ is a reader, too. Christ's divine breath and the reader's breath are interchangeable. The voicing of the words is another form of incarnation, as the words need to resonate with the help of a body in order to come into existence. Voicing the words lends life to them, just like – according to the *botte*'s rationale – the life-giving breath of God vivifies and saves the reader.

When breath and breathing are mentioned in connection with the act of reading, voicing is implied. Words that are articulated through an imaginary voice are a form of imaginary materiality.[102] Once more, the mystical thought of the fourteenth-century Dominican friar Henry Suso is helpful to understand the *botte*. Regarding sensory perception in Suso's devotional programme, Steven Rozenski has pointed out that 'the auditory often occupies a place of privilege *vis-à-vis* the visual: music and voice are frequently treated as both more powerful and more trustworthy than images, visions, or texts'.[103] In research on senses in the Middle Ages, some attention has been paid to hearing, 'that sense ranked second only to sight'.[104] Medieval thinkers, especially theologians, stressed the special status of hearing in the light of salvation history as humans were thought to be able to 'hear God'.[105] The emphasis on reading in the *botte* is linked to the importance of salvation through hearing.

The heightened sensibility for the act of reading as a form of communication also plays out in imaginary settings, that is, reading situations as depicted in visions. The awareness for an imaginary reading becomes more subtle after the *botte*'s beginning. At one instance the narrator speaks directly to the recipients calling on them to 'perceive' (*Nemet war*) a vision in which Christ presides over the joyful convent in lieu of the abbess.[106] With the narrator's appeal to take notice of the vision, the reader becomes a participant in it – in so far as they are invited to identify with the mystic. The participatory mystical experience is collective in the diegetic world too where both *Frowe Cantrix* (probably Mechthild of Hackeborn) and *Truta* (Gertrude of Helfta) have the desire to see God. In the account of the vision, Christ repeats the narrator's words telling the nuns to 'perceive' that his most beloved friends have arrived.[107] Later the narrator uses the same expression (*Nemet war*) again to point to an object in the vision: a golden board (*tofel*) is carried towards God and on it are written all the words that the convent 'had sung, read, or prayed' appearing like multicoloured 'living gems', each of which makes a 'sweet tone'.[108] The different colours are said to signify the various intentions and the desire with which the nuns had sung or read the words of the Office. The colour-coding and the sound of the gems evoke sensory qualities that the reader is called upon to recognise. Mnemonic processes, in which a medieval reader would be trained, are at work.[109] Introduced in the imperative mode (*Nemet war*), the account of the vision, though told retrospectively, becomes an active process of envisioning and embodying through the inner sensorium, with imagination enabling this process.

Similarly, in a vision that Gertrude has after the convent's abbess dies, she sees the latter adorned with many jewels in sundry colours holding a golden book in which are written all the things that she had taught 'her daughter' Gertrude. Furthermore, the book lists all the nuns who had improved them-selves through the abbess's words or example.[110] The beneficial teaching of the abbess translates into a written account, the golden book evoking the Book of Life from the beginning of the *botte*. This vision operates with book imagery borrowed from material manuscript culture in order to illustrate the salvific effects of collective learning. Embedded in the *botte*, where reading and salvation are closely connected, this imagery is self-reflective as it operates on the notion of the incarnated word.

ONTOLOGICAL EFFECTS

When we extend this idea – that the incarnated word is further embodied in any reader's engagement with the *Legatus*, Latin or vernacular – to the *botte* as a dynamic text, we find that any redactor, who is essentially a reader, presents a written form of re-enactment of what has 'flown from the divine rivers' into his chosen bride, Gertrude.[111] The salvific mechanism in the materiality of the book is set up programmatically at the beginning of the *botte*, but the under-standing of the book as material object with an immaterial influence is traditional and can be seen in numerous textual examples. For example, *The Exeter Book* composed around 1000, contains 95 Old English riddles, so-called *aenigmata*, some of which use book imagery as self-reflective devices. One of them depicts a moth which by eating a book's words becomes wiser.[112] Another, relatively long (28 lines), *aenigma* in *The Exeter Book* tells the story of medieval book production from the perspective of parchment. The culmination of the finished book is its illumination, as decoration with gold is mentioned as one of the last processes.[113] The book's materiality comes to life in this riddle, where parchment has the ability to reflect on its own use.

That the reader should follow these words on a parchment itself is not merely coincidental but heightens the importance of materiality in the reading process. Other medieval examples show that the touch of the book is important during the act of reading.[114] In the *botte*, the book presents itself as a form of embodied salvation, multipliable through the acts of copying and reading.

With these acts, the reader and the copyist, who if the text is edited becomes a redactor, can advance to become the bride of Christ. Just as the book's narrative about its coming into being is stylised as a reiteration of the incarnated word, so the soul becomes the bride through the book's reception. The reader – as I argued at the outset of this chapter – is confronted with a finished book right at the beginning of the *botte*. This book appears to be a transformed object already; it has achieved the status of 'holy matter'. Yet, the fluidity of the text material – its potential to be copied, rewritten, and read – places the finished book in a dynamic manuscript culture.[115] The dynamic nature of the text invites processes of transformation of both the text and the reader. The reader's transformation is thus embedded in the book's self-reflectivity. The *botte*'s first visions, thick with writing imagery, are set during mass; in this way, the transubstantiation with its Eucharistic notion of the incarnated word is aligned with the acts of writing and reading. The transformation of the book as told in the visions translates to the mystical idea that the soul becomes God's bride.

Looking at the literary environment of the *botte* – that is at late medieval religious texts received in the same historical contexts – we find that the idea of becoming Christ's bride relies on reading habits. Reading 'the book' is akin to the becoming the bride in the mystical tradition of Meister Eckhart. The ontology of the mystical bride – or, the maturation of the soul enabling it to become the bride of Christ – is a speculative issue that interested lay and religious people in late medieval Germany alike.[116] One of its most prominent advocates was the Dominican scholar and preacher Meister Eckhart, who lived shortly after Gertrude of Helfta, and whose writings (principally sermons) were read *inter alia* by the same late medieval readers who were interested in the *botte*. Almost all of the identified places where the *botte* was kept and read, had access to the writings (and/or sermons) of Meister Eckhart as well as to those of Henry Suso, who stands in an Eckhartian tradition.[117] Eckhart, though, was sceptical of processes of imagination, in so far as God, for him, was imageless and could hence not be mediated via images: 'God needs no image and has no image', and consequently 'it is impossible for you to be beatified by any image whatsoever'.[118] This was different for Suso, for whom, in addition to the auditory, 'images play a crucial role in the process of mystical transformation even if, in the same way as language, they cannot lead to a perfect understanding of divine realities'.[119] As Hans M. Pech argues, salvation through figurative reception is highly relevant for Suso, who in his *Life* sets up a mode of distribution of mystical insight through the reader's participation;[120] and Ingrid Falque puts it succinctly: 'The *Life* is thus based on an open and figurative writing process that perpetually solicits the reader's imagination.'[121] The possible influence of these contemporary mystical thoughts on the redactor of the *botte* leads us to suspect that the *botte*'s programmatic beginning is a deliberate arrangement which reflects Suso's fourteenth-century ideas on imagination and mental images. The *Legatus* then appears not just reworked and rearranged but entirely reconceived in the *botte*.[122] Reading the *botte* thus bears ontological effects as it aims to embody the bride.

That Gertrude is presented as lacking any nameable family ties, and as only being relatable through Christ, augments the potential for ontological effects pertaining to the embodiment of the bride.[123] One scene develops the idea of Gertrude's revelations being worthy of further communication; an unnamed person having prayed for Gertrude is told by Christ that she was chosen by himself to be loved only for his works: 'And that is why I have alienated her from all her relatives so that no one in her biological family would like her, because I want to be the only thing about her that is likeable.'[124] Apart from providing an explanation for why Gertrude is not affiliated with any existing family, most succinctly marked by her missing family name, her detachment from a family installs Christ as her only relative. Could this scene be read as a rhetorical strategy to explain the lack of a family provenance? Historically we know nothing about Gertrude; considering that the convent of Helfta was an aristocratic foundation that continuously attracted girls from the highest ranks of the region and beyond, it is rather surprising that Gertrude's family name should remain unmentioned.[125] Rather than looking at the historical motives, when studying the effect of this account, we ought to understand it as insinuating Gertrude's special relationship to Christ. Where she is from remains unknown, she has no history prior to her entry into the convent; Gertrude comes from nowhere, her coming into being is in her relationship to Christ. This relational notion of the subject means that the soul's mystical path is governed by its connexion to the divine. It also means that any soul's capacity to become the bride is underscored: Gertrude as the protagonist offers a role that can be embodied by a reader who re-envisions Gertrude's mystical life.

The *botte* redactors themselves are recipients and enactors who embody the role of the bride. Reception and creation go hand in hand, or, in other words, the mystical maturation happens in a mode of creative reception. With any redaction, a reader has fulfilled the ontological claim of the mystical programme by recreating 'the book'.[126] Although the *botte* shows a clear conceptual shift by moving from a material book copy to the 'corporeal image' of the book, its textuality is not only part of a mystical programme but remains embedded within a manuscript culture through a writing imagery which includes redactorial processes.

★ ★ ★

When Gertrude is said to be the mouthpiece of the Holy Spirit, what she communicates is deified.[127] Different layers of strategical approbation – the *commendatio*, the visions of the first chapters, an interlocution between Frowe M. Kantrix (probably Mechthild of Hackeborn) and Christ, in which Gertrude's significance for the salvation of the community is further reinforced – corroborate the idea that Gertrude's relationship with the divine is never private. The collective and participatory nature of this relationship is what, in the diegetic world, has led to 'the book', which in turn continues its own life as a dynamic text. The sanctifying effects of Gertrude's words become conflated with any present text containing the same claim to salvific benefits. The self-reflective strategy of presenting a finished book, ready to be copied and rewritten, is a strong statement, which leaves the notion of original authorship behind: there is no such thing as unique authorship but only the distribution of salvation through reception. Both the scribal work that led to the physical book, which the diegetic nun holds when she sits in mass, and the copyist's work, are blessed to bring eternal salvation; they have equal weight. As such the *botte* is self-referential in terms of its own literacy attempting to create extra-diegetic links to the material book and its Eucharistic notion as the incarnated word. Writing and voicing in the act of reading become acts that aim to embody the bride of Christ underlining the ontological effects of the book's self-reflectivity.

FIVE

THE SCRIPTORIAL HEART

The image of 'writing from the heart' – the subject of this chapter – is central to the texts produced by the Helfta nuns, and is prominent in both Mechthild of Hackeborn's *Liber specialis gratiae* and Gertrude of Helfta's *Legatus divinae pietatis*. Instances of the Sacred Heart need to be seen in a wider context, including scholastic texts as well as mystical traditions, which consider processes of wounding and their affinity with writing. In this sense, it is important to look at where the *Legatus* may have found inspiration for the motif of the heart, exploring resemblances to Victorine ideas, and texts by writers such as Bernard of Clairvaux, Alan of Lille, and Mechthild of Magdeburg. The influence of Mechthild of Magdeburg's *Flowing Light of the Godhead*, which was composed before the *Liber* and the *Legatus*, has gone largely unnoticed. The following investigation addresses this issue and shows that ideas central to 'the scriptorial heart' – in Helfta, related to Christ's Passion – are to be found in Mechthild's *Flowing Light*. Indeed, 'writing from the heart' is more of a compositional principle for the Helfta nuns than a mere literary trope, as I show in this chapter.[1] Imaginary texts in visions are intertwined with imagery of writing connected to the heart; in this way, repeated references to the productive heart, on the basis of the medieval understanding of the heart as seat of the soul, illustrate how the mystical union is communicated in bodily terms.

Textual images connected to the heart in the *botte* adapt imagery from the *Legatus*. The motif of the heart has been extensively explored in research on the *Legatus*. For example, Laura Grimes emphasises the rapport between heart and book metaphors as a way to condition the reader's heart to Gertrude's writing. The background for Grimes' reading is the Augustinian understanding of the heart as the site of memory, and of confessional writing and reading as therapeutic to the soul.[2] Eve Jenkins also stresses the heart metaphor as a textual image which mediates between the mystic and the reader in the *Legatus*.[3] While the 'heart' in the *Legatus* has garnered much attention, its counterpart in the *botte* has not been researched – it has even incorrectly been declared not to be extant.[4] I examine the connection between 'writing' and 'the heart' in this study even though it is not specific to the *botte* and is already central in the *Legatus*, because it underlines the emphasis on corporeal images in the *botte*: it forms part of the book's self-reflectivity, and it also reverberates with other vernacular devotional texts in late medieval Germany. In an excursus at the end of this chapter, I explore this reception context of the *botte*, which is of great importance when considering how heart motifs are adapted in the *botte* and how they led to new meanings.

This chapter's argumentative structure leads from images of the heart related to Christ's Passion, via the heart as a gateway to salvation, the heart as a musical organ, and writing imagery connected to the heart, to the figure of John the Evangelist as someone writing from the divine heart. Studying passages central to the *botte* and its wider literary context, I argue that throughout the *botte*, images of the divine heart sustain the notion of an organic scriptorium, the textual outcomes of which promise sacramental redemption. The book as emanating from the divine heart is treated in different registers in the *botte*. On one level, Christ's heart is depicted as a scriptorium mirrored in the mystic's body; on another, the heart is depicted as a musical organ brought to life through the respiratory process of breathing. The corporeality of the image of the heart is closely tied to Christ's Passion, and the idea that Christ's side wound forms the gateway to the divine heart.[5] In the *botte*, writing derived from Christ's bodily heart is the preserve of John the Evangelist who, in one of Gertrude's visions, records the nuns' behaviour in a quasi-book-of-life. The *botte*'s portrayal of Christ's side wound as an ink well for John the Evangelist, who is involved in visionary writing, is thus connected to the divine heart and scriptorial mnemonic devices. Consequently, the idea of salvific writing takes on a prophetic dimension, which harks back to other mystical and devotional texts in late medieval Germany, in particular to texts that circulated among lay communities in South Germany, a social milieu that was especially interested in the *botte*. The correlation between John the Evangelist and visionary mysticism stands in dialogue with urban devotion in late medieval Germany which was pragmatic in its approach to educating the layperson to become the bride of Christ, as can be seen in Otto of Passau's mystagogical treatise *Die Vierundzwanzig Alten* (*The Twenty-Four Elders*, short

The Elders). As I discuss in this chapter, Passau's *Elders* functions as a backdrop for the late medieval readership that was also interested in the *botte*. The study of heart imagery in the *botte* allows us thus to draw connections to the *botte*'s historical and literary contexts. With the exploration of these topics, I demonstrate that the *botte*, composed and copied in devotional contexts that developed bridal mystical concepts for a wider audience, exploits the book's self-reflectivity for a programme of mystical edification centred around the heart.

THE HEART OF THE PASSION

Ever since patristic reflections were made on the meaning of the heart, theologians have treated this central organ as the place where God reveals himself to the human soul; for Augustine it was the inner place where one connects to the deity (*sursum leuans cor ad Dominum*).[6] In high medieval scholastic theology, the heart becomes a metaphor for rational knowing. Thomas Aquinas (c. 1225–1274) wanted to distinguish the formal from the material qualities of the heart, describing their causal relationships; 'Aquinas was one of the scholars who sought to maintain a clear distinction between the soul and the spirit', but later generations of scholars (including physicians) would use his neat categories to blur the lines between them.[7] The divine heart allowed for an overlapping of the material with the spiritual because of the idea of the humanity of Christ. From the second half of the twelfth century, the image of the divine heart was increasingly used in spiritual writings, where it was generally employed to speak about an otherwise hard to depict inwardness.[8] Bernard of Clairvaux refers to the divine heart in his *Sermons on the Song of Songs*, interpreting it as a sign of sacrificial love. Taking the opening (*foramen*) mentioned in the Song of Songs (*dilectus meus misit manum suam per foramen et venter meus intremuit ad tactum eius*, Ct 5:4), Bernard evokes the spear that, as he explains, by piercing Christ's side, revealed the secret of his heart.[9] The Latin word *viscera*, used by Bernard for 'heart', can also refer to any internal organ (similar to *sinus* or *venter*). The multitude of terms that existed in medieval Latin to refer to the heart reveals how flexible the motif of the heart really was at this stage in literary history. Although it kept a figurative value through its metaphorical nature, the 'heart' was not yet a settled trope accompanied by a cult; the Sacred Heart devotion fully ripened only in the seventeenth century.[10]

In medieval texts, the motif of the divine heart is often connected to the crucifixion, as for example in *The Flowing Light of the Godhead* by Mechthild of Magdeburg, an important source for the visionary world of the *Legatus*. In a passage concerned with the Passion, Mechthild of Magdeburg's reader is told to remember 'the spear's wound' in Christ's side, which accessed his heart:

Gedenk ŏch in des spere wunde, das dur die siten gieng ze sines herzen grunde.[11] Although the divine heart in the *Flowing Light* is not as prominent as in both the *Liber specialis gratiae* and the *Legatus divinae pietatis*, Mechthild of Magdeburg appears to have anticipated the understanding of the divine heart that we encounter in Mechthild of Hackeborn and Gertrude of Helfta's visions.[12]

The *Liber* and the *Legatus* are both acclaimed for a strong presence of the divine heart and have thus repeatedly served as objects of study of this motif.[13] Both were influenced by Bernard of Clairvaux's mystical theology and possibly by other spiritual thinkers such as Hugh of St Victor, who puts the 'heart' in relation to the divine incarnation in the word.[14] Surprisingly, Mechthild of Magdeburg – the oldest of the Helfta mystics – has been left out of research concerning the divine heart,[15] although Hans Neumann has hinted at the possibility of Mechthild of Magdeburg having influenced the later 'Cult of the Heart of Jesus' ('Herz-Jesu-Kult') in Helfta.[16] While one can scarcely speak of a 'cult', which would entail dedicated practices and rituals, a deeper look into the *Flowing Light* reveals that, here already, aspects of writing are connected to the divine heart – a nexus which would become accentuated in the *Liber* and the *Legatus*. However, in the *Flowing Light*, the divine heart is not yet fully fleshed out to mean Christ's heart, its semantic designation being also applicable to God and the Holy Spirit. In Kurt Ruh's work on the composition of the *Legatus*, the divine heart as found in the *Flowing Light* is an indicator of the scribal and authorial work of Sister N. Mechthild's work would have been picked up by Sister N's hand as she completed the seventh and final book. Ruh's argument is based on the closing phrases of Book VI:

> This Writing Flowed out of God
> The writing in this book flowed out of the living Godhead into sister Mechthild's heart and has been as faithfully set down here as it was given by God, out of her heart and written by her hand. Thanks be to God.[17]

For Ruh, the convent of Helfta – and Sister N in particular – was already responsible for the description of the writing having 'flown into the heart' as found in the colophon of Book VI. Mechthild is called a '*swester*' indicating her presence in the convent where the nuns took up the writing project that she had started before she joined the community at Helfta. In the *Liber*, expressions of fluidity are also used in connection with the mystic's heart:

> Finally, he united his honey-sweet heart to the Soul's heart, granting her all his exercise of meditation, devotion, and love; and he enriched her abundantly with every good. Thus her whole soul was incorporated into Christ. Melting in divine love like wax before the fire, she put on his likeness, being wholly absorbed in God just as wax is imprinted with the seal. In this way, that blessed soul became completely one with her Beloved.[18]

The language of flowing is – also according to Ruh – not strong enough evidence to assume the same author behind this introductory passage from the *Liber* and the colophon of the *Flowing Light*, Book VI.[19] Rather, the language of flowing – and in the case of the *Liber* of melting – shows a productive reception of the Song of Songs, more precisely of the verses in which the soul is liquefied (*anima mea liquefacta est*, Ct 5:6) and where the heart can be 'stamped' with a seal (*pone me ut signaculum super cor tuum*, Ct 8:6). In this sense, the motif of the heart as connected to processes of flowing and writing forms part of a larger tradition of bridal mysticism.[20] Nevertheless, following Ruh's observation, the question arises as to whether the colophon of Book VI of Mechthild of Magdeburg's *Flowing Light* really is a 'Helfta ingredient'. Passages earlier in the *Flowing Light*, that is, the parts written by Mechthild before her time in Helfta, insinuate a presence of the divine heart. The manifestation of the motif of the heart in the books predating Helfta means that, in fact, Mechthild might have presaged the later development of the motif in Helfta. For example, the flowing 'blood of the heart', the 'heart's blood', can already be found in Book V:

> Our Lord said this as well: 'I hereby send this book as a messenger to all religious people [...] in this book my heart's blood is written, which I shall shed again in the last times.'[21]

The book as messenger of the divine is a common trope in visionary accounts and reappears in the later writings of Helfta.[22] The heart in connection with writing in a physical book that functions as a messenger, is commonplace, found not just in Helfta but indeed a century earlier in the writings of Alan of Lille, where the description of personified Arithmetic – as the first discipline in the quadrivium of the seven liberal arts – is said to have a face which is 'the book, the writing of the heart, the messenger, faithful interpreter and image of the mind'.[23] Far from the notion of Arithmetic, Mechthild of Magdeburg, at any rate, foreshadows ideas expressed in the *Liber* and in the *Legatus* about the flowing 'heart-blood'.[24]

Concerning the Latin writings from Helfta, Rosalynn Voaden has analysed the motif of the heart aligning it to 'female biology'; flowing blood images are treated as metaphors for menstruation which the nuns, according to Voaden, regarded as analogous to the blood flowing from Christ's side wound.[25] Indeed, medieval images of Christ's side wound evoke a figurative proximity to the vagina (and sometimes vulva), as has been frequently discussed in scholarship.[26] However, the flowing-blood metaphor cannot be reduced to a biological argument. As Voaden acknowledges too, 'Mechthild of Magdeburg's visions of the Sacred Heart, even those she recorded after coming to Helfta, reveal little of the female imagery which is so much a part of the revelations of Gertrude and Mechthild of Hackeborn.'[27] Instead, Voaden assigns a more 'traditional' understanding of the

'Sacred Heart' to Mechthild.[28] A comparison of Mechthild of Magdeburg's divine heart to her Dominican and Premonstratensian contemporaries shows her theological involvement in questions concerning the divine heart, which fuelled by an increasing Corpus Christi devotion in the thirteenth century, were still being negotiated.[29] Mechthild of Magdeburg's divine heart is not merely 'concrete and graphic rather than symbolic';[30] rather, it expresses ideas of mystical union through the Eucharist. Mechthild is up to date with the theological deliberations on the divine heart in connection with the Eucharist as comparison with related material, as, for example, written by Albert the Great (1200–1280), reveals.[31] The flowing element of the 'heart-blood' is also central to the status of Mechthild's book as 'God-created', because it aligns the sacrament of the Eucharist to the book's writing, both of which 'flow' from God and are his 'heart-blood'.[32] We can conclude that Mechthild of Magdeburg's complex understanding of the divine heart predates her entrance to Helfta and has thus certainly influenced the two younger mystics Mechthild of Hackeborn and Gertrude of Helfta who little later would pick up the motif and deepen its significance for how their books came into being.

The divine heart as a motif correlating to the book is a larger cultural phenomenon of the High and late Middle Ages and can of course be seen beyond Mechthild of Magdeburg.[33] Similarly to Mechthild, where 'the book' can represent the crucified Christ, for Henry Suso, Christ's martyred body is 'opened' like a book and can be read like one.[34] In the revelations of Adelheid Langmann, the correlation of writing, Trinity, and Christ's suffering is doubly complex as an analogy is drawn between the five letters of Jesus' name as standing for his five wounds and the mystic as mirroring the Trinity.[35] Dorothea of Montau 'presses' Christ's martyrdom into her heart where she can recall it 'like in a book'.[36] In the *botte*, Christ appears to the scribe in a vision and says he has 'pressed the book onto my heart' (*Das bůch han ich gedrucket in min hertz*).[37] This is an image which was surely inspired by the image of the seal from the Song of Songs 8:6 ('set me as a seal upon your heart').[38]

Nevertheless, the central image of the divine heart in the *Legatus* has a lot more in common with Mechthild of Magdeburg's understanding than is often assumed. *Legatus* Book II, especially, which presents itself as having been written by Gertrude herself, reveals the motif of the heart to be closely aligned with Christ's side wound and to generally appear as the locus of love.[39] While with the latter notion, Gertrude seems affiliated with Richard of St Victor, who develops a philosophy of love based on the heart,[40] the notion of the five wounds reminds us of the heart-Passion complex found in the *Flowing Light*. For Ruh, the motif of the heart found in the other books of the *Legatus* (Books III–V) – marked by an intimate relationship between soul and God, and put into nuptial terms – is influenced either by Sister N or by Mechthild of

Hackeborn. Mechthild of Hackeborn's mysticism, according to Ruh, differs from Gertrude's in that that it prepares a Sacred Heart devotion because of its ecstatic and emotionally charged approach to the divine heart, whereas Gertrude maintains a more sober relationship to the divine heart.[41] However, Ruh's conclusions are based on the assumption that Gertrude was the sole author of *Legatus* Book II, by which he assigns her an original and individual spirituality. Even though the style of the Latin language in Book II differs from the other books, this cannot be taken as a guarantee of single authorship, as has been discussed in Chapters 1 and 2. Furthermore, Gertrude and her coauthors might well have changed and developed their ideas of the divine heart over the writing period of the *Legatus* which spanned at least twelve years.

It seems then that the motif of the heart is already complicated in the *Legatus* where multiple understandings are associated with it; but how much of the divine heart in the *Legatus* (whether from Book II or the other four books is irrelevant for this question) is retained in the *botte*? Is the *botte* as stripped of this motif as has been assumed in the comparison between the *botte* and the *Legatus*? Lewis posited that the Sacred Heart was missing in the *botte* 'because of [the] inherent notion of intimacy' found in the *Legatus*.[42] Ruh, by contrast, was opposed to the idea that intimacy between soul and God was expressed in images of the heart in Gertrude's spiritual thinking.[43] The divided opinions in research are partly due to differing academic cultures, Ruh being interested in manuscripts and transmission history as well as spiritual history while Lewis focuses on theological matters. Yet, they are also a sign of the rich spectrum of interpretations that can be applied to the *Legatus* and to the *botte* as an early example of an interpretation of the *Legatus* by a cocreative readership.

Despite the fact that a superficial inventory may list far fewer examples of the motif of the heart in the *botte* than in the *Legatus*, a deeper reassessment is necessary to evaluate how the divine heart was understood, reformulated, and adapted in the vernacular redaction. This is important because the treatment of the motif in the *botte* is multilayered. For example, a vivid vision from *Legatus* Book II, Chapter 4, in which Gertrude leads God to write his wounds into her heart, is missing in the German text altogether.[44] At the same time, an audition – that is, a vision that is purely auditory – in which Christ wants to incline his heart to the devout believer who recalls the crucifixion and meditates with the help of relics (*Legatus* IV, 52), is similarly rendered in the *botte*, ascribing to Christ a desire that mirrors that of the mystic.[45] The mirroring effect is more evident in the *botte* because another *Legatus* chapter which mentions Gertrude's heart (*Legatus* IV, 24), is combined with the audition, so that the *botte* chapter names both the human heart and the divine heart. The context in the German text is that of the Holy Cross, the chapter even being entitled *Von dem heilgen crútz Cristi*.

This labelling, and the combination of Gertrude's veneration of the cross and Christ's words about how to remember his martyrdom while repeatedly referring to his divine heart, reaffirm a juxtaposition between the heart and the Passion, which is also at the core of Mechthild of Magdeburg's understanding of the divine heart. That this particular *botte* chapter – which is also worked into the shorter *Trutta*-legend – was understood to be connected to the Passion is underlined by its partial inclusion in a Passion treatise as transmitted in a miscellany of the Buxheim Charterhouse.[46]

THE HEART AS GATEWAY TO SALVATION

According to Christian theology, the Passion itself is the prerequisite of salvation, and, according to the *botte*'s rationale, reading Gertrude's life means salvation through the divine heart. In an extended vision which unfolds during mass, Gertrude sees her guardian angel bringing a chalice filled with her own 'pain'. As in the narrated time the priest blesses the communion, Christ blesses Gertrude's chalice, after which he sings the opening dialogue to the preface of the Eucharistic prayer, the *sursum corda* ('Lift up your hearts'). Gertrude then sees that all the saints lift up their hearts to 'the golden altar of the divine heart', their hearts appearing as golden tubes that draw drops from the chalice, 'that they may be more rewarded and dignified from it'.[47] This flamboyant image of saints receiving a bonus from Gertrude's Passion-like pain has been described by Ringler as the unification of the divine heart with Gertrude's heart.[48] Carrying strong Eucharistic notions, Gertrude's suffering becomes like Christ's Passion, and it literally trickles into the saints. This kind of emanation, a flowing mercy, is usually attributed to the deity. With Gertrude's pain being sacrificed for the salvation of others she is deified to the degree that her life is a distributor of salvation. The passing on of salvation is already laid out in the beginning of the *botte*, where reading with devout intentions is said to bring spiritual gain: consuming Christ's blood in the Eucharist and reading Gertrude's life become analogous. The Eucharistic blood, though generally meant to embody Christ's martyrdom, takes its iconographic and certainly biblical roots in the image of his bleeding side wound, his *herzeblůt*, to use a term Mechthild of Magdeburg applies.

Christ's side as the gateway into the divine heart opens up a 'corporeal understanding' of salvation. Through Christ as the incarnation of God's Word, the body becomes the place of spiritual deliverance. Medieval devotional practices which aimed to meditate on the Passion were occupied with the question of embodiment as Christ was contemplated in his humanity – rather than in his divinity.[49] Could reflections of this be seen in the *Legatus*, which arguably showcases the side wound more than the divine heart? Ruh saw only traces of a Sacred Heart theme in the *Legatus*, in contrast to the *Liber*, and, scrutinising the relevant passages, came to the conclusion that in the *Legatus* there is a veneration of Christ's side wound but not of his heart.[50] Yet the line between Christ's side wound and his heart is not clear-cut when considering how interconnected the two images are in textual as well as pictorial sources. Barbara Newman, in the context of her work on violence in love poetry, has shown how Christ's heart and his pierced side are connected in textual images, noticeably in mystical texts such as the Daughter Zion allegory, and in figurative art, as, for example, in an early fourteenth-century stained glass from Wienhausen which depicts the Virtues crucifying Christ.[51] Similarly, a thirteenth-century lectionary, which belonged to the Dominican nuns in Regensburg who oversaw its production, contains a miniature of the Virtues crucifying Christ (see Plate XV). Here, the *sponsa*, the mystical bride, pierces Christ's side with a spear: the mystical union is illustrated as a result of the contemplation of Christ's Passion.[52]

In the *botte*, too, the side wound and the divine heart are like two sides of one coin, the wound opening up the passage to the heart. In an extended visionary image of Christ's heart, Gertrude sees that 'many' (*etlich*) humans are able to 'stick their tubes' – in some kind of a drinking straw manner – into Christ's body parts. The tubes are said to stand for the human will; the German term used in the *botte* to describe an egocentric will, *eigenwille*, echoes the Eckhartian concept of the 'own will' suggesting that the *botte* redactor might have been influenced by Meister Eckhart.[53] The closer the humans in Gertrude's vision stick their tubes to the divine heart, the more they have abandoned their own will for the sake of following God's will only. Those who are thankful for this kind of will suck on golden tubes; but those who stick their straws away from the heart correspond to people who follow their own will, the further away they are, the 'more sour' is the content they draw from Christ's body. Reacting to this vision, Gertrude sacrifices her heart voluntarily – literally, 'with her free will' (*mit frigem willen*). Her words connect Christ's side with his heart via a stream of liquids, namely the Eucharistic liquids of water and blood:

> Lord, I offer you my heart on the basis of my free will and independent from any creature's influence. And I beg you to wash it in the strong water of your side, and to adorn it with the rose-coloured blood of your divine heart, and to be unified with you in your divine love.[54]

Gertrude's wish to be washed in the water of the side wound reminds us of a miniature from Hildegard of Bingen's lost *Scivias* manuscript, the *Rupertsberg Codex*, where a female figure (possibly the *sponsa*?) by the crucifix catches the blood from Christ's side in a chalice while another stream splashes (or washes?) her face (see Plate XVI).[55] Based on the central vision of the *Scivias* – the sixth vision of the second part – the image of *Christ's Sacrifice and the Church* portrays a complex understanding of the Church as the joining element between God and humans with the communion being the crucial method to connect the past with the eschaton. Here, remembering the Passion in the Eucharistic celebration occurs in the visual recalling of Christ's side. Gertrude's words pleading to be united with the divine heart are undoubtedly embedded in a visionary tradition connected to the Eucharistic notion of Christ's side wound.[56] In the vision's final narrative phrase as recounted in the *botte*, Gertrude sees 'instantly' that Christ unifies his heart with hers and takes it to his 'celestial father': *Zůhant sach sú, das der gottessůn ir hertze vereinete mit dem sinen und es broht sinem himmelschen vatter.*[57] How one is supposed to picture this union of the hearts remains unspecified in the *botte* while it is expounded in the *Legatus*, where the image of a two-part chalice joined with wax is evoked.[58] In the *botte*, the corporeal aspect of the entire vision and of the vision that precedes it – in which Gertrude's suffering is offered in a chalice – nonetheless proposes an alignment of her quasi-Eucharistic distribution of salvation with the 'tapable' divine heart. This juxtaposition, achieved through the visions being presented one after the other, is unique to the *botte*, since no known *Legatus* source transmits these two visions in immediate proximity.[59]

The intriguing imagery of Christ's 'heart-blood' being accessed by a straw is very likely based on a rare Eucharistic practice in which the consecrated wine was consumed via a straw from the chalice to prevent spilling even a drop of it. An example of such a straw from a monastery near Freiburg im Breisgau dating back to the second quarter of the thirteenth century forms part of an ensemble of elements needed for the celebration of the Eucharist: next to the straw, there is the paten for the bread and the chalice for the wine (see Fig. 37 and Plate XVII). Gertrude's vision therefore carries a pictorially established Eucharistic connotation; its specific imagery also allows us to glimpse what the celebration of the communion at Helfta might have looked like as material culture influenced the mystical vision.

In Gertrude's vision of the joint hearts, water and blood are evoked. The liquids streaming from Christ's side form the basis for the consecration of the wine for the Eucharist, the background for which are the Gospel stories of the Passion (John 19:33–35 and again 1 John 5:6–8). Connecting the Eucharistic liquids to the motif of the divine heart is a device, however, already employed by Mechthild of Magdeburg. In the first book of the *Flowing Light*, the mystical embrace of soul and bridegroom happens in the 'burning' divine heart and is compared to the union of water and wine.[60] Mechthild's thoughts reverberate with the celebration of the Eucharist, which in its essence serves as a commemoration of Christ's martyrdom. Accessing Christ's spiritual heart in this context happens through the remembrance of the Passion, for which the corporeal wound is crucial.

37 Ensemble for the celebration of the Eucharist. German (c. 1230–50)
New York, The Metropolitan Museum of Art
The Cloisters Collection, 1947 (accession nr. 47.101.28)
Image Copyright: The Metropolitan Museum of Art. Image source: Art Resource, NY

The liturgy and patristic and hagiographic literature are other sources for a
salvific spirituality of the divine heart. Visions and narratives of the wounded
heart in mystical texts reverberate with the phrase *Vulneraverat caritas Christi cor
meum* which – inspired by Augustine's *Confessions* – came to form the incipit of
the responsory for the third nocturn on the feast of St Augustine.[61] The image
of the pierced heart achieved a broad reception through this liturgical text but
also through the integration of the phrase into Jacobus de Voragine's *vita* of
Augustine in his *Legenda aurea*.[62] In the *botte*, Christ calls Gertrude to wound
his heart with her 'glance' – literally with her 'eye'.[63] This 'glance' refers to a

contemplative practice, the mechanisms of which work on the basis of a multiple mirroring act of remembering the Passion, renewing Christ's pain in this act of recollection, and forcing Christ to have compassion for the contemplating devotee.[64] Why eyesight should be able to wound Christ's heart becomes apparent when considering the underlying medieval and Aristotelian influenced theory of optics according to which the eye emits light beams in order illuminate objects.[65] Hugh of St Victor understood the physiology of eyesight as a movement from inner to outer.[66] The exegesis of the Song of Songs contributed to this theory the specification that eyesight can wound the heart, referring to the verse *vulnerasti cor meum* [. . .] *in uno oculorum tuorum* (Cant 4:9).[67] In the *botte*, the penetrative power of sight corresponds to the spear piercing Christ's heart. This correlates with the moment of the Eucharist, when Christ teaches Gertrude how to wound his heart, so that the Passion is renewed in the act of commemoration.

Given the penetrative spearlike force of Gertrude's contemplative sight, it is all the more surprising that a vision from the *Legatus* (II, 5), in which a golden arrow representing love exits Christ side and enters into her heart, is not included in the *botte*.[68] Yet, since we do not know what kind of source(s) the *botte* redactor had at hand, it is hard to draw any firm conclusions as to why this vision is missing. The notion that love causes pain is still prominent in the *botte* as different visions involving the divine heart suggest. As Christ's martyrdom is remembered in the celebration of the Eucharist, so Gertrude's suffering is said to transform into spiritual reward and be passed on to others.[69] Her martyrdom is − like in many late medieval texts − not exclusively an external one but also evolves within the soul; it is an interior, as well as exterior, act of imitation:[70] Gertrude's suffering emulates Christ in his martyrdom, the *imitatio Christi* working towards her own salvation and by the virtue of sharing her revelations with the reader, theoretically serving others.

THE HEART AS A MUSICAL ORGAN

Thus far, this chapter has focused primarily on the Christological aspects of a spirituality of the heart. Christ's heart as the gateway to his Passion is negotiated in the *botte* in another register, too, one which alludes to the heart as a respiratory organ thereby evoking a kind of sonic instrument. In the *botte*, the divine heart is depicted as an 'organ-instrument', one defined through the acts of writing and breathing. This specific heart imagery forms a cycle of creation (writing) and reception (breathing) that has a bearing on the *botte*'s ontological effects. While the motif of the heart is necessarily attached to an idea of the body, it is more flexible and supple than a strictly human-corporeal conception would allow. Paul Zarowny has argued that Mechthild of Hackeborn and Gertrude of Helfta were influenced by a medical model of the heart that had

changed in the late thirteenth century in consequence of the introduction of
Aristotelian biological treatises to Western Europe in the first quarter of that
century. Taking into account that for Aristotle, animal anatomy and physiology were cardiocentric, Zarowny interprets the motif of the heart in the
Liber and the *Legatus* in the light of this cardiological tradition. The divine heart
becomes the centre of Christ's mystical body, a circumstance termed 'visionary
cardiocentricism' by Zarowny.[71] This quasi-biological argument is built on a
medical understanding of the human body. Yet, the heart's corporeal imagery
also includes a broader understanding of 'body', more precisely the understanding of a body which, in musical terms, can function as a soundboard.

Breathing – as a prerequisite to an externalised act of reading – and singing
are practices associated with the heart in the *botte*, attributing the qualities of a
musical instrument to this organ. Sometimes the divine heart is more specifically linked to singing; for example, Gertrude's song pierces Christ's heart 'like a
sharp spear' reaching as deep as his backbone (*marg*). The spear's point has
beams that reach to the saint whose feast day it is (the particular saint is not
specified). The spear's lower part has 'spiritual mercy' flowing to the humans
and to all of the souls in purgatory 'like a moist, wet rain' which 'comes
secretly'. The moment in which this act of violent mercy is initiated is when
Gertrude sings the words *in acutis*. However, it is 'all the words that she sings'
that form the cutting spear which creates a direct connection between the
body of Christ and the souls on earth and in purgatory. Moreover, the salvific
character of Gertrude's singing is functionalised in the chapter's title 'What her
singing was good for' (*Wie nútz ir gesang was*).[72] The spear in the *Legatus* – as
the vision is based on *Legatus* III, 24 – connects Gertrude's heart to Christ's,
whereas in the *botte*, only Christ's heart is mentioned. Another distinct difference lies within the words of the song themselves. *In acutis*, the words that in
the *botte* trigger the vision, cannot be found in any medieval song repertoire,
and neither of the known Latin *Legatus* sources actually specifies an *incipit* for
the hymn in question. Instead, the *Legatus* has Gertrude 'piously' sing a
canonical chant to an unspecified saint, not mentioning *in acutis* at all: *In festo
cujusdam Sancti, dum intenderet horas canonicas in laude Dei ejusdemque Sancti
devotius decantare.*[73] The Latin words *in acutis* in the *botte* cover a range of
meanings, from 'sharply' to 'suddenly emerging'. Could they go back to a
Legatus source lost to us today? Are they a copy mistake derived from the
responsory for the Visitation of Mary which starts on the comparative form of
Latin *acutus* (*Acutius matre Joannes audivit*)? Or are they a sign of the redactor
who interpreted the passage since *acutis* means shrill, sharp, and dangerous –
like the spear – as well as a trigger action (activation), and Gertrude's song is
activating? The *Legatus* does not employ the word *acutus* in this passage but uses
peracuta to describe the pointy spear. The *botte,* on the other hand, doubles
the suddenness of the action with the vernacular *nů*, meaning 'now' or

'immediately', followed by the Latin *in acutis*, the use of which seems therefore more likely to have been a choice, rather than a mistake. Another possible explanation for a deliberate inclusion of *in acutis* is that in medieval Latin musical treatises, *in acutis* and *in gravis* are used to describe high and low singing voices respectively; so *in acutis* here could describe Gertrude singing at a high pitch. The integration of the words *in acutis* has manifold effects as the multilingual portrayal of Gertrude's liturgically prompted vision adds a sonic aspect to the image it portrays. The image in itself is synesthetic as the way to reach Christ's heart is to form a spearlike bridge consisting of liturgical song.[74] Celebrating a feast day becomes a window to the celestial sphere, as can be seen at other instances, too. In a vision at Christmas, for example, Christ sends a bright beam from his divine heart to the celebrants of the mass to build a path on which those who give up their own will can walk on to reach him.[75] In the *botte*, as in the *Legatus*, Christ's heart responds to music.

The 'musical heart' of Christ is rendered in a uniquely entertaining way in another vision; transmitted in the *botte* as well as the *Trutta*-legend, it is embedded in the context of Gertrude's unhappiness about her insufficient singing. Gertrude is distracted in her celebration of the Office, asking herself 'how can one hope for perfection with such unsteadiness?'[76] In the narrative account, Christ cannot endure her sadness and shows her his heart, which he holds in both hands as a burning light saying: 'Behold, my heart is a sweet organ [*orgel*] of the honourable Trinity. You shall see it with the eyes of your mind. And whatever you cannot achieve because of human imperfection you shall leave to me, and be reassured that you will gain it through me.'[77] By the time the *botte* was composed, Middle High German *orgel*, which could originally encompass any kind of sound produced by driving pressurised air through pipes (from Lat. *organum*), had come to denote specifically the musical instrument played with a keyboard known to us as an organ today.[78] As such, Christ's heart is not only susceptible to musical sound but actually figures as what is often called 'the king of instruments'.[79] In the account of the vision, Gertrude is surprised by the generosity offered to her in the face of her 'negligence' (*versúmikeit*) as she understands Christ's heart to be 'a divine treasure chamber' (*ein schatzkamer der gotheit*). The narrator goes on to frame Christ's response to Gertrude's astonishment as a simile for his promise to complete what she leaves imperfect.[80] Christ's direct speech then follows:

> Supposed that you had a good voice to sing with and you enjoyed singing very much, but there was someone else singing with you quite poorly and not being able to follow you. You would get very angry about why this other voice does not leave all the singing up to you since they are not capable of it. In the same way my divine heart recognises well human imperfection and unsteadiness [. . .].[81]

Christ opening his heart to Gertrude is put in relation to an embarrassing situation occurring when singing in a community where some sing better than others. The desire to 'fix the song', expressed by the good singer's anger, is taken as analogous to the divine generosity, which is moved by 'unspeakable desire'.[82] The double epistemological layer of vision and simile within the vision again creates the impression of violent mercy in conjunction with the divine heart.

With this understanding of the divine heart as malleable source of mercy, the *botte* moves within late medieval conceptions of this theologically loaded image. As for Suso where 'the heart represents the juncture of the soul and body which allows divine experience to spill over into physical gesture',[83] so for Gertrude, Christ is forced to act and correct what is neglected or done badly through the gesture of opening his heart. Gertrude's vision concludes with Christ admonishing Gertrude to have at least the will and the desire to fulfil her work if she cannot accomplish it with words. Augustine's understanding of volition as key to redemption underlies this mechanism of salvation. Christ's heart is a central image for the mechanism of salvation as it concocts affection and volition in corporeal and spiritual terms. The heart as an organ-instrument is moved and moves.

Behind these visions stands a medieval understanding of the heart as a porous organ. As Heather Webb has shown, one important model of the medieval heart is that of a respiratory organ.[84] It allows several meanings: 'the only circulations "through" the heart were not of blood but of air, breath, spirit', as pointed out by Jocelyn Wogan-Browne.[85] Basing her observations on Webb's work, Wogan-Browne highlights that 'the medieval heart is a breathing heart' which always stands in relation to the external world.[86] The interiorised subjectivity brought forward through the heart image in a devotional vision can in this way be seen as 'a reciprocal and potentially generative mixing of external and innate spirits within the heart of the viewer'.[87] In Gertrude's visions involving Christ's heart as a musical instrument, a reciprocity, which evolves on a sonorous plane, exists between the visionary and Christ. The musical dimension of the monastic community is equally evoked in the mentioning of hymns and varying singing capabilities. As liturgy provided 'a means of relating [to] one another through regular musical performances',[88] this aspect of Gertrude of Helfta's spiritual life and thought was equally important in the reception of the *Legatus*.

WRITING FROM THE HEART

The reception of Gertrude's life takes us back to the book's self-reflectivity. What does the book have to do with the divine heart and its accessibility through Christ's side wound? In the *botte*'s programmatic beginning,

Christ hands out arrows from his heart to those who copy the book in devotion, creating another kind of interchange that is linked to the act of reading. Scribal activity is kindled by arrows shot from the divine heart:

> But to him who devoutly and mercifully writes/copies it [the book], I shall send from the sweetness of my divine heart as many arrows of my divine love as things that he writes, that the desire of divine sweetness may be moved and enlivened in his soul.[89]

As discussed in the previous chapter, the 'book', in turn, is read within a process of breathing, which is joined by Christ who 'sucks' in the reader's breath.[90] More importantly for this analysis, emissions from the divine heart, which initiate love, follow an act of writing.

The complex of writing and the divine heart involves Christ's side wound, or, as I have referred to it above, the heart of the Passion. Already at the beginning of the *botte*, Christ's side wound is evoked: Gertrude sees a 'crystal river' (*kristallen bach*) flowing from Christ's left side, in which two colours – gold and 'rose-red' – are mixed. The meanings of the colours are given by Christ in his address to Gertrude: gold and red stand for her words and deeds to her neighbours.[91] The stream's like nature and the additional colours hint at medieval theories about gemstones and precious metals, and their meanings. Ancient Greek ideas about the transparency, colour, and light of gems were interpreted and adapted by Christian theologians. For Pseudo-Dionysius for example, a crystal's transparency represented the concept of divine transcendence.[92] Gold was thought to be the colour of divine light, perfectly translucent but also reinforcing anything visible by making it shine more intensely. Red came not only to signify the colour of Christ's martyrdom, but was also associated with light, as it became 'a surrogate for white or gold'.[93] These two specific colours, gold and red, are also used to mark special words, letters, and other elements in medieval manuscripts. The graphical correlation with Christ's martyrdom is not incidental, as a later vision makes evident, where Christ's streaming side presents concrete phenomena of medieval book culture such as illumination and rubrication. Visions containing books in the *Legatus* invoke salvific topoi, but in their details of how script is adorned they also echo the production of liturgical manuscripts.[94]

Colour coding in the *botte* forms part of its self-reflectivity as it pertains to a salvific programme of the 'scriptorial heart'. This claim is best illustrated with a vision in which John the Evangelist appears as a scribe, consolidating the conjunction of script and heart. Gertrude sees John the Evangelist at the feet of Christ as a *Majestas Domini* figure writing down all the things that the convent's nuns had been doing.[95] John dips his quill frequently into a black ink horn (literally 'little horn') that he is holding in his hand. From time to time he dips the quill into the 'wound of the heart' of Jesus 'as it stood open towards him':

> And whenever he wrote from the black horn the letters became black, but when he wrote from the rose-coloured wound of Jesus Christ, the script was red. The same red script was interlaced with black and at some spots with golden colour.

The narrator explains that Gertrude understands 'the script written in black colour' to represent – literally 'to be' – the works that the nuns do habitually, and the 'script written in red letters' to be all the good deeds that the nuns do with 'special devotion'. Wherever the rubrication is highlighted with golden colour it means that they act in the 'remembrance of the suffering of Jesus Christ'.[96] The explicit textual details of a manuscript *mise-en-page* put the visions' material allusions into the foreground. In this iconographical vision, colour-coded interiority is externalised in textual images (as such, it is akin to visionary textiles and their materiality – the topic of Chapter 6). The red ink in particular is vividly connected to a corporeal conception of the divine heart as it appears to be drawn from Christ's side wound.

The colour scheme of the streaming side of Christ evokes medieval manuscripts, making his wound serve as a gateway to the divine heart tangible in the form of the book. The *botte* exploits its own manifestation as a 'book' by relating mystical spirituality to the material culture it is embedded in. With the 'fixation on the body' in the narratives of how books – even visionary ones like the one on the nuns' conduct – come into being, the *botte* diminishes the distance to Christ.[97] Tropes of touching the script are aligned to touching the body of Christ so that the actual script creates proximity and intimacy.[98]

The analogy between heart and book has a long tradition. Augustine 'portrayed the heart as a place of "writing", "erasure", "reading", "interpretation", and other textual operations'.[99] Interior conditions and spiritual concepts rendered in textual terminology 'reached [their] apex in the later Middle Ages' when Christ's wounded body was depicted as vellum inscribed with ink, specifically red ink to signify the martyrdom, in the images known as the Charter of Christ.[100] The Helfta mystics are in good company when they make claims of a divine script from Christ's 'heart-blood' with, for example, Bruno of Würzburg (d. 1045), who asserts that Christ is a scribe, who writes 'faith, hope, and charity in the hearts of the faithful', and Alan of Lille, who writes 'that the son of God may be called a pen [*calamus*] because through him the will of God is made manifest'.[101] The incarnated word encompasses both the carnality of the book and the spirituality of the body. The vernacular reception of the *Legatus* in late medieval Germany is surrounded by examples of objectified spirituality, more precisely of book and text metaphors expressing a salvific programme.[102]

Most notable is the manifestation of 'bookish flesh' in the *Life* (*Leben*) of Henry Suso, who lived in the fourteenth century and understood himself to be influenced by Meister Eckhart. He authored several books that he edited into one volume called the *Exemplar*. The oldest *Exemplar* copy dates from the second half of the fourteenth century and very likely belonged to the Strasbourg convent Zum grünen Wörth, a community which was founded by the city merchant Rulman Merswin in 1367 on a site where a Benedictine house once stood.[103] In the book recounting Suso's life, the *Leben*, the devout servant desires to own a manifest sign of love, a contract (*urkúnde*) of some sort. In the heat of a 'glowing love' he takes a quill and carves the monogram of Jesus' name, IHS, on his chest at the height of his heart. The rushing blood eases his 'fiery love' and the pain is forgotten.[104] This corporeal inscription is a concrete application of the Bible verse *pone me ut signaculum super cor tuum* (Cant 8:6), 'set me as a seal upon your heart'; it turns the skin and flesh into a medium for the certification of the relationship between Suso and God.[105] The resulting scars turn 'the body into an artefact'.[106] Script attests an immaterial condition; it externalises the interior. Even though Suso remains an extreme case, this episode illustrates to what degree material culture became a catalyst for the innermost of beliefs. Suso's audience is the kind of – and in some places the same – audience that read the *botte*. It is this reception context in which existed an overlapping understanding of textual book culture and Christ's martyrdom that vivified Gertrude's visions and gave them new life in the vernacular context. The German reception of the *Legatus* adapted to the demands of this late medieval 'mystical culture'.[107]

Correlations between the heart and the book were expounded in many spiritual writings of the Middle Ages.[108] The *botte*, too, draws connections between textual imagery based on a medieval manuscript culture and a salvific programme founded in Christ's martyrdom. The graphical variances of colouring script in black, red, and gold are conventional in late medieval religious manuscripts; according to the rationale of Gertrude's vision, the colours correspond to hierarchical spiritual levels, in which the practice of remembering the Passion is set highest. Drawing the red colour from the wound clearly refers to Christ's blood, or, more detailed, to his 'heart-blood'. The very act of rubricating – John dipping his quill into the wound – means a reactivation of the Passion on the basis of *memoria*: whenever the nuns act in remembrance of the Passion, John has a reason to introduce his quill, a sharp instrument, into Christ's heart to create red writing.[109] Remembering Christ's martyrdom and writing down this act of remembrance are coupled and visually intensified to describe the intrinsic relationship between the devotee and the object of devotion. This is a mnemonic process which leads to – and is illustrated in – the visionary manuscript written by John.

Developing a similar stress on mnemonic writing and contemplation, the thirteenth-century Carthusian nun Marguerite d'Oingt uses scriptorial images that – like in Gertrude's vision – employ a colour-coded allegorical system.[110] In the first chapter of her *Speculum*, Christ appears to Marguerite holding a book which is described in great detail including the ink colours which come to represent different aspects of the Passion; at the same time Marguerite comes to understand that the volume symbolises her own written work. Sergi Sancho Fibla discusses this passage extensively, showing that the visionary book 'illustrates many basic principles of the medieval mnemonic tools'.[111] Based on Mary Carruthers' concept of 'mnemonic criticism',[112] Fibla contends that the mystic expresses the grace she experienced by visually reconstructing it in her readers' minds: 'the physical book and the metaphorical one are linked and articulated through the reader's mind, providing him a useful tool for meditation'.[113] Other medieval texts and stories containing colour-coded book imagery further expose the elaborate visual-mnemonic system underlying the understanding of such scriptorial images.[114] For the late medieval reception of Gertrude's visions this cultural background means that we deal with a late-medieval readership that is practiced in recognising and performing such mnemonic processes.

In contrast to the book mentioned at the beginning of the *botte*, the manuscript in Gertrude's vision of John the Evangelist is not meant to signify the same book that the readers hold in their hands; but there is an interrelation. According to the diegetic world, the vision's rubricated and illuminated manuscript presents a report commissioned by Christ to record the nuns' behaviour:

> Then she asked the Lord what John was writing. He answered, 'All the good that you have done yesterday and that you will do in the coming two days I have collected and given to St John to write in a letter'.

The three days mentioned in Christ's response to Gertrude are the days immediately before Lent, the vision occurring on the day before Shrove Tuesday as the chapter's title specifies (*An dem geilen mentag ist das*). In the narrative account, the manuscript written by John is described as a book, but in his speech Christ repeatedly refers to it as a letter. Taking the term 'letter' to mean a zealous message, John's writing follows an apostolic mission. The title of the actual book held by the historical readers captures such a mission, *botte* meaning 'messenger'. In this way, John's letter, as recounted in the vision, coalesces on some level with the *botte* itself as it likewise gives an account of Gertrude's and other sisters' lives. The mechanism of salvation through remembrance hence expands to the reception of the *botte*.

The manuscript John is preparing in Gertrude's vision has another special feature: there is blank space to be potentially filled in. Gertrude sees empty lines in the 'book', and wonders about their meaning. Christ answers that while the sisters know how to honour his suffering with devout desire and with prayer, they have not yet learned to praise and honour it in all their works. What follows is an instruction for how to praise and honour his suffering in everything including fasting and holding vigil. However, it is the 'right kind' of prayer that is described in great detail, during which the praying person shall imitate the crucifixion by stretching out their arms: *Du súllent ir krützewis betten mit ufgespanneten armen der mine, in der ich ufgespannet stunt an dem heilgen crútze!* The chapter closes rather brusquely with a final sentence referring to John's writing: 'and next to each prayer were recorded the names of those who had prayed them or were going to pray them'.[115] While the vision as told in the *botte* largely relies on the *Legatus*, it is the futuristic connotation of Middle High German *wollen* (imperfect *wolten*) which contrasts the vernacular redaction from the Latin by making the meaning of John's writing multi-layered: the prayers in the *botte* have not all been said in the past.[116] Empty lines and a glimpse of prophetic writing – future prayers are mentioned – give this vision a ring of participation, and the potential to fill the empty space, that aims to be enacted in the practical execution of Christ's instructions. The vision's overall pedagogical element plays with the notion of the book as the Book of Life, and with the act of reading as an insight into how to gain salvation.

EXCURSUS: JOHN THE EVANGELIST AS MYSTICAL SCRIBE

Bookish mechanisms, in the wider cultural and literary context in which the *botte* was embedded, imply a mystical understanding of John the Evangelist. Based on the initial verse of John's Gospel, the first and foremost of medieval Johannine associations was the doctrine of Christ as the Word of God. As an 'inner hearing' of God's word was thought to be a prerequisite to salvation by medieval theologians,[117] fourteenth-century mystical writings stressed the ability to 'hear God'. This aptitude was translated in terms of emptiness and passivity, and correlated with Marian fertility. To hear God's word was next to being 'impregnated' with it.[118] John the Evangelist is a central figure in this concept as the medieval tradition took him also to be the same John who is said to have written the Book of Revelation, who was able to literally hear God's word, record it, and through this account 'impregnate' it into his readers' minds.[119]

Passing down God's word follows a participatory economy of salvation. The scriptural presence in which past or future can be narrated in a vision forms the ground for this economy of salvation. In this sense, it is not coincidental that it should be John who as the scribe of God writes up the nuns' behaviour in Gertrude's vision. His traditional role as an eyewitness to the Crucifixion is here extended to include official reporting on the community.[120] As Annette

Volfing has shown, sermons and religious treatises from late medieval Germany use John the Evangelist to control devotional practices. At the same time, more poetologically orientated texts set John up as a lyrical persona, deploying his character as a visionary author.[121] In the aforementioned visionary scene that Gertrude depicts, John is someone who in the first place writes a report about the service in the community. Yet the cultural background of him as author of the Apocalypse lends this vision a prophetic dimension, which is taken up in the *botte*'s chapter's final phrase about future prayers and their assignment. The salvific consequences of the sisters' behaviour during the days before Lent, when the devotee prepares themselves for a period of repentance and intense remembrance of Christ's Passion, are translated into the visual appearance of a page layout in a medieval book. This visual programme is already contained in the account as described in the *Legatus*,[122] but the vernacular environment of the late medieval reform, as I would like to argue, augments the significance of bookishness for the *botte*'s self-reflectivity.

The affinities between the prophetic tone in *The Flowing Light of the Godhead* and the Apocalypse of John the Evangelist have been remarked upon in previous research.[123] Rather than attempting a similar typological reading, I intend to align the *botte* with a text which, framed by an episode of the Apocalypse, was actually produced roughly at the same time that the *botte* was circulating in late medieval Germany: Otto of Passau's *Die vierundzwanzig Alten (The Elders)*. John the Evangelist features as a scribe in this mystical text, a florilegium – that is, a compilation of excerpts from other writings – which instructs the 'loving soul' through the gradual advice of the so-called Twenty-Four Elders of the Apocalypse. *The Elders* was finished in the early 1380s by the Basel-based Franciscan Otto of Passau and soon sparked interest in religious women and men – lay people as well as monks and nuns – in the Upper Rhine area.[124] Its particular rendering of John the Evangelist as a prophetic writer relevant to everyone's salvation helps us to understand the context in which the *botte* was received.

The Elders is more than just a frame for a collection of sentences, which attempts to make canonical sources known to vernacular readers;[125] it develops a mystagogical curriculum, a guide to how to live as a mystic. Otto's text was extremely popular; it was quickly disseminated, with more than a hundred manuscripts surviving today, and in 1480 the text was printed for the first time. Based on John's apocalyptic vision of the Twenty-Four Elders surrounding God's throne (Revelation 4:4), in Otto's composition each of the Elders instructs the so-called 'loving soul' – an allegory for the human soul – in her spiritual life. Accordingly, each of the twenty-four chapters – ordered alphabetically according to their initial letters – is dedicated to a distinct step in a spiritual process. Chapter topics include the meaning of sins, penance, confession, and the search for God. Although *The Elders* is set up as a dialogue, the continuous dialogue partner, the loving soul, is mute, while only the other side, the Elders, has a voice. What each one of them actually says to the soul consists of sentences from Church Fathers as well as ancient thinkers, quoted directly and indirectly. Large parts also offer genuinely new ideas, probably stemming from Otto's pen. As such *The Elders* is a formidable example for the late medieval creative reception of existing texts.[126]

Being concerned with mysticism as it developed in the Upper Rhine area in the fourteenth century, it is rather striking that neither Eckhart, Tauler, or Suso gets mentioned in *The Elders*. Wieland Schmidt, whose work on this florilegium's transmission remains the foundation of scholarship in the field, debunked previous assumptions that the three aforementioned Dominican mystics would have been known to the text's recipients anyway and would therefore not have been needed to be named.[127] Schmidt explains that the compiler Otto of Passau deliberately chose not to mention Eckhart, Tauler, and Suso because he wanted to base his work on acknowledged Church authorities. Eckhart would not have appeared orthodox enough, while Tauler and Suso did not possess the necessary authority that comes with the passing of time ('autorative Alterspatina') for they would still have been in living memory.[128] The idea that *The Elders* was primarily intended for the so-called Gottesfreunde ('Friends of God') stands on shaky ground,[129] mainly because this group of supposedly devout lay people gathered around fourteenth-century German mystics and only found in vague literary allusions may not have existed in reality.[130] Their fictitious character might have been even deliberate, intended as a purely made-up, quasi-spiritual community not to be found 'in the flesh'.[131] While we have to doubt the existence of the Gottesfreunde, the assumed reception context in South-West Germany remains real: that of a growing monastically inspired lay audience interested in all things concerning the mystical education of the soul. The liminal areas between monasticism and lay spirituality were increasingly served by monastic authors, such as Otto of Passau who functioned as a custodian, confessor, and reformer for his order.[132] The largest group of readers of *The Elders*, as of the *botte*, were nuns. Studying how Otto's text uses John as a scribal figure elucidates the interplay of textual images and book production, and helps us to further expose the book's self-reflectivity, which is so poignantly served in the *botte*.

The Elders and the *botte* were both read in Strasbourg at the same time. In fact, there is an Alsatian recension (transmission line) of *The Elders*: one of the manuscripts belonging to this South-West-German recension of Otto's text is San Marino, Huntington Library, HM 1082.[133] This codex was copied by one scribe alone on a coherent stock of paper; it was rebound in the nineteenth century; its medieval ownership remains unidentified. Huntington Library, HM 1082, originates from Alsace, judging from the text's Alemannic dialect and the style of its illustrations. The miniatures reveal that the codex was produced at the Strasbourg workshop of Diebold Lauber.[134] There are other examples of illustrated Alsatian manuscript copies of Otto of Passau's *The Elders* (for example, Sélestat, Bibliothèque humaniste, ms. 69).[135] Huntington Library, HM 1082, was copied in the first half of the fifteenth century; this can be construed from the manuscript's very last words: after the colophon and the finishing AMEN follows the indication *Anno xxxi Jor et cetera* (fol. 320ra, see Fig. 38). The date mentioned in the colophon on the other hand (1386) is the alleged date on which Otto of Passau finished his composition.[136] The abbreviation for *et cetera* used by the copyist in his final remark could therefore indicate the following century; one may translate: 'in the 31st year of the next', which would result in the year 1431.[137] Otto's colophon plays a key role when it comes to the material aspects of this codex in connection to its prophetic claim, which is first set up in the prologue to the text.

In illustrated copies of *The Elders*, the prologue functions in two different registers, a textual one and a visual one, by introducing a miniature of John the Evangelist in his traditional iconographic pose, that is in a scribal pose. The interplay of image and text in the manuscript is dynamic since the two registers are not only complementary but also in competition. '[I]nterartistic rivalries on the parchment' are part of the 'manuscript matrix', as pointed out by Nichols.[138] A reader of illuminated manuscripts thus requires a 'double literacy' of 'reading text and interpreting visual signs'.[139] Reading the first miniature in Huntington Library, HM 1082, we see that John the Evangelist is portrayed as writing a book (fol. 3vb, see Fig. 39). The lines above the miniature (fols. 1r–3v) are the index, a detailed table of contents. The miniature of John belongs to and mirrors the subsequent textual contents, which forms the prologue (fols. 4r–6r). The prologue starts with an invocation of John the Evangelist and his vision of the Apocalypse, described as the 'book of secrets' (*tögen bůche*), with a special emphasis on the section on the Twenty-Four Elders.[140] An exegetical interpretation of this visionary scene ties John's vision to the current text of spiritual instructions by highlighting the importance of praising and serving God. The object of interpretation is referred to as a figure: *Dise figure betûtet uns daz...* The term *figure* highlights a pictorial value of narrative images. Sentences drawn from Church authorities are interspersed into the prologue, which ends with another reference to John's vision for which the same word – with common scribal variance – *fygure* is employed. The narrator urges the reader to 'look at the figure that John saw', that is, at the enthroned deity: *So sihe an die fygure das Johannes sach/Jn dem himel sitzen vnser herren uf deme trone sinre Almehtikeit...* (fol. 5va). There then follows the author's recommendation and a plea to guard his memory for all the future, whether he is alive or dead (fol. 6ra). The prologue to Otto's work frames the advice

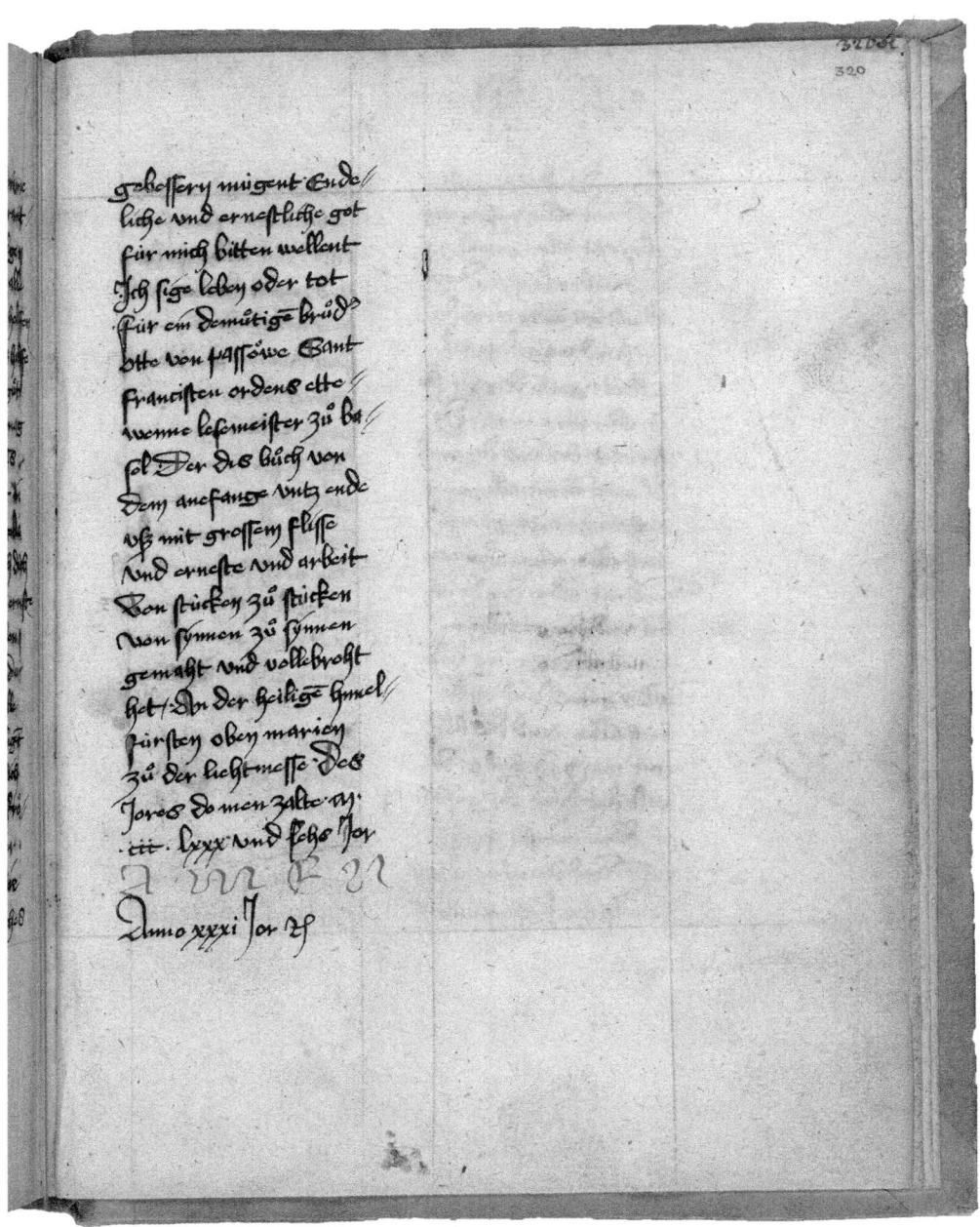

38 Scribal colophon to Otto of Passau, *Die Vierundzwanzig Alten*, with copy date (1431)
San Marino, Huntington Library, HM 1082, fol. 320r
Image Credit: The Huntington Library, San Marino, California

given by the Twenty-Four Elders as a quasi-prophecy passed down from John
as he taps into the latter's authority, and as he is – quite concretely – inspired by
the imagery of the Twenty-Four Elders being in the circle closest to God.
Introducing a miniature of John as a scribe sends the visual message that the

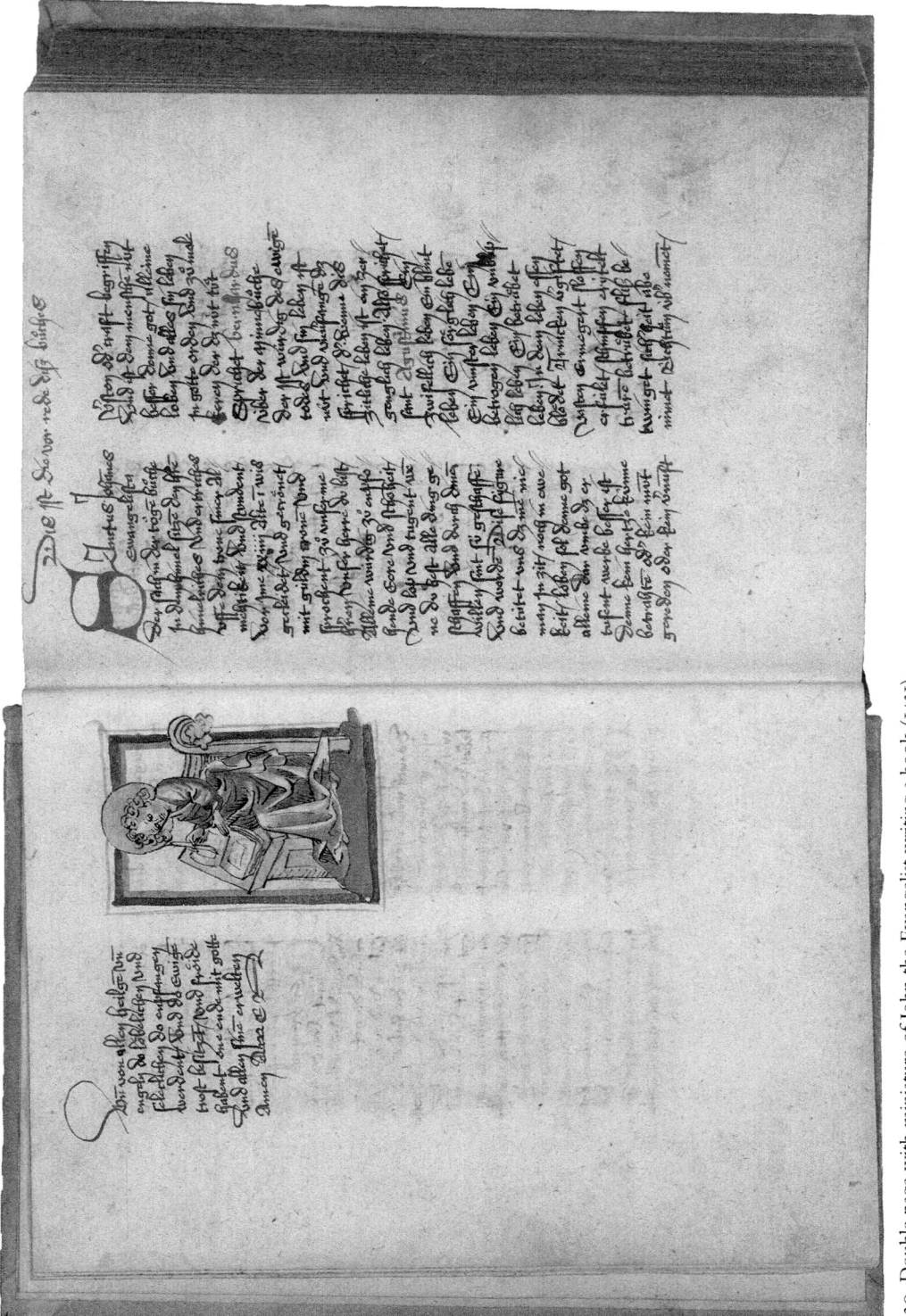

39 Double page with miniature of John the Evangelist writing a book (1431)
San Marino, Huntington Library, HM 1082, fols. 3v–4r
Image Credit: The Huntington Library, San Marino, California

Evangelist is the one who endorses Otto's writing. In this way, Otto borrows the claim to a quasi-visionary prophecy with a salvific quality.

Some manuscripts depict John amongst the Twenty-Four; others portray him on Patmos in front of a background of rocks and trees.[141] In the majority of miniatures, John sits at a pulpit equipped with writing instruments. He writes into a book, a codex. That John is writing into a book rather than on a scroll is not a mere anachronism but a self-referential device hinting at the physical manuscript in the reader's hands. It highlights the work of the author as a sacred task, recording what the divine communicates. John's pose does not represent just any scribal work but specifically that of the author: Otto of Passau's imprint is so prominent that the copy – apart from the additional date at the very end – disappears entirely behind the book's conception. The authorial colophon outlines Otto of Passau's endeavour and mission in writing the book (fols. 319vb–320ra). This is not a scribe's colophon but the compiler's final remarks as he calls once more to practice his *memoria*. As such it is a variation of the prologue, where with the depiction of John especially, we see an interplay between the imagery of scribal activity and the physical material. The book production is pictorially evoked. Like Gertrude's vision of John recording the nuns' conduct, John in Otto of Passau's *The Elders* is used as a figure to authorise what is written.

The miniature of John is one of a series of images as in illustrated codices every chapter is usually accompanied by an illustration of the soul's interlocution with one of the Elders. The initial illustration stands out since it is not part of the picture cycle of the female-gendered soul portrayed with each Elder. For example, in San Marino, Huntington Library, HM 1082, the chapter starting on 'P' contains an illustration in which the 'loving soul' keeps her arm crossed as a sign of her shyness while the Elder points his finger at her in the iconographic gesture of instruction (fol. 166va, see Plate XVIII). Each miniature depicting the soul in her meetings with the Elders is a variation of the same theme. This is a case of intermedia rivalry on the manuscript page because a conversation is depicted in the visual register, whereas the soul remains silent in the text. This tension means that the miniature does not directly transpose a scene 'from the verbal to the visual medium'.[142] The transposition, however, works if we accept the reader's engagement with the text as an embodied practice. The 'loving soul' is the direct addressee of the text as reinforced in the colophon (fol. 319vb), but as an allegory she stands for the reader. The visually depicted soul becomes hence a proxy for the reader who silently absorbs the advice offered to them. The pictorial strategy picks up a dialogical character, which itself is not actually on the textual surface. At the same time, the pictorial strategy of visualising a dialogue is a translation of the reading process to a material level: the text itself is the wisdom shared with the reader. The reader is the 'loving soul'; each Elder is the personification of the text's wisdom. In this way, the direct address to the 'loving soul' within the text is pitched to the reader.

While the advantage of a visual miniature is a multilayered mode of reception (reading images and reading text), Gertrude's visions are never illustrated in manuscripts. Here, images are immaterial and they unfold in visionary accounts. The process of reading is evoked in textual images that are found in a physical book copy, a manuscript. No known *botte* copy contains images; and even where textual images are so strong that one would expect them to be reflected on the material manuscript surface, no extraordinary layout choices stand out in any of the transmitted manuscripts. Instead, the *botte* relies heavily on imaginary acts of visualisation, negotiating thus an 'embodied book' in the reading process. With this method, the *botte* manages to let the book come into being, not just on the narrative basis of Gertrude's visions, but, with the participation of the readers who supposedly maintain an active interest in doing so – as they are told that it is profitable for their salvation. The late medieval reader of the *botte* was an involved one, who through mystagogical texts – such as Otto of Passau's *Elders* – was habitualised to contemplate immaterial images.

★ ★ ★

Imagining corporeal images is the key concept in the *botte* and it is set up as the foundation for the understanding of the text, which is said to have flown from Christ's side wound. Christ's side as the gateway to the divine heart presents – in compliance with patristic and scholastic texts – a corporeal image in itself. The heart was understood to be a porous organ, one that could both breathe and react to sound. The linking of the heart to scribal activity in the *botte* conveys the message of God, the author, and his many scribes, among whom figures John the Evangelist as an illustrious example and foil for any redactor. Operating on different sensorial channels such as auditory, visual, and haptic, the motif of the scriptorial heart thus becomes an embodied promise of redemption.

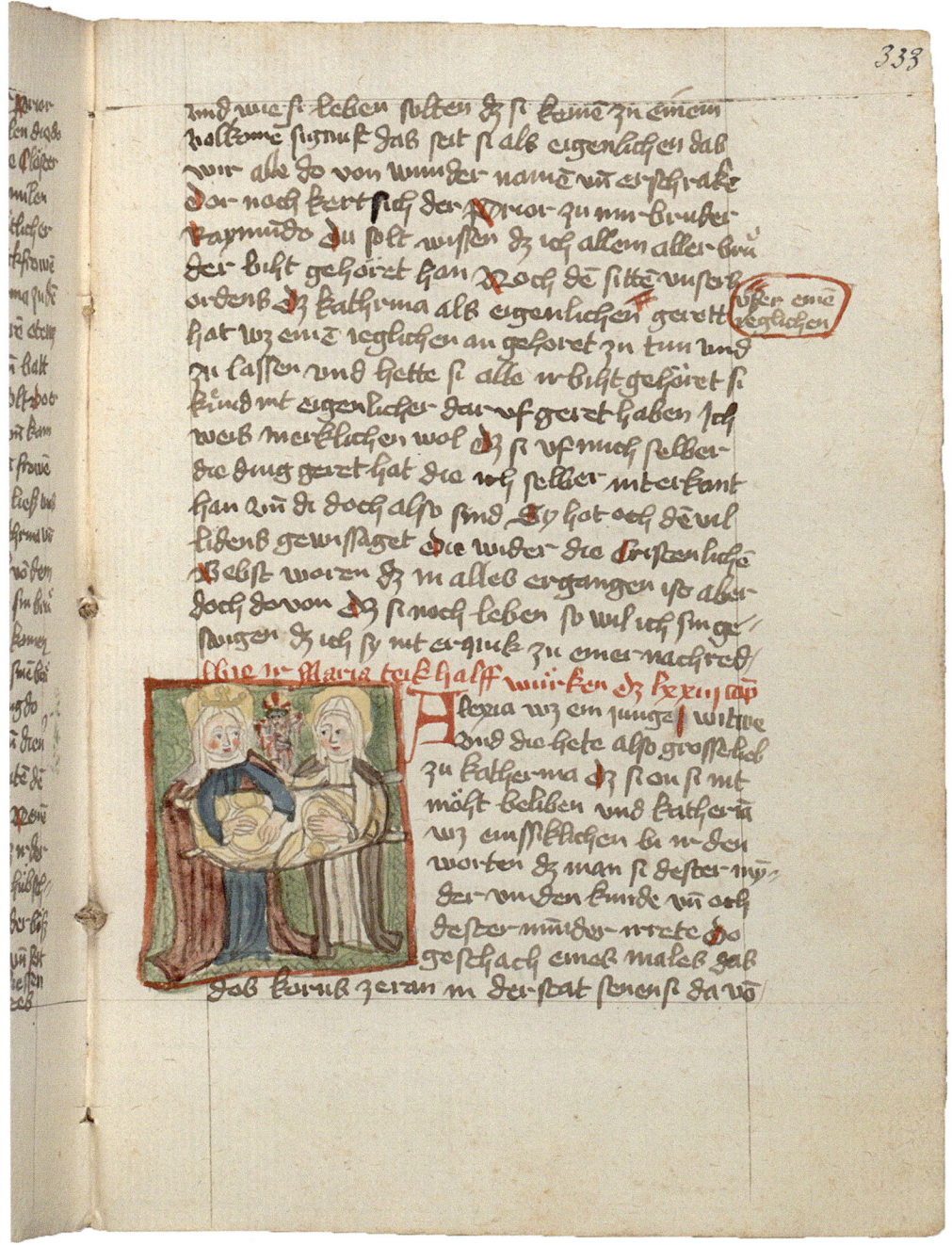

PLATE 1 Miniature: Mary and Catherine of Siena working the dough with Christ crucified in the background (1450–1500)
Brussels, Bibliothèque Royale, cod. 8507–09, fol. 333r

46

ne noch stot wie du denkel
gen wienacht oben solt bezzrn
mit andacht vn ist genomen vss
dem buch der seligen jncfrowe
Sant mechtilden zů dem ersten vo
dem grossen capitel

ndem
oben der
fůssen ge
luwet jhn
xpi̅ hat
tes sin
do der
comient
zů dem
capitel
siems do

sich sy ein grosse schar engsten mit
hechten zwen vn zwen rechlicher
psonen dienende vn vnser herrn

PLATE III Text corresponding to *das búch geistlicher gnaden* [Mechthild of Hackeborn's *Liber specialis gratiae*],
Book I, Ch. 5 (1507)
Solothurn, Zentralbibliothek, Cod. S 458, fol. 46r
Copyright: Zentralbibliothek Solothurn

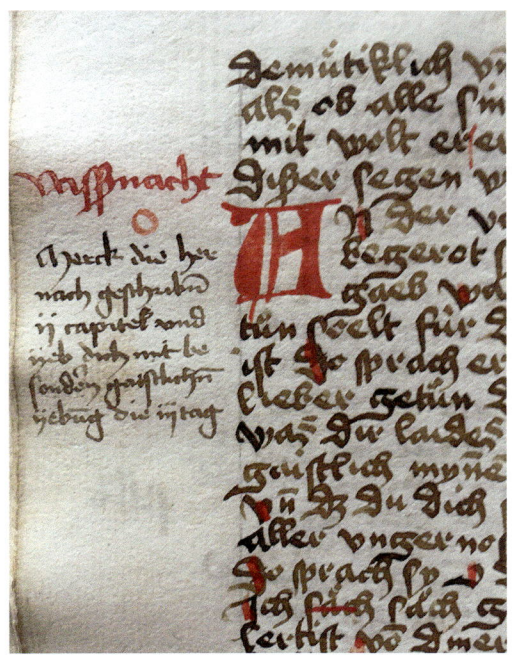

PLATE V Marginal note corresponding to *botte*, Ch. 77: *vaßnacht*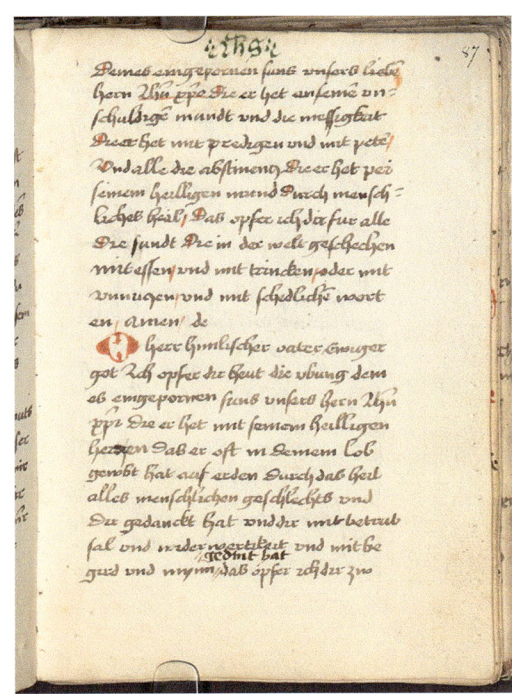

Merck die her nach geschriben ij capitel vnd üeb dich mit besonderen gaistlichen üebung die iij tag (c. 1450)

Augsburg, Benediktinerabtei St Stephan, Hs 38, fol. 46v

Copyright: Klosterbibliothek Abtei St Stephan Augsburg. Photo: Racha Kirakosian

PLATE VI Second prayer corresponding to *botte*, Ch. 77: *O herr himlischer vater, Ewiger got...*
(1480–1520)

Munich, Bayerische Staatsbibliothek, Cgm 843, fol. 87r

Copyright: Bayerische Staatsbibliothek München/Bildarchiv

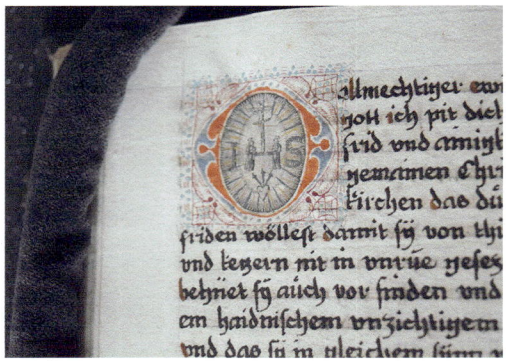

PLATE VII Inserted coloured copper-plate: IHS monogram with the two Marys at the cross forming the H, with crucifix, and Sacred Heart-motive, O-initial (1611)
Eichstätt, Abtei St Walburg, Ms germ. 23, fol. 60v
Copyright: Abtei St Walburg Eichstätt. Photo: Racha Kirakosian

PLATE VIII Inserted coloured copper-plate: Sacred Heart-motif with IHS monogram and instruments of Christ's martyrdom, Lamb of God-motif, O-initial (1611)
Eichstätt, Abtei St Walburg, Ms germ. 23, fol. 270r
Copyright: Abtei St Walburg Eichstätt. Photo: Racha Kirakosian

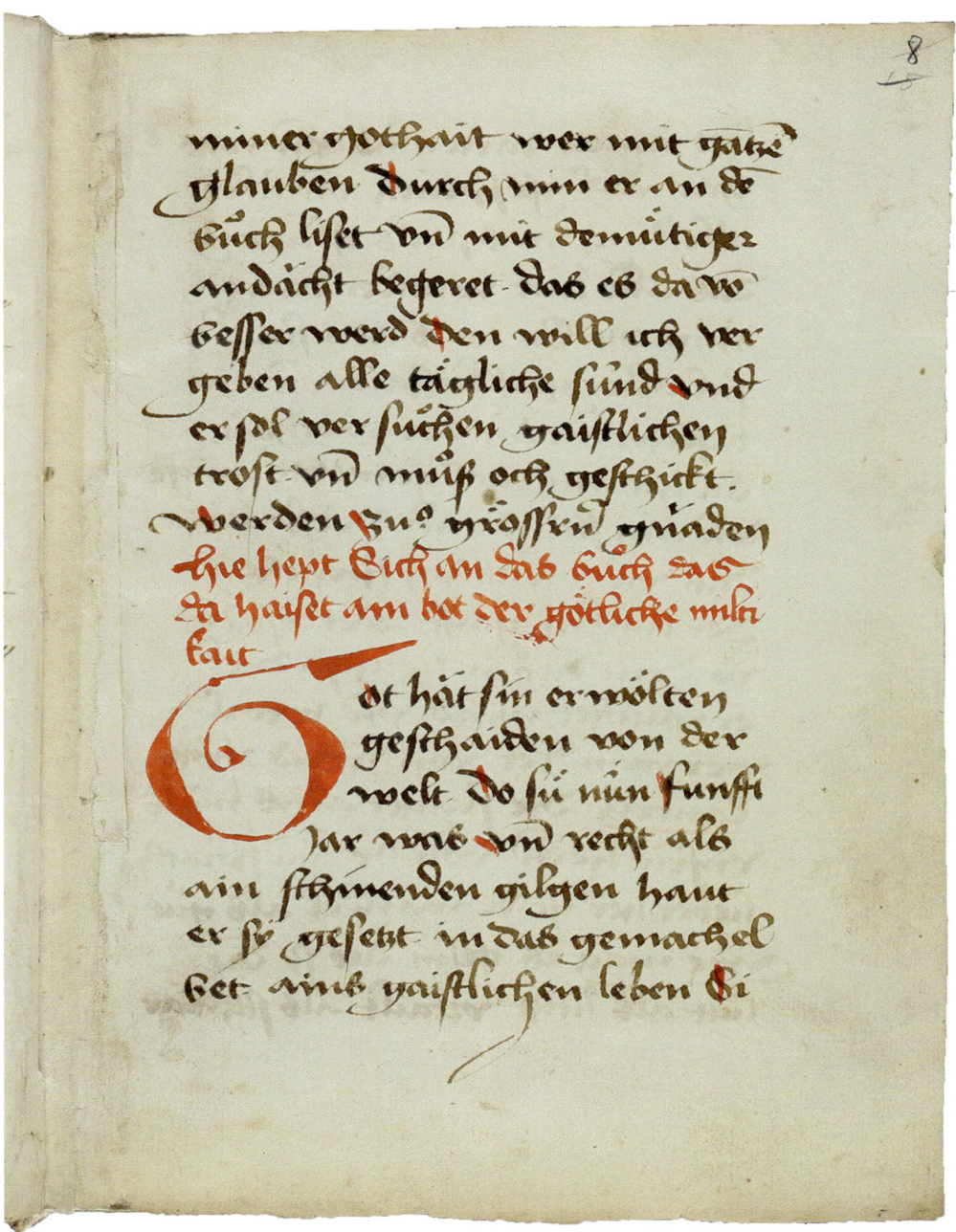

miner gothait wer mit gate
glauben durch inn er an de
buch lyset vn mit demuticger
andacht besseret das es da w
besser werd den will ich ver
geben alle taglicke sund vnd
er sol ver suchen gaistlichen
trost vn muß ock gestickt
werden zu grossen gnaden
hie hept sich an das buch das
da haiset am bet der gotlicke mlst
kait

ot hat sin erwolten
gesthaiden von der
welt do sii nun funff
iar was von recht als
ain stimenden gilgen haut
er sy gesett in das gemachel
bet ains gaistlichen leben si

PLATE IX   G–lombard (1474–76)
Freiburg im Breisgau, Universitätsbibliothek, Hs. 202, fol. 8r
Copyright: Universitätsbibliothek Freiburg i. Br. / Historische Sammlungen

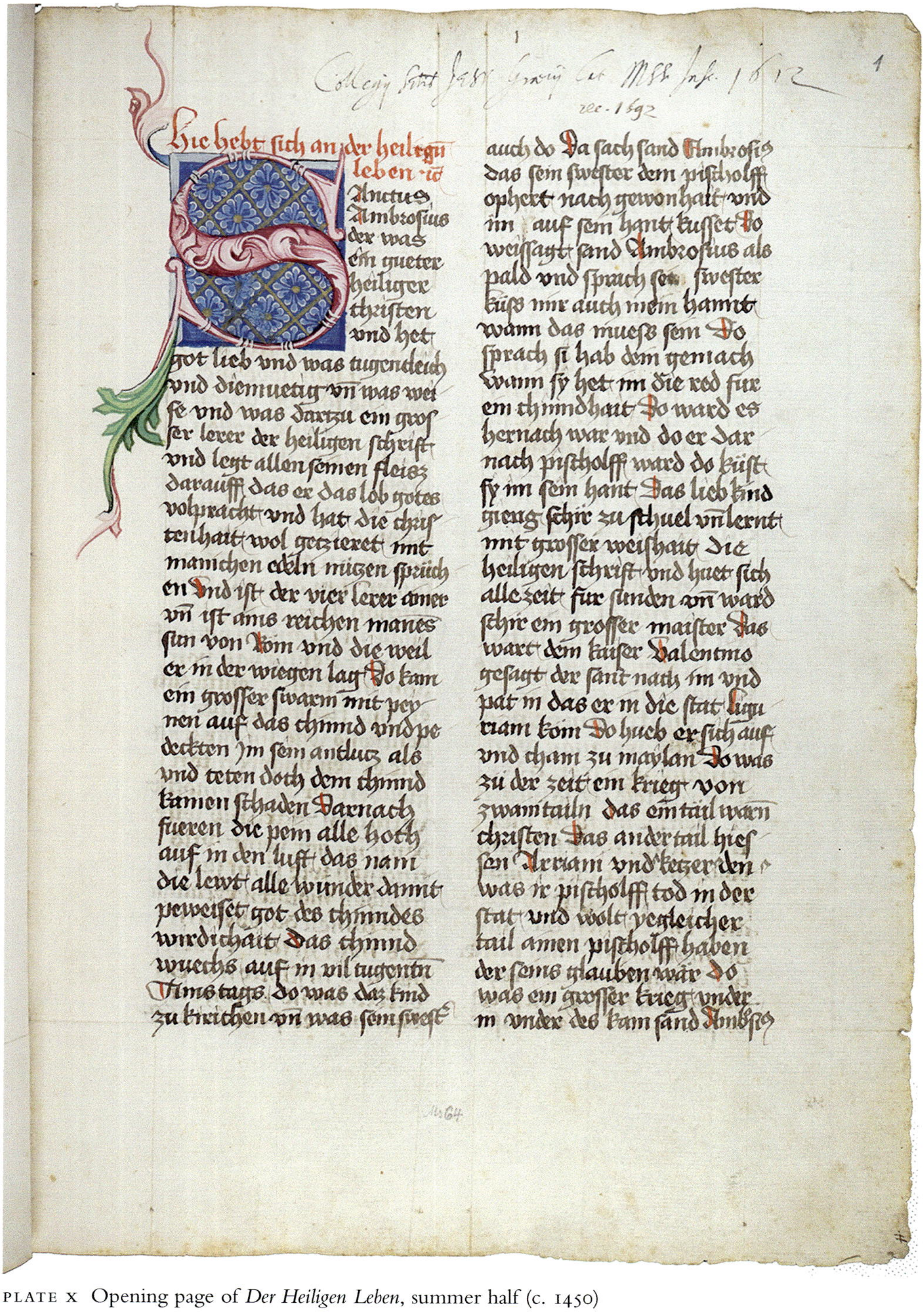

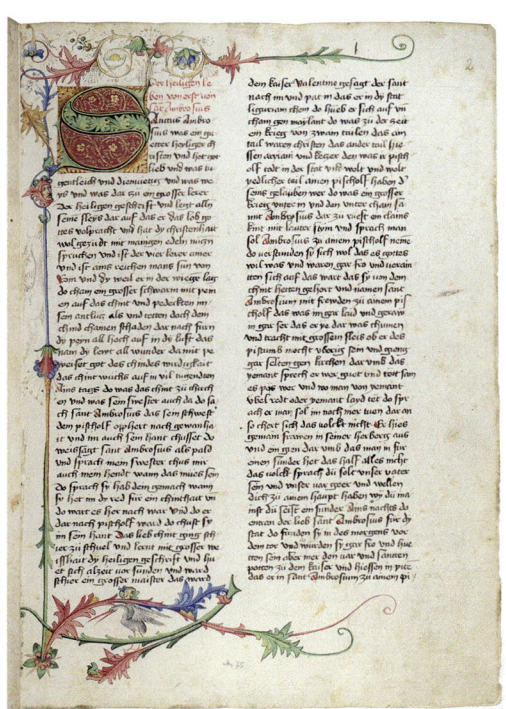

PLATE XII Binding front cover, with coats of arms of the chief commander Johann Siebenhirter
(d. 1508) of the Military Order of St George in Millstadt (c. 1450)
Graz, Universitätsbibliothek, Ms. 64
Copyright: Universitätsbibliothek Graz / Sondersammlung

PLATE XIII Binding front cover (c. 1450)
Graz, Universitätsbibliothek, Ms. 75
Copyright: Universitätsbibliothek Graz / Sondersammlung

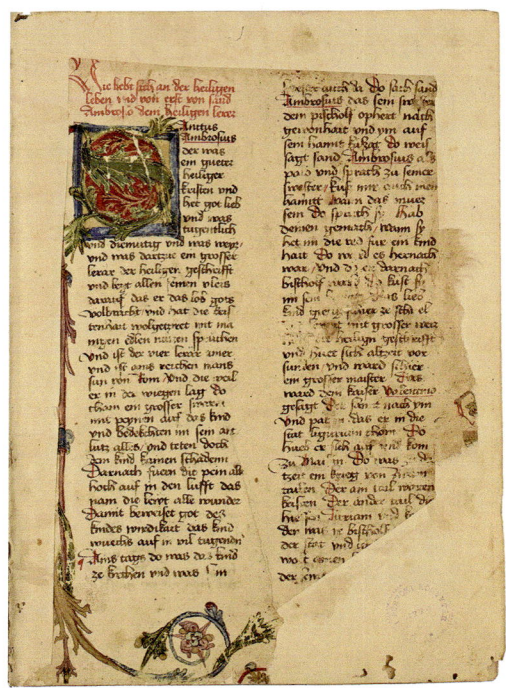

PLATE XIV Opening page of *Der Heiligen Leben*, summer half (1455)
Pécs, Egyházmegyei Könyvtár – Diocesan Library, AA. II. 21, fol. 1r
Copyright: Pécsi Egyházmegyei Könyvtár

PLATE XV Miniature: *Virtues Crucifying Christ* (1270–1276)
Lectionary, Dominican nunnery Zum Heiligkreuz in Regensburg
Oxford, Keble College, MS 49, fol. 7r
Photo Credit: Bridgeman Images

PLATE XVI Miniature: *Christ's Sacrifice and the Church* (also *imago muliebris*), depicting Vision 6 of Part II of Hildegard of Bingen's *Scivias*

Parchment manuscript facsimile (1927–33) of the lost original, plate 15; based on the lost Rupertsberg Scivias Codex (c. 1175), fol. 86rb

Copyright: Benediktinerinnenabtei St. Hildegard Rüdesheim am Rhein

PLATE XVII Straw for the celebration of the Eucharist. German (c. 1230–50)
New York, The Metropolitan Museum of Art
The Cloisters Collection, 1947 (accession nr. 47.101.28)
Image Copyright: The Metropolitan Museum of Art. Image source: Art Resource, NY

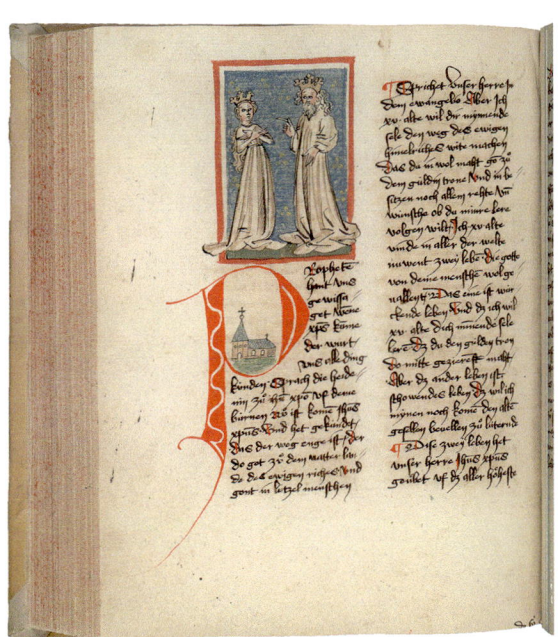

PLATE XVIII Miniature: 'loving soul' being instructed by one of the Twenty-Four Elders (1431)
San Marino, Huntington Library, HM 1082, fol. 166v
Image Credit: The Huntington Library, San Marino, California

PLATE XIX Antependium: *Crowning of Mary* (c. 1300)
Halberstadt, Cathedral Treasury, Inv. nr. 203
Image Copyright: Landesamt für Denkmalpflege und Archäologie Sachsen-Anhalt, Juraj Lipták

PLATE XX Detail: Antependium, *Crowning of Mary* (c. 1300)
Halberstadt, Cathedral Treasury, Inv. nr. 203
Image Copyright: Landesamt für Denkmalpflege und Archäologie Sachsen-Anhalt, Juraj Lipták

PLATE XXI Chasuble back: Scenes of The Baptism of Christ and the Veneration of the Magi (1230–40)
Halberstadt, Cathedral Treasury, Inv. nr. 209
Image Copyright: Landesamt für Denkmalpflege und Archäologie Sachsen-Anhalt, Juraj Lipták

PLATE XXII Reliquary cloth with stones, pearls, and metal
Lower Saxony/Lower Harz (1270–1300)
Halberstadt, Cathedral Treasury, Inv. nr. 17
Image Copyright: Landesamt für Denkmalpflege und Archäologie Sachsen-Anhalt, Juraj Lipták

PLATE XXIII Detail: Chasuble with eagles, silk with gold embroidery
Fabric Byzantium (?), gold orphrey Sicily, embroidery Lower Saxony (1200–50)
Halberstadt, Cathedral Treasury, Inv. nr. 210
Image Copyright: Landesamt für Denkmalpflege und Archäologie Sachsen-Anhalt, Juraj Lipták

PLATE XXIV Ensemble for clothing a Madonna with Christ Child group, with emblems of the Holy Names
Lower Saxony (c. 1480)
Hannover, Museum August Kestner, Inv. nr. WM XX 24–30
Image Source: Landeshauptstadt Hannover, Museum August Kestner. Photographer: Chr. Tepper

SIX

IMAGINARY TEXTILES

The visions of Gertrude of Helfta have been said to exhibit '[v]irtually all the vestments that are deployed in the various forms of monastic liturgies'.[1] In one of Gertrude's visions, on Easter Monday, the transforming image of a dress charts a dizzying superimposition of liturgical celebration and textile culture. The imagery derives from a phenomenological spectrum which evokes knowledge of medieval handicraft and visual traditions. Imaginary textiles build upon a material culture in which devotion and craftmanship go hand in hand.[2] Exegetical notions of textiles such as Birgitta of Sweden's understanding of Scripture as clothing – 'Law is like clothing'[3] – come into play when considering visionary textiles. Descriptions of women's clothing offer us the possibility to understand the self-image of medieval religious women.[4] In the study of textile images in the *botte*, various aspects of textile imagery – visibility, performativity, craftsmanship, and imperfection necessitating transformation – come together, underlining the intricate interlacing of material and devotional cultures. Mapping between historical textiles, medieval allegories such as Alan of Lille's twelfth-century prosimetrum *De planctu naturae*, and Gertrude's Easter Monday vision, I show how in the *botte* material aspects and immaterial concepts merge into a powerful narrative about vision and salvation, and how the *botte* exploits vernacular language to the advantage of a mystically orientated textile culture.

The oldest known text portion from the *botte*, transmitted in Gotha, Forschungsbibliothek, Chart. B 269, recounts the aforementioned Easter

Monday vision.[5] At the centre of this paschal vision stands an imaginary garment and its allegorical meaning for Gertrude's life and salvation. Material culture and (immaterial) divine grace interweave in the fabric of a visionary dress. This earliest text witness of the *botte* provokes investigation of the vision it contains. Elements of textile culture and theological concepts such as forgiveness and grace, in addition to philosophical questions of time and temporality, are combined in it. The full version of the *botte* contains many textile images, but this one vision condenses the many types of textile images employed in the *botte* into a single narrative that stresses the material nature of a temporal presence through the use of imaginary textiles. By analysing Gertrude's Easter Monday vision and its different elements, I prepare the ground for a more in-depth study of textile images in the *botte*, which showcases the strength of the vernacular text. In this chapter, I argue that imaginary textiles are foils against which a medieval material culture can be probed and that they also serve as forms of visualisation for immaterial concepts such as temporality and grace.

The basic vision is common to both the Latin and German texts: on Easter Monday at the Eucharist, Gertrude asks the Lord to complete through the 'highest sacrament' whatever she has neglected to do in her religious life.[6] At this, Christ presents her to God the Father in a specially adorned dress. The construction of the dress is described in detail: it is composed of as many parts as Gertrude has spent years in the nunnery. Words and deeds from every moment, and the intentions with which they were uttered or committed, are distinctly visible. Gertrude is worried to see that some gems are loosely attached; these gems stand for deeds committed with an ulterior motive, and not in earnest devotion. Christ then covers the dress with a golden plate (or metal) making it entirely transparent: *splendidissima et perspicacissima; dúrchsúhtig also ein luter cristalle*. Everything shines even brighter and more colourfully, with even sins 'glorifying God'.[7]

Gertrude's vision presents a dress which marks devotional conduct over time and which also represents the promise of an eternal state outside time when the soul becomes the *sponsa Christi*. It is not a nun's habit that is evoked here, but rather a sumptuous and richly worked dress, a bridal gown. This also alludes to the robes of John's Apocalypse.[8] However, the dress is not simply an example for 'her [Gertrude's] use of metaphors from the sphere of clothing'. By contrasting clothes with a – supposedly spiritually superior – nakedness of the soul, it has been argued that Gertrude only uses 'garment metaphors' to serve as expressions for imperfect spiritual processes.[9] The underlying assumption here is that textile images are metaphors; their material character becomes secondary. Yet they are intricate images in which monastic life, the reception of Scriptures, and textile craftmanship are interwoven.[10] Also, it is the textiles' very materiality that stands in the foreground of the visions in which they appear, allowing us to study connections to historical textiles. Therefore, rather than imposing a metaphorical understanding, the images' material aspect itself deserves a closer look first, before exploring any allegorical implications.

This chapter unites topics discussed in previous chapters by leading from a discussion of material culture to codicological issues and questions about how the transmission context may have influenced those who read the *botte*. I first highlight medieval textile culture, exploring extant textiles from the area around Helfta and discussing the ritualistic use of textiles in the ceremony of profession. Investigating the concepts of 'time' and 'temporality', I argue that visionary textiles served to visualise immaterial notions of time in a way that allowed for multilayered understandings of temporality. A participatory visibility invites the reader or beholder to engage in the textile's interpretative deployment as both material and allegory facilitate a collective dimension to the vision. Textiles for Gertrude are rarely static; instead textiles move and transform, thus externalising manifestations of mystical embodiment (such as the bride of Christ). Technical terms pertaining to craftmanship validate the vernacular redactions and reveal them to be particularly reflective of a textile culture which bore devotional meaning. At the time when the *botte* was continuously redacted, piety was drenched in contemplative practices involving imaginary material objects, above all textiles. In this way, what is already present in the *Legatus* and harks back to allegorical traditions of textile imagery (such as in the writings of Boethius and Alan of Lille), was further developed and continued to unfold new layers of meaning in the late Middle Ages. The Gotha codex, which transmits the oldest portion of the *botte*, heightens the aspects of time and temporality in conjunction with textiles by embedding Gertrude's vision in a collection that bears the title *Book of Purgatory*; purgatory, a time-defined space extending beyond a human's life offers yet an additional lens to understanding Gertrude's Easter Monday vision as centred around the forgiveness of sins with a glimpse of the afterlife.

TEXTILE CULTURE

No textiles from the convent of Helfta survive, but we can be certain that the nuns took great care in spinning, sewing, and stitching textiles. On the basis of the many textile images in the *Legatus* we can infer that Gertrude and her coauthors were involved in such craftsmanship, which was common in medieval nunneries.[11] The production of high quality clothing and other textiles in medieval female convents has in recent decades been of interest to art historians.[12] In the case of the community of Wienhausen in Lower Saxony, discoveries of sewing equipment and remains of the produced objects led to the investigation into links between devotion and material production in medieval nunneries.[13] Kathryn M. Rudy reminds us that '[t]extiles often mediate between the secular and the divine, between the down-to-earth and the otherworldly. Threads, clothes, and vestments mark, absorb, and transmit holy status.'[14] Textiles were also used as contemplative objects, often conferred with the power to create a sense of collective identity.[15] Gertrude's many visionary textiles behave like such *ars sacra*, meaning that they carry sacred significance in their iconographic programme as well as allusions to precious materials.[16] Her 'resort to textiles, specifically vestments, as allegorical objects and vehicles for mystagogy is anything but arbitrary'; rather, as Hamburger and others point out, this textile-orientated iconographical imagination is grafted to a historical practice of embroidery which 'provided enclosed women with a way to participate actively in the shaping of liturgical rites'.[17] Moreover, the circumstance that the cathedral of the diocese to which Helfta belonged – Halberstadt – 'has preserved one of the richest collections of vestments from the Middle Ages' is another strong indicator for a vibrant textile culture with which Gertrude's lifeworld was infused.[18] As I show in this chapter, extant textiles from Halberstadt insinuate that textiles may have inspired a great number of Gertrude's visions.

Gertrude's Easter Monday vision provokes an investigation of possible historical sources for imaginary textiles. Correlations and affinities between extant textiles and the visions of Mechthild of Magdeburg, Mechthild of Hackeborn, and Gertrude of Helfta have already been hinted at by Renate Kroos.[19] For example, the *Descent from the Cross*, as depicted on a medallion of a curtain dating to the early fourteenth century, kept in the Brandenburg Cathedral, is reminiscent of Gertrude's vision of the crucifix in *Legatus* III, 45.[20] Some of Gertrude's visions mention textiles embroidered with gold, pearls, and gems. Pearl stitching is a technique we encounter in Lower Saxony and even in Halberstadt during Gertrude's lifetime.[21] The years around 1300 were the heyday of pearl stitching, and freshwater pearls were abundant in North and Central Germany in those days, that is before overexploitation exhausted the stock in the eighteenth century.[22] Several magnificent pearl-stitched textiles (and objects such as chests) from the twelfth to the fourteenth centuries survive today, giving testimony of the vibrant textile culture of the area around Helfta.[23] For example, a large antependium (157 × 70 cm), that is a lateral or – as is the case here – frontal altar cloth,[24] from the Cathedral treasury shows Mary's celestial crowning by Christ. Set in vivid colours with beads and corals, this textile from c. 1300 offers a rich depiction of different-coloured garments (see Plates XIX and XX).[25] Gold threads woven into silks and linen can also be found in Halberstadt in the thirteenth century, such as in an orphrey (*Kaselstab*) – the pictorial vertical back part of a chasuble – which (on two registers) depicts the Baptism of Christ and the Veneration of the Magi (see Plate XXI).[26] Many other extant textiles from the treasury of Halberstadt testify to the highly skilled embellishment of fabrics, which were often imported (from Byzantium) and then stitched and mounted with pearls, gems, gilded metal strips, threads, and other precious materials in the Harz area, on the eastern edges of which Helfta is situated.[27]

Although we cannot positively attribute any extant textile to Helfta, many medieval textiles from the area and specifically from female convents have come down to us, revealing technical skill combined with liturgical knowledge;[28] for example, the so-called *Magdalenendecke*, one of the oldest large-scale embroidered cloths (94 × 143 cm) in existence, preserved at the Sankt Silvestri church of Wernigerode (see Fig. 40).[29] Dated stylistically to the mid-thirteenth-century, the *Magdalenendecke* was likely intended as an antependium. From the second half of the thirteenth century and into the fourteenth century, embroidered linen cloth was primarily made in the area between the Harz and the Lüneburg Heath.[30] Little is known about the providence of the *Magdalenendecke* – it was donated to the Hospitalkapelle of St Georg of Wernigerode before 1864 – but comparison to an altar cloth from the Augustinian canonesses of Heiningen gives clues to its historical context (Fig. 41).[31] The canonesses of Heiningen 'were famous (and infamous) for their talents with the needle'.[32] Indeed, the canonesses are a good example of how far a culture of textile mastery could be taken. The Cistercian abbot Arnold von Riddagshausen describes in a visitation report from 1240 how the sisters of Heiningen 'dress themselves up in the finest habits and occupy themselves with

40 Antependium of Mary Magdalene, *Magdalenendecke* (c. 1250)
Wernigerode, Parish Church Sankt Silvestri
Image Credit: www.kunstverlag-peda.de

41 Altar cloth, *Majestas Domini and Saints, Crowning of Mary and Apostles*, Augustinian Canonesses in Heiningen (c. 1260)
Helmstedt, Domina Kloster St Marienberg
Copyright: Salge

embroidering their silk veils in gold.'[33] The canonesses, 'reprimanded by the "cura monialium" (ecclesiastical visitor) for their fairly "worldly" lifestyle behind the convent walls' became prolific in the production of embroidered white linen, and accepted commissions from other convents.[34] Where exactly the Wernigeroder *Magdalenendecke* comes from, and for whom it was initially made, must still remain unknown but there are indications that it was either made for penitent converts, such as the Magdalenes of Goslar, or for the Augustinian choir sisters of St Marienberg in Helmstedt. Barbara Baert highlights the interaction between the antependium and its beholder as '[t]he viewer enacts the devotional object'.[35] Based on the medieval theory of optics, according to which a light beam sent out from the object enters the eye,[36] Baert argues that 'medieval seeing is a complex choreography that involves the whole body and even the sense of tactility'.[37] In the same way, the spatial, that is, three-dimensional, quality of textiles is exploited in visionary textiles as the narrative accounts are often based on existing, real-life material culture.

Further material and historical inspiration for Gertrude's textile imagery in the *Legatus* can be found in the liturgy and its ritualistic use of textiles, which with their performative and embodying effects function like costumes. Gertrude's Easter Monday vision notably recalls the medieval ceremony of a novice's profession, when the consecration of the habit changes her status, 'clothing' her as bride of Christ.[38] Being dressed, veiled, and crowned in this rite of initiation is a ceremonial form of embodiment, as the consecrated nun puts on the robe which is meant to transform her into the allegorical bride of the Song of Songs.[39] The rite of the so-called *Consecratio sacrae virginis* in the *Pontificale Romano-Germanicum* – the relevant pontifical for Helfta – lists prayers with a multitude of textile imagery, including references to the *indumentum aeternae*, the robe of eternity. The consecration is to be held at Epiphany, during the paschal week, or on the feast day of the apostles Peter and Paul. After the nun has received the new clothes and the veil, the antiphon *Induit me dominus cyclade auro* is sung.[40] Stemming from the liturgical day of St Agnes, its first line – *Induit me dominus cyclade auro texta et immensis monilibus ornavit me* / 'The Lord has clothed me in a robe woven of gold and has adorned me with innumerable jewels' – picks up the nuptial motif and details that the bridal gown is interlaced with gold and laden with gems.[41] Because no convent statutes survive for Helfta, the Benedictine profession rites of the convent Lüne in North Germany may serve as another point of comparison.[42] Eva Schlotheuber, who has discussed the late medieval liturgy of the consecration ceremony in Lüne, shows that different Bible verses are employed in the acts of veiling and crowning to confer a sacred status to the nun who was undergoing a spiritual marriage to Christ.[43]

In Gertrude's vision, the dress visualising her religious life winds itself up from the bottom, suggesting that it goes beyond an initiation; rather, it is a continuation of her convent life. Nonetheless, the notion of being clothed as *sponsa Christi* evokes the profession, and would certainly have done so for late medieval readers such as nuns, monks, and priests who were familiar with the consecration rite. Gertrude's dress, heightened by Christ's interaction with it, bears the kind of temporal connotation that can also be found in the crowning section of the consecration where '[t]he crowning is reciprocal, both present and future. Christ and the nun each enfold the other in love, but the final crowning is in heaven, when the mortal body is created anew in the gifts of the resurrection.'[44] In the profession rite, materiality – more specifically, textile culture – comes thus to embody aspects of temporality.

Taken altogether, Gertrude's Easter Monday vision reads like an artistic and commemorative reflection on this rite: Gertrude's visionary robe begins with her entry into the convent albeit not with her profession; like the garment in the antiphon *Induit me dominus cyclade auro*, it is (eventually) overlaid with gold and contains gems; she is thus clothed and presented to God by Christ – the way a nun is led to the altar by the bishop during her consecration – and the temporal frame is the same, too, since the vision – just like a nuns' consecration – takes place during an Easter week mass. At the same time, the sumptuous description of Gertrude's visionary dress, decorated with gold and gems, does not mirror the nun's habit put on at the consecration; rather, it resembles medieval paraments including ecclesiastical vestments which were studded with pearls and precious stones, and interlaced with precious metals. In this sense, Gertrude's visionary textiles, similar to actual textiles, may function like *ars memorativa* activating references to both ceremonial and allegorical textiles.[45]

With Gertrude's rich textile imagery, and with her vivid vision on Easter Monday specifically, we see how the material and liturgical lifeworld impacted the visionary world of the medieval nun.[46] Next to the aspects of *ars sacra* and *ars memorativa*, the cyclic character of textiles in the Middle Ages is very likely to have informed Gertrude's vision. Paraments, tapestries, and other textiles – to clothe sculptures, for example[47] – rotating in the course of the church calendar, present different iconographic programmes. Easter and Christmas cycles are renowned for their festive textile decoration, in which salvation and allegory are figuratively visualised. During Lent, altars and sculptures would be shrouded – sometimes in cloths decorated with specific Lenten image cycles.[48] In some places, these covers were only lifted on Easter Monday,[49] after which splendidly embellished textiles would be hung in sacramental spaces. Gertrude's paschal vision of a robe in which she is presented to God reflects the cyclical temporality of ceremonial textiles whose use was tied to the liturgical year.

TIME AND TEMPORALITY

Mystical and hagiographic texts, especially those from late medieval convents, connect textuality with aspects of temporality.[50] In debates in research about temporality and visions, however, imaginary textiles have not been considered despite their strong presence in medieval visionary accounts.[51] Gertrude's paschal dress offers a paradigmatic case for how textiles render concepts of time and temporality palpable in material or – to use the language of the *Legatus* and the *botte* – 'corporeal images'. On the narrative level, the dress of Gertrude's Easter vision renders fleeting time visible. The earliest portion of the *botte*, compared to the Latin *Legatus*, places an emphasis on presenting the material character of the dress as something lasting outside time, even as the narrative frame of the vision supposes a chronological linearity. This juxtaposition interlocks the material with the immaterial, the dress and its components with religious practices and mystical devotion. Other images in the *botte* also present material manifestations of invisible concepts. Starting from the Easter Monday vision transmitted earliest in the Gotha manuscript, the present analysis includes other passages in the text where the immaterial is made visible within a frame of temporality.

Gertrude's Easter Monday dress is composed of her past life, and while it presents her current state in the narrated world, it gives a glimpse to the eschaton in so much as it is an allegory for the gown of the mystical bride, who is only everlastingly united with her groom, Christ, once her body is deceased. Temporality is at the centre of the mystical union and of visions dealing with the mystical marriage. Gertrude's dress converts the complexity of temporality into textile imagery as her religious life is the fabric from which the dress is woven up, from the bottom up, year for year.[52] This 'pattern of the dress' is set up in a circular manner, and this correlates to the seasons and more importantly to the cyclical liturgical calendar.[53] Time and temporality in the Middle Ages were matters for academic debate and furthermore 'problems of moral philosophy'.[54] Astrology, and within that the movement of celestial bodies, was thought essential for time-reckoning, and the circular zodiac informed the medieval concept of time. As early as in Rabanus Maurus' *De computo* we find the idea of circular time, where the year, the months, and other parts of time revolved on the circular path of the zodiac.[55] The efforts put into astrological endeavours were closely linked to religious life. Diagrammatic rotae illustrations in religious manuscripts, and depictions of the heavens and the universe on liturgical objects show that time as a circular recurrent pattern was the basis on which Christian liturgical rhythm developed.[56] Although neither the *botte* nor the *Legatus* engage explicitly with these astrological theories, medieval ideas about the fabric of time underlie Gertrude's vision of a gown composed of circular time and yet pointing to an after-time. Gertrude's visionary dress helps us to understand the connection between material culture and immaterial thought, especially conceptions of time and temporality. Time as a circular phenomenon, along with the contrasting linearity of measured time, are combined and represented in the image of a dress which itself overcomes this conflict by leading the eye of the spectator to another mode of temporality, that of eternity.

How then is time visualised in the textile image? The German redaction of Gertrude's Easter Monday vision emphasises the importance of understanding the dress as a material image. It is needless to say that, philologically seen, the German text will diverge from the Latin. Consequences of linguistic choices that can also be theologically relevant have been emphasised, for example, in scholarship on Meister Eckhart's German and Latin writing.[57] In this case, however, a richer variety of words used in the *botte* to describe how Gertrude's dress is composed means that textual layers are added to the visionary fabric of the dress. In the *Legatus*, parallel constructions are made in order to describe the time spent by Gertrude as depicted in the dress:

> but in each [year] there appeared, separately noted, all the days and hours, and in addition all the thoughts, words, and deeds, both good and evil, that she had accomplished day after day, hour after hour, thought after thought, word after word, deed after deed.[58]

Syntactic repetitions, neat anaphora – *omnes dies et horae ... quae illo anno peregerat de die in diem, de hora in horam...* – create the circular effect of the dress' composition. Where temporal categories are evoked several times and with repeated words in the *Legatus*, the *botte* concentrates the description of the dress in one instance but uses two different words for Lat. *hora* rather than repeating the same word:

> The dress was marked and stretched in such a way that in each year one could well see how she had spent each single day and each moment and hour. She also saw all her deeds and all her thoughts and all her words and everything that she had ever done from day to day, good or bad.[59]

In the *botte*, time is divided into years and days and also into 'times (or moments)' and 'hours' within the composition of the dress. The oldest transmitted witness suggests that this may well allude to the distinction between normal time and liturgical time. The Gotha *botte* specifies the visible temporality in the following terms: *daz man sah wol wi si in ainem iglichen ior iglichen tag besunder verzeret het vnd ain iglicher hor und stund.*[60] Like Latin *hora*, Middle High German *stund* can mean an hour as a quantitative measure of time and a monastic hour. On the surface, the Gotha text witness seems to repeat the same understanding in two different registers, using the Latin *hora* first, followed by *stund*. Still, this is not just a hendiadys, since both known German versions (the Gotha witness and the other witnesses transmitting this portion) shift the emphasis from repetition to differentiation, therefore refining the textile constructed in the vision by adding textual layers to the marking of time. In the *Legatus* this kind of differentiation between concepts of time appears only after the dress is transformed by the 'application of gold'. Only then it is said to represent 'time as well as hour' (*tempore vel hora*).[61] The awareness of a temporality for which the dress stands happens here in retrospect. In contrast, in the *botte*, the two different modes of temporality are constituent in the dress in the first place: the monastic and liturgical *hora* being the sacred one, which recurs in a rhythm marked by circular time, whereas *stund* with its profane notion may be distinguished as quantifiable linear time. In this way, the distinction of what Jacques Le Goff has termed 'merchant's time' and 'church's time' is in the *botte* reflected on a morphological level.[62] Different words for measuring time stand for Gertrude's life as a nun within the 'church's time' on the one hand, and as a person subjected to the continuum of profane time on the other.

The notion of linear time implies the possibility of change. Although Gertrude's dress has the timeless quality of an image, a transformation – the gilding – takes place in the course of the vision, the result of which is visible:

> And whoever looked at the dress could see all at once, how she [Gertrude] had spent every hour of her life. And thus she was given to understand from God that our course is known to God and all the saints because the stains of sins are shining eternally on us in praise of God, that one may recognise how gracious he is to them who regret their sin and that he rewards us as if we had never trespassed against his will.[63]

This perception of the dress is accessible to anyone in the visionary celestial realm, but implicitly also to the reader's imagination. The impersonal and open formulation of the spectator (*wer den rog ansach*) unlocks a potential act of imagination. The vision's explanation clarifies that with the dress both temporalities are seen: change in linear time (*unser aller wandel*) and eternity (*schinen ewiklich*). Imagining the dress makes a material grasp of time possible. Sensory perception, according to medieval thinking, however, meant that the vision itself is embedded in a frame defined by temporality, or in other words: space is always translated into time. Because of the visionary image there is a 'temporal persuasion', a 'rhetorical attribution of eternity'.[64] Although the dress is a material token of quantifiable time – however circular – the stress on its visual apparition catapults it out of time. Figurative language becomes a way to elude the continuum of time by referring to the concept of eternity.[65] In Gertrude's vision, the ultimate transformation of the dress – Christ applying a golden metal to it – alludes to the transubstantiation as the whole episode unfolds at the moment of communion, pointing to an eschatological time of salvation.

The fulfilment of the eschaton for Gertrude is her mystical wedding to Christ. An eschatological dimension following bridal preparation also appears in another vision in the *botte*. On her deathbed, Gertrude is told that her ailments are material arrangements for her mystical wedding. A musical bridal parade as inspired by the Psalms (drum, harps, string instruments, and organ)[66] plays and precious little weddings gifts are said to be the diseases she suffers before dying: 'During this time, many people came to see her. She gave them the very most beautiful little prayers and the most beautiful instructions.'[67] Gertrude is thus prepared for her nuptial celebration by a promise given while she is still active in real life. In a subsequent vision of her own death, Christ appears to Gertrude as the mystical spouse. On his garments are as many translucent flowers as there are virgins standing around him; the flowers have golden hooks which attach to hooks on roses worn by the virgins. The floral additions that turn the textile into an ornamented robe remind us of historical textiles such as the aforementioned antependium of the *Crowning of Mary* from Halberstadt (see Plates XIX and XX). The hooks mentioned in Gertrude's vision could refer to a specific stitching technique. The unification of many souls with Christ is here externalised in the image of a union of flowers.[68] An utterly spiritual condition is rendered in corporeal images loaded with secondary meaning, such as the rose for the martyr's soul or more broadly for the loving soul. The interlocking of hooks hints at a disposition for a future purpose, the celestial nuptials.

The *botte* presents time as measured in a sensual manner and achieves this through the use of images which evoke an affective engagement with past, present, and future. In medieval narratives more generally, manipulations of perspective are employed to produce a distinctive temporal experience. Gabrielle Spiegel has discussed how in prose narratives kinetic practices articulate, beyond language, a uniquely configured consciousness of history and the past, based on the presupposition that prose was conceived of as the 'language of history'.[69] Etymological resonances of prose compared to poetry convey a dichotomy of straight vectors and circular ones: prose signifies the idea of ancestry (from the Roman Goddess Prosa), Latin *prosus* designating what is 'straightforward and direct'.[70] Yet, the act of reading a plot inevitably creates a doubling effect that is not 'straightforward': on the one hand the reader observes someone undergoing an experience (here, Gertrude seeing the dress); on the other, the use of impersonal pronouns introduces perspectival ambiguities forcing the reader to accommodate a certain set of conceptual inclinations, such as observing themselves imagining the dress. Direct addresses in narratives are also ambiguous, or as Monika Fludernik puts it: 'you is an unstable referent'.[71] An impersonal and implicit command might be incorporated into a third person statement of fact – as, for example, to look at Gertrude's dress in the open form 'whoever looked at it' – so that the reader is asked to inhabit multiple spheres of imagination, moving between narrated space and visionary space. The kinetic element of displacement is also a performative way to entice the reader into an Orphic turn: to look at Gertrude's past depicted in the dress and at her future at the same time since the dress is transformed to be fitting for the mystical wedding.

PARTICIPATORY VISIBILITY

The act of looking, no matter how imaginary, is a key aspect in the kinetic strategy of manipulating the reader. Concerning Gertrude's vision as transmitted in the *botte*, the question arises, how is one supposed to imagine the full visibility of a three-dimensional object at one glance? The *botte*, in contrast to the *Legatus*, stresses such a possibility. What underlies this perception is the status of the dress as being 'gilded', a condition which makes the dress transparent (*splendidissima et perspicacissima; dúrchsúhtig also ein luter cristalle*). This transparency speaks to the long catalogue of associations with gold in medieval craftwork: gold was used for highlighting what was judged to be important. Its reflecting quality meant that it was deemed to be of the nature of light and therefore able to render everything – to quote Alan of Lille's *Anticlaudianus* – 'to appear more clearly'.[72] In the Middle Ages, gold was associated with the divine; it was thought to be divine light and hence a colour of salvation. Its application to Gertrude's dress therefore speaks to her becoming God-like as she advances to take on the role of the mystical bride. Seen from the perspective of material culture, the process of gilding is meant to render the textile translucent and therefore visible through and through in itself.[73] This would also entail enhanced visibility at first sight.[74] Similarly, the gold-silver robe of personified Theology in Alan's *Anticlaudianus* makes what is invisible become visible, endowing form to what is formless.[75]

The translucency of Gertrude's Easter Monday dress therefore pertains to both the material condition of visibility and the spiritual moment of divine recognition. In the moment of full recognition, the narrator mentions that Gertrude understands what the visibility stands for (*do verstund sie*): that everything remains visible forever, that the past is captured and enhanced in the transformative process of grace.

The image's totality is reflected in the *botte* and the *Legatus*, but in different ways.[76] The discursive strategies used in both versions respectively reveal different takes on the relationship between image and representation. Gertrude's visionary cloak is a map with details about her inner and outer life, fabricated in a specific and personal pattern. In the *botte*, the many colours of Gertrude's dress as a coded system are expounded: 'and each colour, with which her deeds were distinguished, was clearly visible and each spot of her deeds, whether good or bad, was lucidly visible'.[77] The detail of the colourfulness is missing in all known *Legatus* sources, where in contrast to the *botte*, however, the fall of the folds and the absence of shadows is mentioned: 'This dress appeared expanded and stretched in such a way that no shadows of any fold could have covered anything.'[78] In Gertrude's dress everything is visible at all times, even before it is enhanced by Christ's application of a golden sheen.[79]

What else is specified about the dress's visible materiality? The fixing of the gemstones appears not to be the gown's only imperfection. In the *Legatus*, hypothetical specks of dust that stay visible even after the gilding of the dress are mentioned: 'Not even the smallest speck of dust or the smallest spot would have remained hidden, would have been invisible in the lucid recognition of God's unfailing truth and heavenly hosts'.[80] Only one of the German text witnesses transmits the equivalent speck of dust on Gertrude's imaginary dress: the Gotha witness.[81] The Easter Monday vision as it is transmitted in this codex is largely consistent with other *botte* text witnesses except for one marginal correction, a phrase added by the scribe (in the following transcription the marginal note is marked in angle brackets, abbreviations are solved, punctuation and strikethrough are taken from the manuscript):

> Und ain iglichev varb mit der irev werch unterschaiden waren . di sah man clerlich vnd ainen iglichen puncht irer werch guter oder poser . <vnd ain klaines steublein maht niht verholen werden wann daz> ~~di~~ sah man alles lauterlich . vnd waren do offen vor got . vnd vor allen himlischen her [. . .][82]

> And one could see clearly each colour distinguishing her deeds and each spot of her deeds, whether good or bad ones; <and not even a small speck of dust could be hidden because> one could see everything lucidly, and they [the deeds] were revealed to God and to the entire heavenly hosts.

The added phrase in the margin meant that the scribe had to correct the main text (see Fig. 2) as the sentence's grammar changed to reflect the causality between the gown's condition and its visibility (the translation above takes the correction into account). The corrections were undertaken by the same scribe but after they had written the main text. Perhaps the scribe had consulted a Latin source only after they had copied their text since the marginal addition undoubtedly goes back to the *Legatus*.[83] It is also possible that several redactions, Latin as well as German ones, circulated and were exchanged at the same time. In any event, the scribe deemed it important to change the text at this point, highlighting once more the stark visibility of the imaginary dress.

In contrast to the *botte*'s emphasis on visibility, in the *Legatus* the point of reference for the vision is exegetical. The respective chapter in the *Legatus* is longer as the vision is followed by an interpretation quoting the Bible (Ezekiel 18, 21–22) and explaining in an exegetical manner what Gertrude understood in consequence of her vision:[84]

> She understood from this by divine grace that anyone's condition is similarly obvious to God and all the saints throughout eternity. But what the Lord says through the prophet, 'In what hour so ever the sinner turns,' and so on, should be understood in this way: the Lord will not remember sins any longer, to judge them, if they have been wiped clean by suitable penitence.[85]

Gertrude's personal comprehension of the dress is extended to a general knowledge of how 'every stain of our sins shall perpetually appear on us, to the praise and glory of his sweetest mercy': *apparebunt in nobis singulae maculae peccatorum nostrorum ad laudem et gloriam dulcissimae misericordiae ejus*.[86] It is the exegesis at the end of this chapter that makes the textile in the Latin a metaphor that needs to be interpreted by a theological method. A theological interpretation is delivered which places Scripture and its understanding as the ultimate goal for the use of the textile image.

The German *botte*, too, mentions Gertrude's own understanding of the vision – *dovon verstunt sú von got, das unser aller wandel got bekant ist und allen heilgen* ('thus she was given to understand from God that our course is known to God and all the saints') – but unlike the *Legatus*, the understanding remains on a visual level. This is achieved in two ways: firstly, on a discursive level, there is no Biblical reference and hence no exegesis; secondly, on a quasi-visual level, there is a re-emphasis on the textile's visibility: 'and whoever looked at the dress could see all at once, how she [Gertrude] had spent every hour of her life' (*wer den rog ansach, der sah uf eine stunde, wie sú alle die zit ires lebens ie verzert hette*).[87] Both the *Legatus*' theologically orientated explanation and the *botte*'s reinstatement of the iconographic programme follow a similar idea, which is that of everything being known to God but they pursue different rhetorical strategies. In this last part of the *Legatus* chapter (IV, 28), the Latin text offers a very clear interpretation of the vision, which is distanced from the owner of the vision as Gertrude is last mentioned before the Bible quote and its interpretation. The exegetic part, placed at a prominent place at the end of the passage, is the part that is presented as general truth, derived from Gertrude's vision and relevant to anyone: the repeated use of the first-person plural underlines a universal claim (e.g. *in nobis, nostrorum. . .*, *in omnibus nobis*). By contrast, the *botte* introduces a first-person plural only in the very last phrase (*also ob wir . . .*). The perception of the dress is open to anyone. This is a participatory visibility available to any reader. Here, imagining the dress becomes a material grasp of time just as 'looking also involves a temporal aspect'.[88] The *botte* exploits the complexity of the temporal, yet timeless quality of the image by constantly underlining its visibility.

The *botte* does not include an exegetical explanation. Equally, the invitation to view the textile and hence Gertrude's life cannot be found in any Latin source.[89] The impersonal viewer suggests that the method of visualisation is an allegory rather than a metaphor. In the *botte*, Gertrude's gown is a densely coded image with an abstract depth which does not nullify its materiality. Here, the collective act of looking includes both reader and narrator as the final first-person plural address makes this seem an eye-witness account.

TRANSFORMATIVE EMBODIMENT

Garments in the *botte* come to present acts of transformation through embodiment; the material components of crafted objects – no matter how imaginary – are central for transformative embodiments. In the medieval understanding of mnemonic systems, images are charged 'with a physical re-collective force, which alters the beholder or believer and brings him or her into a state of internalizing and experiencing the truth through the embodiment of memories'.[90] From this vantage point, memory and imagination work similarly in that they activate the inner and outer sensorium, making perceivable what is invisible.[91] For example, Gertrude is an observer, together with the reader, gaining insight into Augustine's life via the visibility of his garments. In the relevant vision, Augustine offers his heart to God in the shape of a delicate rose. After Christ's confirms to Gertrude that Augustine is forgiven his former turbulent life, she sees and notices the jewels on the bishop as:

> his garments were covered by a crystal clarity underneath of which were woven in many colours all the virtues that he had ever practiced on earth. They were shining through his garments with miraculous joy just as gold shines through a crystal.[92]

Just like in the vision of her own gown, Gertrude associates the qualities of gold with that of crystal. In general, the *botte* uses the many images of gemstones from the *Legatus* to enhance a programme of material images.

Traditionally, gemstones stand for a multitude of abstract concepts; in medieval Europe, they came to symbolise Christian virtues.[93] Following ancient Greek ideas about transparency, colour, and light refraction, gemstones were charged with metaphysical meaning in medieval Europe.[94] Transparency is an important principle in both the *Legatus* and the *botte*, where Gertrude's visionary paschal dress becomes entirely translucent 'like a pure crystal' (*aurea lamina splendidissima et perspicacissima*).[95] It is the *botte*, however, which assigns a specific nature to the crystal which derives from the process of purifying gold: *dúrchsúhtig also ein luter cristalle* ('transparent as a pure [or: purified] crystal').[96] Here, gold and crystal are associated symbolically; and what is more, this connection plays out on a morphological level, since the Middle High German adjective *luter* derives from the verb used to designate the process of refining gold, *lutern*. While gold can be refined by different processes, crystals cannot be changed. The intricate morphological conflation of different qualities inherent to precious metals and precious stones – a relationship that we may term medium-mnemonic – emphasises the material culture in which the *botte* is embedded. Certainly by the fourteenth century, the time of the *botte*'s composition, *luter* had become a faded metaphor, but its use is nonetheless marked since the material quality of abstract concepts is repeatedly highlighted in this passage. Gold as divine light and crystal as divine transcendence are combined to maximum effect, this can only be achieved through an acute awareness of the actual materials. The vernacular *botte* redactors were extremely skilful in joining material expertise with linguistic finesse.

The status of textiles in the *botte* itself and more generally at the time of its reception helps us to understand how material culture and symbolism are unpacked in the recounted visions. Textiles were valuable gifts in the Middle Ages; they were objects with agency, as seen in the case of ceremonial textiles that announce a certain authority. For example, a priest's garments bear various meanings at different times during the liturgical year. The circumstance that Gertrude sees herself in a richly decorated garment at the time of the communion on Easter Monday may convey her quasi-priesthood since vestments have strong liturgical implications. Although most liturgical textiles were made by women, the same craftswomen were strictly prohibited from touching the vestments once they were consecrated, except when laundering them.[97] Thus, that Gertrude sees herself in a richly decorated garment underscores her own sacred status, which is confirmed through textiles. Clothes are also important at Easter because the Gospels have Christ leave his garments behind in the tomb (John 20:6–7), and appear in new, heavenly clothes (Matthew 28:3). Gertrude's dress comes to signify a form of sacred representation which encompasses both disguise and embodiment, which are, in fact, two approaches to the ritual use of textiles in the Middle Ages. Mateusz Kaputska and Warren T. Woodfin have pointed out 'the iconological value of vestments and paraments as tools of ritual practice' in the Christian liturgy. Textiles mediated between the visible and invisible, the manifest and the absent as '[o]ne of the most important medieval codifications of liturgy of the West', as *the Rationale divinorum officiorum* (c. 1286), by Guillaume Durand of Mende (c. 1230/31–1296), shows.[98] Drawing on mystagogical traditions, Durand explores the quadruple interpretations – literal, allegorical, tropological, anagogical – of vestments offering multiple symbolic meanings.[99] A textile was 'simultaneously a fabric, a form, and a metaphor', it 'enabled participants in liturgical actions to see through surfaces and images and to bring opposite notions together: disguise and revelation, delimitation and transparency, hierarchical subordination and general invitation to witness.'[100] Bearing this complex framework in mind, we may think of Gertrude's Easter dress and its transformation as a manifestation of a double-layered process: first the soul is disguised as a bride and then it comes to embody the bride. The textile is crucial in this shift from representation to personification. The liturgical frame heightens the sacramental character of this process, as 'textiles helped to unfold in visual terms the transition from "having a body" to "becoming a body" through the re-enactive aspect ("anamnesis") of the liturgy.'[101]

When the textile comes to manifest the act of embodiment, image and representation collapse. Such a process has been described by Louis Marin as the 'auto-representative' function of an image being enhanced to a point where the image comes to possess 'the power of the original'.[102] In the *botte*, as in other bridal mystical texts, textile images are used to reveal embodiment and possession. At one instance, for example, Gertrude receives a delicate blanket which is said to signify the virtues that she is not going to lose; here, ownership of the textile signifies the appropriation of virtues – or in other words, the virtues have become a part of Gertrude.[103] The thirteenth-century Premonstratensian mystic Christina of Hane also sees herself wearing different fabrics with symbolic meaning; she is clothed with virtues.[104] In the *botte*, virtues often appear as gems, for example put into a brooch pinned on one of Gertrude's visionary dresses above her heart.[105] This brooch appears in a vision which is about Gertrude's death, aligning the visionary gown to that of the *Sponsa Christi*, similar to Catherine of Siena's 'wedding garment of charity, adorned with many true virtues' as mentioned in the prologue to *The Dialogue*.[106] Dating from the last quarter of the thirteenth century (that is, Gertrude's lifetime), a surviving reliquary cloth from the Halberstadt treasury suggests that Gertrude's visionary images of gemstones studded onto fabric and externalising sanctity, is related to material culture and its meditative function (see Plate XXII).[107] Its exact origin is unknown but the technique, materials, and composition locate it in Lower Saxony and the edges of the Harz, that is near Helfta. This reliquary cloth is a material expression of holiness as gemstones and sculptured metal plates (depicting the crucifixion) surround and accompany a collection of studded relics. One can easily imagine such 'shiny' objects creating a sense of movement when they were touched in prayer and lit by candlelight.

What do such references mean for the visionary world of Gertrude? Material aspects of textiles, such as Gertrude's visionary brooch, are used as narrative devices that highlight the performative character of a transformation. In this way a visionary garment functions like a costume in a ritualised frame. In visionary texts, the imagined space works like a stage on which certain textiles evoke cultural meaning. In a dream vision from a late medieval German sisterbook, for example, a sister called Adelheit of Gotteszell sees 'a recently deceased sister dressed in rich robes, emblazoned with liturgical passages from Offices for martyrs on the front and back'.[108] Comparing this dream vision to one of Henry Suso's, Jones concludes that there are 'significant manifestations of gender difference in access to saintly status and in experience of the liturgy' since for the Dominican sister it is only after her death that her spiritual state as a holy woman is confirmed (through the liturgically loaded garment), whereas Suso's dream affirms his present holy status.[109] This marked difference between a present sanctity and one in the afterlife is unleashed in textile images. Reconsidering Adelheit's vision in terms of transformative embodiment, the collapse between prayers and their object becomes evident: the soul of the deceased sister is clothed in a garment adorned with the prayers that were said during the Office for the dead. This is an example of the practice of craft-praying in which piety and devotion were translated into textile images. The sister in question has already died and her status is only confirmed, not changed, but the prayers are transformed to embody this status. Gertrude's visionary Easter Monday garment differs from Adelheit's vision in that it reflects upon her present state as the chosen bride while opening other time levels by depicting her conduct in the past as a dress and by transforming her garment to be suitable for a celestial show in front of God's throne.

That visionary garments hold some kind of supernatural meaning deriving from a divine origin becomes more evident when taking into account that celestial figures in Gertrude's visions also wear certain types of textiles. We find out, for instance, that angels are 'beautifully clothed' (*ziemlich gekleidet*);[110] the Virgin Mary appears to Gertrude in purple garments (rather than in her traditional iconographical blue gown) taking on the colour that was considered most precious in the Middle Ages;[111] and in one vision, Christ, walking to the throne of his Father is described as robed in an imperial cloak.[112] When in another vision Gertrude receives a golden dress after pleading for a dyed robe instead of her nondescript gown, she is singled out.[113] In this vision, other souls wear coloured gowns signifying the multiplicity of the bride's embodiment.[114] Gertrude stands out among this group as her desire to be one of the chosen brides confers on her the golden garment; here her desire leads to the transformation of the imaginary textile, which makes manifest the end of her journey to become an embodied bride of Christ.

It is not only desire that leads to Gertrude obtaining a dress suitable for the bride of Christ. In one vision Christ explains to her that if the spouse does not please herself, if she has self-doubts and despises herself, she puts on a dress that makes his heart incline to her.[115] Here, we can fathom an aesthetic principle for textiles, a sense of fashion. But this fashion is inverted: it is not beauty but suffering and self-loathing that appeal to Christ as a suitable gown for his bride. Accordingly, in one vision, Gertrude sees that her own sadness about being despised by her peers turns into 'shining golden flowers' that 'miraculously' clothe her: *Zůhant do sach sú, das sú von der trůbsal wunderlich gekleidet wart mit schinenden gůldenen blůmen.*[116] Being clothed thus appears to be an act of being honoured and rewarded. Self-loathing and insecurity are interpreted as virtues; negative qualities are converted into bonuses and this is made manifest in floral textile images. When considering the liturgical character of Gertrude's visions, one may start to understand her textile visions as a commentary on the liturgy, as a kind of 'liturgical aesthetic'.[117]

Contrary to Michael Bangert's idea that Gertrude's mysticism favours nakedness over being clothed, we find that textiles are more complex in their employment than that, because they exceed the function of spiritual markers as they call upon the reader to imagine material manifestations. Generally, the idea of purity applied to the body is often associated with nakedness, yet Gertrude's visions are saturated with textiles to a degree that an understanding of textiles as signs of an imperfect state falls short. Instead, they show the nuances of the different stages of the soul as she first 'dresses up' as a bride before she embodies one. In this sense, the aesthetic importance of textiles is in line with Winckelmann's thoughts on drapery when he stresses the role of garments in his search for the ideal beauty. Indeed, Winckelmann's interest in costume and drapery has been understated in scholarship, as Fiona Gatty has shown.[118] The expressive charge clothing could take in the form of drapery provided for Winckelmann an interface for the spiritual components of beauty. Gatty points out that 'drapery was a key part of Winckelmann's expressive vocabulary, and it was able to signify attitudes and attributes which were not possible through facial features or when the body was undressed'.[119] Textiles are not mere decoration but expansions to a person. Religious textiles, similar to costumes, represent status, but they also go beyond representation in the mystical text: textiles manifest, they enact the idea of embodiment.

The *botte* presents nakedness as a state that the soul needs to overcome. On the one hand, Gertrude asks Christ to accept her naked as she denies all her good deeds (her nakedness is explained as meaning that she has no cloth of virtue to put on).[120] On the other hand, she wants to be wrapped up in the linen that Mary uses for the Christ Child after his birth.[121] The cloth is said to be the taffeta of innocence. Then the bundle of Gertrude and the Christ Child is tied up with a golden ribbon which is said to signify love.[122] This latter vision, occurring on the Feast of Purification (also known as Candlemas), has parallels to another instance in which Christ, who celebrates a visionary mass, holds up the host, literally 'the body of God' (*gottes lichnam*), in the form of a curtain (*fúrhang*), which he uses to wrap himself and his spouse up in: *Den want er umb sin gemahel und umb sich selber.* This scene of intimacy externalises the communion and the mystical *connubium* as bride and groom are united and become one 'thing': *Also gemehelt er sich zů ir und vereinet sú mit im, das sú ein ding wurden.*[123] The textile, here a token for the Eucharist, becomes a catalyst, a facilitator for the union of soul and deity as both are clothed in it.

In another vision, Gertrude gets to wear Christ's garments. During the Kyrie, she sees herself presented as a child to God who does not heed her, after which she is 'adorned with reflecting and shining garments': *gezieret mit widerglestenden und mit schinenden cleideren.* Precious stones are laid into the fabric: *durchleit mit edelen gymmen.* With the garment on, Gertrude grows to the age of Christ. As she is recognised by God the Father as wearing his son's clothes she receives his 'threefold blessing' (*drivaltiger segen*). Up to this point, all the transformative processes are bestowed on Gertrude. She is only an agent in blushing and feeling embarrassed. After she receives the blessing, however, she thanks God and offers him 'the life of his begotten son'. 'At this, the gems on her dress started moving, all together and against each other, resounding in honour of God with the sweetest and clearest chime that has ever been heard by a human.'[124] Gertrude's offering is reflected in the garment gaining new, that is auditory and kinetic, qualities. Her dress is described as marking her sisterhood to Christ rather than her spousal engagement to him.[125] Textiles thus mark hierarchies and relationships, and they can be transformed in different ways. They are employed to a great and complex variety which exploits material and symbolic nuances alike.

Returning to the robe in Gertrude's paschal vision and the aspect of transformative embodiment: the emphasis on a movement from the lower part of the dress upwards to her current state, aligns this textile beautifully with Boethius' robe of personified Philosophy in his *Consolation of Philosophy*. Here, between the lower part of Philosophy's dress, woven with the Greek letter Π (P), and the upper part, marked with the letter Θ (Th), 'steps were marked like a ladder, by which one might climb from the lower letter to the higher'.[126] With these letters standing for the two branches of philosophy, Practical and Theoretical, climbing the steps from one to the other was, in the Middle Ages, interpreted as a mystical advancement. This devotional reading of Boethius' sixth-century *De consolatione philosophiae* inspired Chaucer and others to appropriate the textile image for a visualisation of 'the transition from active to contemplative'.[127] Arguably, Gertrude's imaginary dress embodies her own spiritual progression to a *vita contemplativa*.[128]

Lastly, on the textual surface too, Gertrude's Easter Monday textile emphasises a double character of material and symbolic, showing that the immaterial is linked to the material through performative language. The dress comes to stand for Gertrude's all-encompassing religious life but there is a subtle difference between the *Legatus* and the *botte* when it comes to how the dress refers to the past. The visionary dress winds itself from the bottom upwards in annual circles (whether as a spiral or as a column is unstipulated); the *Legatus* specifies: 'The lower part of the dress represented the first year, the second [part] the second year, and so forth, up to the year in which she was at that moment'.[129] The first substantial difference to the *botte* is the mode that the dress is presented in: *reputabatur*, an imperfect passive indicative, creates a representative relation between the image and what it stands for (the years of Gertrude's life). In the *botte*, the indicative active use in this crucial passage means that there is no surficial distinction between the material and its meaning: 'And at the hem started the first year, and this continued upwards until the last year, in which she was amidst'.[130] Furthermore, the lower part of the dress, Latin *inferior pars tunicae*, is specified differently in the *botte*, where it is named more specifically *sŏm*. The technical term *sŏm*, meaning hem or hemline, testifies to a handicraft knowledge of needlework and embroidery; moreover, it reverberates with another key term in the passage. In the introduction to the vision, Gertrude admits to having been neglectful in her religious practice. In the *Legatus*, we read that 'she was beseeching the Lord that through that most worthy sacrament he would deign to compensate for everything that she had neglected in the observance of the religious life'.[131] In the *botte*, the verb for 'to neglect', *versumen* (Latin *neglegere*),[132] sounds akin to the word used to name the hem (*sŏm*). Here, Gertrude wishes for fulfilment *wo sú sich an regelicher ordenung ie versumet het*.[133] The Middle High German word *versûmen* has the notion of falling short or abridging.[134] While the two words *sŏm* and *versûmen* are etymologically unrelated, their resemblance when spoken out loud is striking, even more so in the Gotha witness where the diphthong is identical (*versavment-savm*). The Franconian dialectical variance enhances a phonetic effect making the two terms intersect acoustically.

Thus when read aloud, we can hear that the language performs the notion of fixing the past in a sensory perception by the hem (*sŏm/savm*) echoing what is described as failure (*versumet/versavment*).[135] The reverberation of sound creates a circular, rather than linear, sonic temporality. In the *botte*, fleeting time is thus decelerated in a circular movement by the sonority of the spoken word. On top of the homophony between *sŏm/savm* and *versumet/*

versavment, there is also a material and technical connection: usually when sewing a hemline fabric is heaped and shortened in order to thread the needle through. The homophony means that on a performative level, the technical composition of the dress resonates with Gertrude's religious comportment. What she takes to lie in the past is embodied in her dress, her own failing comportment begins as she enters the convent. In the image this translates to precisely where the textile begins, at the hemline. A sonic echo reactivates what was bound to time in an image that exists outside time. More importantly, this is medium-mnemonic language: the words are imitating what they stand for and take on a sensory dimension. Language in its performativity achieves this embodying effect. In other words: the mere sound of what the dress is composed of (conduct in the past) leads to a sonorous collapsing of present state and past time.

VISIONARY CRAFTMANSHIP

The *botte*'s sensory re-enactment links back to the late medieval tradition of weaving imaginary dresses through spoken prayers and sung hymns. When studying Gertrude of Helfta's visions we deal with different historical moments: there is the Helfta nuns' engagement with textile culture and there are the many different reception contexts, one of which is the late medieval reform movement. It is hard to elicit the historical realities in the convent of Helfta since almost all artefacts have been lost − only a few architectural elements remain on site − but the texts that the nuns have left and that have been transmitted in various manuscript copies, in addition to the larger historical, textile, and literary environment, give us a sense of what the material culture in Helfta would have been like in the thirteenth century. The cultural environment in which the vernacular *botte* was received maintained a symbolically heightened relationship to textiles, meaning that textile imagery was never isolated but placed into a larger understanding of materials and their status as holy objects. The *botte* − although its performative strategy of combining visual textiles with an auditory textuality is special − needs to be explored within the context of late medieval devotional practices, when contemplative prayers − so-called craft-prayers − increasingly came to make use of textile imagery.[136] Before we turn to the *botte* and its reception, however, new insights into how textile craftmanship may have influenced the Latin *Legatus* elucidate the relationship between material culture and language.

Many passages from the Latin texts could be cited to explore the textile understanding the Helfta nuns might have had. One example, however, is particularly intriguing. The newly discovered *Leipzig Legatus*, the oldest known *Legatus* source with hitherto unknown text portions, contains a sentence pertaining to textile culture in a visionary conversation which is unknown in the 'standard' *Legatus*. While the passage is mostly congruent with the *Legatus* and also the *botte*, in both of which Gertrude prays for the soul of a deceased converted brother,[137] the 'new' portion in the *Leipzig Legatus* mentions a special type of gown in order to depict the spiritual state of the dead person's soul (Leipzig, Universitätsbibliothek, Ms 827, fol. 130r; see Fig. 42). The word used for this specific textile derives from the vernacular language but appears within the Latin text. The narrative context is a dialogue between Gertrude and the soul of the recently deceased person for whom she and the convent had prayed.

> Tunc illa: Quid prodest tibi, quod desiderauimus tibi a Deo dari, quitquit boni ipse in nobis perfecit? Anima: Valde bene prodest, quia ubi proprium michi deest, ex uestris ornor meritis, sicut qui starrochium non habet in uiridi siue brunato, ornatur quo melius potest.[138]

> Then she [Gertrude] said, 'What benefit do you gain because we have asked God that you should be granted whatever good he has performed in us?' The soul replied, 'A very great benefit indeed. For where my own merits are deficient, I am adorned by yours, like someone who does not have a garment in green or brown adorns himself as best he can.'[139]

Nowhere else attested, *starrochium* (which Alexandra Barratt translates as 'garment') is very likely a Latinised word derived from German, although its German form (**starroch*) is equally unattested. I suggest that it is a compound whose second (determinative) element is German *roch/rock* meaning garment or dress. For example, in Gertrude's Easter vision, Latin *tunica* is rendered as *rock* in the *botte*; *starrochium* is then some kind of a special garment. The first (qualifying) part of the compound might be derived from German *starr*, meaning rigid, in which case *starrochium* would denote a starched garment. One way to obtain coloured garments in the Middle Ages was, in fact, to dye the fabric with the help of wheat starch which would make the colour come out stronger.[140] The context of the dialogue favours this understanding of *starrochium*, since the wearing of a coloured garment is made explicit.[141] With the Leipzig manuscript having been copied in the fourteenth century, this would be a comparably early reference for the practice of starching cloth. It would mean that the Helfta nuns – or at least very closely related contacts – were advanced in methods of making coloured textiles. Indeed, medieval nunneries in Lower Saxony, such as Wienhausen, dyed fabrics using different raw materials such as saffron and galangal.[142] Be it as it may, in the *Leipzig Legatus*, the vernacular was deemed more suitable for describing the type of garment than Latin. This observation shows that textile knowledge was well developed in the vernacular, and that there was some kind of a textile tradition that expressed itself in the vernacular not just during the late medieval reception of the *Legatus*, but already very close to or at the time of its own composition.

130

42 Text from the *Leipzig Legatus* corresponding to *Legatus* V, 12 (1300–20)
Leipzig, Universitätsbibliothek, Ms 827, fol. 130r (1300–20)

Many passages in the *botte* connect devotional practice to the production and manufacturing of textiles (and also jewels), highlighting awareness and knowledge of craftsmanship and handiwork. The vernacular redaction is stupendously detailed in this technical regard as seen in Gertrude's Easter Monday vision, where her faulty behaviour is rendered in the way gems are attached to the dress. The method of how the gemstones are affixed on the dress is specified in the *botte* while the *Legatus* remains non-descript. The Latin text has the gemstones being simply poorly affixed: *gemmulae luto fragili infixae*.[143] The corresponding Middle High German word *klëben* has the same generic meaning of affixing, but also carries the connotation of gluing. Together with the explicit mentioning of glue, however, a precise method is indicated, which is that of gluing gemstones to the fabric: *gymmen, die mit leymen an den rock gekleibet weren*.[144] The mentioning of glue as adhesive testifies to profound knowledge of at least the vocabulary, when it comes to textile craftsmanship. Securely attaching any jewels to fabric would necessitate several processes including mounting the stone and stitching it to the tissue rather than gluing it (an example for which is the aforementioned reliquary cloth from Halberstadt, see Plate XXII). When the *botte* refers to glue it presupposes prior knowledge in material culture that there are different ways of working gemstones into fabrics some of which are inferior to others. Here, Gertrude's poor behaviour is mirrored in the poor craftmanship.

The 'devotional technicality' of the *botte*'s language resonates with its late medieval reception context. That textiles were understood to be valuable objects loaded with the conceptual potential to embody abstract states and feelings, can be seen in the practice of the so-called craft-prayers. When craft-praying, spoken – or meditated – words and non-verbal thoughts create imaginary textiles turning the auditory – or emotional – into the visual and tactile. Immateriality transformed into an imaginary materiality is part of a devotional programme that was exercised and propagated in the late medieval reform movement, the dominant context for the *botte*'s historical reception. In late medieval accounts, such as those from female communities in Strasbourg, nuns would imaginatively create jewels, accessories, and dresses by saying prayers, singing hymns, fasting, and behaving obediently.[145] This practice was directly linked to material objects which would, in their turn, trigger the creation of immaterial, imaginary objects. In this way, physical devotional objects functioned 'not simply as material accessories to prayer, but also as mnemonic devices for more elaborate meditations'.[146] Textiles came to express interior feelings or states. In some medieval legends, there is a 'metaphoric equivalence between praying and textile manufacture'.[147] Like actual textiles, in which '[w]omen imbued their needlework with commemorative and even documentary functions, thereby transforming communal works into personal memorials',[148] imaginary textiles and accessories also functioned as symbols of self-reflection.[149]

Contemplative prayers were treated as mental exercises of visual piety; prayers were imagined visually and immaterial images were brought into life through devotional practice. Thomas Lentes understands these kinds of creative devotional practices as a prayerful contemplation, a 'praying in images' ('Beten in Bildern'), which linked imaginative devotion to the ordered practice of the liturgical prayer.[150] Yet, even in the reform movement, despite a programme of visual piety as propagated in *The Book of the Reformation* by Johannes Meyer, the attitude towards religious art and devotional images was ambivalent, though not iconoclastic: 'Meyer is less concerned about the presence of the image per se than how the nuns use (or abuse) it.'[151] Both Hamburger and Lentes argue that visions inspired by privately owned images created spiritual problems that the reformers tried to avoid.[152] One way to get around this problem was to emphasise the immaterial value of images and to encourage a practice detached from actual objects. In the reform movement, the programme of visual contemplation meant that the pious imagination of materialities was considered an orthodox and quasi-liturgical practice in line with the reformers aim of a pious imagination. For example, Johannes Meyer 'praises the sister Elisabeth Griss for her contemplative practice of imagining that each of the prayers represented a stitch in a garment she was imaginatively sewing for St Anthony'.[153] The *botte*, with its programme of corporeal images, fitted the late medieval devotional culture very well, the retention of textual imagery from the *Legatus* serving it formidably.

When we look at the vernacular redaction of Gertrude's visions we can detect a deep interest in textile images as the *botte* emphasises material objects, especially when they appear in connection with garments, fabrics more generally, and precious stones. Gems set in gold are compared to the heavenly reward when faced with the loss of a beloved person, God being described as a craftsman in this regard: *hantwergmann*.[154] Various techniques of craftsmanship are specified in the *botte*; apart from gluing pearls and setting gems in gold, we also find spinning wool, weaving, sewing, stitching, wreath-binding, braiding, crocheting with hooks, and nailing. Different materials are worked in imaginary objects such as wool, gold, gems, and thread. Only rarely do fabrics carry purely symbolic meaning in the *botte*. One of these cases concerns the robes of John the Evangelist as a 'blossoming young man' (*blügende júngeling*). In Gertrude's vision of a celestial celebration of the mass, she sees John in a sky-blue gown that is embroidered with delicate white and golden eagles.[155] Here, embroidery is emblematic as the eagle is the iconographic signifier of John the Evangelist. Even this symbolic visionary textile has a material counterpart: a chasuble from the Halberstadt treasury dating from the first half of the thirteenth century has striking similarities to Gertude's vision, with its saturated blue silk and delicate golden embroidered eagles (see Plate XXIII).[156]

During the reception history of the *botte*, meditative prayer practice and the production of textiles continued to go hand in hand. Surviving textiles from late medieval German convents give testimony to the embroidery of emblems and even words on garments, which were sometimes meant to clothe sculptures (see Plate XXIV).[157] The reception of textile images in the *botte* could be linked to such devotional objects. In South Germany, where the *botte* was read, we find another form of textile culture in reformed circles, one that evolves on an imaginary level. The *botte* manages to unravel the encounter with the divine in immaterial imagery while meeting the strict principles of the observant movement which was sceptical of material images and objects, by exploiting the flexibility that a visionary corporeality allowed for. Both the divine and the human become active in handiwork. In the *botte,* spiritual exercises are compared to handiwork such as braiding or setting jewels. Similarly, Christ is said to possess golden hooks with which he can nail the soul to himself 'as a precious stone is set in gold': *reht also do man ein edele gymme in ein golt verwürcket;*[158] evoking once more the extant reliquary cloth from Halberstadt (Plate XXII). At another instance, handiwork and spiritual processes are even more intrinsically interlinked. Gertrude spins wool whilst contemplating and dedicating her work to God. The spiritual and material work process is disturbed by a demon who snatches away any excess wool that is thrown away. This is not merely a technical description of how to spin wool; rather, it connects Gertrude's inattentive prayer with her spinning.[159] In a preceding encounter with a Titivillus-like demon, all the syllables that were not sung or spoken with full attention are collected by the demon causing Gertrude to reflect upon her prayer practice as an ephemeral exercise with eternally regretful effects.[160] Gertrude's spinning whilst praying – rather than the other way around – thus highlights the spiritual value of even the seemingly most mundane tasks.[161]

Most instances and mentions of handiwork concern, however, imaginary crafted objects. One of these immaterial objects is a wreath made of roses. During a nocturnal mystical embrace between Christ and Gertrude, Christ expounds on the allegory of a floral wreath made by the bride for her groom. The meaning of the allegory is laid out too: a loyal soul does not care which roses will be broken and worked into a wreath; with the roses being ailments and death, she happily binds the wreath, which is referred to as a 'rosary' (*rosenkrantz*).[162] The rose is a metaphor in itself as it comes with the pictorial connotation of a virtuous and virginal life (but also of a manifestation – generally, though not in the case of the *botte* – of the Ave Maria).[163] The rosary as a religious exercise developed gradually and was fully shaped only by the late fifteenth century with the pope confirming an official version as late as 1569, but by the twelfth century 'prayer exercises already consisted of the repetitive recitation of Pater Nosters or Ave Marias as acts of devotion or penance, or as a substitute for the prayers of the Divine Office'.[164] The rose came to symbolise Mary as well as Christ from the fourteenth century onwards.[165] In late medieval legends and exempla, devotees create imaginary garments and headgear such as flower chaplet or crowns for saints and in particular for Mary by praying the rosary.[166] Gertrude's wreath of roses aligns with this craft-praying practice.[167] By the time of the *botte*'s reception in the late fourteenth and fifteenth centuries, the word *rosenkrantz* had come to designate a prayer practice that would have been recognisable to the reader as underlying the image of a wreath. In this way, we can infer that the reception of the *botte* continued to unfold practical meaning from various images.[168]

Devotional aspects can be taken even further when exploring the 'spiritual materiality' of rosaries as they were practiced in the late Middle Ages. Materiality and spirituality become palpably close 'as the interchangeability of objects and prayers came to stand for the prayer itself', as Hamburger puts it, and '[n]o object of devotion was more familiar than the rose'.[169] Considering that books were bound with either sewing or stitching, the notion of the thread keeping the rosary together and forming a real connection between each prayer/bead, takes us back to book culture. As Hanneke van Asperen has shown in her study on a small sixteenth-century Middle Dutch rosary prayer book, '[t]he use of thread to attach objects refers to the practice of praying, especially in convents where textile work was an important part of the daily practice.'[170] While Asperen works on actual stitching that was effectuated on the manuscript's paper pages, meaning 'that the rosary devotion actually translates the manual act of stringing into a spiritual exercise',[171] the link between practical devotion and the conceptually sacred is not always as tangible as a physically surviving thread or textile, but is still important.[172]

Book crafting also comes into play when we study imaginary objects and references to culturally defined tropes. For example, the colour coding in one of Gertrude's vision as retold in the *botte* could allude to an illuminated medieval manuscript page. In the vision in question, the names of devotees turn into golden, black, or illegible (literally 'darkened', *vinster*) letters in God's eyes, depending on whether the words of their prayer were spoken in special devotion (gold), out of habit (black), or unhappily, that is, despite oneself.[173] Intentions correspond to script in different coloured inks but also to scribal mistakes, as the dark and illegible letters could be imagined as blotted-out lines. The reader of the pious people's names is God, whilst the text's reader is invited to imagine the letters as a written record.[174] This vision – like most of Gertrude's visions – occurs during the liturgy; as the procession begins on the feast of St Mark and the litany is sung, Gertrude has her vision of Christ sitting on a throne and eventually recognising the pious devotees. Gertrude's realisation that prayers matter (and that names materialise) before God, is an imaginative form of intellectual engagement with the liturgy.[175] This kind of productive practice – unpacked in liturgical visions – surpassed 'mere illustrations of dogmatic content to perform independent and creative theological work'.[176]

Like in the medieval courtly world, where the giving of textiles marked a socially coded gifting, in Gertrude's visionary world, textiles are tokens of transactions. In one instance, for example, we read that Gertrude understands that just deeds and words 'clothe the lord with a graceful dress': *kleidet unseren herren mit einem zierlichen kleide*. In return God will 'pay back' a just person with 'a dress of joy' and a 'crown of honours', 'according to his [God's] royal honour'.[177] Human actions and divine grace are expressed in textile images that correlate to the social practice of a handing over textiles as a form of bonding. In her work on textiles in medieval German texts, Kathryn Starkey has shown that clothing is only ever given down the social hierarchy and that, if it is worn, it demonstrates the bond between donor and receiver.[178] In the devotional practice of craft-praying, we see that the transaction of imaginary textiles works also in the other direction: the hierarchically inferior human can create immaterial objects out of praise and worship to clothe the deity. In the *botte*, Christ adorns himself with prayers that are offered in the form of garments, a process which results in a transaction: those who have offered him their prayers are rewarded with 'dignity' (*würdikeit*) in the afterlife. A double transaction takes place as prayers turn into garments, after which God gives grace in return.[179] There is an awareness of the fact that the gifting of textiles follows a social code defined among humans, as becomes clear in a simile that Christ offers to Gertrude: praying for someone else is like giving one's biological sister one's own beautiful dress adorned with gems and pearls so that the parents and all family members and servants may praise the benefactor while the beneficiary earns respect from all people.[180] Aristocratic social codes underlie the presented praying scheme, and both complexes are connected via the use of textiles, whether material or immaterial. Good behaviour and virtuous intentions are exchangeable goods and resemble textiles in this regard.

The scheme of prayer that pursues a collective function is equally directed to individual reward; metaphorically speaking, it correlates to clothing oneself in imaginary garments. This process can be seen in one vision which follows Gertrude's ardent devotion in the Night Office (Matins) as she helps an ill person to celebrate the Nocturns despite her own afflictions; during the subsequent mass, Gertrude recognises that she is clothed with a sumptuous gown adorned with translucent gems. She is taught by God that she deserves this dress because she read the Matins with 'righteous love and humility' (*in rehter mine und demütikeit*). God 'enlightens' (*erlühtet*) her with as many adornments as she has read words, her imaginary gown being described as the 'dress of love' (*kleid der mine*). At the same time the dress is said to cover her sins. Gertrude, upset about her sins soiling her (*verunreiniget*), is then told that love extinguishes the 'neglect caused by daily sins' (*versúmnis der tegelichen súnden*).[181] The temporal aspect of sins, qualified here with the shortcoming of Gertrude's daily practice, reminds us of her Easter Monday vision, where the textile, however, records her entire behaviour. The difference between the sins disappearing or the sins shining forever in glory, as is the case in the paschal vision, does not mean that the *botte* is incoherent, but rather that textile images were used flexibly for various concepts.

IMPERFECT TEXTILES AND THE FORGIVENESS OF SINS

Whether textiles appear clean and perfect, or translucent in their imperfection in Gertrude's visions, the intentions of one's thoughts, words, and deeds matter when they are visualised in textile images. The psychological dimension is stressed and explained in Gertrude's Easter Monday vision. We read that the loosely attached gemstones that are about to fall from her imaginary dress are the deeds she committed with an ulterior motive, literally hypocritically (*glichsenlich*). Gertrude, trying to take leave from a certain task, orchestrates a permission from the abbess that makes her own neglect look like obedience.[182] This twisted behaviour is subsequently shown in the visionary dress as gems that are glued and thus poorly affixed. The material techniques of fabricating a precious textile are juxtaposed with human behaviour, a qualitatively less worthy technique is aligned to guileful and immoral conduct. The imperfect state of Gertrude's dress requires a transformation, which is eventually performed by Christ gilding the fabric. The image of an imperfect textile marked by human sinful behaviour leads us to consider a prominent medieval text which illustrates the fall from a perfect state with textile images, Alan of Lille's *De planctu naturae* (*The Complaint of Nature*).[183]

Alan's allegory of the Goddess Nature, written around 1165, shows us – although it does not explicitly present Christian theology – that in the High Middle Ages, textiles were used to visualise how the use of language correlates to the mechanisms of salvation. At the centre of the philosophical treatise *The Complaint of Nature* stands Nature, embodying a macrocosmic and encyclopaedic course of time. Her richly adorned garments constantly find new shapes depicting narrative and allegorical themes, one of which is that of human sexuality.[184] The ecstatic vision of Nature evolves in a diegetic frame which configures the poet as narrator and visionary. While in Alan's text the visionary is an observer and interlocutor, in Gertrude's Easter Monday vision the visionary is also the one who wears the imaginary dress and comes to embody an allegorical role, that of the mystical bride. Despite these differences, the discursive comparison between the two visions reveals a similar use of textile images.[185]

The Complaint of Nature begins with the poet (more or less implicitly) lamenting homosexuality, upon which the Goddess Nature appears to him. Nature, to whom God has given responsibility for all transformation in the world, passes human sexuality on to Venus. Venus, by betraying her spouse (Hymenäus) with a lover (Antigenius or Antigamus), introduces corruption into the world. In the last part of *The Complaint of Nature*, Genius, Nature's priest, emerges to correct the iniquity in the world by punishing sinful humans. In Alan's dream vision, Nature appears as a virgin brilliantly decorated with precious garments and jewellery. Her upset about human corruption leaves stains on her dress, a dress that is composed of time and virtues. The dress' materiality is impacted by the corrupt use of language. For Alan, moral decay and disintegration are consequences of poets abusing language in order to obscure truth. The art of rhetoric appears then akin to that of drapery, where several layers can create space to hide things in. The term *integumentum*, used by Alan and literally meaning covering, was indeed not only employed to describe the folds of a garment; it also referred to a literary device, which led to creative spaces in the poets' attempts to represent truth.[186] The Christian reception of Alan's allegory of Nature has favoured a Mariological interpretation more than the rhetorical dimension, understanding Nature to stand for Mary as the cosmic queen and coredemptrix. Although not explicit in the text, *The Complaint of Nature* has a quasi-mystical dimension when considering that Nature's dress is that of a bride: the terminology used to describe her dress, evokes a nuptial context (*ad nuptia gradiens ... maritus ... coniugia*).[187] This dress, like Gertrude's, undergoes a process of gilding, as Nature reveals how with humble words she intends to cover the ghastly smell of vice with a golden cover on her gown.[188] Here, the synesthetic quality of the textile underlines its material conception. The 'fixing' of the dress happens through a divine intervention. Creation, deviation, and reparation all happen on an allegorical level.

An integral component of the allegory is the material quality of Nature's dress; Michael Stolz has pointed out that the material aspect is just as important as its interpretation.[189] Despite its character as a visionary textile, the image repeatedly refers to corporeal aspects when it comes to embodying abstract concepts. Nature's dress is made of fine wool, the images on her gown are silken, and layers of fabric symbolise concentric cosmic spheres.[190] The garments of Genius, too, are symbolic and highly ritualised as they define his priesthood.[191] Taking *The Complaint of Nature* as an allegorical text and as a polemical opinion about allegory, its own literary construction is emphasised. The semiotic constitution of Nature points to the distinction between verbal and metaphorical expressions as Alan finds a way to discuss and exploit semiotic representation through language while criticising it at the same time.[192]

The semiotic quality of language and even objects is also laid out in Gertrude's visionary Easter Monday dress, where the textile is described as composed of her conduct in and over time. The relationship between the past and the textile is a semiotic one as every year that Gertrude has spent in her life, how, and in what intention she has spent it, is 'distinguished and signified' in the fabric (*underscheiden und gezeichent*).[193] The allegory itself also hints at a future in which Gertrude embodies the mystical bride. However, the representation of her life is imperfect as her dress is in need of transformation, which occurs during the vision with the golden illumination of the dress. Gertrude's vision, taking place during the communion, at the centre of which stands a most significant transformation, the transubstantiation, carries thus a strong Eucharistic connotation. The Eucharistic notion further confers a salvific and eschatological dimension to the textile image. Although Alan of Lille's *Complaint of Nature* is more of a poetological text and has little explicit theological content, it was read in line with Christian salvation history.[194] In its reception history, the need for Nature's rehabilitation was understood to be part of a divine plan.[195] The idea of the fall of the human reverberated remarkably in the German reception of Alan of Lille's writings (the *Planctus*, and also the *Anticlaudianus*).[196] That Gertrude's visionary dress should be equally understood to be a complex image for time (nature's course) and salvation (divine intervention), stands therefore in a certain tradition of a textile culture laden with symbolic meaning. For Alan, the images on Nature's dress can be read 'like a book' (*In picture etenim libro umbratiliter legebatur...*), the textile teaching humility with letters (*In uestibus uero pictura suarum litterarum fidelitate docebat*).[197] Repeated connections between writing and textile images make *The Complaint of Nature* self-referential and at the same time a useful foil against which Gertrude's Easter Monday vision can be read: in both texts, albeit to different ends, textiles become the vehicle for representing different modes of time. Both Nature's gown and Gertrude's dress carry the notions of past (intention), present (need to be fixed), and future (transformation). As such – whether intended or not – the textile image externalises the abstract notion of salvation history, not despite but enhanced by realities of material culture.

The *botte* negotiates the mechanism of salvation in imaginary textiles that can be transformed and bathed in the 'golden light of divine grace'. At the core of this transformation lies the theological notion of forgiveness and redemption. In Gertrude's Easter Monday vision, there is a need to transform the dress before the bride can be perfected. This transformation is preceded by Gertrude's remorse which is expressed in her worry about the badly attached gems. These three steps to salvation – remorse, forgiveness, and completion – are integral to the *botte*'s philosophy.

Remorse in Gertrude's paschal vision is a moment of presence and immediacy with the textile image illustrating the shortcomings in her daily and religious conduct. This temporal aspect of remorse can also be seen in theological treatises of the late Middle Ages. During the fourteenth century, when the *Legatus* was redacted in the vernacular, the Dominican scholar Meister Eckhart preached about the meaning of presence at the moment of the recognition of sins. In the so-called *Talks of Instruction*, he elaborates that 'God is a God of the present' (*Got ist ein got der gegenwerticheit*), and that hence, when the sinner turns to him, the path he has left behind is acknowledged, but only present affairs are considered: *Ob er in anders nû bereit vindet, sô ensihet er niht ane, waz er vor gewesen ist.*[198] Sins can lead to a higher love for God and are therefore good as long as 'one regrets them' (*ob sie leit sint*): 'That is why God gladly accepts the harm of sins and has often tolerated it and allowed it to come to those whom He has chosen to prepare for great things'.[199] A similar theological value of sin is reflected in Gertrude's Easter Monday vision. Remorse is a key to divine grace (*militkeit*) and functions successfully as long as the conscience is truly regretful.[200] The *Legatus* engages with a merciful forgiveness for repented sins on an exegetical level, while the *botte* briefly wraps up the theological dimension in the final sentence of the chapter, enhancing the visibility of the sins shining in glory on Gertrude's visionary gown instead: 'Because the stains of sins eternally shine on us in praise of God, that one may recognise how gracious he is to those who regret their sins, and that he still does so many good things to us as if we had never acted against his will.'[201] Here we find a late medieval mystical view of the image producing what Niklaus Largier terms 'a sphere of immanence'.[202]

After remorse comes forgiveness, which is for Gertrude often portrayed in textile images. For example, at one instance, Gertrude sees that a deceased person's soul receives a red dress, to mark both the reward for and the distinction of her suffering in life.[203] As sins come to be represented as stains in one's spiritual garment, forgiveness through God only covers the blemishes with a golden plate; considering gold as an intensifier for anything visible, this means that the sins remain and become more visible, but they no longer disfigure the gown.[204]

The *botte* carries the message that human deeds are flawed, and need to be completed and perfected by divine grace.[205] Remorse, a good will, and enduring ailments are enough to 'clothe' the soul with reward as clothing in the *botte*'s visual language means salvation.[206] In this sense, when in a vision a deceased convent sister dressed in 'rose-coloured garments' (*rosevarben kleideren*) appears to Gertrude, the salvation status of the dead sister is marked by her garments in addition to her being accompanied by an adolescent Christ. Seeing the deceased in this outfit confirms to the entire convent from the visionary's perspective that the dead sister's soul is saved. Attempting a historical leap to the sisters of Helfta, Gertrude's vision of the textile, a visual marker of salvation, could have mediated a message that would have been comforting for the convent sisters who grieved for their loss.[207]

In contrast to the vision of a deceased person's status of salvation, Gertrude's own Easter Monday robe appears to her in a vision during her lifetime; and when it is transformed it illustrates the promise of an eventual reward, that of becoming the bride of Christ in the afterlife. Gertrude's vision of a clothed deceased sister offers, however, a different understanding of temporality as the confirmation of salvation occurs after the sister's death. The mechanism of remorse, forgiveness, and transformation initiated in the immediacy of the recognition of one's sins cannot be determined by Gertrude for someone else. She receives the confirmation only afterwards.

Yet, according to high and late medieval conceptions of temporality, there existed the possibility of post-mortem atonement. Purgatory as a topographical and mental space of punishment and purification offered the possibility of a prolonged process of penitence, extending the path to salvation beyond the actual death of the human body. Atonement in purgatory, though removed from the realm of the world, remained a corporeal form of purification. Yet internal remorse still played an important role. Both concepts – penance and purgatory – are arguably part of an increasingly theologically debated, and religiously practised, focus on the individual soul and the modality of suffering within an eschatological order. In thirteenth- and fourteenth-century bridal mysticism, penance, and purgatory are recurrent themes.[208] Purgatory is also present in the *botte* where it features as a gateway to heaven on which Gertrude can have influence through her prayer. She is said to release uncountable souls from purgatory.[209] Souls are released according to a pay-back principle: just as Gertrude can craft-pray garments for her friends, she can help souls with her prayers. In a vision of the mystical nuptials, Gertrude sees Christ sitting at a wedding table distributing gifts to everyone present, including those who are in purgatory. The gifts consist of words and letters that Gertrude has sung during Matins 'in divine love' (*in der götlichen liebe*): 'and the ineffable sweetness of the divine knowledge flowed into their souls from the latter [words and letters], and from the psalms, and responsories, and from each specific word.'[210] Gertrude's celebration of the daily office affects the souls in purgatory directly and seemingly immediately.[211]

The theme of forgiveness and purgatory in particular takes us back to where this chapter started, to the oldest transmitted portion of the *botte*, Gotha, Forschungsbibliothek, Chart. B 269. Considering the given manuscript context, aspects of temporality in connection to salvation in Gertrude's Easter Monday vision take on a codicological significance. The Gotha codex is given a distinct title by a late fourteenth-century medieval scribe: *fegfewr puch*, *Book of Purgatory*.[212] The timeframe of purgatory is an eschatological one. With visions and instructions to visions contained in the codex, the collection of texts deals with the possibility of imagining an end-time via a process of reading. Such an act of imagination is also what happens in Gertrude's vision of the dress as she is able to see at once, in the presence of the image, how all her time was spent and ordered from an end-of-time perspective.

The placement of Gertrude's vision in the Gotha codex just before *The Revelation of the Monk of Eynsham*, in which purgatory and the repentance of sins are central themes, means that the Easter Monday vision prepares the topic of the recognition of sins. Yet, its insertion between a didactic guide on visions and a narrative on purgatory makes it stand out, its iconographic programme allowing it to appear like a vignette. Its figurative programme of time and temporality is a significant strategy to represent linear time in a timeframe of salvation. Although '[t]ime, for much of the Middle Ages, was conceived as repetitive and circular, based on life cycles, seasonal change, liturgical routine',[213] the Christian notion of an end-time and an eternal afterlife made purgatory a space hard to fathom and even harder one to represent. Gertrude's visionary robe manages to represent time progressing towards an end in juxtaposition to the Last Judgement, 'at which time would be abolished and be replaced by eternity'.[214] The vision, however, is more than just prophetic by its foreshadowing of a final salvation in the future; rather, the momentary union between Christ and the bride of Christ during the paschal mass describes a state of 'contemplative consciousness of God's presence', one which mystics such as Hadewijch and Beatrice of Nazareth understood to be an 'eternity without time'.[215] The insertion of Gertrude's vision in a book entitled *Book of Purgatory* is not coincidental, as the vision's pictorial value translates time into space whilst undermining boundaries between linear time and circular time as well as no-time. The corporeal image of time, the visionary textile, is linked to an eschatological notion of redemption. The overall topic of the codex being declared as that of purgatory means that Gertrude's vision renders the idea of human imperfection (her neglectful behaviour is sinful) into the potential of grace (sins still shine and are integral components of the dress).

★ ★ ★

Gertrude's Easter Monday vision as recounted in the German tradition deploys the material aspects of the imaginary textile. Together with the dress being a proxy for a present which contains the past, in its textual presence, it performs what the *botte* declares to be its programme of *bildunge*, the process of imagination. Imagining Gertrude's life, the reader has an example in the visionary textile for the proclaimed salvific effects of the *botte*: corporeal images – and with them their textual performativity – turn into agents for divine grace.[216] The calendric structure of Gertrude's dress, marked by the repetitiveness of years, days, and hours, reflects the regular celebration of the liturgy; and it becomes clear that for Gertrude, liturgy is linked to the understanding of time.[217] Since the narrative composition of the *botte* follows a liturgical structure,[218] the imaginary material of the dress has a counterpart in the corporeal presence of the book, which likewise records Gertrude's life;[219] in this sense, the imaginary textile is structured and composed like the *botte*.[220] The multilayered fusion of bridal mysticism, scholastic theology, aspects of temporality, and monastic practice thus powerfully conveys the appeal of Gertrude's visionary programme, which was rooted in material culture.

FINAL REMARKS

In this book I have suggested that the vernacular corpus of Gertrude's visions challenges the long-standing idea that translations do not bear the same literary or historical weight as the supposed originals upon which they are based. Instead, the independent value and depth of redactions, especially those in other languages, has been highlighted, contributing to debates on vernacularity and manuscript culture. Hagiographic texts that have been redacted, especially when viewed in context of the reform movement, elicit a shadow history of late medieval piety wherein material culture infused mystical devotion. With redactors assimilating hagiographic traditions of rewriting saints' dossiers,[1] they offer us a better understanding of the social history of text production; we may speak of a social history here because we can observe the behaviour of scribes in a milieu united by common interests in matters concerning devotion. Practices of text production shaped reading practices in return, as many devotees became active redactors in the reception process. Studying the variety of manuscript transmission brings out the creative collaboration that medieval textuality entailed. It also shows how mystical devotion operated within a lifeworld in which material objects were charged with sacred power.

In many cases of multilingual redactions, we may not have transmitted text material until the late fourteenth or fifteenth centuries; yet what has come down to us deserves unpacking. By doing so in this study – with the *Legatus* and *botte/Trutta* material – we have found a highly-developed network of redactors who embedded their text material flexibly into new contexts. The earliest vernacular reception of the *Legatus divinae pietatis*, *ein botte der götlichen miltekeit*, demonstrates how religious texts were constantly reshaped to fit the multifaceted ways in which mystical devotion was practiced in the late Middle Ages. Just as the Helfta sisters formed a community that was governed by a multidimensional collective writing culture (expounded in Chapter 1), so did redactors – women and men alike – uphold a textual fluidity of the text material.

I hope to have contributed to research on medieval visionary texts and medieval devotion more broadly, by revealing that late medieval processes of translation, abbreviation, redaction, and rewriting were not perversions, but rather extensions, of the kinds of writing cultures that produced the Latin texts upon which they drew. As I have suggested in Chapter 2, redactors took on various functions in a dynamic manuscript culture, as their writing activities encompassed compiling, adapting, translating, recycling, integrating, omitting, and adding. They partook in the shaping of piety, as vernacularity with its tendency to performative and sensory language enabled a devotional culture of participation.[2]

The refractions of the manuscript transmission (as demonstrated in Chapter 3) reveal that redactors were cultural agents: they recast textual material, reacted to changes of piety, and generated new forms of devotional practice. As imaginative readers, they followed the call of Gertrude's mystical programme, which intended to facilitate encounters with the divine.

> Although in springtime the rose is far more delightful when, fresh and blooming, it gives off a sweet scent than it is in winter when, long since withered, people say that it did once smell sweet, nonetheless recalling the past does seem to kindle some small pleasure. For this reason I too long to offer a description, with what imagery I can muster, of what my littleness perceived in that most delightful vision, with your praise in mind. Then if some of my readers have perhaps received similar or greater favors, my account may stimulate them to give thanks. May I myself, by frequently recalling it, keep in check a little, through thanksgiving, the dark cloud of my negligence by this reflecting mirror which glitters with the sun.[3]

Multisensory mnemonic devices, which help to recall divine favours and stimulation, remained central in the vernacular reception history of the *Legatus*, even more so in an environment that was theoretically sceptical of material images when it came to contemplating the divine. The texts bear traces of the material cultures that surrounded them: 'corporeal images' continued to develop new meanings and reflecting on new interactions with material objects, both physical and imaginary. Vernacular (re)writings moved within a dynamic textuality which enabled and nurtured these processes.

Unprecedented attention to the German *ein botte der götlichen miltekeit* reflects historical contexts in which – and pragmatic functions with which – medieval redactors worked; moreover, it relates this practical framework to rhetorical techniques in the text itself by emphasising visionary vignettes that deal with contemplative and salvific writing and reading exercises. As I emphasise in my last three chapters, the performative potential of vernacular language becomes particularly evident in book and textile images, which stand in dialogue with a late medieval devotional culture in which expert craftsmanship was highly valued as part of a spiritual and quasi-monastic routine. The *botte*'s self-reflectivity facilitates a dynamic oscillation between the devotional book object and a fluid textuality. Following the idea of a redactorial culture, I hope that other translations based on Latin writings – such as the Old Swedish or the Middle English versions of the *Liber specialis gratiae* – can be similarly reassessed.[4]

One lingering problem in research on late medieval devotion is that mysticism and material culture are rarely considered together – one deals with the supposedly immaterial, the other with physical reality. In this book, I have examined correlations between the material and the mystical, analysing how the *Legatus* prepares the ground for a programme of 'corporeal images' that was fully embraced by the redactors of the *botte* and landed on fertile ground in reformed circles, in growing lay communities, and with single devotees. With the *botte*'s reception we see new frames of understanding added to the Helfta mysticism. The *botte*'s popularity among sisters of reformed late medieval German nunneries worked in two ways: on the one hand, the *botte* echoed a hagiographic tradition of personal convent mysticism similar to that of sisterbooks; on the other hand, it was in line with the new regime of contemplative reading practices, which aimed at salvific effects through a text's reception in reading and copying. The *botte* redactors acknowledged that processes of imagination are crucial for this aim by implementing a programmatic self-reflectivity of the book, which is based on a participatory principle and is aligned with the reader's mystical education. Imagination (*bildunge*) and 'corporeal images' (*lipliche bilder*) prove key concepts in the *botte*'s treatment of visions. This nexus of visions and 'corporeal imagery' is entwined with material culture, as seen in the *botte*'s treatment of textile images.

We sometimes think about women as barred from sacred material, when my analysis has demonstrated that, in fact, they often produced it. Women were scribes and/or copyists and/or redactors, and women were embroiderers, not just sewing textiles in their prayers, but in reality. Redacting texts according to material concerns and textile production, for instance, behave similarly: both these activities were creative processes in which women engaged with and even produced divine or sanctified artefacts – whether this be a sanctified mystical text or a liturgical book or vestments. Surviving textiles from the

Middle Ages show us that the synergies between contemplative practices and handicraft impacted the artistic outcomes. Thanks to extant religious textiles from Halberstadt (discussed in Chapter 6), we can in some cases even map between Gertrude's visionary world and the sacred fabrics originating from her diocese. But even for the late medieval reception history of the *Legatus*, we find that rituals for clothing sacred sculptures and imaginary craft-prayers echo the same visionary world in new ways: ways that a late medieval piety, which was governed by observant tendencies and increasing lay devotion, would even promote.

The *Legatus* had many different resonances in late medieval vernacular contexts. Moving from a review of historical research on the status and function of text and textiles within late medieval monastic culture to the way in which such cultures form the basis for an imaginary transformation within the literary creation, Chapters 3 to 6 have shown that the *botte*'s emphasis on embodied writing and reading actively shaped the late medieval devotional landscape. Both book and textile production were processes in which the medieval readers of the *botte*, predominantly women, engaged. The importance of material culture was heightened and sensitised in late medieval piety.

Texts dealing with mystical visions are certainly primarily religious, but as they reflect on material objects – textiles, gems, flowers, books, and other objects – in relation to how language is applied to describe the spirituality of these objects, they may also be read as a form of art critique: visions invite the reader to contemplate imaginary objects in the same way that an art object compels an act of contemplation. Material culture informs a mystical programme and invites processes of imagination by employing a medium-mnemonic language. In the earliest transmission of the *botte*, the fabrication of a garment comes to embody a spiritual status and a transformation. The scribal work of a redactor mirrors this textile image: a redactor is a craftsman working the given material into a new text.

APPENDIX I

MANUSCRIPT TRANSMISSION WITH CATALOGUES

The following list contains all known manuscripts belonging to the medieval transmission of the *Legatus*, both Latin and German. It also lists the dates and provenances, as far as known, and indicates the library catalogues. If applicable, the conventional abbreviation for the manuscript is indicated in square brackets following the manuscript shelf mark and the folios. The manuscripts are categorised by the text they contain and ordered by chronology.[1]

EIN BOTTE DER GÖTLICHEN MILTEKEIT

Gotha, Forschungsbibliothek, Chart. B 269, fol. 25r–v

Late 14th century, North Bavaria

> Eisermann, Falk. 'Chart B 269.' *Katalog der deutschsprachigen mittelalterlichen Handschriften der Forschungsbibliothek Gotha.* http://bilder.manuscripta-mediaevalia.de/hs//projekt-Gotha-pdfs/Chart_B_269.pdf.

Dresden, Sächsische Landesbibliothek, Hs M 243, fols. 2r–193r, 222v–224r, 236r–252r, 252v–262r
[Wieland: D]

c. 1435, Augustinian nunnery Inzigkofen

Hoffmann, Werner J. 'Mscr.Dresd.M.243.' *Tiefenerschließung und Digitalisierung der deutschsprachigen mittelalterlichen Handschriften der Sächsischen Landesbibliothek, Staats- und Universitätsbibliothek (SLUB) Dresden.* www .manuscripta-mediaevalia.de/dokumente/html/obj31600080.

Schnorr v. Carolsfeld, Franz. *Katalog der Handschriften der Sächsischen Landesbibliothek zu Dresden.* Vol. 2. 2nd edition. Dresden: Sächsische Landesbibliothek, 1981. 509.

Munich, Bayerische Staatsbibliothek, Cgm 5292, fols. 2r–104v, 132r–150r, 154r–211r
[Wieland: M]

1448, Augustinian nunnery Inzigkofen

Fechter, Werner. *Deutsche Handschriften des 15. und 16. Jahrhunderts aus der Bibliothek des ehemaligen Augustinerchorfrauenstifts Inzigkofen.* Arbeiten zur Landeskunde Hohenzollerns Vol. 15. Sigmaringen: Thorbecke, 1997. 80–83.

Schneider, Karin. *Die datierten Handschriften der Bayerischen Staatsbibliothek München Pt. 1: Die deutschen Handschriften bis 1450.* Datierte Handschriften in Bibliotheken der Bundesrepublik Deutschland Vol. 4. Stuttgart: Hiersemann, 1994. 52–53.

Wunderle, Elisabeth. *Die deutschen Handschriften der Bayerischen Staatsbibliothek München. Die mittelalterlichen Handschriften aus Cgm 5255–7000 einschließlich der althochdeutschen Fragmente Cgm 5248.* Catalogus codicum manu scriptorum Bibliotheca Monacensis Vol. 5: Editio altera Pt 9. Wiesbaden: Harrassowitz, 2018, 56–60.

Vienna, Schottenstift, Cod. 308, fols. 44r–71v, 72v–74r
[Wieland: w2; Ringler: W]

1451, library of Augustinian nunnery Inzigkofen (provenance not fully determined)

Horninger, Heidelinde, and Franz Lackner. *Die datierten Handschriften in Wien außerhalb der Österreichischen Nationalbibliothek bis zum Jahre 1600.* Vol. 1. Katalog der datierten Handschriften in lateinischer Schrift in Österreich. Vienna: Verlag der Österreichischen Akademie der Wissenschaften, 1981. 144.

Hübl, Albert. *Catalogus codicum manu scriptorum qui in Bibliotheca Monasterii B.M.V. ad Scotos Vindobonae servantur.* Vienna: Braumüller, 1899. 254–56.

Freiburg im Breisgau, Universitätsbibliothek, Hs. 202, fols. 1r–125r, 157r–177v

[Wieland: F1]

1474–1476, East Swabian nunnery

Hagenmaier, Winfried. *Die deutschen mittelalterlichen Handschriften der Universitätsbibliothek und die mittelalterlichen Handschriften anderer öffentlicher Sammlungen.* Kataloge der Universitätsbibliothek Freiburg im Breisgau Vol. 1: Die Handschriften der Universitätsbibliothek und anderer öffentlicher Sammlungen in Freiburg im Breisgau und Umgebung Pt. 4. Wiesbaden: Harrassowitz, 1988. 190–91.

Freiburg im Breisgau, Erzbischöfliches Archiv, Hs. 31, fols. 1r–163v, 210r–237v

1476–1478, East Swabia

Hagenmaier, Winfried. *Die deutschen mittelalterlichen Handschriften der Universitätsbibliothek und die mittelalterlichen Handschriften anderer öffentlicher Sammlungen.* Kataloge der Universitätsbibliothek Freiburg im Breisgau Vol. 1: Die Handschriften der Universitätsbibliothek und anderer öffentlicher Sammlungen in Freiburg im Breisgau und Umgebung Pt. 4. Wiesbaden: Harrassowitz, 1988. 238.

Brussels, Bibliothèque Royale, cod. 8507–09, fols. 1r–132v

[Wieland: B]

Second half of the 15th century, Dominican nunnery St Nikolaus in undis Strasbourg

Bodemann, Ulrike. *Katalog der deutschsprachigen illustrierten Handschriften des Mittelalters.* Vol. 6 Pt. 3/4. Munich: Beck, 2005. 266–68.

Van den Gheyn, J. *Catalogues des manuscrits de la Bibliothèque Royale de Belgique.* Vol. 6: Histoire – Hagiographie. Brussels: Lamertin, 1905. 381.

Nuremberg, Stadtbibliothek, Cent. VII, 62, fols. 98r–100r

[Wieland: n]

Second half of the 15th century, Dominican nunnery, St Katharina Nuremberg

Schneider, Karin, and Heinz Zirnbauer. *Die deutschen mittelalterlichen Handschriften.* Die Handschriften der Stadtbibliothek Nürnberg Vol. 1. Wiesbaden: Harrassowitz, 1965. 367–70.

London, University College, MS Germ. 24, fol. 12v

1493, Charterhouse Buxheim

> Coveney, Dorothy K. *A Descriptive Catalogue of Manuscripts in the Library of University College, London.* London: Printed for University of London, University College, 1935. 72–79.

Überlingen, Leopold-Sophien-Bibliothek, Ms. 26, fols. 84vb–85vb

1497/98, Dominican nunnery Zoffingen

> Heitzmann, Christian. 'Die mittelalterlichen Handschriften der Leopold-Sophien-Bibliothek in Überlingen.' *Schriften des Vereins für Geschichte des Bodensees und seiner Umgebung* 120 (2002): 65–69.

St Gall, Stiftsbibliothek, Cod. Sang. 973, pp. 476–480
[Wieland: ga2]

> 1498, Franciscan Tertiaries Wonnenstein near St Gall

> von Scarpatetti, Beat Matthias, Rudolf Gamper, and Marlis Stähli. *Die Handschriften der Bibliotheken St Gallen – Zürich in alphabetischer Reihenfolge.* Katalog der datierten Handschriften in der Schweiz in lateinischer Schrift vom Anfang des Mittelalters bis 1550 Vol. 3. Dietikon-Zürich: Graf, 1991. 83

> Scherrer, Gustav. *Verzeichnis der Handschriften der Stiftsbibliothek von St Gallen.* Halle: Verlag der Buchhandlung des Waisenhauses, 1875. 368–69.

Augsburg, Benediktinerabtei St Stephan, Hs 38, fols. 2r–65r, 84v–97r, 100r–144r
[Wieland: A]

> 15th century, Charterhouse Buxheim

> Wieland, Otmar. *Gertrud von Helfta. ein botte der götlichen miltekeit.* Studien und Mitteilungen zur Geschichte des Benediktiner-Ordens und seiner Zweige. Ergänzungsband 22. Ottobeuren: Bayerische Benediktinerakademie, 1973. 13–14.

Augsburg, Universitätsbibliothek, Cod. III. 1. 4° 30, fols. 104v–106r

Late 15th century, Fransiscan nunnery Memmingen/Kirchheim

> Schneider, Karin. *Deutsche mittelalterliche Handschriften der Universitätsbibliothek Augsburg. Die Signaturengruppen Cod. I.3 und Cod.*

III.1. Die Handschriften der Universitätsbibliothek Augsburg Vol. 2: Die deutschen Handschriften Pt. 1. Wiesbaden: Harrassowitz, 1988. 314–18.

Wrocław, Biblioteka Kapitulna (no shelf mark), fols. 1r–154v/ 155r [lost]

Late 15th century, Augustinian nunnery Inzigkofen? (belonged to prioress Countess Anna Dorothea von Hohenzollern-Haigerloch in the 17th century, might have contained the *Trutta*-legend)

Klapper, Joseph. 'Breslau, Diözesanarchiv, 9 (ohne Signatur).' www .bbaw.de/forschung/dtm/HSA/breslau_700292490000.html.

Munich, Bayerische Staatsbibliothek, Cgm 843, fols. 86v–90r
[Wieland: m1]

Late 15th/early 16th century, Northern-Bavarian nunnery

Schneider, Karin. *Die deutschen Handschriften der Bayerischen Staatsbibliothek München. Cgm 691–867.* Catalogus codicum manu scriptorum Bibliothecae Monacensis Vol. 5: Editio altera Pt. 5: Codices Germanicos 691–867 complectens. Wiesbaden: Harrassowitz, 1984. 584–92.

Munich, Bayerische Staatsbibliothek, Cgm 861, fols. 72r–76v
[Wieland: m2]

1504, Dominican nunnery St Ursula Augsburg

Schneider, Karin. *Die deutschen Handschriften der Bayerischen Staatsbibliothek München. Cgm 691–867.* Catalogus codicum manu scriptorum Bibliothecae Monacensis Vol. 5: Editio altera Pt. 5: Codices Germanicos 691–867 complectens. Wiesbaden: Harrassowitz, 1984. 692–93.

Solothurn, Zentralbibliothek, Cod. S 458, fols. 63v–64v, 70v–71v, 96v–98v, 101r–105r

1507, Dominican nunnery St Michael Bern

von Scarpatetti, Beat Matthias, Rudolf Gamper, and Marlis Stähli. *Die Handschriften der Bibliotheken St Gallen – Zürich in alphabetischer Reihenfolge.* Katalog der datierten Handschriften in der Schweiz in lateinischer Schrift vom Anfang des Mittelalters bis 1550 Vol. 3. Dietikon-Zürich: Graf, 1991. 134–35.

Heidelberg, Universitätsbibliothek, Heid. Hs. 33, fols. 221r–266v
[Wieland: H]

1516/1517, South-Rhine Franconian?

Bartsch, Karl. *Die altdeutschen Handschriften der Universitätsbibliothek in Heidelberg*. Katalog der Handschriften der Universitäts-Bibliothek in Heidelberg Vol. 1. Heidelberg: Koester, 1887.

Sarnen, Benediktinerkollegium, Cod. chart. 215, fols. 59v–66r

First quarter of the 16th century, North-East High Alemannic

Bretscher-Gisiger, Charlotte, and Rudolf Gamper. *Katalog der mittelalterlichen Handschriften der Klöster Muri und Hermetschwil*. Dietikon-Zürich: Graf, 2005. 350–3. www.urs-graf-verlag.com/pdf/MSMuriK.pdf.

St Gall, Stiftsbibliothek, Cod. Sang. 506, fols. 2r–27v, 42r–54r
[Wieland: ga1]

First half of the 16th century, South-Alemannic

Scherrer, Gustav. *Verzeichnis der Handschriften der Stiftsbibliothek von St Gallen*. Halle: Verlag der Buchhandlung des Waisenhauses, 1875. 159-60.

von Scarpatetti, Beat Matthias, and Philipp Lenz. *Die Handschriften der Stiftsbibliothek St Gallen*. Vol. 2: Abt. III/2: Codices 450–546: Liturgica, Libri precum, deutsche Gebetbücher, Spiritualia, Musikhandschriften. 9.–16. Jahrhundert. Wiesbaden: Harrassowitz, 2008. 222–25.

Rastatt, Historische Bibliothek der Stadt im Ludwig-Wilhelm-Gymnasium, Cod. K 152, Hs 3, fols. 1r–55r

First half of the 16th century, Cistercian nuns Lichtenthal?

Köhler, Jakob. 'Die Handschriften und Inkunabeldrucke der Rastatter Gymnasiumsbibliothek.' *Großherzogliches Gymnasium Rastatt. Jahresbericht für das Schuljahr 1885–1886*. Rastatt: Vogelin, 1886. 3.

Eichstätt, Abtei St Walburg, Ms germ. 23, fols. 58r–60r
[Wieland: e]

1611, Benedictine nun Eugenie Peiserin (convent name: Magdalena) Eichstätt

Lechner, Joseph. *Die spätmittelalterliche Handschriftengeschichte der Benediktinerinnenabtei St Walburg/Eichstätt (By.)*. Eichstätter Studien Vol. 2. Münster: Aschendorff, 1937. 81–82.

Freiburg im Breisgau, Universitätsbibliothek, Hs. 186, pp. 1–101, 134–154, 161–258

[Wieland: F2]

1643, Augustinian nunnery Inzigkofen?

> Hagenmaier, Winfried. *Die abendländischen neuzeitlichen Handschriften der Universitätsbibliothek Freiburg im Breisgau.* Kataloge der Universitätsbibliothek Freiburg im Breisgau Vol. 1: Die Handschriften der Universitätsbibliothek und anderer öffentlicher Sammlungen in Freiburg im Breisgau und Umgebung Pt. 5. Wiesbaden: Harrassowitz, 1996. 37.

OTHER GERMAN REDACTION OF THE *LEGATUS*

Karlsruhe, Badische Landesbibliothek, Cod. Lichtenthal 89, fols. 4r–758v

1566, Cistercian nuns Lichtenthal

> Heinzer, Felix, and Gerhard Stamm. *Die Handschriften von Lichtenthal. Mit einem Anhang: Die heute noch im Kloster Lichtenthal befindlichen Handschriften des 12. bis 16. Jahrhunderts.* Die Handschriften der Badischen Landesbibliothek in Karlsruhe Vol. 9. Wiesbaden: Harrassowitz, 1987. 210.

> Längin, Theodor. *Deutsche Handschriften.* Die Handschriften der Badischen Landesbibliothek in Karlsruhe. Beilage Vol. 2 Pt. 2. Wiesbaden: Harrassowitz, 1974. 91 and 174–785.

TRUTTA-LEGEND

Vienna, Österreichische Nationalbibliothek, Cod. 3042, fols. 405ra–419vb

Single visions in other saints' entries: fols. 33va–34ra, 311va–312vb, 330ra–332ra

[Williams-Krapp: W3; Wieland: w1]

1442, Dominicans Vienna?

> Menhardt, Hermann. *Verzeichnis der altdeutschen literarischen Handschriften der Österreichischen Nationalbibliothek.* Vol. 2. Veröffentlichungen des Instituts für deutsche Sprache und Literatur Vol. 13. Berlin: Akademie-Verlag, 1961. 836–37.

> Unterkircher, Franz. *Die datierten Handschriften der Österreichischen Nationalbibliothek von 1401 bis 1450.* Vol. 1. Katalog der datierten Handschriften in lateinischer Schrift in Österreich Vol. 2. Vienna: Verlag der Österreichischen Akademie der Wissenschaften, 1971. 47–48.

Graz, Universitätsbibliothek, Ms. 64, fols. 389rb–404ra

Single visions in other saints' entries: fols. 29vb–30rb, 294va–295vb, 312va–314va

[Williams-Krapp: Gr1; Wieland: gr 1]

Mid-fifteenth century, Military Order of St George Millstadt

Kern, Anton. *Die Handschriften der Universitätsbibliothek Graz.* Vol. 1. Verzeichnis der Handschriften im deutschen Reich Vol. 2. Leipzig: Harrassowitz, 1942. 29.

Kern, Anton, and Maria Mairhold. *Die Handschriften der Universitätsbibliothek Graz.* Vol. 3. Handschriftenverzeichnisse Österreichischer Bibliotheken. Steiermark Vol. 3. Vienna: Prachner, 1967. 25.

Graz, Universitätsbibliothek, Ms. 75, fols. 237rb–246rb

Single visions in other saints' entries: fols. 18ra–18rb, 175ra–175vb, 187va–189ra

[Williams-Krapp: Gr2; Wieland: gr 2]

Mid-fifteenth century, Military Order of St George Millstadt

Beier, Christine. *Die illuminierten Handschriften und Inkunabeln der Universitätsbibliothek Graz: Die illuminierten Handschriften 1400 bis 1550.* Vol. 1. Österreichische Akademie der Wissenschaften, phil.-hist. Klasse, Denkschriften 390; Institut für Kunstgeschichte der Universität Wien; Veröffentlichungen der Kommission für Schrift und Buchwesen des Mittelalters Vol. 5 Pt. 1. Vienna: Verlag der Österreichischen Akademie der Wissenschaften, 2010. 25–27.

Kern, Anton. *Die Handschriften der Universitätsbibliothek Graz.* Vol. 1. Verzeichnis der Handschriften im deutschen Reich Vol. 2. Leipzig: Harrassowitz, 1942. 34.

Kern, Anton, and Maria Mairhold. *Die Handschriften der Universitätsbibliothek Graz.* Vol. 3. Handschriftenverzeichnisse Österreichischer Bibliotheken. Steiermark Vol. 3. Vienna: Prachner, 1967. 26.

Klosterneuburg, Stiftsbibliothek, cod. 711, fols. 460va–477rb

Single visions in other saints' entries: fols. 41va–42ra, 359va–360vb, 379vb–382ra

[Williams-Krapp: Kl1]

Second half of the fifteenth century, Augustinian convent or nunnery Klosterneuburg?

Zeibig, Hartmann J. 'Die deutschen Handschriften der Stiftsbibliothek zu Klosterneuburg.' *Serapeum* 11 (1850): 101–9, 123–25, at 103.

Pécs, Klimo Könyvtàr Bibliothek, AA. II. 21, fols. 450rb–466vb

Single visions in other saints' entries: fols. 31vb–32rb, 330va–332rb, 355va–358ra

[Williams-Krapp: Pc1]

1455, Vienna? (diocesan library of Pécs in the 18th century)

Vizkelety, András. *Beschreibendes Verzeichnis der altdeutschen Handschriften in ungarischen Bibliotheken.* Vol. 2: Budapest, Debrecen, Eger, Esztergom, Györ, Kalocsa, Pannonhalma, Pápa, Pécs, Szombathely. Wiesbaden: Harrassowitz, 1973. 247–49.

LEIPZIG LEGATUS

Leipzig, Universitätsbibliothek, Ms 827, fols. 25v–148r

First quarter of the 14th century, Benedictine Abbey Pegau

Märker, Almuth. 'Ms 827.' *Tiefenerschließung und Digitalisierung der deutschsprachigen mittelalterlichen Handschriften der Sächsischen Landesbibliothek, Staats- und Universitätsbibliothek (SLUB) Dresden.* www.manuscripta-mediaevalia.de/dokumente/html/obj31571101.

LEGATUS DIVINÆ PIETATIS, ALSO 'STANDARD' *LEGATUS*

Bonn, Universitätsbibliothek, S 726, fols. 361ra–364vb

1410/20, Erfurt, Mathias Pahe

Finger, Heinz. *Handschriftencensus Rheinland. Erfassung mittelalterlicher Handschriften im rheinischen Landesteil von Nordrhein-Westfalen mit einem Inventar.* Vol. 1: Aachen (Diözesanarchiv) bis Köln (Diözesan- und Dombibliothek) (Nr 1–1327). Schriften der Universitäts- und Landesbibliothek Düsseldorf Vol. 18. Wiesbaden: Reichert, 1993. 166.

Geiß, Jürgen. *Katalog der mittelalterlichen Handschriften der Universitäts- und Landesbibliothek Bonn.* Berlin: De Gruyter, 2015. 234–46.

Gildemeister, Johann, Anton Klette, and Joseph Staender. *Chirographorvm in Bibliotheca Academica Bonnensi servatorvm catalogvs.* Vol. 2: Quo libri descripti svnt praeter orientales relicvi. Bonn: Weber, 1858–76. 190.

Munich, Bayerische Staatsbibliothek, Clm 15332

[Solesmes-edition: B]

1412, Charterhouse Buxheim (later Premonstratensian Monastery Roggenburg)

Halm, Karl Felix, Georg von Laubmann, Wilhelm Meyer, and Johann Andreas Schmeller. *Catalogus codicum latinorum Bibliothecae Regiae Monacensis.* Vol. 2 Pt. 3: Codices num. 15121–21313 complectens. Catalogus codicum manu scriptorum Bibliothecae Regiae Monacensis Vol. 4 Pt. 3: Codices latinos continens. Munich: Bayerische Staatsbibliothek, 1878. 14.

Trier, Stadtbibliothek, Cod. 77/1061, fols. 1r–135r

[Solesmes-edition: T]

15th century

Keuffer, Max. *Beschreibendes Verzeichnis der Handschriften der Stadtbibliothek zu Trier.* Vol. 1: Bibel-Texte und Kommentare. Trier: Lintz, 1888. 60–61.

Cambridge, MA, Houghton Library, Ms. Riant 90, fols. 71r–182v

c. 1450, Charterhouse Cologne

De Germon, L., and L. Polain. *Catalogue de la bibliothèque de feu M. Le Comte Riant.* Pt. 2 Vol. 1. Paris: Picard, 1899. LXIII–LXIX.

Moscow, Rossijskaja Gosudarstvennaya Biblioteka, Fonds 183/281, fols. 181r–183v

Mid-15th century, Charterhouse Erfurt

Barow-Vassilevitch, Daria, and Marie-Luise Heckmann. *Abendländische Handschriften des Mittelalters und der frühen Neuzeit in den Beständen der Russischen Staatsbibliothek (Moskau).* Wiesbaden: Harrasswitz, 2016. 94–98.

Würzburg, Universitätsbibliothek, M. ch. f. 241, fols. 113v–129v

1459, East Franconia

Thurn, Hans. *Die Handschriften aus St. Stephan zu Würzburg.* Die Handschriften der Universitätsbibliothek Würzburg Vol. 2 Pt. 2: Handschriften aus Benediktinischen Provenienzen II. Wiesbaden: Harrassowitz, 1986. 90–2.

Mainz, Stadtbibliothek, Hs I 13, fols. 136ra–225va

[Solesmes-edition: Z]

Third quarter of the 15th century, Charterhouse Mainz

List, Gerhard, and Gerhardt Powitz. *Die Handschriften der Stadtbibliothek Mainz*. Vol. 1: Hs I 1 – Hs I 150. Wiesbaden: Harrassowitz, 1990. 40–42.

Darmstadt, Universitäts- und Landesbibliothek, Hs 84, fols. 27v–176v

[Solesmes-edition: K]

1473, Charterhouse Cologne

Staub, Kurt Hans, and Hermann Knaus. *Jüngere theologische Texte*. Die Handschriften der Hessischen Landes- und Hochschulbibliothek Darmstadt Vol. 5 Pt. 1. Wiesbaden: Harrassowitz, 2001. 26–28.

Berlin, Staatsbibliothek Preußischer Kulturbesitz, Ms. theol. lat. oct. 89, fol. 201r

Fourth quarter of the 15th century, Charterhouse Erfurt

Braun-Niehr, Beate. *Die theologischen lateinischen Handschriften in Octavo der Staatsbibliothek zu Berlin Preußischer Kulturbesitz*. Vol. 1 Staatsbibliothek zu Berlin Preußischer Kulturbesitz. Kataloge der Handschriftenabteilung. Erste Reihe: Handschriften, Vol. 3 Pt. 1. Wiesbaden: Harrassowitz, 2007. 138–57.

Vienna, Österreichische Nationalbibliothek, Cod. 4224, fols. 83r–282v

[Solesmes-edition: W]

1482–1490, Benedictine Abbey Donauwörth

Academia Caesarea Vindobonensis. *Tabulae codicum manu scriptorum praeter graecos et orientales in Bibliotheca Palatina Vindobonensi asservatorum*. Vol. 3: Cod. 3501–5000. Vienna: Gerold, 1869. 209.

Unterkircher, Franz. *Die datierten Handschriften der Österreichischen Nationalbibliothek von 1451 bis 1500*. Vol. 1. Katalog der datierten Handschriften in lateinischer Schrift in Österreich Vol. 3. Vienna: Verlag der Österreichischen Akademie der Wissenschaften, 1974. 119–20.

Weimar, Herzogin Anna Amalia Bibliothek, Q 49, fols. 163r–208v

1490–1494, Benedictine Abbey Erfurt OSB

Eifler, Matthias, and Betty C. Bushey. *Die lateinischen Handschriften bis 1600*. Vol. 2: Quarthandschriften (Q). Bibliographien und Kataloge der

Herzogin Anna Amalia Bibliothek zu Weimar. Die lateinischen Handschriften bis 1600 Vol. 2. Wiesbaden: Harrassowitz, 2012. 249–63.

Uppsala, Universitetsbibliotek, Cod. C 517m, fols. 30v–173v

Late 15th century, South Germany

Andersson-Schmitt, Margarete, and Hagan Halberg. *Mittelalterliche Handschriften der Universitätsbibliothek Uppsala. Katalog über die C- Sammlung.* Vol. 5: C 401–550. Acta Bibliothecae R. Universitatis Upsaliensis Vol 26 Pt. 5 Stockholm: Almqvist u. Wiksell International, 1992. 306–07.

Augsburg, Staats- und Stadtbibliothek, 8° Cod. 203, fols. 55r–57v

First quarter of the 16th century, Charterhouse Buxheim

Spilling, Herrad. *Die Handschriften der Staats- und Stadtbibliothek Augsburg 2° Cod 101–250.* Handschriftenkataloge der Staats- und Stadtbibliothek Augsburg Vol. 3. Wiesbaden: Harrassowitz, 1984. 193–96.

PRAYERS FROM *LEGATUS* II, 4[2]

Darmstadt, Universitäts- und Landesbibliothek, Hs 2772, fols. 61r, 90r

c. 1425, Charterhouse Collogne

Achten, Gerard, Leo Eizenhöfer, and Hermann Knaus. *Die lateinischen Gebetbuchhandschriften.* Die Handschriften der Hessischen Landes- und Hochschulbibliothek Darmstadt Vol. 3. Wiesbaden: Harrassowitz, 1972. 71–79.

Munich, Universitätsbibliothek, 8° Cod. ms. 193, fol. 75v

Second third of the 15th century, Swabia

Daniel, Natalia. *Die lateinischen mittelalterlichen Handschriften der Universitätsbibliothek München. Die Handschriften aus der Oktavreihe.* Die Handschriften der Universitätsbibliothek München Vol. 4. Wiesbaden: Harrassowitz, 1989. 136–37.

Kornrumpf, Gisela, and Paul-Gerhard Völker. *Die deutschen mittelalterlichen Handschriften der Universitätsbibliothek München.* Die Handschriften der Universitätsbibliothek München Vol. 1. Wiesbaden: Harrassowitz, 1968. 236–37.

St Gall, Stiftsbibliothek, Cod. Sang. 519, pp. 77–78

Before 1439, Benedictine Abbey St Gall

> von Scarpatetti, Beat Matthias, and Philipp Lenz. *Die Handschriften der Stiftsbibliothek St. Gallen.* Vol. 2: Abt. III/2: Codices 450–546: Liturgica, Libri precum, deutsche Gebetbücher, Spiritualia, Musikhandschriften. 9.–16. Jahrhundert. Wiesbaden: Harrassowitz, 2008. 282–303.

Weimar, Herzogin Anna Amalia Bibliothek, Oct 52, fol. 224v

First half of the 15th century, Charterhouse Erfurt

> Bushey, Betty C., and Hartmut Broszinsky. *Die lateinischen Handschriften bis 1600.* Vol. 1: Fol max, Fol und Oct. Bibliographien und Kataloge der Herzogin Anna Amalia Bibliothek zu Weimar. Die lateinischen Handschriften bis 1600 Vol. 1. Wiesbaden: Harrassowitz, 2004. 267–87.

Weimar, Herzogin Anna Amalia Bibliothek, Oct 62, fol. 54v

15th century, Charterhouse Erfurt

> Bushey, Betty C., and Hartmut Broszinsky. *Die lateinischen Handschriften bis 1600.* Vol. 1: Fol max, Fol und Oct. Bibliographien und Kataloge der Herzogin Anna Amalia Bibliothek zu Weimar. Die lateinischen Handschriften bis 1600 Vol. 1. Wiesbaden: Harrassowitz, 2004. 363–71.

Frankfurt, Universitätsbibliothek, ms. Praed. 169, fol. 315r

c. 1490, Central Rhine, Cistercians?

> Powitz, Gerhardt. *Die Handschriften des Dominikanerklosters und des Leonhardstifts in Frankfurt am Main.* Kataloge der Stadt- und Universitätsbibliothek Frankfurt am Main Vol. 2 Pt. 1: Die Handschriften der Stadt- und Universitätsbibliothek Frankfurt am Main. Frankfurt a.M.: Klostermann, 1968. 372–80.

Brussels, Bibliothèque Royale, Cod. 21600 (1639), fol. 146v

16th century

> Van den Gheyn, J. *Catalogues des manuscrits de la Bibliothèque Royale de Belgique.* Vol. 3: Théologie. Brussels: Lamertin, 1903. 52–56.

APPENDIX II

TRANSCRIPTIONS AND TRANSLATIONS

The following transcriptions aim to make two uniquely transmitted texts in the German reception of the *Legatus* available. The Carnival Prayers, transmitted in Munich, Bayerische Staatsbibliothek, Cgm 86, are inspired by the German redaction *ein botte der götlichen miltekeit* (Ch. 77 in Wieland's edition); the short treatise on the benefits of contemplating Christ's Passion quotes a passage from the *botte* (Ch. 89) and appears in London, University College, MS Germ. 24, a fifteenth-century codex from the Buxheim Charterhouse.

In the following transcriptions, folio numbers are indicated in square brackets ([...]). Paragraph breaks are adopted (which only occurs once, in the London codex). The variances u/v, u/ŭ, u/ü, ŭ/ü, j/i, j/y, y/ÿ are retained, but long ſ is always transcribed as round s. German sz is spelled ß. Rubricated words are printed in **bold**. Abbreviations are silently resolved. Verbs with prefixes that are written apart in the manuscripts but that morphologically belong together, are written as one word (for example, *er zirnet* becomes *erzirnet* in the transcription). Similarly, words with suffixes or prefixes are written together (for instance, *ernst lichen* is, in the transcription, *ernstlichen*). In order to facilitate the reading, I have introduced minimal modern punctuation. Capitalisation has been introduced at the beginning of sentences, for the word *Creutz*, which is mostly capitalized, and for proper names, while it has been suppressed for conjunctions that are sometimes capitalized in the manuscripts. All major editorial emendations are marked in the footnotes, which function as an apparatus. Additions to otherwise fragmentary sentences are made in angled brackets (<example>) and noted in the apparatus. Manuscript spellings are diplomatically transcribed in the apparatus, including the indication of line breaks represented with a single bar (|). Scribal corrections are also displayed, meaning that erased words in the manuscripts are presented as crossed out (~~example~~).

The principal purpose of the translations is to make the transcribed texts intelligible to non-specialist readers, which means that some ambiguous passages had to be interpreted for the sake of comprehensibility. I have attempted to translate every word in the primary source in order to give an accurate account of the texts. However, the English idiom has been given preference over a literal translation. In contrast to the original texts, paragraph breaks have been introduced to facilitate the reading.

CARNIVAL PRAYERS

Munich, Bayerische Staatsbibliothek, Cgm 861

[72r] Ain selige[1] yvnckfraw trŭt genant, die[2] bat zŭ ainer vasnacht zeit vnsern heren vnd sprach, her, was sol ich dir die zeit zŭ lob vnd ze denst volbringen, das ich dich gŭtes mütes mug machen, so dich die welt also ser erzirnet mit [72v] jrem sintlichen leben? Da antwurt vnser her, dŭ solt die drey tag beten, alle tag iij pater noster fir die grosen vuer, die mir enboten wirt in disen iij tagen. Das erst sprich zŭ lob der yebŭng meinens[3] hertzen in [73r] einem[4] hailigen[5] gedencken meinem mitleiden, meinem hertzen, meiner grose lieb, die ich gehebt hab zŭ menschlichem geschlecht von ebigkait vnd besunder xxxiij yar, die weil ich aŭf disem [73v] ertrich was; vnd opfer das erst pater noster meinem himlischan vater fir alle die besen denck vnd bos lust vnd bos willen vnd valsche bose liebin, die ietz die menschen[6] zŭ ain ander haben vnd volbringen in disen iij tagen in yren hertzen. [74r] Das ander pater noster sprich zu lob[7] der yebüng meines mundes, meiner ler vnd bredig, meinem ernstlichen bot, meinen vasten vnd abrechenlichait; vnd[8] opfer das meinem himlichen vater fur all die yrige [74v] verlasne wort vnd schantliche liad[9], die gesüngen vnd geret werden, vnd für die[10] grose freserey vnd vnmesigkait, die die welt volbringt in disen iij tagen. Das[11] drit pater noster [75r] sprich zŭ lob dem hailigen gaist, wercken vnd der grosen yebüng, vnd alle meinem pitern leiden vnd marter vnd ellenden tod, das ich xxxiij yar geliten hon; vnd opfer das pater noster meinem himlischen [75v] vater fur die grosen vnweys vnd vngebert vnd abgeterey mit verkeren yr klaider in mans bild, in weibs bild vnd her widerûm. Vnd wer mir diese dreÿ pater noster spricht dise iij tag ze fasnacht, demselben [76r] menschen wil ich belonen nach meinen kingklichen eren vnd nach seynem nütz. Dŭ waist wol, wen man ainen verschmelich

haltet, vnd wer in die er buytet vnd grieset, das ist im gar genem. Wan nün mich der mertail dise zeyt auftraiben, [76v] das ist auf yrem hertzen, so ist mir gar genem, wer mir dise iij tag in sunderhait denet. Ich wil im sunderlich denen mit sundern gnaden vergelten. Amen.

BENEFITS OF CONTEMPLATING THE PASSION

London, University College, MS Germ. 24

[11r] **Albertus Magnus spricht**: Wer do gleich uberlauffet das leÿden des herren als der, do erbeis oder bauen zelet, der empfecht do von dreÿ nütze. **Der erste nutz**: Das eß jme nutzer ist dan das er ein gantz jare fast, alle freïtag. **Der ander nutz**: Eß ist jm nutzer dan das er alle wochen eines geschlagen vnd gehauwen wurde biß auff vergiessunge des pluttes. **Der dritte nutz**: Eß ist im nützer dan ob er in der wochen eines ein psaltter lese[12]. Du solt mercken, entpfinge der mensch solche andacht von dem gebeth des leidens Christi, das die treuwe oder zeher erschienen in seinen augen vnd doch niht außflussen. Der nütz, der von sollicher andechtiger bewegunge dem menschen bekomet, jst so groß, das alle menschen eß nicht erzelen mogen oder konnen. Zu vertreiben schedliche anfechtunge, zu vergeben die sunde, außzutreiben die vrsach der sunde, gnadenreiche tugent zu erwerben, zu enthaltten vnd zu gemerunge der tugent, eß ist keÿnerleÿ, das so wircklichen, duiftlichen vnd fruchtbarlichen in der sele wircket die widerbringunge der seligkeit vnd die [11v] freüntliche untbarliche geselschafft der lieben heiligen vnnd engel als das bestetliche gebeth des heiligen leidens Christi vnsers herren. **Das leiden Christi macht gelert den ungelertten**. Es macht den tummen vngelirnigen menschen zu einem meister in der demüt. Eß ist ein büch des lebens, do man alles das innen geschriben vindet, das do not ist zu der sele seligkeit. Das selbe buch geet fur alle bucher der weisen meister, der philosophen, mit seiner sussigkeit. Sage mir, werden dir dem lefftzen vnnd dein mondt ubergossen mit vnausprechlicher sussigkeit uber alle honigsame von dem uberlesen dis buchs des lebens? Geben dir nicht alle buchstaben desselben buchleins jglicher besondern edeln ruch, des do ubertritt alle geruch aller kostbarlichen edeln wurz? Seligk ist der, der liset in dem selben buchlein, wan er nÿmpt do von zu jn der liebin gottes vnnd in verschinehunge der werlt in allen tugenden vnnd genaden. Amen. **Santus Bernhardus spricht**: Das leÿden Christi ist ein schule, do[13] man alle tugent in gelernen magk; vnd gebenedeÿet ist der mensch, der hier sinen [12r] lernet vnnd studirt. Wiltu lernen armut, du vindest in nackent an dem Creutz. Wiltu lernen stetigkeit, er ist genagelt an das Creutz. Wiltu lernen herttigkeit, er hanget bloß an dem hertten holtz. Wiltu lernen demutigkeit, er hat das haupt geneigt an dem Creutz[14]. Wiltu lernen miltigkeit, jm seint die hende durchlochert, er kan nicht behaltten. Er

gab den rittern sein cleider, vnnd Iohanni sein liebe müter, vnnd dem morder
das paradeis, vnnd der erden sein plut dem sonder zu besserunge, ob er anders
selber wil, dem vatter sein sele. **Also schreibet Santus Bernhardus** jn dem
buch von dem testament Christi: Wiltu lernen gotliche liebe, das hertz steet jm
offen. Er ließ sich verspeÿen, geisseln vnd krouen vor liebe. **Santus
Bernhardus spricht**: Alles das gut, das mir got gethan hat, das thet er mir,
wan ich lase oder bethe das leiden Christi. Man sol nicht daruber lauffen mit
einem kalten gemuthe. Sonder man sol staidt vnnd zeit darezu nemen vnd ein
lautter vnd friedsame hertz, als dan so begynnet eß dem menschen zu
schmecken. **Bernhardus spricht**: Besser ertzney magk [12v] man nicht geben
dem sonder. Keinerley dinge so sere tottet vnd außslecht die sunde, vnnd
bekerunge bringet. **Die heilige jungkfrauwe Sant Gertraut** stonde mit
gantzer begirde vnnd mit grossem vleis darnach, ob ir des heilthums von
dem Creutz Christi werden mocht, vnnd vermeint das in grosser ere vnnd
wurde zu halten. Vnnd zu einer zeit was sie entzunt in grosser liebe vnd
andacht, vnnd hette grossen verlangen nach sollichem heilthume. Also wardt jr
durch Christus vnsern herren geantwurt: Gerdraut, wiltu haben, das mein
hertz mit grosser begirde zu dir zeuhet vnnd alle zeit bey dir beleibt, so uberlise
den passion meines leidens, vnnd darjnnen bethe mit vleis die werck, die ich
mit grosser hitziger liebe volbracht. Vnnd die selben werck schrib an die
selbigen stat des heilthums vnnd verneuw das offt mit gebethe. Vnnd biß
gesichert, das du dardurch mein genade vberflussigklich vor allem heilthume
herwurbest. **Santus Bernhardus spricht**: Jhesus Christus mein lieber herre,
verwunt das hertze [13r] mein mit deinen heiligen wunden vnd trenck mein
gemüthe mit deinen trenen, <mit deinem> teuren[15] kostenlichen rosenfarben
blut; also wo ich mich hynkere, das ich dich sichtiglich sehe gekreuziget; vnnd
was ich ansehe, das mir das erscheine gerottet mit deinem rosenfarben plut;
also das ich gantz in dich mit meinem gemuth gee vnd an dich nicht anders
vinden moge vnnd auch anders angesehen mŏge dan deine heilige wünden.
Vnd das seÿ mir ein trost, das ich mit dir lieber herre verwundet werde, oder
das sey mir ein pein, das ich an dich icht bedencke. Ich bit dich guttiger Jhesu,
das mein hertz nicht ruwe hab, eß vinde dich; dan do selbest muß eß ruwenn
vnnd enden sein begerunge. Alle die, die in nutz wollen machen das leiden
Christi vnsers lieben herren, die sollen dem leiden Christi nachfolgen. Er hat
gelitten, du hast gotlich leben, das ist Christus. Wes woltten wir dan gemessen,
das wir nit soltten leÿden? Darumb mallen <wir> vnsern[16] anfechtungen
vnnd sollen[17] wir fliehen zu dem leiden Christi, vnd gedencken, hat der herre
aller herren vnnd der [13v] seligmecher alle geleubigen menschen gelitten.
Warumb wollten wir nicht auch leÿden vnnd das leiden Christi vnser regel
<machen>[18], darnach wir sollen leben? Vnnd <eß> ist[19] vnser bilde, in das
wir vns sollen eintrucken alle zeit, vnnß zu trostunge vnd sterckunge. Ye mer
wir vnns in das leiden Christi trucken mit andechtigem gebethe, ye mer wir

getrost werden in guttem willen. Recht wie si<ch>[20] Christus vnser her hat gehalten in seinem leiden durch vnsern willen mit gedult vnnd lieb, also sollen wir vns auch haltten vnnd im nachfolgen durch seinen willen. So kompt vns die nachgeschriben lere der gebethe des leidens Christi zu einer reinigunge vnnd leidunge zu den genaden. Die mitleidunge zu seinem lobe vnnd erhebünge des hertzen, vnd das zufliessen seines leidens herwercke vnser hertz, das wir vnns bilden gentzlich nach jm, vnnd wirt in vnns volbraht alle andacht mit genaden. **Als Santus Bernhardus spricht**: Ich vmbgee hymmel vnnd wasser vnnd alle tale vnnd vindt dich Jhesus lieber herre nirgent baß dan [14r] an dem Creutz. Do schleffest du, do ruwest do; so speisest du alle, die die dich suchen in rechter reuwe. Vnnd welche sele sich henckt zu dir an das Creutz in mitleidünge, die wirt hoch erhaben von der erden vnnd vindet an jrem letzten ende die apfel[21] des lebendigen holtzes, den vater, den sone, den heiligen geist in einem spiegel der ewigen almechtigkeit. Amen. **Albertus Magnus spricht**: Der sein hertz got ergibet eines Pater Nosters langck, das ist got beheglicher vnnd seiner selen nutzlicher dan das er also vile vmb ablaß ginge, das jm die solen von den fussen vielen vnnd sein plut vergosse in einem iglichen fußstapffen.

Als balde der mensch widerkeret mit seinem gemuthe vnnd mit gantzem willen vnnd seinen geist keret jn gottes geist, so wirdet das alles widerbracht in einem augenplick, was ÿe verloren wart. Vnnd mocht das der mensch zu tausent male am tage gethan, so wurde da alle zeit ein ware verneuwunge; vnd in disem lieplichen werck, da ist die warest vnnd die leüterste vereÿnünge, die gesein magk.

TRANSLATIONS

CARNIVAL PRAYERS

Munich, Bayerische Staatsbibliothek, Cgm 861

Once, before Lent, a blessed virgin called Gertrude prayed to our Lord, saying, 'Lord, what service and praise can I offer to you during this period, when the world infuriates you with its sinful behaviour, so that I may raise your spirits?' Then our Lord replied to her, 'On each of these three days, you shall pray three Pater Nosters for the great flames with which I am confronted during these three days.

'Recite the first one in praise of the practices of my heart: in holy remembrance of my compassion, of my heart, and my great love that I have always had for humankind, especially during the thirty-three years that I dwelled on this earth. And offer this first Pater Noster to my celestial Father for all the evil thoughts and evil desires and evil intentions and evil false affections that the people now share among one another and consummate in their hearts during these three days.

'Recite the second Pater Noster in praise of the practices of my mouth: my teaching and preaching, my earnest commandment, and my fasting and abstinence. And offer this to my celestial Father for all the people's forlorn words and shameful songs both sung and spoken, and for the immense gluttony and immodesty in which the world indulges in these three days.

'The third Pater Noster say in praise of the Holy Spirit, its works and its great power, and of my bitter suffering and martyrdom and the wretched death that I suffered when I was thirty-three years old. And offer this Pater Noster to my celestial Father for the immense stupidity and misbehaviour and idolatry committed by those who pervert their clothing: by women who assume a man's attire, and men who dress in a woman's garb.

'And I will reward the person who says these three Pater Nosters during these three days before Lent, in keeping with my royal honour and redounding to their benefit. You know well that when someone is mocked, it does him well when he is honoured and greeted. Because the majority angers me during this period of time – it is marked on their hearts – that person does me well who serves me especially during these three days. I will serve him especially, rewarding him with special grace.'

Amen.

BENEFITS OF CONTEMPLATING THE PASSION

London, University College, MS Germ. 24

Albert the Great says: whoever traverses the Passion of the Lord, with the view that it is labour or edification, receives three benefits from it. The first benefit is that it is more beneficial to him than fasting every Friday for a whole year. The second benefit is that it is more beneficial than his being beaten and hit once every week until the blood flows. The third benefit is that it is more beneficial than reading the entire psalter once a week. You ought to note that one may experience such devotion from the contemplation of Christ's Passion that faith or tears appear in one's eyes, yet not flow. The human benefit resulting from such devotional stirring is so great that no one is able to or could speak of it. There is nothing that works so effectively, beautifully, and fruitfully in the soul towards the recovery of beatitude and the friendly, welcoming community of the dear saints and angels, than the regular contemplation of the holy Passion of Christ our Lord, which drives away vicious temptation, forgives sin, expels the cause of sin; which leads to acquiring merciful virtue, to preserving and augmenting virtue.

Christ's Passion makes the unlearned learned. It turns the unlearned and stupid person into a master of humility. It is a book of life in which one finds everything written that is needed for the soul's beatitude. The same book – with its sweetness – stands above all the books by the wise masters, the philosophers. Tell me, does not the reading of this book of life steep your lips and your mouth in an ineffable sweetness, sweeter than any honey? Do not all the letters of the same little book bestow on you – each one separately – a noble smell, better than the fragrances of any precious and noble spice? Blessed is he who reads the same little book because he takes into himself God's love and the world grows dead to him because of all virtues and grace. Amen.

Saint Bernard says: Christ's Passion is a school in which one can learn all the virtues; and blessed is he who studies here and instructs his senses. If you want to learn poverty, you will find him naked on the cross. If you want to learn steadfastness, he is nailed to the cross. If you want to learn resilience, he hangs exposed on the hardened wood. If you want to learn humility, he has cast down his head on the cross. If you want to learn generosity, his pierced hands cannot clasp anything. He gave his garments to the knights, his dear mother to John, paradise to the murderer, his blood to the earth in order to improve the sinner (whether the sinner wants it or not), and his soul to the Father. Thus writes Saint Bernard in the book of the testament of Christ: if you want to learn divine love, the heart is open to him. He permitted himself to be scorned, whipped, and gouged for love.

Saint Bernard says: everything good that God has ever done to me he did whenever I read or contemplated the Passion of Christ. One should not go through it with a cold demeanour. Rather one should take the space and time for it, and have a pure and peaceful heart. Then it begins to taste good to the human. Bernard says: there is no better medicine that one can give to the sinner. Nothing else will so well kill and extinguish sin, because it brings conversion.

The blessed virgin Saint Gertrude directed all her desire and great diligence towards receiving a relic of Christ's Cross, wishing to keep it in great honour and dignity. And at one time she was kindled with great love and devotion, and she had great desire for such a relic. This is how Christ our Lord replied to her: 'Gertrude, if you want that my heart draw near to you with great desire and stay with you at all times, read the Passion of my martyrdom, and contemplate diligently the works you find therein, which I have performed with great and ardent love. And write down the same works on the same place of the relic and renew it often with contemplation. And rest assured that by doing so, you earn my mercy abundantly above any relic.'

Saint Bernard says: Jesus Christ my dear Lord, wound my heart with your holy wounds and drown my spirit with your tears, with your worthy and precious rose-coloured blood; so that I see you clearly crucified wherever I turn; and so that anything I see is reddened in my eyes by your rose-coloured blood; so that I enter fully into you with my mind and cannot find anything else or see anything else in you other than your holy wounds. And that shall be my comfort, that I, dear Lord, am wounded with you, and it shall be agony for me when I think of you. I beg you gracious Jesus, that my heart may not find rest until it finds you. Only then must it find rest and an end to its desire.

All those who wish to benefit from the Passion of Christ, our dear Lord, shall follow Christ's Passion. He has suffered, you have divine life – that is Christ. How could we assume that we should not suffer? Therefore, we shall crush our temptations, taking refuge in the Passion of Christ. And we shall remember that the Lord of Lords and the saviour of all believing humans has suffered. Why would we not also suffer and make Christ's Passion our rule of life? And the Passion is our image which we shall impress upon us at all times to be a comfort and a support. The more we impress ourselves onto Christ's Passion with devotional contemplation, the more we are comforted with goodwill. Just as Christ our Lord behaved patiently and lovingly in his martyrdom for our sake, so shall we behave and follow him for his sake. In this way the following instruction for the contemplation of Christ's Passion serves us as purgation and suffering to obtain mercy. Compassion in honour of his praise, the lifting up of hearts, and the inflow of his martyrdom shall awaken our hearts that we may model ourselves in his image and that all devotion be mercifully performed in us.

Thus says Saint Bernard: I scan sky and waters and all valleys, but find you, dear Lord Jesus, nowhere more present than on the cross. There you sleep, there you rest. In this way you nourish all those who search for you in true remorse. And that soul that hangs itself on the cross in compassion for you, will be lifted up high above the earth; and at the end of its days, it will find the apples of the living wood, the Father, the Son, the Holy Spirit, in the mirror of eternal omnipotence. Amen.

Albert the Great says: whoever surrenders his heart for the period of just one Pater Noster derives more benefit for his soul and pleases the Lord more than his going on so lengthy a pilgrimage that the soles of his feet come off and he spills blood with each and every footstep.

As soon as the human reverts his mind and all his will, turning his spirit into God's spirit, all the things that ever were lost will be recovered in one instant. And were the human able to do this a thousand times per day, there would follow a true renewal at all times; and in this lovely work is the truest and purest union that could ever be.

NOTES

INTRODUCTION

1 On the correlation of female authorship and visionary writing, see Barbara Newman, 'The Visionary Texts and Visual Words of Religious Women'. *Crown and Veil: Female Monasticism from the Fifth to the Fifteenth Centuries.* Ed. Jeffrey F. Hamburger and Susan Marti. New York: Columbia University Press, 2008, 151–71, at 153.

2 On the 'liturgical and sacramental focus' of the Helfta writings, see Newman, 'The Visionary Texts', 160 [article appeared first in German:] 'Die visionären Texte und visuellen Welten religiöser Frauen.' *Krone und Schleier: Kunst aus mittelalterlichen Frauenklöstern: Ruhrlandmuseum: Die frühen Klöster und Stifte 500-1200: Kunst- und Ausstellungshalle der Bundesrepublik Deutschland: die Zeit der Orden 1200-1500.* Ed. Kunst- und Ausstellungshalle der Bundesrepublik Deutschland Bonn and Ruhrlandmuseum Essen. Munich: Hirmer, 2005, 104–17, at 111.

3 *Legatus* II, 21. In *Gertrude d'Helfta, Œuvres spirituelles.* Vol. 2: *Le Héraut* (Livre I et II). Ed. Pierre Doyère. Sources chrétiennes. Série des textes monastiques d'Occident Vol. 25. Paris: Éditions du Cerf, 1968, 322: *Omnino etiam injustum judicavi recolens gratuita beneficia tuae amicabilis clementiae erga me valde indignam, si in hoc quasi ingrata oblivione pertransirem quod in quadam quadragesima accepi mira dignatione tuae amicissimae pietatis.* Translation by Alexandra Barratt, *Gertrude the Great of Helfta: The Herald of God's Loving-Kindness, Books One and Two.* Cistercian Fathers Vol. 35. Kalamazoo, MI: Cistercian Publications, 1991, 157.

4 *Legatus* II, 21. *Gertrude d'Helfta: Œuvres spirituelles* II, 322: *In secunda ergo dominica dum ad missam ante processionem cantaretur responsorium 'Vidi Dominum facie ad faciem', etc., mirabili quodam et inaestimabili coruscamine illustrata anima, in luce divinae revelationis apparuit mihi tanquam faciei meae applicata facies quaedam, secundum quod Bernardus dicit: 'Non formata sed formans, non perstringens oculos corporis, sed faciem laetificans cordis, grata amoris munere non colore.' Ex hac melliflua visione cum solares oculi tui oculis meis directe oppositi viderentur, qualiter tu suavis dulcedo mea tunc afferceris non solum animam meam, verum etiam cor meum cum omnibus membris, cum tibi soli sit notum, proinde quoad vixero tibi persolvam famulatum devotum.* Translation by Barratt, *The Herald of God's Loving-Kindness,* 1&2, 157–8.

5 Extremely aware of the scholastic stance defended by Bernard on the ways of seeing God, Gertrude quotes a lengthy passage of his thirty-first sermon in a condensed way, reaffirming the vision's inward nature; see Sermon 31, 6; Bernard de Clairvaux, *Sermons sur le cantique.* Ed. Jean Leclercq, Henri Rochais, and Charles Hugh Talbot. Vol. 2. Sources Chrétiennes Vol. 472. Paris: Éditions du Cerf, 1996, 436–8, § 223.

6 The dominant presence of light in Gertrude's vision also reverberates with Bernard's Sermon 31 (see previous note).

7 *Legatus* II, 21. *Gertrude d'Helfta: Œuvres spirituelles* II, 322–4: *Sed quamvis longe aliter placeat rosa tempore vernali cum virens et florens dat odorem, quam tempore hiemali, cum diu arefacta dicitur redoluisse suaviter, aliquantulum tamen excitare videtur delectationem recordatio praelibatorum. Unde et ego quali possum similitudine proferre desidero quid parvitas mea in illa praejucundissima visione tui senserit ad laudem amoris tui; ut si quis legentium forte similia vel majora acceperit, per recordationem ad gratiarum actionem excitetur. Et egomet saepius recolendo etiam caliginem negligentiarum mearum aliqualiter reprimam per gratitudinem, hoc speculo solari vibrato.* Translation by Barratt, *The Herald of God's Loving-Kindness,* 1&2, 158.

8 On the interconnected aspects of remembering and reading in Gertrude's theology, see Ella Johnson, *This Is My Body: Eucharistic Theology and Anthropology in the Writings of Gertrude the Great of Helfta.* Cistercian Studies Vol. 280. Collegeville, MN: Liturgical Press, 2020, 135–59.

9 This mode of speculative perception has been described as 'figuraler Realismus' by Niklaus Largier, *Spekulative Sinnlichkeit: Kontemplation und Spekulation im Mittelalter.* Mediävistische Perspektiven Vol. 7. Zurich: Chronos, 2018, especially 26–9.

10 See Robert Javelet, *Image et ressemblance au XIIe siècle: de saint Anselme à Allain de Lille.* Vol. 1. Paris: Letouzey et Ané, 1967, 377: 'Le mot spéculation n'est pas réservé à l'introspection spirituelle: la spéculation concerne l'observation spirituelle de tous les simulacres de la nature et de la grâce. Elle embrasse tout le monde visible en tant qu'il ressemble à l'invisible. La spéculation, c'est la vision de la vérité par le moyen d'un miroir, par la médiation des ressemblances. Toute spéculation est sacramentelle au sens large.' Quoted after Largier, *Spekulative Sinnlichkeit,* 81, n. 39.

11 See Largier, *Spekulative Sinnlichkeit,* 32–3.

12 *Legatus* II, 21. *Gertrude d'Helfta: Œuvres spirituelles* II, 324: *O quid amplius decam de ista, ut ita dicam, dulcissima visione?* Translation by Barratt, *The Herald of God's Loving-Kindness,* 1&2, 158.

13 *Legatus* II, 21. *Gertrude d'Helfta: Œuvres spirituelles* II, 324: *ex deificis oculis tuis sensi per oculos meos intrantem lucem quamdam inaestimabilem, suavificam, quae transiens omnia interiora mea supra modum mirabilem virtutem in omnibus membris meis videbatur operari.* Translation by Barratt, *The Herald of God's Loving-Kindness,* 1&2, 158.

14 *Legatus* II, 21. *Gertrude d'Helfta: Œuvres spirituelles* II, 324: *quia ut verum fateor secundum quod mihi videtur, omnium linguarum eloquentia per omnes dies vitae meae mihi hunc praeclarum modum videndi te, etiam in coelesti gloria, nunquam persuasisset, si dignatio tua, Deus meus, unica salus animae meae, per experientiam me ad illam non induxisset.* Translation by Barratt, *The Herald of God's Loving-Kindness,* 1&2, 158.

15 *Legatus* II, 21. *Gertrude d'Helfta: Œuvres spirituelles* II, 326: *Pro quo et etiam pro aliis, quorum effectum tu solus nosti, sit tibi exhibitio suavitatis illius quam in supercoelesti apotheca divinitatis supra omnem sensum praejucunde persona personae instillat.* Translation by Barratt, *The Herald of God's Loving-Kindness,* 1&2, 159.

16 This has been remarked by Siegfried Ringler, 'Einführung: Die Mystik der Gertrud von Helfta – Aufbruch zu neuer Gottesrede.' *Aufbruch zu neuer Gottesrede: Die Mystik der Gertrud von Helfta.* Ed. Siegfried Ringler. Ostfildern: Grünewald, 2008, 8–14, at 14.

17 Both Mechthild of Hackeborn and Gertrude of Helfta were influential models for late medieval and early modern piety all across Europe and eventually in the Americas. Their ideas quickly found a broad reception; Burkhard Hasebrink, "'Das fließende Licht der Gottheit' Mechthilds von Magdeburg. Eine Skizze.' *Bete und Arbeite! Zisterzienser in der Grafschaft Mansfeld: Begleitband zur Ausstellung im Sterbehaus Martin Luthers in Eisleben, 24.10.1998 – 24.6.1999.* Ed. Esther Pia Wipfler, Rose-Marie Knape, and Stiftung Luthergedenkstätten in Sachsen-Anhalt. Halle (Saale): Stekovics, 1998, 149–61, at 151, remarks that the 'broad dissemination' ('weite Verbreitung') of the Latin writings of Mechthild of Hackeborn and Gertrude of Helfta is 'extraordinary' ('ungewöhnlich'), contrasting it from the reception of Mechthild of Magdeburg's *Flowing Light of the Godhead* which only became known in modern days through the edition of Gall Morel in the nineteenth century.

18 See in particular the work of Balázs J. Nemes, *Von der Schrift zum Buch – vom Ich zum Autor: Zur Text- und Autorkonstitution in Überlieferung und Rezeption des 'Fliessenden Lichts der Gottheit' Mechthilds von Magdeburg.* Bibliotheca Germanica Vol. 55. Tübingen: Francke, 2010; 'Text Production and Authorship: Gertrude of Helfta's "Legatus divinae pietatis".' *A Companion to Mysticism and Devotion in Northern Germany in the Late Middle Ages.* Ed. Anne Simon, Elizabeth A. Andersen, and Henrike Lähnemann. Brill's Companions to the Christian Tradition Vol. 44. Leiden: Brill, 2014, 103–30. See also Balázs J. Nemes and Almuth Märker, '"Hunc tercium conscripsi cum maximo labore occultandi": Schwester N von Helfta und ihre "Sonderausgabe" des "Legatus divinae pietatis" Gertruds von Helfta in der Leipziger Handschrift Ms 827.' *Beiträge zur Geschichte der deutschen Sprache und Literatur* 137 (2015): 248–96.

19 The most explicit studies on the vernacular redaction of the *Legatus* are: Gertrud Jaron Lewis, 'Gertrud of Helfta's "Legatus divinae pietatis" and "ein botte der götlichen miltekeit": A Comparative Study of Major Themes.' *Mysticism: Medieval & Modern.* Ed. Valerie M. Largorio. Salzburg Studies in English Literature, Elizabethan & Renaissance Studies Vol. 92:20. Salzburg: Institut für Anglistik und Amerikanistik, Universität Salzburg, 1986, 58–71; Siegfried Ringler, 'Die Rezeption Gertruds von Helfta im Bereich süddeutscher Frauenklöster.' *'Vor dir steht die leere Schale meiner Sehnsucht': Die Mystik der Frauen von Helfta.* Ed. Michael Bangert and Hildegund Keul. Leipzig: Benno, 1998, 134–55; Beatrice Trînca, 'Schriftliche Berührung – gedruckte Süße: Zum "bot der gotlichen mildigkeit".' *Zeitschrift für deutsche Philologie* 135 (2016): 349–66; Racha Kirakosian, '"Wie man got verwunden sol mit einem ougen": Zur passionsmystischen Buchschriftlichkeit und Liebesverwundung durch das Auge im "botten der götlichen miltekeit".' *Verletzungen und Unversehrtheit in der deutschen Literatur des Mittelalters. XXIV. Anglo-German Colloquium.* Ed. Nine Miedema, Stephen Mossman, and Sara Bowden. Tübingen: Francke, 2020, 83–96. Kirakosian, 'The Earliest Transmitted German Legatus: Gotha, Forschungsbibliothek, Chart. B 269.' *Analecta Cisterciensa* 69 (2019): 178–97. Kirakosian, 'Intertextuelle Textilien: Imaginäre Kleider und Temporalität bei Alanus ab Insulis und Gertrud von Helfta.' *Beiträge zur Geschichte der deutschen Sprache und Literatur* 142.2 (2020): 236–66.

20 Ringler, 'Einführung: Die Mystik der Gertrud von Helfta', 9. Most recently, Johnson's study, *This Is My Body*, examines theological doctrine in the devotional and visionary writings attributed to Gertrude of Helfta.

21 The main assumption about vernacular religious writings was most succinctly formulated by Nicholas Watson, 'Visions of Inclusion: Universal Salvation and Vernacular Theology in Pre-Reformation England.' *Journal of Medieval and Early Modern Studies* 27 (1997): 145–87, at 145: 'The assumption is that ideas expressed by such writings [Middle English religious writings] are merely simplified versions of ideas developed in Latin by clerics, and that vernacular culture was characterized by feeling, not thought, and by practical rather than speculative approaches to truth.'

22 For more details, see Catherine Squires, 'Das Moskauer Mechthild-Fragment. Neues zur Lesung und zur Zusammenstellung des Kodex.' *Deutsch-russische Arbeitsgespräche zu mittelalterlichen Handschriften und Drucken in russischen Bibliotheken: Beiträge zur Tagung des deutsch-russischen Arbeitskreises vom 14. bis 16. September 2011 an der Lomonossov-Universität Moskau aus Anlass des 300. Geburtstages des Universitätsgründers Michail Lomonossov.* Ed. Natalija Ganina, Klaus Klein, Catherine Squires, and Jürgen Wolf. Akademie gemeinnütziger Wissenschaften zu Erfurt Sonderschriften Vol. 45. Erfurt: Verlag der Akademie gemeinnütziger Wissenschaften, 2014, 57–90; Nigel F. Palmer, 'Ein Zeugnis deutscher Kunstprosa aus dem späten 13. Jahrhundert: Zu den sonst nicht nachgewiesenen Textabschnitten der Moskauer Mechthild-Überlieferung.', ibid., 97–138.

23 Virginia Blanton, Veronica O'Mara, Patricia Stoop, "Introduction." *Nuns' Literacies in Medieval Europe: The Antwerp Dialogue.* Medieval Women – Texts and Contexts Vol. 28. Turnhout: Brepols, 2017, xxi–lxvi, at lv.

24 Notably works by the reformers Johannes Nider (1380–1438) and Johannes Meyer (1422/23–1485) are evaluated, most recently by Claire Taylor Jones, *Ruling the Spirit: Women, Liturgy, and Dominican Reform in Late Medieval Germany.* Philadelphia: University of Pennsylvania Press, 2017.

25 That the study of religious vernacular texts has long suffered from the devaluation of religious texts as non-literary is critically demonstrated by Burkhard Hasebrink and Peter Strohschneider, 'Religiöse Schriftkultur und säkulare Textwissenschaft: Germanistische Mediävistik in postsäkularem Kontext.' *Poetica* 46 (2014): 277–92.

26 So-called 'secular' vernacular literature has always been treated with special care so that today there are established areas of inquiry; on German vernacular poetry as an independent field of study, see Beate Kellner, *Spiel der Liebe im Minnesang.* Munich: Fink, 2018, 14–15.

27 Such as the late medieval English redactions of *The Booke of Gostlye Grace of Mechtild of Hackeborn.* Ed. Theresa A. Halligan. Studies and Texts Vol. 46. Toronto: Pontifical

Institute of Mediaeval Studies, 1979. For an overview of the English transmission, see also Nicholas Watson, 'Censorship and Cultural Change in Late-Medieval England: Vernacular Theology, the Oxford Translation Debate, and Arundel's Constitutions of 1409.' *Speculum* 70 (1995): 822–64, at 835, n. 33 and 863. More recently on the English redaction of the *Liber*, see Naoë Kukita Yoshikawa, 'Mechthild of Hackeborn as Spiritual Authority: the Middle English Translation of the "Liber Specialis Gratia".' *Translation and Authority: Authorities in Translation*. Ed. Pieter De Leemans and Michèle Goyens. Turnhout: Brepols, 2017, 241–53. Yoshikawa, 'Post-mortem care of the soul: Mechtild of Hackeborn's the Book of Gostlye Grace.' *Medieval and Early Modern Literature, Science and Medicine*. Ed. Rachel Falconer and Denis Renevey. Swiss Papers in English Language and Literature Vol. 28. Tübingen: Narr Verlag, 2013, 157–70.

28   See Werner Williams-Krapp, 'Das geistliche Schrifttum des Spätmittelalters vom Anfang des 14. bis zum Ende des 15. Jahrhunderts: Veränderungen nach der Mitte des 14. Jahrhunderts.' *Deutsches Literatur-Lexikon: Das Mittelalter, Autoren und Werke nach Themenkreisen und Gattungen*. Vol. 2: Das geistliche Schrifttum des Spätmittelalters. Ed. Wolfgang Achnitz. Berlin: De Gruyter, 2011, xi–xx. See also Jeffrey F. Hamburger, Eva Schlotheuber, Susan Marti, and Margot Fassler, *Liturgical Life and Latin Learning at Paradies bei Soest, 1300–1425: Inscription and Illumination in the Choir Books of a North German Dominican Convent*. Vol. 1. Münster: Aschendorff, 2016, 4.

29   On vernacular theology, see Bernard McGinn, 'Meister Eckhart and the Beguines in the Context of Vernacular Theology.' *Meister Eckhart and the Beguine Mystics: Hadewijch of Brabant, Mechthild of Magdeburg, and Margerite Porete*. New York: Continuum, 1994, 1–14; *The Flowering of Mysticism: Men and Women in the New Mysticism, 1200–1350*. The Presence of God: A History of Western Christian Mysticism Vol. 3. New York: Crossroad, 1998, 19–24. See also Barbara Newman, *God and the Goddesses: Vision, Poetry, and Belief in the Middle Ages*. Philadelphia: University of Pennsylvania Press, 2003, 295–6; Marleen Cré, *Vernacular Mysticism in the Charterhouse: A Study of*

London, British Library, MS Additional 37790. The Medieval Translator Vol. 9. Turnhout: Brepols, 2006. Nicholas Watson, who uses the term 'vernacular theology' with explicit reference to Bernard McGinn, develops the concept further to emphasise that the vernacular was a platform for an intellectually dynamic culture; see 'Censorship and Cultural Change', 823–4, n. 4 (see also below). For a discussion on 'mystical life' in contrast to the term of 'Gnadenvita', see Racha Kirakosian, *Die Vita der Christina von Hane: Untersuchung und Edition*. Hermaea. Neue Folge Vol. 144. Berlin: De Gruyter, 2017, 51–71.

30   Newman, 'The Visionary Texts', 152, describes that '[a]ll monastics were to some extent bilingual, knowing at least one local vernacular or mother tongue in addition to Latin'. In recent years, the literacy of medieval nuns has increasingly been portrayed as more nuanced in contrast to the conventional belief that they were exclusively or mainly monolingual, see for example Virginia Blanton, Veronica O'Mara, and Patricia Stoop, eds. *Nuns' Literacies in Medieval Europe: The Hull Dialogue*. Medieval Women – Texts and Contexts Vol. 26. Turnhout: Brepols, 2013; *Nuns' Literacies in Medieval Europe: The Kansas City Dialogue*. Medieval Women – Texts and Contexts Vol. 27. Turnhout: Brepols, 2015.

31   On the 'self-reflectiveness' of vernacular religious texts and the call for detailed analyses of case studies, see Burkhard Hasebrink, 'Grenzverschiebung: Zu Kongruenz und Differenz von Latein und Deutsch bei Meister Eckhart.' *Zeitschrift für deutsches Altertum und deutsche Literatur* 121 (1992): 369–98, in particular at 398. See also Kirakosian, 'Intertextuelle Textilien'.

32   See Watson, 'Visions of Inclusion'; see also 'Censorship and Cultural Change'. While the general statement about vernacular theology applies to the German situation too, there are crucial differences to the situation in England – the focus of Watson's study – where theological writing was censored and regulated after 1409, the time at which a piece of ecclesiastical legislation known as Arundel's Constitutions was implemented: Arundel's Constitutions influenced, as Watson has shown, vernacular writing in so far as they

introduced an element of censorship into a formerly thriving vernacular literary culture, which from thenceforth had to operate 'underground'. Watson calls for 'a more nuanced account of fifteenth-century vernacular theology' which is continued 'through the processes of translation and compilation themselves' (ibid., 836). While the same call may be followed for the continent, I still want to mark that the English situation – which in addition was highly politicised due to the concurrence of the 'kynde langage' English to French 'as a foreign tongue'; see Watson, 'Visions of Inclusion', 169 – remains specific and distinct from the German one, which is the focus of this study.

33 *L'image de la noblesse figurée sur la vie de Saincte Gertrude & de ses Parens*. Trans. Guillaume de Rebreviettes Seigneur d'Escoeuures. Paris: Huby, 1612; Johannes Justus Landsberg, *Vita della beata vergine Gertruda*. Trans. Vicenzo Buondi. Venice: Giolito de Ferrari, 1562.

34 For a discussion of anachronistic and obscuring criteria applied to medieval translations leading to 'substitute terms as 'adaptation,' 'paraphrase,' or 'imitation', see Jeanette Beer, 'Introduction.' *Medieval Translators and Their Craft*. Ed. Jeanette Beer. Studies in Medieval Culture Vol. 25. Kalamazoo, MI: Medieval Institute Publications, 1989, 1–7, at 2–3.

35 The *botte*'s inclusion in manuscripts containing vernacular writings attributed to Henry Suso and Meister Eckhart highlights the status of the German redaction of the *Legatus* alongside the two Dominicans, and it points to the flexible adaptation of Gertrude's visions; for detailed information about the manuscript contexts see Chapter 2 'Manuscript Transmission History'.

36 My use of 'material' and 'materiality' does not refer to a Marxist understanding of these terms; rather it concerns the sensorial aspects of material objects, as discussed in studies on material culture; see subsequent note.

37 The supposed semiotic dimension of material objects is usually put in the foreground. Studies on material culture highlight by contrast the notion that material expressions carry meaning within themselves and that they generate meaning when they are situated in specific cultural contexts, see Carl Knappett, *Thinking through Material Culture: An Interdisciplinary Perspective*. Philadelphia: University of Pennsylvania Press, 2015. In this regard, the method of material history offers new ways to study the past, as shown by Beth Williamson, 'Material Culture and Medieval Christianity.' *The Oxford Handbook of Medieval Christianity*. Ed. John H. Arnold. Oxford: Oxford University Press, 2014, 60–75. Thinking through material culture tries to overcome entrenched dualisms, highlighting the fluidity between the everyday and the aesthetic, the real and the imaginary. In addition, the study of Christian materiality must be tied to more broadly conceived implications that touch on theological as well as practical concerns, as called for by Caroline Walker Bynum, *Christian Materiality: An Essay on Religion in Late Medieval Europe*. New York: Zone Books, 2011. As much as debates on material culture seem current and recent, medieval scholars too were concerned about the relation between matter, form, and meaning. The interplay between form and matter was argued about by medieval scholars in a vivid intellectual discussion on Aristotelian principles; see Kellie Robertson, 'Medieval Materialism. A Manifesto.' *Exemplaria* (2010): 99–118. Although this intellectual discussion has been recognised in scholarship, the implications it had for material culture have not been fully studied yet, despite the call for the integration of material sources into the traditional canon of historical studies in order to understand how humans relate to their objects; see Leora Auslander, 'Beyond Words.' *The American Historical Review* 110 (2005): 1015–45. Reflections on material culture also concern language. The methodological and epistemological discourses of the past ten years have demanded a hermeneutical text-interpretative approach that links to material culture; see Markus Hilgert, 'Text-Anthropologie: Die Erforschung von Materialität und Präsenz des Geschriebenen als hermeneutische Strategie.' *Mitteilungen der Deutschen Orient-Gesellschaft* 142. Special Issue: *Altorientalistik im 21. Jahrhundert: Selbstverständnis, Herausforderungen, Ziele* (2010): 85–124; see also the volume *Schriftträger – Textträger: Zur materialen Präsenz des Geschriebenen in frühen Gesellschaften*. Ed. Annette Kehnels and Diamantis Panagiotopoulos. Materiale Textkulturen Vol. 6. Berlin: De Gruyter, 2015.

38 On the practice of sensory stimulation through meditative reading, see Niklaus Largier, 'Inner Senses – Outer Senses: The Practice of Emotions in Medieval Mysticism.' *Codierung von Emotionen im Mittelalter / Emotions and Sensibilities in the Middle Ages.* Ed. C. Stephen Jaeger and Ingrid Kasten. Trends in Medieval Philology Vol. 1. Berlin: De Gruyter, 2003, 3–15.

39 In the prologue to the *Legatus divinae pietatis,* the compiler of the textual material makes a point of the necessity to use 'seemingly corporeal images' (*tam per imaginationes corporearum similitudinum*) to render the things described and revealed to Gertrude more 'intelligible for the human reader', see *Legatus* I, prologue. *Gertrude d'Helfta: Œuvres spirituelles* II, 114. The German *botte* based on the Latin *Legatus* takes up this passage but makes a significant change: not 'seemingly corporeal images' appear to Gertrude but she is unified with God through figures or images (*durch bildunge*) with divine miracles revealed to her 'that we would not understand were they not created with corporeal images', see *Gertrud von Helfta: ein botte der götlichen miltekeit.* Ed. Otmar Wieland. Studien und Mitteilungen zur Geschichte des Benediktiner-Ordens und seiner Zweige. Ergänzungsband 22. Ottobeuren: Bayerische Benediktinerakademie, 1973 [*botte*], Ch. 2, 86. All translations are provided by Racha Kirakosian if not indicated otherwise. For a discussion of these passages, see Chapter 4 'The Book's Self-Reflectivity'.

40 That stemmatological hierarchies can be problematic for complex transmissions has been discussed by Hans-Jochen Schiewer, 'Fassung, Bearbeitung, Version und Edition.' *Deutsche Texte des Mittelalters zwischen Handschriftennahe und Rekonstruktion: Berliner Fachtagung 1–3 April 2004.* Ed. Martin J. Schubert. *Beihefte zu Editio* Vol. 23. Tübingen: Niemeyer, 2005, 35–50.

1 THE HELFTA SCRIPTORIUM

1 Alastair J. Minnis, *Medieval Theory of Authorship: Scholastic Literary Attitudes in the Later Middle Ages.* London: Scolar Press, 1984.

2 For an overview of this feminist history, see Barbara Newman, 'Liminalities: Literate Women in the Long Twelfth Century.' *European Transformation: The Long Twelfth Century.* Ed. Thomas F. X. Noble and John Van Engen. Notre Dame, IN: University of Notre Dame Press, 2012, 354–402, in particular at 354.

3 For a general overview of the spirituality in Helfta, see Anna Harrison, '"I Am Wholly Your Own": Liturgical Piety and Community among the Nuns of Helfta.' *Church History* 78 (2009): 549–83.

4 On the historically retraceable life and writing of Mechthild of Magdeburg, see Ernst Hellgardt, 'Das 'Fließende Licht der Gottheit': Mechthild von Magdeburg und ihr Buch.' *Literatur in der Stadt: Magdeburg in Mittelalter und Früher Neuzeit.* Ed. Michael Schilling. Beihefte zum Euphorion Vol. 70. Heidelberg: Winter, 2012, 97–119. The dating of Mechthild's death is contested; some scholars opt for the early 1280s, while others trace her existence in later Helfta mystical writings, hence advocating the mid-1290s as a more likely time of death.

5 For the dating of the convent's translation to Helfta, see Cornelia Oefelein, *Das Nonnenkloster St. Jacobi und seine Tochterklöster im Bistum Halberstadt.* Studien zur Geschichte, Kunst und Kultur der Zisterzienser Vol. 20. Berlin: Lukas, 2004. Mathias Köhler, *Kloster Helfta: Zisterzienserinnenpriorat St. Marien.* Kleine Kunstführer Vol. 2219. Regensburg: Schnell & Steiner, 2013, 4, still indicates 1258.

6 Gerlinde Schlenker, 'Helfta, Sachsen.' *Repertorium der Zisterzen in den Ländern Brandenburg, Mecklenburg-Vorpommern, Sachsen, Sachsen-Anhalt und Thüringen.* Langwaden: Bernardus, 1998, 287–91, at 288. Eisleben is where, 200 years later, Martin Luther would be born.

7 See Fritz Junkte, 'Die Inkunabeln der St. Andreaskirche zu Eisleben.' *Beiträge zur Inkunabelkunde* III. Folge Vol. 8 (1983): 50–68; Konrad von Rabenau, 'Die Geschichte der Kirchenbibliothek von St. Andreas in Eisleben als Spiegel der Kirchengeschichte des Mansfelder Landes.' *Herbergen der Christenheit* 15 (1985/86): 91–103. On the identification of the incunabula, see Oefelein, *Das Nonnenkloster St. Jacobi,* 135.

8 Cornelia Oefelein, 'Gründung und mittelalterliche Geschichte des Klosters St. Marien zu Helfta – ein Überblick unter Berücksichtigung

neuer Funde.' *Beihefte zur Zeitschrift für deutsche Philologie* 17 (2019). Special Issue: *Mechthild und das Fließende Licht der Gottheit im Kontext. Eine Spurensuche in religiösen Netzwerken und literarischen Diskursen im mitteldeutschen Raum des 13.–15. Jahrhunderts*. Ed. Caroline Emmelius and Balázs J. Nemes, 41–65.

9 The relevant texts of Spangenberg are: Cyriacus Spangenberg, *Quernfurtische Chronica*. Erfurt: Bawman, 1590. Repr. in *Mansfelder Blätter* 28 (1913); *Mansfeldische Chronica*. Vol. 1. Eisleben: Petri, 1572. Repr. in *Mansfelder Blätter* 27 (1912). Ed. Rudolph Leers. The Helfta convent chronicle was probably lost in the ravages of the Peasants' War of 1525; see Oefelein, 'Gründung und mittelalterliche Geschichte des Klosters St. Marien zu Helfta,' 2.

10 Most recently about the 1503 Leipzig imprint and its Cologne reprint from 1557, see Volker Honemann, 'Sächsische Fürstinnen, Patrizier, Kleriker, Kaufleute und der Dominikaner Marcus von Weida als Förderer geistlicher Literatur um 1500.' *Bürgers Bücher: Laien als Anreger und Adressaten in Sachsens Literatur um 1500*. Ed. Christoph Fasbender and Gesine Mierke. Würzburg: Königshausen & Neuman, 2017, 130–59, at 137–42.

11 Oefelein, 'Gründung und mittelalterliche Geschichte des Klosters St. Marien zu Helfta,' 4. See also Oefelein, *Das Nonnenkloster St. Jacobi*, 96. The letter by Sophia of Stolberg is transmitted as: Niedersächsisches Hauptstaatsarchiv Hannover, Depositum 76, C113. A copy is transmitted as: Copial I (dated 1681), Depositum 76, MS 7/1, 1337–51. The edition uses yet another copy which is lost today: Max Krühne, *Urkundenbuch der Klöster der Grafschaft Mansfeld*. Geschichtsquellen der Provinz Sachsen und angrenzender Gebiete Vol. 20. Halle: Hendel, 1888, 223–6, nr. 148.

12 Although the General Chapter of the Cistercian Order had put an official stop to the incorporation of women's convents in 1220, many women's convents continued to live under the order's rule 'without being bound by the jurisdiction of an abbot'; Regina Dorothea Schiewer, 'Books in Texts – Texts in Books: The "St. Georgener Predigten" as an Example of Nuns' Literacy in Late Medieval Germany.' *Nuns' Literacies in Medieval Europe: The Hull Dialogue*. Ed. Virginia Blanton, Veronica O'Mara, and

Patricia Stoop. Medieval Women – Texts and Contexts Vol. 26. Turnhout: Brepols, 2013, 223–37, at 224.

13 On the reform of Bursfelde, see Kaspar Elm, 'Monastische Reformen zwischen Humanismus und Reformation.' *900 Jahre Kloster Bursfelde: Reden und Vorträge zum Jubiläum 1993*. Ed. Lothar Perlitt. Göttingen: Vandenhoeck & Ruprecht, 1994, 59–111. See also Heike Uffmann, *Wie in einem Rosengarten: Monastische Reformen des späten Mittelalters in den Vorstellungen von Klosterfrauen*. Religion in der Geschichte Vol. 14. Bielefeld: Verlag für Regionalgeschichte, 2008; Matthias Eifler, *Die Bibliothek des Erfurter Petersklosters im späten Mittelalter: Buchkultur und Literaturrezeption im Kontext der Bursfelder Klosterreform*. 2 vols. Veröffentlichungen der Historischen Kommission für Thüringen. Kleine Reihe Vol. 51. Cologne: Böhlau, 2017, in particular Vol. 1, 52–79.

14 See Oefelein, 'Gründung und mittelalterliche Geschichte des Klosters St. Marien zu Helfta,' 15.

15 See Nemes, *Von der Schrift zum Buch*, 164, n. 8.

16 For an overview of the convent during the reform and the introduction of observance, see Oefelein, 'Gründung und mittelalterliche Geschichte des Klosters St. Marien zu Helfta,' 17. On the convent of Helfta and its status as Cistercian foundation possibly following the Benedictine rule, see Cornelia Oefelein, 'Grundlagen zur Baugeschichte des Klosters Helfta.' *'Vor dir steht die leere Schale meiner Sehnsucht': Die Mystik der Frauen von Helfta*. Ed. Michael Bangert and Hildegund Keul. Leipzig: Benno, 1998, 12–28. Michael Bangert, 'Die sozio-kulturelle Situation des Klosters St. Maria in Helfta.' Ibid., 29–47. See also Oefelein, *Das Nonnenkloster St. Jacobi*, 98. Alexandra Barratt, 'Introduction.' *Gertrude the Great of Helfta: The Herald of God's Loving-Kindness, Book Four*. Cistercian Fathers Vol. 85. Collegeville, MN: Cistercian Publications, 2018, 11–43, at 11, calls Helfta 'a powerful Benedictine house' drawing evidence from Gertrude's visions of St Benedict.

17 See Hildegund Keul and Siegfried Ringler, 'In der Freiheit des lebendigen Geistes: Helfta als geohistorischer Ort der deutschen Mystik.' *Aufbruch zu neuer Gottesrede*, 21–35. Margot Schmidt, 'Mechthild von Hackeborn.' *Die deutsche Literatur des Mittelalters: Verfasserlexikon: Begründet von Wolfgang*

Stammler, fortgeführt von Karl Langosch. Vol. 6. Ed. Kurt Ruh and Burghart Wachinger. 2nd edition. Berlin: De Gruyter, 1987, 251–9, at 252, sees the Dominicans in Halle in charge of the nuns' supervision.

18   That an official belonging to the Cistercian Order did not affect Helfta's own understanding of a relatively flexible convent, had already been discussed by Markus Dombi, 'Waren die hll. Gertrud und Mechtild Benediktinerinnen oder Cistercienserinnen?' *Cistercienser-Chronik* 25 (1913): 257–68, at 268.

19   See Oefelein, 'Gründung und mittelalterliche Geschichte des Klosters St. Marien zu Helfta,' 20. See also Antje Rüttgardt, *Klosteraustritte in der frühen Reformation: Studien zu Flugschriften der Jahre 1522 bis 1524.* Quellen und Forschungen zur Reformationsgeschichte Vol. 79. Gütersloh: Gütersloher Verlagshaus, 2007.

20   Eva Schlotheuber, *Klostereintritt und Bildung: Die Lebenswelt der Nonnen im späten Mittelalter: Mit einer Edition des 'Konventstagebuchs' einer Zisterzienserin von Heilig-Kreuz bei Braunschweig (1484–1507).* Spätmittelalter und Reformation. Neue Reihe Vol. 24. Tübingen: Mohr Siebeck, 2004.

21   Kaspar Elm, 'Frömmigkeit und Ordensleben in deutschen Frauenklöstern des 13. und 14. Jahrhunderts.' *Ons geestelijk erf* 66 (1992): 28–45, at 39.

22   For a critical discussion on how many members belonged to the Helfta community at the end of the thirteenth century (sixty members at the most), see Michael Bangert, *Demut in Freiheit: Studien zur Geistlichen Lehre im Werk Gertruds von Helfta.* Studien zur systematischen und spirituellen Theologie Vol. 21. Würzburg: Echter, 1997, 30–1; Oefelein, 'Gründung und mittelalterliche Geschichte des Klosters St. Marien zu Helfta,' 10–11.

23   Mechthild of Hackeborn, 'Liber specialis gratiae.' *Revelationes Gertrudianæ ac Mechtildianæ Vol. II: Sanctæ Mechtildis virginis ordinis sancti Benedicti Liber specialis gratiæ, accedit sororis Mechthildis ejusdem ordinis Lux divinitatis. Opus ad codicum fidem nunc primum integre editum Solesmensium O. S. B. monachorum cura et opera.* Ed. Louis Paquelin. Paris: Oudin, 1877, 1–421, here at Book VI (which gives a hagiographic account of Gertrude of Hackeborn), Ch. 1, 374–5: *Divinam Scripturam valde studiose*

et mira delectatione quandocumque poterat legebat, exigens a subditis suis ut lectiones sacras amarent, et jugi memoria recitarent. Unde omnes bonos libros quos poterat, ecclesiæ suæ comparabat, aut transcribi a Sororibus faciebat. Studiose et hoc promovebat, ut puellæ in liberalibus artibus proficerent, ita dicens, si studium scientiæ deperierit, cum amplius divinam Scripturam non intellexerint, Religionis simul cultus interibit. Unde et juniores minus litteratas amplius addiscere sæpe cogebat, et magistras eis providebat.* Mechthild of Hackeborn, *The Book of Special Grace.* Trans. Barbara Newman. New York: Paulist Press, 2017, 204: 'Whenever she could, she read the divine Scripture studiously and with wonderful delight, requiring her subordinates to love the sacred lessons and recite them from memory. She bought her church all the good books that she could, or else had the sisters copy them. She also zealously promoted education so the girls would acquire knowledge of the liberal arts. If zeal for learning were to perish, she used to say, once they no longer understood the divine Scripture, religious devotion would perish too. So she required the younger nuns who were less learned to study more, and she provided them with female teachers.'

24   *Legatus divinae pietatis* I, 4. *Gertrude d'Helfta: Œuvres spirituelles* II, 142–4: *Laborabat etiam crebrius in colligendis et scribendis omnibus quae alicui unquam credebat esse proficua; [. . .] et etiam in quibus majorem locis inopiam Scripturae sacrae sciebat ibi libentius quae poterat utilia procurabat, ut omnes Christo posset lucrari.* Translation by Barratt, *The Herald of God's Loving-Kindness*, 1&2, 50–1: 'She also devoted a good deal of effort to collecting and writing down everything which she thought might sometime be of use to anyone. [. . .] Also, where she knew there was a special shortage of the sacred books, she willingly did what she could to get hold of the necessary copies, so as to win everyone for Christ.' For Gertrude of Helfta's own editorial work on Latin texts, see *Legatus* I, 7.

25   For a discussion of writing utensils in the *Legatus*, see Ulrike Wiethaus, 'Collaborative Literacy and the Spiritual Education of Nuns at Helfta.' *Nuns' Literacies in Medieval Europe: The Kansas City Dialogue.* Ed. Virginia Blanton, Veronica O'Mara, and Patricia Stoop. Medieval Women – Texts and Contexts Vol. 27. Turnhout: Brepols, 2015, 27–46, at 32–3.

26 The text of the 1503 preamble is printed in: Joseph Müller, *Leben und Offenbarungen der heiligen Mechtildis und der Schwester Mechtildis (von Magdeburg), Jungfrauen aus dem Orden des heiligen Benediktus.* Regensburg: Manz, 1880, XXXIIa–g, here at XXXIIa: *Graf Herman von Manssfeldt hat keinen menlichen Erben gehabt, aber drey Toechter: Zwey, als Sophiam and Elisabeth, hat er in das Closter Helpede gethan, welche gantz Gottseliglich gelebt: Eine ist gewesen eine gute Schreiberin, die vil guter und nutzlicher Bücher dem Closter geschriben hat und hernach Abtissin gewesen: Die ander ist eine lange Zeit gewesen Priorin, und ein gute Malerin, die mit ihrem Malen die Bücher und anders das zu dem Goettlichen Dienst gehoeret, fleissig gezieret.* Oefelein, 'Gründung und mittelalterliche Geschichte des Klosters St. Marien zu Helfta,' 9, clarifies that the Sophia mentioned cannot be identified with the abbess Sophia of Querfurt-Mansfeld. The Elisabeth mentioned, however, may well be the same prioress who is mentioned in a charter from 19 June 1323, see Krühne, *Urkundenbuch der Klöster der Grafschaft Mansfeld*, 172, nr. 81.

27 Gertrude is looking at the crucified Christ in an illuminated book (*in folio*, meaning 'on the manuscript page') and describes his side wound; see *Legatus* II, 5. *Gertrude d'Helfta: Œuvres spirituelles* II, 248–50. For a discussion of this vision, see Henning Laugerud, '"And how could I find Thee at all, if I do not remember Thee?" Visions, Images and Memory in Late Medieval Devotion.' *The Materiality of Devotion in Late Medieval Northern Europe: Images, Objects, Practices.* Ed. Henning Laugerud, Salvador Ryan, and Laura Katrine Skinnebach. European Network on the Instruments of Devotion Vol. 3. Dublin: Four Courts Press, 2016, 50–69, at 53.

28 That Mechthild of Magdeburg wrote in her vernacular tongue while the established Helfta sisters preferred Latin for their writings led to conflicts in the scriptorium cannot be ruled out; but it is hard to underpin this supposition with historical evidence.

29 The only evidence for Mechthild having lived in Magdeburg is the mentioning of a deacon in the *Flowing Light* (VI, 3) whose name, Dietrich of Dobin, is attested in other historical documents. For a critical discussion about whether Mechthild can be located in Magdeburg, see Hellgardt, 'Das 'Fließende Licht der Gottheit',' 107–8.

30 Only one full vernacular version has come down to us: Einsiedeln, Stiftsbibliothek, Codex 277 (1014). Were we to believe the Latin prologue to the *Flowing Light* about its production, the aged and nearly blind Mechthild received scribal help from the Helfta nuns to complete her work, that is to finish the final chapters of the ultimate book. The translation of the vernacular *Flowing Light* into Latin, *Lux divinitatis*, does not include the seventh book and is also missing a few chapters from the *Flowing Light* (III, 23; VI, 22, and VI, 43). Other divergences suggest that the Latin text was based on an earlier non-extant version of the *Flowing Light*, see Ernst Hellgardt, 'Latin and the Vernacular: Mechthild of Magdeburg—Mechthild of Hackeborn—Gertrude of Helfta.' *Companion to Mysticism and Devotion*, 131–55.

31 See Nemes, *Von der Schrift zum Buch*, 115–6. On structuring in scholastic texts, see Nigel F. Palmer, 'Kapitel und Buch: Zu den Gliederungsprinzipien mittelalterlicher Bücher.' *Frühmittelalterliche Studien* 23 (1989): 43–88; specifically on the *Flowing Light*, see 77–8.

32 For the notion of Mechthild as author who disseminates her work and reacts to readers, see Gisela Vollmann-Profe, 'Mechthild – auch "in Werktagskleidern": Zu berühmten und weniger berühmten Abschnitten des "Fließenden Lichts der Gottheit".' *Zeitschrift für deutsche Philologie* 113 (1994): 144–58.

33 A Dominican friar called Henricus presents himself in the prologue as having translated it from the vernacular into Latin, see Mechthild von Magdeburg, 'Lux divinitatis.' *Revelationes Gertrudianæ ac Mechtildianæ Vol. II: Sanctæ Mechtildis virginis ordinis sancti Benedicti Liber specialis gratiæ, accedit sororis Mechtildis ejusdem ordinis Lux divinitatis. Opus ad codicum fidem nunc primum integre editum Solesmensium O. S. B. monachorum cura et opera.* Ed. Louis Paquelin. Paris: Oudin, 1877, 435–710, at 437. See also the new edition *'Lux Divinitatis' – 'Das Liecht Der Gotheit': Der Lateinisch-frühneuhochdeutsche Überlieferungszweig des 'Fließenden Lichts Der Gottheit'. Synoptische Ausgabe.* Ed. Ernst Hellgardt, Balázs J. Nemes, and Elke Senne. Berlin: De Gruyter, 2019, 15.

34 For an extensive description of the production and transmission of the *Lux divinitatits*, see Hellgardt, Nemes, and Senne, eds. *'Lux Divinitatis' – 'Das Liecht Der Gotheit'*, xvii–lxxxii.

35 While the precise circumstances of the production of the Einsiedeln manuscript are subject to debate – and in particular the Dominican Heinrich of Nördlingen's role in this process – 'individual amendments to the translation [. . .] and its reception in the fourteenth century indicate that its transmission occurred primarily within Dominican circles', Nemes, 'Text Production and Authorship,' 103–30, at 114. For a comprehensive list of all manuscripts containing the *Flowing Light* see Nemes, *Von der Schrift zum Buch*, 487–8; transcriptions of otherwise not edited excerpts related to the *Flowing Light* on 397–483.

36 For a long time, the idea that Mechthild's work was composed in Middle Low/Central German stood on hypothetical ground, since the transmitted manuscripts were all in either Latin or Middle High German. The recently discovered fragment (Moscow, Lomonosov-University Library, Collection Gustav Schmidt, Fonds 40/1, nr. 47), however, proves the Middle Low German/Central composition; see Palmer, 'Ein Zeugnis deutscher Kunstprosa aus dem späten 13. Jahrhundert,' 97–138; see also Catherine Squires, 'Das Moskauer Mechthild-Fragment,' 57–90.

37 On the Dominican influences, see Hasebrink, '"Das fließende Licht der Gottheit" Mechthilds von Magdeburg,' 149–61.

38 The debate about the attribution of authorship to Mechthild of Magdeburg is long standing; it is discussed by Sara S. Poor, *Mechthild of Magdeburg and Her Book and the Making of Textual Authority*. Philadelphia: University of Pennsylvania Press, 2004, and Nemes, *Von der Schrift zum Buch*.

39 On the stylistic difference of the seventh book, marking also a certain spiritual maturity, see Hasebrink, '"Das fließende Licht der Gottheit" Mechthilds von Magdeburg,' 150 and 157–8.

40 Kurt Ruh, 'Gertrud von Helfta: Ein neues Gertrud-Bild.' *Zeitschrift für deutsches Altertum und deutsche Literatur*, 121 (1992): 1–20. Whether Sister N can be identified as Sophia of Mansfeld, one of the daughters of Count Hermann II of Mansfeld, who was active as a scribe in Helfta (see above), is impossible to determine.

41 See Nemes and Märker, 'Hunc tercium conscripsi cum maximo labore occultandi,' 248–96.

42 On the writing process of the *Liber*, see Claudia Kolletzki, '"Über die Wahrheit dieses Buches": Die Entstehung des "Liber Specialis Gratiae" Mechthilds von Hackeborn zwischen Wirklichkeit und Fiktion.' *'Vor dir steht die leere Schale meiner Sehnsucht': Die Mystik der Frauen von Helfta*. Ed. Michael Bangert and Hildegund Keul. Leipzig: Benno, 1998, 156–79.

43 See Barbara Newman, 'Annihilation and Authorship: Three Women Mystics of the 1290s.' *Speculum* 91 (2016): 591–630.

44 For an overview of Gertrude of Helfta's life, see Barratt, 'Introduction,' 12. For a slightly different account, see Johnson, *This Is My Body*, 3–8.

45 Ruh, 'Gertrud von Helfta,' 4–5.

46 Given the collective nature of learning and writing at Helfta, it is not entirely inconceivable that two sisters would share a similar Latin style. What Kurt Ruh termed 'Sister N' could therefore be less seen as a single person than an epitome for a consistent editorial work enabled by the Helfta scriptorium.

47 Barratt, 'Introduction,' 16.

48 Gertrudis [de Helfta], *Insinuationes divinae pietatis libri quinque*. Ed. Johannes Justus von Landsberg. Cologne: Melchior von Neuß, 1536.

49 Nemes therefore suggests excising the *Exercitia Spiritualia* from the Helfta corpus, see 'Text Production and Authorship,' 105. More recently Nemes adds linguistic reasons for the hypothesis that the *Exercitia* were not produced in Helfta, see '"ut earundem testimonio conprobatur": Schwester Mechthild in der Offenbarungliteratur von Helfta (mit einem Textabdruck aus der Leipziger Handschrift Ms 827.' *Beihefte zur Zeitschrift für deutsche Philologie* 17 (2019). Special Issue: *Mechthild und das Fließende Licht der Gottheit im Kontext. Eine Spurensuche in religiösen Netzwerken und literarischen Diskursen im mitteldeutschen Raum des 13.–15. Jahrhunderts*. Ed. Caroline Emmelius and Balázs J. Nemes, 89–123, at 96, n. 30.

50 Nonetheless, scholars repeat the assumption that Gertrude was the author of the *Spiritual Exercises*; for example Anna Harrison, '"Oh! What Treasure Is in This Book?" Writing,

Reading, and Community at the Monastery of Helfta.' *Viator* 39 (2008): 75–106, at 76; Michael Bangert, 'The Metaphor of the Vestment in the Writings of Gertrud of Helfta (1256–1302).' *Iconography of Liturgical Textiles in the Middle Ages*. Ed. Evelin Wetter. Riggisberger Berichte Vol. 18. Riggisberg: Abegg-Stiftung, 2010, 129–39, at 131; and more recently Claire Taylor Jones, '"Hostia jubilationis": Psalm Citation, Eucharistic Prayer, and Mystical Union in Gertrude of Helfta's "Exercitia spiritualia".' *Speculum* 89 (2014): 1005–39, at 1006; Ella Johnson, 'To Taste ("Sapere") Wisdom ("Sapientia"): Eucharistic Devotion in the Writings of Gertrude of Helfta.' *Viator* 44 (2013): 175–99, at 176; Barratt, 'Introduction,' 11, formulates more hypothetically that Gertrude was 'possibly' the source of the *Spiritual Exercises*.

51 Ruh, 'Gertrud von Helfta,' 6–7.

52 An example for the transmission of altered prayers from the *botte der götlichen miltekeit*, is presented in Chapter 3 'Manuscript Transmission History'.

53 Ruh, 'Gertrud von Helfta,' 7: 'in Wirklichkeit ein Konglomerat von Texten'.

54 See *Legatus* I, prologue. *Gertrude d'Helfta: Œuvres spirituelles* II, 108: *Unde et liber iste diversis temporibus est conscriptus, ita ut pars una conscriberetur post octavum annum acceptae gratiae et pars altera circa vicesimum annum perficeretur*. Translation by Nemes, 'Text Production and Authorship,' 122: 'this book was written down at various times: one part written down eight years after her reception of grace and the second part completed about twenty years later'.

55 On the *Liber* and the *Legatus* as 'glosses' to the liturgy, see Bruce Holsinger, *Music, Body, and Desire in Medieval Culture: Hildegard of Bingen to Chaucer*. Stanford: Stanford University Press, 2001, 242–3.

56 The hypothesis that the *Liber* was originally composed in German and only later translated into Latin, as formulated by Schmidt, 'Mechthild of Hackeborn,' 252, is generally dismissed in scholarship today. Given the confident handling of Latin in Helfta, there is no reason to assume that the nuns needed an intermediary step of writing. However, this does not rule out that the oral report of visions would have been in the nuns' vernacular mother tongues, that is, dialects of German.

57 Nemes, 'Text Production and Authorship,' 114. Johnson, *This Is My Body*, 201, stresses the difference between Mechthild of Magdeburg's 'literary context' and that of Gertrude of Helfta. In contrast to Nemes, who concentrates on the manuscript transmission, Johnson looks at the historically imaginable production scenarios.

58 For a list of manuscripts considered in the Solesmes edition (with their scholarly abbreviation) and for further manuscripts identified to contain portions of the *Legatus*, see 'Manuscript Transmission with Catalogues' in the Appendix. I thank Balázs Nemes for generous sharing of the list of Latin manuscripts.

59 For further details on the transmission, see Nemes, 'Text Production and Authorship,' 108–10. Certainly Erfurt's Benedictine Abbey and its Charterhouse played pivotal roles in the dissemination of the Helfta writings; see also Eifler, *Die Bibliothek des Erfurter Petersklosters*, Vol. 1, 533–4; Nemes, *Von der Schrift zum Buch*, 227–8; Kirakosian, 'The Earliest Transmitted German Legatus' 181–4. On the two Erfurt convents and their book management, see Matthias Eifler, 'Bücher in den Händen von Klosterbibliothekaren: Befunde aus dem 15. und frühen 16. Jahrhundert am Beispiel der Kartause und des Benediktinerklosters in Erfurt.' *Manuscripts Changing Hands: Handschriften wechseln von Hand zu Hand*. Ed. Corine Schleif and Volker Schier. Wolfenbütteler Mittelalter-Studien Vol. 31. Wiesbaden: Harrassowitz, 2016, 207–53. A Freiburg-based project led by Balázs J. Nemes and Antje Kellersohn reconstructs the mystical holdings in the medieval library of the Erfurt Charterhouse, for more information see online: https://making-mysticism.org (last accessed 03.06.2019).

60 See Nemes and Märker, 'Hunc tercium conscripsi cum maximo labore occultandi,' 257 and 251, n. 21.

61 On this prayer community, see Oefelein, 'Gründung und mittelalterliche Geschichte des Klosters St. Marien zu Helfta,' 15.

62 See Kirakosian, 'The Earliest Transmitted German Legatus,' 183.

63 See Balázs J. Nemes, 'Scenes of Writing, Figurations of Authorship: A Literature Historian's Reflections on the Veracity of the

Passages Recounting the Textual Genesis of the Special Edition of Gertrude of Helfta's "Legatus divinae pietatis".' *Analecta Cisterciensia* 69 (2019): 145–60.

64 Translations by Nemes, 'Text Production and Authorship,' 122–6, based on *Legatus* I, prologue, 108–14.

65 Translations by Nemes, 'Text Production and Authorship,' 126–7, based on *Legatus* I, prologue, 116.

66 Following Kurt Ruh's suggestion that this anonymous scribe is Sister N, Nemes ascertains that this Sister N 'could most readily be called an author', Nemes, 'Text Production and Authorship,' 116. Barratt, 'Introduction', 14, allots Sister N 'a noticeable presence in book 4' of the *Legatus*.

67 *Legatus* V, 1. In *Gertrude d'Helfta, Œuvres spirituelles* Vol. 5: *Le Héraut* (Livre V). Ed. Jean-Marie Clément and Bernard de Vregille. Sources chrétiennes Vol. 331. Paris: Éditions du Cerf, 1986, 36: *quae tamen causa brevitatis transcurro*; *Legatus* IV, 27. In *Gertrude d'Helfta, Œuvres spirituelles*. Vol. 4: *Le Héraut* (Livre IV). Ed. Jean-Marie Clément, Sources chrétiennes. Série des textes monastiques d'Occident 48. Paris: Éditions du Cerf, 1978, 266: *quae tamen omnia, sicut et alia plura, causa brevitatis omitto, ne forte prolixitas fastidium* generet. See Barratt, 'Introduction,' 15, for a discussion of 'trimming' the material by Sister N in Book IV of the *Legatus*.

68 Nemes, 'Text Production and Authorship,' 117. Barratt, 'Introduction,' 15, characterises Sister N as 'a privileged intermediary who grants or refuses access to Gertrud's experiences'.

69 The final chapters of the *Legatus* especially draw the attention to Sister N's editorial work; for a discussion in the context of the German *botte der götlichen miltekeit*, see Chapter 4 'The Book's Self-Reflectivity'.

70 For a discussion of this new material, see Alexandra Barratt, 'The Chronological Priority of the Memoriale abundantiae suavitatis divinae in Leipzig, Universitätsbibliothek, MS 827.' *Analecta Cisterciensa* 69 (2019): 198–209.

71 *Est enim liber iste diuisus in tres partes, quarum primam partem ipsa, que hec a largitore omnium graciarum accipere meruit, suis manibus scripsit post octauum annum accepte gracie in sancto die cene dominice.* Edition of the Latin prologue in:

Nemes and Märker, 'Hunc tercium conscripsi cum maximo labore occultandi,' 248–96 (edition on 268–71), at 269.

72 [. . .] *ut aliquam personam eligeret, cui ad lucrum laudis diuine secreta sua detegeret.* Ibid., 269.

73 *Dehinc cum diuine magis quam proprie uoluntati consentiendum iudicaret, in quadragesima die quadam deo regente opportunitate, cum ego licet indigna sola sibi adessem, aliqua mihi detexit tam inuoluto sermone et tam miserabili tremore singulorum membrorum, quod omni uidenti manifeste daretur intelligi, quam nimis contra suam humanam uoluntatem fiebat, si quid de talibus manifestauit.* Ibid., 269.

74 *Contigit domino ut spero prouidente, cuius nutu uniuersa reguntur et disponuntur, ut hec ad noticiam spiritualium prelatorum nostrorum deuenirent, ita omnino tam contra meam quam contra suam uoluntatem, quod uere ambe pocius mortem elegissemus, quam hoc uoluntarie fieri consensissemus. Quod ipsa euidenti testimonio probauit, quia in ipso momento inter uerba huiusmodi notum facientis, quod scilicet aliqua scripta de ea prodita essent, tam acri febre correpta est, quod post ea per multum tempus decubuit. Que eciam pars mei grauaminis inde fuerit, illi committo, qui solus probat renes et corda.* Ibid., 269–70.

75 *Tercium vero libellum, ultimos scilicet quinque quaternos, hac occasione conscripsi.* Ibid., 270.

76 *Nam cum dilectissima et tam deo quam hominibus fidelissima predulcis memorie G abbatissa tali infirmitate laboraret, quod diffidebam de pro-ductiori adiutorio ipsius, quo in hoc negocio nihil tum per omnem modum fueram promota, indignum iudicans tam eleganti et dilecto mihi libro talem imponere finem, qui non plurimorum testimonio manifestiori probabilior redderetur.* Ibid., 270.

77 *Unde commendo eum cordi diuino usque post mortem ipsius deside-rans et exoptans, ut deus restituat conseruatori, si plene fideliter seruauerit, talem remuneracionem, qualem restituere uellet, si tot graues labores pertulis-set pro fidelitate nominis dei, quot littere sunt in libro isto conscripte. Amen.* Ibid., 271.

78 On the importance of obedience to the abbess in women's convents, see Katie Ann-Marie Bugyis, *The Care of Nuns: The Ministries of Benedictine Women in England during the Central Middle Ages.* Oxford: Oxford University Press, 2019.

79 The *Legatus'* compilation spans across different periods and the involved abbesses might have had varying agendas; for a historical overview,

see Nemes and Märker, 'Hunc tercium conscripsi cum maximo labore occultandi,' 250–2.

80 Alexandra Barratt argues that chronological priority is to be given to the *Leipzig Legatus*, hence criticising its denomination as a special edition, and using instead the Latin title conferred on it in the manuscript: *Memoriale abundantiae suavitatis divinae*. According to Barratt, additional paragraphs in the *Leipzig Legatus* and its compositional principle, much more coherent both chronologically and content-wise, mean that it was produced earlier than the more disseminated 'standard' *Legatus*. More evidence may suggest that this manuscript, which was never completed, could be an early version of Gertrude's revelations, perhaps even produced during Mechthild of Hackeborn's lifetime; Barratt, 'The Chronological Priority of the Memoriale'.

81 See Nemes, *Von der Schrift zum Buch*; see also Barbara Newman, 'New Seeds, New Harvests: Thirty Years of Tilling the Mystical Field.' *Traditio* 72 (2017): 9–20. Harrison, 'I Am Wholly Your Own,' 553, draws attention to the Helfta corpus as 'the largest body of female-authored writings of the thirteenth century'; Poor, *Mechthild of Magdeburg and Her Book*, 1, calls authorship a 'central problem' in the case of Mechthild Magdeburg.

82 According to thirteenth-century literary theory, Gertrude – like both Mechthilds – figures as coauthor with God: God, in this sense, is the *causa efficiens movens* while the prophet is the *causa efficiens operans*; these terms are applied to the prophet Isaiah by the Dominican scholar Guerric of Saint-Quentin; see Beryl Smalley, 'A Commentary on Isaias by Guerric of Saint-Quentin.' *Miscellanea Giovanni Mercati*. Vol. 2. Studi e Testi Vol. 122. Vatican: Biblioteca Apostolica Vaticana, 1946, 383–97, at 389. See also Minnis, *Medieval Theory of Authorship*, 79; and Nigel F. Palmer, 'Das Buch als Bedeutungsträger bei Mechthild von Magdeburg.' *Bildhafte Rede in Mittelalter und früher Neuzeit. Probleme ihrer Legitimation und ihrer Funktion*. Ed. Wolfgang Harms. Tübingen: Niemeyer, 1992, 217–35, at 219. Moreover, the notion of a visionary passing on God's message to a third instance, a scribe, was traditional (see Palmer, 'Das Buch als Bedeutungsträger bei Mechthild von Magdeburg,' 224), meaning that prophetic

writing is somewhat tied up with collective authorship.

83 The fact that all three use the scholastic entities *liber* and *capitulum* to structure the material reinforces the notion of conceptually reflected and long-term processes of skilful recording, compiling, and editing. It also means that, in Helfta, knowledge of compositional principles as based on Latin writing was strong. On the scholastic background of such ordering principles, see Palmer, 'Kapitel und Buch'. See also Nemes, *Von der Schrift zum Buch*, 125–6.

84 For Mechthild of Magdeburg as neither 'author' nor 'editor' but 'medium or instrument', see Frank Tobin, *Mechthild von Magdeburg: A Medieval Mystic in Modern Eyes*. Columbia: Camden House, 1995, 108–10.

85 Because of the intricate transmission history of the *Flowing Light*, Nemes, *Von der Schrift zum Buch*, 380, embraces the notion of an 'open concept regarding the author' as first suggested by Margarete Hubrath, 'The "Liber specialis gratiae" as a Collective Work of Several Nuns.' *Jahrbuch der Oswald von Wolkenstein-Gesellschaft* 11 (1999): 233–44, at 238.

86 In this sense, the named writers of Helfta were certainly not alone but formed part of a 'Helfta school of theology' ('Helftaer Theologinnenschule'), which was at the same time a 'laboratory of language' ('Sprachwerkstatt'); Keul and Ringler, 'In der Freiheit des lebenden Geistes,' 29.

87 See Poor, *Mechthild of Magdeburg and her book*, 6–7; see also Nicholas Watson, *Richard Rolle and the Invention of Authority*. Cambridge: Cambridge University Press, 1991. Problems with reporting mystical experiences have, in the long term, led to the attempt of finding 'hard ways' to prove a vision wrong or right; on the so-called discernment of spirits, see Rosalynn Voaden, *God's Words, Women's Voices: The Discernment of Spirits in the Writing of Late-Medieval Women Visionaries*. Woodbridge: York Medieval Press, 1999; Niklaus Largier, 'Rhetorik des Begehrens: Die "Unterscheidung der Geister" als Paradigma mittelalterlicher Subjektivität.' *Inszenierungen von Subjektivität in der Literatur des Mittelalters*. Ed. Martin Baisch, Jutta Erning, Hendrijke Haufe, and Andrea Sieber. Königstein im Taunus: Helmer, 2005, 249–70.

88 Poor, *Mechthild of Magdeburg and Her Book*, 3, for example, argues that Mechthild of

Magdeburg's gender contributes decisively to the 'unstableness' of the text since 'anxiety about authorship expressed in the text [*Flowing Light of the Godhead*] has much to do with women's perceived inadequacy to the task. Medieval female authorship in this case thus seems to be characterized by an absence rather than an assertion of authority.' At the same time, Poor highlights the fact that authorship in medieval texts is generally a difficult matter, also for male theologians, 3–6. Rüdiger Schnell, 'Gender und Rhetorik in Mittelalter und früher Neuzeit: Zur Kommunikation der Geschlechter.' *Rhetorik* 29 (2010): 1–18, at 7, generally states that 'female authors are inclined or see themselves forced to justify their status as authors much more explicitly' ('Autorinnen neigen dazu oder sehen sich gezwungen, sehr viel expliziter ihren Status als Autor zu legitimieren').

89   For a discussion of collaborative literacy at Helfta, see Wiethaus, 'Collaborative Literacy and the Spiritual Education,' 34: 'the norm for medieval Helfta's textual productivity was collaborative anonymous authorship'. See also Laura Maria Grimes, *Wisdom's Friends: Gertrud of Helfta's Conversational Theology*. Saarbrücken: VDM Verlag, 2009.

90   Peter Strohschneider, *Höfische Textgeschichten: Über Selbstentwürfe vormoderner Literatur*. Germanisch-Romanische Monatsschrift. Beihefte Vol. 55. Heidelberg: Universitätsverlag Winter, 2014, in particular 25–7.

91   See Michel Foucault, 'Qu'est-ce qu'un auteur?' *Dits et écrits*. Vol. 1: 1954–1975. Ed. Daniel Defert and François Ewald. Paris: Gallimard, 1994: Repr. 2008, 817–49, in particular 828: '"Hippocrate a dit", "Pline raconte" n'étaient pas au juste les formules d'une argument d'autorité; c'étaient les indices dont étaient marqués des discours destinés à être reçus comme prouvés.' The discursive quality of authorship in medieval literature has been discussed by Klaus Grubmüller, 'Verändern und Bewahren: Zum Bewußtsein vom Text im deutschen Mittelalter.' *Text und Kultur: Mittelalterliche Literatur 1100–1450*. Ed. Ursula Peters. Germanistische Symposien Berichtsbände Vol. 22. Stuttgart, Weimar: J.B. Metzler'sche Verlagsbuchhandlung und Carl Ernst Poeschel Verlag GmbH, 2001, 8–33.

92   Ursula Peters, 'Ordnungsfunktion – Textillustration – Autorkonstruktion: Zu den Bildern der romanischen und deutschen Liederhandschriften.' *Zeitschrift für deutsches Altertum und deutsche Literatur* 130 (2001): 392–430, at 399: 'Aura persönlich-biographischer "auctoritas"'.

93   Some scholars study visionary hagiography as historically accurate biographical accounts; this approach is, for example, defended by Peter Dinzelbacher, 'Zur Interpretation erlebnismystischer Texte des Mittelalters.' *Zeitschrift für deutsches Altertum und deutsche Literatur* 117 (1988): 1–23, at 1–4. Cristina Mazzoni, 'Angela of Foligno.' *Medieval Holy Women in the Christian Tradition, c. 1100–c. 1500*. Ed. Alastair J. Minnis and Rosalynn Voaden. Brepols Essays in European Culture Vol. 1. Turnhout: Brepols, 2010, 581–600, at 591, speculates about a vision of Angela of Foligno that its source of inspiration builds upon personal experience: 'This vision is regularly evoked for its beauty and its positive representation of the body, for its realism and for the confirmation that a married woman who knows what the body of a man feels like will have an experience of Christ's presence different from a virgin.' Generally, research on so-called somatic mysticism has been quick in judging tropes of desire as an outlet for sexuality, especially when female mystics are concerned, see for example Grace M. Jantzen, *Power, Gender and Christian Mysticism*. Cambridge Studies in Ideology and Religion Vol. 8. Cambridge: Cambridge University Press, 1995, 133: 'The sexuality is explicit, and there is no warning that it should not be taken literally.' Understanding authorship as a purely literary construct stands opposed to the idea of finding biographical evidence in the respective writings; for this literary argument see in particular Ursula Peters, *Religiöse Erfahrung als literarisches Faktum: Zur Vorgeschichte und Genese frauenmystischer Texte des 13. und 14. Jahrhunderts*. Tübingen: Niemeyer, 1988; Peters, 'Werkauftrag und Buchübergabe: Textentstehungsgeschichten in Autorbildern volkssprachiger Handschriften im 12. bis 15. Jahrhunderts.' *Autorbilder: Zur Medialität literarischer Kommunikation in Mittelalter und Früher Neuzeit*. Ed. Gerald Kapfhammer, Wolf-Dietrich Löhr, and Barbara Nitsche. Tholos

Kunsthistorische Studien Vol. 2. Münster: Rhema, 2007, 25–62. Several scholars have opted for a third way between these extreme positions, accepting literary constructs as based on historical contexts, for example Susanne Köbele, *Bilder der unbegriffenen Wahrheit: Zur Struktur mystischer Rede im Spannungsfeld von Latein und Volkssprache.* Bibliotheca Germanica Vol. 30. Tübingen: Francke, 1993, at 22 and 198; Susanne Bürkle, *Literatur im Kloster: Historische Funktion und rhetorische Legitimation frauenmystischer Texte des 14. Jahrhunderts.* Bibliotheca Germanica Vol. 38. Tübingen: Francke, 1999.

94 Poor, *Mechthild of Magdeburg and Her Book*, 10, 193–9. See also Sara S. Poor, 'Mechthild von Magdeburg, Gender, and the "Unlearned Tongue".' *Journal of Medieval and Early Modern Studies* 31 (2001): 213–50, in particular 213–21.

95 On discrepancies between Latin and vernacular and the impact the choice made, see Stephen Mossman, *Marquard von Lindau and the Challenges of Religious Life in Late Medieval Germany.* Oxford: Oxford University Press, 2010, 25–6; Susanne Köbele: 'Primo aspectu monstruosa.' Schriftauslegung bei Meister Eckhart.' *Zeitschrift für deutsches Altertum und deutsche Literatur* 122 (1993): 62–81; Almut Suerbaum, 'Sprachliche Interferenz bei Begriffen des Lassens: "Lux Divinitatis" und das "Fließende Licht der Gottheit".' *Semantik der Gelassenheit: Generierung, Etablierung, Transformation.* Ed. Burkhard Hasebrink, Susanne Bernhardt, and Imke Früh. Historische Semantik Vol. 17. Göttingen: Vandenhoeck & Ruprecht, 2012, 33–47. More generally on theological implications due to the choice of language, see Nicholas Watson, 'Conceptions of the Word: The Mother Tongue and the Incarnation of God.' *New Medieval Literatures* 1 (1997): 85–124.

96 This is the case for Mechthild of Magdeburg as shown by Palmer, 'Das Buch als Bedeutungsträger bei Mechthild von Magdeburg,' at 223–4; see also Susanne Köbele, *Bilder der unbegriffenen Wahrheit*, 33–7; and Poor, 'Mechthild von Magdeburg, Gender, and the 'Unlearned Tongue'', 217–18. Yet, Mechthild of Magdeburg, who identifies herself as an uneducated woman, must have been 'anything but uneducated', reasons Elizabeth

A. Andersen, ''Das Fließende Licht der Gottheit' und der Psalter: Dialogische Beziehungen.' *Dialoge: Sprachliche Kommunikation in und zwischen Texten im deutschen Mittelalter: Hamburger Colloquium 1999.* Ed. Nikolaus Henkel, Martin H. Jones, and Nigel F. Palmer. Tübingen: Niemeyer, 2003, 225–38, at 231. The thirteenth-century Premonstratensian mystic Christina of Hane provides a case where a theological tension between divine knowledge communicated in Latin and its vernacular report by the mystic is presented by the hagiographer, see Kirakosian, *Die Vita der Christina von Hane,* 224–5. For the translation of the *Life*, see Racha Kirakosian, ed. *The Life of Christina of Hane: Introduction and Translation.* New Haven: Yale University Press, 2020.

97 Poor, *Mechthild of Magdeburg and Her Book*, 58.

98 Ibid., Chapter 2 'Visions of Authorship: Cloaking the Body in Text,' 57–78. See also Rosalynn Voaden, 'All Girls Together: Community, Gender and Vision at Helfta.' *Medieval Women in their Communities.* Ed. Diane Watt. Cardiff: University of Wales Press, 1997, 72–91, who explains images of the bleeding divine heart found in the *Liber* and *Legatus* with the specific nuns' female bodies, namely with their menstruation. Dyan Elliott, 'Flesh and Spirit: The Female Body.' *Medieval Holy Women in the Christian Tradition, c. 1100–c. 1500.* Ed. Alastair J. Minnis and Rosalynn Voaden. Brepols Essays in European Culture Vol. 1. Turnhout: Brepols, 2010, 13–46, at 21, explores more generally the implications of a body-centred mysticism concluding that experiences of 'embodiment had the effect of rendering the female body a special medium for communication with the incarnate Christ, ushering in forms of religious expression grounded in physicality.'

99 See now also the discussion in Johnson, *This Is My Body*, xx–xxii.

100 Caroline Walker Bynum, *Holy Feast and Holy Fast: The Religious Significance of Food to Medieval Women.* Berkeley: University of California Press, 1987; *Fragmentation and Redemption: Essays on Gender and the Human Body in Medieval Religion.* New York: Zone Books, 1991, in particular at 194. Many studies stand in Bynum's tradition, to name but a couple: Kathleen E. Garay, '"A Naked Intent

unto God": Ungendered Discourse in some Late Medieval Mystical Texts.' *Mystics Quarterly* 23 (1997): 36–51; Rebecca L. R. Garber, *Feminine Figurae: Representations of Gender in Religious Texts by Medieval German Women Writers, 1100–1375*. Studies in Medieval History and Culture Vol. 10. New York: Routledge, 2003.

101 Jantzen, *Power, Gender, and Christian Mysticism*, 108.

102 Amy Hollywood, *Sensible Ecstasy: Mysticism, Sexual Difference and the Demands of History*. Chicago: University of Chicago Press, 2002, 8.

103 Amy Hollywood, *The Soul as Virgin Wife: Mechthild of Magdeburg, Marguerite Porete, and Meister Eckhart*. Notre Dame Studies in Spirituality and Theology Vol. 1. Notre Dame, IN: University of Notre Dame Press, 1995, 16–17.

104 Patricia Dailey, *Promised Bodies: Time, Language, & Corporeality in Medieval Women's Mystical Texts, Gender, Theory, and Religion*. New York: Columbia University Press, 2013, 61.

105 In Dailey's opinion, the question of gender and its relation to embodiment can be studied on different levels defined by techniques of reading, style of writing, presenting, and working through exegesis, Dailey, *Promised Bodies*, 61.

106 See for example, Kirakosian, *Die Vita der Christina von Hane*, 59–64.

107 Such mix-gendered networks and family ties are explored in Fiona J. Griffiths, *Nuns' Priests' Tales: Men and Salvation in Medieval Women's Monastic Life*. Philadelphia: University of Pennsylvania Press, 2018.

108 This is hardly surprising when taking into account that 'men were a constant presence within female religious communities, whether as priests, as authors of spiritual tracts for women, or as monks engaged with women in a shared religious life'; Fiona J. Griffiths and Julie Hotchin, 'Women and Men in the Medieval Religious Landscape.' *Partners in Spirit: Women, Men, and Religious Life in Germany, 1100–1500*. Ed. Fiona J. Griffiths and Julie Hotchin. Medieval Women: Texts and Contexts Vol. 24. Turnhout: Brepols, 2014, 1–45, at 6.

109 For example, texts designed for the *cura monialium*, the male pastoral care of nuns, were characterised by 'diversity, negotiation, and

dialogue', see Griffiths and Hotchin, 'Women and Men in the Medieval Religious Landscape,' 22.

110 Jessica A. Boon, 'Trinitarian Love Mysticism: Ruusbroec, Hadewijch, and the Gendered Experience of the Divine.' *Church History: Studies in Christianity and Culture* 72 (2003): 484–503, at 487.

111 Meister Eckhart's vernacular sermon Q2, 'Intravit Iesus' explores the feminine notion of the soul, Meister Eckhart, *Die deutschen und lateinischen Werke*: DW 1. Ed. Josef Quint. Stuttgart: Kohlhammer, 1958 (repr. 1986), 24–45. On aspects of body and gender in Richard Rolle's writings, see Christopher M. Roman, *Queering Richard Rolle: Mystical Theology and the Hermit in Fourteenth-Century England*. Cham, Switzerland: Palgrave Macmillian, 2017.

112 Claire Elizabeth McIlroy, *The English Prose Treatises of Richard Rolle*. Studies in Medieval Mysticism Vol. 4. Woodbridge: Boydell & Brewer, 2004, 19.

113 Ibid., 65.

114 Ibid., 100.

115 For example Garay, 'A Naked Intent unto God,' 42–4, where differences in gendered discourses are circumscribed with the concept of 'anti-illectualism'.

116 Ibid., 43.

117 Elizabeth A. Andersen, *The Voices of Mechthild of Magdeburg*, Oxford: Lang, 2000, at 30. The commendation of the *Legatus* – transmitted in three extant manuscripts – mentions the Saxon Dominican Dietrich of Apolda as someone who 'held frequent conversations' with Gertrude 'and gave his complete approval to her discourses and their general import'. *Legatus* I, *Gertrude d'Helfta: Œuvres spirituelles* II, 104: *Frater quoque Theodoricus dictus de Apoldia saepius cum ea colloquium habens sermones et sensum illius per omnia approbavit.* Here translated after Barratt, *The Herald of God's Loving-Kindness*, 1&2, 29.

118 On gendered complementation rather than conflict, see Caroline Walker Bynum, 'Women Mystics in the Thirteenth Century: The Case of the Nuns of Helfta.' *Jesus as Mother: Studies in the Spirituality of the High Middle Ages*. Publications of the Center for Medieval and Renaissance Studies Vol. 16. Berkeley: University of California Press, 1982, 170–261. The historical possibility that

the Helfta nuns, and in particular Gertrude of Helfta, took on priestly responsibilities because of a lack of clerical oversight in the convent – reflected in the many liturgical passages of the *Legatus* – is explored by Wiethaus, 'Collaborative Literacy and the Spiritual Education,' 30.

119 More generally, all texts are best understood when studied within their respective historical contexts; for such an approach regarding mystical texts see: Dee Dyas, Valerie Edden, and Roger Ellis, *Approaching Medieval English Anchoritic and Mystical Texts*. Christianity and Culture Vol. 2. Woodbridge: Boydell & Brewer, 2005. See also the approach proclaimed in the series *Lectura Eckhardi: Predigten Meister Eckharts von Fachgelehrten gelesen und gedeutet*. Vol. 2. Ed. Georg Steer and Lors Sturlese. Stuttgart: Kohlhammer, 2003, VII. Based on Kurt Ruh's call for close readings of historical sermons, Georg Steer, 'Die Interpretation der deutschen und lateinischen Predigten Meister Eckharts – eine unendliche Aufgabe.' *Per perscrutationem philosophicam: Neue Perspektiven der mittelalterlichen Forschung. Loris Sturlese zum 60. Geburtstag gewidmet*. Ed. Alessandra Beccarisi, Ruedi Imbach, and Pasquale Porro. Hamburg: Meiner, 2008, 184–203, at 202, demands the 'integration of all historical knowledge available' ('Integration allen verfügbaren historischen Wissens') in order to supply any interpretation.

120 Poor, *Mechthild of Magdeburg*, 83. Poor finds that the Latin version of Mechthild's text, the *Lux divinitatis*, effaces 'her [Mechthild of Magdeburg's] particular agency in writing it' when it 'ignores the human author Mechthild' in the prologue (88). By contrast, Nemes, *Von der Schrift zum Buch*, 342–57, holds that this is a short reading of the *Lux divinitatis*, which in its totality attributes a 'gendered voice' to its author, and that although Mechthild is only marginally named in the Latin version, there is a 'quasi-biographical' understanding of her person (349). While Poor argues that Mechthild's authorship is firmly established in the production of the *Flowing Light*, Nemes is more critical of authenticity regarding authorial agency, taking the position that the reception of the text material creates its authorial functions more than the production does; see Nemes, *Von der Schrift zum Buch*, 317–42, in particular

321. Both views have their advantages but they are not mutually exclusive: Mechthild could have seen herself as an author and been recognised as one in later transmissions of her text.

121 Susanne Bürkle, 'Weibliche Spiritualität und imaginierte Weiblichkeit: Deutungsmuster und -perspektiven frauenmystischer Literatur im Blick auf die Thesen Caroline W. Bynums.' *Zeitschrift für deutsche Philologie* 113 (1994): 116–43, at 138, speaks of 'collective authorial projects' ('Gemeinschaftsprojekten eines wie auch immer zusammengesetzten Autorenkollektivs'). On female collective authorship, see also Caroline Emmelius, 'Verborgene Wahrheiten offenbaren: Verschriftlichungsprozesse in frauenmystischen Texten zwischen Subversion und Autorisierung.' *Offen und Verborgen: Vorstellungen und Praktiken des Öffentlichen im Privaten in Mittelalter und Früher Neuzeit*. Ed. Caroline Emmelius, Fridrun Freise, Rebekka von Mallinkroth, Claudius Sittig, and Regina Töpfer. Göttingen: Wallstein, 2004, 47–65.

122 Julian of Norwich and Margery Kempe, for example, have been identified as the main authors of their respective writings, but while Julian's own literacy is 'unquestionable', Margery needed someone 'to record and read back her dictation for correction'. However, 'employment of a scribe was a sign of prestige, not necessarily an indication of illiteracy', outlines Josephine Koster Tarvers, '"Thys ys my mystrys boke": English Women as Readers and Writers in Late Medieval England.' *The Uses of Manuscripts in Literary Studies: Essays in Memory of Judson Boyce Allen*. Ed. Charlotte C. Morse, Penelope Reed Doob, and Marjorie Curry Woods. Studies in Medieval Culture Vol. 31. Kalamazoo, MI: Western Michigan University, Medieval Institute Publications, 1992, 305–27, 308. Like medieval Germany, late medieval England offers examples for the dynamics of religious books in female communities, where reading and writing went hand-in-hand and were closely connected, and where the role of social networks was very important in the distribution and reception of books: women owned manuscripts and 'frequently bequeathed them to other women' (315).

123 Nemes, 'Text Production and Authorship,' 117.

124 Questions of gendered authority and writing are most recently explored by Johnson, *This Is My Body*, 160–212. Else Marie Wiberg Pederse, 'Gottesbild – Frauenbild – Selbstbild: Die Theologie Mechthilds von Hackeborn und Gertruds von Helfta.' *'Vor dir steht die leere Schale meiner Sehnsucht': Die Mystik der Frauen von Helfta*. Ed. Michael Bangert and Hildegund Keul. Leipzig: Benno, 1998, 48–66, links gendered mystical experience with the nuns' self-understanding as theologians. That female scribes in monastic scriptoria worked alone and collectively with other women as well as also with men has been discussed by Alison I. Beach, *Women as Scribes: Book Production and Monastic Reform in Twelfth-century Bavaria*. Cambridge Studies in Palaeography and Codicology Vol. 10. Cambridge, UK; New York: Cambridge University Press, 2004.

125 Bangert, 'Die sozio-kulturelle Situation,' 45.

126 Barratt, 'Introduction,' 16.

2 REDACTIONS WITHIN A DYNAMIC TEXTUALITY

1 For example, Walther Kofler, 'Zu den Handschriftenverhältnissen des "Nibelungenliedes": Die Verbindungen zwischen den Redaktionen I, d, n und k.' *Zeitschrift für deutsche Philologie* 130 (2011): 51–82; Jan-Dirk Müller, 'Vulgatfassung? Zur Fassung *C des "Nibelungenliedes" und den sog. kontaminierten Fassungen.' *Beiträge zur Geschichte der deutschen Sprache und Literatur* 138 (2016): 227–63; Uta Goerlitz, 'Mittelalterliche Literatur im Medienwandel von der Handschrift zum gedruckten Buch: Das Beispiel des "Herzog Ernst".' *Das Mittelalter* 22 (2017): 13–38, at 16–17; Florian M. Schmid, *Die Fassung *C des "Nibelungenlieds" und der "Klage": Strategien der Retextualisierung*. Hermae. Neue Folge Vol. 147. Berlin, Boston: De Gruyter, 2018, 3, 41–44; Angila Vetter, *Textgeschichte(n): Retextualisierungsstrategien und Sinnproduktion in Sammlungsverbünden: Der "Willehalm" in kontextueller Lektüre*. Philologische Studien und Quellen Vol. 268. Berlin: ESV, 2018; Antonella Calaresu, 'Die Wolfenbütteler Fassungen der Dorothealegende.' *Zeitschrift für deutsches Altertum und deutsche Literatur* 148 (2019): 351–76.

2 The article 'Redaktion' in the *Reallexikon der deutschen Literaturwissenschaft* refers to the entry 'Fassung' by Bodo Plachta: 'Fassung.' *Reallexikon der deutschen Literaturwissenschaft*. Vol. 1. Eds. Klaus Weimar et al. Berlin: De Gruyter, 1997, 567–68. The terms are interchangeably used by Sebastian Holtzhauer, *Die Fahrt eines Heiligen durch Zeit und Raum: Untersuchungen ausgewählter Retextualisierungen des Brandan-Corpus von den Anfängen bis zum 15. Jahrhundert: Mit einer Edition der Münchener Prosafassung der Reise des hl. Brandan (Pm)*. Göttingen: V & R Unipress, 2019, for example at 33; Michael Rupp, 'Unterweisung in Vers und Prosa: Zu den verschiedenen Erscheinungsformen der lateinischen Predigten Bertholds von Regensburg in der Volkssprache.' *Beiträge zur Geschichte der deutschen Sprache und Literatur* 140 (2018): 51–73, at 56–57; Michael Hopf, *Mystische Kurzdialoge um Meister Eckhart: Editionen und Untersuchungen*. Meister-Eckhart-Jahrbuch. Beiheft Vol. 6. Stuttgart: Verlag W. Kohlhammer, 2019, 41, 47–48.

3 See Holtzhauer, *Die Fahrt eines Heiligen durch Zeit und Raum*; Calaresu, 'Die Wolfenbütteler Fassungen der Dorothealegende'. See also Michael Stolz, 'Early Versions in Medieval Textual Traditions: Wolfram's Parzival as a Test Case.' *Dating Egyptian Literary Texts: Göttingen, 9–12 June 2010* Vol. 1. Ed. Gerald Moers et al. Lingua Aegyptia Studia Monographica Vol. 11. Hamburg: Widmaier, 2013, 561–87.

4 Used thus by Mark Chinca et al., 'The "Kaiserchronik" and its Three Recensions.' *Zeitschrift für deutsches Altertum und deutsche Literatur* 148 (2019): 141–208.

5 Joachim Bumke, *Die Vier Fassungen der "Nibelungenklage": Untersuchungen zur Überlieferungsgeschichte und Textkritik der höfischen Epik im 13. Jahrhundert*. Quellen und Forschungen zur Literatur- und Kulturgeschichte Vol. 8. Berlin; New York: De Gruyter, 1996.

6 The discussion is summarised by Schiewer, 'Fassung, Bearbeitung, Version und Edition'. See also the attempt to differentiate the terms by Ralf-Henning Steinmetz, 'Bearbeitungstypen in der Literatur des Mittelalters: Vorschläge für eine Klärung der Begriffe.' *Texttyp und Textproduktion in der deutschen Literatur des Mittelalters*. Ed. Elizabeth Andersen et al. Trends in Medieval Philology Vol. 7. Berlin, New York:

De Gruyter 2005, 41–61, especially at 45 and 52.

7   Werner Williams-Krapp, 'Die überlieferungsgeschichtliche Methode: Rückblick und Ausblick.' *Internationales Archiv für Sozialgeschichte der deutschen Literatur* 25 (2000): 1–21.

8   Schiewer, 'Fassung, Bearbeitung, Version und Edition', 50.

9   Specifically Martin Baumann et al., 'An Interactive Visualization for the Analysis of Annotated Text Variance in the Legendary "Der Heiligen Leben, Redaktion".' *Leipzig symposium on Visualization In Applications* (LEVIA) 19 (2019), online: https://doi.org/10.31219/osf.io/wd9yz (last accessed on 10.07.2020). See also Nemes, *Von der Schrift zum Buch*, 81–82.

10 Monica Hedlund, 'Nuns and Latin, with Special Reference to the Brigittines of Vadstena.' *Nuns' Literacies in Medieval Europe: The Hull Dialogue*. Ed. Virginia Blanton, Veronica O'Mara, and Patricia Stoop. Medieval Women – Texts and Contexts Vol. 26. Turnhout: Brepols, 2013, 97–118, 100.

11 On women's literary activities, including processes of rewriting and rearranging, in the fifteenth century, with a particular focus on the Augustinian nun Anna Eybin (sometimes Ebin), who was the provost of Pillenreuth from 1461 to 1476, see Sara S. Poor, '"Life" Lessons in Anna Eybin's Book of Saints (c. 1465–1482).' *Taxonomies of Knowledge: Information and Order in Medieval Manuscripts*. Ed. Emily Steiner and Lynn Ransom. The Lawrence J. Schoenberg Studies in Manuscript Culture Vol. 2. Philadelphia: Schoenberg Institute for Manuscript Studies, University of Pennsylvania Press, 2015, 136–53, here quoted from 137.

12 See Andrew Taylor, 'Vernacular Authorship and the Control of Manuscript Production.' *The Medieval Manuscript Book: Cultural Approaches*. Ed. Michael Johnston and Michael Van Dussen. Cambridge: Cambridge University Press, 2015, 199–214, at 201.

13 In more recent research, translations, especially those made by nuns, are seen as outcomes of literary activities which rely on a solid knowledge of Latin – that is to say, a bilingual literacy – and which demonstrate considerable compositional achievements. Studying how nuns 'read, interpreted, copied, wrote, translated, edited, acted as patrons of, or intermediaries in, intellectual and literate practices', the three volumes on 'Nuns' Literacies', edited by Virginia Blanton, Veronica O'Mara, and Patricia Stoop, explore an array of literary activities exercised by religious women in Europe; here quoted from the introduction to the first volume, *Nuns' Literacies in Medieval Europe: The Hull Dialogue*, Texts and Contexts Vol. 26. Turnhout: Brepols, 2013, xiii–xxxiii, at xix. For code-switching between Latin and vernacular by medieval nuns and their bilingual literary activities, such as translations, see in particular the contributions in the same volume by Hedlund, 'Nuns and Latin'; and Cynthia J. Cyrus, 'Vernacular and Latinate Literacy in Viennese Women's Convents.' Ibid., 119–32.

14 For general overviews of translation processes in the Middle Ages, see Minnis, *Medieval Theory of Authorship*; Tim William Machan, *Techniques of Translation: Chaucer's Boece*. Norman, OK: Pilgrim Book, 1985; Rita Copeland, 'Rhetoric and vernacular translation.' *Studies in the Age of Chaucer* 9 (1987): 44–75; Copeland, *Rhetoric, Hermeneutics, and Translation in the Middle Ages: Academic Traditions and Vernacular Texts*. Cambridge: Cambridge University Press, 1991; Jocelyn Wogan-Browne, 'General Introduction: What's in a Name? The 'French' of 'England'.' *Language and Culture in Medieval Britain: The French of England. c.1100–c.1500*. Ed. Jocelyn Wogan-Browne. Woodbridge: York Medieval Press, 2009, 1–13. For discussions on vernacular theory and writing processes, see Walter Haug, *Literaturtheorie im deutschen Mittelalter: Von den Anfängen bis zum Ende des 13. Jahrhunderts*. 2nd edition. Darmstadt: Wissenschaftliche Buchgesellschaft, 1992; Ruth Evans, 'The notion of vernacular theory.' *The Idea of the Vernacular: An Anthology of Middle English Literary Theory, 1280–1520*. Ed. Jocelyn Wogan-Browne, Nicholas Watson, Andrew Taylor, and Ruth Evans. University Park, PA: Pennsylvania State University Press, 1999, 314–30; Ruth Evans, 'Vulgar eloquence? Cultural Models and Practices of Translation in Late Medieval Europe.' *Translating Others*. Vol. 2. Ed. Theo Hermans. Manchester: Routledge, 2006, 296–313; Emma Campbell and Robert Mills, *Rethinking Medieval*

Translation: Ethics, Politics, Theory. Cambridge: Brewer, 2012.

15   There is a debate in German scholarship as to whether vernacular mystical texts have a 'spiritual surplus value' ('spirituelle[r] Mehrwert der Volkssprache') in comparison to Latin; the term was coined by Kurt Ruh, *Meister Eckhart: Theologe, Prediger, Mystiker*. 2nd edition. Munich: Beck, 1989, 194, and based on observations made by Alois Maria Haas, 'Mechthild von Magdeburg.' *Sermo mysticus: Studien zu Theologie und Sprache der deutschen Mystik*. Dokimion Vol. 4. Fribourg: Universitätsverlag, 1979, 67–135, at 81. Sometime later Kurt Ruh, *Geschichte der abendländischen Mystik, vol. 1: Die Grundlegung durch Kirchenväter und die Mönchstheologie des 12. Jahrhunderts*. Munich: Beck, 1990, 18, n. 10, downplayed his former opinion on the 'spiritual surplus value' of vernacular mystical texts, but the debate initiated then remains active to this day. Instead of comparing Latin and vernacular texts in a hierarchical manner, Hasebrink, 'Grenzverschiebung,' 398, suggests exploring the 'self-reflectiveness' of vernacular texts in independent in-depth analyses.

16   Dating by Falk Eisermann, 'Chart B 269.' *Katalog der deutschsprachigen mittelalterlichen Handschriften der Forschungsbibliothek Gotha*. http://bilder.manuscripta-mediaevalia.de/hs//projekt-Gotha-pdfs/Chart_B_269.pdf (last accessed on 04.06.2019).

17   Hellgardt, 'Latin and the Vernacular,' 141.

18   Hellgardt, 'Latin and the Vernacular,' 143. The headings are translated into German, and not – as Hellgardt states (142) – provided in Latin.

19   'Die Straffung des Textes der lateinischen Vorlage kann man auch bei den restlichen Kapiteln der Übersetzung [Ch. 11–61 in his edition of the *botte*] feststellen. Allerdings läßt sich hier die Absicht des Übersetzers nicht immer ganz erkennen.' Wieland, *Gertrud von Helfta: ein botte der götlichen miltekeit*, 60. For a synoptic view of the Latin *Legatus* Books and the *botte* chapters, including the *Trutta*-paragraphs/chapters, see ibid., 54–7.

20   Ringler, 'Die Rezeption Gertruds von Helfta,' 144–6.

21   Ibid., 144–5.

22   *Legatus* III, 18. In *Gertrude d'Helfta, Œuvres spirituelles*. Vol. 3: *Le Héraut (Livre III)*. Ed. Pierre Doyère. Sources chrétiennes. Série des textes monastiques d'Occident Vol. 27. Paris: Éditions du Cerf, 1968, 96. Translation by Alexandra Barratt, *Gertrude the Great of Helfta: The Herald of God's Loving-Kindness, Book Three*. Cistercian Fathers Vol. 63 Kalamazoo, MI: Cistercian Publications, 1999, 77: 'The love of one's own heart makes a friend's words delightful'.

23   *botte* 108, 175.

24   I follow the definition of performative language as it has first been developed in speech act theory and picked up in theatre studies; for an extensive discussion of this interdisciplinary use of the concept 'performativity', see Kirakosian, *Die Vita der Christina von Hane*, 28–36.

25   *botte* 2, 86. For a discussion of this image programme, see Chapter 4 'The Book's Self-Reflectivity'.

26   'Wer auf diese Weise mit seiner Vorlage umgeht, will nicht Kürzungen vornehmen, sondern Akzente setzen.' Ringler, 'Die Rezeption Gertruds von Helfta,' 145.

27   'Der Weg verläuft geradlinig zum Höhepunkt; ist dieser erreicht, entfaltet sich das Leben in die Breite und in die Tiefe; hier wird dann eher der Lebensraum als der Lebensweg gezeigt.' Ibid., 148.

28   Ibid.,149. Ringler's observation is remarkable as it seems a strikingly generalising statement on the grounds of highly personal experiences. At the same time, there is undeniably a literary as well as religious trope which celebrates the age of 30 or a little thereafter as the culmination of one's life, just to name a few: the stories of Buddha, Jesus Christ, and Catherine of Siena in her imitation of the latter; in literature, Ingeborg Bachmann's *Das dreißigste Jahr*, and Robert Musil's *Der Mann ohne Eigenschaften*.

29   In order to address more underlying assumptions in Ringler's ideas, we need to turn to his secondary sources. In particular, we must look at the work of Gertrud Jaron Lewis, on which Ringler's conclusions rely (especially: Lewis, 'Gertrud of Helfta's "Legatus divinae pietatis" and "ein botte der götlichen miltekeit",' 58–71).

30   'In Hinblick auf "Mystik" erscheint uns "echt" und "ursprünglich", was von unmittelbarem Erleben und individueller Sprache zeugt'; Ringler, 'Die Rezeption Gertruds von Helfta,' 142.

31 Ringler, *Viten- und Offenbarungsliteratur in Frauenklöstern des Mittelalters: Quellen und Studien.* Münchener Texte und Untersuchungen zur deutschen Literatur des Mittelalters Vol. 72. Munich: Artemis, 1980. It remains questionable how the compound word 'Gnadenvita', which combines the concept of grace (*gnade*) with the category of a genre, should be any less vague. The word '*gnade*' is explicitly derived from medieval German sources, making this a term defined by and restricted to vernacular texts.

32 Ursula Peters, 'Das 'Leben' der Christine Ebner: Textanalyse und kulturhistorischer Kommentar.' *Abendländische Mystik im Mittelalter: Symposium Kloster Engelberg 1984.* Ed. Kurt Ruh. Germanistische Symposien. Berichtsbände Vol. 7. Stuttgart: Metzler, 1986, 402–22, at 418.

33 Ruh, 'Gertrud von Helfta,' 7–8.

34 Any communication of a mystical experience is going to be removed from the actual experience, see Pierre Hadot, 'Apophatisme et théologie négative.' *Exercices spirituels et philosophie antique.* Ed. Pierre Hadot. Paris: Études augustiniennes, 1981, 185–93, at 192; it is hence hard to fathom what an unmediated form of mysticism in texts could be. The way the *Legatus* is collated does certainly convey the impression of a less traditionally arranged and planned hagiography. Arguing from another point of view, the discrepancies and the disorder in the *Legatus* could be read as signs of an early composition, close to an oral communication; on early compositions of mystical texts, see Peters, *Religiöse Erfahrung als literarisches Faktum,* 109; and Caroline Emmelius, 'Begnadung und Zweifel. Zur Interaktion von Innen- und Außenraum in den "Offenbarungen" der Adelheid Langmann.' *Innenräume in der Literatur des deutschen Mittelalters: XIX. Anglo-German Colloquium Oxford 2005.* Ed. Burkhard Hasebrink, Hans-Jochen Schiewer, Almut Suerbaum, and Annette Volfing. Tübingen: Niemeyer Verlag, 2008, 309–25, at 311.

35 'Der Verfasser des "botten" hat zweifellos die im mystischen Sinn überzeugendste Lösung gefunden.' Ringler, 'Die Rezeption Gertruds von Helfta,' 150. This statement seems to contradict the subsequent claim that the *botte* 'author' wholly understood Gertrude's mysticism, unless the reception is seen as a separate engagement with her mysticism.

36 In Ringler's opinion, the *botte* was written in the wake of the observant movement with South-German female convents in mind, see ibid. The updated transmission history challenges this standpoint since the *botte* must have existed before the reform got implemented.

37 Most recently this has been reiterated by the modern translator of the *Legatus*: Barratt, 'Introduction,' 11–43. The collective writing situation is something that Ruh had observed and that led him to name the anonymous sister 'Sister N' (following the medieval convention for anonymous names); see Ruh, 'Gertrud von Helfta: Ein neues Gertrud-Bild'. See also, Chapter 1 'The Helfta Scriptorium'. Sister N coproduced the *Legatus* as well as the *Liber*, in whose centre stand Mechthild of Hackeborn's revelations. Only Book II of the *Legatus* presents itself from a first-person perspective.

38 This assumption leaves Gertrude's voice unaffected: *Legatus* Book II is written differently from the rest of the 'standard' *Legatus*; Barratt has studied the Latin text and finds that there are stylistic differences that single out Book II: 'Sister N's prose style is quite distinctive, and different from that of Gertrud. Although learned and correct, it is somewhat labored and not as fluent as Gertrud's, as it appears in book 2'; see Barratt, 'Introduction,' 15.

39 *Legatus* III, 20. *Gertrude d'Helfta: Œuvres spirituelles* III, 110–12.

40 *botte* 38, 105–6.

41 For Ringler, this means that the *Legatus* does not simply undergo a process of curtailment but of distortion or misrepresentation in the transformation to the *botte*: 'Dies ist nicht mehr Kürzung der Vorlage, dies ist eine Verfälschung'; Ringler, 'Die Rezeption Gertruds von Helfta,' 152. That Mary should not be a great figure of identification in the German redaction is for Ringler yet another indicator to place its genesis and intended readership in South-German convents, where female Dominicans did not aspire to spiritually become the Mother but rather attempted to be the companion of Christ. While this is generally an accurate assessment, there is in fact one other medieval German mystical text, neither Dominican, nor from the German South, in which the female mystic consciously abandons Mary's favour: *The Life of Christina of Hane.* The mystic in question is Christina of

Hane, a thirteenth-century Premonstratensian whose late medieval life is transmitted in only one manuscript; on Christina of Hane's mariologicial understanding, see Kirakosian, *Die Vita der Christina von Hane*, 195–220.

42   Watson, 'Visions of Inclusion,' 146; the statement applies to vernacular religious texts in general.

43   See Chapter 4 'Manuscript Transmission History'.

44   The veneration of Mary can be observed in other chapters, some of which highlight the communion gained through Marian devotion: *botte* 64, 127; 69, 134; 74, 138–9.

45   Ringler, 'Die Rezeption Gertruds von Helfta,' 150: 'Ich vermisse ebenso die Stellen, die mich bei Gertrud besonders ansprechen: wo sie nicht mehr in hieratischen Bildern spricht, sondern realistische Szenen des Alltags zeichnet'. In terms of seriousness, Trinca, 'Schriftliche Berührung - gedruckte Süße,' 350, attributes the early imprint of the *botte* in comparison to Latin, a 'greater stylistic sobriety' ('größere stilistische Nüchternheit').

46   See Lewis, 'Gertrud of Helfta's "Legatus divinae pietatis" and "ein botte der götlichen miltekeit",' 70: 'There is nothing in the 'botte' to convey the great inner happiness of this saint'.

47   Ibid., 67.

48   For a discussion on Gertrude's visionary *Missa* as a short commentary on the mass, see Hamburger, Schlotheuber, Marti, and Fassler, *Liturgical Life and Latin Learning at Paradies bei Soest*. Vol. 1, 329 and 644–5.

49   *botte* 62, 120–5.

50   Lewis discusses in particular the *Legatus'* image of the Sacred Heart with 'tubes' emanating from Christ to nurture people whereby the mystic becomes the mediator; see Lewis, 'Gertrud of Helfta's "Legatus divinae pietatis" and "ein botte der götlichen miltekeit",' 64–6.

51   *botte* 62 goes beyond the descriptions in *Legatus* IV, 59; the imagery is still that of the *Legatus* altogether.

52   *botte* 62 includes elements from *Legatus* III, 30.

53   It is rather astonishing that these two chapters should have escaped Lewis's attention – especially Ch. 62, which Ringler later esteemed to be the culmination of a skilfully calibrated mystical path.

54   *botte* 135, 206–8, at 207. The golden cups are specified to be a prayer, in which the praying person supplicates to be heard and loved by God. Thus, the words create a connection to Christ's heart and the praying person receives mercy from it; the prayer and prayer and the Eucharist collide in this image.

55   This wave of interest, in Ringler's view, was detached from a medieval interest in mysticism, as it had turned into more of a 'combination of religious sensibility and dynastic interest' ('Verquickung von religiösem Empfinden und dynastischem Interesse'); Ringler, 'Die Rezeption Gertruds von Helfta,' 136.

56   So-called female mystical literature is often generally subsumed under 'vernacular theology' – a categorisation which inadvertently led to the language of a mystical text counting as the primary genre characteristic. This derivation is dangerous because of the implicit distinction between Latin discourses of a male-dominated scholastic world and vernacular texts about supposedly practical experiences as reactions to the Scriptures and the Daily Office. Such binary views do not hold up against the complexity of medieval culture.

57   Lewis tends to speak of a 'translator' (e.g. Lewis, 'Gertrud of Helfta's "Legatus divinae pietatis" and "ein botte der götlichen miltekeit",' 66 and 69) but also uses the word 'author' (70).

58   Ibid., 70.

59   Ibid., 71. Lewis's reading of the *botte* has influenced Ringler in his judgement about it; interestingly, she harks back to Ringler's earlier work, when declaring that the *botte* is more of a 'Gnadenvita' than a mystical text, and that it can only be studied under this condition. Following Ringler, she understands 'Gnadenvita' to be 'a distinct form of mystical literature next to the well-established genres of sermons, treatises and revelation literature'; in contrast to the genres of legends or the *Saints' Lives*, it is 'a book of instructions in religious practices or in the mystical realm rather than an account of first-hand mystical experiences; the lessons are conveyed by relating the life of a much gifted saint or mystic; and the book is written with moral intent'. Indeed, Ringler had left it subject to further inspection just how the *botte* may be considered a Gnadenvita: 'Auch die deutschsprachige Redaktion des "Legatus divinae

pietatis", die unter dem Titel "ein botte der götlichen miltekeit" als eigenständiges Werk zu gelten hat, wäre unter diesem Aspekt einer Untersuchung wert.' Ringler, *Viten- und Offenbarungsliteratur*, 356.

60 Lewis, 'Gertrud of Helfta's "Legatus divinae pietatis" and "ein botte der götlichen miltekeit",' 70.

61 The stereotype that the 'mother tongue' is particularly suited to women can already be found in Jerome's writing, but this view – as Watson, 'Censorship and Cultural Change', 843–4, shows – was already contested in the Middle Ages.

62 'Als Gefahren sieht er [the author of the *botte*] – vielleicht 100 Jahre nach Gertrud – eine übersteigerte Marien- und Heiligenverehrung ebenso wie eine allzu sinnliche Minnemetaphorik.' Ringler, 'Die Rezeption Gertruds von Helfta,' 154.

63 Ibid., 154.

64 There is no doubt that internal acts such as personal penance and confession were increasingly favoured over bodily and hence exterior means, see John W. Baldwin, 'From the Ordeal to Confession: In Search of Lay Religion in Early-Thirteenth-Century France.' *Handling Sin: Confession in the Middle Ages*. Ed. Peter Biller and Alastair J. Minnis. York Studies in Medieval Theology Vol. 2. Woodbridge: York Medieval Press, 1998, 191–209, at 198–205. Yet, these developments evolved over the course of centuries and can even be traced back to the Carolingian period, see Sarah Hamilton, *The Practice of Penance, 900–1050*. Royal Historical Society Studies in History: New Series. Woodbridge: Boydell Press, 2001.

65 Hellgardt, 'Latin and the Vernacular,' 143.

66 These and all other manuscripts of the vernacular transmission are discussed in Chapter 3 'Manuscript Transmission History'.

67 That the 'standard' *Legatus* contains material which is not transmitted in the *Leipzig Legatus* and vice versa, suggests that a direct interdependence between the two text witnesses is difficult to establish, and that textual and even layout parallels (respective manuscripts contain identical marginal notes) may instead due to common source material that both drew upon. One example for such a procedure is documented by the sources connected to the *Life* of Elsbeth of Oye (c. 1289–1339): her

anonymous Dominican hagiographer refers to a booklet that Elsbeth wrote herself and that may be consulted for verification of his account; see Wolfram Schneider-Lastin, 'Leben und Offenbarungen der Elsbeth von Oye: Textkritische Edition der Vita aus dem "Ötenbacher Schwesternbuch".' *Kulturtopographie des deutschsprachigen Südwestens im späteren Mittelalter*. Ed. Barbara Fleith and René Wetzel. Kulturtopographie des alemannischen Raums Vol. 1. Berlin: De Gruyter, 2009, 395–467, at 396. Elsbeth's heavily revised and much used 'booklet' survives as Zurich, Zentralbibliothek, Ms. Rh. 159, and served indeed as source for the hagiographer who included her *Life* in the Sisterbook of Ötenbach. The Sisterbook of Ötenbach – as part of a larger miscellany also containing the Sisterbooks of Töß, St Katharinenthal, and St Michael in Bern – was separated at the end of the sixteenth century and survives as Nuremberg, Stadtbibliothek, Cod. Cent. V, 10, and Wrocław, Bibliotheka Uniwersytecka, Ms. IV F 194. Wolfram Schneider-Lastin assumes that there must have been more such booklets that are lost today (Schneider-Lastin, 'Leben und Offenbarungen der Elsbeth von Oye,' 397); in any case, Elsbeth's extant autograph itself shows a multistage process of rewriting, correcting, and emending, which already eludes the notion of a stable text. Regarding the composition of the *Legatus*, I would like to put forth the hypothesis that the first written documents by Sister N and Gertrude herself – probably on different detachable quires – would have been the source material, from which different scribes and redactors compiled, revised, and edited various *Legatus* versions. This hypothesis would entail that more versions could have come into existence in this way (that is drawing from a collection of texts rather than from one single original book), one of which could well have been a direct German redaction, or the Latin basis for the German *botte*. This would also mean that the 'most original' version itself was a dynamic text and never stable.

68 Nemes and Märker, 'Hunc tercium conscripsi cum maximo labore occultandi,' 248–96.

69 In the same century, the *Leipzig Legatus* was bound together with a *Life of St Barbara*, which – copied approximately 25 years later – imitated the *Legatus* portion in its layout.

70 I have made this claim first in Kirakosian, 'The Earliest Transmitted German Legatus,' 181–4.

71 See Sara S. Poor, '"Ich Schreyberin": Rethinking Female Authorship: Anna Eybin's Table of Contents.' *Journal of Medieval Religious Culture* 42.2 (2016): 201–23, here quoted from 202; Poor responds to a discussion of these traditional assumptions, especially to the study by Hans-Jochen Schiewer, 'Literarisches Leben in dominikanischen Frauenklöstern des 14. Jahrhunderts: Das Modell St. Katharinental bei Diessenhofen.' *Studien und Texte zur literarischen und materiellen Kultur der Frauenklöster im späten Mittelalter: Ergebnisse eines Arbeitsgesprächs in der Herzog August Bibliothek Wolfenbüttel, 24.–26. Febr. 1999.* Ed. Falk Eisermann, Eva Schlotheuber, and Volker Honemann. Studies in Medieval and Reformation Thought Vol. 99. Leiden: Brill, 2004, 285–311.

72 Werner Williams-Krapp has argued that observants intervened in fourteenth-century mystical texts stripping from them any potentially dangerous thought that would promote spirituality outside the realm of ecclesial control. Werner Williams-Krapp, 'Frauenmystik und Ordensreform im 15. Jahrhundert.' *Literarische Interessenbildung im Mittelalter: DFG-Symposion 1991.* Ed. Joachim Heinzle. Germanistische Symposien. Berichtsbände Vol. 14. Stuttgart: Metzler, 1993, 301–13, at 312. See also Williams-Krapp, 'Observanzbewegungen, monastische Spiritualität und geistliche Literatur im 15. Jahrhundert.' *Internationales Archiv für Sozialgeschichte der deutschen Literatur* 20 (1995): 1–15; 'Ordensreform und Literatur im 15. Jahrhundert.' *Jahrbuch der Oswald von Wolkenstein-Gesellschaft* 4 (1986/ 87): 41–51.

73 For an overview of the research, see Jones, *Ruling the Spirit*, 2017, 61.

74 Anne Winston-Allen, *Convent Chronicles: Women Writing about Women and Reform in the Late Middle Ages.* University Park, PA: Pennsylvania State University Press, 2004, 204.

75 Antje Willing, ed., *Die Bibliothek des Klosters St. Katharina zu Nürnberg: Synoptische Darstellung der Bücherverzeichnisse.* 2 vols. Berlin: Akademie Verlag, 2013. Simone Mengis, *Schreibende Frauen um 1500: Scriptorium und Bibliothek des Dominikanerinnenklosters St. Katharina St. Gallen.* Scrinium Friburgense Vol. 28. Berlin: De Gruyter, 2013.

76 Jones, *Ruling the Spirit*, 61–2.

77 Thus argues Hans Fromm, 'Volkssprache und Schriftkultur.' *The Role of the Book in Medieval Culture: Proceedings of the Oxford International Symposium. 26 September–1 October 1982.* Vol. 1. Ed. Peter Ganz. Bibliologia Vol. 3–4. Turnhout: Brepols, 1986, 99–108, at 100, for Hildegard of Bingen. This assumption ignores two facts, one being that women referred to God as a rhetorical humility topos, the other that men too used this trope to authorise their writing.

78 Women were generally more likely to be literate than men, see Dennis Howard Green, *Women Readers in the Middle Ages.* Cambridge Studies in Medieval Literature Vol. 65. Cambridge: Cambridge University Press, 2007.

79 See, for example, Lucie Doležalová, 'Multilingualism and Late Medieval Manuscript Culture.' *The Medieval Manuscript Book: Cultural Approaches.* Ed. Michael Johnston and Michael Van Dussen. Cambridge Studies in Medieval Literature Vol. 94. Cambridge: Cambridge University Press, 2015, 160–80, on the deliberate overlapping receptions in Czech and German manuscripts.

80 Schiewer, 'Books in Texts – Texts in Books: The "St. Georgener Predigten",' 237.

81 Ibid., 235.

82 Hamburger, Schlotheuber, Marti, and Fassler, *Liturgical Life and Latin Learning at Paradies bei Soest.* Vol. 1, 293: 'All the texts associated with Gertrude of Helfta, whether those that can be attributed to her or those composed by her followers, take the liturgy as their point of departure.' See also Sabine B. Spitzlei, *Erfahrungsraum Herz: Zur Mystik des Zisterzienserinnenklosters Helfta im 13. Jahrhundert.* Mystik in Geschichte und Gegenwart. Texte und Untersuchungen. Abteilung I Christliche Mystik Vol. 9. Stuttgart: Frommann-Holzboog, 1991, 62–80; Harrison, 'I Am Wholly Your Own,' 549–83.

83 Jones, *Ruling the Spirit*, 121.

84 There is no hard evidence for assuming a male observant to have composed the *botte*, especially since German translations effectuated by reformers were mostly not anonymous, and also since the reform in Teutonia only took off in the first half of the fifteenth century, that is at a time when the *botte* had already existed in one form or another.

85 Ibid., 57.

86 Erika Lauren Lindgren, *Sensual Encounters: Monastic Women and Spirituality in Medieval Germany*. New York: Columbia University Press, 2009, 127.

87 Marie-Luise Ehrenschwendtner notes that women were expected to be *litterata* upon entrance to the Dominican novitiate, see *Die Bildung der Dominikanerinnen in Süddeutschland vom 13. bis 15. Jahrhundert*. Stuttgart: Steiner, 2004. See also Ehrenschwendtner, 'Puellae Litteratae: The Use of the Vernacular in the Dominican Convents of Southern Germany.' *Medieval Women in Their Communities*. Ed. Diane Watt. Toronto: University of Toronto Press, 1997, 49–71.

88 See Jeffrey F. Hamburger and Eva Schlotheuber, 'Books in Women's Hands: Liturgy, Learning, and the Libraries of Dominican Nuns is Westphalia.' *Entre stabilité et itinérance: livres et culture des orders mendicants XIIIe–XVe siècle*. Ed. Nicole Bériou, Marin Morard, and Donatella Nebbiai. Turnhout: Brepols, 2014, 129–57. See also the volumes Hamburger, Schlotheuber, Marti, and Fassler, *Liturgical Life and Latin Learning at Paradies bei Soest*, especially Vol. 1, 49–55.

89 Eva Schlotheuber insists that the medieval notion of *litteratus/litterata* always meant language aptitude and not just phonetic literacy, which would have been required to somewhat follow the liturgy; see Eva Schlotheuber, 'Bücher und Bildung in den Frauengemeinschaften der Bettelorden.' *Nonnen, Kanonissen und Mystikerinnen: Religiöse Frauengemeinschaften in Süddeutschland: Beiträge zur interdisziplinären Tagung vom 21. bis 23. September 2005 in Frauenchiemsee*. Ed. Eva Schlotheuber, Helmut Flachenecker, and Ingrid Gardill. Göttingen: Vandenhoeck & Ruprecht, 2008, 241–62, at 249 and 257–61. See also Schlotheuber, *Klostereintritt und Bildung*, 268–96. Building on this body of scholarship, Jones, *Ruling the Spirit*, 7, argues that the paucity of Latin texts in late medieval nunneries 'does not necessarily reveal any information about the sisters' ability to understand liturgical Latin.' The reform movement in particular emphasised that the liturgy should be understood, see Claire Taylor Jones, 'Rekindling the Light of Faith: Hymn Translation and Spiritual Renewal in the Fifteenth-Century Observant Reform.'

Journal of Medieval and Early Modern Studies 42 (2012): 567–96.

90 Jones, *Ruling the Spirit*, 8.

91 In the *Legatus*, Gertrude as a person stands for a community more than for an individual. This has been stressed by Harrison, 'I Am Wholly Your Own.'

92 See Keul and Ringler, 'In der Freiheit des lebendigen Geistes,' 21–35; Oefelein, 'Grundlagen zur Baugeschichte des Klosters Helfta,' 29–47.

93 It has been argued that if there are still echoes of the Helfta mysticism to be found in Christine Ebner's or Adelheid Langmann's accounts – sometime later, that is, around 1340 – then this should be seen as extraordinary and only possible through the mediation of male figures such as Heinrich of Nördlingen; see Ringler, 'Die Rezeption Gertruds von Helfta,' 137.

94 Individuality is acknowledged similarly to nuns' stories in convent sisterbooks as the balance between individual and community forms part of hagiographic writing; see Richard Kieckhefer, *Unquiet Souls: Fourteenth-century Saints and Their Religious Milieu*. Chicago: University of Chicago Press, 1984.

95 Criticising the edition for its length, Ringler argues that the *botte*'s 'correct end' ('richtiges Ende') is Ch. 170; Ringler, 'Die Rezeption Gertruds von Helfta,' 149.

96 *botte* 170, 242: *Also umgap er sú und durchfür sú gentzlich, also das sú im glich wart und ein ding wart mit im, reht also sich das ysen verkert in dem für*. The final word 'fire' (*für*) struck Ringler as a particularly strong ending, his poetic reading of the *botte* leading him to judge its endpoint on aesthetic grounds.

97 See Wieland, *Gertrud von Helfta*, 5.

98 Gregory told the story of Romula, a disciple to Redempta, in the *Dialogues* as well as in his *Homilies on the Gospel*, see Matthew Dal Santo, *Debating the Saints' Cults in the Age of Gregory the Great*. Oxford: Oxford University Press, 2012, 75.

99 *botte* 173, 245: *Hie hat das buch der götlichen miltikeit ein ende. Lobent und danckent wir unserm lieben herren umb sin rilichen goben und gnoden, die er sinen userwelten fründen so gar miltiklich mitgeteilet het, und bitten wir in, das er uns armen öch begnode und begobe us dem richen schatz siner gnoden und barmhertzikeit, also das wir hie in zit*

erwerben vergebung aller unser súnde und mitteilung siner götlichen gnoden, und uns verlihe noch disem leben das ewige leben! Dis verlihe uns sin grundelose barmhertzikeit, gútikeit und militkeit zů aller zit! Amen.

100   Wieland who had identified two transmission lines (recensions) X and Y (Wieland, *Gertrud von Helfta*, 47–52), operated with the notion of reconstructed text versions in his critical apparatus. Although this means that some of the critical notes refer to data that has not come down to us in the same form as it is cited, the edition is still a valuable scholarly source since it follows one copy in particular: Leithandschrift is Brussels, Bibliothèque Royale, cod. 8507–09, the copy that was held by the Dominican nuns in Strasbourg (St Nikolaus in undis). The edition of 1973 predates the paradigms New Historicism and New Philology, but it still diligently records any variants. Indeed, the fact that Wieland included the additional material, that is, the finale *botte* 171–173, shows the edition's tendency towards the new-philologist call to fully grasp the manuscript matrix.

101   See Chapter 3 'Manuscript Transmission History'.

102   See Dennis D. Martin, 'Carthusians as Advocates of Women Visionary Reformers.' *Studies in Carthusian Monasticism in the Late Middle Ages*. Ed. Julian M. Luxford. Medieval Church Studies Vol. 14. Turnhout: Brepols, 2008, 127–53, 144.

103   See Glyn Coppack, '"Make straight in the desert a highway for our God": The Carthusians and community in late medieval England.' *Monasteries and Society in the British Isles in the Later Middle Ages*. Ed. Janet Burton and Karen Stöber. Woodbridge: Boydell & Brewer, 2008, 168–79, at 173.

104   On the important role that Carthusians played in the production and circulation of vernacular literature, see Volker Honemann, *Deutsche Literatur in der Laienbibliothek der Basler Kartause 1480–1520*. Habilitationsschrift, Freie Universität Berlin, 1982. See also Nigel F. Palmer, 'The German Prayers in their Literary and Historical Context.' *The Prayer Book of Ursula Begerin*. Vol. 2. Ed. Jeffrey F. Hamburger and Nigel F. Palmer. Dietikon-Zurich: Graf, 2015, 377–488, at 483.

105   See Chapter 3 'Manuscript Transmission History'.

106   On the Carthusian tradition of meditational texts, see Palmer, 'The German Prayers,' 404–5.

107   Ibid., 382–3.

108   Sarah McNamer, *Affective Meditation and the Invention of Medieval Compassion*. Philadelphia: University of Pennsylvania Press, 2010, 95. Michelle Karnes, *Imagination, Meditation, and Cognition in the Middle Ages*. Chicago: University of Chicago Press, 2011, 13, n. 49.

109   Parts of the *botte* can be found in the following Buxheim manuscripts: London, University College, MS Germ. 24; Augsburg, Benediktinerabtei St. Stephan, Hs 38. The *Legatus* transmission also includes two extant Buxheim manuscripts: Munich, Bayerische Staatsbibliothek, Clm 15332; Augsburg, Staats- und Stadtbibliothek, 8° Cod. 203. Nemes and Märker, 'Hunc tercium conscripsi,' 275 (n. 87), mention an entry in the medieval catalogue of Buxheim's library which lists a book of 'Gertrude's Revelation' assigned to shelf mark letter F, which stands for devotional texts. This book could well have been one of the extant copies of the *Legatus*, or even an additional one; see Paul Ruf, *Mittelalterliche Bibliothekskataloge Deutschlands und der Schweiz*. Vol. 3 Pt. 1: Bistum Augsburg. Munich: Beck, 1932.

110   Berlin, Staatsbibliothek Preußischer Kulturbesitz, Ms. theol. lat. oct. 89.

111   Bonn, Universitäts- und Landesbibliothek, S 726.

112   See Matthias Eifler, 'Zur Rezeption von mystischen Viten und Offenbarungen bei den Kartäusern und Benediktinern in Erfurt in der zweiten Hälfte des 15. Jahrhunderts.' *Beihefte zur Zeitschrift für deutsche Philologie* 17 (2019). Special Issue: *Mechthild und das Fließende Licht der Gottheit im Kontext. Eine Spurensuche in religiösen Netzwerken und literarischen Diskursen im mitteldeutschen Raum des 13.–15. Jahrhunderts*. Ed. Caroline Emmelius and Balázs J. Nemes. 303–36. An important indicator of an exchange between the Benedictines and the Carthusians are the notes contained in Eisleben, Stiftung Luthergedenkstätten, H 546, a copy of the *Liber specialis gratiae* that originated from the Erfurt Charterhouse (ibid., 318–20); on the Eisleben manuscript, see Nemes, *Von der Schrift zum Buch*, 226.

113 The library of the Erfurt Charterhouse assigned shelf mark letters specifically for mystical theology (D), revelations (I/J), and diverse devotional texts (for example E/F and G), see Almuth Märker, *Das 'Prohemium Longum' des Erfurter Kartäuserkatalogs aus der Zeit um 1475: Edition und Untersuchung*. Lateinische Sprache und Literatur des Mittelalters Vol. 35. Bern: Lang, 2008.

114 The late medieval library catalogue lists Gertrude's revelations several times, see Paul Lehmann, *Mittelalterliche Bibliothekskataloge Deutschlands und der Schweiz*. Vol. 2: Bistum Mainz, Erfurt. Munich: Beck, 1928, 433. The extant copies are: Berlin, Staatsbibliothek Preußischer Kulturbesitz, Ms. theol. lat. oct. 89; Moscow, Rossijskaja Gosudarstvennaya Biblioteka, Fonds 183/281; Weimar, Herzogin Anna Amalia Bibliothek, Oct 52; Weimar, Herzogin Anna Amalia Bibliothek, Oct 62. For the list of manuscripts of the *Legatus* transmission, see Appendix.

115 Erfurt, Bistumsarchiv, Hs. Hist. 6, fol. 118v. On this note by *Frater N* see Nemes, 'ut earundem testimonio conprobatur,' at 96, n. 30. Another note (under shelf mark D5) in the library catalogue refers to Eisenach, it is also written by *Brother N*; on this see Eifler, 'Zur Rezeption von mystischen Viten und Offenbarungen,' 312, n. 29.

116 The hypothesis presented certainly needs further exploration, especially in terms of comparing manuscript collections and investigating textual evidence. As it stands, it could also be possible that the Benedictines were engaged in the redaction of the *botte*. I would like to thank Balázs Nemes for his counsel in this matter.

117 Sabine Janssen points out the burgeoning interest in spiritual texts meant that personal and group interests emerged in shaping the material, which were not necessarily or solely attributed to the reform programme. On the heterogenous aspects of the reform and the literary landscape at large, see Sabine Jansen, *Die Texte des Kirchberg-Corpus': Überlieferung und Textgeschichte vom 15. bis zum 19. Jahrhundert*. Doctoral dissertation, University of Cologne, 2005, 138–41.

118 If one applies a 'more broadly conceived idea of authorship' to the redactions, translations, and various revisions women made, the image of literary activities in the Middle Ages would be drawn in a refreshingly new way; see Poor, 'Re-thinking Female Authorship,' 203; see also 219.

119 Minnis, *Medieval Theory of Authorship*, 5. See also Grubmüller, 'Verändern und Bewahren'.

120 For a discussion on the relationship between an 'author' and their 'work' in medieval text compositions, see Elizabeth A. Andersen, Manfred Eikelmann, and Anne Simon, 'Einleitung.' *Texttyp und Textproduktion in der deutschen Literatur des Mittelalters*. Ed. Elizabeth A. Andersen, Manfred Eikelmann, and Anne Simon. Trends in Medieval Philology Vol. 7. Berlin: De Gruyter, 2005, XI–XXV, at XII–XIII.

121 The relevant texts are: Bonaventura da Bagnoreggio, 'Legenda maior.' *Opera omnia*. Vol. 8. Quaracchi: Collegii S. Bonventura, 1898. 504–65; 'Legenda minor.' *Opera omnia*. Vol. 8. Quaracchi: Collegii S. Bonventura, 1898. 565–79; 'Legenda maior Sancti Francisi.' *Analacta Franciscana*. Vol. 10. Quaracchi: Collegii S. Bonventura, 1926–40. 555–652; 'Legenda maior sancti Francisci, Legenda minor sancti Francisci.' *Fontes Franciscani*. Ed. Enrico Menestò, et al. Assisi: Edizioni Porziuncola, 1995.

122 The redaction had been completed in 1261; the letter of the Paris General Chapter accepting it and calling for the destruction of all earlier accounts was issued in 1266. For a quote of the passage in question and its discussion, see Jay M. Hammond, 'Bonaventure's "Legenda Major".' *A Companion to Bonaventure*. Ed. Jay M. Hammond, Jared Goff, and Wayne Hellmann. Leiden: Brill, 2013, 453–507, at 456. Many *causae scribendi* (reasons for writing) had moved the Order to ask Bonaventure for an authoritative account of the Order's founder, ranging from liturgical needs to political instabilities, which cannot be expounded here but are well researched by Hammond.

123 Ibid., 505.

124 Ibid., 494.

125 For a contextualised close-reading of the collection of miracles, see George F. Rambow, 'The Function and Spirituality of Bonaventure's "Treatise" on the Miracles of St. Francis.' *Franciscan Studies* 75 (2017): 323–41.

126 Albert Haase, *Bonaventure's 'Legenda maior': A Redaction Critical Approach*. Doctoral

127 dissertation, New York, Fordham University, 1990, 180.

127 Hammond, 'Bonaventure's "Legenda Major",' 481 (n. 149).

128 On this latter text, see Timothy J. Johnson, 'The "Legenda Minor." *A Companion to Bonaventure*. Ed. Jay M. Hammond, Jared Goff, and Wayne Hellmann. Leiden: Brill, 2013, 435–52.

129 *Analecta Franciscana* 10, lxxiv and lxxvi: *Hec maior Vita sive Legenda B. Francisci pro edificatione Fratrum in loco quolibet habeatur; et potest legi ad mensam per totam octavam Natalis B. Francisci. Minor autem Legenda, que de hac excerpta est; poni debet in libris choralibus et legi secundum suas distinctiones in festivitatibus B. Francisci et per octavam Natalis eius; et in Breviariis portatilibus potest poni. Scriptores ergo compellantur tenere punctationes et litteram exemplaris; et eorum errores iuxta ipsum exemplar per fratrum diligentiam corrigantur.* Original and translation quoted from Hammond, 'Bonaventure's "Legenda Major",' 460 (n. 38).

130 Ibid., 462.

131 Blanton, O'Mara, Stoop, 'Introduction,' xxi–lxvi, at xxxvi.

132 See also the scholarship on the hagiographic concept *réécriture*: Monique Goullet and Martin Heinzelmann, 'Avant-propos.' *La réécriture hagiographique dans l'occident médiéval: Transformations formelles et idéologiques.* Beihefte der Francia Vol. 58. Ed. Monique Goullet and Martin Heinzelmann. Ostfildern: Thorbecke, 2003, 7–15; François Dolbeau, 'Transformations des prologues hagiographiques, dues aux réécritures.' *L'hagiographie mérovingienne à travers des réécritures.* Ed. Monique Goullet, Martin Heinzelmann, and Christiane Veyrard-Cosme. Beihefte der Francia Vol. 71. Ostfildern: Thorbecke, 2010, 103–24; Monique Goullet, 'Vers une typologie des réécritures hagiographiques, à partir de quelques exemples du Nord-Est de la France: Avec une édition synoptiquedes deux Vies de Saint Èvre de Toul.' *La réécriture hagiographique*, 109–44. For a discussion of the concept *réécriture* in comparison to other hagiographic elements, see Kirakosian, *Die Vita der Christina von Hane*, 45–50.

133 Wybren Scheepsma, 'Writing, Editing, and Rearranging: Griet Essinchges and her Version of the Sister-Book of Diepenveen.' *Nuns' Literacies in Medieval Europe: The Hull Dialogue*, 275–92, at 290.

134 On these changes, see Hasebrink, '"Das fliessende Licht der Gottheit" Mechthilds von Magdeburg,' 151. A cross-linguistic comparison between the *Lux divinitatis* and the *botte der götlichen miltekeit* in contrast to their Latin models could potentially lead to interesting insights into redactions that are also translations. The new edition of the *Lux divinitatis* contains a synoptic presentation of the Early New High German transmission, see Hellgardt, Nemes, and Senne, eds. *'Lux Divinitatis' – 'Das Liecht Der Gotheit'*.

135 Poor has demonstrated that Eybin's work, in comparison to other witnesses, resulted in a legendary which 'is a cleaner and neater text that is easier to navigate, due to the more fulsome organizing markers and rubrications, as well as a more polished prose'; Poor, '"Life" Lessons in Anna Eybin's Book of Saints,' 140–1.

136 In the case of Anna Eybin and her *Book of Saints*, Poor concludes that the created book, a legendary, 'bears witness to a woman's active and creative literary hand in shaping the literature of her day as well as the lives of its readers', underscoring the communal importance of editing and rewriting; Poor, '"Life" Lessons in Anna Eybin's Book of Saints,' 150.

137 Sara S. Poor, 'Stimmen schreibender Frauen in der Mystik des 15. Jahrhunderts: Der Fall Anna Eybins.' *Zeitschrift für Literaturwissenschaft und Linguistik* 171 (2013): 104–21, at 116–17, in particular at 116: 'Eybins Verbesserungen [umfassen] Versuche, den Text sinnvoller zu machen'.

138 Haase, *Bonaventure's 'Legenda maior'*, 178–80.

139 Whether changes were taken deliberately or not, cannot and shall not be answered for the reasons laid out above. Wherever discrepancies between the versions can be traced, however, the effects that such changes entail, may be analysed.

140 In a collective text production environment, even an authorial agent like Gertrude would have had the assistance of a scribe and editor, who occasionally advanced to take on the role of a coauthor. We may call this multifaceted job description that of a redactor. In this sense, Fromm's assumption that it is only in vernacular writings that a 'Redaktor' is placed between author and scribe needs to be

extended to Latin texts too; Fromm, 'Volkssprache und Schriftkultur,' 103.

141 Nemes argues that in the case of the transmission of Mechthild of Magdeburg's *Flowing Light*, the 'redactor' is misleading and a more open approach to authorship would be more helpful; see Nemes, *Von der Schrift zum Buch*, 380. Nemes refers to the suggestion of Johannes Janota, 'Mittelalterliche Texte als Entstehungsvarianten.' *In Spuren gesehen. . .: Festschrift Helmut Koopmann*. Ed. by Andrea Bartl, Jürgen Eder, Harry Fröhlich, Klaus Dieter Post, and Ursula Regener. Tübingen: Niemeyer 1998, 65–80, at 73, to speak of an 'extended authorship' rather than a 'redaction' or 'reworking' whenever more than one person participated in the genesis of a text ('Statt von Bearbeitungen oder Redaktionen sollte man bei Textgenesen, an denen mehrere Personen beteiligt sind, von erweiterter Autorschaft sprechen'). Given that my definition of redactor comprises authorial activities, I argue that it is still useful to speak of a redactor, because in this way the editorial relationship to an existing text is underscored.

142 The full passage in the prose prologue, after the recent edition of *Anticlaudianus*, in Alan of Lille [Alanus ab Insulis], 'Anticlaudianus.' *Literary Works*. Ed. and trans. Winthrop Wetherbee. Dumbarton Oaks Medieval Library Vol. 22. Cambridge, MA: Harvard University Press, 2013, 219–516, at 220, reads as follows: *In quo lector non latratu corrixationis insaniens, verum lima correctionis emendans, circumcidat superfluum et compleat diminutum quatenus illimatum revertatur ad limam, impolitum reducatur ad fabricam, inartificiosum suo referatur artifici, male tortum propriae reddatur incudi.* Winthrop Wetherbee, ibid., 221, translates this as: 'Let the reader not rage against it with quarrelsome snarling; let him rather emend it with the file of correction, trimming what is superfluous, filling out what is insufficient; let what is rough be subjected again to the file, what is imperfect be sent back to the workshop, what is unskilfully done be returned to the artisan, what is badly forged be placed again on his anvil.'

143 See Alan of Lille, 'Anticlaudianus,' 222: *Hoc igitur opus fastidire non audeant qui adhuc nutricum vagientes in cunis inferioriis disciplinae lactantur uberibus.* Wetherbee, *Alan of Lille: Literary Works*, 223: 'Therefore let none dare to scorn this work who are still squalling in the nurse's cradle, still being suckled at the breasts of the lesser arts.' The very last lines of the poem pick up the menace of scorn for the poet, see Alan of Lille, 'Anticlaudianus,' Book 9, lines 424–26, 516.

144 Kurt Ruh described the *Legatus* to be 'in Wirklichkeit ein Konglomerat von Texten'; Ruh, 'Gertrud von Helfta,' 7. In contrast to Ruh, Ulrike Wiethaus, 'Collaborative Literacy and the Spiritual Education of Nuns at Helfta,' at 34–5, recognises a compositional 'scaffolding' to the *Legatus*. However, Wiethaus refers in once instance to the production stages as 'scaffolding', in another to the text-internal structure, which she finds to be echoed in late medieval Dominican sister-books (34, n. 20). Also, she sees 'a lack of overarching rhetorical structure' in the *Legatus* (40).

145 The term 'to redact' was used in this way in fifteenth-century England; c. 1475, Churchill Babington, ed., *Polychronicon Ranulphi Higden maonachi Cestrensis: together with the English translations of John Trevisa and of an unknown writer of the fifteenth century*. Vol. 2. London: Longmans, Green and Co., 1869, 273: *Octauianus Augustus, his successor and nevewe, redacte in to oon monarchy the realmes of alle the worlde*; c. 1475, Joseph Rawson Lumby, ed., *Polychronicon Ranulphi Higden maonachi Cestrensis: together with the English translations of John Trevisa and of an unknown writer of the fifteenth century*. Vol. 3. London: Longmans, Green and Co., 1871, 251: *yere, laborede and founde the arte of logike; þe rewles of whom and causes of þe begynnenge Plato fyndenge encreasede hit moche; but Aristotille redacte hit in an arte.*

146 'Der Handschriftenkundler findet hier noch beieinander, was der Philologe später auseinanderreißt – den Lebenszusammenhang der Schriftlichkeit.' Fromm, 'Volkssprache und Schriftkultur,' 108.

147 Ralph Hanna, 'Middle English Manuscripts and the Study of Literature.' *New Medieval Literatures* Vol. 4. Ed. Wendy Scase, Rita Copeland, and David Lawton. Oxford: Oxford University Press, 2001, 243–64, at 248.

148 Stephen Nichols, in his essay on philology in manuscript culture, had reminded scholars of history that 'medieval culture did not simply

live with diversity, it cultivated it', and so he called for situating the diversity of medieval culture 'squarely within our methodology'. This 'New Philology' aimed to study 'the language of texts not simply as discursive phenomena but in the interaction of text language with the manuscript matrix and of both language and manuscript with the social context and networks they inscribe' ('Introduction: Philology in a Manuscript Culture.' *Speculum* 65 [1990]: 1–10, at 9). The manuscript culture was to be put at the forefront of a philology of textual studies considering the 'medieval artefact itself' ('Philology and its discontents.' *The Future of the Middle Ages: Medieval Literature in the 1990s*. Ed. William D. Paden. Gainesville: University Press of Florida, 1994, 113–41, 117). For Nichols it was a 'philological skepticism' which 'privileges the manuscript as a primary locus of meaning production' ('Why material philology? Some thoughts.' *Zeitschrift für Deutsche Philologie* 116 [1997]: 10–30, at 17). Although the 'manuscript matrix' includes 'marginal voices' (that is, the 'poetic text' represented only 'one of several discourses within the manuscript'; 'Philology and its discontents,' 117) the main texts in question were termed poetic and 'beautiful' while, for Nichols, 'the linguistic emphasis on textual study' was to be put into the background ('Why material philology?' 13).

149 Freimut Löser, 'Postmodernes Mittelalter? New Philology und Überlieferungsgeschichte.' *Kulturen des Manuskriptzeitalters: Ergebnisse der amerikanisch-deutschen Arbeitstagung an der Georg-August-Universität Göttingen vom 17. bis 20. Oktober 2002. Transatlantische Studien zu Mittelalter und Früher Neuzeit – Transatlantic Studies on Medieval and Early Modern Literature and Culture Vol. 1*. Ed. Arthur Groos and Hans-Jochen Schiewer. Göttingen: V&R Unipress, 2004, 215–36, poses the critical question, why it is that theoretical discourses led by American and French scholars have completely ignored the hands-on research of so-called *Altgermanisten*. Löser delivers three reasons for such an imbalance: (1) the texts covered by the Wurzburg school, predominantly from the religious sphere, were not canonical, (2) German research imposes a language barrier, and lastly but for Löser most convincingly, (3) there was

no manifesto in German studies, which would have promoted the methodology of *Überlieferungsgeschichte*. In Löser's view, the three main aspects of New Philology – criticising some old editions for their lack of variance, the liberation of the reader, and the emphasis on manuscript culture or Material Philology – had already been practiced in German scholarship before the American paradigm was declared (as developed from Bernard Cerquiglini, *Éloge de la Variante: Histoire critique de la philologie*. Paris: Seuil, 1989). See also Williams-Krapp, 'Die überlieferungsgeschichtliche Methode'.

150 The views posited by defenders of New Philology have met with extensive criticism on behalf of medieval Germanists; this debate is summarised by Kellner, *Spiel der Liebe im Minnesang*, 29–31.

151 Christopher Baswell, 'Talking Back to the Text: Marginal Voices in Medieval Secular Literature.' *The Uses of Manuscripts in Literary Studies: Essays in Memory of Judson Boyce Allen*. Ed. Charlotte C. Morse, Penelope Reed Doob, and Marjorie Curry Woods. Studies in Medieval Culture Vol. 31. Kalamazoo, MI: Western Michigan University, Medieval Institute Publications, 1992, 121–60, at 121.

152 Ibid., 122–3. Images too are part of the 'manuscript matrix' and may hence enter a similar conflicting conversation with the central text; see Nichols, 'Philology and its Discontents,' 132, for examples of interaction and nearly rivalry between manuscript illuminations and texts.

153 'What is "new" in the philology common to all the contributions [of the journal issue] may be found in their insistence that the language of texts be studied not simply as discursive phenomena, but in the interaction of text language with the manuscript matrix and of both language and manuscript with the social context and networks they inscribe'. Nichols, 'Introduction: Philology in a Manuscript Culture,' 9.

154 Baswell, 'Talking Back to the Text,' 124.

155 Ibid., 134.

156 ibid., 124: 'From ancient Rome and earlier, and until fairly recently, the lines between reading and speaking, and reading and interpretation, were not very clearly drawn if they were drawn at all.'

157 Ibid., 149, argues that many centres of authority, which would like to appear natural, are constructed.

158 Ibid., 130. In his research on marginalia in *Aeneid* manuscripts and commentaries on the *Aeneid* (such as that of Anselm of Laon), Baswell shows that whenever the voice shifts in an oration there is a 'dramatic immediacy to that moment of *lectio* and it doubles it, mirroring the *auctor* in the margin.' (127) Baswell operates with the term 'author' referring to the 'authority' of a text on the manuscript page: 'The written author or author's character is enacted and even extended by the speaking reader and (where they are, as often in the classroom, separate) the inscription of his reading. Such a culture generates inscribed marginal sites of readerly interaction with and response to authority – a talking next to and back to the text – and simultaneously produces expanded, potentially varied versions of authority' (130).

159 Marie de France, for example, alludes to 'interpretation [as] collaboration through time by authors or philosophers in one period and reader–interpreters in subsequent eras'; reading, commenting, and revisiting belonged to the cultural process of transmitting artefacts, a standpoint shared also by Hugh of St Victor in his reflections on the study of reading, his didactic *Didascalicon*; see Nichols, 'Philology and its Discontents,' 128.

160 Ibid., 136.

161 Poor, 'Stimmen schreibender Frauen,' 105, uses the term to designate female authorship in the case of Anna Eybin: 'weibliche Autorschaft [ist] weniger durch Schweigen als vielmehr durch eine schrifliche "multivocality" gekennzeichnet'.

162 Ibid., 107. For Poor, this kind of writing may be understood as a legitimate form of female authorship. The gender argument is important since Poor reacts to a long-standing but erroneous position in scholarship about the relative absence (or 'silence') of female authors in the late Middle Ages.

163 Poor, 'Re-thinking Female Authorship,' 211–12, highlights the personalised copy of Anna Eybin and what it tells us about her self-identification 'as scribe/writer of the book'.

164 Klaus Grubmüller, 'Die Viten der Schwestern von Töß und Elsbeth Stagel (Überlieferung und Literarische Einheit).' *Zeitschrift für deutsches Altertum und deutsche Literatur* 98 (1969): 171–204.

165 On the aspect of intentionality despite collective writing settings, see Johanna Thali, *Beten – Schreiben – Lesen: Literarisches Leben und Marienspiritualität im Kloster Engelthal.* Bibliotheca Germanica Vol. 42. Tübingen: Francke, 2003, 59.

166 Nichols, 'Philology and its Discontents,' at 129.

167 See also the study of Bürkle, *Literatur im Kloster*, especially 213.

168 See Stephen Kelly and John J. Thompson, 'Imagined Histories of the Book: Current Paradigms and Future Directions.' *Imagining the Book.* Ed. Stephen Kelly and John J. Thompson. Medieval Texts and Cultures of Northern Europe Vol. 7. Turnhout: Brepols, 2005, 1–14, at 11. See also Michael Johnston and Michael Van Dussen, 'Introduction: Manuscripts and Cultural History.' *The Medieval Manuscript Book: Cultural Approaches.* Cambridge Studies in Medieval Literature Vol. 94. Ed. Michael Johnston and Michael Van Dussen. Cambridge: Cambridge University Press, 2015, 1–16, at 4–5.

169 Copeland, *Rhetoric, Hermeneutics, and Translation in the Middle Ages.*

170 Paul Zumthor, *Essai de poétique médiévale.* Paris: Éditions du Seuil, 1972, 70–5. The concept of *mouvance* is particularly useful for discussing devotional texts as shown by Almut Suerbaum, '"Es kommt ein schiff, geladen": Mouvance in mystischen Liedern aus Straßburg.' *Schreiben und Lesen in der Stadt: Literaturbetrieb im spätmittelalterlichen Straßburg.* Ed. Stephen Mossman, Nigel F. Palmer, and Felix Heinzer. Kulturtopographie des alemannischen Raums Vol. 4. Berlin: De Gruyter, 2012, 99–116.

171 Taylor, 'Vernacular authorship,' 210.

172 *botte* 98, 166.

3 MANUSCRIPT TRANSMISSION HISTORY

1 The dynamic aspects of a manuscript culture are discussed by Kelly and Thompson, 'Imagined Histories of the Book,' 11. See also Johnston and Van Dussen, 'Introduction: Manuscripts and Cultural History,' 4–5.

2   Nichols, 'Why material philology?' 13. See also Nichols, 'Introduction: Philology in a Manuscript Culture,' 1–10; 'Philology and its discontents,' 113–41.

3   I combine the two approaches because historical philology and source criticism are two sides of one coin. While the methods are similar, the end to which the two approaches work are different in so far as one highlights the transmission details of a particular text while the other aims to comprehend a text more globally, that is, in all its facets, so that the material environment of a text witness is studied rather than focusing on the history of its transmission alone. For a comparison between Material Philology and *Überlieferungsgeschichte*, see Löser, 'Postmodernes Mittelalter?' 215–36.

4   In his survey of the study of manuscripts, Hanna, 'Middle English Manuscripts and the Study of Literature,' 248, asserts that 'the ultimate question manuscript studies needs to face' is 'the cultural move'.

5   Sara S. Poor, 'The Countess, the Abbess, and their Books: Manuscript Circulation in a Fifteenth-Century German Family.' *Nuns' Literacies in Medieval Europe: The Antwerp Dialogue*. Ed. Virginia Blanton, Veronica O'Mara, and Patricia Stoop. Medieval Women – Texts and Contexts Vol. 28. Turnout: Brepols, 2017, 341–65, at 343.

6   See Oefelein, 'Gründung und mittelalterliche Geschichte des Klosters St. Marien zu Helfta,' 17.

7   For the documentation of the reform process at Helfta and the affiliated convents, see also Oefelein, *Das Nonnenkloster St. Jacobi*, 51–3.

8   For an overview of the observant reform movement, see Winston-Allen, *Convent Chronicles*, 81–6.

9   For a historical overview of the late medieval reform movement, see Uffmann, *Wie in einem Rosengarten*, 40–61.

10   I follow Klaus Graf in the call for caution to see monocausal relationships between the reform and increased literary activity in the fifteenth century, because there is a 'danger' of mistaking historical tendencies for observant tendencies; and, as Graf stresses, the reform itself might have used existing dispositions rather than creating them; see Klaus Graf, 'Ordensreform und Literatur in Augsburg während des 15. Jahrhunderts.'

Literarisches Leben in Augsburg während des 15. Jahrhunderts. Ed. Johannes Janota and Werner Williams-Krapp. Studia Augustana Vol. 7. Tübingen: Niemeyer, 1995, 100–59, at 112–15.

11   See Jansen, *Die Texte des Kirchberg-Corpus',* 138–41.

12   In his publications on the observant reform movement, Williams-Krapp has highlighted strong connections between the reform and literary production, see 'Ordensreform und Literatur im 15. Jahrhundert,' 41–51; 'Frauenmystik und Ordensreform im 15. Jahrhundert,' 301–13; 'Observanzbewegungen, monastische Spiritualität und geistliche Literatur im 15. Jahrhundert,' 1–15.

13   See for example, the recent studies of Mengis, *Schreibende Frauen um 1500*; Astrid Breith, *Textaneignung: Das Frauenlegendar der Lichtenthaler Schreibmeisterin Schwester Regula*. Studien und Texte zum Mittelalter und zur Frühen Neuzeit Vol. 17. Münster: Waxmann, 2010, in particular 23–31; Uffmann, *Wie in einem Rosengarten*, 228–53; Antje Willing, *Literatur und Ordensreform im 15. Jahrhundert: Deutsche Abendmahlsschriften im Nürnberger Katharinenkloster*. Studien und Texte zum Mittelalter und zur Frühen Neuzeit Vol. 4. Münster: Waxmann, 2004.

14   For further details, see Oefelein, 'Gründung und mittelalterliche Geschichte des Klosters St. Marien zu Helfta,' 55.

15   The library of the Erfurt Charterhouse assigned shelfmark letters specifically for mystical theology (D), revelations (J), and diverse devotional texts (for example E/F and G), see Almuth Märker, *Das 'Prohemium Longum' des Erfurter Kartäuserkatalogs aus der Zeit um 1475*, 357–8.

16   See Almuth Märker, 'Schweigen und Lesen – Das Prohemium longum' des Erfurter Kartäuserkatalogs als Wissenschaftpropädeutik am Ende des 15. Jahrhunderts. *Bücher, Bibliotheken und Schriftkultur der Kartäuser: Festgabe zum 65. Geburtstag von Edward Potkowski*. Ed. Sönke Lorenz. Contubernium Vol. 59. Stuttgart: Steiner Verlag, 2002, 383–97, in particular 393–4.

17   Watson, 'Censorship and Cultural Change,' 860.

18   Eva Schlotheuber, 'Daily Life, "Amor Dei", and Politics in the Letters of the Benedictine Nuns of Lüne in the Fifteenth and Sixteenth

Centuries.' *Nuns' Literacies in Medieval Europe: The Kansas City Dialogue.* Ed. Virginia Blanton, Veronica O'Mara, and Patricia Stoop. Medieval Women – Texts and Contexts Vol. 27. Turnhout: Brepols, 2015, 249–67, at 250–1.

19 Wieland, *Gertrud von Helfta*, 47; see also Ringler, *Viten- und Offenbarungsliteratur in Frauenklöstern des Mittelalters*, 60–1.

20 The provenance is also verified by Balázs Nemes through the analysis of scribal hands active in St Nikolaus in undis in the fifteenth century, see: Ulrike Bodemann, Siegfried Ringler, and Balázs Nemes, Handschriftencensus, Brüssel, Königl. Bibl., ms. 8507-09 (Kat.-Nr. 3407), online: www .handschriftencensus.de/7334 (last accessed 26.11.2019).

21 For a synopsis of her life, see Anneke B. Mulder-Bakker, 'Gertrude of Ortenberg.' *Women and Gender in Medieval Europe: An Encyclopedia.* Ed. Margaret Schaus. The Routledge Encyclopedias of the Middle Ages Vol. 14. New York: Routledge, 2006, 323. For the edition of the *Life of Gertrude of Ortenberg*, see Hans Derkits, ed., *Die Lebensbeschreibung der Gertrud von Ortenberg, Die Lebensbeschreibung der Gertrud von Ortenberg*. 2 Vols. Doctoral dissertation, University of Vienna, 1990. For a study and translation of the *Life*, see Anneke B. Mulder-Bakker, *The Dedicated Spiritual Life of Upper Rhine Noble Women: A Study and Translation of a Fourteenth-Century Spiritual Biography of Gertrude Rickeldey of Ortenberg and Heilke of Staufenberg.* Brepols: Turnhout, 2017. On Gertrude of Ortenberg, see also Hans Derkits, 'Die Vita der Gertrud von Ortenberg – Historische Aspekte eines Gnaden-Lebens.' *Die Ortenau: Veröffentlichungen des Historischen Vereins für Mittelbaden* 71 (1991): 77–125, in particular at 78–9; Martin Ruch, *Offenburg, die Ortenau und die Literatur: Ein Lesebuch zur Literaturgeschichte Mittelbadens.* Norderstedt: Books on Demand, 2004; Eugen Hillenbrand, 'Heiligenleben und Alltag. Offenburger Stadtgeschichte im Spiegel eines spätmittelalterlichen Beginenlebens.' *Die Ortenau* 90 (2010): 157–76; Martina Backes, 'Eine Stadt voll der Gnaden: Straßburg aus der Perspektive Gertruds von Ortenberg.' *Schreiben und Lesen in der Stadt: Literaturbetrieb im spätmittelalterlichen Straßburg.* Ed. Stephen Mossman, Nigel F. Palmer, and Felix Heinzer.

Kulturtopographie des alemannischen Raums Vol. 4. Berlin: De Gruyter, 2012, 29–38.

22 On this text witness of the German *Life of St. Catherine of Siena*, see Thomas Brakmann, *'Ein Geistlicher Rosengarten': Die Vita der heiligen Katharina von Siena zwischen Ordensreform und Laienfrömmigkeit im 15. Jahrhundert: Untersuchungen und Edition.* Frankfurt a.M.: Lang, 2011.

23 For a full description of the manuscript, see catalogue entry by Ulrike Bodemann, *Katalog der deutschsprachigen illustrierten Handschriften des Mittelalters.* Vol. 6 Pt. 3/4. Munich: Beck, 2005, 266–8, nr. 51.18.2. See also Brakmann, *Ein Geistlicher Rosengarten*, 75–81; Wieland, *Gertrud von Helfta*, 3–5.

24 Mulder-Bakker, 'Gertrude of Ortenberg,' 323.

25 How Catherine's spiritual authority and sanctity were linked with contemporary political and cultural developments, is the subject of F. Thomas Luongo's work, *The Saintly Politics of Catherine of Siena.* Ithaca, NY: Cornell University Press, 2006.

26 Nigel Palmer, 'Die Münchner Perikopenhandschrift Cgm 157 und die Handschriftenproduktion des Straßburger Reuerinnenklosters im späten 15. Jahrhundert.' *Kulturtopographie deutschsprachigen Südwestens im späteren Mittelalter: Studien und Texte.* Ed. Barbara Fleith and René Wetzel. Kulturtopographie des alemannischen Raums Vol. 1. Berlin: De Gruyter, 2009, 263–300, at 265, counts St Nikolaus among the top three 'bisher bekannten Zentren einer literarischen Buchkultur in der Reichsstadt Straßburg am Ende des 15. Jahrhunderts'. See also Anne Winston-Allen, Networking in Medieval Strasbourg: Cross-Order Collaboration in Book Illustration among Women's Reformed Convents.' *Schreiben und Lesen in der Stadt: Literaturbetrieb im spätmittelalterlichen Straßburg.* Ed. Stephen Mossman, Nigel F. Palmer, and Felix Heinzer. Kulturtopographie des alemannischen Raums Vol. 4. Berlin: De Gruyter, 2012, 197–212; Thomas Lentes, *Gebetbuch und Gebärde: Religiöses Ausdrucksverhalten in Gebetbüchern aus dem Dominikanerinnen-Kloster St. Nikolaus in undis zu Straßburg (1350–1550).* Doctoral dissertation, University of Münster, 1996.

27 For a full description of the manuscript, see the catalogue by Elisabeth Wunderle, *Die*

deutschen Handschriften der Bayerischen Staatsbibliothek München: Die mittelalterlichen Handschriften aus Cgm 5255–7000 einschließlich der althochdeutschen Fragemente Cgm 5248. Catalogus codicum manu scriptorum Bibliotheca Monacensis Vol. 5: Editio altera Pt 9. Wiesbaden: Harrassowitz, 2018, 56–60.

28 On Chrstine Ebner, see Susanne Bürkle, 'Die 'Gnadenvita' Christine Ebners: Episodenstruktur – Text-Ich und Autorschaft.' *Deutsche Mystik im abendländischen Zusammenhang.* Ed. Walter Haug and Wolfram Schneider-Lastin. Tübingen: Niemeyer, 2000, 483–513.

29 For a full manuscript description and a discussion on the providence including the links between the family of Probst and the convent Inzigkofen, see Jansen, *Die Texte des Kirchberg-Corpus'*, 37–45.

30 On the history of the nuns of Inzigkofen, see Werner Fechter, *Deutsche Handschriften des 15. und 16. Jahrhunderts aus der Bibliothek des ehemaligen Augustinerchorfrauenstifts Inzigkofen.* Arbeiten zur Landeskunde Hohenzollerns Vol. 15. Sigmaringen: Thorbecke, 1997, 5–47.

31 Dating and provenance according to Kurt Ruh, *Bonaventura deutsch: Ein Beitrag zur deutschen Franziskaner-Mystik und -Scholastik.* Bibliotheca Germanica Vol. 7. Bern: Francke, 1956, 126.

32 Full catalogue descriptions in Gustav Scherrer, *Verzeichnis der Handschriften der Stiftsbibliothek von St. Gallen.* Halle: Verlag der Buchhandlung des Waisenhauses, 1875, 368–9; Beat Matthias von Scarpatetti, ed. *Katalog der datierten Handschriften in der Schweiz in lateinischer Schrift vom Anfang des Mittelalters bis 1550.* Vol. 3: Die Handschriften der Bibliotheken St. Gallen–Zürich. Dietikon-Zürich: Urs Graf, 1991, 83, nr. 231.

33 On the amorphous order identity of Franciscan Tertiaries, especially seen from the perspective of late medieval textual culture, see Alison More, 'Religious Order and Textual Identity: The Case of Franciscan Tertiary Women.' *Nuns' Literacies in Medieval Europe: The Antwerp Dialogue.* Ed. Virginia Blanton, Veronica O'Mara, and Patricia Stoop. Medieval Women – Texts and Contexts Vol. 28. Turnhout: Brepols, 2017, 43–59.

34 On the history of Wonnenstein in the late Middle Ages, see Ekkehard Borries,

Schwesternspiegel im 15. Jahrhundert: Gattungskonstitution, Editionen, Untersuchungen. Berlin: De Gruyter, 2008, 31–2.

35 The binding itself was probably done at the Dominican convent workshop in Bern; for a full manuscript description, see Ian Holt, *Solothurn, Zentralbibliothek, Cod. S 458.* Solothurn: Zentralbibliothek Solothurn, 2009. www.e-codices.unifr.ch/en/description/zbs/S-0458 (last accessed 04.06.2019).

36 On the dynamics between manuscript and print culture, see the volume Gerd Dicke and Klaus Grubmüller eds., *Die Gleichzeitigkeit von Handschrift und Buchdruck.* Wolfenbütteler Mittelalter-Studien Vol. 16. Wiesbaden: Harrassowitz, 2003.

37 The scribe most famous for producing such initials was Nicolas Spierinc, see Antoine de Schryver, 'Nicolas Spierinc: Calligraphe et enlumineur des Ordonnances des états de l'hôtel de Charles le Téméraire.' *Scriptorium* 23 (1969): 434–58. Another example of this style can be found in the so-called *Gothic Alphabet of Mary of Burgundy*, for which François Avril has suggested Pierre Coustain (c. 1420–1497) as scribe, see Eberhard König, *Das Kalligraphiebuch der Maria von Burgund: Brüssel, Bibliothèque Royale de Belgique, Ms. II 845.* Luzern: Quaternio Verlag, 2015. I thank Jeffrey Hamburger for the art historical conformation on Solothurn, Zentralbibliothek, Cod. S 458, fol. 46r.

38 Bernhard Bischoff associates the leaves with ninth-century Tours, see Alfons Schönherr, 'Katalogisierung mittelalterlicher und neuzeitlicher Handschriften.' *30. Bericht der Zentralbibliothek Solothurn über das Jahr 1959* (1960): 31–2.

39 On Carthusian book culture, see the volume, Sylvain Excoffon and Coralie Zermatte, eds., *Sammeln, kopieren, verbreiten: Zur Buchkultur der Kartäuser gestern und heute.* Analecta Cartusiana Vol. 337. Saint-Étienne: CERCOR, 2018.

40 For a study of a theological miscellany from Buxheim and its material composition, including an overview of the library in the late fifteenth century, see Racha Kirakosian, 'Watermarks and Watersheds: The Dating of Ms. Riant 80 and the Overlapping Production of Manuscripts and Printed Books.' *Harvard Library Bulletin* 25 (2014): 108–19.

41 Ruf, *Mittelalterliche Bibliothekskataloge Deutschlands und der Schweiz*, 95.

42 See Chapter 2 'Redactions within a Dynamic Textuality' and the Appendix for a list of manuscripts pertaining to the reception history of the *Legatus*. On the library of Buxheim, see René Wetzel, "Spricht maister Eberhart': Die Unfestigkeit von Autor, Text und Textbausteinen im Cod. Bodmer 59 und in der Überlieferung weiterer mystischer Sammelhandschriften des 15. Jahrhunderts. Mit einem Exkurs zur Buch- und Bibliotheksgeschichte der Kartause Buxheim.' *Kulturtopographie des deutsch-sprachigen Südwestens*. Ed. Barbara Fleith and René Wetzel. Kulturtopographie des Alemannischen Raums Vol. 1. Berlin: De Gruyter, 301–25, in particular at 316–25. On the Buxheim library around 1500, see Oliver Auge, 'Frömmigkeit, Bildung, Bücherliebe – Konstanten im Leben des Buxheimer Kartäusers Hilprand Brandenburg (1442–1514).' *Bücher, Bibliotheken und Schriftkultur der Kartäuser: Festgabe zum 65. Geburtstag von Edward Potkowski.* Ed. Lorenz Sönke and Edward Potkowski. Contubernium Vol. 59. Stuttgart: Steiner, 2002, 399–422. On the history of Buxheim, see Friedrich Stöhlker, *Die Kartause Buxheim. 1402–1803.* 7 vols. Buxheim: Heimatdienst Buxheim, 1974–8.

43 For a general description of the manuscript, see Dorothy K. Coveney, *A Descriptive Catalogue of Manuscripts in the Library of University College, London.* London: Printed for University of London, University College, 1935, 72–9.

44 Similarly, in the Vadstena sermons, preachers frequently used material from Birgitta of Sweden's *Revelations* as an authoritative source of theology; see Roger Andersson, 'Birgitta and her Revelations in the Sermons of the Vadstena Brothers.' *A Companion to Birgitta of Sweden and Her Legacy in the Later Middle Ages.* Ed. Maria H. Oen. Brill's Companions to the Christian Tradition Vol. 89. Leiden: Brill, 2019, 159–85; 'Messenger Manuscripts and Mechanisms of Change.' *Continuity and Change: Papers from the Birgitta Conference at Dartington 2015.* Ed. Elin Andersson, Claes Gejrot, Eddie Jones, and Mia Åkestam. Stockholm: Kungl. Vitterhets Historie och Antikvitets Akademien, 2017, 24–39.

45 For a full manuscript description see Wieland, *Gertrud von Helfta*, 13–14; see also Ringler,

Viten- und Offenbarungsliteratur in Frauenklöstern des Mittelalters, 60; Freimut Löser, Robert Steinke, and Günter Hägele, eds., *Meister Eckhart in Augsburg: Deutsche Mystik des Mittelalters in Kloster, Stadt und Schule. Katalog zur Handschriftenausstellung in der Schatzkammer der Universitätsbibliothek Augsburg (18. Mai bis 29. Juli 2011).* Augsburg: Universitätsbibliothek, 2011, 206–8, nr. IV.

46 The letter X is not a shelf mark signature assigned in Buxheim; for Buxheim's medieval library catalogue, see Ruf, *Mittelalterliche Bibliothekskataloge Deutschlands und der Schweiz*, 81–101.

47 We know that the Buxheim monks had at least one manuscript with excerpts from the *Legatus*, which survives as Augsburg, Staats- und StB, 8° Cod. 203, fols. 55r–57v.

48 Since this manuscript was likely not only kept at Buxheim but also produced there, we may conclude that male scribes worked on it; I hence use the pronoun 'he' (rather than 'they', which I use whenever gender is unspecific).

49 The full text reads: *Jtem in dem büchlin stant daz wort gÿme vnd ist so vil gÿme oder kÿme, edelstain oder die ersten ougen an den baumen die sich erzaigent oder regen im glentz grünen oder broßen* (Augsburg, Benediktinerabtei St. Stephan, Hs 38). For a general study on gems in the Christian literary tradition, see Christel Meier, *Gemma spiritualis: Methode und Gebrauch der Edelsteinallegorese vom frühen Christentum bis ins 18. Jahrhundert.* Münstersche Mittelalter-Schriften Vol. 34. Munich: Fink, 1977.

50 See Chapter 6 'Imaginary Textiles' for a discussion on material objects and devotional prayer, including so-called craft-praying.

51 '*Wer mir drú Pster noster sprichet, der důt mir gar vil liebes. Zů dem ersten Pater noster sol er opferen minem himmelschen vatter die ůbung mines unschuldigen mundes...*'; botte 77, 142.

52 McNamer, *Affective* 73, treats written prayers as a 'script for the performance of prayer'.

53 These three prayers may be connected to the three modes of prayer, each in turn associated with three types of prayer gestures, described in the Gospels and depicted in the *Cursus Sanctae Mariae* at the Pierpont Morgan Library, M. 739, fol. 22v; for discussion, with references to a prayer book from the Benedictine convent of Engelberg and other

allied material, see Jeffrey F. Hamburger, *Nuns as Artists: The Visual Culture of a Medieval Convent*. Berkeley: University of California Press, 1997, 85–8.

54   For a full description of the manuscript, see Karin Schneider and Heinz Zirnbauer, *Die deutschen mittelalterlichen Handschriften*. Die Handschriften der Stadtbibliothek Nürnberg Vol. 1. Wiesbaden: Harrassowitz, 1965, 367–70.

55   On the reform history of the St Gall Dominican nuns, see Mengis, *Schreibende Frauen um 1500*. On the friendship between the St Gall and Nuremberg Dominican nuns in particular, see Willing, *Die Bibliothek des Klosters St. Katharina zu Nürnberg*, especially Vol. 1, CIII–CXIV.

56   Mengis, *Schreibende Frauen um 1500*, 88. Regina Sattler copied at least two more books for the convent in Zoffingen, see ibid., 87.

57   Christian Heitzmann, 'Die mittelalterlichen Handschriften der Leopold-Sophien-Bibliothek in Überlingen.' *Schriften des Vereins für Geschichte des Bodensees und seiner Umgebung* 120 (2002): 41–103, at 65.

58   For a full description of Augsburg, Universitätsbibliothek, Cod. III. 1. 4° 30, see Karin Schneider, *Deutsche mittelalterliche Handschriften der Universitätsbibliothek Augsburg: Die Signaturengruppen Cod. I.3 und Cod. III.1*, Die Handschriften der Universitätsbibliothek Augsburg II,1. Wiesbaden: Harrassowitz, 1988, 314–18. The watermarks of the paper used for Augsburg, Universitätsbibliothek, Cod. III. 1. 4° 30, date to 1476, meaning that – considering that paper was normally used within three years of its production – this manuscript predates the Überlingen copy, suggesting that Regina Sattler copied an existing collection rather compiling one herself. The prayer texts from the *botte* starts in the Augsburg manuscript in the same way as in the Überlingen copy (with spelling variance): *Ain sälige klosterjunkfrow genant Truta...* (fol. 104v).

59   Überlingen, Leopold-Sophien-Bibliothek, Ms. 26, fol. 84vb: *Ain sälge closter frow genant Trutta...*; Augsburg, Universitätsbibliothek, Cod. III. 1. 4° 30, fol. 104v: *Ain sälige klosterjunkfrow genant Truta...*

60   Christ's prayers at Gethsemane were the model of penitential prayer in the monastic tradition; see Hamburger, *Nuns as Artists*, 85–7.

61   Werner J. Hoffmann determined that these two manuscripts from Inzigkofen transmitting the *botte* complement each other and form together a nearly complete *botte*-text; Hoffmann, 'Mscr. Dresd.M.243.' *Tiefenerschließung und Digitalisierung der deutschsprachigen mittelalterlichen Handschriften der Sächsischen Landesbibliothek, Staats- und Universitätsbibliothek (SLUB) Dresden*. www.manuscripta-mediaevalia.de/dokumente/html/obj31600080 (last accessed 26.11.2019).

62   The full shelfmark reference is: Stiftsarchiv Muri-Gries, Benediktinerkollegium Sarnen, Sarnen, M. Cod. chart. 215 (Depot im Staatsarchiv des Kantons Obwalden, Sarnen). For the catalogue entry, see Charlotte Bretscher-Gisiger and Rudolf Gamper, *Katalog der Mittelalterlichen Handschriften der Klöster Muri und Hermetschwil*. Dietikon-Zürich: Graf, 2005, 350–3; online: www.urs-graf-verlag.com/pdf/MSMuriK.pdf (last accessed 04.06.2019).

63   The date 1504 appears on Munich, Bayerische Staatsbibliothek, Cgm 861, fol. 71r. For a full description of the manuscript, see Karin Schneider, *Die deutschen Handschriften der Bayerischen Staatsbibliothek München. Cgm 691–867*. Catalogus codicum manu scriptorum Bibliothecae Monacensis Vol. 5: Editio altera Pt. 5: Codices Germanicos 691–867 complectens. Wiesbaden: Harrassowitz, 1984, 78–81, nr. I, 3.

64   On medieval cross-dressing, see Valerie R. Hotchkiss, *Clothes Make the Man: Female Cross Dressing in Medieval Europe*. Florence: Routledge, 1996. The cross-dressing mentioned in the prayers of Munich, Bayerische Staatsbibliothek, Cgm 861, however, does not speak to a practice of saints as, for example, that of Thecla; for a discussion on cross-dressing saints, see Crystal Lynn Lubinsky, *Removing Masculine Layers to Reveal a Holy Womanhood: The Female Transvestite Monks of Late Antique Eastern Christianity*. Studia Traditionis Theologiae Vol. 13. Turnhout: Brepols, 2013. Rather, late medieval carnival practices in which cross-dressing occurred as a way to destabilise social hierarchies, are meant here; generally on carnival practices and their cultural dimension as encountered by the Church, see Siegfried Wagner, *Der Kampf des Fastens gegen die Fastnacht: Zur Geschichte der Mäßigung*. Kulturgeschichtliche Forschungen Vol. 5. Munich: Tuduv, 1986; Werner

Mezger, *Narrenidee und Fastnachtsbrauch: Studien zum Fortleben des Mittelalters in der europäischen Festkultur.* Konstanzer Bibliothek Vol. 15. Konstanz: Universitätsverlag, 1991.

65 For a full description of the manuscript, see Schneider, *Die deutschen Handschriften der Bayerischen Staatsbibliothek München: Cgm 691–867,* 584–92.

66 The passage in his *Life* (*Leben Seuses,* Ch. IV), as contained in his collected work called *The Exemplar,* documents his ardent desire to incorporate Christ into his own flesh: Heinrich Seuse, *Deutsche Schriften im Auftrag der Württembergischen Kommission für Landesgeschichte.* Ed. Karl Bihlmeyer. Stuttgart: Kohlhammer, 1907, 15–16. For a discussion of this passage, see Chapter 5 'The Scriptorial Heart'.

67 For a discussion of these inscriptions, see Jeffrey F. Hamburger, *The Visual and the Visionary: Art and Female Spirituality in Late Medieval Germany.* New York: Zone Books, 1998, 262–8, especially at 268.

68 For a detailed list of all the excerpts from Suso's texts in Munich, Bayerische Staatsbibliothek, Cgm 843, see Wieland, *Gertrud von Helfta,* 37–8.

69 On the theological development of the idea of spiritual compensation through prayer, see Ane Bysted, *The Crusade Indulgence: Spiritual Rewards and the Theology of the Crusades, c. 1095–1216.* History of Warfare Vol. 103. Leiden: Brill, 2015, 117–21. On substitution and satisfaction, see Racha Kirakosian, 'Penitential Punishment and Purgatory: A Drama of Purification through Pain.' *Punishment and Penitential Practices in Medieval German Writing.* Ed. Sarah Bowden and Annette Volfing. King's College London Medieval Studies Vol. 26. London: Boydell & Brewer, 2018, 129–54; Gavin Fort, 'Suffering Another's Sin: Proxy Penance in the Thirteenth Century.' *Journal of Medieval History* 44 (2018): 202–30.

70 The transposition into the first-person perspective is in line with what McNamer, *Affective Meditation,* 58–85, calls an 'impassioned "I"'.

71 Josef Höcherl, *Das Rebdorfer Anniversar.* Rebdorf: Kloster Rebdorf, 1995, 55.

72 St Walburg had an active scriptorium from which numerous late medieval manuscripts survive; see Joseph Lechner, *Die spätmittelalterliche Handschriftengeschichte der Benediktinerinnenabtei St. Walburg/Eichstätt.*

Eichstätter Studien Vol. 2. Münster: Aschendorff, 1937.

73 St Walburg never strictly joined a reform congregation but maintained strong ties to other convents such as the Dominicans in Eichstätt and the Augustinian canons in Rebdorf; for an overview of the reform in St Walburg with ample reference to source material, see Maria Magdalena Zunker, *Geschichte der Benediktinerinnenabtei St. Walburg in Eichstätt von 1035 bis heute.* Lindenberg: Fink, 2009, 19–24. On Rebdorf see Norbert Backmund, *Die Chorherrenorden und ihre Stifte in Bayern. Augustinerchorherren, Prämonstratenser, Chorherren vom Hl. Geist, Antoniter.* Passau: Neue-Presse-Verlags-Gesellschaft, 1966, 119–23.

74 Hamburger, *Nuns as Artists,* 99. The drawing in question is that of the *Agony in the Garden*; for a reproduction see ibid., plate 89.

75 Full manuscript description by Eisermann, *Katalog der deutschsprachigen mittelalterlichen Handschriften der Forschungsbibliothek Gotha.*

76 Gotha, Forschungsbibliothek, Chart. B 269, fol. 1r. For a discussion of the manuscript collection, see Chapter 6 'Imaginary Textiles'.

77 Winfried Hagenmaier, *Die deutschen mittelalterlichen Handschriften der Universitätsbibliothek und die mittelalterlichen Handschriften anderer öffentlicher Sammlungen: Kataloge der Universitätsbibliothek Freiburg im Breisgau.* Vol. 1: *Die Handschriften der Universitätsbibliothek und anderer öffentlicher Sammlungen in Freiburg im Breisgau und Umgebung* Pt. 4. Wiesbaden: Harrassowitz, 1988, 46 and 238. The binding stamps on Freiburg im Breisgau, Erzbischöfliches Archiv, Hs. 31, point to a binding workshop in South Wurttemberg, see ibid., 238. On the codex's last leaf a crossed out and blackened fifteenth-century Bastarda inscription is still partly visible reading as much as: *das bl bůch* <...> *ist* <...*awe* ...> *ze ysni* (fol. 237v). Although there existed a Benedictine abbey in the East-Swabian community of Isny (current spelling) the inscription may not be taken as a valid provenance since it is crossed out and made illegible.

78 Judging from the feminine forms in the prayers contained Freiburg im Breisgau, Universitätsbibliothek, Hs. 202, it was kept at a nunnery.

79 Prayers translated into imaginary jewels and flowers form part of the late medieval

devotional culture; for example, the role of a celestial dress and jewels, with Mary as the queen of heavens, can be seen in a *contemplatio deuota de vestibus Beatae Mariae reginae coeli* in a fifteenth-century German prayer book (Berlin, Staatsbibliothek zu Berlin – Preußischer Kulturbesitz, Ms. germ. oct. 593, fol. 1r), for a discussion see Hermann Degering, *Kurzes Verzeichnis der germanischen Handschriften der Preußischen Staatsbibliothek*. Vol. III: Die Handschriften in Oktavformat und Register zu Band I-III. Mitteilungen aus der Preußischen Staatsbibliothek Vol. 9. Leipzig: Hiersemann, 1932. Repr. Graz: Akademische Druck- und Verlagsanstalt, 1970, 228.

80   Wieland, *Gertrud von Helfta*, 47.

81   Nevertheless, the catalogue entry does not mention the strong affinity to Munich, Bayerische Staatsbibliothek, Cgm 5292; see Winfried Hagenmaier, *Die abendländischen neuzeitlichen Handschriften der Universitätsbibliothek Freiburg im Breisgau*, Kataloge der Universitätsbibliothek Freiburg im Breisgau Vol. 1 Pt. 5. Wiesbaden: Harrassowitz, 1996, 37–8.

82   Ringler, *Viten- und Offenbarungsliteratur in Frauenklöstern des Mittelalters*, 60–3.

83   Ringler, 'Die Rezeption Gertruds von Helfta,' 141–2, points out that the Heidelberg codex presents the only instance where the *botte* is transmitted alongside mystical literature in the narrow sense. Of course, the overall transmission shows that Gertrude is quite often transmitted with Mechthild; still, Ringler's point is valid as he highlights the overall collection found in the Heidelberg codex.

84   The Leipzig 1503 imprint (*Das buch geistlicher gnaden, offenbarunge, wunderliches vnde beschawlichen lebens der heiligenn iungfrawen Mechtildis vnd Gertrudis, Closter iungfrawen des closters Helffede*. Ed. Marcus von Weida. Leipzig: Lotter, 1503 [VD 16, M 1784]) was printed by Melchior Lotter and commissioned by the same duchess Sidonie of Meißen, who would later have the *botte* printed with Lotter. In 1508, another print of the German *Liber* was effected (VD 16, M 1786), generally leading to misconception that the Gertrude mentioned alongside Mechthild of Hackeborn in the title was her sister Gertrude of Hackeborn – a confusion which lasted until the second half of the nineteenth century, see Ulrich Köpf,

'Gerhard Tersteegen und die Frauen von Helfta: Zur Rezeption der Helftaer Mystik im Protestantismus.' *'Vor dir steht die leere Schale meiner Sehnsucht': Die Mystik der Frauen von Helfta*. Ed. Michael Bangert and Hildegund Keul. Leipzig: Benno-Verlag, 1998, 202–18, at 214. The Dominican Marcus von Weida, who lived in Leipzig, overviewed these editions, see Volker Honemann, 'Predigt und geistliches Schrifttum im Leipziger Dominikanerkloster um 1500.' *Johann Tetzel und der Ablass: Begleitband zur Ausstellung 'Tetzel – Ablass – Fegefeuer' in Mönchenkloster und Nikolaikirche Jüterbo*. Ed. Enno Bünz, Hartmut Kühne, and Peter Wiegand. Berlin: Lukas, 2017, 161–77, at 167. The close working relationship between Duchess Sidonie, Melchior Lotter, and Marcus von Weida attests the ties between monasticism, devout lay people, and printers; on Melchior Lotter's printing activities, see Thomas Döring, 'Der Leipziger Buchdruck vor der Reformation.' *Bücher, Drucker, Bibliotheken in Mitteldeutschland: Neue Forschungen zur Kommunikations- und Mediengeschichte um 1500*. Ed. Enno Bünz. Leipzig: Leipziger Universitätsverlag, 2006, 87–98, at 94–6.

85   See stemma in Wieland, *Gertrud von Helfta*, 47.

86   This link was first established by Wieland, *Gertrud von Helfta*, 74. See also catalogue description Felix Heinzer and Gerhard Stamm, *Die Handschriften von Lichtenthal: Mit einem Anhang: Die heute noch im Kloster Lichtenthal befindlichen Handschriften des 12. bis 16. Jahrhunderts*, Die Handschriften der Badischen Landesbibliothek in Karlsruhe Vol. 9. Wiesbaden: Harrassowitz, 1987, 210, L 89.

87   It is unclear whether the text is copied from another manuscript or whether it is a new translation, see Maria Pia Schindele, 'Der heiligen Getrud von Helfta "both der göttlichen myltigkeit" in einer Lichtenthaler Handschrift von 1566.' *Freiburger Diözesan-Archiv* 120 (2000): 53–107, at 54. For an edition of Book 1 (fols. 4r–87r), see ibid., 55–107. For an edition of Book 2, Chapter 1 and Book 3, see Pius Reiß, 'Die Bücher des Legatus divinae pietatis II und III in einer Lichtenthaler Handschrift von 1566.' *Freiburger Diözesan-Archiv* 125 (2005): 69–217.

88   Wieland's assumption that the book was bound in the late nineteenth or early

twentieth century, when all components were made to fit the same format (18.2×14.5 cm), is incorrect, as shown by Heinzer and Stamm, *Die Handschriften von Lichtenthal*, 33.

89 Wieland, *Gertrud von Helfta*, 18.

90 Felix Heinzer, *Aus Handschriften und Inkunabeln der Historischen Lehrerbibliothek des Ludwig-Wilhelm-Gymnasiums*. Vortragsreihe der Historischen Lehrerbibliothek des Ludwig-Wilhelm-Gymnasiums in Rastatt Vol. 1. Rastatt: Stadtverwaltung Rastatt, 1989, 53.

91 Dating according to Beat von Scarpatetti, *Die Handschriften der Stiftsbibliothek St. Gallen*. Vol. 1: Abt. IV: Codices 547–669. Hagiographica, Historica, Geographica, 8.–18. Jahrhundert. Wiesbaden: Harrassowitz, 2003, 222–5, at 222. Library provenance in the Early Modern period according to *Frauen im Galluskloster: Katalog zur Ausstellung in der Stiftsbibliothek St. Gallen (20. März–12. November 2006)*. Ed. Theres Flury, et al. St. Gallen: Verlag am Klosterhof, 2006, 103.

92 For manuscript descriptions and historical context, see von Scarpatetti, *Die Handschriften der Stiftsbibliothek St. Gallen*, Vol. 1, 162–6; Mengis, *Schreibende Frauen um 1500*, 333–7, nr. 47. Some of the codex's fascicles were written by Regina Sattler, the same scribe who copied Überlingen, Leopold-Sophien-Bibliothek, Ms. 26.

93 Andreas Kraß, *Stabat mater dolorosa: Lateinische Überlieferung und volkssprachliche Übertragungen im deutschen Mittelalter*. Munich: Fink, 1998, 183, does not indicate a provenance, but Richard F. Fasching, *Die 'Vierzig Myrrhenbüschel vom Leiden Christi': Untersuchungen, Überlieferung und Edition*. Scrinium Friburgense. Berlin: De Gruyter, 2020, 233, indicates the Dominican nunnery St Katharina in St Gall as place of provenance. Zurich, Zentralbibliothek, Ms. C 162, is a neatly copied prayer book into which hand-coloured woodblocks with scenes of Christ's Passion have been pasted on fols. 58v, 97v, 146v, 152v, 155v, 176r (torn out 'ecce homo' depiction), 179v, 192v (fragmented, mostly torn out 'cross' depiction), 198r, 201v.

94 Wieland, *Gertrud von Helfta*, 22, indicates *botte* 118 to be the final text portion in St Gall, Stiftsbibliothek, Cod. Sang. 506, where, in fact, material from Ch. 119 and 120 follows in a relatively shortened form.

95 See transmission stemma in Wieland, *Gertrud von Helfta*, 47.

96 See Schlotheuber, *Klostereintritt und Bildung*, 268–96; 'Daily Life, 'Amor Dei', and 'Politics,' 250–1.

97 For a full manuscript description with a detailed list of the texts contained in Dresden, Sächsische Landesbibliothek, Hs M 243, see Werner J. Hoffmann, 'Mscr. Dresd.M.243.' The appearance of inserted texts into the *botte* portion is due to a binding mistake, where quires have been mixed up, see Wieland, *Gertrud von Helfta*, 5.

98 Ibid., 6.

99 Ibid., 5; Ringler, *Viten- und Offenbarungsliteratur*, 61; Hoffmann, *Die deutschsprachigen mittelalterlichen Handschriften der Sächsischen Landesbibliothek - Staats- und Universitätsbibliothek (SLUB) Dresden*.

100 This network is most recently described by Mengis, *Schreibende Frauen um 1500*, 204–41. See also the secondary literature on the links between Inzigkofen, St Gall, Pillenreuth, and Nuremberg noted by Poor, 'Stimmen schreibender Frauen,' 114 (n. 25). On the late medieval scribal activity in Zoffingen and the practice of book production within a 'network of lending, borrowing, and donating of manuscripts', see Sarah Glenn DeMaris, 'Anna Muntprat's Legacy for the Zoffingen Sisters: A Second Copy of the Unterlinden Schwesternbuch 1.' *Zeitschrift für deutsches Altertum und deutsche Literatur* 144.3 (2015): 359–78.

101 Fechter, *Deutsche Handschriften des 15. und 16. Jahrhunderts*, 9.

102 Ringler, *Viten- und Offenbarungsliteratur*, 53–5.

103 Willing, *Die Bibliothek des Klosters St. Katharina zu Nürnberg*, XCII–CI. On Rebdorf and St Walburg, see Zunker, *Geschichte der Benediktinerinnenabtei St. Walburg*, 23.

104 Gabriele Hirsch, who wrote a dissertation on the *Trutta*-legend in 1921, and Wieland were aware of only the first three manuscripts in this list. For the transmission history and a synopsis of the extracts taken from the Latin *Legatus*, see Wieland, *Gertrud von Helfta*, 47–77; see also the edition of the legend as part of the dissertation of Gabriele Hirsch ed., *Die Legende der Heiligen Trutta*. Doctoral dissertation, University of Graz, 1921, 239–300. About the South-German legendaries containing the *Trutta*-legend, see

Werner Williams-Krapp, *Die deutschen und niederländischen Legendare des Mittelalters: Studien zur ihrer Überlieferungs-, Text- und Wirkungsgeschichte*. Texte und Textgeschichte Vol. 20. Tübingen: Niemeyer, 1986, 259–301.

105   For a fifteenth-century example of a collection of the *Lives of Saints* (Nuremberg, Germanisches Nationalmuseum, Hs. 2261), which shows the malleability of the text material, see Sara S. Poor, 'Ich Schreyberin,' 204–5.

106   Wieland, *Gertrud von Helfta*, 73. For a discussion of the term 'redactor' see Chapter 2 'Redactions within a Dynamic Textuality'.

107   How exactly *kunig Gotfridus* made it into the legend's *commendatio* is unclear. The redactors might have used a Latin copy of the *Legatus* or a *botte* witness which lists a '"King Gottfried"'.

108   Graz, Universitätsbibliothek, Ms. 64, was later kept at the Jesuit College in Graz, see note on fol. 1r (see Plate X). On the library of the Military Order, see Maria Mairold, 'Die Millstätter Bibliothek.' *Carinthia I* 170 (1980): 87–106; see also Fritz Peter Knapp, *Die Literatur des Spätmittelalters in den Ländern Österreich, Steiermark, Kärnten, Salzburg und Tirol von 1273 bis 1439.* Vol. 2: Die Literatur zur Zeit der habsburgischen Herzöge von Rudolf IV. bis Albrecht V. (1358–1439): Geschichte der Literatur in Österreich Vol. 2. Graz: Akademische Druck- u. Verlagstanstalt, 2004, 321.

109   On the decoration of Graz, Universitätsbibliothek, Ms. 64, see Susanne Rischpler, *Der Illuminator Michael*. Codices Manuscripti. Supplementum Vol. 1. Purkersdorf: Hollinek, 2009, 90–1, nr. 48; for Graz, Universitätsbibliothek, Ms. 75, see Christine Beier, *Die illuminierten Handschriften und Inkunabeln der Universitätsbibliothek Graz: Die illuminierten Handschriften 1400 bis 1550*. Vol. 1. Österreichische Akademie der Wissenschaften, phil.-hist. Klasse, Denkschriften Vol. 390; Institut für Kunstgeschichte der Universität Wien; Veröffentlichungen der Kommission für Schrift und Buchwesen des Mittelalters Vol. 5 Pt. 1. Vienna: Verlag der Österreichischen Akademie der Wissenschaften, 2010, 25–7, nr. 8.

110   Another *Der Heiligen Leben* from the same workshop also transmits the *Trutta*-legend, but the exact place of conservation is unknown since this codex was sold by a dealer in Hamburg in 1979; for further details, see Williams-Krapp, *Die deutschen und niederländischen Legendare*, 205.

111   Ute Bergner, 'Wasserzeichen in der Handschrift UBG-Ms 64.' *Der Handschriftenkatalog der UB Graz: Papierforschung*. http://sosa2.uni-graz.at/sosa/katalog/index.php (last accessed 04.06.2019).

112   On this scribe, see Elisabeth Wunderle, *Katalog der mittelalterlichen lateinischen Papierhandschriften*. Die Handschriften der Forschungsbibliothek Gotha Vol. 1. Wiesbaden: Harrassowitz, 2002, 126.

113   Williams-Krapp, *Die deutschen und niederländichen Legendare*, 230.

114   Ibid., 210.

115   For a manuscript description, see András Vizkelety, *Beschreibendes Verzeichnis der altdeutschen Handschriften in ungarischen Bibliotheken*. Vol. 2: Budapest, Debrecen, Eger, Esztergom, Györ, Kalocsa, Pannonhalma, Pápa, Pécs, Szombathely. Wiesbaden: Harrassowitz, 1973, 247–9.

116   For a list of texts in Vienna, Österreichische Nationalbibliothek, Cod. 3042, see Hermann Menhardt, *Verzeichnis der altdeutschen literarischen Handschriften der österreichischen Nationalbibliothek*. Vol. 2. Veröffentlichungen des Instituts für deutsche Sprache und Literatur Vol. 13. Berlin: Akademie-Verlag, 1961, 836.

117   Klaus Grubmüller, 'Gertrud von Helfta.' *Die deutsche Literatur des Mittelalters: Verfasserlexikon: Begründet von Wolfgang Stammler, fortgeführt von Karl Langosch*. Vol. 3. Ed. Kurt Ruh and Burghart Wachinger. 2nd edition. Berlin: De Gruyter, 1981, 7–10, at col. 9.

118   Williams-Krapp, *Die deutschen und niederländichen Legendare*, 258–9.

119   For an analysis of the library catalogue, see Willing, *Die Bibliothek des Klosters St. Katharina zu Nürnberg*. Vol. 1, XIX–XXXI.

120   For a full list of references to the *Trutta*-legend, see ibid., 529–31, here 530.

121   Also, women who joined St Katharina often brought books with them because it was expected of Dominican novices to be literate upon entering a convent; on Dominican recruits, see Jones, *Ruling the Spirit*, 6. For example, the Nuremberg widow Katharina Tucher joined the nunnery in 1433 with twenty-four manuscripts containing religious and mystical texts, and she also recorded her

own visions; see Karin Schneider, 'Die Bibliothek des Katharinenklosters in Nürnberg und die städtische Gesellschaft.' *Studien zum städtischen Bildungswesen des späten Mittelalters und der frühen Neuzeit: Bericht über Kolloquien der Kommission zur Erforschung der Kultur des Spätmittelalters. 1978 bis 1981.* Ed. Bernd Moeller, Hans Patze, Karl Stackmann, and Ludger Grenzmann. Abhandlungen der Akademie der Wissenschaften in Göttingen. Philologisch-Historische Klasse 3. Folge 137. Göttingen: Vandenhoeck & Ruprecht, 1983, 70–82, at 73–5. The complexity of the literary management in and the book traffic between convents, including personal property, means that in many cases we can only speculate about where, when, and for whom certain texts were produced.

122 Ursula Geiselherin identifies herself on fol. 173v and fol. 238r of New Haven, Yale University, Beinecke Rare Book and Manuscript Library, MS 968.

123 On these two scribes, see Schneider, *Die deutschen mittelalterlichen Handschriften*, XVI–XVII. On the scribal culture at St Katharina, see also Anne Winston-Allen, 'Outside the Mainstream: Women as Readers, Scribes, and Illustrators of Books in Convents of the German-Speaking Regions.' *Nuns' Literacies in Medieval Europe: The Kansas City Dialogue.* Ed. Virginia Blanton, Veronica O'Mara, and Patricia Stoop. Medieval Women – Texts and Contexts Vol. 27. Turnhout, Brepols, 2015, 191–206, at 196–203.

124 The spelling for *supriorin* in the manuscript is rather peculiar; a direct transcription would suggest sup*er*<iori>bus. Although individual abbreviations for the Latin -bus ending are attested elsewhere (see Beach, *Women as Scribes*, 88–91), the reading *superioribus* would be grammatically wrong.

125 Mengis, *Schreibende Frauen um 1500*, 53–8.

126 In an interview in September 2017, Józef Pater, archival director of the Wrocław diocesan library, confirmed with no further details that the manuscript has been lost since World War II.

127 Joseph Klapper's 1910 description of the manuscript for the archival catalogue is available online: www.bbaw.de/forschung/

dtm/HSA/breslau_700292490000.html (last accessed on 04.06.2019).

128 For a short synopsis of the last Hohenzollern-Haigerloch generation, see Eduard Schwarzmann, *Karl I., Graf zu Hohenzollern-Sigmaringen und Veringen, herr zu Haigerloch und Werstein, des Heiligen Römischen Reichs Erbkämmerer, und Markgräfin Anna von Baden und Hochberg.* Sigmaringen: Verlag der P. Liehner'schen Buchhandlung, 1859, 27.

4 THE BOOK'S SELF-REFLECTIVITY

1 Brussels, Bibliothèque Royale, cod. 8507–09; Dresden, Sächsische Landesbibliothek, Hs M 243; Munich, Bayerische Staatsbibliothek, Cgm 5292; Augsburg, Benediktinerabtei St Stephan, Hs 38; Freiburg im Breisgau, Universitätsbibliothek, Hs. 202; Freiburg im Breisgau, Erzbischöfliches Archiv, Hs. 31; Freiburg im Breisgau, Universitätsbibliothek, Hs. 186; imprint of 1505, commissioned by Lady Sidonie Duchess of Meißen and printed in Leipzig by Melchior Lotter [VD16 M 1785].

2 The main source for Wieland's edition is the text witness which the Strasbourg Dominican nuns kept in the fifteenth century: Brussels, Bibliothèque Royale, cod. 8507–09. It stands in close relationship to at least three other major text witnesses: Dresden, Sächsische Landesbibliothek, Hs M 243; 1505 imprint by Leipzig printer Melchior Lotter; Heidelberg, Universitätsbibliothek, Heid. Hs. 33. Wieland's edition of the *botte* did not take Freiburg im Breisgau, Erzbischöfliches Archiv, Hs. 31, into account; but since the latter is strongly related to Freiburg im Breisgau, Universitätsbibliothek, Hs. 202, there are no pertinent variances, which would affect Wieland's text. As such, the edition is a reliable source for studying the *botte*.

3 Hasebrink and Strohschneider, 'Religiöse Schriftkultur und säkulare Textwissenschaft,' 289.

4 See Christian Kiening, *Zwischen Körper und Schrift: Texte vor dem Zeitalter der Literatur.* Frankfurt a.M.: Fischer Taschenbuch Verlag, 2003.

5 See Christian Kiening, *Mystische Bücher.* Mediävistische Perspektiven Vol. 2. Zurich: Chronos, 2011, 38–9. See also the volume *Medialität des Heils im späten Mittelalter.* Ed. Carla

Dauven-van Knippenberg, Cornelia Herberichs, and Christian Kiening. Medienwandel, Medienwechsel, Medienwissen Vol. 10. Zurich: Chronos, 2009.

6   For the text strategy in which 'intended readers' are set up 'to inhabit' the position of a figure in the text, see Poor, 'Ich Schreyberin,' 218.

7   The correlation between meditation and manuscript culture is also embedded in the *Legatus*, where at one instance Gertrude is looking at an image of Christ on the cross in an illuminated book (*Legatus* II, 5). For a discussion of this instance in which material culture and vision are indistinguishable, see Laugerud, 'And how could I find Thee at all, if I do not remember Thee?' 53.

8   For example, Hamburger, Schlotheuber, Marti, and Fassler, *Liturgical Life and Latin Learning at Paradies bei Soest*. Vol. 1, 763, highlight that while '[t]he corpus of writings attributed to Gertrude cannot be claimed to reproduce, let alone transcribe, her experience', they were meant 'to provide exemplary models of reading and repsonse'. Most recently, Johnson, *This Is My Body*, 135–59, has addressed aspects of reading, 're-membering', and ritual.

9   See Harrison, "Oh! What Treasure Is in This Book?" 101. Harrison's work is invested in the historical context of text production in Helfta.

10   Jessica Barr, 'Imagined Bodies: Intimate Reading and Divine Union in Gertrude of Helfta's "Legatus".' *Journal of Medieval Religious Cultures* 43 (2017): 186–208, at 196–7.

11   Barr, 'Imagined Bodies,' 188.

12   McNamer, *Affective Meditation*. Mark Amsler, *Affective Literacies: Writing and Multilingualism in the Late Middle Ages*, Late Medieval and Early Modern Studies Vol. 19. Turnhout: Brepols, 2011.

13   Karnes, *Imagination, Meditation, and Cognition*, 16.

14   Barr, 'Imagined Bodies,' 195.

15   See Köbele, *Bilder der unbegriffenen Wahrheit*, 119–20.

16   Barr, 'Imagined Bodies,' 187.

17   Karin Littau, *Theories of Reading: Books, Bodies, and Bibliomania*. Cambridge: Polity, 2006, 8–12 and 154–8.

18   Barr, 'Imagined Bodies,' 204.

19   For a thorough structural comparison between the *botte* and the *Legatus*, respecting the manuscript transmission as known in 1973, see Wieland, *Gertrud von Helfta*, 54–72.

20   Only Brussels, Bibliothèque Royale, cod. 8507–09, transmits this full title. That Gertrude's unnamed community should be categorised as Benedictine may not be surprising considering the place that St Bernard takes in the *Legatus*. At the same time, historically, too, Helfta oscillated between the Benedictine and the Cistercian rule, see Oefelein, *Das Nonnenkloster St. Jacobi*, 98; see also , Chapter 1 'The Helfta Scriptorium'. The 1505 Leipzig imprint, however, mentions Gertrude's particular convent Helfta and locates it geographically near Eisleben – a detail that must have been interesting to the contemporary reader since Martin Luther, by 1505 a major public figure, originated from Eisleben.

21   Wieland, *Gertrud von Helfta*, Ch. 2, 86. On studies addressing the relationship between image and text, see the volume *Pragmatische Schriftlichkeit im Mittelalter: Erscheinungsformen und Entwicklungsstufen*. Ed. Hagen Keller, Klaus Grubmüller, and Nikolaus Staubach. Münstersche Mittelalter-Schriften Vol. 65. Munich: Fink, 1992.

22   *Von dem nutze dis bůches ist dis Capitel*; *botte* 3, 87.

23   See *botte* 3, 87–88.

24   Hence, this fourth chapter bears the title 'This is about how God himself conferred this book a name, and he called it a herald of divine grace' (*Dis ist, wie got selber dissem bůch einen namen gabe und hies es ein botte der gottlichen miltekeit*; *botte* 4, 88).

25   The divine justification therefore operates on different levels, to which belong the list of approvers as well as the visionary mode of confirmation. On such 'strategies of legitimization' ('Geltungssicherungstrategien') in the *Flowing Light*, see Nemes, *Von der Schrift zum Buch*, 378.

26   *botte* 5, 89.

27   *botte* 6, 89.

28   *Wie sú einen júngeling sach in einer gesiht. / Nů ret sú aber von ir selber und sprichet*; *botte* 7, 89.

29   For example, Trînca, 'Schriftliche Berührung – gedruckte Süße,' 349–66; Lewis, 'Gertrud of Helfta's "Legatus divinae pietatis" and "ein botte der götlichen miltekeit",' 58–71.

30   Wieland, *Gertrud von Helfta*, 72: 'Der Übersetzer wollte (wahrscheinlich für Ordensfrauen) das umfangreiche lateinische

Werk in ein kleines geistliches Büchlein umgießen und er ging dabei alles andere als sklavisch und schematisch übersetzend vor.'

31 On the *commendatio* in the *Legatus*, see an explanatory note in the Latin edition: *Gertrude d'Helfta: Œuvres spirituelles* III, 349–50.

32 *Legatus* I. *Gertrude d'Helfta: Œuvres spirituelles* II, 104: *Frater quoque Theodoricus dictus de Apoldia saepius cum ea colloquium habens sermones et sensum illius per omnia approbavit.* Barratt, *The Herald of God's Loving-Kindness*, 1&2, 29, translates: 'Brother Theodoricus, too, known as "of Apoldia", held frequent conversations with the author and gave his complete approval to her discourses and their general import.'

33 Clearly, this editorial choice is less informed by the manuscript transmission than by an argumentative logic. This choice marks once more the need for a new and critical edition of the *Legatus*.

34 Although this is a structural commonality with the Trier *Legatus*, a direct dependence of the *botte* on Trier, Stadtbibliothek, Cod. 77/1061, cannot be drawn: there is a time discrepancy in the transmission, the *botte* transmission being partly older than the Trier copy. That the *botte*'s arrangement might actually have influenced some later Latin sources is not impossible but remains to be clarified.

35 The prologue of the 'standard' *Legatus* summarises the five books and states that Christ himself ordered this structure 'for the reader's estimation and comprehension' (translated by Nemes, 'Text Production and Authorship,' 126). For more details on the *Legatus*' production, see Chapter 1 'The Helfta Scriptorium'.

36 See Nemes, *Von der Schrift zum Buch*, 223–4, who has worked extensively on the Latin transmission, describes the discourse on the genesis of the *Legatus* within the different text sources as 'particularly complex'.

37 *botte* 3, 87: *In der minne, in der ich dir zů důnde geben han, das du das bůch schribest, in derselben minne wil ich es ŏch inflehten dem, der es von dir hŏret. Und wer es aber schribet, das wil ich selbes rihten und orden, das alle ding geschriben werdent noch minem wolgefallen.*

38 Translation by Nemes, 'Text Production,' 128, based on *Legatus* V. *Gertrude d'Helfta: Œuvres spirituelles* V, 266.

39 *botte* 2, 86.

40 *Legatus* I, prologue. *Gertrude d'Helfta: Œuvres spirituelles* II, 114: *Et quamvis tam ferialibus quam festivis diebus pius Dominus continue indifferenter gratiam suam huic infuderit, tam per imaginationes corporearum similitudinum quam etiam per puriores illuminationes cognitionum; si quid tamen de imaginationibus corporearum similitudinum ad intellectum humanum in libello isto describi voluit, ad discretionem legentium et capacitatem divisum est in quinque.* Translation by Barratt, *Gertrude the Great of Helfta: The Herald of God's Loving-Kindness*, 1&2, 34.

41 Hamburger, Schlotheuber, Marti, and Fassler, *Liturgical Life and Latin Learning at Paradies bei Soest.* Vol. 1, 763.

42 Laugerud, 'And how could I find Thee at all,' 56. On the corporeal and spiritual understanding of the senses in the *Legatus*, as indebted to scholastic traditions, see Johnson, *This Is My Body*, 58–134.

43 *botte* 2, 86: *und sin erwelte het er uffgefůret zů siner heimlicheit durch bildunge, reht also uff staffelen, das sú darús schŏppfen solte als hohe ding gŏtlicher wunder, der wir nit mŏhten verstanden haben, het er sú nit erzŏiget mit liplichen bildern.*

44 The text itself is the product of the 'flowing of the divine rivers' into his chosen bride (*flussz der gŏtlichen beche [. . .] geflossen in sine erwelte*; *botte* 2, 86), meaning that through the sharing of the text the reader is able to partake in the divine grace experience by Gertrude.

45 Medieval theory on imagination trades on analogy and similitude. Imagination is often figured in medieval discussions on vision, see Karnes, *Imagination, Meditation, and Cognition*, 5–8.

46 Jeffrey F. Hamburger, 'A "Liber precum" in Sélestat and the Development of the Illustrated Prayer Book in Germany.' *Art Bulletin* 73 (1991): 209–36, at 232.

47 See Alan of Lille, 'Anticlaudianus,' Book 5, ll. 124–7; translation by Winthrop Wetherbee, ed. and trans. *Alan of Lille: Literary Works*, 371; see also Alan of Lille, 'Anticlaudianus,' Book 5, ll. 86–8. In the ascent of Prudentia/Fronesis trying to reach God, the encountered robe of Faith takes the appearance of a book; see ll. 32–4. The book metaphor serves here as a figuration of immaterial thoughts.

48 See Jeffrey F. Hamburger, 'A Plenitude of Pictures: A Picture Book from Late Fourteenth-Century Strasbourg.' *The Prayer Book of Ursula Begerin*. Vol. 1. Ed. Jeffrey

F. Hamburger and Nigel F. Palmer. Dietikon-Zürich: Graf, 2015, 15–110, at 16. On Gertrude's 'image-orientated theology' ('bildorientierte Theologie'), see Michael Bangert, 'In Bildern Gott denken: Das Christusbild in den Visionen Gertruds von Helfta.' *Aufbruch zu neuer Gottesrede*, 93–107, at 105.

49   This programme folds into the vernacular composition of the *botte*, although no single text witness is actually illustrated. Michael Curschmann has drawn attention to the close connection between manuscript illustrations and the vernacular in the High and Late Middle Ages, '"Pictura laicorum litteratura"? Überlegungen zum Verhältnis von Bild und volksprachlicher Schriftlichkeit im Hoch- und Spätmittelalter bis zum Codex Manesse.' *Pragmatische Schriftlichkeit im Mittelalter: Erscheinungsformen und Entwicklungsstufen.* Ed. Hagen Keller, Klaus Grubmüller, and Nikolaus Staubach. Münstersche Mittelalter-Schriften Vol. 65. Munich: Fink, 1992, 2–11. Repr. *Wort – Bild – Text: Studien zur Medialität des Literarischen in Hochmittelalter und früher Neuzeit.* Vol. 1. Saecula Spiritalia Vol. 43. Baden-Baden: Koerner, 2007, 253–81. However, Curschmann's observations do not necessarily extend to late medieval religious texts, where mental images were emphasised. Despite the lack of actual images in the transmitted manuscripts, the *botte* is in line with other devotional texts of the fourteenth and fifteenth centuries, because with its programme of 'corporeal images' it employs a figurative mode of devotional practice without stressing physical images.

50   On the figurative programme of 'corporeal images', see Racha Kirakosian, 'Intertextuelle Textilien'.

51   *botte* 2, 86: *Die hette die gotlich miltekeit übergenüglichen bewiset an dissem buch zu dem heil der suchen, das in dovon gemeret wurde hundertvaltige fruht, das sú dester würdeklicher geschriben werdent an das buch des lebens.*

52   *botte* 2, 86: *Wann alle, die es lesen, die mogent nit gelossen, sú müssent lust haben in dissem buch der gotlichen miltekeit.*

53   Mary McDevitt, "The Ink of Our Mortality': The Late-Medieval Image of the Writing Christ Child.' *The Christ Child in Medieval Culture: Alpha es et O!* Ed. Mary Christine Dzon and Theresa Marie Anne Kenney.

Toronto: University of Toronto Press, 224–53, at 236.

54   On the traditional notion of Christ and the Church as *materia* of a work, see Palmer, 'Das Buch als Bedeutungsträger bei Mechthild von Magdeburg,' 219.

55   Bynum, *Christian Materiality*, 25.

56   *botte* 2, 86: *Das buch ist volbroht mit also gar wunderlicher hilff der gotlichen erbarmhertzkeit.*

57   *botte* 4, 88: *Aber wer es von andaht und von gnoden schribet, dem wil ich senden von der süssikeit mines gotlichen hertzen also manig schos miner gotlichen minne, die in siner sel bewegen und erqúicken die wolust der gotlichen süssikeit, also manig ding er schribet. Wenn ich reisse in und bring es darzú, das man es schriben müs. Und dovon so wil ich getruwelich darzú helffen und min werg wil ich unverwert behúten.*

58   At the end of Suso's mystical treatise we find similar copying processes mentioned in the text's colophon: *Swer dis büchli, daz mit fliss geschriben und geriht ist, well ab schriben, der sol es alles sament eigenlich an worten und sinnen schriben, als es hie stat, und nút dar zú noh dur von legen noh dú wort verwandlen, und sol es denne einest oder zwirunt hier ab durnehtklich rihten, und sol nút sunders dar us schriben, denne die hundert betrahtung ze hindrost; die schrib dar us, ob er well. Wer im út anders tút, der sol vúrchten gottes rach, wan er beróbet got des wirdigen lobes und dú menschen der bessrung und den, der sich dar zú gearbeit hat, siner arbeit. Und dar umb, wer es hier umb nit well lassen, das müss gerochen werden von der EWIGEN WISHEIT.* Heinrich Seuse: 'Büchlein der ewigen Weisheit'. *Heinrich Seuse: Deutsche Schriften*, 196–325, at 325.

59   McDevitt, 'The Late-Medieval Image of the Writing Christ Child,' 230. McDevitt refers specifically to Hugh of St Victor's formulation of the whole world as a book 'written by the finger of God': *Universus enim mundus iste sensibilis quasi quidam tiber est scriptus digito Dei,* Hugh of St Victor, '[De tribus diebus=]De eruditione docta, liber VII.' *Opera Omnia.* Vol. 2. Ed. Jacques-Paul Migne. Patrologiae Latinae Cursus Completus Vol. 176 (PL 176). Paris: Migne, 1854, 811–38, ch. 4, at 814.

60   This is one of the instances at which we see that the mysticism of the Helfta nuns 'transforms the structure, practice, and meaning of Christian liturgy practically beyond recognition.' Holsinger, *Music, Body, and Desire in Medieval Culture*, 242.

61 *botte* 3, 87: *Das bůch han ich gedrucket in min hertz, dorumb das ich durchziehe einen iegelichen bůchstaben besunder, der an dem bůch geschriben stet, mit der sůssikeit miner gõtlichen miltekeit, reht also der ein weich sůmel duncket in einen sůssen metten, also das alle, die an dem bůche lesen mir zů lobe mit demůtiger andaht, den sol nochvolgen die fruht des ewigen heiles.*

62 See Ann Marie Caron, 'The Continuum of Time and Eternity in the "Liber specialis gratiae" of Mechthild of Hackeborn (1241–99).' *Time and Eternity: The Medieval Discourse.* Ed. Gerhard Jaritz and Gerson Moreno-Riaño. International Medieval Research Vol. 9. Turnhout: Brepols, 2003, 251–69, especially at 255–65.

63 For some late medieval examples, see Watson, 'Censorship and Cultural Change in Late-Medieval England,' 849.

64 On the processual transmission of the German versions of Mechthild of Hackeborn's *Liber,* see the doctoral dissertation by Linus Ubl, *Manifestation und Konstruktion von Frauenmystik. Prozessuales Schreiben in der oberdeutschen Überlieferung der Mechthild von Hackeborn.* Doctoral dissertation, University of Oxford, 2019.

65 *botte* 3, 88.

66 It is hard to say whether all of the readers of the *botte* would have known about the Latin *Legatus* – in other words, whether they were aware that they were reading a translation – but they would have surely understood that there had been a supposed first scribal outcome from Helfta, which was not the physical copy they were holding in their hands.

67 See Mechthild von Magdeburg, *Das fließende Licht der Gottheit: Nach der Einsiedler Handschrift in kritischem Vergleich mit der gesamten Überlieferung.* Ed. Hans Neumann. Vol. 1: Text. Ed. Gisela Vollmann-Profe. Münchener Texte und Untersuchungen zur deutschen Literatur des Mittelalters Vol. 100. Munich: Artemis, 1990, Book II, Ch. 26, 69. The manuscript Einsiedeln, Stiftsbibliothek, Codex 277 (1014), has a singular for the scribe; nonetheless some editors have conjectured from the Latin *Lux divinitatis* that Mechthild must have meant more than one scribe (hence 'scribes' appears in the editions and translations of the text). Palmer, 'Das Buch als Bedeutungsträger,' 225, discusses the question of singular or plural scribe/s.

68 Mechthild von Magdeburg, 'Lux divinitatis,' 436, ll. 12–15. See also the new edition by Hellgardt, Nemes, and Senne, eds. '*Lux Divinitatis' – 'Das Liecht Der Gotheit',* 15–17, ll. 24–26: *Sic eciam omnes, qui hunc librum scripturi uel lecturi sunt, si tamen pia mente intenderint incrementum consolaciones et gracie spiritus, sicut in ipso promissum est a domino, consequentur.*

69 Palmer, 'Das Buch als Bedeutungsträger,' 225, discusses the prologue of the *Lux divinitatis* and concludes that in it every future scribe and reader is included in the salvific programme manifested in the book.

70 *botte* 3, 87: *Die arbeit des schribers, der das bůch schribet, ist mir also lůstlichen, also der mir also manig zartes bysemfesselin gebe, also manig bůchstabe doran geschriben stet; wann von einem iegelichen besunder han ich drůfaltigen lust, wann darinne smecke ich die unussprechliche sůssikeit miner gõtlichen mine, us der geflossen sind alle die wort, die an dem bůch geschriben stuont.*

71 See *botte* 3, 87: *wann der gůte wille des schribers reisset mich dozů, und das bilde miner unverdineten miltekeit spilet gegen mir.*

72 See Trînca, 'Schriftliche Berührung – gedruckte Süße,' 362–63.

73 Corresponding to *botte* 3 – Christ pressing the book against his heart – Trînca stresses that Christ, when holding the product of a female-gendered scribal work to his body, 'impregnates' it (Trînca, 'Schriftliche Berührung – gedruckte Süße,' 361), a process she links to the printed book (365).

74 See Trînca, 'Schriftliche Berührung – gedruckte Süße,' 365: 'Es ist, als fungierten der Text, die Übersetzungen und die Abschriften als Ersatzkörper eines immer schon verschwundenen Originals bzw. als lauter gleichursprüngliche Originale.' Trînca develops the idea that salvation is conferrable from copy to copy in a footnote (366, n. 56).

75 Ibid., 366: 'Dabei erweist sich kein Exemplar – auch nicht das im Text thematisierte – als besonders privilegiert, die besondere Bedeutung des ersten Buches wird zurückgenommen.'

76 The reinforcement of the copied version is present in the text itself, and the *botte* even begins with it, as the *commendatio* builds upon a supposed – portrayed as certain – early reception. Through the use of deictic particles, for example in 'this book' (*dis bůch*), a direct link to the physical manifestation of the book is

established. The link to the material existence of the book is a way to manifest the existence of the book as one within and without the text, both conceptual and corporeal. The title of the book, which in the *botte* precedes the first chapter, claims that 'in the name of God almighty we are going to say how this book was acknowledged by great masters' (*botte* 1, 86). Introduced with the indication of the *nomen sacrum*, the first sentence locates the book's composition in the year of 1289 in a nunnery in Saxony. 'There lived a blessed woman, on which God fulfilled so many great wonders that one can barely believe it' (*botte* 1, 85: *Do man zalte von Crists geburt tusent jor und zweihundert jor und in dem nünden und ahtzigesten jor, do wart angefangen von der überflissigen gnoden gottes das bůch, das do geschah in Sachsen in einem frowenkloster. Dorinne was ein selige frowe, mit der det got also grosse wunder, das es kume zů glôben ist*). It is uncertain what 'there' or 'therein' (*dorinne*) refers to; on a diegetic level, 'there' could be a local indicator (that is, meaning 'in the nunnery'). However, the direct context allows us to think of the adverb 'there' as another deictic particle hinting at the present text copy. The text would then refer to itself as the locus where Gertrude 'lives'. The next phrase is introduced with another adverb 'therefore' (*dovon*). This adverb makes a causal claim since 'many masters approved that everything was quite possible' (*botte* 1, 85: *Dovon ist es bewert worden von vil meistren, das es alles wol mügelichen ist*). In the *commendatio*, the *botte*'s first chapter, any miraculous event recounted in the book ('one can barely believe it') is declared plausible ('everything was quite possible') by the judgement of those who have the power to authorise or condemn it ('many masters'). Subsequently we read that the book has been approved by clerics of her own order (*von den prelaten irs ordens*), Dominicans (*von namhafften gelerten meistren der heiligen geschrift brediger ordens*), and lay brothers (*der mineren brůder*). The list also contains names of scholars (*lesemeister*) and even a certain king called Gottesfrid; but the strongest statement about the book's benefits remains nonetheless anonymous. This final person endorses what is written and declares 'in utmost truth that not one who has a divine spirit will dare to question this book' (*botte* 1, 86: *Ich vergihe in worer worheit, das dis bůch nieman getürsteklichen widersprechet, der einen götlichen geist het*). Strengthened by the Holy Spirit ('the truthful spirit of the lover of human mankind'), this reader takes to defend the book that to him is worth as much as his own life. The salvific effects of the reading here take on an existential dimension. What exactly is read is always what is in 'this book', that is in any text copy. The conceptual shift from a specific copy to any copy includes the *botte*, the beginning of which is set up authoritatively justifying not simply Gertrude's spirituality as having 'flown out of God's grace' but also any reworked redaction to be equally holy and salvific.

77 *botte* 2, 86: *das sú versůchen werdent, wie süesse der herre ist*.

78 On 'voice' as a phenomenological category with an ontological dimension, see Poor, 'Stimmen schreibender Frauen,' 104–5.

79 Zumthor, *Essai de poétique médiévale*.

80 The term 'voice' is here used differently from the discussion in the previous chapter where it stands in the tradition of scholars of New Philology, who have used 'voice' to denote textual variants.

81 Henning Laugerud, Salvador Ryan, and Laura Katrine Skinnebach, 'Introduction.' *The Materiality of Devotion in Late Medieval Northern Europe, Images, Objects, Practices*. European Network on the Instruments of Devotion Vol. 3. Ed. Laugerud, Ryan, and Skinnebach. Dublin: Four Courts Press, 2016, 1–9, at 2.

82 Karnes, *Imagination, Meditation, and Cognition*, 4.

83 On corporeal and spiritual imagery in the *Spiritual Exercises* which are based on the *Legatus*, see Ella Johnson, 'Bodily Language in the Spiritual Exercises of Gertrude the Great of Helfta.' *Magistra* 14.1 (2008): 79–107.

84 Wiethaus, 'Collaborative Literacy and the Spiritual Education of Nuns at Helfta,' 31.

85 Cyrus, 'Vernacular and Latinate Literacy in Viennese Women's Convents,' 131.

86 Reading and community building via visionaries' accounts is discussed in the medieval German sermon collection *St. Georgener Predigten*, as shown by Schiewer, 'Books in Texts – Texts in Books' especially at 228–32, quote at 229.

87 On the Eucharist and the sense of taste in the *Legatus*, see Ella Johnson, 'To Taste ("Sapere")

Wisdom ("Sapientia")'; *This Is My Body*, 118–32.

88 *botte* 3, 87: *Also ich húte in der messz verwandelt han minen heiligen fronlichamen in den win und in das brote, also segen ich alle die wörter, die an dissem búch geschriben stont, mit minem himelschen segen all den, die doran lesen, zú einem ewigen heil.*

89 *botte* 3, 87–88: *Und wer in miner minne doran lisset, bi dem wil ich sin, also ob ich sitze in siner schossz und im mit dem vinger zeige, was im das nútzeste ist.*

90 For example, books get mentioned to be used by authors, such as Konrad of Würzburg, Helbrecht, and Brandan; we may add Gottfried of Strasbourg and Wolfram of Eschenbach to this list, and books are depicted on authors' portraits as seen in the Codex Manesse (Heidelberg, Universitätsbibliothek, Cpg. 848). See André Schnyder, 'Das Buch im Buch: Von lehrreicher, erfreulicher und gefährlicher Lektüre in mittelalterlichen Texten.' *Buchkultur im Mittelalter: Schrift, Bild, Kommunikation.* Ed. Michael Stolz and Adrian Mettauer. Berlin: De Gruyter, 2005, 123–43.

91 This relationship is inter alia discussed by Michael Curschmann, 'Hören – Lesen – Sehen: Buch und Schriftlichkeit im Selbstverständnis der volkssprachlichen literarischen Kultur Deutschlands um 1200.' *Beiträge zur Geschichte der deutschen Sprache und Literatur* 106 (1984): 218–57; Horst Wenzel, *Hören und Sehen, Schrift und Bild: Kultur und Gedächtnis im Mittelalter.* Munich: Beck, 1995. See also the volume Jan-Dirk Müller, ed. *'Aufführung' und 'Schrift' in Mittelalter und Früher Neuzeit.* Germanistische Symposien. Berichtsbände Vol. 17. Stuttgart: Metzler, 1996.

92 *botte* 3, 88: *und also nohe wil ich mich zú im haben, also ob ich in kússen welle, und wil in anblosen mit dem öttem miner sússen gotheit reht als ein mönsche, das gesattet ist mit wolsmeckender spetzerige.* I have kept the masculine pronoun in the translation since the original Middle High German word for 'reader' is grammatically gendered male.

93 Translation of the words in *Legatus* V, 34, by Nemes, 'Text production,' 129: '[...] someone who has been sated by both species of the Eucharist breathes onto the one who wishes to kiss him [...]'.

94 The olfactory formulation found in the *botte* might be a reference to Bernard of Clairvaux who uses images of digestion, namely such of breath having a pleasing fragrance when well-spiced food has been consumed. In Bernard's *Sermons on the Song of Songs*, the bride, whose belch smells of a well-spiced dish, is connected to apophatic speech after the mystical union; see Philip Liston-Kraft, 'Bernard's Belching Bride: The Affectus That Words Cannot Express.' *Medieval Mystical Theology* 26 (2017): 54–72.

95 Mary Carruthers, 'Sweetness.' *Speculum* 81 (2006): 999–1013, at 999.

96 *botte* 7, 90: *Und von der zit wart ich fúrbas erfrouwet mit einer nuuwen fröide mines geistes und wart im nochlöffen noch dem gesmack siner gúten salben.*

97 *botte* 7, 90: *Du bist ein lústliches lut alles sússen seitenspúles, du bist ein lebelich widerbringung mit dinem sússen anotmen wolgesmag úber alle wurtz.*

98 For an overview of affect theory in the modernist tradition from Spinoza to Deleuze, see Anne Enderwitz, *Modernist Melancholia: Freud, Conrad and Ford.* New York: Palgrave Macmillan, 2015, 2–19.

99 On emotive aspects of affective readings, see McNamer, *Affective Meditation*, 12–13. See also Ayoush Sarmada Lazikani, *Cultivating the Heart: Feeling and Emotion in Twelfth- and Thirteenth-Century Religious Texts.* Cardiff: University of Wales Press, 2015.

100 *botte* 4, 88: *Wer begert, das er mit andaht an dem búch lese, des otem wil ich in mich ziehen, also ob er es zwischen minen henden lese, und in dem werck wil ich mich zú im gesellen, also do zwei lesen an einem búch, also das einer des anderen otem entpfindet, also wil ich in mich ziehen den otem siner begirde also lange, bitz das die inneren miner militkeit úber in beweget werden. Darzú wil ich den otem miner gotheit also lange an in blosen, bitz er inwendig von minem geist ernuwet wurt.*

101 All Bible quotes are from the fifth edition of the *Vulgata.* Bonifatius Fischer, Robert Weber, and Roger Gryson, eds. *Biblia sacra: iuxta Vulgatam versionem.* 5th edition. Stuttgart: Deutsche Bibelgesellschaft, 2007.

102 On the materiality of communication in medieval texts more generally, see the volume *Materialität der Kommunikation.* Ed. Hans Ulrich Gumbrecht and Karl Ludwig Pfeiffe. Suhrkamp-Taschenbuch Wissenschaft Vol. 750. Frankfurt a.M: Suhrkamp, 1988.

103 Steven Rozenski, 'The Visual, the Textual, and the Auditory in Henry Suso's "Vita" or "Life of the Servant".' *Mystic's Quarterly* 34 (2008): 35–72, at 36.

104 Elizabeth Sears, 'The Iconography of Auditory Perception in the Early Middle Ages: On Psalm Illustration and Psalm Exegesis.' *The Second Sense: Studies in Hearing and Musical Judgement from Antiquity to the Seventeenth Century*. Ed. Charles Burnett, Michael Fend, and Penelope Gouk. Warburg Institute Surveys and Texts Vol. 22. London: The Warburg Institute, 1991, 19–42, at 38. See also Rainer Warning, 'Seeing and Hearing in Ancient and Medieval Epiphany.' *Rethinking the Medieval Senses: Heritage, Fascinations, Frames*. Ed. Stephen G. Nichols, Andreas Kablitz, and Alison Calhoun. Baltimore: Johns Hopkins University Press, 2008, 102–16, at 102. Medieval philosophers did not only make a hierarchical distinction between senses but also distinguished them according to their qualities and functioning; Albert the Great and Thomas Aquinas differentiated between different sensory perceptions and effects; see Robert Jütte, *Geschichte der Sinne: Von der Antike bis zum Cyberspace*. Munich: Beck, 2000, 60–62.

105 Jütte, *Geschichte der Sinne*, 77–79.

106 *botte* 66, 130: *Nement war, do sach sú, das Ihesus Cristus sas an der Eptissen stat und des conventes wartet mit grossen unsegeklichen frǒiden.*

107 *botte* 66, 130: *Nemet war, nů sint sú kumen, min allerliebsten frúnt.*

108 *botte* 66, 131: *Do sach sú, das an der tofelen student alle die wort, die der convent gesungen oder gelesen hette oder gebettet hette. Die stundent allesamt an der tofelen reht also die lebendigen gymmen. Und die gymmen woren wunderlich underscheiden mit wunderlicher varbe, und ein iegliche gimme besunder hette einen wunderlichen, cloren schin, und ein iegliche klang mit einem sǔssen ton.*

109 See Mary Carruthers, 'Reading with Attitude, Remembering the Book.' *The Book and the Body*. Ed. Katherine O'Brien O'Keeffe and Dolores Warwick Frese. Ward-Phillips Lectures in English Language and Literature Vol. 14. Notre Dame, IN: University of Notre Dame Press, 1997, 1–33; 'Inventional Mnemonics and the Ornaments of Style: The Case of Etymology.' *Connotations* 2 (1992): 103–14. See also the volume *Jeux de mémoire: Aspects de la mnémotechnie médiévale: Recueil d'études*. Ed. Bruno Roy and Paul Zumthor. Montréal: Presses de l'Université de Montréal/Librairie Philosophique J. Vrin, 1985.

110 *botte* 132, 204: *Sú sach ǒch ein gúlden bǔch, daran stunt geschrieben alles, das sú ir dohter ie geleret und gemanet hette. Zǔ einer merung ires lones was alles das geschriben, wer sich von ir ler oder von irem gǔten bilde ie gebessert hette.*

111 *botte* 2, 86: *Der flussz der gǒtlichen beche ist in keine wise gar usgeschǒppfet noch geflossen in sine enwelte.* Editor Otmar Wieland opts here for a reading from the Dresden and Leipzig text witnesses, although, in my opinion, Brussels, Bibliothèque Royale, cod. 8507–09, offers a sound variant in this phrase: *ist ǔberflisseklichen* instead of *noch*.

112 *The Exeter Book*. Ed. George Philip Krapp and Eliott van Kirk Dobbie. Anglo-Saxon Poetic Records Vol. 3. New York: Columbia University Press, 1936, 205, riddle nr. 47. The riddle alludes to Rev. 10, 9–10.

113 *The Exeter Book*, 193, riddle nr. 26.

114 For such examples, see Margaret Bridges, 'Mehr als ein Text: Das ungelesene Buch zwischen Symbol und Fetisch.' *Buchkultur im Mittelalter: Schrift, Bild, Kommunikation*. Ed. Michael Stolz and Adrian Mettauer. Berlin: De Gruyter, 2005, 103–21, at 105–06.

115 On the copying culture and transmission history of medieval manuscripts, see Löser, 'Postmodernes Mittelalter?' 219.

116 On the ontology of the soul and the becoming God as a text-receptive mode, see Ben Morgan, *On Becoming God: Late Medieval Mysticism and the Modern Western Self*. New York: Fordham University Press, 2013.

117 Suso makes numerous cross-references to the teachings of Meister Eckhart; an important one is found in his *Büchlein der Wahrheit*. *Heinrich Seuse: Deutsche Schriften*. Ed. Karl Bihlmeyer. Stuttgart: W. Kohlhammer, 1907 (repr. 1961), 326–59, Ch. VI, at 355–57.

118 Eckhart's stance against images is most succinctly formulated in his Sermon S 101; Meister Eckhart, *Die deutschen und lateinischen Werke*, DW 4,1: Meister Eckharts Predigten IV, 1. Ed. Georg Steer. Stuttgart: Kohlhammer, 2003, 334–67. Quotes: *got bedarf keines bildes noch enhât kein bilde* (350, l. 82); *des bilde ez ist, sô wære daz unmügelich, daz dû iemer möhtest sælic werden von keinem bilde* (353, ll. 103–04). For a discussion on the transmission of the sermon, see 279–333. Translation by

Maurice O'C. Walshe, *The Complete Mystical Works of Meister Eckhart*. New York: Crossroad, 2009, Sermon 1, 29–38 (at 32).

119 Ingrid Falque, '"Daz man bild mit bilde us tribe": Imagery and Knowledge of God in Henry Suso's Exemplar.' *Speculum* 92.2 (2017): 447–92, at 458. See also Richard Fasching F., '"aber so soll man die bilde schiere lossen varn": Zum Konzept der "Bildlosigkeit" bei Johannes Tauler.' *Die Predigt im Mittelalter zwischen Mündlichkeit, Bildlichkeit und Schriftlichkeit – La prédication au Moyen Age entre oralité, visualité et écriture.* Ed. René Wetzel and Fabrice Flückiger. Medienwandel – Medienwechsel – Medienwissen Vol. 13. Zurich: Chronos, 2010, 397–410.

120 For a discussion on Suso's participatory mode of mystical knowledge, see Pech, 'Persuasion from Nothing? On the Pedagogical Scope of Henry Suso's Vita and beyond.' Paper at the Stanford/Berkeley/Princeton/Toronto/ Harvard Medieval German Graduate Colloquium, Berkeley (May 2017). See also Niklaus Largier, 'The Poetics of the Image in Late Medieval Mysticism.' *Image and Incarnation: The Early Modern Doctrine of the Pictorial Image.* Ed. Walter S. Melion and Lee Palmer Wandel. Intersections Vol. 39. Leiden: Brill, 2015, 173–86.

121 Falque, 'Daz man bild mit bilde us tribe,' 459.

122 The strict enclosure in the reformed convents, where the *botte* was received, would enhance an established tradition of the contemplative reading of mystical and visionary accounts. See also Almut Suerbaum, '"A Room with a view": Zur Spannung zwischen Kontemplation und Leben in der Welt in den Dorotheenviten des Johannes Marienwerder.' *Muße im kulturellen Wandel: Semantisierungen, Ähnlichkeiten, Umbesetzungen.* Ed. Burkhard Hasebrink and Peter Philipp Riedl. Linguae & Litterae Vol. 35. Berlin: De Gruyter, 2014, 131–51.

123 Johnson, *This Is My Body*, 3, explores the historical scenario of Gertrude having been an orphan who was brought to Helfta; see also Mary Jeremy Finnegan, *The Women of Helfta: Scholars and Mystics.* Athens, GA: University of Georgia Press, 1991.

124 *botte* 6, 89: *Und darumb han ich sú ellende gemaht von allen iren fründen, das sú nieman liep het von sypteil, wenn ich wil selber die sache sin, darumb man sú liep hat.*

125 Maybe this was a way to elude speaking about an embarrassing topic: was her provenance shameful or was she shameful for her family? Rather than speculating about historical possibilities, I suggest looking at the effects of such a narrative.

126 Remarkably, the *Trutta*-legend ends on the vision of the finished book. This arrangment structurally aligns with the order presented in the known *Legatus* versions. More importantly though, the manuscript contexts convey this order: in all legendaries that transmit the *Trutta*-legend, it is the last one in the collection. In this way, the very last story in the legendary is one about a finished book being sanctified by Christ. Here, the visionary image of the diegetic book applies to the entire codex. The relevant manuscripts are: Graz, Universitätsbibliothek, Ms. 64; Graz, Universitätsbibliothek, Ms. 75; Vienna, Österreichische Nationalbibliothek, Cod. 3042; Klosterneuburg, Stiftsbibliothek, cod. 711; Pécs, Klimo Könyvtàr Bibliothek, AA. II. 21.

127 *botte* 5, 89.

5 THE SCRIPTORIAL HEART

1 On the topic of writing and composing in the *Legatus*, see also Barratt, 'Introduction'. *The Herald of God's Loving-Kindess,* 4, xi–xliii, at xxxv–xxxviii.

2 Laura M. Grimes, 'Gender and Confession: Guibert of Nogent and Gertrud of Helfta as Readers of Augustine.' *Magistra* 18.2 (2012): 3–19.

3 Eve Jenkins, 'St. Gertrude's Synecdoche: The Problem of Writing the Sacred Heart.' *Essays in Medieval Studies* 14 (1997): 29–37.

4 See Lewis, 'Gertrud of Helfta's "Legatus divinae pietatis" and "ein botte der götlichen miltekeit",' 64.

5 For a discussion of the devotional musicality embedded in the *Legatus* and the *Liber*, see Holsinger, *Music, Body, and Desire in Medieval Culture*, 242, specifically on 'pulse-music' as the sensation of Christ's heartbeat.

6 Humility is the core virtue for Augustine which allows the human soul to orientate one's heart towards God, see Augustine of Hippo, *Sancti Aurelii Augustini Episcopi de civitate dei libri XXII.* Ed. Bernhard Dombart and Alfons Kalb. Berlin: De Gruyter, 2013, Liber XVI, Caput 4: *Quid denique noceret Deo*

quantacumque uel spiritalis uel corporalis elatio? Tutam ueramque in caelum uiam molitur humilitas, sursum leuans cor ad Dominum, non contra Dominum, sicut dictus est gigans iste uenator contra Dominum.

7   Heather Webb, *The Medieval Heart*. New Haven: Yale University Press, 2010, 100–5, at 102.

8   Jean Leclercq, 'Le Sacré-Coeur dans la Tradition Bénédictine au Moyen Âge.' *Cor Jesu: Commentationes in litteras encyclicas P II PP. XII 'Haurietis Aquas'*. Vol. 1. Ed. Augustinus Bea and Hugo Rahner. Rome: Herder, 1959, 2–28, at 13.

9   Sermon 61, 4: Bernard de Clairvaux, *Sermons sur le cantique*, 250: *Ferrum pertransiit animam eius, et appropinquavit cor illius, ut non iam non sciat compati infirmitatibus meis. Patet arcanum cordis per foramina corporis, patet magnum illud pietatis sacramentum, patent viscera misericordiae Dei nostri, in quibus visitavit nos oriens ex alto. Quidni viscera per vulnera pateant? In quo enim clarius, quam in vulneribus tuis eluxisset, quod tu, Domine, suavis et mitis, et multae misercordiae?*

10   It is only in the seventeenth century that a Sacred Heart devotion operating on a theologically negotiated understanding of the divine heart emerges, when Margaret Mary Alacoque (1547–1690) develops a spirituality of the divine heart; see David Morgan, 'Rhetoric of the Heart: Figuring the Body in Devotion to the Sacred Heart of Jesus.' *Things: Religion and the Question of Materiality*. Ed. Dick Houtman and Birgit Meyer. New York: Fordham University Press, 2012, 90–111.

11   Mechthild von Magdeburg, *Das fließende Licht der Gottheit: Nach der Einsiedler Handschrift in kritischem Vergleich mit der gesamten Überlieferung*, Book VII, Ch. 27, ll. 30–46.

12   Ruh, *Geschichte der abendländischen Mystik*. Vol. 2, 311, stresses Mechthild of Hackeborn's 'imaginative power' ('Einbildungskraft') in anything concerning the heart of Christ.

13   For example: Hugo Rahner, 'Grundzüge einer Geschichte der Herz-Jesu-Verehrung.' *Zeitschrift für Aszese und Mystik* 18 (1943): 61–83; Cyprien Vagaggini, 'La devotion au sacré-coeur chez Sainte Mechtilde et Sainte Gertrude.' *Cor Jesu: Commentationes in litteras encyclicas P II PP. XII 'Haurietis Aquas'*. Vol. 1. Ed. Augustinus Bea and Hugo Rahner,

Rome: Herder, 1959, 31–48; Nigel F. Palmer, 'Herzeliebe, weltlich und geistlich: Zur Metaphorik vom "Einwohnen im Herzen" bei Wolfram von Eschenbach, Juliana von Cornillon, Hugo von Langenstein und Gertrud von Helfta.' *Innenräume in der Literatur des deutschen Mittelalters: XIX. Anglo-German Colloquium Oxford 2005*. Ed. Burkhard Hasebrink, Hans-Jochen Schiewer, Almut Suerbaum, and Annette Volfing. Tübingen: Niemeyer, 2008, 197–224. Karl Richstätter, *Die Herz-Jesu-Verehrung des deutschen Mittelalters*. Munich: Kösel & Pustet, 1924, offers an overview of the motif of the heart of Christ; but this study needs to be viewed critically, since Richstätter interprets the sources from a teleogical and nationalist-ideological perspective advocating for a supremacy of German catholicism.

14   See Hugh of St Victor, 'De verbo incarnato collationes tres.' *Opera Omnia*. Vol 3. Ed. Jacques-Paul Migne. Patrologiae Latinae Cursus Completus Vol. 177 (PL 177). Paris: Migne, 1854, 315–23, at 318D.

15   For a study towards re-evaluating the significance of Mechthild of Magdeburg's influence on the *Liber* and the *Legatus* in terms of the motif of the divine heart, see Racha Kirakosian, 'Das göttliche Herz im "Fließenden Licht der Gottheit" Mechthilds von Magdeburg: Eine motivgeschichtliche Verortung.' *Euphorion* 111 (2017): 257–75.

16   Hans Neumann, 'Mechthild von Magdeburg.' *Die deutsche Literatur des Mittelalters: Verfasserlexikon*. Vol. 6, 260–70, at col. 267.

17   Mechthild of Magdeburg, *The Flowing Light of the Godhead*. Ed. and trans. Frank Tobin. Classics of Western Spirituality. New York: Paulist Press, 1998, 267. *Das fließende Licht der Gottheit: Nach der Einsiedler Handschrift in kritischem Vergleich mit der gesamten Überlieferung*, VI 43, ll. 2–5: *Disú schrift ist us got geflossen / Dise schrift, die in diesem búche stat, die ist gevlossen us von der lebenden gotheit in swester Mechtilden herze und ist also getrúwelich hie gesetzet, alse si us von irme herzen gegeben ist von gotte und geschriben mit iren henden. Deo gratias.*

18   Mechthild of Hackeborn, 'Liber specialis gratiae,' here at Book I, Ch. 1, 9: *Postremo Cor suum mellifluum cordi animæ adunavit, tribuens illi omnem exercitationem meditationis, devotionis et amoris, omnibusque bonis abunde ditavit.*

Sicque anima tota Christo incorporata et amore divino liquefacta, tamquam cera a facie ignis, totaque absorpta in Deo, sicut cera sigillo impressa, similitudinem illius prætendit. Sic beata illa anima tota cum dilecto unum est effecta. Trans. Barbara Newman, *Mechthild of Hackeborn: 'The Book of Special Grace',* I, 39.

19　Ruh, 'Gertrud von Helfta,' 5.

20　On flowing as a metaphor of writing, see Freimut Löser, '"Schriftmystik": Schreibprozesse in Texten der deutschen Mystik.' *Finden – Gestalten – Vermitteln: Schreibprozesse und ihre Brechungen in der mittelalterlichen Überlieferung. Freiburger Colloquium 2010.* Ed. Eckart Conrad Lutz. Wolfram-Studien Vol. 22. Berlin: Schmidt, 2012, 155–201.

21　*Das Fließende Licht der Gottheit,* V 34, ll. 41–5: *Dis sprach öch únser herre: 'Dis bůch sende ich nu ze botten allen gesitlichen lúten [...] in disem bůche stat min herzebůt geschriben, das ich in den jungesten ziten anderwarbe wil giessen.'* Translation by Tobin, *The Flowing Light,* 217.

22　For a study of this trope in women's visionary writing, see Diane Watt, *Medieval Women's Writing: Works by and for Women in England, 1100–1500.* Cambridge: Polity, 2009.

23　Alan of Lille, 'Anticlaudianus,' Book 3, lines 278–9, 312: *Nam vultus noster liber est et littera cordis, / nuncius, interpres verax animique figura.* Translation by Wetherbee, *Alain of Lille,* 313.

24　See Mechthild of Hackeborn, 'Liber specialis gratiæ,' Book II, Ch. 43; *Legatus* V, 33–34. *Gertrude d'Helfta: Œuvres spirituelles* V, 264–8.

25　Voaden, 'All Girls Together,' 83–5.

26　Hamburger, *Nuns as Artists,* esp. at 219; Bynum, *Christian Materiality,* 89–101; Ruth Mazo Karras, *Sexuality in Medieval Europe: Doing unto Others.* 2nd edition. Abingdon: Routledge, 2012, 67–8; Silke Tammen, 'Blick und Wunde – Blick und Form: Zur Deutungsproblematik der Seitenwunde Christi in der spätmittelalterlichen Buchmalerei.' *Körper und Bild im Mittelalter.* Ed. Kristin Marek, Raphaèle Preisinger, Marius Rimmele, and Katrin Kärcher. Munich: Fink, 2006, 85–114; Kirakosian, 'Penitential Punishment and Purgatory,' 129–54.

27　Voaden, 'All Girls Together,' 83.

28　Ibid., 82: 'Mechthild of Magdeburg had a more traditional approach to the devotion of the Sacred Heart, and images of the heart and the wounded side do not feature prominently in her work. When such images do appear, they are often concrete and graphic rather than symbolic, and serve to provoke identification with Christ's pain and suffering.' However, during the thirteenth century, there was not yet such a thing as a traditional understanding of the Sacred Heart. Moreover, the concept of the heart of Jesus was not yet detached from that of the divine heart.

29　See Kirakosian, 'Das göttliche Herz,' 267–74.

30　Voaden, 'All Girls Together,' 82.

31　See Albertus Magnus, 'De Eucharistia.' *Opera Omnia.* Vol. 38. Ed. Auguste and Émile Borgnet. Paris: Vivès, 1899, Dist. I, 1, 193.

32　Tobin, *Mechthild von Magdeburg,* 110, stresses that 'the Trinity is named sole author and that Mechthild is completely ignored'. Similarly, see Wiethaus, 'Collaborative Literacy and the Spiritual Education of Nuns at Helfta,' at 36–7.

33　Her 'book' at one instance is said to be Trinitarian; see Mechthild von Magdeburg, *Das fließende Licht der Gottheit,* Book II, Chapter 26, l. 10–11: *Daz buoch is drivaltig und bezeichent alleine mich.* On this passage in the *Flowing Light,* see Horst Wenzel, 'Die Verkündigung an Maria: Zur Visualisierung des Wortes in der Szene oder: Schriftgeschichte im Bild.' *Maria in der Welt: Marienverehrung im Kontext der Sozialgeschichte 10.–18. Jahrhundert.* Ed. Claudia Opitz, Hedwig Röckelein, Gabriela Signori, and Guy P. Marchal. Clio Lucdenensis Vol. 2. Zurich: Chronos, 1993, 23–52, at 43; and Palmer, 'Das Buch als Bedeutungsträger bei Mechthild von Magdeburg,' 231.

34　See Seuse, 'Büchlein der ewigen Weisheit,' Ch. 3, 209: *Daz ist der anevang in der schůle der wisheit, den man liset an dem ufgetanen zertenneten bůch mines gekrúzgeten libes.*

35　Adelheid Langmann, *Die Offenbarungen der Adelheid Langmann: Klosterfrau zu Engelthal.* Ed. Philipp Strauch. Quellen und Forschungen zur Sprach- und Kulturgeschichte der Germanischen Völker Vol. 26. Strasbourg: Trübner, 1878, 16, ll. 15–26.

36　See Johannes Marienwerder, 'Das Leben der heiligen Dorothea von Montau.' *Scriptores rerum Prussicarum: Die Geschichtsquellen der preußischen Vorzeit bis zum Untergange der Ordenherrschaft.* Vol. 2. Ed. Theodor Hirsch, Max Töppen, and Ernst Strehlke. Leipzig:

Hirzel, 1863; repr. Frankfurt a.M.: Minerva, 1963, 197–350, here Book 1, Chapter 17, 213: *In sulchir wyse, mit so grosin wundin, smertzen und castyunge druckte sy in ire sele eyn stete gedechtnis der heiligen wunden und narwen Crist des herren, in den sy als in eynem buche laz di libe und das lyden Cristi unsers herren.*

37   *botte* 3, 87.

38   The German word for 'to print', *drucken*, is derived from the word 'to press', *drücken*, both of which have the same past participle with no Umlaut: *gedrucket*. In context, this means that the material production of the printed book and Christ's blessing through a corporeal gesture coalesce phonetically and create a third, new meaning, that of Christ's printing the book in his heart. This association remains – as appealing as it is – interpretative, and it is hypothetical to assume that a late medieval reader would have made the same connection. Trînca, 'Schriftliche Berührung - gedruckte Süße,' 365, has hinted at the potential implications of this passage for the notion of 'original' and 'mulitple copies' fostered by the print culture.

39   For a full analysis of *Legatus* Book II regarding the motif of the heart, see Ruh, 'Gertrud von Helfta: Ein Neues Gertrud-Bild'.

40   On Richard of St Victor's spiritual theology of love and its impact on later mystics and authors, see Newman, *God and the Goddesses,* 148–51.

41   Ruh highlights a 'new image' of Gertrude, which is now 'liberated from the catholic Baroque coating that was attached to it' ('ein neues Gertrud-Bild, befreit von der katholisch-"barocken" Patina, die ihr anhaftete'), Ruh, 'Gertrud von Helfta,' 16–19, at 19.

42   See Lewis, 'Gertrud of Helfta's "Legatus divinae pietatis" and "ein botte der götlichen miltekeit",' 58–71, at 64.

43   Ruh, 'Gertrud von Helfta,' 16–19.

44   See *Legatus* II, 4. *Gertrude d'Helfta: Œuvres spirituelles* II, 242–8.

45   *Legatus divinae pietatis* IV, 52. *Gertrude d'Helfta: Œuvres spirituelles* IV, 434; *botte* 89, 158.

46   London, University College, MS Germ. 24, fol. 12v; see the transcription in the Appendix.

47   *botte* 62, 120–5, here at 123: *Den kelch segent der herre in aller wise, also der priester gottes licham segent. Darnoch sang er mit süsser stimme: 'Sursum corda.' Dovon wurden alle heilgen erquicket und*

rihten uf ir hertzen zů dem gůldenen altar des götlichen hertzen in der form gůldener rören, darumb das etwas darin tropfete us dem gůldenen kelch, den er mit grossem flis gesegenet hette und geheilget, das ir aller lon und ir wůrdikeit öch dovon gemeret wurde.

48   See Ringler, 'Die Rezeption Gertruds von Helfta,' 147–8.

49   Giles Constable has drawn attention to the shift from the imitation of the divinity of Christ to the imitation of the humanity of Christ, see 'The ideal of the imitation of Christ.' *Three Studies in Medieval Religious and Social Thought.* Cambridge: Cambridge University Press, 1995, 143–248. For more literature on Passion piety and meditation connected with Christ in his humanity, and the imitation of Christ, see Palmer, 'The German Prayers,' at 402 (n. 3).

50   Ruh, 'Gertrud von Helfta,' 9–10.

51   Newman, *God and the Goddesses*, 160–6.

52   For a description of the miniature *Virtues Crucifying Christ* in the lectionary (1270–1276) of the Dominican nunnery Zum Heilig-Kreuz in Regensburg, Oxford, Keble College, MS 49 (fol. 7r), see *Krone und Schleier*, 402–3 (nr. 301). See also the same motif – without the *sponsa* though – in a Cologne manuscript (Historisches Archiv der Stadt Köln, Best. 7010 (W★) 255, fol. 117v); *Krone und Schleier*, 460–1 (nr. 390).

53   The concept of the own will (*eigenwille*) is connected to Eckhart's idea of detachment (*gelassenheit*), see Friedrich-Wilhelm von Herrmann, '"Gelassenheit" bei Heidegger und Meister Eckhart.' *From Phenomenology to Thought, Errancy, and Desire: Essays in Honor of William J. Richardson, S.J.* Ed. Babette E. Babich. Phaenomenologica Vol. 133. Dordrecht: Kluwer Academic, 1995, 115–27, at 119–21. See also Udo Kern, '"Der Mensch sollte werden ein Gott Suchender." Zum Verständnis des Menschen in Eckharts "Rede der underscheidunge".' *Meister Eckhart in Erfurt.* Ed. Andreas Speer and Lydia Wegener. Miscellanea Mediaevalia Vol. 32. Berlin: De Gruyter, 2005, 146–77, at 158–9.

54   *botte* 63, 126: *Herre, ich opfer dir min hertz mit frigem willen, lidig von aller creatur, und bitte dich, das du es weschest in dem kreftigen wasser diner syten und zieren wöllest mit dem rosarvarben blůt dines götlichen hertzen und mit dir vereinen in diner götlichen minne.*

55 The Rupertsberg Codex was hand copied between 1927 and 1933 before it was lost during World War II. The Benedictines of St Hildegard (near Rüdesheim in Hesse) still own this facsimile. The current reproduction (Plate XVI) is courtesy of the nuns of the abbey St Hildegard in Rüdesheim-Eibingen. For another reprint of the miniature in question, see Hildegardis Bingensis. *Hildegardis Scivias*. Ed. Adelgundis Führkötter. Corpus Christianorum. Continuatio Mediaevalis Vols. 43–43A. Turnhout: Brepols, 1978, vol. 1, table 15, 228–9.

56 Mechthild of Magdeburg employs the image of the communicated woman at the crucifix (here Virgin Mary), see *Das Fließende Licht der Gottheit*, Book I, Chapter 22, ll. 54–8; for how this image plays into the overall motif of the heart in the *Flowing Light*, see Kirakosian, 'Das göttliche Herz,' 265–7. In the mystical allegory *Daughter Zion*, personified Caritas collects blood drops from Christ's wound to give them to the Daughter to be healed from love sickness, see Lamprecht von Regensburg, *Sanct Francisken Leben und Tochter Syon*. Ed. Karl Weinhold. Paderborn: Schöningh, 1880, 289. Volfing hypothesises that Mechthild of Magdeburg was acquainted with this text, see Annette Volfing, *'Daughter Zion' in Medieval German Literature*. Abingdon: Routledge, 2017, 35: 'This thematic overlap testifies to Mechthild's awareness, if not of the Daughter Zion allegory itself, then at least of a pool of mystical and allegorical top related to the Song of Songs.'

57 *botte* 63, 126.

58 *Legatus* III, 30. *Gertrude d'Helfta: Œuvres spirituelles* III, 134: *Apparuit Filius Dei, offerens illud Deo Patri unitum Cordi suo divino in similitudine calicis, qui ex duabus partibus cera esset compactus.*

59 *botte* 62 is based on the so-called *Missa* which is transmitted in only one manuscript (Vienna, Österreichische Nationalbibliothek, Cod. 4224) as an addition to the *Legatus* after the conclusion of Book V; it is edited as an appendix to the fifth book, see *Legatus Missa*. *Gertrude d'Helfta: Œuvres spirituelles* V, 284–308. *botte* 63 draws from *Legatus* III, 30 (in particular paragraphs 1–2). The vision corresponding to the 'standard' *Legatus* III, 30, nr. 1–2, can also be found in the *Leipzig Legatus*: Leipzig, Universitätsbibliothek, Ms 827, fols. 110r–111r.

60 See *Das Fließende Licht der Gottheit*, Book I, Chapter 4, ll. 1–8: *Von der hovereise der sele, an der sich got wiset / Swenne die arme sele kumet ze hove, so ist si wise und wol gezogen. So siht si iren got vrôlichen ane. Eya, wie lieplich wirt si da enpfangen! So swiget si und gert unmessenlich sines lobes. So wiset er ir mit grosser gerunge sin gôtlich herze. Das ist gelich dem roten golde, das da brinnet in einem grossen kolefûre. So tût er si in sin glûgendes herze. Alse sich der hohe fûrste und die kleine dirne alsust behalsent und vereinet sint als wasser und win, so wirt sie ze nihte und kumet von ir selben.*

61 See Jones, *Ruling the Spirit*, 84. The wording itself does not appear in Augustine's *Confessions*.

62 For an extensive study on the reception of the wounded-heart iconography, see Barbara Newman, '"Love's Arrows": Christ as Cupid in Late Medieval Art and Devotion.' *The Mind's Eye: Art and Theological Argument in the Middle Ages*. Ed. Jeffrey F. Hamburger and Anne-Marie Bouché. Princeton, NJ: Princeton University, 2006, 263–86.

63 See *botte* 48, 110.

64 For a study on sight that wounds, see Kirakosian, 'Wie man got verwunden sol mit einem ougen'.

65 On medieval optics, see Henryk Anzulewicz, 'Perspektive und Raumvorstellung.' *Raum und Raumvorstellung im Mittelalter*. Ed. Jan A. Aertsen and Andreas Speer. Miscellanea Mediaevalia Vol. 25. Berlin: De Gruyter, 1997, 249–86, at 262–3.

66 See Hugh of St Victor, 'De tribus diebus'. *PL* 176, 818A–B: *Supremum locum obtinet visus in oculis [. . .]. Scimus autem, quod reliqui omnes sensus foris intro veniunt, solus visus intus foras exit, et eminus posita mira prae ceteris agilitate percipit.*

67 Referring to I Cor 2, see Hugh of St Victor, 'Commentaria in hierarchiam coelestem.' *Opera Omnia*. Vol. 1. Ed. Jacques-Paul Migne. Patrologiae Latinae Cursus Completus Vol. 175 (PL 175). Paris: Migne, 1854. 923–1154, at III, 7, 975A; see also 'De sacramentis christianae fidei.' *Opera Omnia*. Vol. 2. Ed. Jacques-Paul Migne. Patrologiae Latinae Cursus Completus Vol. 176 (PL 176). Paris: Migne, 1854. 173–618, at I, 10.

68 The *botte*'s editor Otmar Wieland remarked on the inexplicable absence of the 'love-arrow' vision; see Wieland, *Gertrud von Helfta*, 57. On love and violence, especially

69 in tropes of archery, see Newman, *God and the Goddesses*, 159–89.

69 A series of chapters in the botte is dedicated to the meaning of suffering, which appears to be sanctified by Christ as a spiritual reward, see *botte* 21, 22, 26–28 (97–101).

70 On the inner martyrdom of the bride in late medieval texts, see Volfing, '*Daughter Zion*', 176–8.

71 Paul Zarowny, *The Heart of Christ at Helfta: The Influence of Aristotelian Cardiology on the Visions of Saint Gertrude the Great and Saint Mechthilde of Hackeborn*. Doctoral dissertation, New York, Fordham University, 1999.

72 *botte* 41, 107: *An eines heilgen tag sang sú gar begirlich in der ere gottes und des heilgen. Und do sú nů sang 'In acutis', do gingen alle die wort, di sú sang, also ein snidendes sper durch das hertz Ihesu Cristi und fůrent im bitz durch das marg. Und von dem ŏberen teil des speres fůrent ytel schine [. . .], die fůrent zů einem ieglichen heilgen, des hochzit man beging [. . .]. Und von dem nyderen teil des speres, darus flos allen irdenschen mŏnschen geistlich gnode und den selen in dem vegefúr hilf reht also ein fůhter nasser regen, der gehelingen kummet.*

73 *Legatus* III, 24. *Gertrude d'Helfta: Œuvres spirituelles* III, 118.

74 For a study on liturgical song as visionary and mystical catalyst, see Racha Kirakosian, 'Musical Heaven and Heavenly Music: At the Crossroads of Liturgical Music and Mystical Texts.' *Viator* 48 (2017): 121–44.

75 See *botte* 64, 127; based on *Legatus* IV, 1.

76 *botte* 42, 108; Hirsch, Ed. *Die Legende der Heiligen Trutta*, Ch. 12, 249.

77 *botte* 42, 108: *Nim war, min hertze ist ein sůsse orgel der ersamen drúvalitkeit. Das soltu schowen mit den ŏgen dines gemůtes! Und was du von mŏnschlicher blŏdikeit nit volbringen maht, das soltu mir entfelhen und solt gentzlich getruwen, du erwerbest es durch mich!*

78 In 1361, the episcopal city of Halberstadt (diocese in which Helfta was situated) received the first permanently installed organ; see Karl Bormann, *Die gotische Orgel zu Halberstadt: Eine Studie über mittelalterlichen Orgelbau*. Veröffentlichung der Gesellschaft der Orgelfreunde Vol. 27. Berlin: Merseburger, 1966. *Legatus* III, 25. *Gertrude d'Helfta: Œuvres spirituelles* III, 125, also uses the word *organum*, but what kind of an air-piped instrument we have to picture for the late thirteenth century is unclear.

79 This expression is often falsely attributed to Guillaume de Machaut; for example by William Leslie Sumner, *The Organ: Its Evolution, Principles of Construction and Use*. 3rd, rev., and enl. edition. London: MacDonald, 1964, 39. See Pierre Bec, 'Note musico-philologique sur l'orgue et l'aile de Guillaume de Machaut.' *Et c'est la fin pour quoy sommes ensemble: hommage à Jean Dufournet: littérature, histoire et langue du Moyen Age.* Vol. 1. Ed. Jean-Claude Aubailly, Emmanuèle Baumgartner, Francis Dubost, and Marcel Faure. Nouvelle Bibliothèque du Moyen Age Vol. 25. Paris: Champion, 1993, 149–61, for proving this attribution to be erroneous.

80 See *botte* 42, 108: *Er beweret es noch bas mit diser glichnis und sprach [. . .].*

81 The whole passage reads (ibid.): *Ob das wer, das du ein gůte stimme hettest zů singen und dich singens wol lustet und das denn eines mit dir singe, das gar úbel singe und dir nit gevolgen mŏhte. Dovon so wurdestu gar zornig, das es dir es nit allein lies, so es sin doch nit vermŏht. Also bekennet min gŏtliches hertze wol mŏnschlich blŏdikeit und unstetiket, und dovon beger ich zů allen ziten mit unsegelicher begirde, was du von mŏnschlicher blŏdikeit nit erreichen maht, das du es nuwen entpfelhest mit minem gŏtlichen hertzen, das es das fúr dich volbringe und erfúlle. Mahtu es nit gesprechen mit den worten, so tů es nuwen mit dem willen und mit der begirde! –* For a discussion on the equivalent passage in the *Legatus*, see Holsinger, *Music, Body, and Desire*, 248–9.

82 See *botte* 42, 108.

83 Jones, *Ruling the Spirit*, 56.

84 Webb, *The Medieval Heart*, esp. Ch. 2 'The Porous Heart,' 50–95.

85 Jocelyn Wogan-Browne, 'The Tongues of the Nightingale: "hertely redyng" at English Courts.' *New Directions in Medieval Manuscript Studies and Reading Practices: Essays in Honor of Derek Pearsall*. Ed. Kathryn Kerby-Fulton, John J. Thompson, and Sarah Baechle. Notre Dame, IN: University of Notre Dame Press, 2014, 78–98, at 85.

86 Ibid. See also Webb, *The Medieval Heart*, 4.

87 Wogan-Browne, 'The Tongues of the Nightingale,' 85.

88 Holsinger, *Music, Body, and Desire*, 252: '[. . .] like Hildegard of Bingen's "Symphonia", liturgy provided the Helfta nuns with a means of relating with one another through regular

musical performance.' The same community-building effects are given in any monastic group setting.

89 *botte* 4, 88: *Aber wer es von andaht und von gnoden schribet, dem wil ich senden von der süssikeit mines götlichen hertzen also manig schos miner götlichen minne, die in siner sel bewegen und erqúicken die wolust der götlichen süssikeit, also manig ding er schribet.*

90 Ibid., see also Chapter 4 'The Book's Self-Reflectivity'.

91 See *botte* 8, 90. Christ's 'bleeding streams' (*beche*) are also portrayed in a vision that 'another person' ('*Ein ander person*') has on New Year's Day (Feast of Circumcision): The unnamed nun sees the infant Jesus as if he had been circumcised just then, squiggling around and beating with his hands and feet 'as children do' and 'bleeding so much that real rivers were flowing from his body', see *botte* 70, 135.

92 See Erkinger Schwarzenberg, 'Colour, Light and Transparency in the Greek World.' *Medieval Mosaics: Light, Color, Materials.* Ed. Eve Borsook, Fiorella Gioffredi Superbi, and Giovanni Pagliarulo. Cinisello Balsamo: Silvana Editoriale, 2000, 15–34, at 29.

93 John Gage, *Color and Meaning: Art, Science, and Symbolism.* Berkeley: University of California Press, 1999, 71

94 For a discussion of Gertrude's visions and their bookish quality including comparison to certain types of books such as a 'gradated calendar, in which the most important feasts are written in gold, red letter days marked in red, and ordinary feast days in unadorned script', see Hamburger, Schlotheuber, Marti, and Fassler, *Liturgical Life and Latin Learning at Paradies bei Soest.* Vol. 1, 764–5, quote at 765.

95 For a discussion of this vision as transmitted in the *Legatus*, see Hamburger, Schlotheuber, Marti, and Fassler, *Liturgical Life and Latin Learning at Paradies bei Soest.* Vol. 1, 764–5.

96 *botte* 78, 144: *Und do Johannes also schreip, do tunkete er die vederen ie ein wil in das swartze hörnelin, das er in siner hant het. Do dunckete er sú ein wil in die wunden des hertzen unseres herren Ihesu Cristi, wen die stunt gliches gegen im offen. Und wenn er schreip us dem swartzen hoernelin, so wurden die buochstaben swartz. Wenn er aber schreip us der rosevarben wunden Ihesu Cristi, so wart die geschrift rot, und dieselbe rote geschrift was*

etwo underscheiden mit swartzer varbe, etwo mit gúldener. Do verstunt sú: Die geschrift, die mit swartzer varbe geschriben was, das worent die werg, die sú nuwent von gewonheit geton hetten [...]. Aber die geschrift, die mit roten buochstaben geschriben was, das worent die guoten werg, die sú von besunder andaht doten. Und dieselbe rote varbe was etwo mit golde underscheiden. Das bedútet, das sú es geton hetten in der meinung des lidens Ihesu Cristi.

97 Trînca, 'Schriftliche Berührung – gedruckte Süße,' 351: 'Fixierung auf den Körper'. Although Trînca's analysis of the *botte*'s awareness for its material quality is primarily focused on the first imprint (1505), the remarks she makes are not specific to the printed book as they concern the *botte*'s textual imagery.

98 Ibid., 352; Trînca speaks of an 'intradiegetic script' ('intradiegetische Schrift').

99 Eric Jager, *The Book of the Heart.* Chicago: University of Chicago Press, 2000, 13–14.

100 McDevitt, 'The Ink of Our Mortality,' 224–53, at 231.

101 Ibid., 234. For Bruno of Würzburg, see Sanctus Bruno Herbipolensis Episcopus. 'Expositio in psalmos.' *Opera Omnia.* Vol. 1. Ed. Jacques-Paul Migne. Patrologiae Latinae Cursus Completus Vol. 142 (PL 142). Paris: Migne, 1853, 50–530, at 187: *Calamus scribae, scriba ipse Christus est, qui scripsit fidem, spem, et charitatem, in cordibus sanctorum, Expositio psalmorum*; for Alan of Lille, 'Liber in Distinctionibus dictionum theologicalium.' *Opera Omnia.* Ed. Jacques-Paul Migne. Patrologiae Latinae Cursus Completus Vol. 210 (PL 210). Paris: Migne, 1853, 687–1012, at 725: *Dicitur propheta David, unde in Psalmo: Lingua mea calamus scribae, velociter scribentis, quia sancti Spiritus fuit scriptor. Dicitur Filius Dei, ut in eodem exemplo secundum aliam expositionem, quia per eam nobis manifestatur et demonstratur voluntas Patris sui omnipotentis, Liber in distinctionibus dictionum theologicalium.*

102 For studies on objectified spirituality in late medieval Germany, see Bruno Quast, '"drücken und schieben": Passionsmystische Frömmigkeit in den Offenbarungen der Margarethe Ebner.' *Gewalt im Mittelalter: Realitäten – Imaginationen.* Ed. Manuel Braun and Cornelia Herberichs. Munich: Fink, 2005, 293–306; Christian Kiening, *Mystische Bücher*, 59–86.

103 On the fifteenth-century history of the Haus zum Grünen Wörth, see Barbara Fleith, '"Remotus a tumultu civitatis?" Die Johanniterkommende "zum Grünen Wörth" im 15. Jahrhundert.' *Literaturbetrieb im spätmittelalterlichen Straßburg*. Ed. Felix Heinzer, Stephen Mossman, and Nigel F. Palmer. Kulturtopographie des alemannischen Raums Vol. 3. Berlin: De Gruyter, 2012, 411–65.

104 Heinrich Seuse, 'Leben.' *Heinrich Seuse, Deutsche Schriften im Auftrag der Württembergischen Kommission für Landesgeschichte*. Ed. Karl Bihlmeyer. Stuttgart: Kohlhammer, 1907, Chapter IV, 15–16: *In den selben ziten ward neiswaz unmeziges fúres in sin sel gesendet, daz sin herz in gotlicher minne gar inbrúnstig machete. Eins tages, do er sin bevand in ime und sere wart kalende in gotlicher minne, do gie er in sin celle an sin heinlichi und kam in ein minneklich betrahtunge und sprach also: 'ach, zarter got, wan kond ich etwas minnezeichens erdenken, daz ein ewiges minnezeichen weri enzwischan mir und dir ze einem urkúnde, daz ich din und du mins herzen ewigú minne bist, daz kein vergessen niemer me verdilgen mohti!' In disem inbrúnstigen ernste warf er vornan sinen schapren uf und zerlies vornan sinen búsen, und nam einen grifel in die hand und sach sin herz an und sprach: 'ach, gewaltiger got, nu gib mir hút kraft und macht ze volbringen min begirde, wan du múst hút in den grund mins herzen gesmelzet werden.' Und vie an und stach dar mit dem grifel in daz flaisch ob dem herzen die richti, und stach also hin und her und uf und ab, unz er den namen IHS eben uf sin herz gezeichent. Von den scharpfen stichen wiel daz blút vast uss dem fleische und ran úber den lip abe in den búsen. Daz waz ime als minneklich an ze sehent von der fúrinen minne, daz er dez smerzen nit vil ahtete.*

105 On the material notion of Suso's relationship to Christ, see Urban Küsters, 'Narbenschriften: Zur religiösen Literatur des Spätmittelalters.' *Mittelalter: Neue Wege durch einen alten Kontinent*. Ed. Jan-Dirk Müller and Horst Wenzel. Stuttgart: Hirzel, 1999, 81–109, at 106.

106 Ludger Lieb and Michael R. Ott, 'Schrift-Träger: Mobile Inschriften in der deutschsprachigen Literatur des Mittelalers.' *Schriftträger–Textträger: zur materialen Präsenz des Geschriebenen in frühen Gesellschaften*, 16–36, at

29: 'Die Narbenschrift macht den Körper zum Artefakt [. . .]'.

107 For a definition of the term 'mystical culture' in regard to late medieval devotion, see Thom Mertens, 'Mystieke cultuur en literatuur in de Late Middelleeuwen.' *Grote lijnen: Syntheses over Middelnederlandse letterkunde Rijksuniversiteit Te Leiden*. Ed. Frits van Oostrom. Nederlandse literatuur en cultuur in de middeleeuwen Vol. 11. Amsterdam: Prometheus, 1995, 117–35.

108 Richard of St Victor (d. 1173), in a treatise on the Last Judgement, discusses the opened books of Rev. 20, 12: 'Each person carries in his heart a written record, as it were, whereby his conscience accuses or defends him'; quoted from Jager, *The Book of the Heart*, 49. A sermon for the feast of St Augustine gives Richard the opportunity to explain the book motif further, diving into an interpretation of Ps 44, 2 (*eructavit cor meum verbum bonum dico ego opera mea regi lingua mea calamus scribae velociter scribentis*), as he assigns that 'the scribe is the holy spirit, the pen is the teacher's tongue, the inkhorn is Christ, the parchment is the hearts of men'; quoted from McDevitt, 'The Ink of Our Mortality,' 233. In Caesarius of Heisterbach's *Dialogus miracolorum*, the wounds of Christ become an allegory for writing on a piece of parchment; see Caesarius von Heisterbach, *Dialogus miraculorum = Dialog über die Wunder*. Ed. and trans. Nikolaus Nösges and Horst Schneider. Fontes Christiani Vol. 86. Turnhout: Brepols, 2009, Dist. 8, Ch. 35, 1583.

109 For Trînca, 'Schriftliche Berührung – gedruckte Süße,' 354, this vision contains the notion of Christ as man of sorrows ('Schmerzensmann') since John's quill could be interpreted as the spear of Longinus.

110 For the edition of her work, see *Les Oeuvres de Marguerite d'Oingt*. Ed. Antonin Duraffour, Pierre Gardette, and Paulette Durdilly. Paris: Les Belles Lettres, 1965; for a translation into English, see Marguerite d'Oingt, *The Writings of Margaret of Oingt: Medieval Prioress and Mystic*. Ed. Renate Blumenfeld-Kosinski. Newburyport: Focus Information Group, 1990.

111 Sergi Sancho Fibla, 'Colors and Books in Marguerite d'Oingt's "Speculum": Mnemonic Images for Meditation and Vision.' *Commitments to Medieval Mysticism within Contemporary Contexts*. Ed. Patrick Cooper and Satoshi Kikuchi. Bibliotheca Ephemeridum

Theologicarum Lovaniensium Vol. 290. Leuven: Peeters, 2017, 255–71, at 262. See also Fibla's monograph, *Escribir y meditar: La obra de Marguerite d'Oingt, cartuja del siglo XIII.* El árbol Del Paraíso Vol. 93. Madrid: Siruela, 2018, 144–82.

112 Carruthers, 'Inventional Mnemonics and the Ornaments of Style,' 103–14.

113 Fibla, 'Colors and Books,' 259.

114 For example of fourteenth-century French accounts and also the work of Ruusbroec, see Anne-Marie Legaré, 'L'image du livre comme adjuvant mémoriel dans le "Conte des trois chevaliers et des trois livres."' *Medieval Memory: Image and Text.* Ed. Frank Willaert, Herman Braet, Thomas Felix Constantijn Mertens, and Theo Venckeler. Textes et Études du Moyen Âge Vol. 27. Turnhout: Brepols, 2004, 129–43.

115 *botte* 78, 145: *Und by einem ieglichen gebette stunden die nammen der, die das gebet geton hetten oder tůn wolten.*

116 In the *Legatus*, the prayers and the intentions with which they have been said in order to instruct others, are highlighted instead, see *Legatus* IV, 16. *Gertrude d'Helfta: Œuvres spirituelles* IV, 182: *Ad quaelibet etiam scripta intentionem sive orationum videbatur annotata etiam illa persona quae facientem admonitionibus sive exemplis instigaverat.*

117 Jütte, *Geschichte der Sinne,* 77–9.

118 For example, the Dominican John Tauler, standing in an Eckhartian tradition, preached a Christmas sermon that is influenced by the Aristotelian theory of perception according to which the object perceived is literally impressed into the human's cognitive faculty. Medieval theories of optics did not simply serve as illustrations for what happens during contemplation, but were understood literally as if the contemplated image became active within the human who remained passive, see Johannes Tauler, *Die Predigten Taulers: aus der Engelberger und der Freiburger Handschrift sowie aus Schmidts Abschriften der ehemaligen Straßburger Handschriften.* Ed. Ferdinand Vetter. Frankfurt a.M.: Weidmann, 1910, 9–10: *Wan wenne zwei súllent eins werden, so můs sich daz eine halten lidende und daz ander wúrckende; sol min ouge enpfohen die bilde in der want oder waz es sehen sol, so můs es an ime selber blos sin aller bilde, wan hette es ein einig bilde in ime einiger varwen, so gesehe es niemer kein varwe;*

oder hat daz ore ein getóne, so gehórt es niemer enkein getóne; so welich ding enpfohen sol, das můs itel, lidig und wan sin. Translation by Jones, *Ruling the Spirit,* 34: 'For if two should become one, then the one must stay passive and the other active; if my eye is to receive the images on the wall or whatever it is supposed to see, it must in itself be pure of all images, since if it even had one image in it of whatever colour, it would never see any colour; or the ear had a tone, it would never hear any tone; so anything that should be receptive must be empty, passive, and pure.'

119 On John's model for prophetic writing, see Palmer, 'Das Buch als Bedeutungsträger,' 220.

120 See Hamburger, Schlotheuber, Marti, and Fassler, *Liturgical Life and Latin Learning at Paradies bei Soest.* Vol. 1, 764: 'John writes a charter, which lends his notes the authority of an official document and obligation.'

121 Annette Volfing, *John the Evangelist in Medieval German Writing: Imitating the Inimitable.* Oxford: Oxford University Press, 2001.

122 On this vision in *Legatus* IV, 16, see also Alexandra Barratt, 'Introduction', 36. In the *Legatus*, Gertrude notices the editorial work of John, specifically the presence of marginal notes and of a blank space after every second paragraph, see *Legatus* IV, 16. *Gertrude d'Helfta: Œuvres spirituelles* IV, 178–80.

123 Palmer, 'Das Buch als Bedeutungsträger,' 230–1.

124 Although most colophons ascribe 1386 as the finishing date of *Die vierundzwanzig Alten*, Schmidt has proven that the oldest manuscript was composed by 1383, see Wieland Schmidt, *Die vierundzwanzig Alten Ottos von Passau.* Palaestra Vol. 212. Leipzig: Akademische Verlagsgesellschaft, 1938. Repr. New York: Johnson, 1967, 280–1.

125 Ibid., 29.

126 Jens Haustein and Martin Schubert are currently preparing a critical edition of *Die Vierundzwanzig Alten* based on the manuscript Karlsruhe, Badische Landesbibliothek, Cod. St. Georgen 64. The manuscript's digital reproduction can be found online: https://digital.blb-karlsruhe.de/blbhs/content/titleinfo/1933673 (12.06.2020).

127 As previously stated by Wilhelm Wackernagel in 1858 and Philip Strauch in 1887, see Schmidt, *Die vierundzwanzig Alten,* 29.

128 Ibid., 30: 'War aber der Zweck dieser deutschen Sentenzensammlung wirklich der,

die bestehenden kirchlichen Lehren durch die Aussprüche der kirchlichen Autoritäten zu stützen und zu festigen, so mußte der zeitliche Abstand ein größerer sein, die zitierten Persönlichkeiten in der kirchlichen Tradition eine unverrückbare Stellung inne haben und in ihrer Bedeutung für die kirchliche Lehre allgemein anerkannt sein.' As Schmidt specifies for different reasons, florilegia usually tend to use authorities which are long-standingly approved.

129   Ibid., 29.

130   There is no evidence that a real circle of 'Friends of God' existed, as shown by Regina Dorothea Schiewer, '"Vos amici Dei estis": Die "Gottesfreunde" des 14. Jahrhunderts bei Seuse, Tauler, und in den "Engelberger Predigten."' *Religiöse Elite, Verein oder Literaturzirkel?' Oxford German Studies* 36 (2007). Themed Issue: *Amicitia. Friendship in Medieval Culture: Papers in Honour of Nigel F. Palmer.* Ed. Almut Suerbaum and Annette Volfing: 227–46, especially at 245. See also Urban Federer, *Mystische Erfahrung im Literarischen Dialog: Die Briefe Heinrichs von Nördlingen an Margaretha Ebner.* Scrinium Friburgense Vol. 25. Berlin: De Gruyter, 2011, 7–13. Hans M. Pech (Harvard University) is currently preparing a PhD thesis in which he discusses the fictitious character of the Gottesfreunde.

131   Nevertheless, the Gottesfreunde are often portrayed as a group that might have existed, for example by Bernard McGinn, *The Harvest of Mysticism in Medieval Germany, 1300–1500. The Presence of God: A History of Western Christian Mysticism* Vol. 4. New York: Crossroad, 2005. McGinn's chapter includes an overview of late medieval mystical texts using the term 'Friend of God'.

132   See the overview article by André Schnyder, 'Otto von Passau OFM.' *Die deutsche Literatur des Mittelalters: Verfasserlexikon: Begründet von Wolfgang Stammler, fortgeführt von Karl Langosch.* Vol. 7. Ed. Kurt Ruh and Burghart Wachinger. 2nd edition. Berlin: De Gruyter, 1989, 229–34.

133   On the Huntington manuscript, see Seymour de Ricci, *Census of Medieval and Renaissance Manuscripts in the United States and Canada.* Vol. I. New York: Bibliographical Society of America, 1935. Repr. 1962, 90.

134   See Lieselotte E. Saurma-Jeltsch, *Spätformen mittelalterlicher Buchherstellung: Bilderhandschriften aus der Werkstatt Diebold Laubers in Hagenau.* Vol. 2. Wiesbaden: Reichert, 2001, 100–1,

nr. I.68, with a list of the miniatures and a reproduction of the miniature on the eleventh Elder in San Marino, Huntington Library, HM 1082, fol. 79a, see 168.

135   For this copy, see Hamburger, 'A Plenitude of Pictures,' 39: 'What the drawings lack in polish they more than make up for in combination of garrulous detail and quivering animation.'

136   The actual date of completion was 1383; see above, n. 124.

137   As a comparison, *botte* text witness Brussels, Bibliothèque Royale, cod. 8507–09, dates from the second half of the fifteenth century.

138   Nichols, 'Philology in a Manuscript Culture,' 7.

139   Ibid., 8.

140   The bible verse is very descriptive, see Rev. 4:4: *et in circuitu sedis sedilia viginti quattuor et super thronos viginti quattuor seniores sedentes circumamictos vestimentis albis et in capitibus eorum coronas aureas;* 'And round about the throne were four and twenty seats: and upon the seats I saw four and twenty elders sitting, clothed in white raiment; and they had on their heads crowns of gold' (KJB).

141   On other manuscripts of the *Vierundzwanzig Alten* depicting John the Evangelist (in different settings), see Schmidt, *Die vierundzwanzig Alten,* 276–8.

142   Nichols, 'Philology in a Manuscript Culture,' 7, in the context of the interplay between text and image in medieval manuscripts containing poetry.

6 IMAGINARY TEXTILES

1   Bangert, 'The Metaphor of the Vestment,' 133–39 , 129–39, at 131.

2   On the nexus of prayer and imagination, see Thomas Lentes, 'Die Gewänder der Heiligen: Ein Diskussionsbeitrag zum Verhältnis von Gebet, Bild und Imagination.' *Hagiographie und Kunst: der Heiligenkult in Schrift, Bild und Architektur.* Ed. Gottfried Kerscher. Berlin: Reimer, 1993, 120–51.

3   See Birgitta of Sweden. *The Revelations of St. Birgitta of Sweden.* Vol. I: *Liber Caelestis* Books I–III. Trans. Denis Searby. Ed. Bridget Morris. Oxford: Oxford University Press, 2006, Book I, Ch. 47, 132–3.

4   This has recently been argued by Griffiths, *Nuns' Priests' Tales,* 182. Griffiths works with a range of textiles from medieval German

convents, in which women portray themselves alongside depictions of saints and Christ, arguing that textiles provided women with a practical and material way of partaking in the liturgy, see ibid., 182–97.

5 Recent dating of this vernacular rendering of a portion of the *Legatus* to the first quarter of the fourteenth century updates the hitherto assumed dating of its translation to the fifteenth century, see Chapter 3 'Manuscript Transmission and Reception'.

6 The vision as recorded in Gotha, Forschungsbibliothek, Chart. B 269, does not mention Gertrude by name. It corresponds to *botte* 93 which is unmistakably based on *Legatus* IV, 28. *Gertrude d'Helfta: Œuvres spirituelles* IV, 268–72.

7 *Legatus* IV, 28. *Gertrude d'Helfta: Œuvres spirituelles* IV, 270; *botte* 93, 162.

8 Rev 7, 14 'These are the ones coming out of the great tribulation. They have washed their robes and made them white in the blood of the Lamb.' (KJB).

9 Bangert, 'The Metaphor of the Vestment,' 133–9. Bangert, who looks exclusively at the Latin *Legatus*, understands a 'spiritual clothing programme' as a 'kind of textile theology of grace'.

10 For a study, which takes the influence of the liturgy on Gertrude's textile images into account, see Mary Forman, 'Garments of Salvation on the Feast of the Purification in Gertrud's Legatus II. 16.' *Magistra* 16.2 (2010): 62–76.

11 The affinity between texts and textiles has many roots, among which are the Bible and Bible exegesis. Especially curtains and veils appear in canonical texts, see Herbert L. Kessler, 'Through the Temple Veil: The Holy Image in Judaism and Christianity.' *Kairos* 32–3 (1990–1): 53–77; Klaus Krüger, *Das Bild als Schleier des Unsichtbaren: Ästhetische Illusion in der Kunst der frühen Neuzeit in Italien*. Munich: Fink, 2001.

12 For example *Krone und Schleier*; *Iconography of Liturgical*; Hamburger, *Nuns as Artists*, 40–50.

13 See Horst Appuhn and Christian Heusinger, 'Der Fund kleiner Andachtsbilder des 13. bis 17. Jahrhunderts in Kloster Wienhausen.' *Niederdeutsche Beiträge zur Kunstgeschichte* 4 (1965): 157–238; Horst Appuhn, *Der Fund vom Nonnenchor*. Kloster Wienhausen Vol. 4.

Wienhausen: Kloster Wienhausen, 1973; Charlotte Klack-Eitzen, Wiebke Haase, and Tanja Weißgraf, eds. *Heilige Röcke: Kleider für Skulpturen in Kloster Wienhausen*. Regensburg: Schnell & Steiner, 2013; June L. Mecham, *Sacred Communities, Shared Devotions: Gender, Material Culture, and Monasticism in Late Medieval Germany*. Medieval Women–Texts and Contexts Vol. 29. Turnhout: Brepols, 2014; Caroline Walker Bynum, '"Crowned with Many Crowns": Nuns and Their Statues in Late Medieval Wienhausen.' *The Catholic Review* 101 (2015): 18–40. See also the catalogue of tapestries and edgings produced in Wienhausen, Tanja Kohwagner-Nikolai, '*per manus sororum. . .*': *Niedersächsische Bildstickereien im Klosterstich, 1300–1583*. Munich: Meidenbauer, 2006.

14 Kathryn M. Rudy, 'Introduction. Miraculous Textiles in "Exempla" and Images from the Low Countries.' *Weaving, Veiling, and Dressing: Textiles and Their Metaphors in the Late Middle Ages*. Ed. Kathryn M. Rudy and Barbara Baert. Medieval Church Studies Vol. 12. Turnhout: Brepols, 2007, 1–36, at 3.

15 For textiles with collective functions in Wienhausen and other late medieval nunneries, see Tanja Kohwagner-Nikolai, 'Patrons, Saints and Benefactresses: The Use of Tapestries to Create Corporate Identity in Late Medieval Nunneries.' *Iconography of Liturgical Textiles*, 141–52.

16 On the sacramental meaning of textiles, especially liturgical textiles, see Evelin Wetter, *Mittelalterliche Textilien*. Vol. 3: Stickerei bis um 1500 und figürlich gewebte Borten. Textilsammlung der Abegg-Stiftung Vol. 6. Ed. Evelin Wetter. Riggisberg: Abegg-Stiftung, 2012, 11–19 (English translation on 297–302).

17 Hamburger, Schlotheuber, Marti, and Fassler, *Liturgical Life and Latin Learning at Paradies bei Soest*. Vol. 1, 763.

18 Andreas Odenthal, '"Diaconi cum rufis casulis precincti": Traces of Medieval and Early Modern Use of Liturgical Vestments in the Cathedral of Halberstadt.' *Iconography of Liturgical Textiles*, 2010, 19–32, at 19. See also the study of Hans Fuhrmann, 'Three Angels? The Abraham Tapestry or the Tapestry of the Angels in Halberstadt Cathedral: The Correlation between Text and Image.' *Iconography of Liturgical Textiles*, 63–78.

19 Renate Kroos, *Niedersächsische Bildstickereien des Mittelalters*. Berlin: Deutscher Verlag für Kunstwissenschaft, 1970, especially 47 and 79. On 158–9, 161–2, Kroos lists some of the visions of Mechthild of Magdeburg, Mechthild of Hackeborn, and Gertrude of Helfta, in which textiles are described.

20 Kroos, *Niedersächsische Bildstickereien*, 47 and Fig. 103.

21 See Leonie von Wilckens, *Die textilen Künste: Von der Spätantike bis um 1500*. Munich: Beck, 1991, 198–202, especially 201–2.

22 See Barbara Pregla, 'Mitra mit Perlstickerei.' *Kostbarkeiten aus dem Domschatz zu Halberstadt*. Ed. Ute Bednarz et al. Halle an der Saale: Stekovics, 2001, 148–51, here at 148.

23 For example two church cloths with Byzantine motifs, Halberstadt, Domschatz, inventory numbers 87 and 88; for reproductions and description, see Barbara Pregla, 'Zwei Kirchenfahnen mit eucharistischen Tüchern.' *Kostbarkeiten aus dem Domschatz zu Halberstadt*, 110–13. Two mitres are likwise magnificent examples of pearl stitching, Halberstadt, Domschatz, inventory numbers 131 and 132; *Kostbarkeiten aus dem Domschatz zu Halberstadt*, 142–3, 148–51. Objects were studded with pearls, too, for example a ciborium from the second half of the thirteenth century, Halberstadt, Domschatz, inventory number 148; ibid., 136–7.

24 Generally on the composition and use of altar cloths, see Gerhard Weilandt, 'Part of the Whole: Medieval Textile Frontals in Their Liturgical Context.' *Iconography of Liturgical Textiles*, 33–50, at 33–4.

25 Halberstadt, Domschatz, inventory number 203; see Barbara Pregla and Elisabeth Rüber-Schütte, 'Antependium mit der Krönung Mariens in Perlstickerei.' *Der Heilige Schatz im Dom zu Halberstadt*. Ed. Harald Meller, Ingo Mundt, and Boje Schmuhl. Regensburg: Schnell & Steiner, 2008, 288–91.

26 Halberstadt, Domschatz, inventory number 209; see von Wilckens, *Die textilen Künste*, 195. A comparable antependium dated to 1230 from Hildegard of Bingen's convent Rupertsberg combines gold, silver, and silk threads; see ibid., 192.

27 For example, a red dalmatic (red silk from Byzantium) with metal threads (gilded silver threads) stitched in a lion motif (stitching made in Lower Saxony) from the second half of the

twelfth century, Halberstadt, Domschatz, inventory number 117; *Kostbarkeiten aus dem Domschatz zu Halberstadt*, 108–9. Other textiles from the second and final third of the thirteenth century present examples of the art of stitching in the Harz area; see Halberstadt, Domschatz, inventory numbers 208 and 214; ibid., 138–41, 226–31.

28 For an early fifteenth-century example of an antependium of uncertain origin, see Hamburger, Schlotheuber, Marti, and Fassler, *Liturgical Life and Latin Learning at Paradies bei Soest*. Vol. 1, 763.

29 See Kroos, *Niedersächsische Bildstickereien*, 35–7. Another similarly stitched cloth is preserved in the treasury of Halberstadt.

30 See Barbara Pregla, 'Gesticktes Leinentuch.' *Kostbarkeiten aus dem Domschatz zu Halberstadt*. Ed. Ute Bednarz et al. Halle an der Saale: Stekovics, 2001, 144. Another similarly embroidered cloth is preserved in the treasury of Halberstadt, Domschatz, inventory number 94; see ibid., 144–5.

31 See von Wilckens, *Die textilen Künste*, 196 (reproduction) and 198 (discussion). See also Kroos, *Niedersächsische Bildstickereien*, 37–8.

32 Barbara Baert, 'Textile, Tactility, and the Senses: The 13th-century Embroidered Antependium of Wernigerode Revisited.' *Clothing the Sacred: Medieval Textiles as Fabric, Form, and Metaphor*. Ed. Mateusz Kaputska and Warren T. Woodfin. Textile Studies Vol. 8. Emsdetten: Édition Imorde, 2015, 89–119, at 91.

33 Baert, 'Textile, Tactility, and the Senses,' 91; see also von Wilckens, *Die textilen Künste*, 198.

34 Baert, 'Textile, Tactility, and the Senses,' 92.

35 Ibid., 108.

36 See Horst Bredekamp, *Theorie des Bildakts: Frankfurter Adorno-Vorlesungen 2007*. Berlin: Suhrkamp, 2010.

37 Baert, 'Textile, Tactility, and the Senses,' 108.

38 On the profession, including the crowning of the nun, in medieval German convents (in particular in the northern convent of Lüne), see Schlotheuber, *Klostereintritt und Bildung*, 152–67. Bynum, 'Crowned with Many Crowns,' 31–2, argues that for nuns, more than for monks, 'clothes made the person'.

39 On this transformation and the bridal mystical dimension of the rite of consecration, see Evelin Wetter, 'Von Bräuten und Vikaren Christi: Zur Konstruktion von Ähnlichkeit im sakralen Initiationsakt.' *Similitudo: Konzepte der*

Ähnlichkeit in Mittelalter und Früher Neuzeit. Ed. Martin Gaier, Jeanette Kohl, and Alberto Saviello. Paderborn: Fink, 2012, 129–46.

40 See Nikolaus Gussone, '"Die Jungfrauenweihe in ottonischer Zeit nach dem Ritus im Pontificale Romano-Germanicum".' *Frauen, Kloster, Kunst: Neue Forschungen zur Kulturgeschichte des Mittelalters: Beiträge zum internationalen Kolloquium vom 13. bis 16. Mai 2005 anlässlich der Ausstellung 'Krone und Schleier'.* Ed. Jeffrey F. Hamburger and Carola Jäggi. Turnhout: Brepols, 2007, 25–42; see also Wetter, 'Von Bräuten und Vikaren Christi,' 136–7.

41 See René Metz, *La consécration des vierges dans l'église romaine: Étude d'histoire de la liturgie.* Paris: Presses universitaires de France, 1954, 203.

42 Rüttgardt, *Klosteraustritte in der frühen Reformation,* 297–300.

43 See Schlotheuber, *Klostereintritt und Bildung,* 154–74, especially 154–5.

44 Bynum, 'Crowned with Many Crowns,' 37–8.

45 On the commemorative function of medieval textiles, see Kohwagner-Nikolai, '*per manus sororum. . .*', 143–51 and 160–1.

46 Visionary accounts may also have influenced actual textiles as Wetter, 'Von Bräuten und Vikaren Christi,' discusses with the help of a twelfth-century fabric crown which was used for the consecration of nuns. On this particular embroidered textile, see Wetter, ed. *Mittelalterliche Textilien III,* Kat. Nr 1, 41–7.

47 For example, a sculpture of Mary with the Christ Child from Lower Saxony dating from c. 1300, survives with different 'costumes' for Mary and the Infant; see *Krone und Schleier,* 455–6 (nr. 382 a–c). For more examples, see Charlotte Klack-Eitzen, 'Skulpturenkleider in Norddeutschland.' *Heilige Röcke,* 15–25 and 26–47.

48 See Tanja Kohwagner-Nikolai, '*per manus sororum. . .*', 172–9.

49 Reiner Sörries, *Die alpenländischen Fastentücher: Vergessene Zeugnisse volkstümlicher Frömmigkeit.* Klagenfurt: Universitätsverlag Carinthia, 1988, 167–9.

50 Kiening, *Mystische Bücher,* 38, highlights codicological qualities and textual metaphors, which create temporal dynamics, especially in Mechthild of Magdeburg's *Flowing Light of the Godhead.* Daniela Fuhrmann, *Konfigurationen der Zeit: Dominikanerinnenviten des späten Mittelalters.* Philologie der Kultur Vol. 12. Würzburg: Königshausen & Neumann, 2015, discusses narratological aspects and temporality in late medieval *Lives* of Dominican sisters.

51 One particular vision of Mechthild of Magdeburg, for instance, also links textiles to temporality, the visionary being told that the scribes' letters, written in 'this book', appear eternally on their 'highest garments': *Do sprach únser herre: 'Si hant es mit guldinen búchstaben geschriben, also sônt allú disú wort des búches an irem obersten cleide stan ewiklich offenbar in minem riche mit himmelschem lúhtendem golde ob aller ir gezierde wesen geschriben'; Das Fließende Licht der Gottheit,* Book II, Chapter 26, ll. 37–40. Edition: Mechthild von Magdeburg, *Das fließende Licht der Gottheit,* 69. Translation after Frank Tobin, *Mechthild of Magdeburg: The Flowing Light of the Godhead,* 98: 'Our Lord said: "They have written it in golden letters. All these words shall appear written on their outermost garments, forever visible in my kingdom in heavenly shining gold above all their adornment, because to love freely must always be the highest value for people."'

52 See *botte 93,* 161: 'And at the hem started the first year and this continued upwards until the last year, which was her current year.' *Legatus* IV, 28. *Gertrude d'Helfta, Œuvres spirituelles IV,* 268: 'The lower part of the gown represented the first year, the second [part] the second year, and so forth, up to the year in which she was at that moment'. Barratt translates *tunica* as 'habit': 'the lower part of the habit was deemed to represent the first year, the second the second year, and from there on up to the current year'; *The Herald of God's Loving-Kindness,* 4, 149.

53 On the importance of temporal aspects of the liturgy in medieval female convents, see Gisela Muschiol, 'Zeit und Raum: Liturgie und Ritus in mittelalterlichen Frauenkonventen.' *Krone und Schleier,* 40–51 [English version of the article: 'Time and Space: Liturgy and Rite in Female Monasteries of the Middle Ages.' *Crown and Veil,* 191–206].

54 Simona Cohen, *Transformations of Time and Temporality in Medieval and Renaissance Art.* Leiden: Brill, 2014, 96.

55 Ibid., 101–5.

56 Computistic methods helped to determine liturgical fests such as Easter. More generally

on the development of the medieval system of counting time, see Daniel P. McCarthy, 'The Emergence of "Anno Domini".' *Time and Eternity: The Medieval Discourse.* Ed. Gerhard Jaritz and Gerson Moreno-Riano. International Medieval Research Vol. 9. Turnhout: Brepols, 2003, 31–53.

57 See Köbele, 'Primo aspectu monstruosa,' 62–81; Mossman, *Marquard von Lindau*, 25–6.

58 *Legatus* IV, 28. *Gertrude d'Helfta: Œuvres spirituelles* IV, 268: *sed in quolibet anno distinctim apparebant annotati omnes dies et horae, et insuper singulae cogitationes, verba et opera, tam bona quam mala, quae illo anno peregerat de die in diem, de hora in horam, de cogitatione in cogitationem, de verbo ad verbum, de opere ad opus.* Translation by Barratt, *The Herald of God's Loving-Kindness*, 4, 149.

59 *botte* 93, 161: *Der rock was also underscheiden und gespannet, das man in einem ieglichen jor wol sach, wie sú einen ieglichen tag besunder und ein ieglich zit und stunde verzert hette. Sú sach och alle ire werg und alle ir gedencke und alle ir wort und alles, das sú von tag zu tage ie geton het, gůt uder úbel.*

60 Gotha, Forschungsbibliothek, Chart. B 269, fol. 25r (Fig. 1).

61 *Legatus* IV, 28. *Gertrude d'Helfta: Œuvres spirituelles* IV, 270.

62 Jacques Le Goff, 'Merchant's Time and Church's Time in the Middle Ages.' *Time, Work, and Culture in the Middle Ages.* Trans. Arthur Goldhammer. Chicago: University of Chicago Press, 1980, 29–42.

63 *botte* 93, 162: *Und wer den rog ansach, der sah uf eine stunde, wie sú alle die zit ires lebens ie verzert hette. Und dovon verstunt sú von got, das unser aller wandel got bekant ist und allen heilgen. Wenn die mosen der súnden schinen ewiklich an uns got zů einem lobe, das man prúffe, wie milte er gegen den sy, die ruwe haben úber ir súnde, und das er uns dennoch also vil gůtes důt, also ob wir wider sinen willen nie geton hetten.*

64 On temporal rhetoric in art as persuasion strategy, see Peter Nesteruk, 'When Space is Time: The Rhetoric of Eternity: Hierarchy and Narrative in Medieval and Renaissance Art.' *Time and Eternity: The Medieval Discourse.* Ed. Gerhard Jaritz and Gerson Moreno-Riano. International Medieval Research Vol. 9. Turnhout: Brepols, 2003, 403–25, at 405.

65 '[T]he language of metaphor' may be seen as a way to represent the concept of eternity, as argued for the *Liber* which is closely related to the *Legatus*, by Caron, 'The Continuum of Time and Eternity,' 251–69; here quoted from 254.

66 See Ps 150, 4–6.

67 *botte* 169, 239: *Viele mónschen woren dar kummen zů ir, die sú beschoweten. Den seite sú die allerschónsten gebettelin und die schónste ler.*

68 See *botte* 170, 241.

69 Gabrielle Spiegel, *The Theory and Practice of Medieval Historiography.* Baltimore: Johns Hopkins University Press, 1997, 2.

70 Ibid., 57.

71 Monika Fludernik, 'Second-person narrative as a Text Case of Narratology: The Limits of Realism.' *Style* 28.3 (1994): 445–79. Repr. *Narrative Theory: Critical Concepts in Literary and Cultural Studies.* Vol. 2. Ed. Mieke Bal. London: Routledge, 2004, 19–55, at 23.

72 Alan of Lille, 'Anticlaudianus,' Book 1, ll. 483–7, 258, Reason's third mirror is of gold: *Auri nobilitas, auro decoctior omni, / vixque suum dignata genus speciemque fateri / in specuili transit speciem, quae tertia rerum / umbras mentiri nescit, sed singula monstrat / certius et specie meliori ciuncta figurat.* Translation by Winthrop Wetherbee, *Alan of Lille: Literary Works*, 259: 'The nobility of gold, yet more refined than any gold, and hardly deigning to acknowledge its genus and species, spreads over the surface of the third mirror, which cannot offer deceiving shadows of things, but shows all things more exactly, and causes them to appear more clearly.'

73 This does not mean that the beholder can see the body underneath, but rather they can see through the body. In the visions of Christina of Hane, for example, when Christ celebrates the mass, the translucent quality of his vestments allows to look through him: 'Our Lord's chasuble was as translucent as a clear stone so that one could look through him and see from behind him what was happening in front of him.' Kirakosian, *The Life of Christina of Hane*, Ch. 33; Kirakosian, *Die Vita der Christina von Hane*, Ch. 33, 308.

74 One surviving textile (a cope) from the medieval diocese to which Helfta belonged, exemplifies the idea of a 'golden garment' as its pale silk fabric (perhaps originating from Spain) appears as if golden-coloured, Halberstadt, Domschatz, inventory number 218; *Kostbarkeiten aus dem Domschatz zu Halberstadt*, 90–3.

75 See Alan of Lille, 'Anticlaudianus,' Book 5, ll. 109–118, esp. ll. 116–118: *figurat / infornem, locat immensum monstratque latentem, / incircumscriptum describit, visibus offert / invisum*. Translation by Wetherbee, *Alan of Lille*, 371: 'It [the robe of Theology] endows what is formless with form, measures immensity, shows forth what is hidden, describes the umcircumscribed, presents the invisible to sight.'

76 See *Legatus* IV, 28. Gertrude d'Helfta: *Œuvres spirituelles* IV, 270. *botte* 93, 162.

77 *botte* 93, 162: *Und ein ieglich varbe, mit der ir werg wurdent underscheiden, die sach man clerlich, und einen ieglichen punten ir werck, gûter oer bôser, die sach man lûterlich.*

78 *Legatus* IV, 28. Gertrude d'Helfta: *Œuvres spirituelles* IV, 268: *Videbaturque tunica illa ita obpansa et extensa, quod nullius omnino plicae umbra quidquam in ea contegere poterat.*

79 Alan of Lille's *Anticlaudianus* may in this sense serve as an intertext to Gertrude's vision as it is described in the *Legatus*, because in both the absence of shadows is mentioned in connection to the qualities of gold (see n. 72). Further comparison of Alan's *De Planctu Naturae* to Gertrude's vision on Easter Monday (see below and in more detail Kirakosian, 'Intertextuelle Textilien') means that the affinities between the *Legatus* and the works of Alan of Lille may go back to a rigorous scholastic education in Helfta, where the convent library may very well have had comprised the widely circulating books of the twelfth-century poet and philosopher of the School of Chartres.

80 *Legatus* IV, 28. Gertrude d'Helfta: *Œuvres spirituelles* IV, 270: *Nec aliquis saltem minimus pulvis aut punctus latere poterat, qui in luce cognitionis infallibilis veritatis, tam Deo quam etiam omnibus caelicol[a]s, evidentissime non appareret.*

81 Gotha, Forschungsbibliothek, Chart. B 269, is a multilingual miscellany which, judged from the Franconian vernacular, was produced in North Bavaria. As expounded in earlier chapters, the compilation of religious texts hints at a Carthusian origin but the concrete providence remains unidentified. See Chapter 3 'Manuscript Transmission History'.

82 Gotha, Forschungsbibliothek, Chart. B 269, fol. 25v.

83 German and Latin texts also informed each other (that is scribal corrections were undertaken in cross-linguistic consultation of manuscripts) in the transmission of Mechthild of Magdeburg's *Flowing Light*, as shown by Nemes, *Von der Schrift zum Buch*, 365–6.

84 Ez 33, 12: *in quacumque die conversus fuerit ab impietate sua*. See in comparison the wording in *Legatus* IV, 28. Gertrude d'Helfta: *Œuvres spirituelles* IV, 270: *in quacumque hora conversus feurit peccator*. However, the quote in the *Legatus* could refer to Pseudo-Ezekiel as this latter text was widespread in the Middle Ages: *Quacumque hora [die] ingemuerit peccator, omnes iniquitates eius non recordabor amplius*. On Pseudo-Ezekiel see James W. Marchand, 'An Unidentified Latin Quote in "Piers Plowman".' *Modern Philology* 88 (1991): 398–400. I thank Alexandra Barratt for bringing this to my attention.

85 *Legatus* IV, 28. Gertrude d'Helfta: *Œuvres spirituelles* IV, 270: *Unde divinitus intellexit quod cujuslibet hominis status similiter patet Deo et omnibus sanctis per aeterna saecula. Quod autem Dominus dicit per prophetam: 'In quacumque hora conversus fuerit peccator', etc., sic intelligendum est, quod non recordabitur Dominus ultra peccatorum condigna paenitentia deletorum ad vindicandum.* Translation by Barratt, *The Herald of God's Loving-Kindness*, 4, 150.

86 *Legatus* IV, 28. Gertrude d'Helfta: *Œuvres spirituelles* IV, 270–2. The chapter continues and ends as follows: *Verumtamen jugiter apparebunt in nobis singulae maculae peccatorum nostrorum ad laudem et gloriam dulcissimae misericordiae ejus, qua tam benigne paenitentibus peccata dimisit et insuper tam multimodis beneficiis suae divinae pietatis nos circumvenit ac si nunquam contra ipsum in aliquo deliquissemus. Singula etiam opera nostra bona, cogitationes, verba et voluntates quas unquam pro amore et laude Dei perfecimus, similiter in sempiternum efflorebunt in laudem ipsius, cujus dono et cooperatione omnia perfecimus, et ad cumulum gaudiorum nostrorum; sique semper pro invicem laudabimus et amabimus Deum, qui in Trinitate perfecta vivens et regnans operatur omnia in omnibus nobis.* Translation by Barratt, *The Herald of God's Loving-Kindness*, 4, 150.

87 *botte* 93, 162.

88 Beth Williamson, 'Sensory Experience in Medieval Devotion: Sound and Vision, Invisibility and Silence.' *Speculum* 88 (2013): 1–43, at 23, in the context of an inward devotion beyond images.

89 *botte* 93, 162.

90 Laugerud, 'And how could I find Thee at all, if I do not remember Thee?,' 67.

91   On the importance of sensory perception for transformative processes, see Laura Katrine Skinnebach, 'Transfiguration: Change and Comprehension in Late Medieval Devotional Perception.' *The Materiality of Devotion in Late Medieval Northern Europe: Images, Objects, Practices.* European Network on the Instruments of Devotion Vol. 3. Ed. Henning Laugerud, Salvador Ryan, and Laura Katrine Skinnebach, 90–103.

92   *botte* 120, 186: *do woren sine kleider überzogen mit einer cristallen luterkeit. Under den worent gewebet mit manigerle varbe alle die tugen, die er uf erden ie geübet het. Und die schinnet durch sin kleider mit wunderlicher lustikeit, reht also ein golt schinet durch ein crystal.*

93   See Meier, *Gemma spiritalis*, 67–138.

94   Schwarzenberg, 'Colour, Light and Transparency in the Greek World,' 15–34.

95   *Legatus* IV, 28. *Gertrude d'Helfta: Œuvres spirituelles* IV, 270: *Orante autem pro ea Filio Dei et suam innocentissimam ac perfectissimam conversationem Deo Patri offerent, videabtur tota tunica illa veluti quadam aurea lamina splendidissima et perspicacissima obtecta: per quam tamen omnia praedicta cogitationum, verborum et operum, necnon intentionum, necessitatum vel simulationum, quae vel scienter vel negligenter, sponte vel coacte, quolibet tempore vel hora peregerat, ita clare micabant et distincte sicut per purum crystallum quilibet color suppositus potest discerni.*

96   *botte* 93, 162.

97   On the production of liturgical textiles by women and the prohibition of touching them, see Griffiths, *Nuns' Priests' Tales*, 183.

98   Mateusz Kaputska and Warren T. Woodfin, 'Clothing the Sacred: An Introduction.' *Clothing the Sacred: Medieval Textiles as Fabric, Form, and Metaphor.* Ed. Mateusz Kaputska and Warren T. Woodfin. Textile Studies Vol. 8. Emsdetten: Édition Imorde, 2015, 7–11, 8.

99   See Warren T. Woodfin, 'Disjuncture between Text and Image: Mystagogy and the Embroidered Iconography of Byzantine Vestments.' Ibid., 13–32, at 14.

100 Kaputska and Woodfin, 'Clothing the Sacred,' 8–9.

101 Ibid., 9.

102 Louis Marin, *Des pouvoirs de l'image: Gloses.* Paris: Éditions du Seuil, 1993: 'la pussicane d'origine' (236) and 'l'énergie d'autoprésentation' (12).

103 See *botte* 102, 169–70.

104 See Kirakosian, *Die Vita der Christina von Hane*, Ch. 76, 328.

105 See *botte* 165, 235–6.

106 See Catherine of Siena, *The Dialogue.* Ed. and trans. Suzanne Noffke. Classics of Western Spirituality New York: Paulist Press, 1980, 26.

107 Halberstadt, Domschatz, inventory number 17; *Der Heilige Schatz im Dom zu Halberstadt*, 114–15.

108 Jones, *Ruling the Spirit*, 39. For Adelheit's story, see F. W. E. Roth, 'Aufzeichnungen über das mystische Leben der Nonnen von Kirchberg bei Sulz Predigerordens während des XIV. und XV. Jahrhunderts.' *Alemannia* 21 (1893): 103–48, at 131–2.

109 Jones, *Ruling the Spirit*, 39. Henry Suso's vision in: *Vita*, Ch. 38, in: Seuse, *Deutsche Schriften*, 117–118.

110 See *botte* 129, 199.

111 See *botte* 138, 210.

112 See *botte* 128, 197.

113 See *botte* 125, 194.

114 See Mary Carruthers, *Experience of Beauty in the Middle Ages.* Oxford-Warburg Studies. Oxford: Oxford University Press, 2013, for the medieval allegorical understanding of the bride's colourful robe in Ps 45, 10 (Vulgate Ps 44, 10) as the variety within the Church. On the multiple embodiment of the bridal allegory in mystical texts, see Kirakosian, *Die Vita der Christina von Hane*, 187–91.

115 See *botte* 23, 99.

116 See *botte* 61, 120.

117 Hamburger, Schlotheuber, Marti, and Fassler, *Liturgical Life and Latin Learning at Paradies bei Soest.* Vol. 1, 766: 'Underlying Gertrude's writings is what might be called a liturgical aesthetic, one predicated priamrily on a paradisical vision of brilliant, enamel-like colors, glittering gemstones, burnished gold, dazzling light, sweet, pungent smells, and, not least, glorious music.'

118 Fiona K. A. Gatty, *Ideal Beauty in Late Eighteenth- and Early Nineteenth-Century French Art and Art Criticism with Special Reference to the Role of Drapery and Costume.* Doctoral dissertation, University of Oxford, 2014. In previous research, the role of drapery and garments in Winckelmann's concept of beauty has been underplayed, see Alex Potts, *Flesh and the Ideal: Winckelmann and the Origins of Art History.* New Haven: Yale University

Press, 1994, does exclude aspects of clothing. Some other scholars have started to note Winckelmann's interest in drapery, see Alice A. Donohue, *Greek Sculpture and the Problem of Description*. Cambridge: Cambridge University Press, 2005; Katherine Harloe, *Winckelmann and the Invention of Antiquity*. Oxford: Oxford University Press, 2013.

119   Gatty, *Ideal Beauty*, 92.

120   See *botte* 139, 211.

121   On the corresponding vision in the *Legatus*, see Bangert, 'The Metaphor of the Vestment', 138.

122   See *botte* 73, 139.

123   See *botte* 163, 234.

124   *botte* 40, 107: *Do wurdent sich alle die gymmen regen, alle widereinander, die an an irem cleide worent und wurden klingen zů dem lobe gottes mit dem allersůssesten und allerlůstlichsten getȏn, von den ie kein mȏnsch gehorte.*

125   In one vision, Gertrude sees another nun (who was the lead singer that week) being clothed by the same garments Christ is wearing, see *botte* 25, 100.

126   Boethius, *De consolatione philosophiae*, Book 1, ll. 18–22: *Harum in extrema margine Π Graecum, in supremo vero Θ, legebatur intextum. Atque inter utrasque litteras in scalarum modum gradus quidam insigniti videbantur quibus ab inferiore ad superius elementum esset ascensus.* Quoted from Boethius, *Tractates. The Consolation of Philosophy*. Trans. H. F. Stewart, E. K. Rand, and S. J. Tester. Loeb Classical Library Vol. 74. Cambridge, MA: Harvard University Press, 1973, 132–4. Translation by Tester, 133–5.

127   Elisabeth Dutton, 'A neglected witness to Chaucer's "Boece" in a medieval devotional commentary on "The Consolation of Philosophy".' *Carmina Philosophiae: Journal of the International Boethius Society* 24 (2015): 1–34, at 24.

128   I thank Elisabeth Dutton for this suggestion.

129   *Legatus* IV, 28. *Gertrude d'Helfta: Œuvres spirituelles* IV, 268: *ita quod inferior pars tunicae reputabatur pro primo anno, secunda pro secundo anno, et sic deinceps usque ad annum in quo tunc erat.*

130   *botte* 93, 161: *Und an dem sȏm hůp sich an das erste jor und das ging iemer me über sich uf bitz an das letzste jor, in dem sú alle mitten was.* Translation by Barratt, *The Herald of God's Loving-Kindness*, 4, 149.

131   *Legatus* IV, 28. *Gertrude d'Helfta: Œuvres spirituelles* IV, 268: *exoraret Dominum ut per illud dignissimum sacramentum supplere dignaretur omne quod ipsa unquam neglexerat in ordine Religionis.*

132   It might be purely coincidental but nonetheless interesting that in Boethius, *De consolatione philosophiae*, the lines preceding the description of Philosophy's dress being divided into lower and upper parts, the same verb *neglegere* is employed; see Book 1, ll. 16–17: *Quarum speciem, veluti fumosas imagines solet, caligo quaedam neglectae vestustatis obduxerat.* Translation by Tester, 133: 'Its [her dress] was shrouded by a kind of darkness of forgotten years, like a smoke-blackened family statue in the atrium.'

133   *botte* 93, 161: 'where she was neglectful in religious commitment'.

134   See '*versûmen*', in *Mittelhochdeutsches Handwörterbuch*, see online: http://woerterbuchnetz.de/Lexer/?sigle=Lexer&mode=Vernetzung&hitlist=&patternlist=&lemid=LV02709#XLV02709 (last accessed on 11.11.2018).

135   In a way, the vernacular redaction amplifies reading strategies that are at the heart of Helfta's literary activities, as they are described by Ulrike Wiethaus; exploring the 'somatic unity of reading and mystical event', Wiethaus recognizes 'mystical competencies' in Helfta, which 'harnessed the technologies of vocal reading and sing-reading liturgical texts to develop a transformative somato-spiritual experience of the liturgical event'; Wiethaus, 'Collaborative Literacy and the Spiritual Education of Nuns at Helfta,' 39.

136   Björn Buschbeck (Stanford University) is currently preparing a PhD dissertation (*Eintauchen und Auswirken: Rezeptionsangebote und Effektansprüche spätmittelalterlicher Gebets- und Andachtsübungen*) on meditative textiles, and late medieval craft-prayers and their transmission.

137   *Legatus divinae pietatis* V, 12. *Gertrude d'Helfta: Œuvres spirituelles* V, 150–60; *botte* 143, 216–18.

138   Leipzig, Universitätsbibliothek, Ms 827, fol. 130r. Note on the transcription: abbreviations have been solved and a minimal punctuation to facilitate the reading has been introduced.

139   I thank Alexandra Barratt for bringing this passage to my attention (I have slightly modified her translation).

140   See Judith H. Hofenk de Graaff, *The Colourful Past: Origins, Chemistry and Identification of Natural Dyestuffs*. Riggisberg: Abegg-Stiftung, 2004, 358–9.

141 The colour coding of the starched garment being brown or green hints at differences in the social rank of a person.

142 For the procedure of dyeing, see Kohwagner-Nikolai, 'per manus sororum…', 96–8. For technical details and chemical composition, see Hofenk de Graaff, *The Colourful Past.*

143 *Legatus* IV, 28. *Gertrude d'Helfta: Œuvres spirituelles* IV, 270.

144 *botte* 93, 162.

145 See the following medieval German accounts: André Schnyder, *Die Ursulabruderschaften des Spätmittelalters: Ein Beitrag zur Erforschung der deutschsprachigen religiösen Literatur des 15. Jahrhunderts.* Bern: Haupt, 1986, at 199, 225, 228 (*Dyt is sant Vrsulen schiffgen*); at 268 (Johannes von Lindau, *Traktat über die Tullner Ursulabruderschaft*). See also Johannes Meyer, *Buch der Reformacio Predigerordens.* Ed. B. M. Reichert. Quellen und Forschungen zur Geschichte des Dominikanerordens in Deutschland Vols. 2–3. Leipzig: Harrassowitz, 1908–9, at III/14, 73; III/25, 94.

146 Hamburger, *The Visual and the Visionary,* 78.

147 Rudy, 'Introduction: Miraculous Textiles,' 25.

148 Mecham, *Sacred Communities,* 69.

149 See Kohwagner-Nikolai, 'per manus sororum…', 143–51. See also Ella Johnson, 'To Taste ("Sapere") Wisdom ("Sapientia"), at 198: 'Gertrude is particularly innovative in the way that she cultivates liturgical piety, one that is both sensorially rich and sensorially self-aware.' Whether this is an individual trait linked to Gertrude's feminity, as suggested by Johnson, is difficult to answer, since we are dealing with a collaborative textual production.

150 Thomas Lentes, 'Bild, Reform und Cura Monialium: Bildverständnis und Bildgebrauch im Buch der Reformacio Predigerordens des Johannes Meyer (d. 1485).' *Dominicains et Dominicaines en Alsace, XIIIe-XXe siècle.* Ed. Jean-Luc Eichenlaub. Colmar: Archives départementales du Haut-Rhin: 1996, 177–95, at 188.

151 Hamburger, *The Visual and the Visionary,* 445.

152 Lentes, 'Bild, Reform und Cura Monialium,' 185.

153 Jones, *Ruling the Spirit,* 114–15.

154 *botte* 17, 96.

155 *botte* 62, 122.

156 Halberstadt, Domschatz, inventory number 210; *Der Heilige Schatz im Dom zu Halberstadt,* 232–3.

157 For examples, see *Heilige Röcke.* Ed. Klack-Eitzen et al., 11–69, especially 20–1; however, without a reproduction of the coat for the Mary statue on which the names of Jesus, the Virgin Mary, and St Anne are emblematically embroidered; see Hannover, Museum August Kestner, Inv. nr. WM XX 24–30 (here Plate XXIV). I thank Björn Buschbeck for bringing this ensemble to my attention. Another example is Halberstadt, Domschatz, inventory number 165; *Der Heilige Schatz im Dom zu Halberstadt,* 348–9.

158 *botte* 163, 232–3.

159 *botte* 46, 109–10.

160 *botte* 45, 109. On Titivillus, the patron demon of scribes who also collects idle speech during prayers, see Kathleen M. Ashley, 'Titivillus and the Battle of Words in Mankind.' *Annuale mediaevale* 16 (1975): 128–50.

161 Spinning wool and weaving cloth are particularly linked to divine tasks as Mary was portrayed as spending her youth with such activities on apocrypha and medieval legends, see Rudy, 'Introduction: Miraculous Textiles,' 17. In contrast to this notion of craftmanship as that of a female virgin, the *botte* repeatedly highlights God and Christ as craftsmen, for example *botte* 107, 174, has Christ stitch pearls into silk with Gertrude as a child apprentice.

162 *botte* 54, 115.

163 The earliest story of how Aves transformed into flowers dates back to the second half of the thirteenth century, see Hildegard Elisabeth Keller, 'Rosen-Metamorphosen: Von unfesten Zeichen in spätmittelalterlichen Texten: Heinrich Seuses 'Exemplar' und das Mirakel 'Marien-Rosenkranz'.' *Der Rosenkranz: Andacht, Geschichte, Kunst.* Ed. Urs-Beat Frei and Fredy Bühler. Bern: Benteli, 2003, 48–67, at 61–3; and Anne Winston-Allen, *Stories of the Rose: The Making of the Rosary in the Middle Ages.* University Park, PA: Pennsylvania State University Press, 1997. Repr. 1998, 101–3.

164 Anne Margreet W. As-Vijvers, 'Weaving Mary's Chaplet: The Representation of the Rosary in Late Medieval Flemish Manuscript Illumination.' *Weaving, Veiling, and Dressing: Textiles and Their Metaphors in the Late Middle Ages.* Ed. Kathryn M. Rudy and Barbara Baert. Medieval Church Studies Vol. 12. Turnhout: Brepols, 2007, 41–79, at 47.

165 Ibid., 50–1.

166 See ibid., 52 and 79 for specific examples. See also Rudy, 'Introduction: Miraculous Textiles,' 28–36; Hamburger, *Nuns as Artists*, 66–80. In the *botte*, devotion to saints, in particular to St Bernard, is also rendered in textile images including gems and golden jewels, see in particular *botte* 118, 182–3.

167 Although the *botte* does not explicitly refer to spoken prayers in this instance, in another Gertrude's prayers offered to Christ turn into 'many delicate lovely roses' (*in der forme zarter minneklicher rosen*). In a royal-like welcome of the soul at the heavenly king's court, Gertrude is affirmed to be worshipped as Christ's spouse and to be presented 'to the king of kings in royal and pleasing garments of virtue' *(mit kinniglichen und mit zimlichen kleideren der tugent dem kinnige aller kinnige)*, see *botte* 122, 190.

168 Winston-Allen, *Stories of the Rose*, 14–15, highlights that the 'meaning' is not 'in the text' but 'in the context, that is, in the performance of the ritual', when dealing with the rosary. On the enacting quality of tactile sensitivity in the devotional prayer practice of the rosary, see also Hans Henrik Lohfert Jørgensen, 'Prostheses of Pious Preception: On the Instrumentalization and Mediation of the Medieval Sensorium.' *The Materiality of Devotion in Late Medieval Northern Europe: Images, Objects, Practices*. Ed. Henning Laugerud, Salvador Ryan, and Laura Katrine Skinnebach. European Network on the Instruments of Devotion Vol. 3, 146–67, at 154–6.

169 Hamburger, *Nuns as Artists*, 75.

170 Hanneke van Asperen, 'Praying, Threading, and Adorning: Sewn-in Prints in a Rosary Prayer Book (London, British Library, ADD. MS 14042).' *Weaving, Veiling, and Dressing: Textiles and Their Metaphors in the Late Middle Ages*. Ed. Kathryn M. Rudy and Barbara Baert. Medieval Church Studies Vol. 12. Turnhout: Brepols, 2007, 82–120, at 83.

171 Ibid., 113.

172 Interactions between manuscripts and textiles are known from narrative images but there also exist numerous manuscripts that contain various textiles, such as silk veils (or 'curtains') for protecting precious illumination, and manuscripts that are wrapped up in luxurious textiles to protect the books and to enshrine them as relics; see Christine Sciacca, 'Raising the Curtain on the Use of Textiles in Manuscripts.' *Weaving, Veiling, and Dressing: Textiles and Their Metaphors in the Late Middle Ages*. Ed. Kathryn M. Rudy and Barbara Baert. Medieval Church Studies Vol. 12. Turnhout: Brepols, 2007, 161–90. See also the book furnishing of Ottonian Gospel books as object-related metaphors of the Incarnation, where clothing appears as metaphorical concealment: David Ganz, 'Das Kleid der Bücher: Vestimentäre Dimensionen mittelalterlicher Prachteinbände.' *Clothing the Sacred: Medieval Textiles as Fabric, Form, and Metaphor*. Ed. Mateusz Kaputska and Warren T. Woodfin. Textile Studies Vol. 8. Emsdetten: Édition Imorde, 2015, 121–46. Similarly, the inner parts of Ottonian codices play with the notion of textiles as media of concealment, where the corporeal and the spiritual become tactile in textile pages which allegorically highlight the Christian doctrine of the Incarnation in the concrete liturgical object of the book: Anna Bücheler, 'Textile Ornament and Scripture Embodied in the Echternach Gospel Books.' *Clothing the Sacred*, 147–72.

173 *botte* 115, 180.

174 Colour coding as manipulative decoration is also the theme of one of Gertrude's visions in which Christ likes to adorn people in gold (*gúldin gezierde*) and mixes in (*vermúsche*) black colour to designate divine mercy. Colour aesthetics and the practice of underlining (*understrichet*) one colour with another suggests aspects of manuscript book culture again; see *botte* 95, 165.

175 Bruce Holsinger and Anna Harrison have pointed out that the Helfta mystics maintain an intellectual engagement with the liturgy. Holsinger, *Music, Body, and Desire in Medieval Culture*, 242; Harrison, '"I Am Wholly Your Own",' 549–83.

176 Jones, *Ruling the Spirit*, 78.

177 *botte* 76, 141: *Und das wil im got vergelten in dem ewigen leben und wil in begoben noch sinen kinnigklichen eren mit einem kleide der frôiden und wil in krônen mit der kronen der eren.*

178 See Kathryn Starkey, 'On Deer and Dragons: Textiles and the Poetics of Medieval Story-Telling in König Rother.' *Animals in Text and Textile: Story-Telling in the Medieval World*. Ed. Kathryn Starkey and Evelin Wetter. Riggisberger Berichte Vol. 23. Riggisberg: Abegg-Stiftung, 2019, 47–64. On clothing in

medieval German poetry more generally, see Elke Brüggen, *Kleidung und Mode in der höfischen Epik des 12. und 13. Jahrhunderts.* Beihefte zum Euphorion Vol. 23. Heidelberg: Winter, 1989.

179 *botte* 99, 167–8. The vision containing these prayer-crafted garments occurs at Ascension and is followed by another textile vision during the None, the liturgical mid-afternoon prayer (ninth hour after midnight, that is 3 PM), when Christ appears to Gertrude dressed in a green gown and a red coat, decoded as green meaning his abundant virtues in his human life and red meaning his strong love that made him suffer the martyrdom. In the same vision, Christ puts rings on his chosen brides' fingers, symbolising the mystical union.

180 See *botte* 20, 97. Similarly, friends exchange imaginary garments and jewels, see *botte* 106, 174.

181 *botte* 96, 165.

182 *botte* 93, 162: *Sú sach die werck, die sú glichsenlich in der gehorsam geton het, also das sú ein ding von eigenem willen tůn wolt und doch ein urlop von der meisterschaft gewan, also ob sú es in der gehorsam tůn wollte und doch selber veriht het, das man ir es gebieten můst.*

183 See also the imperfect 'workmanship' in art crafted with gold and jewels in relation to Nature, in Alan of Lille, 'Anticlaudianus,' Book 1, ll. 159–64.

184 Previous research held that homosexuality is the main topic of *The Complaint of Nature*. However, this focus falls short when it comes to the many other topics poetically discussed by Alan; see Beate Kellner, 'Allegorien der Natur bei Alanus ab Insulis – mit einem Ausblick auf die volkssprachliche Rezeption.' *Schriftsinn und Epochalität: Zur historischen Prägnanz allegorischer und symbolischer Sinnstiftung.* Germanisch-romanische Monatsschrift. Beihefte Vol. 81. Ed. Bernhard Huss and David Nelting. Heidelberg: Winter, 2017, 113–43, at 123.

185 Whether the Helfta authors had direct acces to Alan's *The Complaint of Nature* or not, is hard to determine. An indirect reception is, however, likely; for a full discussion of the historical reception, see Kirakosian, 'Intertextuelle Textilien'.

186 On the *integumentum* as a creative device, see Frank Bezner, *Vela Veritatis: Hermeneutik,*

Wissen und Sprache in der Intellectual History des 12. Jahrhunderts. Studien und Texte zur Geistesgeschichte des Mittelalters Vol. 85. Leiden: Brill, 2005, 85, similarly 553.

187 See Alanus ab Insulis [Alan of Lille]. *De Planctu Naturae.* Ed. Nikolaus Häring. *Studi Medievali* 19.2 (1978): 806–79 (article starts on 797), here at 825.

188 See *De Planctu Naturae*, ed. Häring, 839: *Ab altiori etenim sumens inicium excellentiorique stilo mee uolens seriem narrationis contexere, nolo ut prius plana uerborum planicie explanare proposita uel prophanis uerborum nouitatibus prophanare prophana, uerum pudenda aureis pudicorum uerborum faleris inaurare uariisque uenustorum dictorum coloribus inuestire. Consequens enim est predictorum uiciorum scorias deauratis locutionibus purpurare uiciorumque fetorem adore uerborum inbalsamare mellifluo, ne si tanti sterquilinii fetor in nimie promulgationis auras euaderet plerosque ad indignationis nauseantis uomitum inuitaret.*

189 Michael Stolz, '"ibi quasi allegorice – ibi tamen ad litteram": Imagined Animals on Nature's Dress in Alan of Lille's De Planctu Naturae.' *Animals in Text and Textile: Story-Telling in the Medieval World.* Ed. Kathryn Starkey and Evelin Wetter. Riggisberger Berichte Vol. 23. Riggisberg: Abegg-Stiftung, 2019, 81–91.

190 For a more detailed description and an analysis, see Kirakosian, 'Intertextuelle Textilien'. On the drapery of rhetorical garments, see Michael Stolz, 'Bewegtes Beiwerk: Ästhetische Funktionen der Kleiderthematik bei Alanus ab Insulis und Giovanni Boccaccio.' *Reflexionsfiguren der Künste in der Vormoderne.* Ed. Annette Gerok-Reiter, Anja Wolkenhauer, Robert Jörg, and Stefanie Gropper. Germanisch-Romanische Monatsschrift. Beihefte Vol. 88. Heidelberg: Winter, 2018, 359–94.

191 See *De Planctu Naturae*, ed. Häring, 877.

192 On the polemic aspects of *The Complaint of Nature*, see Johannes B. Köhler, ed. and trans. *Alain de Lille: Die Klage der Natur. Lateinischer Text, Übersetzung und philologisch-philosophiegeschichtlicher Kommentar = Alani ab Insulis. De planctu naturae. textus, translatio una cum annotationibus.* Texte und Studien zur europäischen Geistesgeschichte. Series A Vol. 2. Münster: Aschendorff, 2013, 31–41.

193 *botte* 93, 161. The earliest transmitted *botte* witness even employs the Latin term *gesignirt*

194 Nevertheless, Alan thought and wrote as someone who connects the poetological with the theological, as pointed out by Johan Huizinga, *Über die Verknüpfung des poetischen mit dem theologischen bei Alanus de Insulis*. Koninklijke Nederlandse Akademie van Wetenschappen. Afd. Letterkunde. Medeleelingen; deel 74, ser. B., no. 6. Y. Amsterdam: Noord-Hollandsche uitgevers-maatschappij, 1932.

195 The Christian interpretation started early, for example with William of Auxerre's commentary. On the theological reception of *The Complaint of Nature*, see Christoph Huber, *Die Aufnahme und Verarbeitung des Alanus ab Insulis in mittelhochdeutschen Dichtungen. Untersuchungen zu Thomasin von Zerklære, Gottfried von Straßburg, Frauenlob, Heinrich von Neustadt, Heinrich von St. Gallen, Heinrich von Mügeln und Johannes von Tepl*. Münchener Texte und Untersuchungen zur deutschen Literatur des Mittelalters Vol. 89. Munich: Artemis, 1988, 386–402.

196 Huber, *Die Aufnahme und Verarbeitung des Alanus ab Insulis*, 160; see also 210 and 284.

197 *De Planctu Naturae*, ed. Häring, 866 and 868.

198 Meister Eckhart, *Die deutschen und lateinischen Werke*, DW 5: Meister Eckharts Traktate. Ed. Josef Quint. Stuttgart: Kohlhammer, 1963 (repr. 1987), 232–3. *The Complete Mystical Works of Meister Eckhart*, trans. Maurice O'C. Walshe, 499–500: 'Provided He finds him now ready, He pays no regard to what he was before.'

199 Walshe, *The Complete Mystical Works*, 500; Meister Eckhart, DW 5, 235: *Dar umbe lídet got gerne den schaden der sünden und hât dicke geliten und aller dickest verhenget über die menschen, die er hât versehen, daz er sie ze grôzen dingen ziehen wolte.*

200 Gertrude has 'pangs of conscience' (*Zů dem júngsten wart sú ir gewissen bissen*), see *botte* 34, 104. For Gertrude's remorse and subsequent gain of divine grace, see also *botte* 36, 104.

201 *botte* 93, 162: *Wenn die mosen der súnden schinen ewiklich an uns got zů einem lobe, das man prúffe, wie milte er gegen den sy, die ruwe haben über ir súnde, und das er dennoch also vil gůtes důt, also ob wir wider sinen willen nie geton hette.*

202 Largier, 'The Poetics of the Image in Late Medieval Mysticism,' 178.

203 See *botte* 134, 206. This vision lends itself for comparison to the thirteenth-century Premonstratensian mystic Christina of Hane, who in a vision sees herself adorned in a red dress about which her mystical bridegroom Christ tells her that it is composed of his precious blood. Then he crowns her with four crowns (justice, divine virtues, divine wisdom, divine love), marking her virtues and divine reward; Kirakosian, *Die Vita der Christina von Hane*, Ch. 63, 321–2.

204 For example, when Gertrude feels ashamed for a non-defined temptation that she cannot withstand, God covers 'the stains with a golden plate of miraculous metal'; *botte* 62, 123: *verdeckte er die mose mit einem gúldenen blech von wunderlichem gesmyde.*

205 See for example *botte* 168, 238–9; 59, 119.

206 *botte* 39, 106.

207 See *botte* 136, 208.

208 The link between female spirituality and purgatory has already been addressed in research, just as female spirituality and its tensions between inner and outer world have also been mentioned. On women and purgatory see: Bynum, *Holy Feast and Holy Fast,* 120–1; Jo Ann McNamara, 'The Need to Give: Suffering and Female Sanctity in the Middle Ages.' *Images of Sainthood in Medieval Europe*. Ed. Renate Blumenfeld-Kosinski and Timea Klara Szell. Ithaca, NY: Cornell University Press, 1991, 199–221, at 213–18; Barbara Newman, *From Virile Woman to WomanChrist: Studies in Medieval Religion and Literature*, Middle Ages Series. Philadelphia: University of Pennsylvania Press, 1995, 109–36; Dyan Elliott, *Proving Woman: Female Spirituality and Inquisitional Culture in the Later Middle Ages*. Princeton: Princeton University Press, 2004, 74–84; Kirakosian, 'Penitential Punishment and Purgatory,' 129–54.

209 See *botte* 92, 161.

210 *botte* 95, 163.

211 Similarly, as mass is sung on the eve before Assumption, Gertrude has a vision of a golden rod that is sent to purgatory to release as many souls as there are hooks on the rod; *botte* 98, 166.

212 Gotha, Forschungsbibliothek, Chart. B 269, fol. 1r.

for 'to signify' in order to underline the technicality, see Gotha, Forschungsbibliothek, Chart. B 269, fol. 25r.

213 Robert Mills, 'God's Time? Purgatory and Temporality in Late Medieval Art.' *Time and Eternity: The Medieval Discourse.* Ed. Gerhard Jaritz and Gerson Moreno-Riano. International Medieval Research Vol. 9. Turnhout: Brepols, 2003, 477–98, at 480.

214 Ibid.

215 Caron, 'The Continuum of Time and Eternity,' 263.

216 See also Largier, 'The Poetics,' 183, as for the late medieval Henry Suso: 'the image itself turns into the agent for divine grace'.

217 See Jones, 'Hostia jubilationis,' 1011: 'Occasionally, Gertrude mentions a psalm or other liturgical text as a way to mark time either by invoking a particular date or celebration or by measuring the length of time by how long it takes to recite a prayer'.

218 The timing of the vision during the celebration of the Eucharist means that there is also a sonorous analogy to the textile. For synaesthetic phenomena in which music triggers images of fabric such as silk, see Luminita Florea, 'Synaesthesia and Textile Analogies in Fourteenth-Century Music Theory.' *Viator* 41 (2010): 317–33. On how nuns experienced spirituality within the physical setting of the monastery, see Lindgren, *Sensual Encounters*; for an introductory overview of sensation in the Middle Ages, see Carruthers, *Experience of Beauty*, 1–13.

219 Thomas Lentes has demonstrated how nuns imagined fictive crowns; see Lentes, 'Die Gewänder der Heiligen'. See also Bynum, 'Crowned with Many Crowns'.

220 On the book production as it is reflected in the visions of Gertrude of Helfta, see Kirakosian, 'Wie man got verwunden sol mit einem ougen'.

FINAL REMARKS

1 On the hagiographic tradition of rewriting, see Goullet, 'Vers une typologie des réécritures hagiographiques'; Dolbeau, 'Transformations des prologues hagiographiques'.

2 See Eleanor Johnson, *Staging Contemplation: Participatory Theology in Middle English Prose, Verse, and Drama.* Chicago: University of Chicago Press, 2018.

3 *Legatus* II, 21. *Gertrude d'Helfta: Œuvres spirituelles* II, 322–4. Translation by Barratt, *The Herald of God's Loving-Kindness*, 1&2, 158.

4 On the Old Swedish translation of the *Liber specialis gratiae* made in a late fifteenth-century Birgittine context, see Hedlund, 'Nuns and Latin, with Special Reference to the Brigittines of Vadstena', 100, especially note 11. On the Middle English redaction, see Halligan, ed. *The Booke of Gostlye Grace by Mechtild of Hackeborn*; Yoshikawa, 'Mechthild of Hackeborn as Spiritual Authority' and 'Post-mortem care of the soul'.

MANUSCRIPT TRANSMISSION WITH CATALOGUES

1 I thank Balázs Nemes for kindly sharing information on the transmission of the Latin sources.

2 A range of manuscripts transmits a prayer generally attributed to Gertrude, quoted in the *Legatus* II, 4 and perhaps originating from a prayer book that Gertrude possessed; see Nemes, 'Text Production,' 109.

TRANSCRIPTIONS AND TRANSLATIONS

1 selige] ~~sey~~ selige
2 die] ~~da~~ die
3 meinens] me | inent
4 einem] einen
5 hailigen] ~~haig~~ hailigen
6 menschen] mench | en
7 lob] ~~lob b bot~~ lob
8 vnd] vn̄]vnd
9 liad] liab
10 die] ~~die~~ die
11 Das] das | das
12 lese] leſe dir
13 do] do | do
14 Creutz] creutz
15 <mit deinem> teuren] teuren
16 <wir> vnsern] vnſern
17 sollen] leiden ſollen
18 regel <machen>] regel
19 <eß> ist] iſt
20 si<ch>] ſie
21 apfel] opfel

BIBLIOGRAPHY

PRIMARY SOURCES

Manuscripts

Augsburg
> Benediktinerabtei St. Stephan, Hs 38
> Universitätsibibliothek, Cod. III. 1. 4° 30
> Staats- und Stadtbibliothek, 8° Cod. 203

Berlin
> Staatsbibliothek Preußischer Kulturbesitz, Ms. germ. oct. 593
> Staatsbibliothek Preußischer Kulturbesitz, Ms. theol. lat. oct. 89

Bonn, Universitäts- und Landesbibliothek, S 726

Brussels
> Bibliothèque Royale, cod. 8507–09
> Bibliothèque Royale, cod. 21600 (1639)

Cambridge, MA, Houghton Library, Ms. Riant 90

Cologne, Historisches Archiv der Stadt, Köln, Best. 7010 (W★) 255

Darmstadt
> Universitäts- und Landesbibliothek, Hs 84
> Universitäts- und Landesbibliothek, Hs 2772

Dresden, Sächsische Landesbibliothek, Hs M 243

Eichstätt, Abtei St. Walburg, Ms germ. 23

Einsiedeln, Stiftsbibliothek, Codex 277 (1014)

Eisleben, Stiftung Luthergedenkstätten, H 546

Erfurt, Bistumsarchiv, Hs. Hist. 6

Frankfurt, Universitätsbibliothek, ms. Praed. 169

Freiburg im Breisgau
> Erzbischöfliches Archiv, Hs. 31
> Universitätsbibliothek, Hs. 186
> Universitätsbibliothek, Hs. 202

Gotha, Forschungsbibliothek, Chart. B 269

Graz
> Universitätsbibliothek, Ms. 64
> Universitätsbibliothek, Ms. 75

Heidelberg
> Universitätsbibliothek, Heid. Hs. 33
> Universitätsbibliothek, Cpg. 848

Karlsruhe
> Badische Landesbibliothek, Cod. Lichtenthal 89
> Badische Landesbibliothek, Cod. St. Georgen 64

Klosterneuburg, Stiftsbibliothek, cod. 711

Leipzig, Universitätsbibliothek, Ms 827

London, British Library, ADD. MS 14042

London, University College, MS Germ. 24

Mainz, Stadtbibliothek, Hs I 13

Moscow
> Lomonosov-University Library, Collection Gustav Schmidt, Fonds 40/1, nr. 47
> Rossijskaja Gosudarstvennaya Biblioteka, Fonds 183/281

Munich
> Bayerische Staatsbibliothek, Cgm 843
> Bayerische Staatsbibliothek, Cgm 861
> Bayerische Staatsbibliothek, Cgm 5292
> Bayerische Staatsbibliothek, Clm 15332
> Universitätsbibliothek, 8° Cod. ms. 193

New Haven, Yale University, Beinecke Rare Book and Manuscript Library, MS 968

New York, The Pierpont Morgan Library, M. 739

Nuremberg
> Germanisches Nationalmuseum, Hs. 2261
> Stadtbibliothek, Cod. Cent. V, 10
> Stadtbibliothek, Cod. Cent. VII, 62

Oxford, Keble College, MS 49

Pécs, Klimo Könyvtàr Bibliothek, AA. II. 21

Rastatt, Historische Bibliothek der Stadt im Ludwig-
    Wilhelm-Gymnasium, Cod. K 152, Hs 3
San Marino, Huntington Library, HM 1082
Sarnen, Benediktinerkollegium, Cod. chart. 215
Solothurn, Zentralbibliothek, Cod. S 458
St. Gall
    Stiftsbibliothek, Cod. Sang. 506
    Stiftsbibliothek, Cod. Sang. 519
    Stiftsbibliothek, Cod. Sang. 603
    Stiftsbibliothek, Cod. Sang. 973
Strasbourg,   Bibliothèque   Nationale   et
    Universitaire, MS 2929
Trier, Stadtbibliothek, Cod. 77/1061
Überlingen, Leopold-Sophien-Bibliothek, Ms. 26
Uppsala, Universitetsbibliotek, Cod. C 517m
Vienna
    Österreichische Nationalbibliothek, Cod. 3042
    Österreichische Nationalbibliothek, Cod. 4224
    Schottenstift, Cod. 308
Weimar
    Herzogin Anna Amalia Bibliothek, Q 49
    Herzogin Anna Amalia Bibliothek, Oct 52
    Herzogin Anna Amalia Bibliothek, Oct 62
Wrocław
    Biblioteka Kapitulna (no shelf mark)
    Bibliotheka Uniwersytecka, Ms. IV F 194
Würzburg, Universitätsbibliothek, M. ch. f. 241
Zurich
    Zentralbibliothek, Ms. C 162
    Zentralbibliothek, Ms. Rh. 159

Archival Materials

Niedersächsisches Hauptstaatsarchiv Hannover
    Depositum 76, C113
    Depositum 76, MS 7/1

PRINTED SOURCES

Alan of Lille [Alanus ab Insulis]. *De Planctu
    Naturae.* Ed. Nikolaus Häring. *Studi Medievali*
    19.2 (1978): 806–79.
    'Liber in Distinctionibus dictionum theologi-
    calium.' *Opera Omnia.* Ed. Jacques-Paul
    Migne.   Patrologiae   Latinae   Cursus
    Completus Vol. 210. Paris: Migne, 1853.
    687–1012.
    'Anticlaudianus.' *Alan of Lille: Literary Works.*
    Ed.   and   trans.   Winthrop   Wetherbee.
    Dumbarton Oaks Medieval Library Vol. 22.

Cambridge,   MA: Harvard   University   Press,
    2013. 219–516.
    *Alain de Lille: Die Klage der Natur. Lateinischer
    Text,   Übersetzung   und   philologisch-
    philosophiegeschichtlicher Kommentar = Alani ab
    Insulis. De planctu naturae. textus, translatio una
    cum annotationibus.* Ed. and trans. Johannes B.
    Köhler. Texte und Studien zur europäischen
    Geistesgeschichte. Series A Vol. 2. Münster:
    Aschendorff, 2013.
Albert the Great [Albertus Magnus]. 'De
    Eucharistia.' *Opera Omnia.* Vol. 38. Ed.
    Auguste and Émile Borgnet. Paris: Vivès, 1899.
Augustine of Hippo [Augustinus Hipponensis,
    Aurelius]. *Sancti Aurelii Augustini Episcopi de
    civitate dei libri XXII.* Ed. Bernhard Dombart
    and Alfons Kalb. Berlin: De Gruyter, 2013.
Babington, Churchill, ed. *Polychronicon Ranulphi
    Higden maonachi Cestrensis: together with the
    English translations of John Trevisa and of an
    unknown writer of the fifteenth century.* Vol. 2.
    London: Longmans, Green and Co., 1869.
Bernard of Clairvaux. *Sermons sur le Cantique.* 5
    vols. Ed. Jean Leclercq, Henri Rochais, and
    Charles Hugh Talbot. Trans. Paul Verdeyen
    and Raffaele Fassetta. Paris: Éditions du Cerf,
    1996–2007.
Boethius. *Tractates: The Consolation of Philosophy.*
    Trans. H. F. Stewart, E. K. Rand, and S. J.
    Tester. Loeb Classical Library Vol. 74.
    Cambridge, MA: Harvard University Press, 1973.
Bonaventure   [Bonaventura   da   Bagnoreggio].
    'Legenda   maior.'   *Opera   omnia.*   Vol. 8.
    Quaracchi: Collegii S. Bonventura, 1898. 504–65.
    'Legenda minor.' *Opera omnia.* Vol. 8.
    Quaracchi: Collegii S. Bonventura, 1898.
    565–79.
    'Legenda maior Sancti Francisi.' *Analacta
    Franciscana.* Vol. 10. Quaracchi: Collegii
    S. Bonventura, 1926–40. 555–652.
    'Legenda maior sancti Francisci, Legenda
    minor sancti Francisci.' *Fontes Franciscani.* Ed.
    Enrico Menestò et al. Assisi: Edizioni
    Porziuncola, 1995.
Birgitta of Sweden. *The Revelations of St. Birgitta
    of Sweden.* Vol. I: *Liber Caelestis* Books I–III.
    Trans. Denis Searby. Ed. Bridget Morris.
    Oxford: Oxford University Press, 2006.
Bruno of Würzburg [Bruno Herbipolensis
    Episcopus] 'Expositio in psalmos.' *Opera*

Omnia. Vol. 1. Ed. Jacques-Paul Migne. Patrologiae Latinae Cursus Completus Vol. 142. Paris: Migne, 1853. 50–530.

Caesarius von Heisterbach. *Dialogus miraculorum = Dialog über die Wunder*. Ed. and trans. Nikolaus Nösges and Horst Schneider. Fontes Christiani Vol. 86. Turnhout: Brepols, 2009.

Catherine of Siena. *The Dialogue*. Ed. and trans. Suzanne Noffke. Classics of Western Spirituality. New York: Paulist Press, 1980.

Derkits, Hans, ed. *Die Lebensbeschreibung der Gertrud von Ortenberg*. Vol. 1: Text edition. Doctoral dissertation, University of Vienna, 1990.

Fischer, Bonifatius, Robert Weber, and Roger Gryson, eds. *Biblia sacra: iuxta Vulgatam versionem*. 5th ed. Stuttgart: Deutsche Bibelgesellschaft, 2007.

Gertrude the Great of Helfta [Gertrude d'Helfta/Gertrud von Helfta]. *Œuvres spirituelles*. Vol. 2: *Le Héraut* (Livre I et II). Ed. Pierre Doyère. Sources chrétiennes. Série des textes monastiques d'Occident Vol. 25. Paris: Éditions du Cerf, 1968.

Œuvres spirituelles. Vol. 3: *Le Héraut* (Livre III). Ed. Pierre Doyère. Sources chrétiennes. Série des textes monastiques d'Occident Vol. 27. Paris: Éditions du Cerf, 1968.

Œuvres spirituelles. Vol. 4: *Le Héraut* (Livre IV). Ed. Jean-Marie Clément, Sources chrétiennes. Série des textes monastiques d'Occident 48. Paris: Éditions du Cerf, 1978.

Œuvres spirituelles. Vol. 5: *Le Héraut* (Livre V). Ed. Jean-Marie Clément and Bernard de Vregille. Sources chrétiennes Vol. 331. Paris: Éditions du Cerf, 1986.

Nemes, Balázs J. and Almuth Märker, ed. '"Hunc tercium conscripsi cum maximo labore occultandi": Schwester N von Helfta und ihre 'Sonderausgabe' des "Legatus divinae pietatis" Gertruds von Helfta in der Leipziger Handschrift Ms 827.' *Beiträge zur Geschichte der deutschen Sprache und Literatur* 137 (2015): 248–96, at 268–271.

Ein botte der götlichen miltekeit. Ed. Otmar Wieland. Studien und Mitteilungen zur Geschichte des Benediktiner-Ordens und seiner Zweige, Ergänzungsband 22. Ottobeuren: Bayerische Benediktinerakademie, 1973.

Das buch der botschafft ader legatio gotlicher guttikeit. Leipzig: Melchior Lotter, 1505 [VD16 M 1785].

Insinuationes divinae pietatis libri quinque. Ed. Johannes Justus von Landsberg. Cologne: Melchior von Neuß, 1536.

'Der heiligen Getrud von Helfta 'both der göttlichen myltigkeit' in einer Lichtenthaler Handschrift von 1566.' Ed. Maria Pia Schindele. *Freiburger Diözesan-Archiv* 120 (2000): 53–107.

'Die Bücher des Legatus divinae pietatis II und III in einer Lichtenthaler Handschrift von 1566.' Ed. Pius Reiß. *Freiburger Diözesan-Archiv* 125 (2005): 69–217.

L'image de la noblesse figurée sur la vie de Saincte Gertrude & de ses Parens. Trans. Guillaume de Rebreviettes Seigneur d'Escoeuures. Paris: Huby, 1612.

The Herald of God's Loving-Kindness, Books One and Two. Trans. Alexandra Barratt. Cistercian Fathers Vol. 35. Kalamazoo, MI: Cistercian Publications, 1991.

The Herald of God's Loving-Kindness, Book Three. Trans. Alexandra Barratt. Cistercian Fathers Vol. 63. Kalamazoo, MI: Cistercian Publications, 1999.

The Herald of God's Loving-Kindness, Book Four. Cistercian Fathers Vol. 85. Collegeville, MN: Cistercian Publications, 2018.

Hildegard of Bingen [Hildegard Bingensis]. *Hildegardis Scivias*. Ed. Adelgundis Führkötter. Corpus Christianorum. Continuatio Mediaevalis Vols. 43–43A. Turnhout: Brepols, 1978.

Hirsch, Gabriele, ed. *Die Legende der Heiligen Trutta*. Doctoral dissertation, University of Graz, 1921.

Hugh of St Victor [Hugo de S. Victore]. 'Commentaria in hierarchiam coelestem.' *Opera Omnia*. Vol. 1. Ed. Jacques-Paul Migne. Patrologiae Latinae Cursus Completus Vol. 175. Paris: Migne, 1854. 923–1154.

Hugh of St Victor 'De sacramentis christianae fidei.' *Opera Omnia*. Vol. 2. Ed. Jacques-Paul Migne. Patrologiae Latinae Cursus Completus Vol. 176. Paris: Migne, 1854. 173–618.

'[De tribus diebus=]De eruditione docta, liber VII.' *Opera Omnia*. Vol. 2. Ed. Jacques-Paul Migne. Patrologiae Latinae Cursus Completus Vol. 176. Paris: Migne, 1854. 811–38.

'De verbo incarnato collationes tres.' *Opera Omnia*. Vol 3. Ed. Jacques-Paul Migne. Patrologiae Latinae Cursus Completus Vol. 177. Paris: Migne, 1854. 315–23.

Kirakosian, Racha, ed. *Die Vita der Christina von Hane: Untersuchung und Edition*. Hermaea. Neue Folge Vol. 144. Berlin: De Gruyter, 2017.

The Life of Christina of Hane: Introduction and Translation. New Haven: Yale University Press, 2020.

Krapp, George Philip, and Eliott van Kirk Dobbie, eds. *The Exeter Book*. Anglo-Saxon Poetic Records Vol. 3. New York: Columbia University Press, 1936.

Krühne, Max. *Urkundenbuch der Klöster der Grafschaft Mansfeld*. Geschichtsquellen der Provinz Sachsen und angrenzender Gebiete Vol. 20. Halle: Hendel, 1888.

Landsberg, Johannes Justus. *Vita della beata vergine Gertruda*. Trans. Vicenzo Buondi. Venice: Giolito de Ferrari, 1562.

Lamprecht von Regensburg. *Sanct Francisken Leben und Tochter Syon*. Ed. Karl Weinhold. Paderborn: Schöningh, 1880.

Langmann, Adelheid. *Die Offenbarungen der Adelheid Langmann: Klosterfrau zu Engelthal*. Ed. Philipp Strauch. Quellen und Forschungen zur Sprach- und Kulturgeschichte der Germanischen Völker Vol. 26. Strasbourg: Trübner, 1878.

Lumby, Joseph Rawson, ed. *Polychronicon Ranulphi Higden maonachi Cestrensis: together with the English translations of John Trevisa and of an unknown writer of the fifteenth century*. Vol. 3. London: Longmans, Green and Co., 1871.

Margaret of Oingt [Marguerite d'Oingt]. *Les Oeuvres de Marguerite d'Oingt*. Ed. Antonin Duraffour, Pierre Gardette, and Paulette Durdilly. Paris: Les Belles Lettres, 1965.

The Writings of Margaret of Oingt: Medieval Prioress and Mystic. Ed. Renate Blumenfeld-Kosinski. Newburyport: Focus Information Group, 1990.

Marienwerder, Johannes. 'Das Leben der heiligen Dorothea von Montau.' *Scriptores rerum Prussicarum: Die Geschichtsquellen der preußischen Vorzeit bis zum Untergange der Ordenherrschaft*. Vol. 2. Ed. Theodor Hirsch, Max Töppen, and Ernst Strehlke. Leipzig: Hirzel, 1863; repr. Frankfurt a.M.: Minerva, 1963.

Mechthild of Hackeborn [Mechthild von Hackeborn]. 'Liber specialis gratiae.' *Revelationes Gertrudianæ ac Mechtildianæ Vol. II: Sanctæ Mechtildis virginis ordinis sancti Benedicti Liber specialis gratiæ, accedit sororis Mechthildis ejusdem ordinis Lux divinitatis. Opus ad codicum fidem nunc primum integre editum Solesmensium O. S. B. monachorum cura et opera*. Ed. Louis Paquelin. Paris: Oudin, 1877. 1–421.

The Booke of Gostlye Grace of Mechtild of Hackeborn. Ed. Theresa A. Halligan. Studies and Texts Vol. 46. Toronto: Pontifical Institute of Mediaeval Studies, 1979.

Das buch geistlicher gnaden, offenbarunge, wunderliches vnde beschawlichen lebens der heiligenn iungfrawen Mechtildis vnd Gertrudis, Closter iungfrawen des closters Helffede. Ed. Marcus von Weida. Leipzig: Melchior Lotter, 1503 [VD16 M 1784].

The Book of Special Grace. Trans. Barbara Newman. New York: Paulist Press, 2017.

Mechthild of Magdeburg [Mechthild von Magdeburg/Mechthildis Magdeburgensis]. *Das fließende Licht der Gottheit: Nach der Einsiedler Handschrift in kritischem Vergleich mit der gesamten Überlieferung*. Ed. Hans Neumann. Vol. 1: Text. Ed. Gisela Vollmann-Profe. Münchener Texte und Untersuchungen zur deutschen Literatur des Mittelalters Vol. 100. Munich: Artemis, 1990.

'Lux divinitatis.' *Revelationes Gertrudianæ ac Mechtildianæ Vol. II: Sanctæ Mechtildis virginis ordinis sancti Benedicti Liber specialis gratiæ, accedit sororis Mechthildis ejusdem ordinis Lux divinitatis. Opus ad codicum fidem nunc primum integre editum Solesmensium O. S. B. monachorum cura et opera*. Ed. Louis Paquelin. Paris: Oudin, 1877. 435–710.

'Lux Divinitatis' – 'Das Liecht Der Gotheit': Der Lateinisch-frühneuhochdeutsche Überlieferungszweig des 'Fließenden Lichts Der Gottheit.' *Synoptische*

Ausgabe. Ed. Ernst Hellgardt, Balázs J. Nemes, and Elke Senne. Berlin: De Gruyter, 2019.

The Flowing Light of the Godhead. Ed. and trans. Frank Tobin. Classics of Western Spirituality. New York: Paulist Press, 1998.

Meister Eckhart. *Die deutschen und lateinischen Werke: Die deutschen Werke*. 5 vols. Ed. Josef Quint and Georg Steer. Stuttgart: Kohlhammer, 1958–2016.

DW 1. Ed. Josef Quint. Stuttgart: Kohlhammer, 1958 (repr. 1986).

DW 4,1: Meister Eckharts Predigten IV, 1. Ed. Georg Steer. Stuttgart: Kohlhammer, 2003.

DW 5: Meister Eckharts Traktate. Ed. Josef Quint. Stuttgart: Kohlhammer, 1963 (repr.1987).

The Complete Mystical Works of Meister Eckhart. Trans. Maurice O'C Walshe. New York: Crossroad, 2009.

Meyer, Johannes. *Buch der Reformacio Predigerordens*. Ed. B. M. Reichert. Quellen und Forschungen zur Geschichte des Dominikanerordens in Deutschland Vols. 2–3. Leipzig: Harrassowitz, 1908-9.

Müller, Joseph, trans. *Leben und Offenbarungen der heiligen Mechtildis und der Schwester Mechtildis (von Magdeburg), Jungfrauen aus dem Orden des heiligen Benediktus*. Regensburg: Manz, 1880.

Schmidt, Wieland, ed. *Die vierundzwanzig Alten Ottos von Passau*. Palaestra Vol. 212. Leipzig: Akademische Verlagsgesellschaft, 1938. Repr. New York: Johnson, 1967.

Spangenberg, Cyriacus. *Mansfeldische Chronica*. Vol. 1. Eisleben: Petri, 1572. Repr. in *Mansfelder Blätter* 27 (1912). Ed. Rudolph Leers.

Quernfurtische Chronica. Erfurt: Bawman, 1590. Repr. in *Mansfelder Blätter* 28 (1913).

Suso, Henry [Seuse, Heinrich]. *Deutsche Schriften im Auftrag der Württembergischen Kommission für Landesgeschichte*. Ed. Karl Bihlmeyer. Stuttgart: W. Kohlhammer, 1907.

'Büchlein der ewigen Weisheit.' *Heinrich Seuse: Deutsche Schriften*. Ed. Karl Bihlmeyer. Stuttgart: W. Kohlhammer, 1907 (repr. 1961). 196–325.

'Büchlein der Wahrheit.' *Heinrich Seuse: Deutsche Schriften*. Ed. Karl Bihlmeyer.

Stuttgart: W. Kohlhammer, 1907 (repr. 1961). 326–59.

Tauler, Johannes. *Die Predigten Taulers: aus der Engelberger und der Freiburger Handschrift sowie aus Schmidts Abschriften der ehemaligen Straßburger Handschriften*. Ed. Ferdinand Vetter. Frankfurt a.M.: Weidmann, 1910.

SECONDARY SOURCES

Academia Caesarea Vindobonensis. *Tabulae codicum manu scriptorum praeter graecos et orientales in Bibliotheca Palatina Vindobonensi asservatorum*. Vol. 3: Cod. 3501–5000. Vienna: Gerold, 1869.

Achten, Gerard, Leo Eizenhöfer, and Hermann Knaus. *Die lateinischen Gebetbuchhandschriften*. Die Handschriften der Hessischen Landes- und Hochschulbibliothek Darmstadt Vol. 3. Wiesbaden: Harrassowitz, 1972.

Amsler, Mark. *Affective Literacies: Writing and Multilingualism in the Late Middle Ages*, Late Medieval and Early Modern Studies Vol. 19. Turnhout: Brepols, 2011.

Andersen, Elizabeth A. *The Voices of Mechthild of Magdeburg*. Oxford: Lang, 2000.

'"Das Fließende Licht der Gottheit" und der Psalter: Dialogische Beziehungen.' *Dialoge: Sprachliche Kommunikation in und zwischen Texten im deutschen Mittelalter: Hamburger Colloquium 1999*. Ed. Nikolaus Henkel, Martin H. Jones, and Nigel F. Palmer. Tübingen: Niemeyer, 2003. 225–38.

Manfred Eikelmann, and Anne Simon, eds. 'Einleitung.' *Texttyp und Textproduktion in der deutschen Literatur des Mittelalters*. Trends in Medieval Philology Vol. 7. Berlin: De Gruyter, 2005. XI–XXV.

Andersson, Roger. 'Messenger Manuscripts and Mechanisms of Change.' *Continuity and Change: Papers from the Birgitta Conference at Dartington 2015*. Ed. Elin Andersson, Claes Gejrot, Eddie Jones, and Mia Åkestam. Stockholm: Kungl. Vitterhets Historie och Antikvitets Akademien, 2017. 24–39.

'Birgitta and her Revelations in the Sermons of the Vadstena Brothers.' *A Companion to Birgitta of Sweden and Her Legacy in the Later*

Middle Ages. Ed. Maria H. Oen. Brill's Companions to the Christian Tradition Vol. 89. Leiden: Brill, 2019. 159–85.

Andersson-Schmitt, Margarete, and Hagan Halberg. *Mittelalterliche Handschriften der Universitätsbibliothek Uppsala. Katalog über die C- Sammlung*. Vol. 5: C 401–550. Acta Bibliothecae R. Universitatis Upsaliensis Vol. 26 Pt. 5. Stockholm: Almqvist u. Wiksell International, 1992.

Anzulewicz, Henryk. 'Perspektive und Raumvorstellung.' *Raum und Raumvorstellung im Mittelalter*. Ed. Jan A. Aertsen and Andreas Speer. Miscellanea Mediaevalia Vol. 25. Berlin: De Gruyter, 1997. 249–86.

Appuhn, Horst. *Der Fund vom Nonnenchor*. Kloster Wienhausen Vol. 4. Wienhausen: Kloster Wienhausen, 1973.

Appuhn, Horst, and Christian Heusinger. 'Der Fund kleiner Andachtsbilder des 13. bis 17. Jahrhunderts in Kloster Wienhausen.' *Niederdeutsche Beiträge zur Kunstgeschichte* 4 (1965): 157–238.

As-Vijvers, Anne Margreet W. 'Weaving Mary's Chaplet: The Representation of the Rosary in Late Medieval Flemish Manuscript Illumination.' *Weaving, Veiling, and Dressing: Textiles and Their Metaphors in the Late Middle Ages*. Ed. Kathryn M. Rudy and Barbara Baert. Medieval Church Studies Vol. 12. Turnhout: Brepols, 2007. 41–79.

Ashley, Kathleen M. 'Titivillus and the Battle of Words in Mankind.' *Annuale mediaevale* 16 (1975): 128–50.

Auge, Oliver. 'Frömmigkeit, Bildung, Bücherliebe – Konstanten im Leben des Buxheimer Kartäusers Hilprand Brandenburg (1442–1514).' *Bücher, Bibliotheken und Schriftkultur der Kartäuser: Festgabe zum 65. Geburtstag von Edward Potkowski*. Ed. Lorenz Sönke and Edward Potkowski. Contubernium Vol. 59. Stuttgart: Steiner, 2002. 399–422.

Auslander, Leora. 'Beyond Words.' *The American Historical Review* 110 (2005): 1015–45.

Backes, Martina. 'Eine Stadt voll der Gnaden: Straßburg aus der Perspektive Gertruds von

Ortenberg.' *Schreiben und Lesen in der Stadt: Literaturbetrieb im spätmittelalterlichen Straßburg*. Ed. Stephen Mossman, Nigel F. Palmer, and Felix Heinzer. Kulturtopographie des alemannischen Raums Vol. 4. Berlin: De Gruyter, 2012. 29–38.

Backmund, Norbert. *Die Chorherrenorden und ihre Stifte in Bayern. Augustinerchorherren, Prämonstratenser, Chorherren vom Hl. Geist, Antoniter*. Passau: Neue-Presse-Verlags-Gesellschaft, 1966.

Baert, Barbara. 'Textile, Tactility, and the Senses: The 13th-century Embroidered Antependium of Wernigerode Revisited.' *Clothing the Sacred: Medieval Textiles as Fabric, Form, and Metaphor*. Ed. Mateusz Kaputska and Warren T. Woodfin. Textile Studies Vol. 8. Emsdetten: Édition Imorde, 2015. 89–119.

Baldwin, John W. 'From the Ordeal to Confession: In Search of Lay Religion in Early-Thirteenth-Century France.' *Handling Sin: Confession in the Middle Ages*. Ed. Peter Biller and Alastair J. Minnis. York Studies in Medieval Theology Vol. 2. Woodbridge: York Medieval Press, 1998. 191–209.

Bangert, Michael. *Demut in Freiheit: Studien zur Geistlichen Lehre im Werk Gertruds von Helfta*. Studien zur systematischen und spirituellen Theologie Vol. 21. Würzburg: Echter, 1997.

'Die sozio-kulturelle Situation des Klosters St. Maria in Helfta.' *'Vor dir steht die leere Schale meiner Sehnsucht': Die Mystik der Frauen von Helfta*. Ed. Michael Bangert and Hildegund Keul Leipzig: Benno-Verlag, 1998. 29–47.

'In Bildern Gott denken: Das Christusbild in den Visionen Gertruds von Helfta.' *Aufbruch zu neuer Gottesrede: Die Mystik der Gertrud von Helfta*. Ed. Siegfried Ringler. Ostfildern: Grünewald, 2008. 93–107.

'The Metaphor of the Vestment in the Writings of Gertrud of Helfta (1256–1302).' *Iconography of Liturgical Textiles in the Middle Ages*. Ed. Evelin Wetter. Riggisberger Berichte Vol. 18. Riggisberg: Abegg-Stiftung, 2010. 129–39.

Barow-Vassilevitch, Daria and Marie-Luise Heckmann. *Abendländische Handschriften des Mittelalters und der frühen Neuzeit in den Beständen der Russischen Staatsbibliothek (Moskau).* Wiesbaden: Harrassowitz, 2016.

Barr, Jessica. 'Imagined Bodies: Intimate Reading and Divine Union in Gertrude of Helfta's "Legatus".' *Journal of Medieval Religious Cultures* 43 (2017): 186–208.

Barratt, Alexandra, trans. 'Introduction.' *Gertrude the Great of Helfta: The Herald of God's Loving-Kindness Book 4.* Cistercian Fathers Vol. 85. Collegeville, MN: Cistercian Publications, 2018. 11–43.

'The Chronological Priority of the Memoriale abundantiae suavitatis divinae in Leipzig, Universitätsbibliothek, MS 827.' *Analecta Cisterciensa* 69 (2019): 198–209.

Bartsch, Karl. *Die altdeutschen Handschriften der Universitätsbibliothek in Heidelberg.* Katalog der Handschriften der Universitäts-Bibliothek in Heidelberg Vol. 1. Heidelberg: Koester, 1887.

Baswell, Christopher. 'Talking Back to the Text: Marginal Voices in Medieval Secular Literature.' *The Uses of Manuscripts in Literary Studies: Essays in Memory of Judson Boyce Allen.* Ed. Charlotte C. Morse, Penelope Reed Doob, and Marjorie Curry Woods. Studies in Medieval Culture Vol. 31. Kalamazoo, MI: Western Michigan University, Medieval Institute Publications, 1992. 121–60.

Baumann, Martin, et al. 'An Interactive Visualization for the Analysis of Annotated Text Variance in the Legendary "Der Heiligen Leben, Redaktion".' *Leipzig Symposium on Visualization in Applications* (LEVIA) 19 (2019), online: https://doi.org/10.31219/osf.io/wd9yz (10.07.2020).

Beach, Alison I. *Women as Scribes: Book Production and Monastic Reform in Twelfth-century Bavaria.* Cambridge Studies in Palaeography and Codicology Vol. 10. Cambridge, UK; New York: Cambridge University Press, 2004.

Bec, Pierre. 'Note musico-philologique sur l'orgue et l'aile de Guillaume de Machaut.' *Et c'est la fin pour quoy sommes ensemble: hommage à Jean Dufournet: littérature, histoire et langue du Moyen Age.* Vol. 1. Ed. Jean-Claude Aubailly, Emmanuèle Baumgartner, Francis Dubost, and Marcel Faure. Nouvelle Bibliothèque du Moyen Age Vol. 25. Paris: Champion, 1993. 149–61.

Bednarz, Ute et al., eds. *Kostbarkeiten aus dem Domschatz zu Halberstadt.* Halle an der Saale: Stekovics, 2001.

Beer, Jeanette, ed. 'Introduction.' *Medieval Translators and Their Craft.* Studies in Medieval Culture Vol. 25. Kalamazoo, MI: Medieval Institute Publications, 1989. 1–7.

Beier, Christine. *Die illuminierten Handschriften und Inkunabeln der Universitätsbibliothek Graz: Die illuminierten Handschriften 1400 bis 1550.* Vol. 1. Österreichische Akademie der Wissenschaften, phil.-hist. Klasse, Denkschriften Vol. 390; Institut für Kunstgeschichte der Universität Wien; Veröffentlichungen der Kommission für Schrift und Buchwesen des Mittelalters Vol. 5 Pt. 1. Vienna: Verlag der Österreichischen Akademie der Wissenschaften, 2010.

Bergner, Ute. 'Wasserzeichen in der Handschrift UBG-Ms 64.' *Der Handschriftenkatalog der UB Graz: Papierforschung.* http://sosa2.uni-graz.at/sosa/katalog/index.php

Bezner, Frank. *Vela Veritatis: Hermeneutik, Wissen und Sprache in der Intellectual History des 12. Jahrhunderts.* Studien und Texte zur Geistesgeschichte des Mittelalters Vol. 85. Leiden: Brill, 2005.

Blanton, Virginia, Veronica O'Mara, and Patricia Stoop, eds. *Nuns' Literacies in Medieval Europe: The Hull Dialogue.* Medieval Women – Texts and Contexts Vol. 26. Turnhout: Brepols, 2013.

Nuns' Literacies in Medieval Europe: The Kansas City Dialogue. Medieval Women – Texts and Contexts Vol. 27. Turnhout: Brepols, 2015.

'Introduction.' *Nuns' Literacies in Medieval Europe: The Antwerp Dialogue.* Medieval Women – Texts and Contexts Vol. 28. Turnhout: Brepols, 2017. xxi–lxvi.

Bodemann, Ulrike. *Katalog der deutschsprachigen illustrierten Handschriften des Mittelalters.* Vol. 6 Pt. 3/4. Munich: Beck, 2005.

Bodemann, Ulrike, Siegfried Ringler, and Balázs Nemes. *Handschriftencensus: Brüssel, Königl. Bibl., ms. 8507-09 (Kat.-Nr. 3407)*, online: www.handschriftencensus.de/7334

Boon, Jessica A. 'Trinitarian Love Mysticism: Ruusbroec, Hadewijch, and the Gendered Experience of the Divine.' *Church History: Studies in Christianity and Culture* 72 (2003): 484–503.

Bormann, Karl. *Die gotische Orgel zu Halberstadt: Eine Studie über mittelalterlichen Orgelbau.* Veröffentlichung der Gesellschaft der Orgelfreunde Vol. 27. Berlin: Merseburger, 1966.

Borries, Ekkehard. *Schwesternspiegel im 15. Jahrhundert: Gattungskonstitution, Editionen, Untersuchungen.* Berlin: De Gruyter, 2008.

Brakmann, Thomas. *'Ein Geistlicher Rosengarten': Die Vita der heiligen Katharina von Siena zwischen Ordensreform und Laienfrömmigkeit im 15. Jahrhundert: Untersuchungen und Edition.* Frankfurt a.M.: Lang, 2011.

Braun-Niehr, Beate. *Die theologischen lateinischen Handschriften in Octavo der Staatsbibliothek zu Berlin Preußischer Kulturbesitz.* Vol. 1. Staatsbibliothek zu Berlin Preußischer Kulturbesitz. Kataloge der Handschriftenabteilung. Erste Reihe: Handschriften Vol. 3 Pt. 1. Wiesbaden: Harrassowitz, 2007.

Bredekamp, Horst. *Theorie des Bildakts: Frankfurter Adorno-Vorlesungen 2007.* Berlin: Suhrkamp, 2010.

Breith, Astrid. *Textaneignung: Das Frauenlegendar der Lichtenthaler Schreibmeisterin Schwester Regula.* Studien und Texte zum Mittelalter und zur Frühen Neuzeit Vol. 17. Münster: Waxmann, 2010.

Bretscher-Gisiger, Charlotte, and Rudolf Gamper. *Katalog der Mittelalterlichen Handschriften der Klöster Muri und Hermetschwil.* Dietikon-Zürich: Graf, 2005.

Bridges, Margaret. 'Mehr als ein Text: Das ungelesene Buch zwischen Symbol und Fetisch.' *Buchkultur im Mittelalter: Schrift, Bild, Kommunikation.* Ed. Michael Stolz and Adrian Mettauer. Berlin: De Gruyter, 2005. 103–21.

Brüggen, Elke. *Kleidung und Mode in der höfischen Epik des 12. und 13. Jahrhunderts.* Beihefte zum Euphorion Vol. 23. Heidelberg: Winter, 1989.

Bücheler, Anna. 'Textile Ornament and Scripture Embodied in the Echternach Gospel Books.' *Clothing the Sacred: Medieval Textiles as Fabric, Form, and Metaphor.* Ed. Mateusz Kaputska and Warren T. Woodfin. Textile Studies Vol. 8. Emsdetten: Édition Imorde, 2015. 147–72.

Bugyis, Katie Ann-Marie. *The Care of Nuns: The Ministries of Benedictine Women in England during the Central Middle Ages.* Oxford: Oxford University Press, 2019.

Bumke, Joachim. *Die Vier Fassungen der 'Nibelungenklage': Untersuchungen zur Überlieferungsgeschichte und Textkritik der höfischen Epik im 13. Jahrhundert.* Quellen und Forschungen zur Literatur- und Kulturgeschichte Vol. 8. Berlin, New York: De Gruyter, 1996.

Bürkle, Susanne. 'Weibliche Spiritualität und imaginierte Weiblichkeit: Deutungsmuster und -perspektiven frauenmystischer Literatur im Blick auf die Thesen Caroline W. Bynums.' *Zeitschrift für deutsche Philologie* 113 (1994): 116–43.

Literatur im Kloster: Historische Funktion und rhetorische Legitimation frauenmystischer Texte des 14. Jahrhunderts. Bibliotheca Germanica Vol. 38. Tübingen: Francke, 1999.

'Die "Gnadenvita" Christine Ebners: Episodenstruktur – Text-Ich und Autorschaft.' *Deutsche Mystik im abendländischen Zusammenhang.* Ed. Walter Haug and Wolfram Schneider-Lastin. Tübingen: Niemeyer, 2000. 483–513.

Bushey, Betty C., and Hartmut Broszinsky. *Die lateinischen Handschriften bis 1600.* Vol. 1: Fol max, Fol und Oct. Bibliographien und Kataloge der Herzogin Anna Amalia Bibliothek zu Weimar. Die lateinischen Handschriften bis 1600 Vol. 1. Wiesbaden: Harrassowitz, 2004.

Bynum, Caroline Walker. 'Women Mystics in the Thirteenth Century: The Case of the Nuns of Helfta.' *Jesus as Mother: Studies in the*

Spirituality of the High Middle Ages. Publications of the Center for Medieval and Renaissance Studies Vol. 16. Berkeley: University of California Press, 1982. 170–261.
Holy Feast and Holy Fast: The Religious Significance of Food to Medieval Women. Berkeley: University of California Press, 1987.
Fragmentation and Redemption: Essays on Gender and the Human Body in Medieval Religion. New York: Zone Books, 1991.
Christian Materiality: An Essay on Religion in Late Medieval Europe. New York: Zone Books, 2011.
'"Crowned with Many Crowns": Nuns and Their Statues in Late Medieval Wienhausen.' *The Catholic Review* 101 (2015): 18–40.

Bysted, Ane. *The Crusade Indulgence: Spiritual Rewards and the Theology of the Crusades, c. 1095–1216.* History of Warfare Vol. 103. Leiden: Brill, 2015.

Campbell, Emma, and Robert Mills. *Rethinking Medieval Translation: Ethics, Politics, Theory.* Cambridge: Brewer, 2012.

Caron, Ann Marie. 'The Continuum of Time and Eternity in the "Liber specialis gratiae" of Mechthild od Hackeborn (1241–99).' *Time and Eternity: The Medieval Discourse.* Ed. Gerhard Jaritz and Gerson Moreno-Riaño. International Medieval Research Vol. 9. Turnhout: Brepols, 2003. 251–69.

Carruthers, Mary. 'Inventional Mnemonics and the Ornaments of Style: The Case of Etymology.' *Connotations* 2 (1992): 103–14.
'Reading with Attitude, Remembering the Book.' *The Book and the Body.* Ed. Katherine O'Brien O'Keeffe and Dolores Warwick Frese. Ward-Phillips Lectures in English Language and Literature Vol. 14. Notre Dame, IN: University of Notre Dame Press, 1997. 1–33.
'Sweetness.' *Speculum* 81 (2006): 999–1013.
Experience of Beauty in the Middle Ages. Oxford-Warburg Studies. Oxford: Oxford University Press, 2013.

Cerquiglini, Bernard. *Éloge de la Variante: Histoire critique de la philologie.* Paris: Seuil, 1989.

Chinca, Mark, Helen Hunter, and Christopher Young. 'The "Kaiserchronik" and its Three Recensions.' *Zeitschrift für deutsches Altertum und deutsche Literatur* 148 (2019): 141–208.

Cohen, Simona. *Transformations of Time and Temporality in Medieval and Renaissance Art.* Leiden: Brill, 2014.

Constable, Giles. 'The ideal of the imitation of Christ.' *Three Studies in Medieval Religious and Social Thought.* Cambridge: Cambridge University Press, 1995. 143–248.

Copeland, Rita. 'Rhetoric and vernacular translation.' *Studies in the Age of Chaucer* 9 (1987): 44–75.
Rhetoric, Hermeneutics, and Translation in the Middle Ages: Academic Traditions and Vernacular Texts. Cambridge: Cambridge University Press, 1991.

Coppack, Glyn. '"Make straight in the desert a highway for our God": The Carthusians and community in late medieval England.' *Monasteries and Society in the British Isles in the Later Middle Ages.* Ed. Janet Burton, and Karen Stöber. Woodbridge: Boydell & Brewer, 2008. 168–79.

Coveney, Dorothy K. *A Descriptive Catalogue of Manuscripts in the Library of University College, London.* London: Printed for University of London, University College, 1935.

Cré, Marleen. *Vernacular Mysticism in the Charterhouse: A Study of London, British Library, MS Additional 37790.* The Medieval Translator Vol. 9. Turnhout: Brepols, 2006.

Curschmann, Michael. 'Hören – Lesen – Sehen: Buch und Schriftlichkeit im Selbstverständnis der volkssprachlichen literarischen Kultur Deutschlands um 1200.' *Beiträge zur Geschichte der deutschen Sprache und Literatur* 106 (1984): 218–57.
'"Pictura laicorum litteratura"? Überlegungen zum Verhältnis von Bild und volksprachlicher Schriftlichkeit im Hoch- und Spätmittelalter bis zum Codex Manesse.' *Pragmatische Schriftlichkeit im Mittelalter: Erscheinungsformen und Entwicklungsstufen.* Ed. Hagen Keller, Klaus Grubmüller, and Nikolaus Staubach. Münstersche Mittelalter-Schriften Vol. 65. Munich: Fink, 1992. 2–11. Repr. *Wort – Bild – Text: Studien zur Medialität des Literarischen in Hochmittelalter und früher Neuzeit.* Vol. 1. Saecula Spiritalia Vol. 43. Baden-Baden: Koerner, 2007. 253–81.

Cyrus, Cynthia J. 'Vernacular and Latinate Literacy in Viennese Women's Convents.' *Nuns' Literacies in Medieval Europe: The Hull Dialogue.* Ed. Virginia Blanton, Veronica O'Mara, and Patricia Stoop. Medieval Women – Texts and Contexts Vol. 26. Turnhout: Brepols, 2013. 119–32.

Dailey, Patricia. *Promised Bodies: Time, Language, & Corporeality in Medieval Women's Mystical Texts, Gender, Theory, and Religion.* New York: Columbia University Press, 2013.

Dal Santo, Matthew. *Debating the Saints' Cults in the Age of Gregory the Great.* Oxford: Oxford University Press, 2012.

Daniel, Natalia. *Die lateinischen mittelalterlichen Handschriften der Universitätsbibliothek München. Die Handschriften aus der Oktavreihe.* Die Handschriften der Universitätsbibliothek München Vol. 4. Wiesbaden: Harrassowitz, 1989.

De Germon, L., and L. Polain. *Catalogue de la bibliothèque de feu M. Le Comte Riant.* Pt. 2 Vol. 1. Paris: Picard, 1899.

DeMaris, Sarah Glenn. 'Anna Muntprat's Legacy for the Zoffingen Sisters: A Second Copy of the Unterlinden Schwesternbuch 1.' *Zeitschrift für deutsches Altertum und deutsche Literatur* 144.3 (2015): 359–78.

De Schryver, Antoine. 'Nicolas Spierinc: Calligraphe et enlumineur des Ordonnances des états de l'hôtel de Charles le Téméraire.' *Scriptorium* 23 (1969): 434–58.

Degering, Hermann. *Kurzes Verzeichnis der germanischen Handschriften der Preußischen Staatsbibliothek.* Vol. III: Die Handschriften in Oktavformat und Register zu Band I–III. Mitteilungen aus der Preußischen Staatsbibliothek Vol. 9. Leipzig: Hiersemann, 1932. Repr. Graz: Akademische Druck- und Verlagsanstalt, 1970.

Derkits, Hans. *Die Lebensbeschreibung der Gertrud von Ortenberg.* Vol. 2: Kommentar. Doctoral dissertation, University of Vienna, 1990.

'Die Vita der Gertrud von Ortenberg – Historische Aspekte eines Gnaden-Lebens.' *Die Ortenau: Veröffentlichungen des Historischen Vereins für Mittelbaden* 71 (1991): 77–125.

Dicke, Gerd, and Klaus Grubmüller, eds. *Die Gleichzeitigkeit von Handschrift und Buchdruck.*

Wolfenbütteler Mittelalter-Studien Vol. 16. Wiesbaden: Harrassowitz, 2003.

Dinzelbacher, Peter. 'Zur Interpretation erlebnismystischer Texte des Mittelalters.' *Zeitschrift für deutsches Altertum und deutsche Literatur* 117 (1988): 1–23.

Dolbeau, François. 'Transformations des prologues hagiographiques, dues aux réécritures.' *L'hagiographie mérovingienne à travers des réécritures.* Ed. Monique Goullet, Martin Heinzelmann, and Christiane Veyrard-Cosme. Beihefte der Francia Vol. 71. Ostfildern: Thorbecke, 2010. 103–24.

Doležalová, Lucie. 'Multilingualism and Late Medieval Manuscript Culture.' *The Medieval Manuscript Book: Cultural Approaches.* Ed. Michael Johnston and Michael Van Dussen. Cambridge Studies in Medieval Literature Vol. 94. Cambridge: Cambridge University Press, 2015. 160–80.

Dombi, Markus. 'Waren die hll. Gertrud und Mechtild Benediktinerinnen oder Cistercienserinnen?' *Cistercienser-Chronik* 25 (1913): 257–68.

Donohue, Alice A. *Greek Sculpture and the Problem of Description.* Cambridge: Cambridge University Press, 2005.

Döring, Thomas. 'Der Leipziger Buchdruck vor der Reformation.' *Bücher, Drucker, Bibliotheken in Mitteldeutschland: Neue Forschungen zur Kommunikations- und Mediengeschichte um 1500.* Ed. Enno Bünz. Leipzig: Leipziger Universitätsverlag, 2006. 87–98.

Dutton, Elisabeth. 'A neglected witness to Chaucer's "Boece" in a medieval devotional commentary on "The Consolation of Philosophy".' *Carmina Philosophiae: Journal of the International Boethius Society* 24 (2015): 1–34.

Dyas, Dee, Valerie Edden, and Roger Ellis. *Approaching Medieval English Anchoritic and Mystical Texts.* Christianity and Culture Vol. 2. Woodbridge: Boydell & Brewer, 2005.

Ehrenschwendtner, Marie-Luise. '"Puellae Litteratae": The Use of the Vernacular in the Dominican Convents of Southern Germany.' *Medieval Women in Their Communities.* Ed.

Diane Watt. Toronto: University of Toronto Press, 1997. 49–71.

Die Bildung der Dominikanerinnen in Süddeutschland vom 13. bis 15. Jahrhundert. Stuttgart: Steiner, 2004.

Eifler, Matthias. 'Bücher in den Händen von Klosterbibliothekaren: Befunde aus dem 15. und frühen 16. Jahrhundert am Beispiel der Kartause und des Benediktinerklosters in Erfurt.' *Manuscripts Changing Hands: Handschriften wechseln von Hand zu Hand.* Ed. Corine Schleifs and Volker Schier. Wolfenbütteler Mittelalter-Studien Vol. 31. Wiesbaden: Harrassowitz, 2016. 207–53.

Die Bibliothek des Erfurter Petersklosters im späten Mittelalter: Buchkultur und Literaturrezeption im Kontext der Bursfelder Klosterreform. 2 Vols. Veröffentlichungen der Historischen Kommission für Thüringen. Kleine Reihe Vol. 51. Cologne: Böhlau, 2017.

'Zur Rezeption von mystischen Viten und Offenbarungen bei den Kartäusern und Benediktinern in Erfurt in der zweiten Hälfte des 15. Jahrhunderts.' *Beihefte zur Zeitschrift für deutsche Philologie* 17 (2019). Special Issue: *Mechthild und das Fließende Licht der Gottheit im Kontext. Eine Spurensuche in religiösen Netzwerken und literarischen Diskursen im mitteldeutschen Raum des 13.–15. Jahrhunderts.* Ed. Caroline Emmelius, and Balázs J. Nemes. 303–36.

Eifler, Matthias, and Betty C. Bushey. *Die lateinischen Handschriften bis 1600.* Vol. 2: Quarthandschriften (Q). Bibliographien und Kataloge der Herzogin Anna Amalia Bibliothek zu Weimar. Die lateinischen Handschriften bis 1600 Vol. 2. Wiesbaden: Harrassowitz, 2012.

Eisermann, Falk. 'Chart B 269.' *Katalog der deutschsprachigen mittelalterlichen Handschriften der Forschungsbibliothek Gotha.* http://bilder.manuscripta-mediaevalia.de/hs//projekt-Gotha-pdfs/Chart_B_269.pdf.

Elliott, Dyan. *Proving Woman: Female Spirituality and Inquisitional Culture in the Later Middle Ages.* Princeton: Princeton University Press, 2004.

'Flesh and Spirit: The Female Body.' *Medieval Holy Women in the Christian Tradition, c. 1100 –*

c. 1500. Ed. Alastair J. Minniss and Rosalynn Voaden. Brepols Essays in European Culture Vol. 1. Turnhout: Brepols, 2010. 13–46.

Elm, Kaspar. 'Frömmigkeit und Ordensleben in deutschen Frauenklöstern des 13. und 14. Jahrhunderts.' *Ons geestelijk erf* 66 (1992): 28–45.

'Monastische Reformen zwischen Humanismus und Reformation.' *900 Jahre Kloster Bursfelde: Reden und Vorträge zum Jubiläum 1993.* Ed. Lothar Perlitt. Göttingen: Vandenhoeck & Ruprecht, 1994. 59–111.

Emmelius, Caroline. 'Verborgene Wahrheiten offenbaren: Verschriftlichungsprozesse in frauenmystischen Texten zwischen Subversion und Autorisierung.' *Offen und Verborgen: Vorstellungen und Praktiken des Öffentlichen im Privaten in Mittelalter und Früher Neuzeit.* Ed. Caroline Emmelius, Fridrun Freise, Rebekka von Mallinkroth, Claudius Sittig, and Regina Töpfer. Göttingen: Wallstein, 2004. 47–65.

'Begnadung und Zweifel: Zur Interaktion von Innen- und Außenraum in den 'Offenbarungen' der Adelheid Langmann.' *Innenräume in der Literatur des deutschen Mittelalters: XIX. Anglo-German Colloquium Oxford 2005.* Ed. Burkhard Hasebrink, Hans-Jochen Schiewer, Almut Suerbaum, and Annette Volfing. Tübingen: Niemeyer Verlag, 2008. 309–25.

Enderwitz, Anne. *Modernist Melancholia: Freud, Conrad and Ford.* New York: Palgrave Macmillan, 2015.

Evans, Ruth. 'The Notion of Vernacular Theory.' *The Idea of The Vernacular: An Anthology of Middle English Literary Theory, 1280–1520.* Ed. Jocelyn Wogan-Browne, Nicholas Watson, Andrew Taylor, and Ruth Evans. University Park, PA: Penn State University Press, 1999. 314–30.

'Vulgar eloquence? Cultural Models and Practices of Translation in Late Medieval Europe.' *Translating Others.* Vol. 2. Ed. Theo Hermans. Manchester: Routledge, 2006. 296–313.

Excoffon, Sylvain, and Coralie Zermatte, eds. *Sammeln, kopieren, verbreiten: Zur Buchkultur der Kartäuser gestern und heute.* Analecta Cartusiana Vol. 337. Louvain-La-Neuve: i6doc.com, 2019.

Falque, Ingrid. '"Daz man bild mit bilde us tribe": Imagery and Knowledge of God in Henry Suso's Exemplar.' *Speculum* 92.2 (2017): 447–92.

Fasching, Richard F. '"aber so soll man die bilde schiere lossen varn": Zum Konzept der 'Bildlosigkeit' bei Johannes Tauler.' *Die Predigt im Mittelalter zwischen Mündlichkeit, Bildlichkeit und Schriftlichkeit – La prédication au Moyen Age entre oralité, visualité et écriture.* Ed. René Wetzel and Fabrice Flückiger. Medienwandel – Medienwechsel – Medienwissen Vol. 13. Zurich: Chronos, 2010. 397–410.

Die 'Vierzig Myrrhenbüschel vom Leiden Christi': Untersuchungen, Überlieferung und Edition. Scrinium Friburgense. Berlin: De Gruyter, 2020.

Fechter, Werner. *Deutsche Handschriften des 15. und 16. Jahrhunderts aus der Bibliothek des ehemaligen Augustinerchorfrauenstifts Inzigkofen.* Arbeiten zur Landeskunde Hohenzollerns Vol. 15. Sigmaringen: Thorbecke, 1997.

Federer, Urban. *Mystische Erfahrung im Literarischen Dialog: Die Briefe Heinrichs von Nördlingen an Margaretha Ebner.* Scrinium Friburgense Vol. 25. Berlin: De Gruyter, 2011.

Fibla, Sergi Sancho. 'Colors and Books in Marguerite d'Oingt's 'Speculum': Mnemonic Images for Meditation and Vision.' *Commitments to Medieval Mysticism within Contemporary Contexts.* Ed. Patrick Cooper and Satoshi Kikuchi. Bibliotheca Ephemeridum Theologicarum Lovaniensium Vol. 290. Leuven: Peeters, 2017. 255–71.

Escribir y meditar: La obra de Marguerite d'Oingt, cartuja del siglo XIII. El árbol Del Paraíso Vol. 93. Madrid: Siruela, 2018. 144–82.

Finger, Heinz. *Handschriftencensus Rheinland. Erfassung mittelalterlicher Handschriften im rheinischen Landesteil von Nordrhein-Westfalen mit einem Inventar.* Vol. 1: Aachen (Diözesanarchiv) bis Köln (Diözesan- und Dombibliothek) (Nr 1–1327). Schriften der Universitäts- und Landesbibliothek Düsseldorf Vol. 18. Wiesbaden: Reichert, 1993.

Finnegan, Mary Jeremy. *The Women of Helfta: Scholars and Mystics.* Athens, GA: University of Georgia Press, 1991.

Fleith, Barbara. '"Remotus a tumultu civitatis?" Die Johanniterkommende "zum Grünen Wörth" im 15. Jahrhundert.' *Literaturbetrieb im spätmittelalterlichen Straßburg.* Ed. Felix Heinzer, Stephen Mossman, and Nigel F. Palmer. Kulturtopographie des alemannischen Raums Vol. 3. Berlin: De Gruyter, 2012. 411–65.

Florea, Luminita. 'Synaesthesia and Textile Analogies in Fourteenth-Century Music Theory.' *Viator* 41 (2010): 317–33.

Fludernik, Monika. 'Second-Person Narrative as a Text Case of Narratology: The Limits of Realism.' *Style* 28.3 (1994): 445–79. Repr. *Narrative Theory: Critical Concepts in Literary and Cultural Studies.* Vol. 2. Ed. Mieke Bal. London: Routledge, 2004. 19–55.

Flury, Theres, et al. eds. *Frauen im Galluskloster: Katalog zur Ausstellung in der Stiftsbibliothek St. Gallen (20. März–12. November 2006).* St. Gallen: Verlag am Klosterhof, 2006.

Forman, Mary. 'Garments of Salvation on the Feast of the Purification in Gertrud's Legatus II. 16.' *Magistra* 16.2 (2010): 62–76.

Fort, Gavin. 'Suffering Another's Sin: Proxy Penance in the Thirteenth Century.' *Journal of Medieval History* 44 (2018): 202–30.

Foucault, Michel. 'Qu'est-ce qu'un auteur?' *Dits et écrits.* Vol. 1: 1954–1975. Ed. Daniel Defert and François Ewald. Paris: Gallimard, 1994: Repr. 2008. 817–49.

Fromm, Hans. 'Volkssprache und Schriftkultur.' *The Role of the Book in Medieval Culture: Proceedings of the Oxford International Symposium. 26 September–1 October 1982.* Vol. 1. Ed. Peter Ganz. Bibliologia Vol. 3–4. Turnhout: Brepols, 1986. 99–108.

Fuhrmann, Daniela. *Konfigurationen der Zeit: Dominikanerinnenviten des späten Mittelalters.* Philologie der Kultur. Vol. 12. Würzburg: Königshausen & Neumann, 2015.

Fuhrmann, Hans. 'Three Angels? The Abraham Tapestry or the Tapestry of the Angels in

Halberstadt Cathedral: The Correlation between Text and Image.' *Iconography of Liturgical Textiles in the Middle Ages*. Ed. Evelin Wetter. Riggisberger Berichte Vol. 18. Riggisberg: Abegg-Stiftung, 2010. 63–78.

Gage, John. *Color and Meaning: Art, Science, and Symbolism*. Berkeley: University of California Press, 1999.

Ganz, David. 'Das Kleid der Bücher: Vestimentäre Dimensionen mittelalterlicher Prachteinbände.' *Clothing the Sacred: Medieval Textiles as Fabric, Form, and Metaphor*. Ed. Mateusz Kaputska, and Warren T. Woodfin. Textile Studies Vol. 8. Emsdetten: Édition Imorde, 2015. 121–46.

Garay, Kathleen E. '"A Naked Intent unto God": Ungendered Discourse in some Late Medieval Mystical Texts.' *Mystics Quarterly* 23 (1997): 36–51.

Garber, Rebecca L. R. *Feminine Figurae: Representations of Gender in Religious Texts by Medieval German Women Writers, 1100–1375*. Studies in Medieval History and Culture Vol. 10. New York: Routledge 2003.

Gatty, Fiona K. A. *Ideal Beauty in Late Eighteenth- and Early Nineteenth-Century French Art and Art Criticism with Special Reference to the Role of Drapery and Costume*. Doctoral dissertation, University of Oxford, 2014.

Geiß, Jürgen. *Katalog der mittelalterlichen Handschriften der Universitäts- und Landesbibliothek Bonn*. Berlin: De Gruyter, 2015.

Gildemeister, Johann, Anton Klette, and Joseph Staender. *Chirographorvm in Bibliotheca Academica Bonnensi servatorvm catalogvs*. Vol. 2: Quo libri descripti svnt praeter orientales relicvi. Bonn: Weber, 1858–76.

Goerlitz, Uta. 'Mittelalterliche Literatur im Medienwandel von der Handschrift zum gedruckten Buch: Das Beispiel des "Herzog Ernst".' *Das Mittelalter* 22 (2017): 13–38.

Goullet, Monique, ed. 'Vers une typologie des réécritures hagiographiques, à partir de quelques exemples du Nord-Est de la France: Avec une édition synoptiquedes deux Vies de Saint Èvre de Toul.' *La réécriture hagiographique dans l'occident médiéval: Transformations formelles et idéologiques*. Beihefte der Francia Vol. 58. Ostfildern: Thorbecke, 2003. 109–44.

Goullet, Monique, and Martin Heinzelmann, eds. 'Avant-propos.' *La réécriture hagiographique dans l'occident médiéval: Transformations formelles et idéologiques*. Beihefte der Francia Vol. 58. Ostfildern: Thorbecke, 2003. 7–15.

Graf, Klaus. 'Ordensreform und Literatur in Augsburg während des 15. Jahrhunderts.' *Literarisches Leben in Augsburg während des 15. Jahrhunderts*. Ed. Johannes Janota, and Werner Williams-Krapp. Studia Augustana Vol. 7. Tübingen: Niemeyer, 1995. 100–59.

Green, Dennis Howard. *Women Readers in the Middle Ages*. Cambridge Studies in Medieval Literature Vol. 65. Cambridge: Cambridge University Press, 2007.

Griffiths, Fiona J. *Nuns' Priests' Tales: Men and Salvation in Medieval Women's Monastic Life*. Philadelphia: University of Pennsylvania Press, 2018.

Griffiths, Fiona J., and Julie Hotchin, eds. 'Women and Men in the Medieval Religious Landscape.' *Partners in Spirit: Women, Men, and Religious Life in Germany, 1100–1500*. Medieval Women: Texts and Contexts Vol. 24 Turnhout: Brepols, 2014.

Grimes, Laura Maria. *Wisdom's Friends: Gertrud of Helfta's Conversational Theology*. Saarbrücken: VDM Verlag, 2009.

'Gender and Confession: Guibert of Nogent and Gertrud of Helfta as Readers of Augustine.' *Magistra* 18.2 (2012): 3–19.

Grubmüller, Klaus. 'Die Viten der Schwestern von Töß und Elsbeth Stagel (Überlieferung und Literarische Einheit).' *Zeitschrift für deutsches Altertum und deutsche Literatur* 98 (1969): 171–204.

'Gertrud von Helfta.' *Die deutsche Literatur des Mittelalters: Verfasserlexikon: Begründet von Wolfgang Stammler, fortgeführt von Karl Langosch*. Vol. 3. Ed. Kurt Ruh and Burghart Wachinger. 2nd edition. Berlin: De Gruyter, 1981. 7–10.

'Verändern und Bewahren: Zum Bewußtsein vom Text im deutschen Mittelalter.' *Text und Kultur: Mittelalterliche Literatur 1100–1450*. Germanistische Symposien Berichtsbände 22.

Ed. Ursula Peters. Stuttgart, Weimar: J.B. Metzler'sche Verlagsbuchhandlung und Carl Ernst Poeschel Verlag GmbH, 2001. 8–33.

Gumbrecht, Hans Ulrich, and Karl Ludwig Pfeiffe. *Materialität der Kommunikation.* Suhrkamp-Taschenbuch Wissenschaft Vol. 750. Frankfurt a.M: Suhrkamp, 1988.

Gussone, Nikolaus. 'Die Jungfrauenweihe in ottonischer Zeit nach dem Ritus im 'Pontificale Romano-Germanicum'.' *Frauen, Kloster, Kunst: Neue Forschungen zur Kulturgeschichte des Mittelalters: Beiträge zum internationalen Kolloquium vom 13. bis 16. Mai 2005 anlässlich der Ausstellung 'Krone und Schleier.'* Ed. Jeffrey F. Hamburger and Carola Jäggi. Turnhout: Brepols, 2007. 25–42.

Haas, Alois Maria. 'Mechthild von Magdeburg.' *Sermo mysticus: Studien zu Theologie und Sprache der deutschen Mystik.* Dokimion Vol. 4. Fribourg: Universitätsverlag, 1979. 67–135.

Haase, Albert. *Bonaventure's 'Legenda maior': A Redaction Critical Approach.* Doctoral dissertation, New York, Fordham University, 1990.

Hadot, Pierre. 'Apophatisme et théologie négative.' *Exercices spirituels et philosophie antique.* Ed. Pierre Hadot. Paris: Études augustiniennes, 1981. 185–93.

Hagenmaier, Winfried. *Die deutschen mittelalterlichen Handschriften der Universitätsbibliothek und die mittelalterlichen Handschriften anderer öffentlicher Sammlungen. Kataloge der Universitätsbibliothek Freiburg im Breisgau.* Vol. 1: Die Handschriften der Universitätsbibliothek und anderer öffentlicher Sammlungen in Freiburg im Breisgau und Umgebung Pt. 4. Wiesbaden: Harrassowitz, 1988.

Die abendländischen neuzeitlichen Handschriften der Universitätsbibliothek Freiburg im Breisgau, Kataloge der Universitätsbibliothek Freiburg im Breisgau Vol. 1 Pt. 5. Wiesbaden: Harrassowitz, 1996.

Halligan, Theresa A., ed. *Mechthild of Hackeborn: The Booke of Gostlye Grace by Mechtild of Hackeborn.* Studies and Texts Vol. 46. Toronto: Pontifical Institute of Mediaeval Studies, 1979.

Halm, Karl Felix, Georg von Laubmann, Wilhelm Meyer, and Johann Andreas Schmeller. *Catalogus codicum latinorum Bibliothecae Regiae Monacensis.* Vol. 2 Pt. 3: Codices num. 15121–21313 complectens. Catalogus codicum manu scriptorum Bibliothecae Regiae Monacensis Vol. 4 Pt. 3: Codices latinos continens. Munich: Bayerische Staatsbibliothek, 1878.

Hamburger, Jeffrey F. 'A 'Liber precum' in Sélestat and the Development of the Illustrated Prayer Book in Germany.' *Art Bulletin* 73 (1991): 209–36.

Nuns as Artists: The Visual Culture of a Medieval Convent. Berkeley: University of California Press, 1997.

The Visual and the Visionary: Art and Female Spirituality in Late Medieval Germany. New York: Zone Books, 1998.

'A Plenitude of Pictures: A Picture Book from Late Fourteenth-Century Strasbourg.' *The Prayer Book of Ursula Begerin.* Vol. 1. Ed. Jeffrey F. Hamburger and Nigel F. Palmer. Dietikon-Zürich: Graf, 2015. 15–110.

Hamburger, Jeffrey F., and Eva Schlotheuber. 'Books in Women's Hands: Liturgy, Learning, and the Libraries of Dominican Nuns is Westphalia.' *Entre stabilité et itinérance: livres et culture des orders mendicants XIIIe–XVe siècle.* Ed. Nicole Bériou, Marin Morard, and Donatella Nebbiai. Turnhout: Brepols, 2014. 129–57.

Hamburger, Jeffrey F., Eva Schlotheuber, Susan Marti, and Margot Fassler. *Liturgical Life and Latin Learning at Paradies bei Soest, 1300–1425: Inscription and Illumination in the Choir Books of a North German Dominican Convent.* Vol. 1. Münster: Aschendorff, 2016.

Hamilton, Sarah. *The Practice of Penance, 900–1050.* Royal Historical Society Studies in History: New Series. Woodbridge: Boydell Press, 2001.

Hammond, Jay M. 'Bonaventure's "Legenda Major".' *A Companion to Bonaventure.* Ed. Jay M. Hammond, Jared Goff, and Wayne Hellmann. Leiden: Brill, 2013. 453–507.

Hanna, Ralph. 'Middle English Manuscripts and the Study of Literature.' *New Medieval*

Literatures Vol. 4. Ed. Wendy Scase, Rita Copeland and David Lawton. Oxford: Oxford University Press, 2001. 243–64.

Harloe, Katherine. *Winckelmann and the Invention of Antiquity*. Oxford: Oxford University Press, 2013.

Harrison, Anna. '"Oh! What Treasure Is In This Book?" Writing, Reading, and Community at the Monastery of Helfta.' *Viator* 39 (2008): 75–106.

———. '"I Am Wholly Your Own": Liturgical Piety and Community among the Nuns of Helfta.' *Church History* 78 (2009): 549–83.

Hasebrink, Burkhard. 'Grenzverschiebung: Zu Kongruenz und Differenz von Latein und Deutsch bei Meister Eckhart.' *Zeitschrift für deutsches Altertum und deutsche Literatur* 121 (1992): 369–98.

———. '"Das fließende Licht der Gottheit" Mechthilds von Magdeburg: Eine Skizze.' *Bete und Arbeite! Zisterzienser in der Grafschaft Mansfeld: Begleitband zur Ausstellung im Sterbehaus Martin Luthers in Eisleben, 24.10.1998 – 24.6.1999*. Ed. Esther Pia Wipfler, Rose-Marie Knape, and Stiftung Luthergedenkstätten in Sachsen-Anhalt. Halle (Saale): Stekovics, 1998. 149–61.

Hasebrink, Burkhard, and Peter Strohschneider. 'Religiöse Schriftkultur und säkulare Textwissenschaft: Germanistische Mediävistik in postsäkularem Kontext.' *Poetica* 46 (2014): 277–92.

Haug, Walter. *Literaturtheorie im deutschen Mittelalter: Von den Anfängen bis zum Ende des 13. Jahrhunderts*. 2nd edition. Darmstadt: Wissenschaftliche Buchgesellschaft, 1992.

Hedlund, Monica. 'Nuns and Latin, with Special Reference to the Brigittines of Vadstena.' *Nuns' Literacies in Medieval Europe: The Hull Dialogue*. Ed. Virginia Blanton, Veronica O'Mara, and Patricia Stoop. Medieval Women – Texts and Contexts Vol. 26. Turnhout: Brepols, 2013. 97–118.

Heinzer, Felix. *Aus Handschriften und Inkunabeln der Historischen Lehrerbibliothek des Ludwig-Wilhelm-Gymnasiums*. Vortragsreihe der Historischen Lehrerbibliothek des Ludwig-Wilhelm-Gymnasiums in Rastatt Vol. 1. Rastatt: Stadtverwaltung Rastatt, 1989.

Heinzer, Felix, and Gerhard Stamm. *Die Handschriften von Lichtenthal: Mit einem Anhang: Die heute noch im Kloster Lichtenthal befindlichen Handschriften des 12. bis 16. Jahrhunderts*. Die Handschriften der Badischen Landesbibliothek in Karlsruhe Vol. 9. Wiesbaden: Harrassowitz, 1987.

Heitzmann, Christian. 'Die mittelalterlichen Handschriften der Leopold-Sophien-Bibliothek in Überlingen.' *Schriften des Vereins für Geschichte des Bodensees und seiner Umgebung* 120 (2002): 41–103.

Hellgardt, Ernst. 'Das "Fließende Licht der Gottheit": Mechthild von Magdeburg und ihr Buch.' *Literatur in der Stadt: Magdeburg in Mittelalter und Früher Neuzeit*. Ed. Michael Schilling. Beihefte zum Euphorion Vol. 70. Heidelberg: Winter, 2012. 97–119.

———. 'Latin and the Vernacular: Mechthild of Magdeburg–Mechthild of Hackeborn–Gertrude of Helfta.' *A Companion to Mysticism and Devotion in Northern Germany in the Late Middle Ages*. Ed. Anne Simon, Elizabeth A. Andersen, and Henrike Lähnemann. Brill's Companions to the Christian Tradition Vol. 44. Leiden: Brill, 2014. 131–55.

Hilgert, Markus. 'Text-Anthropologie: Die Erforschung von Materialität und Präsenz des Geschriebenen als hermeneutische Strategie.' *Mitteilungen der Deutschen Orient-Gesellschaft* 142. Special Issue: *Altorientalistik im 21. Jahrhundert: Selbstverständnis, Herausforderungen, Ziele* (2010): 85–124.

Hillenbrand, Eugen. 'Heiligenleben und Alltag: Offenburger Stadtgeschichte im Spiegel eines spätmittelalterlichen Beginenlebens.' *Die Ortenau* 90 (2010): 157–76.

Hirsch, Gabriele, ed. *Die Legende der Heiligen Trutta*. Doctoral dissertation, University of Graz, 1921.

Höcherl, Josef. *Das Rebdorfer Anniversar*. Rebdorf: Kloster Rebdorf, 1995.

Hofenk de Graaff, Judith H. *The Colourful Past: Origins, Chemistry and Identification of Natural Dyestuffs*. Riggisberg: Abegg-Stiftung, 2004.

Hoffmann, Werner J. 'Mscr.Dresd.M.243.' *Tiefenerschließung und Digitalisierung der deutschsprachigen mittelalterlichen Handschriften der Sächsischen Landesbibliothek, Staats- und Universitätsbibliothek (SLUB) Dresden.* www.manuscripta-mediaevalia.de/dokumente/html/obj31600080.

Hollywood, Amy. *The Soul as Virgin Wife: Mechthild of Magdeburg, Marguerite Porete, and Meister Eckhart.* Notre Dame Studies in Spirituality and Theology Vol. 1. Notre Dame, IN: University of Notre Dame Press, 1995.

Sensible Ecstasy: Mysticism, Sexual Difference and the Demands of History. Chicago: University of Chicago Press, 2002.

Holsinger, Bruce. *Music, Body, and Desire in Medieval Culture: Hildegard of Bingen to Chaucer.* Stanford: Stanford University Press, 2001.

Holt, Ian. *Solothurn, Zentralbibliothek, Cod. S 458.* Solothurn: Zentralbibliothek Solothurn, 2009. www.e-codices.unifr.ch/en/description/zbs/S-0458/.

Holtzhauer, Sebastian *Die Fahrt eines Heiligen durch Zeit und Raum: Untersuchungen ausgewählter Retextualisierungen des Brandan-Corpus von den Anfängen bis zum 15. Jahrhundert: Mit einer Edition der Münchener Prosafassung der Reise des hl. Brandan (Pm).* Göttingen: V & R Unipress, 2019.

Honemann, Volker. *Deutsche Literatur in der Laienbibliothek der Basler Kartause 1480–1520.* Habilitationsschrift, Freie Universität Berlin, 1982.

'Predigt und geistliches Schrifttum im Leipziger Dominikanerkloster um 1500.' *Johann Tetzel und der Ablass: Begleitband zur Ausstellung 'Tetzel – Ablass – Fegefeuer' in Mönchenkloster und Nikolaikirche Jüterbo.* Ed. Enno Bünz, Hartmut Kühne, and Peter Wiegand. Berlin: Lukas, 2017. 161–77.

'Sächsische Fürstinnen, Patrizier, Kleriker, Kaufleute und der Dominikaner Marcus von Weida als Förderer geistlicher Literatur um 1500.' *Bürgers Bücher: Laien als Anreger und Adressaten in Sachsens Literatur um 1500.* Ed. Christoph Fasbender and Gesine Mierke. Würzburg: Königshausen & Neuman, 2017. 130–59.

Hopf, Michael, *Mystische Kurzdialoge um Meister Eckhart: Editionen und Untersuchungen.* Meister-Eckhart-Jahrbuch. Beiheft 6. Stuttgart: Verlag W. Kohlhammer, 2019, 41. 47–48.

Horninger, Heidelinde, and Franz Lackner. *Die datierten Handschriften in Wien außerhalb der Österreichischen Nationalbibliothek bis zum Jahre 1600.* Vol. 1. Katalog der datierten Handschriften in lateinischer Schrift in Österreich. Vienna: Verlag der Österreichischen Akademie der Wissenschaften, 1981.

Hotchkiss, Valerie R. *Clothes Make the Man: Female Cross Dressing in Medieval Europe.* Florence: Routledge, 1996.

Huber, Christoph. *Die Aufnahme und Verarbeitung des Alanus ab Insulis in mittelhochdeutschen Dichtungen: Untersuchungen zu Thomasin von Zerklære, Gottfried von Straßburg, Frauenlob, Heinrich von Neustadt, Heinrich von St. Gallen, Heinrich von Mügeln und Johannes von Tepl.* Münchener Texte und Untersuchungen zur deutschen Literatur des Mittelalters Vol. 89. Munich: Artemis, 1988. 386–402.

Hubrath, Margarete. 'The "Liber specialis gratiae" as a Collective Work of Several Nuns.' *Jahrbuch der Oswald von Wolkenstein-Gesellschaft* 11 (1999): 233–44.

Huizinga, Johan. *Über die Verknüpfung des poetischen mit dem theologischen bei Alanus de Insulis.* Koninklijke Nederlandse Akademie van Wetenschappen. Afd. Letterkunde. Medeleelingen; deel 74, ser. B., no. 6. Y. Amsterdam: Noord-Hollandsche uitgevers-maatschappij, 1932.

Jager, Eric. *The Book of the Heart.* Chicago: University of Chicago Press, 2000.

Janota, Johannes. 'Mittelalterliche Texte als Entstehungsvarianten.' *In Spuren gesehen. . .: Festschrift Helmut Koopmann.* Ed. Andrea Bartl, Jürgen Eder, Harry Fröhlich, Klaus Dieter Post, and Ursula Regener. Tübingen: Niemeyer 1998. 65–80.

Jansen, Sabine. *Die Texte des Kirchberg-Corpus': Überlieferung und Textgeschichte vom 15. bis zum 19. Jahrhundert.* Doctoral dissertation, University of Cologne, 2005.

Jantzen, Grace M. *Power, Gender and Christian Mysticism.* Cambridge Studies in Ideology and Religion Vol. 8. Cambridge: Cambridge University Press, 1995.

Javelet, Robert. *Image et ressemblance au XIIe siècle: de saint Anselme à Allain de Lille.* Vol. 1. Paris: Letouzey et Ané, 1967.

Jenkins, Eve. 'St. Gertrude's Synecdoche: The Problem of Writing the Sacred Heart.' *Essays in Medieval Studies* 14 (1997): 29–37.

Johnson, Eleanor. *Staging Contemplation: Participatory Theology in Middle English Prose, Verse, and Drama.* Chicago: University of Chicago Press, 2018.

Johnson, Ella. 'Bodily Language in the Spiritual Exercises of Gertrude the Great of Helfta.' *Magistra* 14.1 (2008): 79–107.

'To Taste ("Sapere") Wisdom ("Sapientia"): Eucharistic Devotion in the Writings of Gertrude of Helfta.' *Viator* 44 (2013): 175–99.

This Is My Body: Eucharistic Theology and Anthropology in the Writings of Gertrude the Great of Helfta. Cistercian Studies Vol. 280. Collegeville, MN: Liturgical Press, 2020.

Johnston, Michael, and Michael Van Dussen, eds. 'Introduction: Manuscripts and Cultural History.' *The Medieval Manuscript Book: Cultural Approaches.* Cambridge Studies in Medieval Literature Vol. 94. Cambridge: Cambridge University Press, 2015. 1–16.

Johnson, Timothy J. 'The Legenda Minor.' *A Companion to Bonaventure.* Ed. Jay M. Hammond, Jared Goff, and Wayne Hellmann. Leiden: Brill, 2013. 435–52.

Jones, Claire Taylor. 'Rekindling the Light of Faith: Hymn Translation and Spiritual Renewal in the Fifteenth-Century Observant Reform.' *Journal of Medieval and Early Modern Studies* 42 (2012): 567–96.

'"Hostia jubilationis": Psalm Citation, Eucharistic Prayer, and Mystical Union in Gertrude of Helfta's "Exercitia spiritualia".' *Speculum* 89 (2014): 1005–39.

'"Hostia jubilationis": *Ruling the Spirit: Women, Liturgy, and Dominican Reform in Late Medieval Germany.* Philadelphia: University of Pennsylvania Press, 2017.

Jørgensen, Hans Henrik Lohfert. 'Prostheses of Pious Preception: On the Instrumentalization and Mediation of the Medieval Sensorium.' *The Materiality of Devotion in Late Medieval Northern Europe: Images, Objects, Practices.* Ed. Henning Laugerud, Salvador Ryan, and Laura Katrine Skinnebach. European Network on the Instruments of Devotion Vol. 3. Dublin: Four Courts Press, 2016. 146–67.

Juntke, Fritz. 'Die Inkunabeln der St. Andreaskirche zu Eisleben.' *Beiträge zur Inkunabelkunde* III. Folge Vol. 8 (1983): 50–68.

Jütte, Robert. *Geschichte der Sinne: Von der Antike bis zum Cyberspace.* Munich: Beck, 2000.

Kaputska, Mateusz, and Warren T. Woodfin, eds. 'Clothing the Sacred: An Introduction.' *Clothing the Sacred: Medieval Textiles as Fabric, Form, and Metaphor.* Textile Studies Vol. 8. Emsdetten: Édition Imorde, 2015. 7–11.

Karnes, Michelle. *Imagination, Meditation, and Cognition in the Middle Ages.* Chicago: University of Chicago Press, 2011.

Karras, Ruth Mazo. *Sexuality in Medieval Europe: Doing unto Others.* 2nd edition. Abingdon: Routledge, 2012.

Kehnel, Annette, and Diamantis Panagiotopoulos, eds. *Schriftträger – Textträger: Zur materialen Präsenz des Geschriebenen in frühen Gesellschaften.* Materiale Textkulturen Vol. 6. Berlin: De Gruyter, 2015.

Keller, Hildegard Elisabeth. 'Rosen-Metamorphosen: Von unfesten Zeichen in spätmittelalterlichen Texten: Heinrich Seuses 'Exemplar' und das Mirakel 'Marien-Rosenkranz'.' *Der Rosenkranz: Andacht, Geschichte, Kunst.* Ed. Urs-Beat Frei and Fredy Bühler. Bern: Benteli, 2003. 48–67.

Keller, Hagen, Klaus Grubmüller, and Nikolaus Staubach, eds. *Pragmatische Schriftlichkeit im Mittelalter: Erscheinungsformen und Entwicklungsstufen.* Münstersche Mittelalter-Schriften Vol. 65. Munich: Fink, 1992.

Kellner, Beate. 'Allegorien der Natur bei Alanus ab Insulis – mit einem Ausblick auf die volkssprachliche Rezeption.' *Schriftsinn und Epochalität: Zur historischen Prägnanz allegorischer und symbolischer Sinnstiftung.* Ed. Bernhard Huss, and David Nelting. Germanisch-romanische

Monatsschrift. Beihefte Vol. 81. Heidelberg: Winter, 2017. 113–43.

Spiel der Liebe im Minnesang. Munich: Fink, 2018.

Kelly, Stephen, and John J. Thompson. 'Imagined Histories of the Book: Current Paradigms and Future Directions.' *Imagining the Book.* Ed. Stephen Kelly and John J. Thompson. Medieval Texts and Cultures of Northern Europe Vol. 7. Turnhout: Brepols, 2005. 1–14.

Kern, Anton. *Die Handschriften der Universitätsbibliothek Graz.* Vol. 1. Verzeichnis der Handschriften im deutschen Reich Vol. 2. Leipzig: Harrassowitz, 1942.

Kern, Anton, and Maria Mairhold. *Die Handschriften der Universitätsbibliothek der Graz.* Vol. 3. Handschriftenverzeichnisse Österreichischer Bibliotheken. Steiermark Vol. 3. Vienna: Prachner, 1967.

Kern, Udo. '"Der Mensch sollte werden ein Gott Suchender." Zum Verständnis des Menschen in Eckharts "Rede der underscheidunge".' *Meister Eckhart in Erfurt.* Ed. Andreas Speer and Lydia Wegener. Miscellanea Mediaevalia Vol. 32. Berlin: De Gruyter, 2005. 146–77.

Kessler, Herbert L. 'Through the Temple Veil: The Holy Image in Judaism and Christianity.' *Kairos* 32–33 (1990–1991): 53–77.

Keuffer, Max. *Beschreibendes Verzeichnis der Handschriften der Stadtbibliothek zu Trier.* Vol. 1: Bibel-Texte und Kommentare. Trier: Kommissionsverlag der Fr. Lintz'schen Buchhandlung, 1888.

Keul, Hildegund, and Siegfried Ringler. 'In der Freiheit des lebendigen Geistes: Helfta als geohistorischer Ort der deutschen Mystik.' *Aufbruch zu neuer Gottesrede: Die Mystik der Gertrud von Helfta.* Ed. Siegfried Ringler. Ostfildern: Grünewald, 2008. 21–35.

Kieckhefer, Richard. *Unquiet Souls: Fourteenth-century Saints and Their Religious Milieu.* Chicago: University of Chicago Press, 1984.

Kiening, Christian. *Zwischen Körper und Schrift: Texte vor dem Zeitalter der Literatur.* Frankfurt a. M.: Fischer Taschenbuch Verlag, 2003.

Mystische Bücher. Mediävistische Perspektiven Vol. 2. Zurich: Chronos, 2011.

Kirakosian, Racha. 'Watermarks and Watersheds: The Dating of Ms. Riant 80 and the Overlapping Production of Manuscripts and Printed Books.' *Harvard Library Bulletin* 25 (2014): 108–19.

'Das göttliche Herz im 'Fließenden Licht der Gottheit' Mechthilds von Magdeburg: Eine motivgeschichtliche Verortung.' *Euphorion* 111 (2017): 257–75.

Die Vita der Christina von Hane: Untersuchung und Edition. Hermaea. Neue Folge Vol. 144. Berlin: De Gruyter, 2017.

'Musical Heaven and Heavenly Music: At the Crossroads of Liturgical Music and Mystical Texts.' *Viator* 48 (2017): 121–44.

'Penitential Punishment and Purgatory: A Drama of Purification through Pain.' *Punishment and Penitential Practices in Medieval German Writing.* Ed. Sarah Bowden, and Annette Volfing. King's College London Medieval Studies Vol. 26. London: Boydell & Brewer, 2018. 129–54.

'The Earliest Transmitted German Legatus: Gotha, Forschungsbibliothek, Chart. B 269.' *Analecta Cisterciensa* 69 (2019): 178–97.

'"Wie man got verwunden sol mit einem ougen": Zur passionsmystischen Buchschriftlichkeit und Liebesverwundung durch das Auge im "botten der götlichen miltekeit".' *Verletzungen und Unversehrtheit in der deutschen Literatur des Mittelalters. XXIV. Anglo-German Colloquium.* Ed. Nine Miedema, Stephen Mossman, and Sara Bowden. Tübingen: Francke, 2020. 83–96.

'Intertextuelle Textilien: Imaginäre Kleider und Temporalität bei Alanus ab Insulis und Gertrud von Helfta.' *Beiträge zur Geschichte der deutschen Sprache und Literatur* 142.2 (2020): 236–66.

Klack-Eitzen, Charlotte. 'Die Heiligen Röcke in Kloster Wienhausen.' *Heilige Röcke: Kleider für Skulpturen in Kloster Wienhausen.* Regensburg: Schnell & Steiner, 2013. 26–47.

'Skulpturenkleider in Norddeutschland.' *Heilige Röcke: Kleider für Skulpturen in Kloster Wienhausen.* Regensburg: Schnell & Steiner, 2013. 15–25.

Klack-Eitzen, Charlotte, Wiebke Haase, and Tanja Weißgraf, eds. *Heilige Röcke: Kleider für Skulpturen in Kloster Wienhausen*. Regensburg: Schnell & Steiner, 2013.

Klapper, Joseph. 'Breslau, Diözesanarchiv, o. Sign. [9].' www.bbaw.de/forschung/dtm/HSA/breslau_700292490000.html.

Knapp, Fritz Peter. *Die Literatur des Spätmittelalters in den Ländern Österreich, Steiermark, Kärnten, Salzburg und Tirol von 1273 bis 1439*. Vol. 2: Die Literatur zur Zeit der habsburgischen Herzöge von Rudolf IV. bis Albrecht V. (1358–1439). Geschichte der Literatur in Österreich Vol. 2. Graz: Akademische Druck- u. Verlagstanstalt, 2004.

Knappett, Carl. *Thinking through Material Culture: An Interdisciplinary Perspective*. Philadelphia: University of Pennsylvania Press, 2015.

Knippenberg, Carla Dauven-van, Cornelia Herberichs, and Christian Kiening, eds. *Medialität des Heils im späten Mittelalter*. Medienwandel, Medienwechsel, Medienwissen Vol. 10. Zurich: Chronos, 2009.

Köbele, Susanne. *Bilder der unbegriffenen Wahrheit: Zur Struktur mystischer Rede im Spannungsfeld von Latein und Volkssprache*. Bibliotheca Germanica Vol. 30. Tübingen: Francke, 1993.

'"Primo aspectu monstruosa." Schriftauslegung bei Meister Eckhart.' *Zeitschrift für deutsches Altertum und deutsche Literatur* 122 (1993): 62–81.

Kofler, Walther. 'Zu den Handschriftenverhältnissen des "Nibelungenliedes": Die Verbindungen zwischen den Redaktionen I, d, n und k.' *Zeitschrift für deutsche Philologie* 130 (2011): 51–82.

Köhler, Jakob. 'Die Handschriften und Inkunabelndrucke der Rastatter Gymnasiumsbibliothek.' *Großherzogliches Gymnasium Rastatt. Jahresbericht für das Schuljahr 1885–1886*. Rastatt: Vogelin, 1886.

Köhler, Johannes B., ed. and trans. *Alain de Lille: Die Klage der Natur. Lateinischer Text, Übersetzung und philologisch-philosophiegeschichtlicher Kommentar = Alani ab Insulis. De planctu naturae. textus, translatio una cum annotationibus*. Texte und Studien zur europäischen Geistesgeschichte. Series A Vol. 2. Münster: Aschendorff, 2013.

Köhler, Mathias. *Kloster Helfta: Zisterzienserinnenpriorat St Marien*. Kleine Kunstführer Vol. 2219. Regensburg: Schnell & Steiner, 2013.

Kohwagner-Nikolai, Tanja. *'per manus sororum. . .': Niedersächsische Bildstickereien im Klosterstich, 1300–1583*. Munich: Meidenbauer, 2006.

'Patrons, Saints and Benefactresses: The Use of Tapestries to Create Corporate Identity in Late Medieval Nunneries.' *Iconography of Liturgical Textiles in the Middle Ages*. Ed. Evelin Wetter. Riggisberger Berichte Vol. 18. Riggisberg: Abegg-Stiftung, 2010. 141–52.

Mittelalterliche Textilien. Vol. 3: Stickerei bis um 1500 und figürlich gewebte Borten. Ed. Evelin Wetter. Textilsammlung der Abegg-Stiftung Vol. 6. Riggisberg: Abegg-Stiftung, 2012.

Kolletzki, Claudia. '"Über die Wahrheit dieses Buches": Die Entstehung des "Liber Specialis Gratiae" Mechthilds von Hackeborn zwischen Wirklichkeit und Fiktion.' *'Vor dir steht die leere Schale meiner Sehnsucht': Die Mystik der Frauen von Helfta*. Ed. Michael Bangert and Hildegund Keul. Leipzig: Benno-Verlag, 1998. 156–79.

König, Eberhard. *Das Kalligraphiebuch der Maria von Burgund: Brüssel, Bibliothèque Royale de Belgique, Ms. II 845*. Luzern: Quaternio Verlag, 2015.

Köpf, Ulrich. 'Gerhard Tersteegen und die Frauen von Helfta: Zur Rezeption der Helftaer Mystik im Protestantismus.' *'Vor dir steht die leere Schale meiner Sehnsucht': Die Mystik der Frauen von Helfta*. Ed. Michael Bangert and Hildegund Keul. Leipzig: Benno-Verlag, 1998. 202–18.

Kornrumpf, Gisela, and Paul-Gerhard Völker. *Die deutschen mittelalterlichen Handschriften der Universitätsbibliothek München*. Die Handschriften der Universitätsbibliothek München Vol. 1. Wiesbaden: Harrassowitz, 1968.

Kraß, Andreas. *Stabat mater dolorosa: Lateinische Überlieferung und volkssprachliche Übertragungen im deutschen Mittelalter*. Munich: Fink, 1998.

Krone und Schleier: Kunst aus mittelalterlichen Frauenklöstern: Ruhrlandmuseum: Die frühen Klöster und Stifte, 500–1200: Kunst- und Ausstellungshalle der Bundesrepublik Deutschland: die Zeit der Orden, 1200–1500. Ed. Kunst- und Ausstellungshalle der Bundesrepublik Deutschland Bonn and Ruhrlandmuseum Essen. Munich: Hirmer, 2005.

Kroos, Renate. *Niedersächsische Bildstickereien des Mittelalters.* Berlin: Deutscher Verlag für Kunstwissenschaft, 1970.

Krüger, Klaus. *Das Bild als Schleier des Unsichtbaren: Ästhetische Illusion in der Kunst der frühen Neuzeit in Italien.* Munich: Fink, 2001.

Küsters, Urban. 'Narbenschriften: Zur religiösen Literatur des Spätmittelalters.' *Mittelalter: Neue Wege durch einen alten Kontinent.* Ed. Jan-Dirk Müller and Horst Wenzel. Stuttgart: Hirzel, 1999. 81–109.

Längin, Theodor. *Deutsche Handschriften.* Die Handschriften der Badischen Landesbibliothek in Karlsruhe. Beilage Vol. 2 Pt. 2. Wiesbaden: Harrassowitz, 1974.

Largier, Niklaus. 'Inner Senses – Outer Senses: The Practice of Emotions in Medieval Mysticism.' *Codierung von Emotionen im Mittelalter / Emotions and Sensibilities in the Middle Ages.* Ed. C. Stephen Jaeger and Ingrid Kasten. Trends in Medieval Philology Vol. 1. Berlin: De Gruyter, 2003. 3–15.

'Rhetorik des Begehrens: Die 'Unterscheidung der Geister' als Paradigma mittelalterlicher Subjektivität.' *Inszenierungen von Subjektivität in der Literatur des Mittelalters.* Ed. Martin Baisch, Jutta Erning, Hendrijke Haufe, and Andrea Sieber. Königstein im Taunus: Helmer, 2005. 249–70.

'The Poetics of the Image in Late Medieval Mysticism.' *Image and Incarnation: The Early Modern Doctrine of the Pictorial Image.* Ed. Walter S. Melion and Lee Palmer Wandel. Intersections Vol. 39. Leiden: Brill, 2015. 173–86.

Spekulative Sinnlichkeit: Kontemplation und Spekulation im Mittelalter. Mediävistische Perspektiven Vol. 7. Zurich: Chronos, 2018.

Laugerud, Henning, ed. '"And How Could I Find Thee at All, If I Do Not Remember Thee?" Visions, Images and Memory in Late Medieval Devotion.' *The Materiality of Devotion in Late Medieval Northern Europe: Images, Objects, Practices.* Ed. Henning Laugerud, Salvador Ryan, and Laura Katrine Skinnebach. European Network on the Instruments of Devotion Vol. 3. Dublin: Four Courts Press, 2016. 50–69.

Laugerud, Henning, Salvador Ryan, and Laura Katrine Skinnebach, eds. 'Introduction.' *The Materiality of Devotion in Late Medieval Northern Europe: Images, Objects, Practices.* European Network on the Instruments of Devotion Vol. 3. Dublin: Four Courts Press, 2016. 1–9.

Lazikani, Ayoush Sarmada. *Cultivating the Heart: Feeling and Emotion in Twelfth- and Thirteenth-Century Religious Texts.* Cardiff: University of Wales Press, 2015.

Le Goff, Jacques. 'Merchant's Time and Church's Time in the Middle Ages.' *Time, Work, and Culture in the Middle Ages.* Trans. Arthur Goldhammer. Chicago: University of Chicago Press, 1980. 29–42.

Lechner, Joseph. *Die spätmittelalterliche Handschriftengeschichte der Benediktinerinnenabtei St. Walburg/Eichstätt.* Eichstätter Studien Vol. 2. Münster: Aschendorff, 1937.

Leclercq, Jean. 'Le Sacré-Coeur dans la Tradition Bénédictine au Moyen Âge.' *Cor Jesu: Commentationes in litteras encyclicas P II PP. XII 'Haurietis Aquas.'* Vol. 1. Ed. Augustinus Bea and Hugo Rahner. Rome: Herder, 1959. 2–28.

Legaré, Anne-Marie. 'L'image du livre comme adjuvant mémoriel dans le 'Conte des trois chevaliers et des trois livres.'' *Medieval Memory: Image and Text.* Ed. Frank Willaert, Herman Braet, Thomas Felix Constantijn Mertens, and Theo Venckeler. Textes et Études du Moyen Âge Vol. 27. Turnhout: Brepols, 2004. 129–43.

Lehmann, Paul. *Mittelalterliche Bibliothekskataloge Deutschlands und der Schweiz.* Vol. 2: Bistum Mainz, Erfurt. Munich: Beck, 1928.

Lentes, Thomas. 'Die Gewänder der Heiligen: Ein Diskussionsbeitrag zum Verhältnis von Gebet, Bild und Imagination.' *Hagiographie und Kunst: der Heiligenkult in Schrift, Bild und*

Architektur. Ed. Gottfried Kerscher. Berlin: Reimer, 1993. 120–51.

'Bild, Reform und Cura Monialium: Bildverständnis und Bildgebrauch im Buch der Reformacio Predigerordens des Johannes Meyer (d. 1485).' *Dominicains et Dominicaines en Alsace, XIIIe–XXe siècle*. Ed. Jean-Luc Eichenlaub. Colmar: Archives départementales du Haut-Rhin: 1996. 177–95.

Gebetbuch und Gebärde: Religiöses Ausdrucksverhalten in Gebetbüchern aus dem Dominikanerinnen-Kloster St. Nikolaus in undis zu Straßburg (1350–1550). Doctoral dissertation, University of Münster, 1996.

Lewis, Gertrud Jaron. 'Gertrud of Helfta's "Legatus divinae pietatis" and "ein botte der götlichen miltekeit": A Comparative Study of Major Themes.' *Mysticism: Medieval & Modern*. Ed. Valerie M. Largorio. Salzburg Studies in English Literature, Elizabethan & Renaissance Studies Vol. 92:20. Salzburg: Institut für Anglistik und Amerikanistik, Universität Salzburg, 1986. 58–71.

Lieb, Ludger, and Michael R. Ott. 'Schrift-Träger: Mobile Inschriften in der deutschsprachigen Literatur des Mittelalers.' *Schriftträger–Textträger: zur materialen Präsenz des Geschriebenen in frühen Gesellschaften*. Ed. Annette Kehnel and Diamantis Panagiotopoulos. Materiale Textkulturen Vol. 6. Berlin: De Gruyter, 2015. 16–36.

Lindgren, Erika Lauren. *Sensual Encounters: Monastic Women and Spirituality in Medieval Germany*. New York: Columbia University Press, 2009.

List, Gerhard, and Gerhardt Powitz. *Die Handschriften der Stadtbibliothek Mainz*. Vol. 1: Hs I 1–Hs I 150. Wiesbaden: Harrassowitz, 1990.

Liston-Kraft, Philip. 'Bernard's Belching Bride: The Affectus That Words Cannot Express.' *Medieval Mystical Theology* 26 (2017): 54–72.

Littau, Karin. *Theories of Reading: Books, Bodies, and Bibliomania*. Cambridge: Polity, 2006.

Löser, Freimut. 'Postmodernes Mittelalter? New Philology und Überlieferungsgeschichte.' *Kulturen des Manuskriptzeitalters: Ergebnisse der amerikanisch-deutschen Arbeitstagung an der Georg-August-Universität Göttingen vom 17. bis 20. Oktober 2002*. Ed. Arthur Groos and Hans-Jochen Schiewer. Transatlantische Studien zu Mittelalter und Früher Neuzeit – Transatlantic Studies on Medieval and Early Modern Literature and Culture Vol. 1. Göttingen: V&R Unipress, 2004. 215–36.

'"Schriftmystik": Schreibprozesse in Texten der deutschen Mystik.' *Finden – Gestalten – Vermitteln: Schreibprozesse und ihre Brechungen in der mittelalterlichen Überlieferung. Freiburger Colloquium 2010*. Ed. Eckart Conrad Lutz. Wolfram-Studien Vol. 22. Berlin: Schmidt, 2012. 155–201.

Löser, Freimut, Robert Steinke, and Günter Hägele, eds. *Meister Eckhart in Augsburg: Deutsche Mystik des Mittelalters in Kloster, Stadt und Schule. Katalog zur Handschriftenausstellung in der Schatzkammer der Universitätsbibliothek Augsburg (18. Mai bis 29. Juli 2011)*. Augsburg: Universitätsbibliothek, 2011.

Lubinsky, Crystal Lynn. *Removing Masculine Layers to Reveal a Holy Womanhood: The Female Transvestite Monks of Late Antique Eastern Christianity*. Studia Traditionis Theologiae Vol. 13. Turnhout: Brepols, 2013.

Luongo, F. Thomas. *The Saintly Politics of Catherine of Siena*. Ithaca, NY: Cornell University Press, 2006.

Machan, Tim William. *Techniques of Translation: Chaucer's Boece*. Norman, OK: Pilgrim Book, 1985.

Marchand, James W. 'An Unidentified Latin Quote in "Piers Plowman".' *Modern Philology* 88 (1991): 398–400.

Mairold, Maria. 'Die Millstätter Bibliothek.' *Carinthia I* 170 (1980): 87–106.

Marin, Louis. *Des pouvoirs de l'image: Gloses*. Paris: Éditions du Seuil, 1993.

Märker, Almuth. 'Schweigen und Lesen – Das "Prohemium longum" des Erfurter Kartäuserkatalogs als Wissenschaftpropädeutik am Ende des 15. Jahrhunderts.' *Bücher, Bibliotheken und Schriftkultur der Kartäuser: Festgabe zum 65. Geburtstag von Edward Potkowski*. Ed. Sönke Lorenz. Contubernium Vol. 59. Stuttgart: Steiner Verlag, 2002. 383–97.

Das 'Prohemium Longum' des Erfurter Kartäuserkatalogs aus der Zeit um 1475: Edition und Untersuchung. Lateinische Sprache und Literatur des Mittelalters Vol. 35. Bern: Lang, 2008.

'Ms 827.' *Tiefenerschließung und Digitalisierung der deutschsprachigen mittelalterlichen Handschriften der Sächsischen Landesbibliothek, Staats- und Universitätsbibliothek (SLUB) Dresden.* www.manuscripta-mediaevalia.de/dokumente/html/obj31571101.

Martin, Dennis D. 'Carthusians as Advocates of Women Visionary Reformers.' *Studies in Carthusian Monasticism in the Late Middle Ages.* Ed. Julian M. Luxford. Medieval Church Studies Vol. 14. Turnhout: Brepols, 2008. 127–53.

Mazzoni, Cristina. 'Angela of Foligno.' *Medieval Holy Women in the Christian Tradition, c. 1100–c. 1500.* Ed. Alastair J. Minnis and Rosalynn Voaden. Brepols Essays in European Culture Vol. 1. Turnhout: Brepols, 2010. 581–600.

McCarthy, Daniel P. 'The Emergence of "Anno Domini".' *Time and Eternity: The Medieval Discourse.* Ed. Gerhard Jaritz and Gerson Moreno-Riano. International Medieval Research Vol. 9. Turnhout: Brepols, 2003. 31–53.

McDevitt, Mary. '"The Ink of Our Mortality": The Late-Medieval Image of the Writing Christ Child.' *The Christ Child in Medieval Culture: Alpha es et O!* Ed. Mary Christine Dzon and Theresa Marie Anne Kenney. Toronto: University of Toronto Press. 224–53.

McGinn, Bernard. 'Meister Eckhart and the Beguines in the Context of Vernacular Theology.' *Meister Eckhart and the Beguine Mystics: Hadewijch of Brabant, Mechthild of Magdeburg, and Margerite Porete.* Ed. Bernard McGinn. New York: Continuum, 1994. 1–14.

The Flowering of Mysticism: Men and Women in the New Mysticism, 1200–1350. The Presence of God: A History of Western Christian Mysticism Vol. 3. New York: Crossroad, 1998.

The Harvest of Mysticism in Medieval Germany, 1300–1500. The Presence of God: A History of Western Christian Mysticism Vol. 4. New York: Crossroad, 2005.

McIlroy, Claire Elizabeth. *The English Prose Treatises of Richard Rolle.* Studies in Medieval Mysticism Vol. 4. Woodbridge: Boydell & Brewer, 2004.

McNamara, Jo Ann. 'The Need to Give: Suffering and Female Sanctity in the Middle Ages.' *Images of Sainthood in Medieval Europe.* Ed. Renate Blumenfeld-Kosinski and Timea Klara Szell. Ithaca, NY: Cornell University Press, 1991. 199–221.

McNamer, Sarah. *Affective Meditation and the Invention of Medieval Compassion.* Philadelphia: University of Pennsylvania Press, 2010.

Mecham, June L. *Sacred Communities, Shared Devotions: Gender, Material Culture, and Monasticism in Late Medieval Germany.* Medieval Women–Texts and Contexts Vol. 29. Turnhout: Brepols, 2014.

Meier, Christel. *Gemma spiritualis: Methode und Gebrauch der Edelsteinallegorese vom frühen Christentum bis ins 18. Jahrhundert.* Münstersche Mittelalter-Schriften Vol. 34. Munich: Fink, 1977.

Mengis, Simone. *Schreibende Frauen um 1500: Scriptorium und Bibliothek des Dominikanerinnenklosters St. Katharina St. Gallen.* Scrinium Friburgense Vol. 28. Berlin: De Gruyter, 2013.

Menhardt, Hermann. *Verzeichnis der altdeutschen literarischen Handschriften der österreichischen Nationalbibliothek.* Vol. 2. Veröffentlichungen des Instituts für deutsche Sprache und Literatur Vol. 13. Berlin: Akademie-Verlag, 1961.

Mertens, Thom. 'Mystieke cultuur en literatuur in de Late Middelleeuwen.' *Grote lijnen: Syntheses over Middelnederlandse letterkunde Rijksuniversiteit te Leiden.* Ed. Frits van Oostrom. Nederlandse literatuur en cultuur in de middeleeuwen Vol. 11. Amsterdam: Prometheus, 1995. 117–35.

Metz, René. *La consécration des vierges dans l'église romaine: Étude d'histoire de la liturgie.* Paris: Presses universitaires de France, 1954.

Mezger, Werner. *Narrenidee und Fastnachtsbrauch: Studien zum Fortleben des Mittelalters in der europäischen Festkultur.* Konstanzer Bibliothek Vol. 15. Konstanz: Universitätsverlag, 1991.

Mills, Robert. 'God's Time? Purgatory and Temporality in Late Medieval Art.' *Time and Eternity: The Medieval Discourse*. Ed. Gerhard Jaritz and Gerson Moreno-Riano. International Medieval Research Vol. 9. Turnhout: Brepols, 2003. 477–98.

Minnis, Alastair J. *Medieval Theory of Authorship: Scholastic Literary Attitudes in the Later Middle Ages*. London: Scolar Press, 1984.

More, Alison. 'Religious Order and Textual Identity: The Case of Franciscan Tertiary Women.' *Nuns' Literacies in Medieval Europe: The Antwerp Dialogue*. Ed. Virginia Blanton, Veronica O'Mara, and Patricia Stoop. Medieval Women – Texts and Contexts Vol. 28. Turnhout: Brepols, 2017. 43–59.

Morgan, Ben. *On Becoming God: Late Medieval Mysticism and the Modern Western Self*. New York: Fordham University Press, 2013.

Morgan, David. 'Rhetoric of the Heart: Figuring the Body in Devotion to the Sacred Heart of Jesus.' *Things: Religion and the Question of Materiality*. Ed. Dick Houtman and Birgit Meyer. New York: Fordham University Press, 2012. 90–111.

Mossman, Stephen. *Marquard von Lindau and the Challenges of Religious Life in Late Medieval Germany*. Oxford: Oxford University Press, 2010.

Mulder-Bakker, Anneke B. 'Gertrude of Ortenberg.' *Women and Gender in Medieval Europe: An Encyclopedia*. Ed. Margaret Schaus. The Routledge Encyclopedias of the Middle Ages Vol. 14. New York: Routledge, 2006.

The Dedicated Spiritual Life of Upper Rhine Noble Women: A Study and Translation of a Fourteenth-Century Spiritual Biography of Gertrude Rickeldey of Ortenberg and Heilke of Staufenberg. Brepols: Turnhout, 2017.

Müller, Jan-Dirk, ed. 'Aufführung' und 'Schrift' in Mittelalter und Früher Neuzeit. *Germanistische Symposien. Berichtsbände* Vol. 17. Stuttgart: Metzler, 1996.

Müller, Jan-Dirk. 'Vulgatfassung? Zur Fassung ⋆C des "Nibelungenliedes" und den sog. kontaminierten Fassungen.' *Beiträge zur Geschichte der deutschen Sprache und Literatur* 138 (2016): 227–63.

Muschiol, Gisela. 'Zeit und Raum: Liturgie und Ritus in mittelalterlichen Frauenkonventen.' *Krone und Schleier: Kunst aus mittelalterlichen Frauenklöstern: Ruhrlandmuseum: Die frühen Klöster und Stifte, 500–1200: Kunst- und Ausstellungshalle der Bundesrepublik Deutschland: Die Zeit der Orden, 1200–1500*. Ed. Kunst- und Ausstellungshalle der Bundesrepublik Deutschland Bonn and Ruhrlandmuseum Essen. Munich: Hirmer, 2005. 40–51.

'Time and Space: Liturgy and Rite in Female Monasteries of the Middle Ages.' *Crown and Veil: Female Monasticism from the Fifth to the Fifteenth Centuries*. Ed. Jeffrey F. Hamburger and Susan Marti. New York: Columbia University Press, 2008. 191–206.

Nemes, Balázs J. *Von der Schrift zum Buch – vom Ich zum Autor: Zur Text- und Autorkonstitution in Überlieferung und Rezeption des 'Fliessenden Lichts der Gottheit' Mechthilds von Magdeburg*. Bibliotheca Germanica Vol. 55. Tübingen: Francke, 2010.

'Text Production and Authorship: Gertrude of Helfta's 'Legatus divinae pietatis'.' *A Companion to Mysticism and Devotion in Northern Germany in the Late Middle Ages*. Ed. Anne Simon, Elizabeth A. Andersen, and Henrike Lähnemann. Brill's Companions to the Christian Tradition Vol. 44. Leiden: Brill, 2014. 103–30.

'"ut earundem testimonio conprobatur": Schwester Mechthild in der Offenbarungliteratur von Helfta (mit einem Textabdruck aus der Leipziger Handschrift Ms 827.' *Beihefte zur Zeitschrift für deutsche Philologie* 17 (2019). Special Issue: *Mechthild und das Fließende Licht der Gottheit im Kontext. Eine Spurensuche in religiösen Netzwerken und literarischen Diskursen im mitteldeutschen Raum des 13.–15. Jahrhunderts*. Ed. Caroline Emmelius and Balázs J. Nemes. 89–123.

'Scenes of Writing, Figurations of Authorship: A Literature Historian's Reflections on the Veracity of the Passages Recounting the Textual Genesis of the Special Edition of Gertrude of Helfta's "Legatus divinae pietatis".' *Analecta Cisterciensia* 69 (2019): 145–60.

Nemes, Balázs J., and Almuth Märker. '"Hunc tercium conscripsi cum maximo labore occultandi": Schwester N von Helfta und ihre "Sonderausgabe" des "Legatus divinae pietatis" Gertruds von Helfta in der Leipziger Handschrift Ms 827.' *Beiträge zur Geschichte der deutschen Sprache und Literatur* 137 (2015): 248–96.

Nemes, Balázs J., and Antje Kellersohn. *Making Mysticism. Mystical books in the library of Erfurt Charterhouse*, DFG Projekt, 2018–2021: https://making-mysticism.org.

Nesteruk, Peter. 'When Space Is Time: The Rhetoric of Eternity: Hierarchy and Narrative in Medieval and Renaissance Art.' *Time and Eternity: The Medieval Discourse*. Ed. Gerhard Jaritz and Gerson Moreno-Riano. International Medieval Research Vol. 9. Turnhout: Brepols, 2003. 403–25.

Neumann, Hans. 'Mechthild von Magdeburg.' *Die deutsche Literatur des Mittelalters: Verfasserlexikon: Begründet von Wolfgang Stammler, fortgeführt von Karl Langosch*. Vol. 6. Ed. Kurt Ruh and Burghart Wachinger. 2nd edition. Berlin: De Gruyter, 1987. 260–70.

Newman, Barbara. *From Virile Woman to WomanChrist: Studies in Medieval Religion and Literature*. Middle Ages Series. Philadelphia: University of Pennsylvania Press, 1995.

God and the Goddesses: Vision, Poetry, and Belief in the Middle Ages. Philadelphia: University of Pennsylvania Press, 2003.

'Die visionären Texte und visuellen Welten religiöser Frauen.' *Krone und Schleier: Kunst aus mittelalterlichen Frauenklöstern: Ruhrlandmuseum: Die frühen Klöster und Stifte, 500–1200: Kunst- und Ausstellungshalle der Bundesrepublik Deutschland: die Zeit der Orden, 1200–1500*. Ed. Kunst- und Ausstellungshalle der Bundesrepublik Deutschland Bonn and Ruhrlandmuseum Essen. Munich: Hirmer, 2005. 104–17.

'"Love's Arrows": Christ as Cupid in Late Medieval Art and Devotion.' *The Mind's Eye: Art and Theological Argument in the Middle Ages*. Ed. Jeffrey F. Hamburger and

Anne-Marie Bouché. Princeton, NJ: Princeton University Press, 2006. 263–86.

'The Visionary Texts and Visual Words of Religious Women.' *Crown and Veil: Female Monasticism from the Fifth to the Fifteenth Centuries*. Ed. Jeffrey F. Hamburger and Susan Marti. New York: Columbia University Press, 2008. 151–71.

'Liminalities: Literate Women in the Long Twelfth Century.' *European Transformation: The Long Twelfth Century*. Ed. Thomas F. X. Noble and John Van Engen. Notre Dame, IN: University of Notre Dame Press, 2012. 354–402.

'Annihilation and Authorship: Three Women Mystics of the 1290s.' *Speculum* 91 (2016): 591–630.

'New Seeds, New Harvests: Thirty Years of Tilling the Mystical Field.' *Traditio* 72 (2017): 9–20.

Nichols, Stephen G. 'Introduction: Philology in a Manuscript Culture.' *Speculum* 65 (1990): 1–10.

'Philology and its discontents.' *The Future of the Middle Ages: Medieval Literature in the 1990s*. Ed. William D. Paden. Gainesville: University Press of Florida, 1994. 113–41.

'Why material philology? Some thoughts.' *Zeitschrift für Deutsche Philologie* 116 (1997): 10–30.

Odenthal, Andreas. '"Diaconi cum rufis casulis precincti": Traces of Medieval and Early Modern Use of Liturgical Vestments in the Cathedral of Halberstadt.' *Iconography of Liturgical Textiles in the Middle Ages*. Ed. Evelin Wetter. Riggisberger Berichte Vol. 18. Riggisberg: Abegg-Stiftung, 2010. 19–32.

Oefelein, Cornelia. 'Grundlagen zur Baugeschichte des Klosters Helfta.' *'Vor dir steht die leere Schale meiner Sehnsucht': Die Mystik der Frauen von Helfta*. Ed. Michael Bangert and Hildegund Keul. Leipzig: Benno, 1998. 12–28.

Das Nonnenkloster St. Jacobi und seine Tochterklöster im Bistum Halberstadt. Studien zur Geschichte, Kunst und Kultur der Zisterzienser Vol. 20. Berlin: Lukas, 2004.

'Gründung und mittelalterliche Geschichte des Klosters St. Marien zu Helfta – ein Überblick unter Berücksichtigung neuer Funde.' *Beihefte zur Zeitschrift für deutsche Philologie* 17 (2019). Special Issue: *Mechthild und das Fließende Licht der Gottheit im Kontext. Eine Spurensuche in religiösen Netzwerken und literarischen Diskursen im mitteldeutschen Raum des 13.–15. Jahrhunderts.* Ed. Caroline Emmelius and Balázs J. Nemes. 41–65.

Palmer, Nigel F. 'Das Buch als Bedeutungsträger bei Mechthild von Magdeburg.' *Bildhafte Rede in Mittelalter und früher Neuzeit. Probleme ihrer Legitimation und ihrer Funktion.* Ed. Wolfgang Harms. Tübingen: Niemeyer, 1992. 217–35.

'Kapitel und Buch. Zu den Gliederungsprinzipien mittelalterlicher Bücher.' *Frühmittelalterliche Studien* 23 (1989): 43–88.

'Herzeliebe, weltlich und geistlich: Zur Metaphorik vom 'Einwohnen im Herzen' bei Wolfram von Eschenbach, Juliana von Cornillon, Hugo von Langenstein und Gertrud von Helfta.' *Innenräume in der Literatur des deutschen Mittelalters: XIX. Anglo-German Colloquium Oxford 2005.* Ed. Burkhard Hasebrink, Hans-Jochen Schiewer, Almut Suerbaum, and Annette Volfing. Tübingen: Niemeyer, 2008. 197–224.

'Die Münchner Perikopenhandschrift Cgm 157 und die Handschriftenproduktion des Straßburger Reuerinnenklosters im späten 15. Jahrhundert.' *Kulturtopographie deutschsprachigen Südwestens im späteren Mittelalter: Studien und Texte.* Ed. Barbara Fleith, and René Wetzel. Kulturtopographie des alemannischen Raums Vol. 1. Berlin: De Gruyter, 2009. 263–300.

'Ein Zeugnis deutscher Kunstprosa aus dem späten 13. Jahrhundert: Zu den sonst nicht nachgewiesenen Textabschnitten der Moskauer Mechthild-Überlieferung.' *Deutsch-russische Arbeitsgespräche zu mittelalterlichen Handschriften und Drucken in russischen Bibliotheken: Beiträge zur Tagung des deutsch-russischen Arbeitskreises vom 14. bis 16. September 2011 an der Lomonossov-Universität Moskau aus Anlass des 300. Geburtstages des Universitätsgründers Michail Lomonossov.* Eds Natalija Ganina, Klaus Klein, Catherine Squires, and Jürgen Wolf. Akademie gemeinnütziger Wissenschaften zu Erfurt. Sonderschriften Vol. 45. Erfurt: Verlag der Akademie gemeinnütziger Wissenschaften, 2014. 97–138.

'The German Prayers in their Literary and Historical Context.' *The Prayer Book of Ursula Begerin.* Vol. 2. Ed. Jeffrey F. Hamburger and Nigel F. Palmer. Dietikon-Zurich: Graf, 2015. 377–488.

Pech, Hans M. 'Persuasion from Nothing? On the Pedagogical Scope of Henry Suso's Vita and beyond.' Paper at the Stanford/Berkeley/Princeton/Toronto/Harvard Medieval German Graduate Colloquium, Berkeley (May 2017).

Pederse, Else Marie Wiberg. 'Gottesbild – Frauenbild – Selbstbild: Die Theologie Mechthilds von Hackeborn und Gertruds von Helfta.' *'Vor dir steht die leere Schale meiner Sehnsucht': Die Mystik der Frauen von Helfta.* Eds Michael Bangert and Hildegund Keul. Leipzig: Benno, 1998. 48–66.

Peters, Ursula. 'Das 'Leben' der Christine Ebner: Textanalyse und kulturhistorischer Kommentar.' *Abendländische Mystik im Mittelalter: Symposium Kloster Engelberg 1984.* Ed. Kurt Ruh. Germanistische Symposien. Berichtsbände Vol. 7. Stuttgart: Metzler, 1986. 402–22.

Religiöse Erfahrung als literarisches Faktum: Zur Vorgeschichte und Genese frauenmystischer Texte des 13. und 14. Jahrhunderts. Tübingen: Niemeyer, 1988.

'Ordnungsfunktion – Textillustration – Autorkonstruktion: Zu den Bildern der romanischen und deutschen Liederhandschriften.' *Zeitschrift für deutsches Altertum und deutsche Literatur* 130 (2001): 392–430.

'Werkauftrag und Buchübergabe: Textentstehungsgeschichten in Autorbildern volkssprachiger Handschriften des 12. bis 15. Jahrhunderts.' *Autorbilder: Zur Medialität literarischer Kommunikation in Mittelalter und Früher Neuzeit.* Ed. Gerald Kapfhammer, Wolf-Dietrich Löhr, and Barbara Nitsche. Tholos

Kunsthistorische Studien Vol. 2. Münster: Rhema, 2007. 25–62.

Plachta, Bodo. 'Fasung.' *Reallexikon der deutschen Literaturwissenschaft*. Ed. Klaus Weimar et al. Vol. 1. Berlin: De Gruyter, 1997. 567–68.

Poor, Sara S. 'Mechthild von Magdeburg, Gender, and the 'Unlearned Tongue'.' *Journal of Medieval and Early Modern Studies* 31 (2001): 213–50.

Mechthild of Magdeburg and Her Book and the Making of Textual Authority. Philadelphia: University of Pennsylvania Press, 2004.

'Stimmen schreibender Frauen in der Mystik des 15. Jahrhunderts: Der Fall Anna Eybins.' *Zeitschrift für Literaturwissenschaft und Linguistik* 171 (2013): 104–21.

'"Life" Lessons in Anna Eybin's Book of Saints (ca. 1465–1482).' *Taxonomies of Knowledge: Information and Order in Medieval Manuscripts*. Ed. Emily Steiner and Lynn Ransom. The Lawrence J. Schoenberg Studies in Manuscript Culture Vol. 2. Philadelphia: Schoenberg Institute for Manuscript Studies, University of Pennsylvania Press, 2015. 136–53.

'"Ich Schreyberin": Re-thinking Female Authorship: Anna Eybin's Table of Contents.' *Journal of Medieval Religious Culture* 42.2 (2016): 201–23.

'The Countess, the Abbess, and their Books: Manuscript Circulation in a Fifteenth-Century German Family.' *Nuns' Literacies in Medieval Europe: The Antwerp Dialogue*. Ed. Virginia Blanton, Veronica O'Mara, and Patricia Stoop. Medieval Women – Texts and Contexts Vol. 28. Turnhout: Brepols, 2017. 341–65.

Potts, Alex. *Flesh and the Ideal: Winckelmann and the Origins of Art History*. New Haven: Yale University Press, 1994.

Powitz, Gerhardt. *Die Handschriften des Dominikanerklosters und des Leonhardstifts in Frankfurt am Main*. Kataloge der Stadt- und Universitätsbibliothek Frankfurt am Main Vol. 2 Pt. 1: Die Handschriften der Stadt- und Universitätsbibliothek Frankfurt am Main. Frankfurt a.M.: Klostermann, 1968.

Pregla, Barbara. 'Gesticktes Leinentuch.' *Kostbarkeiten aus dem Domschatz zu Halberstadt*. Ed. Ute Bednarz et al. Halle an der Saale: Stekovics, 2001. 144.

'Zwei Kirchenfahnen mit eucharistischen Tüchern.' *Kostbarkeiten aus dem Domschatz zu Halberstadt*. 110–13.

'Mitra mit Perlstickerei.' *Kostbarkeiten aus dem Domschatz zu Halberstadt*. 148–51.

Pregla, Barbara, and Elisabeth Rüber-Schütte. 'Antependium mit der Krönung Mariens in Perlstickerei.' *Der Heilige Schatz im Dom zu Halberstadt*. Ed. Harald Meller, Ingo Mundt, and Boje Schmuhl. Regensburg: Schnell & Steiner, 2008. 288–91.

Quast, Bruno. '"drücken und schieben": Passionsmystische Frömmigkeit in den Offenbarungen der Margarethe Ebner' *Gewalt im Mittelalter: Realitäten – Imaginationen*. Ed. Manuel Braun and Cornelia Herberichs. Munich: Fink, 2005. 293–306.

Rahner, Hugo. 'Grundzüge einer Geschichte der Herz-Jesu-Verehrung.' *Zeitschrift für Aszese und Mystik* 18 (1943): 61–83.

Rambow, George F. 'The Function and Spirituality of Bonaventure's "Treatise" on the Miracles of St. Francis.' *Franciscan Studies* 75 (2017): 323–41.

Ricci, Seymour de. *Census of Medieval and Renaissance Manuscripts in the United States and Canada*. Vol. I. New York: Bibliographical Society of America, 1935. Repr. 1962.

Richstätter, Karl. *Die Herz-Jesu-Verehrung des deutschen Mittelalters*. Munich: Kösel & Pustet, 1924.

Ringler, Siegfried. *Viten- und Offenbarungsliteratur in Frauenklöstern des Mittelalters: Quellen und Studien*. Münchener Texte und Untersuchungen zur deutschen Literatur des Mittelalters Vol. 72. Munich: Artemis, 1980.

'Die Rezeption Gertruds von Helfta im Bereich süddeutscher Frauenklöster.' *'Vor dir steht die leere Schale meiner Sehnsucht': Die Mystik der Frauen von Helfta*. Ed. Michael Bangert and Hildegund Keul. Leipzig: Benno, 1998. 134–55.

'Einführung: Die Mystik der Gertrud von Helfta – Aufbruch zu neuer Gottesrede.' *Aufbruch zu neuer Gottesrede: Die Mystik der Gertrud von Helfta*. Ed. Siegfried Ringler. Ostfildern: Grünewald, 2008. 8–14.

Rischpler, Susanne. *Der Illuminator Michael*. *Codices Manuscripti*. Supplementum Vol. 1. Purkersdorf: Hollinek, 2009.

Robertson, Kellie. 'Medieval Materialism: A Manifesto.' *Exemplaria* (2010): 99–118.

Roman, Christopher M. *Queering Richard Rolle: Mystical Theology and the Hermit in Fourteenth-Century England*. Cham, Switzerland: Palgrave Macmillian, 2017.

Roth, F. W. E. 'Aufzeichnungen über das mystische Leben der Nonnen von Kirchberg bei Sulz Predigerordens während des XIV. und XV. Jahrhunderts.' *Alemannia* 21 (1893): 103–48.

Roy, Bruno, and Paul Zumthor, eds. *Jeux de mémoire: Aspects de la mnémotechnie médiévale: Recueil d'études*. Montréal: Presses de l'Université de Montréal/Librairie Philosophique J. Vrin, 1985.

Rozenski, Steven. 'The Visual, the Textual, and the Auditory in Henry Suso's "Vita" or "Life of the Servant".' *Mystic's Quarterly* 34 (2008): 35–72.

Ruch, Martin. *Offenburg, die Ortenau und die Literatur: Ein Lesebuch zur Literaturgeschichte Mittelbadens*. Norderstedt: Books on Demand, 2004.

Rudy, Kathryn M. 'Introduction: Miraculous Textiles in "Exempla" and Images from the Low Countries.' *Weaving, Veiling, and Dressing: Textiles and Their Metaphors in the Late Middle Ages*. Ed. Kathryn M. Rudy and Barbara Baert. Medieval Church Studies Vol. 12. Turnhout: Brepols, 2007. 1–36.

Ruf, Paul. *Mittelalterliche Bibliothekskataloge Deutschlands und der Schweiz*. Vol. 3 Pt. 1: Bistum Augsburg. Munich: Beck, 1932.

Ruh, Kurt. *Bonaventura deutsch: Ein Beitrag zur deutschen Franziskaner-Mystik und -Scholastik*. Bibliotheca Germanica Vol. 7. Bern: Francke, 1956.

Meister Eckhart: Theologe, Prediger, Mystiker. 2nd edition. Munich: Beck, 1989.

Geschichte der abendländischen Mystik. 4 vols. Munich: Beck, 1990–1999.

'Gertrud von Helfta: Ein Neues Gertrud-Bild.' *Zeitschrift für deutsches Altertum und deutsche Literatur* 121 (1992): 1–20.

Rupp, Michael. 'Unterweisung in Vers und Prosa: Zu den verschiedenen Erscheinungsformen der lateinischen Predigten Bertholds von Regensburg in der Volkssprache.' *Beiträge zur Geschichte der deutschen Sprache und Literatur* 140 (2018): 51–73.

Rüttgardt, Antje. *Klosteraustritte in der frühen Reformation: Studien zu Flugschriften der Jahre 1522 bis 1524*. Quellen und Forschungen zur Reformationsgeschichte Vol. 79. Gütersloh: Gütersloher Verlagshaus, 2007.

Saurma-Jeltsch, Lieselotte E. *Spätformen mittelalterlicher Buchherstellung: Bilderhandschriften aus der Werkstatt Diebold Laubers in Hagenau*. Vol. 2. Wiesbaden: Reichert, 2001.

Scheepsma, Wybren. 'Writing, Editing, and Rearranging: Griet Essinchghes and her Version of the Sister-Book of Diepenveen.' *Nuns' Literacies in Medieval Europe: The Hull Dialogue*. Ed. Virginia Blanton, Veronica O'Mara, and Patricia Stoop. Medieval Women – Texts and Contexts Vol. 26. Turnhout: Brepols, 2013. 275–92.

Scherrer, Gustav. *Verzeichnis der Handschriften der Stiftsbibliothek von St. Gallen*. Halle: Verlag der Buchhandlung des Waisenhauses, 1875.

Schiewer, Hans-Jochen. 'Fassung, Bearbeitung, Version und Edition.' *Deutsche Texte des Mittelalters zwischen Handschriftennahe und Rekonstruktion: Berliner Fachtagung 1–3 April 2004. Beihefte zu Editio 23*. Ed. Martin J. Schubert. Tübingen: M. Niemeyer, 2005. 35–50.

'Literarisches Leben in dominikanischen Frauenklöstern des 14. Jahrhunderts: Das Modell St. Katharinental bei Diessenhofen.' *Studien und Texte zur literarischen und materiellen Kultur der Frauenklöster im späten Mittelalter: Ergebnisse eines Arbeitsgesprächs in der Herzog August Bibliothek Wolfenbüttel, 24.–26. Febr. 1999*. Ed. Falk Eisermann, Eva Schlotheuber, and Volker Honemann.

Studies in Medieval and Reformation Thought Vol. 99. Leiden: Brill, 2004. 285–311.

Schiewer, Regina Dorothea. "'Vos amici Dei estis": Die "Gottesfreunde" des 14. Jahrhunderts bei Seuse, Tauler, und in den "Engelberger Predigten." Religiöse Elite, Verein oder Literaturzirkel?' *Oxford German Studies* 36 (2007). Themed Issue: *Amicitia. Friendship in Medieval Culture: Papers in Honour of Nigel F. Palmer.* Ed. Almut Suerbaum and Annette Volfing. 227–46.

'Books in Texts – Texts in Books: The "St. Georgener Predigten" as an Example of Nuns' Literacy in Late Medieval Germany.' *Nuns' Literacies in Medieval Europe: The Hull Dialogue.* Ed. Virginia Blanton, Veronica O'Mara, and Patricia Stoop. Medieval Women – Texts and Contexts Vol. 26. Turnhout: Brepols, 2013. 223–37.

Schlenker, Gerlinde. 'Helfta, Sachsen.' *Repertorium der Zisterzen in den Ländern Brandenburg, Mecklenburg-Vorpommern, Sachsen, Sachsen-Anhalt und Thüringen.* Langwaden: Bernardus, 1998. 287–91.

Schlotheuber, Eva. *Klostereintritt und Bildung: Die Lebenswelt der Nonnen im späten Mittelalter: Mit einer Edition des 'Konventstagebuchs' einer Zisterzienserin von Heilig-Kreuz bei Braunschweig (1484–1507).* Spätmittelalter und Reformation. Neue Reihe Vol. 24. Tübingen: Mohr Siebeck, 2004.

'Bücher und Bildung in den Frauengemeinschaften der Bettelorden.' *Nonnen, Kanonissen und Mystikerinnen: Religiöse Frauengemeinschaften in Süddeutschland: Beiträge zur interdisziplinären Tagung vom 21. bis 23. September 2005 in Frauenchiemsee.* Ed. Eva Schlotheuber, Helmut Flachenecker, and Ingrid Gardill. Göttingen: Vandenhoeck & Ruprecht, 2008. 241–62.

'Daily Life, "Amor Dei", and Politics in the Letters of the Benedictine Nuns of Lüne in the Fifteenth and Sixteenth Centuries.' *Nuns' Literacies in Medieval Europe: The Kansas City Dialogue.* Ed. Virginia Blanton, Veronica O'Mara, and Patricia Stoop. Medieval Women – Texts and Contexts Vol. 27. Turnhout: Brepols, 2015. 249–67.

Schmid, Florian M. *Die Fassung *C des "Nibelungenlieds" und der "Klage": Strategien der Retextualisierung.* Hermae. Neue Folge Vol. 147. Berlin, Boston: De Gruyter, 2018, 3. 41–44.

Schmidt, Margot. 'Mechthild von Hackeborn.' *Die deutsche Literatur des Mittelalters: Verfasserlexikon: Begründet von Wolfgang Stammler, fortgeführt von Karl Langosch.* Vol. 6. Ed. Kurt Ruh and Burghart Wachinger. 2nd edition. Berlin: De Gruyter, 1987. 251–59.

Schmidt, Wieland. *Die vierundzwanzig Alten Ottos von Passau.* Palaestra Vol. 212. Leipzig: Akademische Verlagsgesellschaft, 1938. Repr. New York: Johnson, 1967.

Schneider, Karin. 'Die Bibliothek des Katharinenklosters in Nürnberg und die städtische Gesellschaft.' *Studien zum städtischen Bildungswesen des späten Mittelalters und der frühen Neuzeit: Bericht über Kolloquien der Kommission zur Erforschung der Kultur des Spätmittelalters. 1978 bis 1981.* Ed. Bernd Moeller, Hans Patze, Karl Stackmann, and Ludger Grenzmann. *Abhandlungen der Akademie der Wissenschaften in Göttingen. Philologisch-Historische Klasse* 3. Folge 137. Göttingen: Vandenhoeck & Ruprecht, 1983. 70–82.

Die datierten Handschriften der Bayerischen Staatsbibliothek München. Pt. 1: Die deutschen Handschriften bis 1450. Datierte Handschriften in Bibliotheken der Bundesrepublik Deutschland Vol. 4. Stuttgart: Hiersemann, 1994.

Die deutschen Handschriften der Bayerischen Staatsbibliothek München. Cgm 691–867. Catalogus codicum manu scriptorum Bibliothecae Monacensis Vol. 5: Editio altera Pt. 5: Codices Germanicos 691–867 complectens. Wiesbaden: Harrassowitz, 1984.

Deutsche mittelalterliche Handschriften der Universitätsbibliothek Augsburg. Die Signaturengruppen Cod. I.3 und Cod. III.1. Die Handschriften der Universitätsbibliothek Augsburg Vol. 2: Die deutschen Handschriften Pt. 1. Wiesbaden: Harrassowitz, 1988.

Schneider, Karin, and Heinz Zirnbauer. *Die deutschen mittelalterlichen Handschriften.* Die

Handschriften der Stadtbibliothek Nürnberg Vol. 1. Wiesbaden: Harrassowitz, 1965.

Schneider-Lastin, Wolfram. 'Leben und Offenbarungen der Elsbeth von Oye: Textkritische Edition der Vita aus dem 'Ötenbacher Schwesternbuch'.' *Kulturtopographie des deutschsprachigen Südwestens im späteren Mittelalter*. Ed. Barbara Fleiths and René Wetzel. Kulturtopographie des alemannischen Raums Vol. 1. Berlin: De Gruyter, 2009. 395–467.

Schnell, Rüdiger. 'Gender und Rhetorik in Mittelalter und früher Neuzeit: Zur Kommunikation der Geschlechter.' *Rhetorik* 29 (2010): 1–18.

Schnorr v. Carolsfeld, Franz. *Katalog der Handschriften der Sächsischen Landesbibliothek zu Dresden*. Vol. 2. 2nd editon. Dresden: Sächsische Landesbibliothek, 1981.

Schnyder, André. *Die Ursulabruderschaften des Spätmittelalters: Ein Beitrag zur Erforschung der deutschsprachigen religiösen Literatur des 15. Jahrhunderts*. Bern: Haupt, 1986.

'Otto von Passau OFM.' *Die deutsche Literatur des Mittelalters: Verfasserlexikon: Begründet von Wolfgang Stammler, fortgeführt von Karl Langosch*. Vol. 7. Ed. Kurt Ruh and Burghart Wachinger. 2nd edition. Berlin: De Gruyter, 1989. 229–34.

'Das Buch im Buch: Von lehrreicher, erfreulicher und gefährlicher Lektüre in mittelalterlichen Texten.' *Buchkultur im Mittelalter: Schrift, Bild, Kommunikation*. Ed. Michael Stolz and Adrian Mettauer. Berlin: De Gruyter, 2005. 123–43.

Schönherr, Alfons. 'Katalogisierung mittelalterlicher und neuzeitlicher Handschriften.' *30. Bericht der Zentralbibliothek Solothurn über das Jahr 1959* (1960): 31–32.

De Schryver, Antoine. 'Nicolas Spierinc: Calligraphe et enlumineur des Ordonnances des états de l'hôtel de Charles le Téméraire.' *Scriptorium* 23 (1969): 434–58.

Schwarzenberg, Erkinger. 'Colour, Light and Transparency in the Greek World.' *Medieval Mosaics: Light, Color, Materials*. Ed. Eve Borsook, Fiorella Gioffredi Superbi, and

Giovanni Pagliarulo. Cinisello Balsamo: Silvana Editoriale, 2000. 15–34.

Schwarzmann, Eduard. *Karl I., Graf zu Hohenzollern-Sigmaringen und Veringen, Herr zu Haigerloch und Werstein, des Heiligen Römischen Reichs Erbkämmerer, und Markgräfin Anna von Baden und Hochberg*. Sigmaringen: Verlag der P. Liehner'schen Buchhandlung, 1859.

Sciacca, Christine. 'Raising the Curtain on the Use of Textiles in Manuscripts.' *Weaving, Veiling, and Dressing: Textiles and Their Metaphors in the Late Middle Ages*. Ed. Kathryn M. Rudy and Barbara Baert. Medieval Church Studies Vol. 12. Turnhout: Brepols, 2007. 161–90.

Sears, Elizabeth. 'The Iconography of Auditory Perception in the Early Middle Ages: On Psalm Illustration and Psalm Exegesis.' *The Second Sense: Studies in Hearing and Musical Judgement from Antiquity to the Seventeenth Century*. Ed. Charles Burnett, Michael Fend, and Penelope Gouk. Warburg Institute Surveys and Texts Vol. 22. London: The Warburg Institute, 1991. 19–42.

Skinnebach, Laura Katrine. 'Transfiguration: Change and Comprehension in Late Medieval Devotional Perception.' *The Materiality of Devotion in Late Medieval Northern Europe: Images, Objects, Practices*. Ed. Henning Laugerud, Salvador Ryan, and Laura Katrine Skinnebach. European Network on the Instruments of Devotion Vol. 3. Dublin: Four Courts Press, 2016. 90–103.

Smalley, Beryl. 'A Commentary on Isaias by Guerric of Saint-Quentin.' *Miscellanea Giovanni Mercati*. Vol. 2. Studi e Testi Vol. 122. Vatican: Biblioteca Apostolica Vaticana, 1946. 383–97.

Sörries, Reiner. *Die alpenländischen Fastentücher: Vergessene Zeugnisse volkstümlicher Frömmigkeit*. Klagenfurt: Universitätsverlag Carinthia, 1988.

Spiegel, Gabrielle. *The Theory and Practice of Medieval Historiography*. Baltimore: Johns Hopkins University Press, 1997.

Spilling, Herrad. *Die Handschriften der Staats- und Stadtbibliothek Augsburg 2° Cod 101–250.* Handschriftenkataloge der Staats- und Stadtbibliothek Augsburg Vol. 3. Wiesbaden: Harrassowitz, 1984.

Spitzlei, Sabine B. *Erfahrungsraum Herz: Zur Mystik des Zisterzienserinnenklosters Helfta im 13. Jahrhundert.* Mystik in Geschichte und Gegenwart. Texte und Untersuchungen. Abteilung I Christliche Mystik Vol. 9. Stuttgart: Frommann-Holzboog, 1991. 62–80.

Squires, Catherine. 'Das Moskauer Mechthild-Fragment: Neues zur Lesung und zur Zusammenstellung des Kodex.' *Deutsch-russische Arbeitsgespräche zu mittelalterlichen Handschriften und Drucken in russischen Bibliotheken: Beiträge zur Tagung des deutsch-russischen Arbeitskreises vom 14. bis 16. September 2011 an der Lomonossov-Universität Moskau aus Anlass des 300. Geburtstages des Universitätsgründers Michail Lomonossov.* Ed. Natalija Ganina, Klaus Klein, Catherine Squires, and Jürgen Wolf. Akademie gemeinnütziger Wissenschaften zu Erfurt Sonderschriften Vol. 45. Erfurt: Verlag der Akademie gemeinnütziger Wissenschaften, 2014. 57–90.

Starkey, Kathryn. 'On Deer and Dragons: Textiles and the Poetics of medieval Story-Telling in König Rother.' *Animals in Text and Textile: Story-Telling in the Medieval World.* Ed. Kathryn Starkey, and Evelin Wetter. Riggisberger Berichte Vol. 23. Riggisberg: Abegg-Stiftung, 2019. 47–64.

Staub, Kurt Hans, and Hermann Knaus. *Jüngere theologische Texte.* Die Handschriften der Hessischen Landes- und Hochschulbibliothek Darmstadt Vol. 5 Pt. 1. Wiesbaden: Harrassowitz, 2001.

Steer, Georg. 'Die Interpretation der deutschen und lateinischen Predigten Meister Eckharts – eine unendliche Aufgabe.' *Per perscrutationem philosophicam: Neue Perspektiven der mittelalterlichen Forschung. Loris Sturlese zum 60. Geburtstag gewidmet.* Ed. Alessandra Beccarisi, Ruedi Imbach, and Pasquale Porro. Hamburg: Meiner, 2008. 184–203.

Steer, Georg, and Loris Sturlese, eds. *Lectura Eckhardi: Predigten Meister Eckharts von Fachgelehrten gelesen und gedeutet.* Vol. 2. Stuttgart: Kohlhammer, 2003.

Steinmetz, Ralf-Henning. 'Bearbeitungstypen in der Literatur des Mittelalters: Vorschläge für eine Klärung der Begriffe.' *Texttyp und Textproduktion in der deutschen Literatur des Mittelalters.* Ed. Elizabeth Andersen Manfred Eikelmann and Anne Simon. Trends in Medieval Philology Vol. 7. Berlin, New York: De Gruyter, 2005. 41–61.

Stöhlker, Friedrich. *Die Kartause Buxheim. 1402–1803.* 7 vols. Buxheim: Heimatdienst Buxheim, 1974–1978.

Stolz, Michael. 'Bewegtes Beiwerk: Ästhetische Funktionen der Kleiderthematik bei Alanus ab Insulis und Giovanni Boccaccio.' *Reflexionsfiguren der Künste in der Vormoderne.* Ed. Annette Gerok-Reiter, Anja Wolkenhauer, Robert Jörg, and Stefanie Gropper. Germanisch-Romanische Monatsschrift. Beihefte Vol. 88. Heidelberg: Winter, 2018. 359–94.

'Early Versions in Medieval Textual Traditions: Wolfram's Parzival as a Test Case.' *Dating Egyptian Literary Texts: Göttingen, 9–12 June 2010* (vol. 1). Ed. Gerald Moers et al. Lingua Aegyptia Studia Monographica Vol. 11. Hamburg: Widmaier, 2013. 561–87.

'"ibi quasi allegorice – ibi tamen ad litteram": Imagined Animals on Nature's Dress in Alan of Lille's De Planctu Naturae.' *Animals in Text and Textile: Story-Telling in the Medieval World.* Ed. Kathryn Starkey and Evelin Wetter. Riggisberger Berichte Vol. 23. Riggisberg: Abegg-Stiftung, 2019. 81–91.

Strohschneider, Peter. *Höfische Textgeschichten: Über Selbstentwürfe vormoderner Literatur.* Germanisch-Romanische Monatsschrift. Beihefte Vol. 55. Heidelberg: Universitätsverlag Winter, 2014.

Suerbaum, Almut. 'Sprachliche Interferenz bei Begriffen des Lassens: 'Lux Divinitatis' und das 'Fließende Licht der Gottheit'.' *Semantik der Gelassenheit: Generierung, Etablierung, Transformation.* Ed. Burkhard Hasebrink, Susanne Bernhardt, and Imke Früh.

Historische Semantik Vol. 17. Göttingen: Vandenhoeck & Ruprecht, 2012. 33–47.

'"Es kommt ein schiff, geladen": Mouvance in mystischen Liedern aus Straßburg.' *Schreiben und Lesen in der Stadt: Literaturbetrieb im spätmittelalterlichen Straßburg*. Ed. Stephen Mossman, Nigel F. Palmer, and Felix Heinzer. Kulturtopographie des alemannischen Raums Vol. 4. Berlin: De Gruyter, 2012. 99–116.

'"A Room with a view": Zur Spannung zwischen Kontemplation und Leben in der Welt in den Dorotheenviten des Johannes Marienwerder.' *Muße im kulturellen Wandel: Semantisierungen, Ähnlichkeiten, Umbesetzungen*. Ed. Burkhard Hasebrink, and Peter Philipp Riedl. Linguae & Litterae Vol. 35. Berlin: De Gruyter, 2014. 131–51.

Sumner, William Leslie. *The Organ: Its Evolution, Principles of Construction and Use*. 3rd, rev., and enl. edition. London: MacDonald, 1964.

Tammen, Silke. 'Blick und Wunde – Blick und Form: Zur Deutungsproblematik der Seitenwunde Christi in der spätmittelalterlichen Buchmalerei.' *Körper und Bild im Mittelalter*. Ed. Kristin Marek, Raphaèle Preisinger, Marius Rimmele, and Katrin Kärcher. Munich: Fink, 2006. 85–114.

Tarvers, Josephine Koster. '"Thys ys my mystrys boke": English Women as Readers and Writers in Late Medieval England.' *The Uses of Manuscripts in Literary Studies: Essays in Memory of Judson Boyce Allen*. Ed. Charlotte C. Morse, Penelope Reed Doob, and Marjorie Curry Woods. Studies in Medieval Culture Vol. 31. Kalamazoo, MI: Western Michigan University, Medieval Institute Publications, 1992. 305–27.

Taylor, Andrew. 'Vernacular Authorship and the Control of Manuscript Production.' *The Medieval Manuscript Book: Cultural Approaches*. Ed. Michael Johnston, and Michael Van Dussen. Cambridge: Cambridge University Press, 2015. 199–214.

Thali, Johanna. *Beten – Schreiben – Lesen: Literarisches Leben und Marienspiritualität im Kloster Engelthal*. Bibliotheca Germanica Vol. 42. Tübingen: Francke, 2003.

Thurn, Hans. *Die Handschriften aus St. Stephan zu Würzburg*. Die Handschriften der Universitätsbibliothek Würzburg Vol. 2 Pt. 2: Handschriften aus Benediktinischen Provenienzen II. Wiesbaden: Harrassowitz, 1986.

Tobin, Frank. *Mechthild von Magdeburg: A Medieval Mystic in Modern Eyes*. Columbia: Camden House, 1995.

Trînca, Beatrice. 'Schriftliche Berührung – gedruckte Süße: Zum "bot der gotlichen mildigkeit".' *Zeitschrift für deutsche Philologie* 135 (2016): 349–66.

Ubl, Linus. *Manifestation und Konstruktion von Frauenmystik: Prozessuales Schreiben in der oberdeutschen Überlieferung der Mechthild von Hackeborn*. Doctoral dissertation, University of Oxford, 2019.

Uffmann, Heike. *Wie in einem Rosengarten: Monastische Reformen des späten Mittelalters in den Vorstellungen von Klosterfrauen*. Religion in der Geschichte Vol. 14. Bielefeld: Verlag für Regionalgeschichte, 2008.

Unterkircher, Franz. *Die datierten Handschriften der Österreichischen Nationalbibliothek von 1401 bis 1450*. Vol. 1. Katalog der datierten Handschriften in lateinischer Schrift in Österreich Vol. 2. Vienna: Verlag der Österreichischen Akademie der Wissenschaften, 1971.

Vagaggini, Cyprien. 'La devotion au sacré-coeur chez Sainte Mechtilde et Sainte Gertrude.' *Cor Jesu: Commentationes in litteras encyclicas P II PP. XII 'Haurietis Aquas.'* Vol. 1. Ed. Augustinus Bea and Hugo Rahner. Rome: Herder, 1959. 31–48.

Van Asperen, Hanneke. 'Praying, Threading, and Adorning: Sewn-in Prints in a Rosary Prayer Book (London, British Library, ADD. MS 14042).' *Weaving, Veiling, and Dressing: Textiles and Their Metaphors in the Late Middle Ages*. Ed. Kathryn M. Rudy, and Barbara Baert. Medieval Church Studies Vol. 12. Turnhout: Brepols, 2007. 82–120.

Vetter, Angila. *Textgeschichte(n): Retextualisierungsstrategien und Sinnproduktion in Sammlungsverbünden: Der "Willehalm" in kontextueller Lektüre*. Philologische Studien und Quellen Vol. 268. Berlin: ESV, 2018.

Vizkelety, András. *Beschreibendes Verzeichnis der altdeutschen Handschriften in ungarischen Bibliotheken*. Vol. 2: Budapest, Debrecen, Eger, Esztergom, Györ, Kalocsa, Pannonhalma, Pápa, Pécs, Szombathely. Wiesbaden: Harrassowitz, 1973.

Voaden, Rosalynn. 'All Girls Together: Community, Gender and Vision at Helfta.' *Medieval Women in their Communities*. Ed. Diane Watt. Cardiff: University of Wales Press, 1997. 72–91.

God's Words, Women's Voices: The Discernment of Spirits in the Writing of Late-Medieval Women Visionaries. Woodbridge: York Medieval Press, 1999.

Volfing, Annette. *John the Evangelist in Medieval German Writing: Imitating the Inimitable*. Oxford: Oxford University Press, 2001.

The Daugher Zion Allegory in Medieal German Religious Writing. Abingdon: Routledge, 2017.

Vollmann-Profe, Gisela. 'Mechthild – auch "in Werktagskleidern": Zu berühmten und weniger berühmten Abschnitten des "Fließenden Lichts der Gottheit".' *Zeitschrift für deutsche Philologie* 113 (1994): 144–158.

Van den Gheyn, J. *Catalogues des manuscrits de la Bibliothèque Royale de Belgique*. Vol. 3: Théologie. Brussels: Lamertin. 1903.

Catalogues des manuscrits de la Bibliothèque Royale de Belgique. Vol. 6: Histoire – Hagiographie. Brussels: Lamertin, 1905.

von Herrmann, Friedrich-Wilhelm. '"Gelassenheit" bei Heidegger und Meister Eckhart.' *From Phenomenology to Thought, Errancy, and Desire: Essays in Honor of William J. Richardson, S.J.* Ed. Babette E. Babich. Phaenomenologica Vol. 133. Dordrecht: Kluwer Academic, 1995. 115–27.

von Lexer, Matthias. *Mittelhochdeutsches Handwörterbuch. Zugleich als Supplement und alphabetischer Index zum mittelhochdeutschen Wörterbuche von Benecke-Müller-Zarnecke*. 3 vols. Leipzig: Hirzel, 1872–1878.

von Rabenau, Konrad. 'Die Geschichte der Kirchenbibliothek von St. Andreas in Eisleben als Spiegel der Kirchengeschichte des Mansfelder Landes.' *Herbergen der Christenheit* 15 (1985/86): 91–103.

von Scarpatetti, Beat Matthias. *Katalog der datierten Handschriften in der Schweiz in lateinischer Schrift vom Anfang des Mittelalters bis 1550*. Vol. 3: Die Handschriften der Bibliotheken St. Gallen-Zürich. Dietikon-Zürich: Urs Graf, 1991.

Die Handschriften der Stiftsbibliothek St. Gallen. Vol. 1: Abt. IV: Codices 547–669. Hagiographica, Historica, Geographica, 8.–18. Jahrhundert. Wiesbaden: Harrassowitz, 2003.

von Scarpatetti, Beat Matthias, and Philipp Lenz. *Die Handschriften der Stiftsbibliothek St. Gallen*. Vol. 2: Abt. III/2: Codices 450–546: Liturgica, Libri precum, deutsche Gebetbücher, Spiritualia, Musikhandschriften. 9.–16. Jahrhundert. Wiesbaden: Harrassowitz, 2008.

von Scarpatetti, Beat Matthias, Rudolf Gamper, and Marlis Stähli. *Die Handschriften der Bibliotheken St. Gallen – Zürich in alphabetischer Reihenfolge*. Katalog der datierten Handschriften in der Schweiz in lateinischer Schrift vom Anfang des Mittelalters bis 1550 Vol. 3. Dietikon-Zürich: Graf, 1991.

von Wilckens, Leonie. *Die textilen Künste: Von der Spätantike bis um 1500*. Munich: Beck, 1991.

Wagner, Siegfried. *Der Kampf des Fastens gegen die Fastnacht: Zur Geschichte der Mäßigung*. Kulturgeschichtliche Forschungen Vol. 5. Munich: Tuduv, 1986.

Warning, Rainer. 'Seeing and Hearing in Ancient and Medieval Epiphany.' *Rethinking the Medieval Senses: Heritage, Fascinations, Frames*. Ed. Stephen G. Nichols, Andreas Kablitz, and Alison Calhoun. Baltimore: Johns Hopkins University Press, 2008. 102–16.

Watson, Nicholas. *Richard Rolle and the Invention of Authority*. Cambridge: Cambridge University Press, 1991.

'Censorship and Cultural Change in Late-Medieval England: Vernacular Theology, the Oxford Translation Debate, and Arundel's Constitutions of 1409.' *Speculum* 70 (1995): 822–64.

'Conceptions of the Word: The Mother Tongue and the Incarnation of God.' *New Medieval Literatures* 1 (1997): 85–124.

'Visions of Inclusion: Universal Salvation and Vernacular Theology in Pre-Reformation England.' *Journal of Medieval and Early Modern Studies* 27 (1997): 145–87.

Watt, Diane. *Medieval Women's Writing: Works by and for Women in England, 1100–1500*. Cambridge: Polity, 2009.

Webb, Heather. *The Medieval Heart*. New Haven: Yale University Press, 2010.

Weilandt, Gerhard. 'Part of the Whole: Medieval Textile Frontals in Their Liturgical Context.' *Iconography of Liturgical Textiles in the Middle Ages*. Ed. Evelin Wetter. Riggisberger Berichte Vol. 18. Riggisberg: Abegg-Stiftung, 2010. 33–50.

Wenzel, Horst. 'Die Verkündigung an Maria: Zur Visualisierung des Wortes in der Szene oder: Schriftgeschichte im Bild.' *Maria in der Welt: Marienverehrung im Kontext der Sozialgeschichte 10.–18. Jahrhundert*. Ed. Claudia Opitz, Hedwig Röckelein, Gabriela Signori, and Guy P. Marchal. Clio Lucdenensis Vol. 2. Zurich: Chronos, 1993. 23–52.

Hören und Sehen, Schrift und Bild: Kultur und Gedächtnis im Mittelalter. Munich: Beck, 1995.

Wetter, Evelin, ed. *Iconography of Liturgical Textiles in the Middle Ages*. Riggisberger Berichte Vol. 18. Riggisberg: Abegg-Stiftung, 2010.

'Von Bräuten und Vikaren Christi: Zur Konstruktion von Ähnlichkeit im sakralen Initiationsakt.' *Similitudo: Konzepte der Ähnlichkeit in Mittelalter und Früher Neuzeit*. Ed. Martin Gaier, Jeanette Kohl, and Alberto Saviello. Paderborn: Fink, 2012. 129–46.

Wetzel, René. '"Spricht maister Eberhart": Die Unfestigkeit von Autor, Text und Textbausteinen im Cod. Bodmer 59 und in der Überlieferung weiterer mystischer Sammelhandschriften des 15. Jahrhunderts. Mit einem Exkurs zur Buch- und Bibliotheksgeschichte der Kartause Buxheim.' *Kulturtopographie des deutschsprachigen Südwestens*. Ed. Barbara Fleith and René Wetzel. Kulturtopographie des Alemannischen Raums Vol. 1. Berlin: De Gruyter. 301–25.

Wieland, Otmar, ed. *Gertrud von Helfta: ein botte der götlichen miltekeit*. Studien und Mitteilungen zur Geschichte des Benediktiner-Ordens und seiner Zweige. Ergänzungsband 22. Ottobeuren: Bayerische Benediktinerakademie, 1973.

Wiethaus, Ulrike. 'Collaborative Literacy and the Spiritual Education of Nuns at Helfta.' *Nuns' Literacies in Medieval Europe: The Kansas City Dialogue*. Ed. Virginia Blanton, Veronica O'Mara, and Patricia Stoop. Medieval Women – Texts and Contexts Vol. 27. Turnhout: Brepols, 2015. 27–46.

Williams-Krapp, Werner. *Die deutschen und niederländischen Legendare des Mittelalters: Studien zur ihrer Überlieferungs-, Text- und Wirkungsgeschichte*. Texte und Textgeschichte Vol. 20. Tübingen: Niemeyer, 1986.

'Ordensreform und Literatur im 15. Jahrhundert.' *Jahrbuch der Oswald von Wolkenstein-Gesellschaft* 4 (1986/87): 41–51.

'Frauenmystik und Ordensreform im 15. Jahrhundert.' *Literarische Interessenbildung im Mittelalter: DFG-Symposion 1991*. Ed. Joachim Heinzle. Germanistische Symposien. Berichtsbánde Vol. 14. Stuttgart: Metzler, 1993. 301–13.

'Observanzbewegungen, monastische Spiritualität und geistliche Literatur im 15. Jahrhundert.' *Internationales Archiv für Sozialgeschichte der deutschen Literatur* 20 (1995): 1–15.

'Das geistliche Schrifttum des Spätmittelalters vom Anfang des 14. bis zum Ende des 15. Jahrhunderts: Veränderungen nach der Mitte des 14. Jahrhunderts.' *Deutsches Literatur-Lexikon: Das Mittelalter, Autoren und Werke nach Themenkreisen und Gattungen*. Ed. Wolfgang Achnitz. Vol. 2: Das geistliche Schrifttum des Spämittelalters. Berlin: De Gruyter, 2011. xi–xx.

Williamson, Beth. 'Sensory Experience in Medieval Devotion: Sound and Vision, Invisibility and Silence.' *Speculum* 88 (2013): 1–43.

'Material Culture and Medieval Christianity.' *The Oxford Handbook of Medieval Christianity*. Ed. John H. Arnold. Oxford: Oxford University Press, 2014. 60–75.

Willing, Antje. *Literatur und Ordensreform im 15. Jahrhundert: Deutsche Abendmahlsschriften im*

Nürnberger Katharinenkloster. Studien und Texte zum Mittelalter und zur Frühen Neuzeit Vol. 4. Münster: Waxmann, 2004.

ed. *Die Bibliothek des Klosters St. Katharina zu Nürnberg: Synoptische Darstellung der Bücherverzeichnisse.* 2 vols. Berlin: Akademie Verlag, 2013.

Winston-Allen, Anne. *Stories of the Rose: The Making of the Rosary in the Middle Ages.* University Park, PA: Pennsylvania State University Press, 1997. Repr. 1998.

Convent Chronicles: Women Writing about Women and Reform in the Late Middle Ages. University Park, PA: Pennsylvania State University Press, 2004.

'Networking in Medieval Strasbourg: Cross-Order Collaboration in Book Illustration among Women's Reformed Convents.' *Schreiben und Lesen in der Stadt: Literaturbetrieb im spätmittelalterlichen Straßburg.* Ed. Stephen Mossman, Nigel F. Palmer, and Felix Heinzer. Kulturtopographie des alemannischen Raums Vol. 4. Berlin: De Gruyter, 2012. 197–212.

'Outside the Mainstream: Women as Readers, Scribes, and Illustrators of Books in Convents of the German-Speaking Regions.' *Nuns' Literacies in Medieval Europe: The Kansas City Dialogue.* Ed. Virginia Blanton, Veronica O'Mara, and Patricia Stoop. Medieval Women – Texts and Contexts Vol. 27. Turnhout: Brepols, 2015. 191–206.

Wogan-Browne, Jocelyn, ed. 'General Introduction: What's in a Name? The "French" of "England".' *Language and Culture in Medieval Britain: The French of England. c.1100 – c.1500.* Woodbridge: York Medieval Press, 2009. 1–13.

'The Tongues of the Nightingale: "hertely redyng" at English Courts.' *New Directions in Medieval Manuscript Studies and Reading Practices: Essays in Honor of Derek Pearsall.* Ed. Kathryn Kerby-Fulton, John J. Thompson, and Sarah Baechle. Notre Dame, IN: University of Notre Dame Press, 2014. 78–98.

Woodfin, Warren T. 'Disjuncture between Text and Image: Mystagogy and the Embroidered Iconography of Byzantine Vestments.' *Clothing the Sacred: Medieval Textiles as Fabric, Form, and Metaphor.* Ed. Mateusz Kaputska and Warren T. Woodfin. Textile Studies Vol. 8. Emsdetten: Édition Imorde, 2015. 13–32.

Wunderle, Elisabeth. *Katalog der mittelalterlichen lateinischen Papierhandschriften.* Die Handschriften der Forschungsbibliothek Gotha Vol. 1. Wiesbaden: Harrassowitz, 2002.

Die deutschen Handschriften der Bayerischen Staatsbibliothek München. Die mittelalterlichen Handschriften aus Cgm 5255–7000 einschließlich der althochdeutschen Fragmente Cgm 5248. Catalogus codicum manu scriptorum Bibliotheca Monacensis Vol. 5: Editio altera Pt 9. Wiesbaden: Harrassowitz, 2018. 56–60.

Woodfin, Warren T. 'Disjuncture between Text and Image: Mystagogy and the Embroidered Iconography of Byzantine Vestments.' *Clothing the Sacred: Medieval Textiles as Fabric, Form, and Metaphor.* Ed. Mateusz Kaputska and Warren T. Woodfin. Textile Studies Vol. 8. Emsdetten: Édition Imorde, 2015. 13–32.

Yoshikawa, Naoë Kukita. 'Mechtild of Hackeborn As Spiritual Authority: The Middle English Translation of the "Liber Specialis Gratia".' *Translation and Authority: Authorities in Translation.* Ed. Pieter De Leemans and Michèle Goyens. Turnhout: Brepols, 2017. 241–53.

'Post-mortem Care of the Soul: Mechtild of Hackeborn's the Book of Gostlye Grace.' *Medieval and Early Modern Literature, Science and Medicine.* Ed. Rachel Falconer and Denis Renevey. Swiss Papers in English Language and Literature 28. Tübingen: Narr Verlag, 2013. 157–70.

Zarowny, Paul. *The Heart of Christ at Helfta: The Influence of Aristotelian Cardiology on the Visions of Saint Gertrude the Great and Saint Mechthilde of Hackeborn.* Doctoral dissertation, New York, Fordham University, 1999.

Zeibig, Hartmann J. 'Die deutschen Handschriften der Stiftsbibliothek zu Klosterneuburg.' *Serapeum* 11 (1850): 101–9, 123–5.

Zumthor, Paul. *Essai de poétique médiévale.* Paris: Éditions du Seuil, 1972.

Zunker, Maria Magdalena. *Geschichte der Benediktinerinnenabtei St. Walburg in Eichstätt von 1035 bis heute.* Lindenberg: Fink, 2009

INDEX

abstinence. *See* fasting
Adelhausen Sisterbook, 50
Adelhausen, convent of, 50
Adelheit of Gotteszell, 192
Aeneid, 267n158
aenigmata, 144–5
affect, 10, 30, 128, 139–44, 242n38, 271n52, 273n70
Agnes, Saint, 43, 181
Alacoque, Margaret Mary, 286n10
Alan of Lille, 58, 134, 137, 148, 152, 164, 175, 177, 186, 204–6
    Anticlaudianus, 58, 134, 186, 206, 299n79, 304n183, *See also* prologue
    De planctu naturae, 175, 204–6, 299n79
Albert the Great, 85, 153, 231, 233, 284n104
    De Eucharistia, 287n31
allegory, 4, 134, 152, 156, 180, 186, 191, 204–6, 289n56, 300n114
Alsace, 170
altar cloth, 178–80, 185, 296n26
Angela of Foligno, 29
Anna Dorothea von Hohenzollern-Haigerloch, Countess, 122
Annunciation, 80, 83, 95
Anselm of Laon, 267n158
antependium. *See* altar cloth
Anthony, Saint, 200
anxiety, scribal, 24
Apocalypse. *See* Revelation of John
apophatic discourse, 2, 4, 30, 208, 257n34, 283n94
approbation, 14, 25, 129–32, 137, 147, *See also* commendatio
Aquinas, Thomas, 150, 284n104
Aristotle, 159–60, 241n37, 293n118
Arnold von Riddagshausen, 179
arrows of love, 135–6, 159, 160, 163
ars memorativa, 181
ars moriendi, 98, 192
ars sacra, 178–82
artefact, xiv, 55, 64, 165, 196, 213, 266n148, 267n159
Ascension, 63, 120, 304n179
Assumption, 305n211
astrology, 183

Augsburg, Benediktinerabtei St. Stephan, Hs 38, 84–93, 97, 103, 218, 262n109, 271n49, 277n1, 307
Augsburg, Staats- und Stadtbibliothek, 8° Cod. 203, 226, 262n109, 271n47, 307
Augsburg, Universitätsbibliothek, Cod. III. 1. 4° 30, 95, 218, 272n59, 307
Augustine (Saint), Bishop of Hippo, 43, 53, 97, 116, 149–50, 158, 164, 189, 292n108
    Confessions, 158
    De civitate dei, 285n6
Augustinians, 57, 65, 70, 99, 101, 116, 179
    Augustinian canonesses, 68, 70, 99, 101, 103
authorship, 7, 10, 12–13, 19, 39, 136, 147, 263n118
    co-authorship, 30, 62, 264n140
    collective authorship, 7, 12, 25–32, 249n49, 250n89, 253n121, 302n149
    gendered authorship, 9, 25–32, 45, 54, 237n1, 250n88, 253n120, 267n162, *See also* gendered writing
    single authorship, 18–19, 62, 154, 253n122
Ave Maria, 201

Basel, 168
Beatrice of Nazareth, 209
Beguines, 44
Benedict, Saint, 53
Benedictines, 14, 51, 65, 68, 165, 181, 262n112, 263n116, 273n77, 278n20
    Benedictine brothers of Solesmes as modern editors of the *Legatus*, 20, 46
    Benedictine nuns, 101, 110, 129, 271n53
    Rule of St Benedict, 140
Berlin, Staatsbibliothek Preußischer Kulturbesitz, Ms. germ. oct. 593, 274n79, 307
Berlin, Staatsbibliothek Preußischer Kulturbesitz, Ms. theol. lat. oct. 89, 225, 262n110, 263n114, 307
Bern, 270n35
Bernard of Clairvaux, 2–3, 19, 29–30, 43, 85, 116, 143, 148, 150–1, 231–3, 283n94
    Sermons on the Song of Songs, 3, 29, 143, 150, 283n94
Bernard, Saint. *See* Bernard of Clairvaux
Biberach, 74